CISTERCIAN STUDIES SERIES: NUMBER TWO HUNDRED THIRTY-FIVE

The *Discourses* of Philoxenos of Mabbug

Translated by Robert A. Kitchen

D1563212

CISTERCIAN STUDIES SERIES: NUMBER TWO HUNDRED THIRTY-FIVE

The *Discourses* of Philoxenos of Mabbug

A New Translation and Introduction

Translated by Robert A. Kitchen

α

Cistercian Publications
www.cistercianpublications.org

LITURGICAL PRESS
Collegeville, Minnesota
www.litpress.org

A Cistercian Publications title published by Liturgical Press

BR
65
.P486
D513
2013

Cistercian Publications
Editorial Offices
Abbey of Gethsemani
3642 Monks Road
Trappist, Kentucky 40051
www.cistercianpublications.org

© 2013 by Order of Saint Benedict, Collegeville, Minnesota. All rights reserved. No part of this book may be reproduced in any form, by print, microfilm, microfiche, mechanical recording, photocopying, translation, or by any other means, known or yet unknown, for any purpose except brief quotations in reviews, without the previous written permission of Liturgical Press, Saint John's Abbey, PO Box 7500, Collegeville, Minnesota 56321-7500. Printed in the United States of America.

1   2   3   4   5   6   7   8   9

Library of Congress Cataloging-in-Publication Data

Philoxenus, Bishop of Hierapolis, approximately 440–523.
    [Discourses on the Christian life. English]
    The Discourses of Philoxenos of Mabbug : a new translation and introduction / translated by Robert A. Kitchen.
        pages cm — (Cistercian studies series ; 235)
    In English; translated from Syriac.
    Includes bibliographical references and index.
    ISBN 978-0-87907-135-6 — ISBN 978-0-87907-749-5 (e-book)
    1. Asceticism—History—Early church, ca. 30–600.   2. Christian life.
3. Philoxenus, Bishop of Hierapolis, approximately 440–523.   I. Kitchen, Robert A.   II. Title.

BR65.P486D5   2013
248.4'814—dc23   2013024332

Contents

Preface

One of the most illustrious theologians and ecclesiastical leaders of the post-Chalcedonian era, Philoxenos (bishop of Mabbug in western Syria), was known for the elegance of his written Syriac in which he wrote all his works. Rarely has he been acknowledged by historians of Christianity or by the memory of the Church. A subtle theologian explaining the One Nature of Christ, Philoxenos was also an imaginative biblical exegete who insisted upon a better translation of the Syriac Bible, a dedicated supporter and guide to the monks and monasteries under his episcopal care, as well as one who could not only play in the rough and tumble of political matters but also be a compassionate reconciler.

Perhaps it was the language. "The devil spoke Syriac" is Theodoret of Cyrrhus's memorable quip and the language certainly faded from the spotlight in the memory of the Western Church where Greek and Latin were the preferred tongues. Philoxenos, whose name means "Lover of Strangers" or "the Hospitable One," spoke and wrote many things worth rescuing from history's forgetfulness. His most copied and circulated work, the *Discourses*, appeals to the broadest audience and is the logical place to begin hearing again a forgotten voice.

The *Discourses* of Philoxenos serves as the companion volume to the *Book of Steps*,[1] although on the surface the two texts appear quite diverse in geographical locations, theological perspectives, social structures and political surroundings, and time. Their connection

---

[1] *The Book of Steps: the Syriac* Liber Graduum, trans. with an introduction and notes, Robert A. Kitchen and Martien F. G. Parmentier, CS 196 (Kalamazoo, MI: Cistercian Publications, 2004).

is in the common infrastructure of the two levels of committed Christian life, uprightness (*kēnūtā*) and perfection (*gmīrūtā*), which only these two works describe at length in subtle detail.

I stumbled across Philoxenos and his *Discourses* nearly four decades ago in the Semitics department of The Catholic University of America, and it must have been Fr. Alexander Di Lella who directed me to the bishop since I surely had never heard of him. The Eastern and particularly Syriac churches were not part of a mainline-Protestant seminarian's worldview at that time. Things have changed. I eventually wrote a master's thesis on the upright and the perfect in the *Book of Steps* and the *Discourses*. Philoxenos back then took center stage, although along the way to a DPhil at the University of Oxford under the guidance of Sebastian Brock, the *Book of Steps* would play the siren and I was seduced.

Now Philoxenos is receiving his due again. The study of this author is reviving, but not with the vibrancy due a prolific author who played a major role in the establishment of a church movement still very much alive. A physical problem is that the critical edition of the *Discourses*, upon which this and previous translations have been based, is E. Wallis Budge's beautifully produced and printed 1894 two-volume set.[2] There are simply too few copies available in North American and European libraries for the access of younger scholars. A new translation enables Philoxenos' voice to be heard in a modern accent, to direct the reader toward recent scholarship and interpretations, and an opportunity to emend the Syriac text en route.

The length of the *Discourses* is daunting, but the most effective and engaging way to access their dynamic tone is to read them aloud, whether in Syriac or in translation. Debate continues whether these *mēmrē* were actually delivered orally by Philoxenos or written in order to be read by someone else—a debate that will not be conclusively resolved. I hope that Philoxenos did preach them himself, for after reading these aloud, what reader would be able to duplicate his voice and passion?

---

[2] E. A. Wallis Budge, *The Discourses of Philoxenus, Bishop of Mabbôgh, A.D. 485–519*, 2 vols. (London: Asher & Co., 1894).

Several decisions have been made in translating and annotating the text that should be clarified. "Discourses" is an appropriate yet flat translation for *mēmrē*, the Syriac term (plural) for this kind of literary vehicle that adopts a wide variety of genres. As I did in the *Book of Steps*, I will identify each unit as a *mēmrā* (singular) so that the reader may come to appreciate the qualities of this unique Syriac genre.

The labels of the two levels of spiritual life remain the same from the *Book of Steps*: the lower, worldly level of uprightness (*kēnūtā*) and its practitioners, the upright (*kēnē*), and those who follow the major commandments of perfection (*gmīrūtā*), or the perfect (*gmīrē*). In earlier translations, *kēnūtā* was rendered as "justice" / "the just," but that can be confusing at certain points, so the suggestion of "uprightness"/"upright" seemed more fitting, and considering the subsequent work done on the *Book of Steps* the term has become fixed. The translations "perfection" and "the perfect" have been challenged from time to time, for although this is a legitimate translation of the terms, the perfect were frequently described as being decidedly not perfect in the modern sense. Suggestions have been offered along the lines of "mature," but the imprecision of that term seems even more ambiguous. I have remained with the renderings perfection/perfect because both authors project an eschatological tone, the idea that one is striving for perfection which will be finally fulfilled in the kingdom of heaven.

Scholarship is never a solitary task; one stands on the shoulders of countless other people who have written and spoken and taught, much of which one records only as a footnote. In the first place, I wish to express my gratitude to Sebastian Brock for his innumerable hours looking over much of what I have done in the last couple of decades. His suggestions have always given me needed direction and his generosity and patience have enabled me to understand how much grace is at play in these endeavors. The people engaged in Syriac studies are indeed a graceful lot, but how could they be otherwise once touched by the personality and example of Sebastian Brock?

My wife, Molly, knows Philoxenos well and can cite his verdict on the lust of the belly at a moment's notice. Her encouragement and participation as a pastoral colleague in a life of study have constituted the less traveled road, but for us that has made all the difference. Our children, Winifred, Sidney, and Thanh, have heard the bishop's name whispered around the table all their lives and they willingly admit they know who he is.

I wish to express my gratitude to the congregation and leadership of Knox-Metropolitan United Church, Regina, Saskatchewan, for their generous and continuing support of my scholarship throughout the years of my pastorate. While they do not always catch on fully to the significance of the Oriental and Syriac churches, they have recognized the importance of my contribution to the study of the Great Church. I was granted a sabbatical leave by the congregation to be a pastor-theologian in residence at the Center of Theological Inquiry (CTI), Princeton, New Jersey, where my work on the *Discourses* really began to take shape. The environment of theological adventure fostered at CTI by William Storrar can only be experienced to fully appreciate.

I have been fortunate to become acquainted with David Michelson, now assistant professor, Vanderbilt Divinity School, whose Princeton dissertation on Philoxenos under Peter Brown has taken the study of the bishop of Mabbug to a deeper and subtler level in much the same way that the dissertation on Philoxenos by André de Halleux did more than a generation ago. We organized the so-called Philoxenos Phest at CTI, cosponsored by the Center for the Study of Religion at Princeton University and Gorgias Press, and were able later to edit a full year's volume of *Hugoye Journal of Syriac Studies* devoted to various aspects of the study of Philoxenos. Our conversations have enabled me to see Philoxenos in significantly new ways, as well as to better understand things about Philoxenos I had known for a good while. It is my desire and intent to transmit many of those things now to the reader.

The introduction begins with an overview of miaphysite theology and ecclesiastical history in which Philoxenos was engaged then reviews what is known about the life and ministry of Philoxenos and his writings. The previous study of the *Discourses* is described, along with the various manuscripts E. W. Budge used to create the critical edition. A summary of the contents of the thirteen *mēmrē* is presented, followed by a note on the versions of Philoxenos' literary work in other languages and a brief review of how Thomas Merton read and interpreted the *Discourses*. Several sections then treat various key terms and issues in the work: a detailed analysis of the upright and the perfect and a reflection on the nature of Syriac asceticism from the vantage point of the *Book of Steps* and the *Discourses*; the use of christological terminology in the *Discourses*; how Philoxenos interpreted the Bible in the *Discourses*; and finally the manner in which Philoxenos utilized the concepts and categories of Evagrius Ponticus.

The English translation of the thirteen *Discourses*, or *mēmrē*, is given with biblical references and occasional notes. For those who may be reading the English translation with Budge's Syriac text at hand, the numbers inside parentheses are the page numbers in Budge's Syriac edition. Notations regarding typographical errors of the Syriac text, as well as the use of variant readings, are recorded in the footnotes.[3]

---

[3] E. A. Wallis Budge admits in his preface to his 1894 critical edition and translation that after some shifting back and forth regarding which readings would be in the text and which in the apparatus and notes, he realized that "as a result of these changes it will be seen that, in some cases, the better readings are given in the notes and the less good in the text." Budge, 2:viii.

Introduction to the *Discourses* of Philoxenos of Mabbug

Post-451 and the One Nature of Miaphysitism

To live in a quiet age was not the luxury of Philoxenos of Mabbug. Persecution and controversy assailed him throughout his entire life. The years following the Council of Chalcedon in 451 were generally troubled times for the Syriac Church, and Philoxenos, it seems, consistently found himself in the eye of the storm.

Celebrated and stigmatized for his role as one of the leaders in the anti-Chalcedonian movement in the late fifth / early sixth centuries, Philoxenos' doctrinal position, along with those of Severus of Antioch and others, is identified by several confusing christological labels—monophysite, miaphysite, and henophysite. The *Discourses* are perhaps the least affected of Philoxenos' writings by christological concerns, but these *mēmrē* do include casual comments and particular questions and refutations that illustrate Philoxenos' theological allegiance.[1] A brief description of the history and concepts of miaphysitism will help in comprehending Philoxenos' orientation, though certainly not fully describe it.[2]

---

[1] See below, "Christological Comments in *The Discourses*," for how and where these casual comments were used.

[2] The starting point for modern interpretation is W. H. C. Frend, *The Rise of the Monophysite Movement: Chapters in the History of the Church in the Fifth and Sixth Centuries* (Cambridge: Cambridge University Press, 1972).

The emergence of Nestorius, bishop of Constantinople, in the late 420s is the usual place to begin. Educated in the Antiochene tradition under Theodore of Mopsuestia, Nestorius emphasized the human nature of Christ, infamously rejecting the popular use of the term for Mary, *Theotokos* or God-bearer, Mother of God. Cyril of Alexandria responded with vehement and articulate refutations, and the controversy eventually led to the calling of the Council of Ephesus in 431 at which Nestorius was condemned and removed from office.

Matters were not settled in Ephesus, similar to the way things had happened a century earlier at Nicaea over the nature of the Trinity, and heated debate continued for twenty years until the Council of Chalcedon was gathered in 451. Cyril's phrase, "one incarnate nature [*mia physis*] of God the Logos/Word," became the central affirmation to describe the incarnation on which Chalcedon would focus.

The Definition of Chalcedon rejected both the two-nature interpretation of Nestorius that seemed to imply two Christs (one human and one divine), and the one-nature interpretation of Eutyches that essentially denied a human element in Christ.[3] The Council affirmed that Christ existed in one person in two natures, fully human and fully divine, without confusion, change, division, or separation.[4] Many Eastern bishops disagreed, believing that Christ had One Nature, out of or from two natures, and refused to sign the Definition. Two Greek prepositions—*en* and *ek*—marked the distinction, the difference of one letter creating a wide chasm between theologies and churches. The debate, which would continue unabated for over a century, showed that the Nicene and post-Nicene decisions about the nature of the Trinity were not finally conclusive.[5]

---

[3] For a vivid narrative regarding Eutyches and the "Gangster" or "Robber" Synod, see Philip Jenkins, *Jesus Wars: How Four Patriarchs, Three Queens, and Two Emperors Decided What Christians Would Believe for the Next 1,500 years* (New York: HarperOne, 2010), 187–97.

[4] The Definition of Chalcedon is recorded in numerous sources. See J. N. D. Kelly, *Early Christian Doctrines* (San Francisco: Harper & Row, 1976), 339–40.

[5] Still the best discussion of the doctrinal intricacies is that of Jaroslav Pelikan, *The Christian Tradition: A History of the Development of Doctrine*, vol.

A significant portion of the Eastern Church—the so-called Oriental Churches of Syria, Egypt, Ethiopia, Armenia, and Georgia—would effectively separate from the Constantinople- and Rome-centered Western churches. Ironically, Cyril's theology was accepted by both sides, especially by the Eastern miaphysite wing after Chalcedon.[6] When the miaphysites wished to caricature the Chalcedonian position, they castigated the majority decision as thinly veiled Nestorianism. In turn, they were incorrectly labeled "monophysite" or "one nature"—the implication being that Christ had simply one divine nature, no human nature, echoing the intellectual excesses of Eutyches.

The miaphysite movement itself was neither uniform nor unified, so it has been uncomfortable for historians and historical theologians to label the theologies and churches with one stroke. In recent years, the accepted academic label for these groups is *anti-Chalcedonian*, which appropriately reflects the political character of the controversy as emperors and empresses and patriarchs, monks, and courtiers wrestled for power and official status of orthodox faith.[7] The vocabulary was theological, but the language was power politics.[8]

1, *The Emergence of the Catholic Tradition (100–600)* (1971), esp. 266–77; and vol. 2., *The Spirit of Eastern Christendom (600–1700)* (Chicago & London: University of Chicago Press, 1974), esp. 49–61.

[6] Pelikan, 2:52: "The Chalcedonian opponents of the Jacobite Christology quoted Cyril against it, and its defenders had to explain away some of Cyril's language." See Susan Wessel, *Cyril of Alexandria and the Nestorian Controversy: The Making of a Saint and of a Heretic* (New York: Oxford University Press, 2004), especially the epilogue, 296–302.

[7] A. H. M. Jones, "Were Ancient Heresies National or Social Movements in Disguise?" JTS 11 (1959): 280–98.

[8] Two recent monographs demonstrate the critical role of the Eastern churches in the history of Christianity in Late Antiquity: Diarmaid MacCulloch, *Christianity: The First Three Thousand Years* (New York: Viking, 2010), especially chapter 7, "Defying Chalcedon: Asia and Africa (451–622)," 233–54; and Philip Jenkins, *Jesus Wars: How Four Patriarchs, Three Queens, and Two Emperors Decided What Christians Would Believe for the Next 1,500 years* (New York: HarperOne, 2010). Interestingly, the two

Philoxenos was involved in all aspects of the controversy, theological and political. The reigns of emperors Zeno and Anastasius, both empathetic to the anti-Chalcedonian movement, enabled Philoxenos to be bishop from 485 to 518 of Mabbug. However, the moment Justin I, a strong supporter of Chalcedon, assumed the throne in 518, it was the end of the miaphysite movement thriving in imperial favor. Justin removed all miaphysite clergy from their positions on Easter, March 31, 519, including Philoxenos. Attempts to reconcile the Chalcedonian Church with the miaphysites failed and the latter were increasingly persecuted. The Second Council of Constantinople in 553 reasserted Chalcedon and condemned various aspects of One Nature theology along with various of the personalities who supported it. In dire straits, the miaphysite church found a different solution as Jacob Baradaeus embarked on an ambitious and charismatic pilgrimage throughout an immense territory, ordaining priests and bishops into the miaphysite fold. His labors infused a renewed vitality to the Syrian Orthodox Church which would be nicknamed "Jacobite" in deference to the contribution of the one who revitalized it.[9]

Philoxenos, Bishop of Mabbug: The Hospitable Stranger

Life

We know Philoxenos mainly through his writings, although there are a few sources that give a systematic, albeit sometimes legendary,

---

authors diverge in terminology. MacCulloch's magisterial work carefully underlines that the subject is *miaphysite* Christianity, while Jenkins's more popular book focused on Chalcedon and its aftermath recognizes that this is the correct term, but apologetically opts for *monophysite* since it is still the more recognizable expression among the general readership.

[9] See Jeanne-Nicole Saint-Laurent, *Apostolic Memories: Religious Differentiation and the Construction of Orthodoxy in Syriac Missionary Literature* (PhD dissertation, Brown University, 2009); and Volker L. Menze, *Justinian and the Making of the Syrian Orthodox Church* (Oxford: Oxford University Press, 2008).

account of his life. The primary source is the anonymous *Chronicle of 846* compiled at the monastery of Qartmīn in the Ṭūr 'Abdīn.[10] From this same monastery a thirteenth-century monk, Elijah, composed a valuable poetical biography.[11] A handful of other manuscripts offer short biographies with some interesting details, about which A. de Halleux[12] and A. Vööbus[13] have published notices.

All indications point to Taḥel in Bet Garmai as the birthplace of Philoxenos, probably in the 440s. His family, as part of the Christian Aramaic-speaking community of Persia, found themselves precariously caught between the hostility of Zoroastrian clergy and the suspicions of the Sassanian monarchy against these reputed allies of Roman Christianity.[14] According to Elijah, a severe persecution took place in Bet Garmai ca. 445–46, forcing Philoxenos' family to migrate to Ṭūr 'Abdīn.[15] De Halleux believes Elijah may have imagined this final location in order to situate Philoxenos geographically closer to the monastery of Qartmīn, although the date of the persecution provides a logical explanation for the family's migration.[16]

---

[10] *Chronicon anonymum ad A.D. 846 oertinens*, ed. E. W. Brooks, trans. J. B. Chabot in *Chronica minora* (CSCO 3–4; Louvain, 1903).

[11] Eli de Qartamin, *Memra sur S. Mar Philoxène de Mabbog*, ed. A. de Halleux (CSCO 233–34/Syr 100–101; Louvain, 1963).

[12] André de Halleux, "Á la source d'une biographie expurgée de Philoxène de Mabboug," *Orientalia Lovaniensia Periodica* 6/7 (1975–76): 253–66. Focuses on variations in Sin. syr. 10 and the relevant section in *Chronicle of 846*.

[13] Arthur Vööbus, "La Biographie de Philoxène: Tradition des Manuscrits," *Analecta Bollandiana* 93 (1975): 111–14. Mss. noted: Vat. syr. 155; Damas Patr. 2/8; Mardin Orth. 270; Mardin Orth. 267; Mardin Orth. 216; Mossoul Orth. F; Midyat Melki 8; Manchester Rylands syr. 45; Deir Za'faran 1/6; Diyarbakir Mar Ja'qob 1/13; Mardin Orth. 264; Sarfeh 5/3; Harvard Har. 47 (now Harvard Syr. 59—contains Elijah of Qartmin, note 11 above).

[14] Andre de Halleux, *Philoxène de Mabboug: Sa vie, ses Écrits, sa Théologie* (Universitas Catholica Louvaniensis Dissertationes ad gradum magistri, Series 3 8; Louvain, 1963), 13–15.

[15] Eli de Qartamin, vv. 39–44.

[16] De Halleux, *Philoxène*, 15.

If there were one quiet period in Philoxenos' life, it was during his youth and education. He attended the School of Edessa while it was still dominated by Antiochene Christology, but Philoxenos was eventually attracted to the Cyrillian/miaphysite perspective. After becoming a head teacher[17] of the School of the Persians he was expelled by Calendio, the patriarch of Antioch, for promoting miaphysite Christology among the monasteries. The controversies concerning the acceptance of the decisions of Chalcedon were to some degree masks hiding the political struggle to keep the Christian empire unified, and in this struggle Philoxenos would prove to be a highly skilled participant.

Calendio was deposed by the Emperor Zeno and Peter the Fuller was reinstated as patriarch of Antioch in 481. The latter ordained Philoxenos as bishop of Mabbug (Hierapolis; currently, Membidj) on 18 Ab of the year 796 of the Seleucids (August 485).[18] Being fundamentally Aramean, little touched by Hellenization, Philoxenos was an excellent choice as pastor for a people of Syriac language and education.[19]

It was apparently at this point that our author adopted his familiar name. His ordination name was *'Aksenāyā*, "the stranger." *Philoxenos* is a Hellenization of this name (φιλόξενος), "lover of strangers," "the hospitable one." Later Syriac works are mixed in using either the original name or its Greek version. Harvard Syr. 59 (formerly Harris 47), however, adds the information that Philoxenos' name prior to ordination was Joseph.[20]

Aside from the furor in the post-Chalcedonian East, Philoxenos had just as serious a problem in his new see with its indigenous paganism. Situated one hundred miles northeast of Antioch, Mabbug was a complex city, being a center of the cult of Atargatis, the

[17] Harvard Syr. 38, folio 113b: lines 6–7. Syriac text edited by S. P. Brock in *Qolo Suryoyo* 110 (1996): 253–54. The related text Rylands Syr. 45 was translated by A. Mingana, "New Documents on Philoxenos of Hierapolis, and on the Philoxenian Version of the Bible," *Expositor* 8.13 (1920): 149–60.

[18] De Halleux, *Philoxène*, 40.

[19] De Halleux, *Philoxène*, 41.

[20] Vööbus, "Biographie," 113–14.

Syrian goddess of fertility. Christians gained the majority in the city only in the fifth century. Numerous temples, especially the principal one in the center of the city, attracted many pilgrims and gave the city its Hellenistic name of Hierapolis or holy city.[21] The insidious feature of the Atargatis cult for Philoxenos, however, was not the thriving business of the temples, but the artistic connections between the dove as the Christian symbol of the Holy Spirit and the dove as the cult's sacred bird. Philoxenos' remedy was a strong iconoclastic program, forbidding the use of eucharistic doves.[22]

Philoxenos' historical reputation, however, is built on his opposition to the theology and politics of Chalcedon and its heirs. His first target was "Nestorianism," with which he aligned Chalcedon as a dyophysite variation. Although he is often portrayed as a fanatical advocate of miaphysitism, Philoxenos was actually very tolerant with the diphysites or Chalcedonians. Pleading indulgence for his opponents, he and Severus of Antioch agreed not to require reiteration of sacramental and liturgical acts by Chalcedonians. He even continued to tolerate the mention of a signer of Chalcedon in the liturgy.[23]

As for the other traditional heresies of the early Christian centuries, Philoxenos' opposition was largely intellectual since he had little actual experience of them. He knew about Gnosticism and Origenism through reading the Church Fathers and through Ephrem he became familiar with the basic systems of Valentinus, Bardaisan, Mani, and Marcion. He opposed the Messalian doctrines, although he was uncertain about whether the movement still existed.[24]

By the late-fifth century, monasticism had established itself as a powerful religious and political force.[25] For Philoxenos, the monks under his episcopal jurisdiction were his favorites, and correspondence with individual monks and communities comprised the

---

[21] De Halleux, *Philoxène*, 41–42.
[22] De Halleux, *Philoxène*, 89–90.
[23] De Halleux, *Philoxène* 86–87. Stephen I of Mabbug.
[24] De Halleux, *Philoxène*, 14.
[25] See David Brakke, *Athanasius and the Politics of Asceticism* (Oxford: OUP, 1995).

majority of his literary output. The largest and most famous monastery at Senun was the recipient of his last letter that urged the monks there to stand by their miaphysite faith.[26] It was to these monks at Senun, De Halleux speculates, that Philoxenos directed his *Discourses*.[27]

Although pastoral toward his monks, Philoxenos was uncompromising in his stand for the integrity of his Church. As a consequence, his power steadily rose over the years, but its decline was rapid and catastrophic. He actively opposed Zeno's *Henoticon*, a compromise document that both sides agreed did not accomplish its purpose.[28] However, it was his ten-year-long battle with Flavian, the successor to Peter the Fuller as patriarch of Antioch, that created enough enemies to eventually crush him. Philoxenos equated Flavian's support of the *Henoticon* with an acceptance of Nestorianism. Fortunately, during this period Philoxenos had a protector in the emperor Anastasius (491–518).

Eventually, Philoxenos would triumph over Flavian when the great miaphysite theologian Severus assumed the patriarchate of Antioch, although the triumph was only to last from 512 to 518. When Anastasius died in 518 and the Chalcedonian Justin replaced him, the buffer for miaphysitism was lost, quickly spelling the ruin of the miaphysite regime in the East.

The reconciliation with Rome took place on Easter Sunday, March 31, 519, with Severian bishops being forced to sign a *libellus* or go into exile. Anticipating the situation, Severus fled in September 518 to Alexandria. Philoxenos, however, resisted for a while, but was forced to give up his seat to a Chalcedonian in 519. He was abandoned even by his own clergy of Mabbug who anathematized him as a heretic and a Manichaean.[29]

[26] *Philoxène de Mabboug. Lettres aux moines de Senoun*, ed. André de Halleux (CSCO 231–32/Syr 98–99; Louvain, 1963).

[27] De Halleux, *Philoxène*, 45.

[28] See Aloys Grillmeier, *Christ in the Christian Tradition*, trans. John Bowden, vol. 2, part 1 (New York: Sheed and Ward, 1965), 269–73.

[29] De Halleux, *Philoxène*, 93–94.

While the last four years of Philoxenos' life were certainly spent in exile, tradition appears confused about the exact location. Jacobite historians named Gangra of Paphlagonia, while the *Chronicle of Seert*, along with three of Philoxenos' letters (including Senun), pinpointed Philippopolis in Thrace.[30] De Halleux concludes that he spent time in both places, remaining at Philippopolis after spending the winter of 519–20 in Gangra.[31]

His last letter to the monks at Senun mentioned two things that have been associated with his death. First, Philoxenos described the uncomfortable conditions in his room above a kitchen from which smoke rose up to him, giving rise in turn to the legend of Philoxenos' martyrdom by asphyxiation.[32] Second, he complained of generally poor health that more likely indicates the eventual cause of death, especially when one considers his eighty-some years. His death took place on the tenth of Kanun, 835 of Alexander, or December 523.[33]

Not doomed to obscurity, Philoxenos was commemorated by an active cult centered at the monastery of Qartmin in Tūr 'Abdīn.[34] There is evidence of the cult's existence as early as the writing of the *Chronicle of 846*.[35] The cult reached its peak in the thirteenth century as Elijah listed three celebrations: 18 August (ordination); 10 December (death); 18 February (translation).[36]

Writings

Divided primarily between doctrinal polemics and monastic spirituality, Philoxenos' literary output was extraordinary both in volume and variety. Homilies, letters, liturgies, biblical commentaries, and

---

[30] De Halleux, *Philoxène*, 95.

[31] De Halleux, *Philoxène*, 97.

[32] De Halleux, *Philoxène*, 95–96.

[33] De Halleux, *Philoxène*, 100–101.

[34] See Philoxenos' links with Qartmin: Andrew N. Palmer, *Monk and Mason on the Tigris Frontier* (Cambridge: Cambridge UP, 1990), 113–16.

[35] De Halleux, *Philoxène*, 104–5.

[36] De Halleux, *Philoxène*, 102.

theological treatises were all part of his repertoire. The only exception appears to be poetry.

Philoxenos has been traditionally associated with a version of the New Testament known to have been compiled by a chorepiscopus, Polycarp, working under Philoxenos' direction at Mabbug in 507–8. Polycarp revised the *Peshitta* in accordance with Greek manuscripts, seeking to give a more theologically correct rendering of the Greek than the *Peshitta* had accomplished.[37] Inconsistent in the quotation of various biblical texts in his own writings, Philoxenos gives us few clues concerning the particular biblical version he used.[38]

As is the case with many spiritual directors of that age, Philoxenos compiled a series of biblical commentaries, exegeting only the significant passages.[39] In addition, he wrote several professions of faith, developing the miaphysite perspective on trinitarian and christological issues and concluding with a list of anathemas.[40] In a pastoral role, he composed funeral sermons, prayers, baptismal and eucharistic liturgies.[41]

The most effective and prolific genre utilized by Philoxenos was the letter. De Halleux lists nineteen letters on dogmatic issues and eight on spiritual and moral issues.[42] One of the longest and most significant letters on the spiritual life is the *Letter to Patricius of Edessa*.[43]

[37] Bruce M. Metzger, *The Early Versions of the New Testament* (Oxford: Clarendon, 1977), 65–68.

[38] De Halleux, *Philoxène*, 118–28. See S. P. Brock, "The Resolution of the Philoxenian/Harclean Problem," in *New Testament Textual Criticism: Its Significance for Exegesis. Essays in Honour of Bruce M. Metzger*, ed. Eldon Jay Epp and Gordon D. Fee (Oxford: Clarendon, 1981), 325–43.

[39] De Halleux, *Philoxène*, 128–62.

[40] De Halleux, *Philoxène*, 168–87.

[41] De Halleux, *Philoxène*, 290–308.

[42] De Halleux, *Philoxène*, 187–223, 253–74.

[43] *Lettre à Patricius d'Édesse de Philoxène de Mabboug*, ed. René Lavenant, *Patrologia Orientalis* 30.5 (1963).

Nevertheless, "probably the most read and recopied work"[44] of Philoxenos was his collection of thirteen *mēmrē* or *Discourses* on the ascetical life.

Scholarship on Philoxenos and the Discourses

Following the magisterial dissertation of André de Halleux in 1963, virtually all scholarship concerning Philoxenos has had to commence from De Halleux's work.[45] Not only did this volume catalogue nearly everything Philoxenian, but the Belgian scholar was producing as well critical editions and translations of a number of unedited treatises and letters by Philoxenos.[46] As his title indicates, De Halleux constructs a life of Philoxenos from a number of disparate sources, followed by a descriptive catalogue of any text in any language associated with the author, and concluding with a synthetic survey of his Christology and soteriology, in which it is not surprising that the *Discourses* provide a substantial portion of the sources. De Halleux epitomizes Philoxenos' understanding of the Christian pilgrimage in a "double becoming"—God becomes human in order that the human being becomes God—the first becoming is the incarnation or Christology and the second is divinization or soteriology.[47]

---

[44] De Halleux, *Philoxène*, 283.

[45] De Halleux, *Philoxène*.

[46] De Halleux, André, "'Nouveaux textes inédits de Philoxène de Mabbog. I: Lettre aux moines de Palestine; Lettre liminaire au synodicon d'Éphèse,'" *Le Muséon* 75.1–2 (1962): 31–62; "'Nouveaux textes inédits de Philoxène de Mabbog. II: Lettre aux moines orthodoxes d'Orient,'" *Le Muséon* 76.1–2 (1963): 5–26; Éli de Qartamin. *Memra sur S. Mar Philoxène de Mabbog*. CSCO 233–34, Syri. 100–101 Louvain: Secrétariat du CSCO, 1963); Philoxène de Mabbog. *Lettre aux moines de Senoun*. CSCO 231–32, Syr. 98–99 (Louvain: Secrétariat du CSCO, 1963); Philoxène de Mabbog. *Commentaire du prologue johannique (Ms. Br. Mus. Add. 14, 534)*. CSCO 380–81, Syr. 165–66. (Louvain: Secrétariat du CSCO, 1977); "La deuxième Lettre de Philoxène aux Monastères du Beit Gaugal," *Le Muséon* 96.1–2 (1983): 5–79.

[47] De Halleux, *Philoxène*, 317, 397–98.

The Oxford dissertation of Roberta C. Chesnut (Bondi), *Three Monophysite Christologies*,[48] presented a rich investigation of the doctrines that made Philoxenos distinctive. Her comparative study, along with the Christologies of Severus of Antioch and Jacob of Serug, centers primarily, though not totally, on the *Discourses* or the *Thirteen Homilies* as the source of Philoxenos' miaphysite Christology. This emphasis goes against the grain of several other scholars who see no evidence of miaphysite theology in the *Discourses*. Chesnut begins with the "double being" of Christ—God by nature, human by a miracle—then moves to the "two births," the birth of the Word from the Father and the birth of the humanity from Mary.[49] Chesnut examines closely Philoxenos' provocative emphasis on the *mixture* of natures and concludes that while he knew that the subtleties would not always be understood, he admitted he was drawing on the vocabulary and tradition of the Syriac biblical exegete Ephrem (d. 373).[50] Chesnut's final section analyzes the character of divine knowledge that according to Philoxenos is perceived by means of faith, a faculty outside of or beyond the natural knowledge of the world. At a deeper level, the content of this knowledge is acquired through *theoria*, "spiritual contemplation," though for all practical purposes not as such in the *Discourses*.[51]

Roberta Chesnut Bondi did not write another major work on Philoxenos, but the bishop did not let her go easily. Mentioning Philoxenos in several other books and essays intended for a more general theological readership, Bondi relates how he was that particular author she encountered in the Bodleian Library who gently ignited in her a renewed spiritual pilgrimage.[52]

---

[48] Roberta C. Chesnut, *Three Monophysite Christologies: Severus of Antioch, Philoxenus of Mabbug, and Jacob of Sarug* (Oxford Theological Monographs; Oxford: OUP, 1976), 57–112.

[49] Chesnut, 57–65.

[50] Chesnut, 65–70.

[51] Chesnut, 102–11.

[52] Roberta Chesnut Bondi, *To Love as God Loves* (Minneapolis: Fortress Press, 1987), 7; *Memories of God: A Reflection on a Theological Life* (Nashville,

A unique study of Philoxenos was undertaken by Guy Lardreau in a small monograph, *Discours philosophique et discours spirituel: Autour de la philosophie spirituelle de Philoxène de Mabboug.*[53] While neither a theologian nor a student of Syriac Christianity, Lardreau recognized that philosophy and theology are frequently discussing the same thing in a particular text. His experimental study approaches the same text first with a philosophical methodology and then from the perspective of spiritual theology, attempting to discover "le point de fracture" between the two approaches. Primarily focusing on the *Discourses* of Philoxenos, Lardreau draws in a number of other Philoxenian texts in translation, as well as academic studies. His experiment aside, Lardreau offers a number of incisive comments on aspects of the *Discourses* which Lavenant lifts out for numerous footnotes to his revised translation of the *Homélies.*[54] Lardreau's analysis notes that the dominant theme of Philoxenos' corpus is that of return and restoration to the original condition of humanity, epitomized by baptism, and that of perfection seen from the vantage of Eden.[55]

Volker Menze's monograph *Justinian and the Making of the Syrian Orthodox Church*[56] begins at the point Philoxenos leaves the stage, focusing on the three decades following Justin I's ascendancy to the emperor's throne and the deposition of Philoxenos and other anti-Chalcedonian bishops and clergy in 519. Menze's study is historical. It chronicles the rise of the Syrian Orthodox Church and its leadership, rather than examining the theological debates during

---

TN: Abingdon Press, 1995), 72, 76, 133; "Monastic Mentors (Luke 20:27-35)," *The Christian Century*, November 2, 2004, 16.

[53] Guy Lardreau, *Discours philosophique et discours spirituel: Autour de la philosophie spirituelle de Philoxène de Mabboug* (Paris: Éditions du Seuil, 1985).

[54] Philoxène de Mabboug, *Homélies*, trans. Eugène Lemoine SCh 44 (Paris: Éditions du Cerf, 1956); new and revised edition, SCh 44bis (Paris: Éditions du Cerf, 2007)—footnotes to text on the following pages of SCh 44bis: 81, 174, 179, 261, 274, 311, 328, 331, 333, 342, 367, 389, 403, 453, 495, 500, 510, 513.

[55] Lardreau, *Discours philosophique*, 79–134.

[56] Volker L. Menze, *Justinian and the Making of the Syrian Orthodox Church* (Oxford: OUP, 2008).

this period. Nevertheless, Menze presents a thorough introduction to the political and ecclesiastical controversies, including Philoxenos' role in the temporary dominance of the anti-Chalcedonian faction. Inevitably, the size and scope of Philoxenos' corpus enticed new students to investigate old assumptions. The 2007 Princeton dissertation of David A. Michelson has challenged and corrected some of these assumptions and moved the study of Philoxenos in fresh new directions.[57] Michelson demonstrates how the christological concerns dominating many of Philoxenos' letters are found as well in the *Discourses*, contrary to the traditional perception that the bishop's most popular work is free of the doctrinal issues and debates of that turbulent period. Essentially, Philoxenos rejects the validity of theological speculation, subtly libeling the content and method of Greek Chalcedonian thought, and insists on the epistemological primacy of faith as a kind of sixth sense. Michelson fills out the increasing attention given to the relationship of Philoxenos to the concepts and writings of Evagrius Ponticus.[58]

A historically significant figure like Philoxenos demands more scholarly attention. The first ever symposium on Philoxenos was organized by David Michelson in May 2008 at the Center of Theological Inquiry (CTI), Princeton, New Jersey, under the auspices of CTI and the Center for the Study of Religion, Princeton University. The papers presented provided the impetus for a double issue of *Hugoye: Journal of Syriac Studies* in 2010.[59] Philoxenos' wide range of interests is reflected in the articles. Michelson initiated both the conference and the *Hugoye* volume with a thorough overview of what has been discovered about Philoxenos in the years since De

---

[57] David A. Michelson, *Practice Leads to Theory: Orthodoxy and the Spiritual Struggle in the World of Philoxenos of Mabbug (470–523)* (PhD dissertation; Princeton University, 2007).

[58] Michelson, 50–72. See the section below on the Evagrian influence on Philoxenos.

[59] *Hugoye: Journal of Syriac Studies* 13.1–2 (2010). Special Issue on Philoxenos of Mabbug, David A. Michelson and Robert A. Kitchen, guest editors. http://www.bethmardutho.org/index.php/hugoye/volume-index/83 .html.

Halleux.[60] Daniel King examines closely early translations of Cyril of Alexandria from Greek into Syriac and notes how the Philoxenian version (507) of the New Testament appears to follow the former's lead in the development of the mirror-image strategy of translation —the Syriac translator attempts to conform precisely to the Greek in morphology and grammatical structure.[61] There is no extant text of the Philoxenian version, except perhaps in the writings of Philoxenos. James E. Walters aligns a number of Philoxenos' biblical citations with the *Peshitta* and reputed Harklean citations to compare theological and philological values.[62]

Fr. Roger-Youssef Akhrass treats Philoxenos' affirmative understanding of Mary as *Theotokos* as a window into the bishop's Christology, moving from the virginal conception and birth to the eternal generation of the Son in the incarnation.[63] The most prolific of Philoxenos' literary genres is the letter, written over a period of forty years. Dana Iuliana Viezure analyzes and groups these letters into four periods, the emphasis shifting from scriptural reasoning and paradox to a strident targeting of the personal background of the heretics rather than the heresies, then finally to a more gracious attitude toward opponents developed through contact with the issues and strategies of Greek miaphysite thought.[64] Adam C. McCollum deals with a recurrent problem in late antique texts, here the false attribution of Philoxenos to a text clearly not written by him.[65]

[60] David A. Michelson, "Introduction to Hugoye 13: A Double Issue on Philoxenos of Mabbug," *Hugoye* 13.1 (2010): 3–8.

[61] Daniel King, "New Evidence on the Philoxenian Version of the New Testament and Nicene Creed," *Hugoye* 13 (2010): 9–30.

[62] J. Edward Walters, "The Philoxenian Gospels as Reconstructed from the Writings of Philoxenos of Mabbug," *Hugoye* 13 (2010): 177–249.

[63] Roger-Youssef Akhrass, "La Vierge Mère de Dieu dans la pensée de Philoxène de Mabboug," *Hugoye* 13 (2010): 31–48.

[64] Dana Iuliana Viezure, "Argumentative Strategies on Philoxenos of Mabbug's Correspondence: From the Syriac Model to the Greek Model," *Hugoye* 13 (2010): 149–75.

[65] Adam C. McCollum, "An Arabic Scholion to Genesis 9:18-21 (Noah's Drunkenness) Attributed to Philoxenos of Mabbug," *Hugoye* 13 (2010): 125–48.

An Arabic scholion on the drunkenness of Noah (Genesis 9:18-21) identified as that of Philoxenos is shown by McCollum probably to be from Ephrem as it matches up with several Ephremic hymns and commentaries on this text.

The *Discourses* receive their due in a double dose. For my part, I demonstrate how the tenth *mēmrā* on gluttony or "the lust of the belly" functions as the critical dividing line for the ascetical development of the upright and perfect in the monastic community. Once one has tamed the lust of the belly, all the other thoughts and temptations are readily vanquished.[66] I also submitted a review article of the revised translation and introduction of the *Discourses* in the French patristic series *Sources Chrétiennes*.[67]

A different perspective to be treated more fully below is the transcription by David Odorisio of a lecture by Thomas Merton to monk novices in 1965 on Philoxenos' spirituality.[68] A fitting conclusion to the volume is a bibliographic clavis to the works of Philoxenos by David Michelson, the most extensive bibliography on this author.[69]

The *Discourses*: The Ascetical Homilies

The starting point for all modern studies of the *Discourses* has been Budge's two-volume edition of the Syriac text with an English

---

[66] Robert A. Kitchen, "The Lust of the Belly Is the Beginning of All Sin. Practical Theology of Asceticism in the Discourses of Philoxenos of Mabbug," *Hugoye* 13 (2010): 49–63.

[67] Robert A. Kitchen, "Philoxène de Mabboug. Homélies. Introduction, traduction et notes par Eugène Lemoine. Nouvelle édition revue par René Lavenant, S.J. *Sources Chrétiennes* 44bis (Paris: les Éditions du Cerf, 2007)," *Hugoye* 13 (2010): 65–73.

[68] David Odorisio, "Thomas Merton's Novitiate Conferences on Philoxenos of Mabbug (April–June 1965): Philoxenos on the Foundations of the Spiritual Life and the Recovery of Simplicity," *Hugoye* 13 (2010): 251–71.

[69] David A. Michelson, "A Bibliographic Clavis to the Works of Philoxenos of Mabbug," *Hugoye* 13 (2010): 273–338.

translation and introduction.[70] Using Budge's Syriac text as its base, the French patristic sources series *Sources Chrétiennes* has produced French translations, initially by Eugène Lemoine and a revision by René Lavenant.[71] This new English translation is also based on Budge's Syriac text.

Budge consulted nineteen manuscripts in the Nitrian collection of Syriac manuscripts in the British Library to construct his critical edition. Nine of the manuscripts have little value since they contain only short passages, but the other ten provide much useful material, dating from the sixth to eleventh centuries. Eight were then chosen to form the critical edition. The seventh- or ninth-century Ms. A (BL Add. 14598), containing all thirteen discourses or *mēmrē*, was selected as the base text by Budge, while the sixth-century Ms. B (BL Add. 14595) operated as a close guide for the last six *mēmrē*. Budge also appealed to the older authority of the sixth-century Ms. C (BL Add. 12163) as well as the ninth-century Ms. D (BL Add. 17153). The other four manuscripts from which variant readings were taken are: sixth- or seventh-century Ms. E (BL Add. 14596); tenth- or eleventh-century Ms. F (BL Add. 14525); ninth-century Ms. G (BL Add. 14601); dated 802 Ms. H (BL Add. 14621).[72] The most significant manuscript that Budge did not utilize is the twelfth-century Bibliothèque Nationale de France Syrus 201: ff. 1–161. This manuscript also includes the primary manuscript of the *Book of Steps/Liber Graduum* (ff. 174–280).

The French translation of the *Discourses* by Lemoine in *Sources Chrétiennes* was the first Syriac text to appear in the new series, and it was this translation that Thomas Merton would pick up and devour. Lemoine believes that the *Discourses* were written to be read in the monastery and were edited specifically for this purpose.[73] Seeing no traces of miaphysitism in the *Discourses*,[74] Lemoine confirmed the

---

[70] *The Discourses of Philoxenos, Bishop of Mabbôgh*, ed. E. A. W. Budge, 2 vols. (London, 1894).

[71] See n. 54; see n. 67, Kitchen, "Philoxène de Mabboug. Homélies."

[72] Budge, *Discourses*, 2:lxvi–lxxiii.

[73] SCh 44bis:12–13.

[74] SCh 44bis:15.

earlier observations of Irenée Hausherr that the christological ideas of the miaphysites had no influence on their ascetical and mystical teachings.[75] In a later article Lemoine characterized Philoxenos' literary style as "often cadenced, rhythmic, clear and limpid,"[76] excelling in symmetrical and well-balanced comparatives and parallelisms.

Organization and Strategies of the Discourses

The thirteen *Discourses* begin with an introductory *mēmrā*, and then proceed with six pairs of *mēmrē*, each pair treating a single topic. The pairs are: Faith (2 and 3); Simplicity (4 and 5); Fear of God (6 and 7); Renunciation of the World (8 and 9); Gluttony (10 and 11); and Fornication (12 and 13).

While maintaining that the *Discourses* are a unified work, Budge noted that "they were frequently divided into two volumes; the first volume contained the first nine, and the second volume the last four of the *Discourses*."[77] Mss. C and D are of the "first volume," while B and E belong to this "second volume."[78]

Budge speculates that Philoxenos intended the *Discourses* to be a supplement or sequel to the twenty-two *Demonstrations* of Aphrahat.[79] To underline the literary connection Budge included a translation of Aphrahat's first Demonstration, also titled "On Faith," in the edition of the *Discourses*.[80]

---

[75] Irénée Hausherr, "Contemplation et Sainteté: Une remarquable mise au point par Philoxène de Mabboug," *Révue d'ascétique et de mystique* 14 (1933): 15.

[76] Eugène Lemoine, "Physionomie d'un moine Syrien: Philoxène de Mabboug," *L'Orient Syrien* 3 (1958): 101.

[77] Budge, *Discourses*, 2:lxxiii.

[78] Budge, *Discourses*, 2:xciv–xcv. A table of the manuscripts and the distribution of the *mēmrē* in each manuscript.

[79] Budge, *Discourses*, 2:lxxiii–lxxiv. See for the Syriac text with Latin translation, *Aphraatis Sapientis Persae Demonstrationes*, ed. J(ean) Parisot, PS 1 & 2 (Paris, 1894, 1907); *The Demonstrations of Aphrahat, the Persian Sage*, trans. Adam Lehto (Piscataway, NJ: Gorgias Press, 2010).

[80] Budge, *Discourses*, 2:clxxv–clxxxvii.

Lemoine attempted to discern a pattern in Philoxenos' organization of the *Discourses* and developed a theory that stimulated a great deal of debate.[81] He observed that in each pair of *mēmrē* written on the same topic the ideas of the first were relatively simple, while the ideas of the second were more sophisticated. Lemoine concluded that Philoxenos combined in his *Discourses* two series of *mēmrē* written at different times for different purposes. Initially, Philoxenos dealt with each topic in a *mēmrā*, but after a certain interval of time he reworked his ideas into a more theologically mature second homily. During this interval Lemoine perceived Philoxenos' thought becoming more mystical.

Filling out the skeleton of his theory, Lemoine showed that usually the first member of each pair was written in a moralistic tone "with the memory of what is said in the Holy Books"; the second member was written in a mystical tone "with the experience of what is said in the Holy Books."[82]

The further Lemoine tried to demonstrate his theory the more it began to unravel. On closer analysis, Lemoine placed two *mēmrē*, the fourth on simplicity and the sixth on the fear of God, out of their expected sequence. Although these two *mēmrē* are the first ones to deal with their respective topics, Lemoine assigned them to the second mystical series because they emphasize mystical ideas and experience. Moreover, Lemoine wrote, Philoxenos himself indicated the original order of the *mēmrē* in the fifth Discourse: "We spoke in our preceding discourse [On Faith] of simplicity and innocence; it is of that useful subject that I wish to speak again now" (m.5.1; 120:13–16). The fifth Discourse, therefore, should have been in the fourth position.[83]

After this analysis, Lemoine's division of the *Discourses* is as follows: moralistic discourses: 2, 5, 7, 8, 10, 12; mystical discourses: 3, 4, 6, 9, 11, 13.

[81] SCh 44bis:20–24.
[82] SCh 44bis:163.
[83] SCh 44bis:90–91.

The major problem with Lemoine's theory is that his classification of moralistic and mystical is too subjective, for depending on the definition of these concepts, one could contest the classification either way of any of the *Discourses*.

This theory was not allowed to rest long. Hausherr quickly responded, highly praising Lemoine's translation but questioning his two-series theory.[84] In particular, Hausherr was puzzled by Lemoine's juggling of the order of the second and third pairs. Observing that Lemoine's analysis relied on the appearance of the mystical conception of experience, Hausherr rejected this concept as a reliable criterion and concluded that neither an internal nor external analysis justifies such a transposition of *mēmrē*. The *Discourses* of Philoxenos, as we have them now, are in the exact order that Philoxenos intended from the first edition.

Nevertheless, Hausherr believed that Philoxenos had developed a spiritual dichotomy in the *Discourses*. In each pair there appears to be a division into two stages or states of life that are different, but in continuity with each other.[85] By implication, these two stages of life are those of the upright (*kēnē*) and the perfect (*gmīrē*).

Jean Gribomont entered the discussion gingerly, responding both to Lemoine's work as well as to Hausherr's reaction. After reviewing the arguments of both scholars, Gribomont tacitly accepted Hausherr's opinion.[86] T. Jansma also published a thorough review article in which he detailed inaccurate translations of terms,[87] which Lavenant would later credit as one of his sources of amendment to Lemoine's translation.[88]

De Halleux also offered a schema of the *Discourses*, observing that the traditional collection of thirteen *mēmrē* is probably an incom-

---

[84] Irenée Hausherr, "Spiritualité Syrienne: Philoxène de Mabboug," OC 23 (1957): 171–85.

[85] Hauser, "Spiritualité Syrienne," 176.

[86] J. Gribomont, "Les Homélies Ascétiques de Philoxène de Mabbog et l'écho du Messalianisme," *OrSyr* 2 (1957): 419–32.

[87] T. Jansma, "[Review of] E. Lemoine, *Philoxène de Mabboug. Homélies*," VC 12 (1958): 233–37.

[88] R. Lavenant, *Homélies* (2007), 7.

plete or unfinished work. In the introductory *mēmrā* De Halleux sees Philoxenos proposing a three-part outline: the second through seventh *mēmrē* deal with the beginning of the spiritual life or the "degree of the body"; the eighth through thirteenth *mēmrē* show the progress of the individual in the struggle against the passions or the "degree of the soul"; while the third part was to examine the "degree of the spirit." A series of ninth- to eleventh-century manuscripts reproduce ascetical florilegia that include extracts of the ninth and thirteenth *mēmrē* along with fragments on humility, penitence, and prayer.[89] These fragments, de Halleux suggests, are from the last *mēmrē* of the third part, the "degree of the spirit."[90]

De Halleux's analysis appears a more comfortable fit to the themes of the existing *mēmrē*. The first three pairs on faith, simplicity, and the fear of God project the sense of a primer in the essentials of the spiritual life. There is a change in tone entering *mēmrā* 8, in which is treated the more concrete issue of worldly renunciation for the monk who has only recently gone out from the world. The passions of the lust of the belly and of the lust of fornication are, as Philoxenos identifies, the two fundamental passions against which one must initially struggle once inside the monastery walls.

Yet despite his rambling and length of argument stretching to 625 pages in the critical text, Philoxenos seems far from finished. Noticeably absent are discussions of some of the other traditional disciplines of the way of life of perfection: humility, prayer, solitude. De Halleux's hunch from the later florilegia fits well into this perception.

However, there is another possible key to Philoxenos' schema, especially in his second section, "the degree of the soul." It has been recognized that Philoxenos knew of and read Evagrius Ponticus.[91]

---

[89] F. Graffin, "Le florilège patristique de Philoxène de Mabbog," I. Ortiz de Urbina, ed., *Symposium Syriacum, 1972* (Rome: Pontificium Institutum Orientalium Studiorum, 1974), OCA 197 (1974): 267–90.

[90] De Halleux, *Philoxène*, 285–86.

[91] See Paul Harb, "L'attitude de Philoxène de Mabboug à l'égard de la spiritualité 'savante' d'Évagre le Pontique," *Mémorial Mgr. Gabriel Khouri-Sarkis (1898–1968)*, ed. F. Graffin (Louvain: Imprimerie orientaliste, 1969),

One of Evagrius' more enduring contributions has been his identifications of the eight vices or "principal thoughts."[92] The first two are gluttony or the lust of the belly and the lust of fornication—the second and third pairs following the renunciation of the world in Philoxenos' so-called second section. It could be construed that Philoxenos intended to complete the series of principal thoughts: love of money, sadness, anger, listlessness, vainglory, and pride. Then he would move on to treat the topics of "the degree of the spirit" of which we have already been afforded a glimpse. However, there are no known selections of Philoxenos' writing lurking in florilegia and other ascetical collections that deal with the other "thoughts."[93]

In the absence of further evidence it is more prudent to agree with the conclusions of Hausherr and Gribomont that the *Discourses* we have received are the intended complete *Discourses*. Attractive and convincing as de Halleux's schema may be, we do not have any manuscripts that exhibit in a recognizable form that they belong to the third part.

The absence of historical references makes the date of the *Discourses* difficult to ascertain. Budge believed they were written between 485 and 508, and complete copies of the *Discourses* were found in Egyptian monasteries in the early sixth century, identifying Philoxenos as the bishop of Mabbug. Budge reasoned, therefore, that 485 must be the earliest date for that is the year of Philoxenos'

135–36. Also, John W. Watt, "Philoxenos and the Old Syriac Version of Evagrius' Centuries," *OrChr* 64 (1980): 65–81.

[92] Jeremy Driscoll, *The 'Ad Monachos' of Evagrius Ponticus: Its Structure and a Select Commentary Studia Anselmiana* 104 (Rome: Benedictina Edizioni Abbazia S. Paolo, 1991), 12–17.

[93] Grigory Kessel has undertaken a research project funded by the German Research Foundation (DFG), "Syriac monastic anthologies as a source for the history of Syriac Christianity: Reception and transmission of Syriac and Greek monastic literature." Kessel reports in a preliminary fashion that there are numerous excerpts from the *Discourses* in these monastic anthologies which have not yet been analyzed.

consecration.[94] On the other hand, Budge assumes that 508, the year of the appearance of the Philoxenian Bible, had to be the latest date because Budge had previously determined that all biblical quotations in the *Discourses* were taken from the *Peshitta*.[95] This assumes too much about Philoxenos' use of Scripture and presumes that Polycarp's version was given immediate canonical status.

The other scholars do not attempt such elaborate reasoning. Lemoine believes the *Discourses* were written before his episcopate, that is, before 485;[96] Gribomont thinks they were written about 485;[97] De Halleux concludes that the *Discourses* were probably written sometime during his episcopate for the monks under his jurisdiction.[98] The latter, general as it may be, makes the most sense for it takes into account most fully Philoxenos' intended audience.

Summary of the Discourses[99]

First mēmrā: *Introduction (3–25).* Philoxenos urges first laying the foundation of wisdom with the appropriate building blocks in the correct order. One needs to be able to recognize the various lusts and passions with which one does battle and against which spiritual masters guide us, prescribing the right medicines or antidotes against these passions. A long list of spiritual antidotes to counter various passions of sin is presented. Philoxenos promises to show the reader/listener how to begin and then advance up through all the grades of the Christian life until one reaches Perfection.

Second mēmrā: *On Faith (26–51).* The first building block is that of faith (ܗܝܡܢܘܬܐ- *haymānūtā*) to which Philoxenos will devote two *mēmrē*. Everyone should have the kind of faith that accepts God,

---

[94] Budge, *Discourses*, 2:lxxiii.

[95] Budge, *Discourses*, 2:ix.

[96] SCh 44bis:14.

[97] Gribomont, 420–21.

[98] De Halleux, *Philoxène*, 288.

[99] The numbers in parentheses following the title of the *Discourse/Mēmrā* are the page numbers in Budge's Syriac text. Other references will indicate a citation as (*mēmrā.* section; page: line numbers).

but neither questions nor challenges him. However, the eye of faith, which one possesses by God's grace, is able to see deeply into the secret things of God. All should approach God with the mind of a child, and so through our second birth, which is baptism, we are taught by God as infants. Faith is the tongue and command of God the Creator. Sometimes faith does not even pray first but gives an authoritative command like God, as was the case with Elijah, Jesus, and others. Jesus made faith the foundation of the Church and we should make faith the beginning of our life in God, for without faith all other spiritual activities are ineffectual.

Third mēmrā: *On Faith (52–73).* Faith is the activity of God in the new creation just as wisdom was utilized in the beginning. Faith is required for the efficacy of baptism and communion. Knowledge is external to created things, while faith, unobservable by the physical senses, is within the thing itself. Without faith the eyes see the things of the Church as common and poor, while the things of the world are perceived as powerful and rich. If one seeks in faith he believes in God; but if he desires in faith he believes in idols. Faith alone should be the cause of one's going forth from the world into the monastery.

Fourth mēmrā: *On Simplicity (74–119).* The second pair of *mēmrē* is on the theme of simplicity (ܦܫܝܛܘܬܐ- *pšīṭūtā*) which Philoxenos defines as the "singleness of one thought." Abraham responded to the call of God with faith and simplicity, as did the apostles, while Adam lived in simplicity until the Enemy made him use cunning and question God's command to him. God is "Simple," for in God there are no structures or parts. The desert is perceived as the source of simplicity: the primary reason for Israel's wandering in the wilderness was to teach them simplicity. If you were cunning (ܚܪܥܘܬܐ - *ḥēr'ūtā*) you would not have followed God who called you to the monastery and eventually you would have despised instruction.

Fifth mēmrā: *On Simplicity (120–58).* Simplicity is fitting for the life of the solitary and ascetic, those who have forsaken the world and become strangers to it, for in the monastery there is no competition, property, or power in which cunning can become involved. In this angelic way of life, cunning is considered a disease since it encourages wickedness to act out its deeds. A simple person should be called in a positive sense "a child." Jesus chose fishermen who were innocent, but since some sought positions of honor he had to teach them more about childlikeness. Just as a king or person of worldly honor denies knowing about lowly crafts, we should not know about the cunning of the world in our simplicity. Those who are simple are more admired and loved by others than the cunning ones. Simplicity is the beginning of the path of Christ, but purity of spirit is its end. The apostles, therefore, began as simple ones, but after receiving the Holy Spirit became pure human beings.

Sixth mēmrā: *On the Fear of God (159–90).* The third pair of *mēmrē* is on the fear of God (ܪܚܠܬ ܐܠܗܐ - *deḥlat 'alāhā*). Meditation on God increases the fear of God in us, by which Philoxenos means an ecstatic feeling in the soul that makes the whole body "tremble." Essential for this fear is the remembrance of God, for if one sins and does not remember or think of God's punishment and disappointment, one's soul is dead. If one is conscious of his sins the fear of God will increase continually within himself. The fear of God is born from faith but is also the preserver of faith. Adam and later Cain cast away their fear and as a consequence lost their faith. The commandments are kept by three things: by fear (servants), by reward (hirelings), by love (spiritual beings and friends).

Seventh mēmrā: *On the Fear of God (191–221).* Philoxenos returns to the methodological admonition to climb Jacob's ladder in proper order, as did the upright of old. We should fear God because we have sinned or so that we may not sin. The creation naturally fears God, but loves God by the grace which comes down in search of creation. The country of fear is mortal life, while the country of love is the other world of immortal life. As God's graciousness is revealed to us, we are urged to become like the Father. The ancient revelations of God belonged to fear showing us that he is our God, while the latter revelation is of friendship and love showing us that he is our Father. God lifted up humanity from the fear of death that belongs to time and laid on us the fear of death for eternity.

Eighth mēmrā: *On Renunciation (222–56).* The world is an obstacle to perfection and so commandments were set apart for those in the world (uprightness) and for those above the world (perfection). Wealth, in particular, is an obstacle to meditation on God. Jesus commanded the wealthy to be masters, not slaves, of their wealth, but the perfect are not to be masters even of inanimate objects. The way to perfection is distinguished through renunciation of the world and its possessions in imitation of Jesus the stranger. The upright are also above the law, not doing evil in order not to provoke God to anger. Before baptism Jesus was obedient to his parents and kept the law; after baptism he taught and lived a rule of life more perfect than this and refused to acknowledge his parents. The righteousness of the law is defined as roughly equal to uprightness in this world.

Ninth mēmrā: *On Renunciation (257–352).* The second *mēmrā* on renunciation is the longest of the *Discourses* and is found in some manuscripts as an epitome and summation of the *Discourses.* A case in point is the recent publication of a lost text ascribed to Gregory of Nyssa, which turned out to be a collection of excerpts from this Ninth Discourse of Philoxenos.[100]

Jesus' going out into the wilderness is considered the primary example of renunciation for those who wish to be perfect. The metaphor presented is of one leaving the natural womb of this world, renouncing all possessions, and going naked into the Christian life. The natural child proceeds out of nonexistence into existence; the child of the Spirit is born into becoming a son of God. An infant cannot be an adult in the womb and so a person cannot be perfect in the world. As the infant casts off the umbilical cord, so the person born from the world must cast off his own passions and physical appetites.

One becomes truly rich by not needing anything, so Philoxenos urges monks to depart from the world possessing nothing. The monk will have two baptisms: one of water and one of one's own free will. On leaving the world the monk has temptations and memories of past transgressions, as well as concerns regarding

---

[100] Martien F. G. Parmentier, "Pseudo-Gregory of Nyssa's Homily on Poverty," *Aram* 5 (1993): 401–26.

the future hardships of asceticism. The monk must divide his austerities as Moses divided the sea, leaving Satan and the demons drowned in the depth of one's tribulations. One now enters a new country with one's enemies vanquished behind him, a new spiritual world of great joy and benefit.

Philoxenos examines the life of John the Baptist as the model of the solitary and ascetic who received the natural innocence (ܫܦܝܘܬ - *šapyūtā*) which Adam possessed before he sinned. Monks are to follow his example and not look back on the separation from family life, looking straight ahead to the new world. A person of God is born three times: from womb into creation; from bondage into freedom (that is, from an ordinary human being into becoming a son of God), accomplished through grace by baptism; and from physical into spiritual life, accomplished through the absolute renunciation of everything. Those who renounce the world are higher than the upright and are dead to the world, while the upright are still alive in the world.

Tenth mēmrā: *On the Lust of the Belly (353–419).* The lust of the belly is the filthiest passion that inhibits rational thought and is the door for all evil, enslaving the soul as well as the body. It inhibits compassion and as the opposite of fasting is the destroyer of prayer and the source of sloth.

The glutton considers doctrine and Scripture idle and superfluous, blaspheming those who practice faith, and calls virtues vices. Yet he unduly criticizes anyone who breaks a fast for necessity. Philoxenos cautions about the connivance of the glutton who tries to counsel an ascetic to be moderate and hears only those Scriptures that support his eating. Philoxenos exhorts the disciples not to be lax in their strenuous asceticism and to beware of falling into the trap of the lust of the belly that will lead to all sorts of vices. Gluttony is the sin of Adam's fall in Eden.

Eleventh mēmrā: *On Abstinence (420–93).*[101] One is not completely worthy of the life of Christ until he extinguishes all appetite for

---

[101] A palimpsest fragment of the eleventh *mēmrā* has recently been discovered in a Melkite manuscript (British Library Oriental 8607), containing

worldly foods. Abstinence gives us birth into the blessing of Christ, which is the beginning of our becoming like the angels.

The lust of the belly contends that food and hunger were given to you by the Creator. Natural hunger needs the power food supplies but should not foster a lust for food. You are god over your own lusts, willing whether they exist or not. If you defeat the first lust (gluttony) you will increase your strength against other lusts. But if you only conquer the rare and expensive foods, you are not completely victorious; defeat common plain foods as well. If possible eat like a dead man; if you eat like one alive, do not taste your food with pleasure which would mean that lust is still alive. Also overcome lust for common garden vegetables, for lust knows it cannot tempt monks with fancy foods. Food itself is not reprehensible, only the lust that eats it. Philoxenos encourages monks to abstain from all kinds of food and to eat without the sensation of taste, seeing the table as a place of struggle rather than pleasure. The apostles did not receive the Holy Spirit until they had led a life of abstinence after leading a life of freedom in Christ.

Twelfth mēmrā: *On Fornication (494–550).* Philoxenos sees the corrupt conversations and stories associated with lustful meals fueling the fire of lust. This lust is placed by God into our bodies for the continuation of the race and in marriage is good, but not for disciples. Defeating this lust is the source of victory and spiritual crowns for the disciples.

An analogy is depicted of a person lured into loving an ugly blind woman, but later he sees the king's beautiful daughter, which is the beauty of Christ. Jesus prohibited disciples from intercourse since God did not place us in the world to perpetuate it, but as a place for spiritual contest in order to gain the crown of victory. The lust of intercourse is left in our members as an adversary. If we lose, it is because of our weakness, not the strength of lust.

---

parts of the text found in pages 480–92 in Budge's edition. See Sebastian P. Brock, "Notulae Syriacae: Some Miscellaneous Identifications," *Le Muséon* 108 (1995): 69–78, esp. 72–73.

The soul must not be mingled with the body and become subject to its lusts. Philoxenos contrasts fornication of body, soul, and spirit with intercourse of the same three. It is not good for the mind to have intercourse with the body, but it is good that the body be an associate with the soul in fortitude. When physical lust arises, the soul must counter with the desire of the soul as an antidote. No crown of glory is achieved if there is no adversary.

Thirteenth mēmrā: *On Fornication (551–625).* If the passion of fornication becomes embedded in the soul for too long it obscures its power of discernment so that the mind does not recognize that it is a passion. The war against hidden lust is more critical than the war waged externally, for external lust is restrained by a number of people and circumstances. We must be inwardly chaste before God. Jesus desired to uproot lust from the soul by not lusting after a woman in one's heart. One should look upon a woman as a beautiful work of God. The reason for monasteries is to avoid distraction, for whoever commits fornication sins against the body of Christ.

Young adulthood (ܥܠܝܡܘܬܐ - *'elaymūtā*) is the primary period of fornication, lust entering one by the sight of women, stories about lust, and meat and drink beyond need. God allowed marriage, lust, riches, and power to remain as originally constituted but commanded the monk to become an alien. Whoever defeats his lusts in the period of early adulthood will become mighty in his soul, for when old and feeble one can redeem the deposits handed over to the soul in young adulthood. But one who has lived entirely in the body will come to a complete end in old age.

In the war against the lust of fornication the best weapon is very little water, for this lust is fed by moisture. The story of Gideon choosing his soldiers to fight against the Midianites through lapping up water is an example of using water sparingly to fight against the sin of fornication symbolized by the Midianites.

Responses to Philoxenos

Philoxenos in Other Tongues

The consensus is that Philoxenos was fluent only in Syriac, although acquainted with a great deal of the Greek christological literature, including Evagrius Ponticus, but almost certainly through translation into Syriac. Nevertheless, at the turn of the sixth century, texts worth reading did not remain monolingual for long. Philoxenos' writings and his reputation were translated into several neighboring languages and cultures which were usually miaphysite.

Syriac literature was being translated at a great pace into Armenian during Philoxenos' period and later, but questions persist about which are authentic translations of Philoxenos' writings and which merely attribute the work of other authors to Philoxenos, a renowned ecclesiastical writer.[102]

The Second Council of Dviv, 555–56, at which Armenian and Syrian clergy met to condemn the Chalcedonianism of the imperial church, Abdisho, a Syrian follower of Julian Halicarnassus, is reputed to have brought with him some unnamed works of Philoxenos, although there is no explicit mention of translation into Armenian in the *Book of Letters*, the record of these meetings and conversations conducted over a number of decades.[103]

A seventh-century Armenian florilegium, the *Seal of Faith*,[104] included four citations of Philoxenos: from the seventeenth Discourse, on "I shall go to my Father" (John 20:17);[105] from the Com-

---

[102] I am grateful for the assistance of Robert W. Thomson in questions of the Armenian Philoxenos.

[103] *Book of Letters* [*Girk' T'lt'oc'*], ed. Y. Ismireanc' (Tiflis, 1901); ed. N. Połarean (Jerusalem, 1994). See N. G. Garsoïan, *L'Eglise arménienne et le grand schisme d'Orient*, CSCO 574, Subsidia 100 (Louvain, 1999), esp. 453, for French translation of some of the letters.

[104] *Seal of Faith* [*Knik' Hawatoy*], ed. K. Tēr-Mkrtč'ean (Ejmiacin, 1914); reprinted as *Sceau de la Foi* (Louvain, 1974).

[105] *Seal of Faith*, 253.

mentary on the Gospel of John (quoting John 10:18);[106] unidentified (concerning Christ's freedom from human passions);[107] reference (not verbal quotation) to his twenty-fifth Discourse (also on Christ's freedom from passions).[108]

The other major Armenian text attributed to Philoxenos was the *Letter on the Three Degrees of the Monastic Life.*[109] An Arabic version circulated as well.[110] This text, widely transmitted under Philoxenos' authorship, has only recently been recognized to be written by the eighth-century Church of the East mystical writer Joseph Ḥazzāyā.[111]

De Halleux indicates that there are no known works attributed to Philoxenos in either Coptic or Georgian.[112] Arabic does not appear to have authentic translations of Philoxenos, though there are several short texts attributed to him.[113] Greek also did not receive Philoxenos openly, as the *Letter to Patricius* was transmitted under the name of Isaac of Nineveh.[114]

A unique Syriac text circulated in Arabic and eventually in Ge'ez was erroneously attributed to Philoxenos: *The Commentary on the Paradise of the Fathers* by Dadīshō' Qaṭrāyā (late seventh century,

---

[106] *Seal of Faith*, 260–61.

[107] *Seal of Faith*, 286.

[108] *Seal of Faith*, 327.

[109] *Vie des saints Pères* [*Vark' srboc' Haranc' ew k'alak'avarowt'iwnk' noc'in est krkin t'argmanouwt'ean naxneac'*], tome 2 (Venice, 1855), 538–62.

[110] See Georg Graf, *Geschichte der Christlichen Arabischen Literatur*, vol. 1, *Studi e Testi* 118 (Cittá del Vaticano: Biblioteca Apostolica Vaticana, 1944), 453, no. 3.

[111] *Joseph Ḥazzāyā. Lettre sur les trois étapes de la vie monastique*, ed. Paul Harb and François Graffin, PO 202 (45.2) (Turnhout: Brepols, 1992); Paul Harb, "Faut-il restituer à Joseph Hazzâyâ la Lettre sur les trois degrés de la vie monastique attribuée à Philoxène de Mabbug?,"*Melto* 4 (1968): 13–36.

[112] A. de Halleux, *Philoxène*, 112.

[113] Graf, 384–85. Thanks to Sidney H. Griffith for this reference.

[114] N. Theotoki, ed., first edition (Leipzig, 1770), second edition (Athens, 1895).

Church of the East).[115] Structured as a series of questions and answers from "the brothers" or novice monks to "the old man" (*sābā*), in some manuscripts consistently identified as Dadīshō' himself, the work treated creatively the stories of the desert fathers collected in Syriac version by an early seventh-century Church of the East author, Ananisho.[116] In one of the question/answer sections, the old man is identified as Philoxenos,[117] possibly to provide a miaphysite writer in place of a Church of the East author for the readership of a particular manuscript. There is no record of explanation, but when translated into Arabic and from Arabic into Ge'ez the reputed author of the collection is Philoxenos. In the Ethiopian Church, the *Filekseyus* had gained the position of one of "The Book of Three Monks" utilized as the ascetical and spiritual manual for novice monks for centuries. The other two books are also translations of Syriac Church of the East authors transmitted through Arabic: Isaac of Nineveh and John Saba of Dalyatha.[118]

---

[115] A critical edition, French translation, and introduction are being prepared by David Phillips and Jean-Claude Haelewyck for the series *Sources Chrétiennes*. See David Phillips, "The Syriac Commentary of Dadisho' Qatraya on the Paradise of the Fathers: Towards a Critical Edition," BABELAO 1 (2012): 1–23. http://www.uclouvain.be/cps/ucl/doc/ir-inca/images/BABELAO_I_2012_1_D._Phillips.pdf.

[116] *The Paradise or Garden of the Holy Fathers, Being Histories of the Anchorites, Recluses, Monks, Coenobites, and Ascetic Fathers of the Deserts of Egypt between A.D. CCL and A.D. CCCC circiter*, trans. Ernest A. Wallis Budge (London: Chatto & Windus, 1907); Syriac text: *The Book of Paradise*, 2 vols., ed. E. W. Budge, Lady Meux Manuscripts 6 (London: Lady Meux, 1904).

[117] Nicholas Sims-Williams, "Dādišo' Qatrāyā's Commentary on the Paradise of the Fathers," A Boll 112 (1994): 33–64; esp. 45–47.

[118] Witold Witakowski, "*Filekseyus,* the Ethiopic Version of the Syriac Dadisho Qatraya's *Commentary on the Paradise of the Fathers*," Walatta Yohanna, *Ethiopian Studies in Honour of Joanna Mantel-Niećko, Rocznik Orientalistyczny* 51.1 (Warsaw: Oriental Institute Warsaw University, 2006); R. A. Kitchen, "Dadisho Qatraya's Commentary on Abba Isaiah: The Apophthegmata Patrum Connection," SP 41 (2006): 35–50.

Two other works circulate in Ge'ez under the name of Philoxenos: a prayer of Philoxenos[119] and a homily on Simeon who carried the baby Jesus.[120]

Thomas Merton on Philoxenos

A surprising student and expositor of Philoxenos was Thomas Merton, OCSO (1915–68), a monk of the Abbey of Gethsemani in Kentucky and widely read author on the spiritual and monastic life. Merton introduced many in the general reading public to the Sayings of the Desert Fathers (*Apophthegmata Patrum*), comparing them with the stories of Zen Buddhist masters.[121] Merton went further into Eastern Church literature, reading Eugène Lemoine's French translation of the *Discourses* of Philoxenos of Mabbug in the 1956 edition in the *Sources Chrétiennes* series, the same text being translated in this volume. Philoxenos would also figure in one of Merton's essays in *Raids on the Unspeakable*.[122] When Merton became novice master at Gethsemani, he began a thorough introduction into the history and character of monastic spirituality. The extensive notes he compiled for these lectures are now being published, the second volume focusing on Eastern spirituality, and in particular

---

[119] A great number of Ethiopic or Ge'ez manuscripts are on microfilm or digitized in the collection of Hill Museum and Manuscript Library (HMML), Saint John's University, Collegeville, Minnesota. The following are in the Ethiopian Manuscript Microfilm Library (EMML): EMML Pr. 1867–3: "Prayer of Philoxenus of Mabbug," ff. 133a–137b; also, EMML 2213 (2) Ff. 169b–175b; EMML 2793 (1) Ff. 1a–4b.

[120] EMML Pr. No. 1763: "Homily by Philoxenus of Mabbug on how Simeon carried Jesus in his arms," ff. 129a–132b.

[121] Thomas Merton, *The Wisdom of the Desert: Sayings from the Desert Fathers of the Fourth Century* (New York: New Directions Publishing, 1960) (Merton translated selected apophthegmata from the Latin version, *Verba Seniorum*); *Zen and the Birds of Appetite* (New York: New Directions Publishing, 1968), especially the chapter "Wisdom in Emptiness. A Dialogue: D.T. Suzuki and Thomas Merton," 99–138.

[122] Thomas Merton, "Rain and the Rhinoceros," *Raids on the Unspeakable* (New York: New Directions Publishing, 1966), 9–23.

a forty-six-page section devoted primarily to his commentary on Philoxenos' *Discourses*.[123] The Thomas Merton Center at Bellarmine University, Louisville, Kentucky, possesses an archive of taped recordings of Merton's novice conferences. David Odorisio has published transcripts of four of these conferences that focus on Philoxenos, delivered from April to June 1965.[124]

Merton also dealt with Aphrahat and Ephrem, the two primary fourth-century Syriac authors, so in his preface to *Pre-Benedictine Monasticism* Sidney H. Griffith worked to locate the Syriac tradition for those primarily interested in reading Merton. Griffith observed, "It is startling to find in his novitiate conferences what one now realizes must have been the first general survey in America of several of the works of the major 'monastic' thinkers among the Syriac-speaking Fathers of the Church."[125]

Merton had no pretensions to a scholarly assessment of Philoxenos, but he was captivated by Philoxenos' engagement with and description of the struggles of the monastic and prayer life. In his conferences Merton read Philoxenos as a student and practitioner of the monastic and spiritual life and art who had something to say directly to the spiritual dilemmas of Merton's novices. Merton sought out other texts and scholarly articles by and about Philoxenos, including several French translations of letters of Philoxenos in *L'Orient Syrien*, a Lebanese journal of Syriac studies not easily accessible.

Proceeding through the thirteen *mēmrē* in order, Merton is especially attracted to the classic traits of simplicity and purity of heart, as well as the importance of silence (ܫܠܝܐ - *šēlyā*) as the way

---

[123] Thomas Merton, *Pre-Benedictine Monasticism: Initiation into the Monastic Tradition 2*, ed. Patrick F. O'Connell, Preface by Sidney H. Griffith, MW 9 (Kalamazoo, MI: Cistercian Publications, 2006), 279–325.

[124] "Thomas Merton's Novitiate Conferences on Philoxenos of Mabbug (April–June 1965): Philoxenos on the Foundations of the Spiritual Life and the Recovery of Simplicity," ed. David M. Odorisio. *Hugoye Journal of Syriac Studies* 13 (2010): 251–71. Odorisio transcribes Tapes #142–4 [recorded 4-11-65], #114–2 [4-25-65], #147–4 [5-27-65], and #148–3 [6-7-65].

[125] MW 9:viii.

to knowledge.[126] The analogy by Philoxenos in the ninth *mēmrā* on renunciation of a fetus exiting the womb into the world and a person exiting the world into the monastery is perceived by Merton as an apt image for his novices still wondering whether they have made the right decision to enter the monastery. "The true maturity of the Christian is in that knowledge of God that is granted only in the desert,"[127] Merton infers and then cites Philoxenos, "The true rich man is not he who has many things but he who has need of nothing."[128] The two *mēmrē* on gluttony (10 and 11) also engage a universal principle of monastic practice and Merton regales his listeners with Philoxenos' long and masterly diatribe against eating and the glutton, adding contributions from John Climacus and Pachomius[129] along the way.

These notes reflect Merton's research and interests, but the transcripts and the audio recording themselves witness to his passion and enthusiasm for Philoxenos' own novice conferences, which Merton projects back to his students. Working through the fourth *mēmrā* on simplicity, Merton is attempting to describe the necessity of becoming simple without trying to be simple:

> So the first thing Adam and Eve *never* did was that they never *tried* to be simple. They never made the slightest effort to be simple. As soon as you try to be simple you're through, you've had it. You're already complicated. So this is a most important point. The thing to do is to absorb this and immediately forget it. When you walk out of this room, don't give simplicity another thought for the rest of your life! Have nothing more to do with simplicity. Simply walk with God in the reality that He has given us, in which we're not thinking about Him— we are immediately united with Him—and we just simply walk with God. We are not aware we are walking with God, because 9/10's of the trouble comes from wanting to *see* that we are walking with God and not with somebody else. How

---

[126] MW 9:289–95.
[127] MW 9:300.
[128] MW 9:301.
[129] MW 9:309–20.

do I know it's you? That's not the question one asks. Adam and Eve didn't think about Him. They didn't say, "Where did you come from? Where were you at 9:00 this morning? You weren't here then, you're coming only in the afternoon!" [Laughter]. And "Who made you?" Well, mind your own business! [Laughter]. I think this is a very excellent expression of what this whole idea of simplicity is and where [Philoxenos] really gets it across is where he speaks about the child being completely mingled with the word of Him who speaks.[130]

I began this introduction to the *Discourses* by saying that the best way to understand Philoxenos is to read his *mēmrē* out loud, and listening to Merton tells one what the benefit of doing that is.

Excurses on the Influences and Sources of Philoxenos in the *Discourses*

The Upright, the Perfect, and the Character of Syriac Asceticism

At least one scribe noticed a long time ago that the *Discourses* of Philoxenos of Mabbug shared something particular and unique with the *Book of Steps / Liber Graduum* written one hundred to one hundred fifty years earlier. The scribe of the manuscript Bibliothèque Nationale de France Syrus 201 included full versions of both lengthy texts in this manuscript.[131] Irenée Hausherr, reviewing Eugène Lemoine's French translation of the *Discourses* in *Sources Chrétiennes*, was alarmed that such a reasonable author as Philoxenos was living so closely on a manuscript folio with the reputed Messalian asceticon of the *Book of Steps*.[132]

Linked by their common usage of the levels of the upright (*kēnē*) and perfect (*gmīrē*), the *Book of Steps* and the *Discourses* distinguish the non-ascetical from the ascetical wings of the church, although

---

[130] "Thomas Merton's Novitiate Conferences," Tape #147–4 [5-27-65], 253–64.

[131] BNF Syrus 201 (12th c.): *The Discourses* of Philoxenos, ff. 1–172; *The Book of Steps*, ff. 172b–281a.

[132] Hausherr, "Spiritualité Syrienne," 181–82.

their sociological and political situations are significantly different. While Philoxenos never appears to directly cite the *Book of Steps*, he is clearly familiar with the institutional tradition of these two levels. Both texts describe the relationship between the upright and the perfect in strikingly similar terms, yet there are subtle and important distinctions.

Traditionally titled *Liber Graduum* in academic circles, the *Book of Steps*, a late fourth-century collection of thirty *mēmrē* appears to be written by an anonymous spiritual leader in a town or village residing in the Persian Empire when memories of Shapur II's persecution of Christians in the 340s as sympathizers to the archrival Roman Empire still haunted the community.[133] Whether the author was the pastor or teacher of this community, or even if he had attained the level of perfection, is not discernible. The author has obvious authority but keeps his personal history out of the text.

This is not an irenic work, for conflict of one sort or another hovers continually in the background and occasionally moves to center stage. The stratification of the upright and perfect produces significant problems that the author persistently addresses—the jealousy of the lower level against the higher, as well as the arrogance of the superior over the inferior.[134]

Monasticism is not yet a reality, although the sharp distinctions between the upright who are married and have families, have jobs and own homes and property, and their counterparts, the perfect,

---

[133] *The Book of Steps: The Syriac Liber Graduum*, trans. and intro. Robert A. Kitchen and Martien F. G. Parmentier, CS 196 (Kalamazoo, MI: Cistercian Publications, 2004); see Gregory Greatrex, "The Romano-Persian Frontier and the Context of *The Book of Steps*" *Breaking the Mind: New Essays in the Syriac Book of Steps*, ed. Kristian S. Heal and Robert A. Kitchen, Studies in Early Christianity 6 (Washington, DC: CUA Press, forthcoming).

[134] "Conflict and Transition," CS 196:li–lvi; also, Shafiq Abou-Zayd, "Violence and Killing the *Liber Graduum*," *Aram* 11–12 (1999–2000): 451–65; and Peter Nagel, "Die 'Martyrer des Glaubens' und die 'Martyrer der Liebe' im syrische *Liber Graduum*," *Religion und Wahrheit. Religionsgeschichtliche Studien. Festschrift für Gernot Wiessner zum 65 Geburtstag*, ed. B. Kohler (Wiesbaden: Harrassowitz, 1998), 127–42.

who are celibate, have renounced all worldly possessions, including a permanent home, and pointedly do not work, prefigure the development of the monastic ideal.

The *Discourses*, a century or more later, is not anonymous but clearly the work of the bishop of Mabbug in West Syria, spoken or read to a monastic audience or audiences during a period when the miaphysites enjoyed imperial favor and security. While elements of the christological controversies did creep into the *Discourses*, these addresses to the monks were not primarily focused on doctrinal issues, but on the methods and problems of the spiritual and monastic life. The audience too was haunted by "remembrance of things past," but for the monks it was the memory of how they had lived in the world.

Both collections are saturated with scriptural citations and extended exegeses, interpreted to suit each author's conception of the ascetic *dūbbārā* (ܕܘܒܪܐ) or way of life. No holy man or woman or saint crosses the pages, only biblical characters are mentioned and examined. In keeping with this subdued tone no hint of excessive and spectacular feats of ascetical prowess is admitted. The author of the *Book of Steps*, with his signature citation that "you must consider everyone else better than you" (Phil 2:3), would conceivably condemn such practices as self-centered and vain glorious.

The *mēmrē* of the *Book of Steps* appear to be occasional pieces addressed in response to circumstances that have risen, although the early *mēmrē* do build a systematic picture of the upright and perfect. Philoxenos, proceeding on a more tightly structured road through the steps of the ascetic and monastic life, does not countenance those who seek their own path (look at what he does to gluttons!). Within the monastic community the primary characteristics of the monk are simplicity and humility, or lowliness.

Both levels, the upright and the perfect, have particular tasks of ministry for their calling. For the author of the *Book of Steps*, the upright feed the hungry, clothe the naked, visit the prisoners, and heal the sick, and provide for the physical needs of the perfect—the latter assignment producing significant tension from time to time. The perfect lead a contemplative life devoted to unceasing prayer, but also wander in the surrounding areas of teaching and mediating conflicts. There is little progression indicated from the lower to higher level, although the author is constantly urging the upright to renounce the world, its possessions, and necessarily to renounce their wives and become celibate. Not surprisingly, this is not a popular option for most of the upright so that while the author agrees to the worthiness of the marriage state, becoming celibate is the major boundary line for the upright to negotiate and enter into the level of the perfect.

The author identifies the division of Jesus' commandments into major and minor commandments. The minor commandments center around physical acts of ministry, tasks reserved for the upright. The perfect have advanced to the major commandments that seek to surpass normal human limits and patterns. Moreover, the perfect are severely admonished in several passages for having slid backward into performing the minor commandments and thereby negating their higher calling.[135]

Philoxenos, by contrast, appears not to have heard of the major or minor commandments. He commences with the fundamentals of Christian spirituality: faith, simplicity, fear of God, renunciation, anti-gluttony, asceticism, and celibacy. These characteristics reflect both the directions of traditional Syriac asceticism as well as the basics of the ascetical agenda of Evagrius of Ponticus with which Philoxenos had become enamored.[136] While Philoxenos' *Discourses* appear to be intended for novice monks newly arrived from the world—celibate by requirement, but often not deeply versed in biblical and Christian spirituality—these basic characteristics will not be abandoned upon attaining the level of perfection but are in a continuing process of development for both upright and perfect. Philoxenos has transformed the institution of the upright and perfect of the *Book of Steps* from almost mutually exclusive ways of life into an open-ended continuum in the *Discourses.*

---

[135] See especially *mēmrā* 2: "About Those Who Want to Become Perfect," CS 196:13–21; and *mēmrā* 3: "The Physical and Spiritual Ministry," CS 196:23–37; *mēmrā* 4: "On the Vegetables for the Sick," CS 196:39–44; and *mēmrā* 5: "On the Milk of the Children," CS 196:45–60.

[136] See section below on Evagrius and Philoxenos, "A Student of Evagrius."

Perhaps the most striking contrast between the two configurations of the upright/perfect dichotomy is that Philoxenos never instructs the perfect not to work. The ideal of not working is the re-entry into the state of perfection in the Garden of Eden before Adam had sinned, a trait that left the *Book of Steps* open to accusations of messalianism prevalent during the fourth and fifth centuries.[137] Philoxenos, however, never specifically mentions work for the upright or perfect. Moreover, he never mentions that the upright are responsible to care for the perfect, a contentious issue in the *Book of Steps*. Work is an assumption in the life of the monastery.

A different pressure point for each author marks the critical entry onto the road toward spiritual maturity and perfection. The author of the *Book of Steps* returns again and again to celibacy or holiness, renouncing one's wife in practical terms. The fifteenth *mēmrā*[138] reveals the tensions in the community primarily from the side of the upright, while the author never hints whether there are problems regarding sexuality with the perfect. Renunciation of the world and its possessions is punctuated by the renunciation of sexuality, an indication of one being dead to the world.

Renunciation and poverty for the perfect are givens in the *Book of Steps*, but for the upright, money is to be used for others, not for self-aggrandizement and comfort, in essence an alternative form of poverty and detachment from a soul bent on possessing things.

A century and a half later, while celibacy is no longer a formal issue with Philoxenos' charges, it is the remembrance of things past—family, wealth, food, comforts, positions of power and authority—as well as anxieties, unresolved passions, and regrets that continue to haunt the monk's soul and potentially could infect his fellow monks. Philoxenos points decisively to the lust of the belly as the beginning of all sin and until one has conquered and controlled this basic impulse progress in the spiritual life will continue

---

[137] "The Decline of Perfection and Messalian Behavior," CS 196:lvi–lxi; and R. A. Kitchen, "Becoming Perfect: The Maturing of Asceticism in the Syriac Book of Steps," *Journal of the Canadian Society for Syriac Studies* 2 (2002): 30–45.

[138] *The Book of Steps, Mēmrā* 15, "On Adam's Marital Desire," CS 196:139–57.

to be inhibited.[139] Just as with celibacy, the taming and elimination of gluttony is a psychosomatic ascetical act that rebels against the social conventions of the normal life. Once one has controlled the drives for sexuality and eating, the road is clear for authentic spiritual development.

A difficulty in interpreting Philoxenos' prescriptions for the upright is that he does not explicitly declare who the upright are. Often his references clearly indicate someone living in the world, married, and with a job, income, and possessions. At other times, the upright are the novices in the monastery who appear to have a minimal background in Christian life and who cannot seem to get the world out of their heads. This situational ambiguity has a benefit, for the monk must come to grips with the real reasons he has entered the monastery rather than remaining in the world and simply doing good with his money, family, and influence.

The upright and perfect in the *Book of Steps* literally live in the world, perhaps on the outskirts of a town or village. The perfect do not renounce their location in the world, but their social connections to society—family, home, and physical stability, participation in the work of a community. In many ways it is a very difficult model to follow and the author points out the instances where the perfect were imperfect in their endeavors. Philoxenos, on the other hand, is emphatic that perfection is attainable only in the monastery or the wilderness/desert.

For those familiar with the patterns of Syriac asceticism, familiarity breeds a certain contempt. The radical excesses reported in many hagiographical texts can easily direct one to draw the conclusion that some athletic ascetics attempted to outdo one another in reducing their bodies to the bare minimum for life.

While the desert fathers were primarily Egyptian, early translations provided ample models for their Syriac readership. The *Historia Religiosa* or the *History of the Monks in Syria* by Theodoret of Cyrrhus was penned in Greek, but established a standard portrait of Syriac

---

[139] R. A. Kitchen, "The Lust of the Belly Is the Beginning of All Sin," 49–63.

ascetics, the most famous of whom was Simeon Stylites.[140] There were other Syriac versions of Simeon's story circulating,[141] as well as Jacob of Serug's *mēmrā* or poetic sermon on the Stylite,[142] none of which shy away from depicting his spectacular and graphic feats of holiness. Hagiographical accounts often narrated the extraordinary efforts of holy men, for instance in the tales of the dendrites or tree-dwellers, who were understood to be forerunners of stylites.[143]

These were the heroes of the Syriac church, but not necessarily the norm or model for budding ascetics. The stories of these spiritual athletes functioned more as literary asceticism driven by the enthusiasm of hagiographical hyperbole. The intensity of these stories may lead one initially to believe that is how one lives as a Christian in Syriac culture. Yet, there are other witnesses to a different way of ascetical life.

Asceticism, which has generally defied a single and universally accepted definition, finds common ground among these authors and their communities. Prayer and fasting are mentioned frequently, and Philoxenos persistently refers to the heavy physical

---

[140] Theodoret of Cyrrhus, *A History of the Monks in Syria*, trans. R. M. Price, CS 88 (Kalamazoo, MI: Cistercian Publications, 1983); Simeon Stylites, 160–76; Paul Naaman, *The Maronites: The Origins of an Antiochene Church, A Historical and Geographical Study of the Fifth to Seventh Centuries*, trans. DIT, Kaslik, Lebanon, CS 243 (Collegeville, MN: Cistercian Publications, 2009), especially chapter 3, "Theodoret of Cyr and the Patriarchate of Antioch after the Council of Ephesus (431–452)," 65–115.

[141] *The Lives of Simeon Stylites*, trans. Robert Doran, CS 112 (Kalamazoo, MI: Cistercian Publications, 1992). Doran includes Theodoret's version, another Greek vita by Antonius, and a much longer anonymous Syriac version.

[142] "Jacob of Serug, Homily on Simeon the Stylite," trans. Susan Ashbrook Harvey, *Ascetic Behavior in Graeco-Roman Antiquity: A Sourcebook*, ed. Vincent L. Wimbush (Minneapolis, MN: Fortress Press, 1990), 15–28.

[143] *The History of the Great Deeds of Bishop Paul of Qentos and Priest John of Edessa*, trans. Hans Arneson, Emanuel Fiano, Christine Marquis, and Kyle Smith (Piscataway, NJ: Gorgias Press, 2010). Kyle Smith, "Dendrites and Other Standers in *The History of the Great Deeds of Bishop Paul of Qentos and Priest John of Edessa*," *Hugoye Journal of Syriac Studies* 12 (2009): 117–34.

toll that rigorous fasting and narrow confinement in one's cell exact on one's health. Notable, however, is that neither author mentions *šēlyā* (ܫܸܠܝܵܐ) or "stillness" in the sense of the advanced technique of wordless, silent prayer practiced in many parts of later Syriac worship. Worship may not be explicitly an ascetical act, but it is an essential aspect of the Christian discipline, especially at the insistence of the *Book of Steps* in *mēmrā* 12 on the necessity of traveling through the earthly church before one can contemplate the heavenly church or church of the heart.[144] Philoxenos often refers to communal worship in the monastery. Knowledge of the Scriptures is the alphabet of the Christian's language and imaginative universe, and both the author and Philoxenos assume that everyone is speaking the same language.

Celibacy and anti-gluttony are both very difficult steps for the aspiring upright to take, requiring both physical and social renunciation. Both boundaries demand absolute commitment to a distinctive way of life which initially engenders misgivings and regrets, as well as physical discomfort. It should be noted that both authors do not condemn food or eating *per se*, nor do they condemn marriage and sexual activity though these are no longer intended or allowed for the perfect or the monk.

The trajectory on which the *Book of Steps* and the *Discourses* travel is a disciplined, methodical way of life, the narrow steep road. It is the strenuous calling of being simple—abject humility, renouncing the world, its possessions and its sexuality, controlling the intake of food, praying and worshiping unceasingly, populating one's mind and spirit with the personalities and words of the Scriptures that still live among us. The two books emerge from very different sociological, political, and theological environments, as well as living in distinctive historical eras, yet they share the inner core of this ascetic discipline. Both authors lament that the perfect life is neither easy nor fully attainable by a significant segment of Christians.

---

[144] *Mēmrā* 12: "On the Hidden and Public Ministry of the Church," CS 196:119–26.

Neither author mentions an instance of the more spectacular ascetic feats, but the regimen of perfection seems significantly rigorous, all-encompassing, and explicitly discouraging of vainglorious behavior to sanction such extraordinary personalities and actions. Despite the size of these two works, a few more comprehensive examples of ascetic communities are needed to draw definitive conclusions about the institutional character of early Syriac asceticism. Nevertheless, what we see in Philoxenos and the *Book of Steps* may well be the genuine norm.

Biblical Exegesis in the Discourses

Philoxenos shows himself to be one more instance of an early Christian writer who lives in the thought-world of the Bible, seldom allowing a page to be turned without some reference to the Scriptures. While Philoxenos does employ the short proof-text, his more striking use of Scripture is through longer narrative units, reading into the narratives rationales for the ascetical and theological themes he is developing. There are over thirteen hundred biblical references in the *Discourses*, so the following will point out only some of the more significant themes.

The Ordered Steps of Asceticism. Philoxenos' introduction emphasizes the necessity of an ordered methodology of asceticism. Jesus' words from the conclusion of the Sermon on the Mount (Matt 7:24-27) regarding the house built on the rock is posited as the requirement for any physical or spiritual development (m 1.1; 4:3–10).

A critical aspect of this development is urged in the explanation of the parable of the person who started building a tower but could not finish it because of lack of funds and materials and was then ridiculed by all (Luke 14:29) (1.3; 7:4–13). The parable of the unfinished tower is revisited in the ninth *mēmrā* as a caution to the monk to fulfill the obligation of his monastic profession, to stay for the long run or to simply stay in the world (9.41–43; 310:13–314:13).

The importance of a rule is therefore uppermost to Philoxenos who also offers the image of Jacob's ladder (Gen 28:12) to symbolize the orderly progression of humans up the ladder one step or rung at a time (7.2; 192:22–193:20). Angels and humans mingle on the ladder in order to teach us that a virtuous way is common to both creatures.

Adam and Eve in the Garden. The themes of Adam's and Eve's natures and their transgression are threaded throughout early Syriac literature. Philoxenos interprets the story primarily to undergird his rule of spiritual development for monks.

In the fourth *mēmrā* on simplicity, Philoxenos demonstrates that the basic characteristic of simplicity is that one never questions the commands of God. Adam and Eve possessed simplicity until they encountered the Enemy who manipulated Adam into exercising judgment on God's command to him—i.e., that he should not eat from the fruit of the tree (4.7; 80:5–81:20). "The advice that was brought to him made that youth and simple one a judge of the commandment of God to him. Because he had lost his simplicity, he also did not prosper by his judgment. He had judged foolishly that he ought to obey an enemy more than a friend" (4.7; 81:1–4).

The simplicity of Adam and Eve allows them to talk directly with God just as with a close acquaintance. During this time their simplicity never thought to ask questions about God's nature or being (4.10–11; 83:17–84:15). In the sixth *mēmrā* on the fear of God, Philoxenos observes that Adam believed in God, but once he cast out the fear of God from his mind he abandoned the faith (6.34; 185:21–186:4).

An intriguing detail about Adam comes from a backhanded reference in the discussion of John the Baptist as the greatest of the prophets. Philoxenos observes that John received the Holy Spirit while still in the womb in order that he might attain the innocence (*šapyūtā*) of Adam before Adam had sinned against the commandment (9.35; 300:10–302:19).

The root of Adam's sin occupies a predictable category. Since our author is keen to demonstrate that the lust of the belly is the root of all sin, as well as the most powerful, he identifies this lust as the real source of the transgression—when he ate the fruit[145] of

---

[145] Scripture does not give us much detail, Philoxenos says, but oral tradition indicates that the fruit Eve ate was from the fig tree (ܬܬܐ - *tētā*) (11.32; 446:17–23).

the tree of the knowledge of good and evil—thus inducing shame at his nakedness and lust (10.59–61; 412:4–414:5).

Simplicity and the Fear of God. Proceeding through the biblical history of salvation, Philoxenos demonstrates that simplicity and the fear of God were the fundamental characteristics of the patriarchs, prophets, and apostles. Simplicity is evidenced in receiving God's command without questioning or analysis. Abraham responded to God's call without hesitation (4.2; 74:13–76:8), as did the apostles to Jesus' summons (4.3; 76:17–77:4). Matthew and Philip are extolled specifically for their immediate response (4.4; 77:23–78:8). Philoxenos focuses on Zacchaeus' triumph of simplicity, a man who had acquired all his possessions through cunning (ܚܐܪܘܬܐ - *ḥē'rūtā*) (4.6; 79:5–80:5).

Those Israelites who were born in the wilderness possessed natural simplicity, while those who whored after the daughters of Midian and worshiped the golden calf came from the generation that came up out of Egypt (m 4.15–18; 86:10–90:9).

Simplicity was evident in the people who followed Joshua around the city of Jericho (m 4.19; 90:9–91:2). David is described as a "beast [of burden]" before God—compliant and simple (Ps 73:22). His shepherding and relationship with Jonathan, as well as lack of cunning regarding Saul proved his simplicity (m 4.22–23; 93:2–95:5).

Jacob is proclaimed as the model person of simplicity, both in his struggles with his brother Esau (m 4.25–28; 96:2–99:10) and with the deception of Laban regarding his daughters (m 4.29–30; 99:10–101:7). God turned these controversies into profit for Jacob (m 4.34; 103:3–104:13).

The simplicity of Abel, apparent in his offering in contrast to the evilness and cunning of Cain, is declared (m 4.40; 109:19–110:13), as well as the simplicity of Joseph in the honor toward his father and love of his brothers that bore the test of adversity (m 4.42; 111:1–112:10).

The other basic characteristic of the Christian, the fear of God, is shown to be the active element in several personalities. Adam, as mentioned above, lost his faith in God when he cast out his fear of God. God surrounded succeeding generations with fear so that they might keep the commandments: Cain was overwhelmed by the fear of everything (m 6.34; 186:6–13); and the commandments given through Moses were embedded with fear (m 6.34; 186:13–22). Philoxenos constructs a long catena of citations from the Psalms to illustrate David the Prophet's expressions of the fear of God (m 7.9–19; 199:14–212:17). The concluding example is demonstrated in the adventures of Jonah who fled toward Tarshish out of the fear of God and it was the fear of the true God which converted the sailors on his ship (m 7.21; 213:18–214:8).

Joseph's resistance to the advances of Potiphar's wife (Gen 39:8-10) is recounted as an exercise of the remembrance of God. The Ten Commandments had not yet been given, but Joseph knew that to sin against his master would be violating the natural law of the Golden Rule, "Whatever is hateful to you, do not do to your neighbor," which in turn would be sinning against God (m 13.62; 607:1–608:5). The example of Joseph would become an inspiration to all the patriarchs, prophets, and forerunners of monks who would follow him (m 13.65; 610:9–21).

Monastic Imperatives. After Philoxenos has established the fundamental characteristics of the ascetic life, he moves to the critical transition from the secular world to the monastery, the renunciation of possessions and passions in order to go out from the world into the desert. Adopting several biblical typologies for this defining experience of the monk, Philoxenos works to reinforce the resolve of his audience to accept and rejoice in their vocation.

The initial scriptural passage is an exegesis of a familiar verse, "Come unto me, all who are weary and are laden with heavy burdens, and I will give you rest" (Matt 11:28). In a lengthy extended discourse, Philoxenos uses the verse to encourage those people burdened with riches and the cares of the world to cast them off and renounce or empty themselves of these things (m 9.12; 270:16–273:15).

The Jordan River becomes a typological landmark for Jesus, that of his passing from the legalism of his prebaptized life into the freedom of the way of life in the wilderness.[146] The Jordan functioned in

---

[146] See Aloys Grillmeier, "Die Taufe und die Taufe der Christen: Zur Tauftheologie des Philoxenos von Mabbug under ihrer Bedeutung für

the same way as the sea did for the Israelites fleeing Egypt: through
it they ended their subjection to Egypt and had their fear of the
Egyptians removed through the return of the waters on Pharaoh's
chariots, and entered into the desert—a land of freedom in which
no one else would rule over them, except God (m 9.13; 274:3–275:2).

The typology of Israel in Egypt is built on further to identify
Egypt with the troubles of this world. "Egypt was making the Hebrews work with mud and bricks and with toils and harsh labors;
and with cares, anxiety, adversities, and groans the world also
works against you. The Jews were washed of the mud of Egypt
once they had crossed over the sea" (m 9.15; 276:10–14).

Creatively, Philoxenos carries the analogy further, observing that
Israel did not automatically enjoy the benefits of freedom once it
had crossed into the wilderness for there were many moments of
doubt. The monk departing from the world to enter the monastery
also is not exempt from these doubts.

> So also, when the disciple has departed from the world and
> wishes to become free of its servitude, he does not imme-
> diately receive joy, nor is he worthy of the taste of spiritual
> pleasures, just as neither had those once they had departed
> from Egypt received joy or were worthy of spiritual pleasure.
> But there will occur to you at first, O disciple, after your tran-
> sition from the world the fear of austerities and the vexation
> of thoughts and repentance concerning your departure from
> the world, and the fact that you have dispersed whatever you
> had possessed, or that you have abandoned your inheritance
> and have moved out of the dwelling of your parents (m 9.16;
> 277:15–278:4).

Just as the Israelites in the wilderness wished at times to be back
amidst the security of the fleshpots of Egypt, the disciple/monk
begins to question his choices. "Such [thoughts] as these begin to
agitate in your thoughts: why have you left the world in which it

---

die Christliche Spiritualität," *Fides Sacramenti Sacramentum Fidei: Studies
in honor of Pieter Smulders*, ed. J. J. Auf der Maur (Assen: Van Gorcum,
1981), 137–75.

would have been easier for you to be justified? Why did you decide to disperse your wealth, for while it was with you, through it you were seen to be an especially compassionate person? Now because you have divided it hastily it happens also that it has been given to those who are not worthy" (m 9.17; 278:9–14).

Wealth may be the first thing to come to mind when renouncing the world, but the next most important possession is that of one's family. Philoxenos recognizes that the monk may often be of weaker resolve in this area, so he presents the biblical precedents and imperatives to fortify his decision.

Philoxenos relates that Mary, the mother of Jesus, attempted to use her parental authority on Jesus at the wedding at Cana (John 2:1-11).

> When the wine was failing for the guests, his mother said to Jesus, "They have no wine." She began here to speak to him authoritatively as a mother would usually do. But Jesus rejected that liberty, teaching that she had been repaid by him the debt of parental honor, and now he is no longer subservient to them as at first. . . . [H]e was giving an example to the perfect through this word, lest they be led by the law of natural parents once they were living outside of the world in which the parents are dwelling. Mary was living in one mode of life and Jesus was in another rule—she according to the law and he according to the spirit (m 8.30; 251:1–6, 9–14).

This teaching is directed to the monk tempted by visiting relatives to return home. Philoxenos includes the later account (John 7:1-10) in which Jesus refused to go up to the feast of the Tabernacles with his brothers and then went up later by himself during the middle of the feast to show them that he was no longer subject to parents/relatives or to the law, which here was the obligation of attending the feast (m 8.31; 252:15–254:7).

In the ninth *mēmrā* on renunciation, Philoxenos points to the example of John the Baptist as the model of the perfect disciple of Christ. "Receive it then as proof for the way of life of this righteous [person], and learn also from it that a person may not become a perfect disciple of Christ unless he has become a stranger from the entire world by the example of this upright person" (m 9.37; 305:3–7). Jesus' advice to the hesitant disciple, "Leave the dead to bury their dead and you, go announce the kingdom of God" (Luke 9:60), is interpreted to mean that one must cast off one's duty to his natural parents (m 9.38; 305:11–306:9).

Against the Lust of the Belly and Fornication. Finally, Philoxenos tackles the two fundamental passions, gluttony and fornication, spending on them just short of half of the length of the *Discourses.* He proceeds on a selected biblical tour of the figures who exemplify the saintly model in the struggle against the lust of the belly and fornication.[147]

Philoxenos rehearses the problem of gluttony by recalling three tragic figures who were controlled by the lust for food and meat. Adam, as noted earlier, fell from innocence through the lust of the belly (m 10.59–61; 412:4–414:5). Esau lost his birthright and blessings on account of his lust for food (m 10.62; 414:18–20). And then the people of Israel forgot God on account of their food and worshiped instead the golden calf (m 10.62; 414:20–22).

In the eleventh *mēmrā* Philoxenos contrasts two cases of eating versus lust. Esau merely ate lentils (Gen 25:29-34) but was condemned because he lusted for food. Elijah, on the other hand, ate meat (1 Kgs 17:6) but was considered spiritual (m 11.38; 452:2–17). Even the drinking of cold water, if done with lust, can bring one down, as nearly happened to David at Bethlehem, before he poured out the water before the Lord to suppress his lust (2 Sam 23:15-17) (m 11.39; 452:17–453:5).

Positively, Philoxenos tells of Daniel and the three young men (Dan 1:3-16) who refused to eat the rich diet of King Nebuchadnezzar for three years and ended being in better physical condition than those who did and were able to receive revelations of divine knowledge (m 11.58; 471:1–473:12). The apostles, however, were exempt from abstinence and fasting while they were with Jesus "the Bridegroom" (m 11.70; 483:22–485:13). Simon broke his fast,

---

[147] For a detailed discussion, see Kitchen, "The Lust of the Belly Is the Beginning of All Sin," 49–63.

but only because he was divinely ordered to do so (m 11.71–72; 486:1–487:13). A short catena of the fasting heroics of several figures is given: Daniel had to fast three weeks to be worthy of the sight of angels (Dan 10:2, 7); Elijah had a forty-day fast on Mount Horeb (1 Kgs 19:8); Ezekiel ate bread by weight and water by measure (Ezek 4); and David ate ashes like bread and drank tears (Ps 102:9) (m 11.74–75; 488:6–490:17).

Philoxenos utilizes the story of Gideon's selection of his attack force against the Midianites (Judg 7:1-23) as one of two principal stories to illustrate the overcoming of the passion of fornication. Whereas Aphrahat had interpreted the story as a typology of how the *bnay/bnāt qyāmā* (ܒܢܝ̈ ܩܝܡܐ ܐܘ ܒܢ̈ܬ ܩܝܡܐ)[148] were selected and consecrated, simply identifying the three hundred who lapped water in their hands as the elite chosen to join the ranks of the *bnay/ bnāt qyāmā*,[149] Philoxenos perceives the test as a struggle against the lust of fornication. Because the Israelites had whored with the daughters of Midian (Num 25:1), the army of Midian now symbolizes fornication. Beginning with an admonition regarding the physiology of fornication, Philoxenos calls on his monks to reduce their liquid intake—for moisture nourishes fornication, especially in tandem with gluttony. Dryness reduces desire by heating it up and burning it off, so to speak. Philoxenos pointed to Gideon's turning away those who drank their fill, but accepted those who with caution "drank a little," and this came not from Gideon's ingenuity, but from God's divine plan. The sound of the horn is the commandment of God; the breaking of the pitchers is the breaking

---

[148] Aphrahat wrote twenty-three "Demonstrations" between 337–45, in the midst of severe persecution of Persian Christians by Shapur II. The *bnay/bnāt qyāmā* ("sons/daughters of the covenant") were premonastic orders of consecrated men and women who led ascetically disciplined and celibate lives in the community.

[149] *The Demonstrations of Aphrahat, the Persian Sage*, trans. Adam Lehtò (Piscataway, NJ: Gorgias Press, 2010), Demonstration Seven: "On the Penitent," 18–22; pp. 210–13; Syriac critical edition: *Aphraatis Sapientis Persae. Demonstrationes*, ed. Ioannes Parisot, PS 1 (Paris: Firmin-Didot, 1894), 7.18–22: columns 341:11–349:27.

of the passion of fornication; and the light inside the pitcher is that of divine knowledge (m 13.53–56; 597:15–601:18). While both Aphrahat and Philoxenos see the lapping of water as the selection of the elite, Aphrahat attaches no specific meaning to the method, but Philoxenos creatively interprets this act as a rejection of fornication—an embracement of celibacy.

Philoxenos understands the narrative as an allegorical model for the new resident monks who are ostensibly celibate, but for whom the distracting ideas of the world are still active in their minds and souls. This is a prescriptive text, outlining how and why one should behave in the ascetic and monastic way of life, moving from worldly uprightness up to the spiritual realm of perfection. Philoxenos interpreted the using of hands to drink as an indication of *how much* one drank as the measure of exactly how the monk should perform in the midst of the struggle. The *Discourses* are seldom directed to the perfect, but to the upright, the newly arrived monks, who may lapse into their worldly ways of thinking, even while living in the monastery.

Christological Comments in the Discourses

One of the appeals of Philoxenos' *Discourses*, his most popular and most copied work, is that it is apparently free from the tensions of contemporary christological debate in which Philoxenos was a well-known and fiery participant. Modern scholarship has generally passed down the assessment that the *Discourses* are not concerned with christological matters. Lemoine believes that the *Discourses* were written to be read in the monastery and were edited specifically for this purpose[150] and sees no traces of miaphysitism in the *Discourses*.[151] Irenée Hausherr had earlier promoted this view that the christological ideas of the miaphysites have no influence on their ascetical and mystical teachings.[152] This view of Lemoine and Hausherr is only partially the case.

---

[150] SCh 44bis:12–13.

[151] SCh 44bis:15.

[152] Hausherr, "Contemplation et Sainteté," 15.

Philoxenos periodically inserts comments and references that reflect his doctrinal and christological perspectives. These casual comments are not intended to construct a systematic theology for his listeners but are spontaneous interjections reflecting Philoxenos' theological worldview and arise out of concerns for the foundational concepts and practices of monastic asceticism. Indeed, as recent studies have demonstrated, particularly that of David Michelson,[153] there is not the great divide once assumed and imagined between the doctrinal letters and the ascetical homilies of this author. While it is true that the *Ascetical Homilies* and/or the *Discourses* are not consumed by doctrinal matters, Philoxenos persistently implies that proper *ascesis* or progress toward spiritual perfection cannot be accomplished without proper doctrinal understanding. While he doesn't name names or even parties, Philoxenos incessantly warns the monks under his episcopal care about those confused, even demented, dyophysites.

His delineation of the basic doctrinal concepts illustrates this pastoral attention. Philoxenos understands faith (ܗܝܡܢܘܬܐ - *haymānūtā*) as the first epistemological faculty that aims to see and hear the knowledge of God. Faith's opponent is error or false doctrine, but broader than simply doctrine. Error derives from trying to analyze and dissect God, Christ, and the truth, rather than simply believing.

Simplicity (ܦܫܝܛܘܬܐ - *pšīṭūtā*) is the characteristic which accompanies and grows out of faith. Philoxenos spends considerable time contrasting simplicity with its opposites—cunning and cleverness. If the monk had been cunning, he would never have departed from the world for the monastery, for he would have imagined too many alternatives. Philoxenos' definition of simplicity is not stupidity or lack of awareness, but "the singleness of one thought." God, for that matter, is "Simple," for in God there are no structures or parts.

The fear of God (ܕܚܠܬ ܐܠܗܐ - *deḥlat 'alāhā*), by which Philoxenos means an ecstatic feeling in the soul which then makes the whole body "tremble," has its basis in the remembrance of God. If one sins and does not remember or think of God's punishment and

---

[153] Michelson, *Practice Leads to Theory*, 2007.

disappointment, one's soul is dead. If one is conscious of his sins the fear of God increases continually within himself. The fear of God is born from faith but is also the preserver of faith. Adam and later Cain cast out their fear and as a consequence lost their faith. Once again, the fear of God is not an analytical tool, but one of experientially knowing God, derived out of faith and its simplicity. All too many do not remember God, being occupied with new conceptions of the nature of God.

The implication for present monks is that the search for the knowledge and experience of God is not accomplished through speculation and discussion of divine attributes, but through states of being that are beyond discussion—perfection/*apatheia* and natural innocence of the Garden of Eden before Adam had sinned.

While a different tone is at play in the *Discourses*, a decidedly more irenic and pastoral approach, Philoxenos does want to bring the nature of Christ into the conversation, for not surprisingly Jesus Christ is the model for the life of the monk, providing what Philoxenos will refer to frequently as the "*oikonomia*/economy of salvation" (ܕܚܝܐ ܕܒܪܢܘܬܐ - *mdabrānūtā dḥayyē*). Description of the true nature of Christ is not the primary subject matter of the *Discourses*, but along the way, Philoxenos finds it instructive to delineate who Jesus really is and what he has accomplished that begs imitation.

There are many instances in which Philoxenos inserts one of the traditional miaphysite formulas, seemingly on reflex and not out of apparent design. In the first *mēmrā*/discourse, Philoxenos declares, "The foundation is solid and laid down, according to the word of Paul, which is Jesus Christ *our God*" (m 1.3; 7:13–14).[154] Philoxenos understands Christ maintaining a single nature, but as he sees it, the dyophysite error is to divide Jesus into human and divine and thereby reduce Jesus' divinity to his humanity. While Chalcedonians may also say that "Jesus Christ is our God," for our

---

[154] "Christ our God" is employed by Philoxenos also at m 2.18 (45:18–19); m 5.40 (158:19); m 8.1 (222:10); m 12.60 (550:1); "Jesus God" at m 9.35 (302:5–6).

author this is a statement of emphasis—Christ is not just human, but in the first place God incarnate.

In the thirteenth and last discourse, a similar epithet slips out almost unnoticed. Speaking about the damage that fornication by a member does to the whole community:

> But here [the baptized ones] become spiritual people from corporeal people. And from the fact that every one of them—with regard to his person is a body of many members—is counted in the body of Christ as a member, because it is constructed invisibly and established in the body ineffably and becomes a spiritual member in the *body of God*, according to the word of the Apostle, "Your bodies are the members of Christ." How then will a member of Christ fight to defeat desire? (m 13.74; 619:24–620:5)

Others arise out of theopaschite vocabulary and theology: that Christ suffered as God on the cross. Two passages in the tenth discourse on gluttony, wickedly humorous in rhetoric against that filthy passion, tuck in familiar formulas.

> Not for this has the Creator created you to eat like animals, but to take nourishment as a rational being and to glorify him as a living being. . . . *You have been ordained to [sing] the Holy [Trisagion] with the seraphim.* Why do you compare your life with a mute beast by your feebleness? You are the master of creation by the will of your Maker. Why have you been made the servant of your belly by your free will? The will of your Creator has committed all of creation to you, and have you subjected yourself to your small belly? (m 10.29; 381:20–22, 382:9–14)

Putting aside the gluttony harangue, the mention of the Trisagion[155] is not meant as a full doctrinal affirmation—though it is an

---

[155] The Trisagion (Greek, "three times holy"; Syriac, ܡܩܕܫܢܐ - *mqadšānā* "that which proclaims 'holy God, holy mighty, holy immortal' ") is a familiar refrain of the Orthodox liturgy, sung before the reading of the Scriptures. The Chalcedonian churches interpreted "holy" to refer to the

affirmation of their miaphysite identity—but as the divine intention for the monks, the end play of the economy of salvation.

The lust of the belly is still a problem for the would-be singers of the Trisagion in a passage cited above, continued further here:

> You have been made a god by the true God, but have you made your belly a god? . . . Your Lord has loved you to such an extent that he should become food for you, but for his love should you not have abstained from vile foods? *The Living One died and was buried in order to save you*, yet have you made yourself a tomb for food? (m 10.29; 382:17–18, 24–383:2)

The "Living One" in Syriac can be a double entendre for the "One Who Saves," both a play on the character of the Mosaic Lord God and the role of Christ as Savior of the world, but clearly in the theopaschite understanding of a Christ who as God dies in order to save and redeem humanity. A critical part of the economy of Christ's incarnation is that as the monks become dead to the world, strangers and aliens, no longer tasting pleasurably their food, they are paralleling Christ's trajectory as the God who dies in order to save humanity, so the monk dies to the world in order to attain this new life or salvation.[156]

Trinity, while the miaphysite understood it to refer to Christ and added the phrase ("and was crucified for us") that became controversial, as well as symbolic of miaphysite theology. See Sebastian P. Brock, "The Thrice Holy Hymn in the Liturgy," *Sobornost/Eastern Churches Review* 7.2 (1985): 24–34; Michael Van Esbroeck, "The Memra on the Parrot by Isaac of Antioch," JTS 47 (1996): 464–76; S. P. Brock, "The Origins of the *Qanona* 'Holy God, Holy Mighty, Holy Immortal' accordion to Gabriel of Qatar (early seventh century)," *The Harp* 21 (2006): 173–85. Philoxenos refers to the Trisagion as well at m 7.2 (193:17–18) and m 9.73 (351.1).

[156] Other christological comments include: " although by nature he is free *because he is God*," m 8.20 (241:2–3); "in the foreknowledge of the Father these things were prepared for us in advance *because he is God*," m 9.34 (299:17–18); "you will resemble God (= Jesus)," m 8.21 (243:2–5); "the way of freedom of Christ, who as God was above the laws," m 10.40 (393:11–12); "Jesus Christ, the Only Begotten One, *God the Word*, to him be glory," m 13.80 (625:6–7).

While these *Discourses* were intended for monks, they replay many of the themes from his other writings dealing more strictly with doctrinal and polemical issues. One cannot practice proper asceticism without correct theology, for theology in this time describes who Christ is and therefore who and what one wishes to become. Incorrect theology can leave one confused, if not actually steered away from the truth by demonic forces. The insertions of christological comments in the *Discourses* are neither programmatic nor accidental. The goal and economy of salvation in Philoxenos is accomplished through imitation of Christ who demonstrates consistently that he is fully involved in the human journey, even while still divine, and through the cross enables his disciples to die to the world and live spiritually, even divinely. It should be kept in mind that Philoxenos, like many controversialists, only sees his side of the story, so in any imagined debate with opponents, he always wins. Ironically, for someone known as an important anti-Chalcedonian theologian, he advises his disciples to avoid theological discussion and accept what the eye of faith abundantly provides.

A Student of Evagrius

Writers in Late Antiquity did not use footnotes and seldom attributed citations and ideas to authors they had read, so we cannot be certain whether a later author was responding to an earlier mentor or appropriating ideas that had acquired common currency in the intellectual culture. In the case of Philoxenos and Evagrius of Pontus, the Greek desert father and theologian of the ascetical life, however, an intellectual relationship is clearly evident.

What is apparent is that Philoxenos had read Evagrius fairly extensively in Syriac translations that started to circulate at an early stage following Evagrius' death. He didn't just read Evagrius; he absorbed Evagrius' thought, and while Philoxenos is quite original, the imprint of the Evagrian method is sewn into all his writings.

Evagrius grew up in Pontus in Asia Minor and as a bright rising theological star served as an archdeacon to Gregory Nazianzen, accompanying him to the Second Ecumenical Council of Constantinople in 381. He fell in love with a married woman and when he came to himself he fled to Jerusalem where he was counseled by Melania the Elder to go into the Egyptian desert. He went down into Nitria and Kellia, apprenticed himself to Ammonas and the two Macarii, the Great and of Alexandria, and eventually acquired a reputation for his intellectual acumen. Evagrius is recorded in a number of *logoi* of the *Apophthegmata Patrum* and the *Lausiac History* of Palladius, as well as in other works. His learning and strenuous prayer resulted in his many literary works often seen in the tradition of Origen—letters and treatises, as well as collections of pithy and enigmatic *logoi* or chapters on the nature of pure prayer, often in sets of "centuries" or one-hundred sayings. But even in enumerating items Evagrius was subtle: the centuries usually had only ninety entries, indicating the imperfection of the human being's attempt to grasp God.

Evagrius' asceticism, unfortunately, so undermined his health that he died prematurely in 399. His literary legacy seemed to accelerate in its influence, and modern scholarship is finding even more evidence of his reception in a variety of spiritual writers in the following centuries—John the Solitary of Apamea, Philoxenos, Isaac of Nineveh, and Joseph Hazzaya in Syriac tradition; John Cassian in the Latin West, Pseudo-Dionysius, Maximus the Confessor, John Climacus, and Symeon the New Theologian among the Greek fathers for a short list. The Second Council of Constantinople in 553 anathematized the thought and writings of Origen, but a century and a half removed it turned out that the works and ideas condemned were the interpretations of Evagrius.

In the process of developing theories about Philoxenos' organization and plan, many scholars see the influence of Evagrius Ponticus factored in.[157]

Evagrius' most enduring contribution has been his identifications of the eight vices or "principal thoughts."[158] The first two are gluttony or the lust of the belly and the lust of fornication—the second

---

[157] See Harb, "L'attitude de Philoxène de Mabboug," 135–36. Also, Watt, "Philoxenos and the Old Syriac Version of Evagrius' Centuries," 65–81.

[158] Driscoll, *The 'Ad Monachos' of Evagrius Ponticus*, 12–17; also, Augustine M. Casiday, *Evagrius Ponticus*, Early Church Fathers (New York: Routledge,

and third pairs of *mēmrē* following the renunciation of the world in Philoxenos' so-called second section. It seems logical that Philoxenos would have intended to complete the series of "principal thoughts"—love of money, sadness, anger, listlessness, vainglory, and pride—and then move on to treat the topics of "the degree of the spirit" of which we may have been afforded a glimpse in the ascetical florilegia. Notwithstanding, there are no extant copies of the *Discourses* with any more than the thirteen *mēmrē* in the canonical list.

Already two important terms of Evagrius, the passions (*ḥašē* - ‪ܚܫܐ‬) and the thoughts (*ḥūšābē* - ‪ܚܘܫܒܐ‬), come to the fore. These two become persistent terms in Philoxenos' vocabulary: the passions represent the destructive desires and lusts of the human being; the thoughts are not just normal ideas, but imply one of the eight principal thoughts that lead one astray.

In the middle of the longest *mēmrā* (ninety-five pages), the ninth on renunciation of the world, Philoxenos discusses the nature and qualities of the kingdom of heaven, but not from a speculative perspective. Renunciation is more than simply abandoning one's possessions, leaving behind one's friends and family and spouse, and departing from the business and conflict of human society and going out into the desert or monastery. All the monks have accomplished this on the surface, but it is the internal struggle that will determine the final salvation of the monk. Philoxenos states plainly, "When a person is freed from the passions of the world, it is as if his dwelling is [already] in the kingdom of heaven" (m 9.31; 297:3–5).

After describing in some detail the benefits of such freedom, Philoxenos cites Evagrius anonymously: "One of the spiritual teachers also correctly said, 'The kingdom of heaven is the soul without passions with the knowledge of these things that are in truth,'[159] which are words and incorporeal movements" (m 9.32; 297:16–19).

2006); Evagrius Pontus, *The Greek Ascetic Corpus*, trans. Robert E. Sinkewicz (New York: OUP, 2003), 66–90, 136–82.

[159] Evagrius Pontus, "The Monk: A Treatise on the Practical Life," *The Greek Ascetic Corpus*, chapter 5, no. 2, p. 97.

This citation appropriately comes from the first volume of Evagrius'
monastic trilogy, *Praktikos*, in which he initiates the monk into the
first level of the ascetical/monastic life, a work quite similar in purpose and situation to the *Discourses*. The phrase "without passions"
is one of Evagrius' most famous technical terms—*apatheia*—or in
Syriac, *lā ḥašūšūtā* (ܠܐ ܚܫܘܫܘܬܐ). This state is nothing to trifle with,
however, as Philoxenos cautions regarding an absence of *apatheia*.
"If freedom from passions is the kingdom of heaven, according to
the word of that wise spiritual [teacher], then also the servitude
of passions is a Gehenna that tortures, the outer darkness and the
worm that gnaws at the heart and thoughts" (m 9.32; 298:10–13).

In the exegesis of Gideon's selection of the three hundred men to
fight against the Midianites, the limitation on drinking water derives
from Evagrius' *Praktikos* in which he observes, "Limiting one's intake of water helps a great deal to obtain temperance. This was well
understood by the three hundred Israelites accompanying Gideon
just when they were preparing to attack Midian" (*Praktikos* 17).[160]

Philoxenos begins his instruction on the ascetical life with the
Evagrian fundamentals of the ascetic life—faith, simplicity, and the
fear of God. In the context of monastic life, these can be understood
as solid catechetical instruction for a novice in the Christian faith,
as no doubt some of his monks were.

Two critical principles in the monk's spiritual progression
emerge: first is the function and importance of simplicity (*pešīṭūtā* -
ܦܫܝܛܘܬܐ) in how Philoxenos approaches the knowledge of God;
second is the crucial role of the defeat of gluttony or lust of the belly
(*rēḥmat karsā* - ܪܚܡܬ ܟܪܣܐ) in the monastic life.

Simplicity here goes well beyond a pleasant naive disposition
as it refers to the divine attribute—God is not made of composite
parts, but is One, complete, unified, integral whole. In his advanced
work, *Antirrhêtikos*, or "talking back," Evagrius notes in his prologue an important definition: "For a monastic man is one who has
departed from the sin that consists of deeds and action, while a

---

[160] Evagrius Pontus, "The Monk: A Treatise on the Practical Life," *The
Greek Ascetic Corpus*, chapter 5, no. 17, p. 101.

monastic intellect is one who has departed from the sin that arises from the thoughts that are in our intellect and who at the time of prayer sees the light of the Holy Trinity."[161] This describes precisely the situation that Philoxenos addresses: monks who have physically but not mentally/spiritually withdrawn from the world, and have come to live in the monastery, and discover that they are no further advanced in the spiritual life, if not further behind. The development of a monastic intellect indicates an inner spiritual faculty that enables one to discern and reject the passions and make a correct judgment. Evagrius' favorite technique is to prescribe an antidote for a spiritual disease. The critical principles Evagrius has emphasized in the monk's spiritual progression take the literary form of a demon's seductive, typically negative idea followed by a fitting scriptural verse that one uses as a sort of antidote to "talk back"[162] to a demon and defeat it. In his introduction, Philoxenos lists fifty-four pairs of diseases/passions and a fitting antidote for each (m 1.13; 22:2–23:18).

Despite the complexity of his thought, Evagrius nevertheless discourages monks from too much speculation. In his *Exhortations to Monks* he advises, "Restrain your curiosity about the Trinity; only believe and offer worship, for one who displays curiosity does not believe."[163] In his overture to the *Discourses*, Philoxenos repeats this idea several times. "Whoever is constant in reading, but far from works, indicts himself through his reading. He is worthy of greater judgment, for he treats contemptuously and despises daily what he hears every day" (m 1.2; 5:10–13). "Whoever approaches God ought to believe that [God] exists, and [God] rewards those who

---

[161] Evagrius Pontus, *Talking Back: Antirrhêtikos: A Monastic Handbook for Combating Demons*, trans. David Brakke, CS 229 (Collegeville, MN: Cistercian Publications, 2009), Prol.5, p. 51.

[162] Brakke credits Clark with this colloquial turn of translation, CS 229:4. See Elizabeth A. Clark, *Reading Renunciation: Asceticism and Scripture in Early Christianity* (Princeton, NJ: Princeton UP, 1999), 128–32.

[163] Evagrius Pontus, "Exhortation to Monks," *The Greek Ascetic Corpus*, chapter 2, no. 33, p. 222.

seek him.[164] Paul commended this law to one who desires to draw near to God and placed this debt on him to pay: to believe only that God exists. Whoever believes that [God] exists, and does not investigate 'when' and 'how,' so also if he obeys his will and word and teaching, he will affirm that it is the will of God and will hear and believe the voice and commandment of God. But as for judging 'why' and 'in which form,' and 'why thus,' this is an audacious investigation for a soul that has not perceived God" (m 2.1; 28:1–11).

Philoxenos becomes more serious when he arrives at "the renunciation of the world." The shift from the physical to the spiritual realm is apparent, for Philoxenos does not need to urge anyone to "depart from the world." However, many have not spiritually renounced the world, still dwelling mentally in the memories of worldly settings of family and marriage, instead of their minds dwelling spiritually in the kingdom of heaven or the Garden of Eden.

All of this theological musing on renunciation is still prolegomena for the monks since it concerns an action and event on which they have already embarked, however imperfectly and incompletely. In the tenth *mēmrā*, Philoxenos drops the shoe and talks bluntly of the beginning of all sin. Gluttony or the lust of the belly is a psychosomatic stumbling block, not only to physical health, but also to spiritual vitality and divine knowledge. In the physiology of asceticism the lust of the belly leads directly to the spirit of fornication, and then to worse spiritual malaise. This is not manichaeistic dualism at play, for nothing is wrong with food, Philoxenos emphasizes, it is a matter of how you eat, of not allowing desire to have control over you.

In *Antirrhêtikos*, Evagrius cites the story in Daniel 1 regarding Daniel and the three other young men who reject the rich food of the Persian court for a diet of seeds and before long they are far more fit than their indulgent compatriots.[165] This is also one of Philoxenos' favorite stories, reviewed at length in the eleventh *mēmrā* (m 11.58; 471:1–473:12), partly to show explicitly how to

---

[164] Heb 11:6

[165] Evagrius Pontus, *Talking Back*, Gluttony 45, p. 62.

practice a proper nongluttonous way of life, but also to demonstrate that it is not food in itself that is the demon, but the tendency and weakness for the wrong kind of food.

In the two long *mēmrā* on gluttony, fasting (ܨܘܡܐ - *ṣawmā*) is not the primary focus, since the most difficult sins develop in situations where the individual does not recognize the dire consequences and sinfulness of what he is doing. Philoxenos warns against the delusion that if the monk believes he has conquered the rich and fancier foods that he has defeated gluttony. Rather, one must be alert even more to the temptations of eating too much plain, regular food. Once one is in control regarding plain food, then the challenge of richer foods is a moot point (m 10.63; 415:11–416:8).

Philoxenos' intention is to tame, transcend, and be victorious over the lust of the belly, which has become the new boundary line for his understanding of the ascetical and monastic life,[166] superseding the requirement of celibacy for entry into perfection for the *Book of Steps*. A decision that leads to an authentic commitment typically is of sufficient stringency that one cannot make it with half measures. "The lust of the belly is the beginning of all sin" and the rejection of its control over one's body and soul necessitates at first a clearly uncomfortable transformation of one's entire being, spirit, soul, and body. The "battle" (ܬܟܬܘܫܐ - *taktūšā* / ܩܪܒܐ - *qrābā*) has moved inwardly, where gluttony plays out its beguiling challenge.

This emphasis on gluttony and then fornication does seem to take us back to the perception that Philoxenos was attempting an Evagrian model of sins and vices in the construction of his *mēmrē*.[167]

The most thorough effort at showing the indebtedness of Philoxenos to Evagrius is in the essay of Robin Darling Young, a Syriac and Evagrian scholar, in the Sidney Griffith festschrift.[168] Darling Young succinctly summarizes the literary and ecclesiastic careers of

---

[166] Kitchen, "The Lust of the Belly Is the Beginning of All Sin."

[167] See David A. Michelson, *Practice Leads to Theory*, chapter 2: "Monastic Practice and Divine Knowledge: The Evagrian Background to Philoxenos' Vision of Christian Faith and Life," 50–72.

[168] Robin Darling Young, "The Influence of Evagrius of Pontus," *To Train His Soul In Books: Syriac Asceticism in Early Christianity*, ed. Robin Darling

both authors, noting that while Evagrius' work would eventually come under fire for its speculative visions, Philoxenos focused solely on the former's theology of monasticism and the spiritual life. Darling Young concentrates on Philoxenos' *Letter to Patricius*[169] to illustrate how Philoxenos understood Evagrius' ideas and intentions, admonishing and amending the interpretation of a monk who had been reading Evagrius erroneously.

Darling Young makes the observation that Philoxenos never seems to have lived in a monastery or to have taken monastic vows.[170] Nevertheless, his monastic deference was formed through the ascetical life of a scholar begun at a young age.[171] Philoxenos' fundamental ethic was to live in imitation of Christ, an essential tenet of Evagrius.[172] He appears to have inherited in some fashion the stratification of the Christian way of life from the *Book of Steps*:[173] uprightness or justice/righteousness and perfection. The first level, Darling Young notes, is more of an exterior imitation of Christ's obedience, while perfection is the true imitation of Christ.[174]

In the *Letter to Patricius*, Philoxenos responds to the inquiries of a monk, Patricius of Edessa, whom he recognizes has read Evagrius in an incorrect way. Patricius wishes to bypass the need to follow the commandments on his way to full contemplation, an immature interpretation of Paul's rejection of the law. Philoxenos insists on the

---

Young and Monica J. Blanchard, CUA Studies in Early Christianity 5 (Washington, DC: CUAP, 2011), 157–75.

[169] *La Lettre à Patricius de Philoxène de Mabboug*, ed. and trans. René Lavenant, PO 3 (Paris: Firmin-Didot, 1963).

[170] See Andrew Palmer, *Monk and Mason on the Tigris Frontier*, 115, regarding the legacy of Philoxenos in the monastery of Qartmin in Ṭur 'Abdin. Eli of Qartmin identifies Philoxenos as a monk of Qartmin (ll. 235–48), but Ignatius Aphram I Barsoum (*The Scattered Pearls: History of Syriac Literature and Sciences*, trans. Matti Moosa [Piscataway, NJ: Gorgias Press, 2005, 297f.]) says Philoxenos only became a monk when he went to Tell'Eda.

[171] Darling Young, "The Influence of Evagrius," 166–67.

[172] Darling Young, "The Influence of Evagrius," 160–66.

[173] CS 196: lxxxii–lxxxiii.

[174] Darling Young, 170.

necessity of suffering and keeping the commandments in the imitation of Christ. Faith precedes and is a prerequisite for knowledge,
and Philoxenos goes further in making faith a form of knowledge,
a kind of sixth sense, a perspective Darling Young believes he may
have acquired from Ephrem and John Chrysostom.[175] Moreover,
in a theme found a number of times in the *Discourses*, Philoxenos
advises Patricius not to read too much for such practice does not
produce the knowledge of Christ and instead will produce many
thoughts in the soul that will lead to trouble.[176] Trouble for Philoxenos means the contortions of christological debate, especially as
conducted by Chalcedonian supporters. Faith and simplicity are
the appropriate and adequate perceptional skills for the monk
aspiring to perfection.

David Michelson's studies of Philoxenos' appropriation of Evagrian *ascesis* and divine knowledge,[177] while paying significant
attention to the *Letter to Patricius*, also draw the *Discourses* into
the bishop's Evagrian hermeneutical approach. He demonstrates
that Philoxenos' purpose in utilizing Evagrius' system of monastic
asceticism was to counter "out of order" theological speculation.
Michelson sees the central concept to be that of simplicity, the essential beginning point for those embarking on the monastic life.
It is not stupidity or dullness of mind, but the singleness of one
thought which hears and does not judge, accepts and does not
investigate the ineffable reality of God. Simplicity is, in fact, one
of the basic characteristics of God, who is simple, not complex,
segmented, or divided. The opposite of simplicity for Philoxenos is
worldly wisdom and craftiness which inevitably lead one toward
the convoluted arguments and controversies of the christological
debates in which Philoxenos both engages and works to disengage
himself. Michelson suggests that the order of Philoxenos' themes

---

[175] Darling Young, 171–72; *Patricius*, 118, 54.
[176] Darling Young, 174; *Patricius*, 62, 65.
[177] Michelson, *Practice Leads to Theory*.

(faith, simplicity, fear of God, renunciation, gluttony, abstinence, fornication) is essentially an Evagrian scheme.[178]

It is apparent that Philoxenos approaches his progression of monastic and spiritual education informed by an Evagrian imagination, but it is not obvious, as might have been with a systematic delineation of the eight thoughts or vices. Philoxenos also participates in the classic Syriac spiritual tradition, so several of his ascetical qualities are not distinguishable from earlier authors. E. W. Budge, in his introduction to the *Discourses*, recognized a kindred spirit between Philoxenos and Aphrahat. The first discourse and demonstration for both authors is "On Faith," which Budge emphasizes by including an English translation of Aphrahat's *Demonstration*.[179] Budge conjectures that Philoxenos might have desired to imitate or continue Aphrahat's *Demonstrations*, but there is no evidence of that scenario. Philoxenos' corpus is more disciplined and directed in its organization, whereas Aphrahat's topics are more occasional. It is Evagrius' theology which Philoxenos is utilizing as a template.

Faith is the first step for Evagrius, not a specific content of doctrine, but a theological "sense." Evagrius states that "faith is the beginning of love; the end of love, knowledge of God,"[180] and then connects faith to one of Philoxenos' other steps, "The fear of the Lord begets prudence; faith in Christ bestows the fear of God."[181] In between faith and the fear of God is simplicity, which as recognized before is a basic concept for Evagrius. "God is universally confessed as simple and uncompounded."[182] The renunciation of the

[178] David A. Michelson, "Philoxenos of Mabbug and the Simplicity of Evagrian Gnosis: Competing Uses of Evagrius in Early Sixth-Century Polemical Theology," *Evagrius and His Legacy*, ed. Joel Kalvesmaki and Robin Darling Young (South Bend, IN: University of Notre Dame Press, forthcoming).

[179] Budge, *The Discourses*, 2:lxxiii–lxxiv.

[180] Evagrius of Pontus, "To the Monks in Monasteries," *The Greek Ascetic Corpus*, no. 3, p. 122.

[181] Evagrius of Pontus, "To the Monks in Monasteries," *The Greek Ascetic Corpus*, no. 69, p. 126.

[182] Evagrius Pontus, "On the Faith," no. 5, Casiday, 47.

world is a universal principal for monastic spirituality—Evagrian, Syrian, and other—while gluttony and fornication are the initial two "thoughts" in Evagrius' system.

A Pastoral Philoxenian Postscript

Quiet Philoxenos was not. The energy and enthusiasm with which he approached and delivered the themes of the *Discourses* can be overwhelming. Whether or not he ever was a monk himself, the bishop cares deeply for the vocation of the novices around him. Nothing is more important than the monastic and ascetical life, a life that is neither extraordinary nor ordinary. It is the way of perfection by which Christ leads one back into the Garden, characterized by the single-minded simplicity of the original couple before they stopped being simple. There is, however, nothing easy about this way, and it is a continual state of struggle for the monk, and Philoxenos cuts no corners for his charges.

Philoxenos is on the side of the monks, encouraging them, bolstering their spirits, cheering them on as the consummate pastor who knows when to insist uncompromisingly and when to reassure his flock so that they may accomplish the humanly improbable. 'Tis a gift to be simple, for the human being is drawn to distractions, irrelevancies, and excesses. Philoxenos points on every page or every minute of his narration to the authentic desire to become fulfilled (ܡܫܠܡܠܘܬܐ - *mšamlyūtā*)—which is a Syriac synonym for perfection. If the monk can keep that goal in mind, he remembers God.

Abbreviations

A Boll	*Analecta Bollandiana*
CS	Cistercian Studies Series
CSCO	*Corpus Scriptorum Christianorum Orientalium*
JTS	*Journal of Theological Studies*
MW	Monastic Wisdom Series
OC	*Orientalia Christiana Periodica*
OCA	*Orientalia Christiana Analecta*
OrChr	*Oriens Christianus*
OrSyr	*L'Orient Syrien*
PO	*Patrologia Orientalis*
PS	*Patrologia Syriaca*
SP	*Studia Patristica*
VC	*Vigiliae Christianae*

Mēmrā 1

Introduction

(3) [These are] the discourses concerning instruction in the ways of life described by the blessed Mar Philoxenos, bishop of Mabbug, who explains through them the entire system of discipline: how one should begin in Christ's discipleship, and by which laws and rules one should journey until one attains the spiritual love from which perfection is born. For through [perfection] we become like Christ, as Paul the Apostle said. This is the first *mēmrā*, the introduction to this entire volume, by the grace of our Lord.

Summary: Philoxenos stresses laying the foundation of wisdom in the correct order with the appropriate building blocks. One needs to be able to recognize the various lusts and passions with which one does battle, and against which spiritual masters guide us, prescribing the right medicines or antidotes against these passions. A long list of spiritual antidotes to counter different passions of sin is presented. Philoxenos promises to show the reader how to begin and then advance through all the grades of the Christian life until one reaches Perfection.

Beginning to Build

1. Our Lord and Savior Jesus Christ invited us through his living gospel to approach wisely the work of keeping his commandments and to establish in us the foundation of his discipline in an orderly fashion, so that the building of our ways of life may ascend straight up and true. Whoever does not know how to begin knowledgeably

in the building of this tower that rises up to heaven is not able to finish and bring it to the perfection of wisdom. For **(4)** knowledge and wisdom direct, order, and accomplish the beginning, completion, and nurturing of all these things.

Whoever begins this way is called wise by our Savior's word: "Everyone who hears these words of mine and does them is like the wise man who digs deeply and establishes his building upon a rock. The rain came down and the torrents came and the winds blew, and [though] they beat against that house it did not fall, for its foundations were established upon a rock. But whoever hears and does not do [these words] is like the foolish man who establishes his building upon the sand. Even if the elements beating against his building are weak, they will tear it down."[1]

Reading and Hearing the Word

2. Therefore, according to the word of our teacher, we must not only become constant hearers of the word of God, but also constant doers. Whoever does [these words]—even though he does not listen—is better than one who constantly listens but is bereft of deeds. As the word of the Apostle Paul teaches us, "It is not the hearers of the law [who] are [considered] upright before God, but the doers of the law [who] are held to be righteous. If the Gentiles, who do not have the law, act lawfully by their nature, they are a law unto themselves, even though they had no law. They show that the doing of the law is written on their heart, their conscience witnessing for them."[2]

Yet, hearing the law is excellent because it brings [one] to works. Reading and study **(5)** of the Scriptures are excellent, purifying our inner mind from the thoughts of evil things. But if a person is constant in reading, hearing, and studying the Word of God, while not carrying through on his reading by performing works[, this is not good]. The Spirit of God foretold against this through the blessed David when he was refuting and reproaching his evilness.

---

[1] Matt 7:24-27.
[2] Rom 2:13-15.

[The Spirit] prohibited him from being able even to pick up the holy book in his filthy hands. God speaks to the sinful person, "What do the books of my commandments matter to you that you take up my covenant with your mouth? Yet you despise my instruction and cast my words behind you,"[3] [along] with the rest of what was written after these [words].

Whoever is persistent in reading, but far from works, indicts himself through his reading. He is worthy of greater judgment, for he treats contemptuously and regularly despises what he hears every day. Therefore, he is like a dead person and a corpse without a soul. If a myriad of trumpets and horns should blow into the ear of a dead person he does not hear. In the same way also, the soul of a person dead in sins and the mind from which the recollection of God has been lost do not hear the sound of shouts of divine voices through the deadly error of thoughts. The loud sound of divine summons and the trumpet of the spiritual word do not stir him, for he is sinking into the sleep of death which he finds pleasurable. Though he is dying, he does not perceive his [own] death, so that he could turn himself around and seek life for himself. Just as the person who has died naturally does not perceive his own death, so also one who is [spiritually] dead, who dies by his own will to the knowledge **(6)** of God, does not suffer at his own death, nor also does he perceive his destruction in order to find a way to recover life for himself.

So when God saw the deadness of the Jews, who willingly stopped up their ears and shut their eyes and hardened their heart from the recollection and knowledge of God, [God] roused Isaiah to awaken them and [God] called to him to shout into their ears, "Shout at the top of your lungs and do not hold back. Raise up your voice like a trumpet and show my people their iniquity and to those of the house of Jacob their sins."[4]

Again in another passage, the prophet said, "He said to me, 'Cry.' I said, 'What shall I cry?' 'All flesh is grass, and all its beauty is like

[3] Ps 50:16-17.
[4] Isa 58:1.

the flower of the field.' "[5] Just as grass and flowers dry up from the sun which the rain and all the irrigation of the springs are not able to make flourish once its natural moisture has been eliminated, such is the case of a people completely dead to the spiritual life. Like grass and flowers they wither and dry up before the noon [sun] of error and from the heat of evil things.

For the soul dies from the recollection of God, and when it has died, all its faculties of discernment die with it, and thoughts on the reflection of heavenly things cease from it. While the soul lives according to its nature, it dies through its will. And while it is found in its form, it perishes in its free will. Then it is necessary for the disciple of God that the recollection of his teacher Jesus Christ become fixed in his soul, and he should meditate on him night and day.

(7) It is appropriate to learn where one should begin, and how and where one should erect the stages of his building, and how one should begin and complete his building, lest one be ridiculed by all the passersby as our Lord said concerning whoever began to build a tower but was not able to finish it, for he became a joke and a mockery to all those seeing him.[6]

The Foundation

3. Who else would begin building the tower about which our Savior spoke, except the disciple who begins on the road of the Gospel of Christ? Here is the beginning of this disciple's own building: his promise and his covenant with God by which he promises to depart from the world and keep the commandments, and to begin to run and accomplish, while gathering and bringing from every place the precious stones of excellent rules for the building of this tower that ascends to heaven.

The foundation is solid and laid down, according to the word of Paul, which is Jesus Christ our God.[7] Every person builds upon that foundation as he desires, because once the foundation [Christ]

---

[5] Isa 40:6.
[6] Luke 14:29-30.
[7] Eph 2:20.

has bent down through his love so that he might accept everything placed upon him until the day of revelation comes, on which the work of every person is examined and tried; [then] he who is the foundation at the base of the building ascends and becomes the judge and the head at the top of the building. As Paul himself said, "If a person builds upon this foundation, [using] gold or silver or **(8)** valuable stones or wood or grass or stubble, the work of every person is revealed. For that Day will reveal it, because it is revealed through fire, and the fire will discern the accomplishment of every person as he is."[8]

Precious Gems

4. Paul compared the rules and virtues of righteousness with gold and silver and precious gems, for faith is in them like gold, and abstinence, fasting, and asceticism with the remainder of the labors of righteousness are like silver. Love, peace and hope, pure minds and holy thoughts are like precious gems; the intellect, pulsating completely in the Spirit, is carried in all its movements by the wonder of God and the marvel at the majesty of his being, and the mind that kept silent with trembling before the unexplained and unspoken mysteries of God.

Therefore, Paul labeled "precious gems" these thoughts and movements and heavenly pulsations and spiritual rules. But he called wood and grass and stubble "error" and "evilness," along with the practice of all these lusts. Insofar as a building is anchored into the ground, every person builds and erects upon it whatever he desires until the day of judgment is revealed, and the one about whom it was said comes: "He holds the winnowing fan in his hand and purifies his threshing floors and gathers grains of wheat into barns and burns the straw in unquenchable fire."[9]

The laborer who has planted the tree of our humanity in the world shows himself to be like a judge, the axe of decision being held **(9)** in his hand. Every tree that does not bear virtuous fruits

[8] 1 Cor 3:12-13.
[9] Matt 3:12, Luke 3:17.

he cuts down and throws into the fire.[10] When the fisher appears, having cast his net into the sea of the world and [the net] is full of large and small fish that are the races and families of humanity, peoples and generations of the sons of flesh, different tongues and nations without measure, [then] at that time he will draw and pull in his net onto the seashore, just as he said, and he will select the good fish and put [them] into his buckets which are the living storehouses of his kingdom. But the bad ones he will cast away into the outer darkness where there shall come to be weeping and gnashing of teeth.[11]

These things are reserved for that time so they may take place when the chief shepherd is revealed in the glory of his kingdom. For one thing is the time of trial, and another that of training, and another that of study, and another that of discernment. Just as there is no trial in this time of training, so also in that time of trial there will be no training.

The Beginning of Discipleship

5. Then, my friends, let us listen to the living voice of God who has called us in order to give us eternal life. His utterances are full of life and give life to whoever listens to them. Living utterances are spoken by life, and life is given by living utterances to those who pay attention to their words with a living ear.

However, because it is right for us to distinguish and speak concerning every one of the matters in its place, we should explain through our word which one is first and which one is after it, and how one after another the virtues are kept **(10)** and are perfected.

An Established Regimen

6. We have written this introduction so that it might encourage the reader [to discover] the wealth in the following discourses. Because it is appropriate for whoever is beginning on the road of

[10] Matt 7:19.
[11] Matt 13:47-50.

the commandments of Christ to know where he should begin and which stone is fitting to become the first [stone] for the building of his discipline, and which stone should be second and which third, lest while not knowing the order, nor learning where one should start, one also does not know where and how one should finish. Without the knowledge of his discipline, one might make the last things first and the first things last, and place some of these things in the middle.

For if the times are known to ploughmen and laborers of the world for seeding and plantings, and other [times] for harvesting and for the picking of fruits, keeping to the order of the seasons lest [the harvests] be damaged and their affairs be troubled—how much more ought the sower and spiritual worker and true disciple know which things are appropriate at first for his discipline, and where he should begin. Once he has set the first stone in its order into the foundation of his discipline, he will correctly erect all the rest of the building. Builders and masons also work in this way, for when they begin on the foundation of their building, [they start with] heavy stones and great solid rocks. Even if they place in the building something inferior, a solid foundation is able to receive and bear inferior materials. But if they place underneath in the foundation **(11)** weak and inferior [materials], and strong and great things above, their entire building will come tumbling down.

Moreover, let us take this example from those teachers who educate youths, who transmit their teaching to them in an order. They do not pass over and mix up the rules and the procedures of human knowledge, but they know which [subjects] they should present first, and which afterward, until the student reaches the completion of his level of education.

This apprenticeship is also familiar to all the worldly crafts according to a norm by which items are given to students to practice when they first begin learning the trade. Their teachers show them how to perform the smaller things in the craft, according to their lowest level. If a defect should occur, there will be [only] a little damage.

It is also standard with these who learn the art of athletics that they first begin with those [elementary] techniques of wrestling and

pay attention to which degrees they will progress through the art
of athletics. Initially, they move into a ready position against one
another. After this they throw their hands upon each other and so
are provoked to wrestle in full competition. Those who are chosen
for military service in the world also learn this art of war **(12)** in this
same order.

Learning in Order

7. For them, the process of learning is neither in a confused nor
disorderly manner. But they learn every one of these things in its
place and in its order with everything else that is in the world, the
beginning and middle and ending of each being evident.

Then, by the examples of these cases we have brought forward,
this order is especially useful for us. The knowledge of the first
mode of life and of the one after it is necessary for us. For here,
spiritual athletics is learned, and we are chosen for the cultivation
of those things that are in heaven, just as those who are chosen to
serve kings in the world learn the royal laws and customs from
those who preceded them regarding, for example, [how to] walk
and [how to] appear and [how to] speak and where one should
be in position to speak before [the king]. Those coming later learn
from [their] predecessors, those who are chosen recently from those
who preceded them. So also here it is necessary for a human being
who is chosen, whether by the discernment of his will or by the
promise of his parents, to serve Christ, to learn this ministry from
those who preceded him, or from the Holy Scriptures, or from a
spiritual person, for they have walked following the law on this
road, people who have commenced in the labors and completed
[them] spiritually and were perfected in love.

Fighting the Passions

8. The lusts that fight with us at the beginning of youth **(13)** are
obvious. It is evident which ones occur in the middle of youth, and
which ones at the end of the stage of youth; and which ones in the
beginning of young adulthood, and which ones in its middle and
which ones at its end; and moreover, which ones in middle age

in the same order as the first until the end of this level; and even more, which passions fight with us in the time of old age until our departure from the world. Then, which are the ones that happen to us in childhood and infancy by movements and natural impulses before the discernment of free will is stirred up in us, and we attain the knowledge that distinguishes good things from the bad.

Again, while we are fulfilling the rules and labors, we should know which passion contends against which one, and which desire strives against which one, and at the completion of the work of that good thing, which evil thing is awakened against us. How, in the defeat of one of the lusts, does another seize victory? How, when we have controlled the lusts of the body, does a battle of the soul's passions become aroused against us? And how, when we cast off an evil thing from the outside, does it turn around against us to clothe us interiorly in our thoughts? When we have killed it from the members of the body, it still lives in the living movements of the soul. When we have cut it off and thrown it away from us, it enters insidiously into us **(14)** in order to live inside us.

Which passion is engendered in the soul from the fasting of the body? Which ones from abstinence, from singing out loud, from prayer in stillness, or from the renunciation of possessions, or by ragged clothing? Which passion is engendered in us from inner compassion toward every person? Which passion is aroused against us when our way of life is greater than that of our brother?

Which passions occur inside us from the knowledge of thoughts? Which ones from the words of instruction, and which ones from the words transmitted in the Scriptures? Into which passion do we fall once we have defeated the lust of the belly in all things? Which one is awakened against us at the final triumph of the war against fornication? Which passion is engendered in us by obedience to superiors, and which one by obedience to every person? What kind of thoughts do we have when we resist obedience? By which teaching is an unruly thought brought to nothing for its teachers? By which way of thinking do we uproot from ourselves the prejudices that we ourselves have? Which passions are defeated by which ones? Which lusts are dissipated by which [passions]?

[It is necessary to know] which [passion] is a battle with physical things, and which one with those of the soul, and which one with spiritual things. What should corporeal [people] do when they wish to defeat the lusts of the body? What should those of the soul do **(15)** in order to defeat and overcome the soul's passions? What should spiritual [people] [do] to be rescued from the faults that beset the spiritual in the spiritual sphere, and how far should the battle be extended into each one of these orders?

Discerning the Passions

9. How do we know when a movement of desire is from us? How and when does it occur in us by the enemy's instigation from outside? Through which [passions] is the desire engendered by us vanquished, and which ones does the enemy awaken against us? Is the same desire vanquished by a single method at all times? Are [certain] ways also necessary for us to triumph according to the circumstances? How and by what do we sense when our lust is defeated by us, [whether it is] by the strength of our patience or by the grace of God?

Which battle is awakened against us [when we are] among [too] many [people]? And which one when we are in solitude, and how especially is the soul cleansed and purified? Which place is helpful for the labor of the body? In which [things] should we begin first when we approach the discipleship of Christ? Which passion is awakened in us by the glory given to us by superiors, either on account of our knowledge, or on account of our way of life? Which passion [is awakened] when we are praised by the great majority of people? By which thoughts do we see the cause of the passions, and how should we be aware in our soul so as not to be disturbed by them when they set upon us? Which **(16)** attitudes should we adopt when we defeat their contention? How are we able to acquire humility? By which thoughts should we eliminate from ourselves pride which is the opposite of humility? By which ideas should we take hold of patience in our soul? What is the renunciation of the body, and what is the renunciation of the world, and what is the renunciation of the soul? When we have renounced the wealth of these visible things, how do we acquire the wealth of the gifts of Christ?

First Steps in the Ascetical Life

10. Which commandments should we keep at the beginning of our discipleship? How should we listen to our teachers, those who advise and teach us virtuous things, while not noticing their faults? Which power wrests our soul away from every one of the good things that are being performed by us? How should we live with excellent manners in the monasteries of our brothers? To what degree is it necessary for one to fast? How in every time like it should we add and subtract from the food for our bodies? How and how much should we eat when the war of desire confronts us? What should we do when we desire to extinguish from ourselves the passions of the soul? With which reflection of thoughts do we uproot enmity from ourselves?

How and from where is pure prayer born inside us? Which examples draw us toward a state of wonder about God? How does the passion for God stir in our soul at every moment? How many passions and examples should there be for this passion for God? How when we come **(17)** to stillness should we guard our thoughts from wandering beyond us? What harm happens to a person from association with heretics? How is our heart hardened and darkened from the recollection and reflection of God through human encounters and meetings?

We should know which is a physical fast, and which is one of the soul, and which is a spiritual [fast]; which one is physical purity, and which is that of the soul and that of the spirit; which one is physical renunciation, and which is [renunciation] of the soul, and which one is spiritual; and which are the distinctions of stillness—physical, soulful, and spiritual.

The Spiritual Art

11. How is the soul taught to fast from evil things, except through the example of the body [fasting] from food?

These [examples] and many others like them the disciple of Christ ought to learn and comprehend in order to journey with confidence on the road of his service and to carry out the desires of the heavenly King before whom he serves. If those who diligently learn the trades of the world learn all the secrets of the trades and are eager to understand all the forms of activities involved in every one of them, how much more for that one chosen for this spiritual art—if it is right to call it an art—is it necessary for him to know all the roads and paths and aims and examples of the mysteries of this divine way of life, and to understand that while a person is a physical being, he has been selected to serve in spiritual matters, and by the grace of God has been deemed worthy of the way of life of heavenly beings. (18) But while he exists in the flesh in the world, he should journey on the road that is above his nature.

Therefore, we ought—if we are disciples—to inquire and learn as disciples all those things in which we find ourselves living. Just as disciples learn the arts from their teachers, so also let us learn and receive from spiritual teachers. For no one is able to become a teacher, unless at first he becomes a disciple.[12] He is not able to assist and help others unless he has accumulated profits for himself from others, subjugating himself to receive and learn from everyone, and considering everyone greater and higher than himself.

Because our nature is created, and even though we did not exist, we live according to the will of the Creator and are able to acquire newly the learning of virtues. Just as we have come into being from nonbeing, so also from being sinful we become righteous.

But when a person has completely taken off the world, then he clothes himself perfectly in the way of Christ. Until he takes off the dirty outer coat and purifies himself through tears of repentance from the stains of evil things, he is not able to put on the purple garments of the knowledge of Christ. For a person who is defiled by thoughts or by deeds of iniquity ought to heal his [own] bruises first, and cleanse the blemishes of his soul and of his body, and then

[12] See Matt 10:24-25a.

come to the banquet hall of the divine mysteries, while putting on the spiritual outer garments [required for] this feast.[13]

Starting from Childhood

12. Because of this it is especially fitting that everyone who becomes a disciple of Christ should establish the foundation of his discipline from the time of his childhood in order that his entire **(19)** upbringing should acquire virtuous habits. He should not approach this new ministry after the world depletes the strength of his soul and of his body, like an old and worn out vessel. But as it was said by our Lord, "Let us put new wine into new skins [so that] both of them will be preserved";[14] so at the beginning of our childhood, while our planting is still new, let us place into our soul the new wine of the teaching of Christ, while our strength is in us and our newness has not become old through sins, in order that we might be able to endure the fervor of the love of holy teaching. Thus, while we preserve it, we will be protected in it from all evil things, especially so that the strength of our soul is not seized and taken for the labor of foreign slaveries.

But whoever begins in his childhood in this way of life needs to live with the admonition of teachers, being obedient to their words and not judging their faults. Moreover, those teachers should place themselves in the rank of tutors to whom the sons of the heavenly King have been entrusted so that they might bring them up: whose father is the king, and whose brother is king, and their mother the queen. Just like those who educate princes in the world, they should demonstrate unending diligence for their [students'] education, along with vigilance and care, so that they might be pleasing through them to their parents, and also to [the princes] when they come to the honor of the kingdom; in the same way also the teacher who has disciples should consider himself to be bringing up princes and should be vigilant and alert, inwardly and outwardly, concerning their precepts and their development.

---

[13] See Matt 22:12.
[14] Matt 9:17; Luke 5:36-38.

It is appropriate, **(20)** moreover, imitating physicians, that we should behave in this way toward ourselves and toward one another, because there is no physician for whom a disease occurs in his [own] body who does not show diligence concerning it before [he attempts] to cure the diseases of others. Moreover, if others become ill, the code of the healing profession requires him to rush to their healing. In the manner of physicians we should first know the causes of diseases, and then offer the medicines that do not make the disease increase. Bearing the soul and the body by the grace of God in the structure of our created being, we are required to have diligence for both of them.

Concerning diseases and physical sufferings, the nature of the body makes its demands on us and for its nourishment and drink and clothing, its natural needs press us to take care of its need.[15] We are not able to turn away, not even if we want to, because the coercion of its sufferings directs us to its cure and to satisfy fully its needs and necessities.

As for the cure of our soul, the commandment of the word of God urges us to cure its diseases and to heal its passions and to satisfy its hunger with the nourishment of doctrine, to give it the drink of the knowledge of God, to clothe it in the clothing of faith, to put on it the shoe of the preparation of hope, and to rear it in good habits and in the fullness of all virtues, and in the obedience that prepares **(21)** [it] for the work of the commandments of God.

For while our inner actions are holy and our outer actions are pure, let us become vessels prepared for the spirit of God, so that it may dwell in us purely and in a holy way, while through knowledge and wisdom we heal the diseases that occur within us, and heal the wounds of sin from our soul.

Spiritual Antidotes

13. There is not one of the lustful diseases for which we are not given a medicine for its healing from the word of God. Similar to how medicines are mixed and prepared by physicians for physical

---

[15] See Matt 6:25ff.

illnesses, medicines against the passions of sins are prepared and made ready by the Spirit of God, in order that whoever is aware of an illness may find the medicine for it at his side and from close by bring aid to himself. Everything for the most part is healed by its opposite, because the opposition of the medicine will fight with the harm of the disease. The diseases that occur from severe cold will receive healing from hot brews. Those that occur from heat, things that quench thirst will be brought to their aid. So also dryness heals those that occur from moisture. Those that happen by moisture, things that dry up [others] are given for their healing. Therefore, take an example from here, O discerning one who wishes to heal the ailments of the soul, and provide for your soul something that performs the art of healing to the body. On account of this, the work of external things is placed before our eyes so that it might be an example of instruction for those things that are internal, and we might heal the soul from **(22)** the diseases of evil things similar to [the way] the body is healed.

Let us prepare against each of the passions of sin the antidote that is the opposite of the disease: against doubt, faith; against error, truth; against supposition, accuracy; against falsehood, integrity; against guile, simplicity; against cunning, innocence; against blurriness, transparency; against harshness, gentleness; against cruelty, kindness; against physical desire, spiritual desire; against pleasure, suffering; against the joy of the world, the joy of Christ.

Against [popular] songs, spiritual melodies; against play, groans and weeping; against intemperance, fasting; against intoxicating drink, the thirst of discernment; against comfort, toil; against pleasure, trouble; against fleshly pleasure, the pleasure of thoughts that exult spiritually; against speaking, stillness; against public conversations, silence; against laxity, tenacity.

Against slowness, quickness; against carelessness of thoughts, acuteness of mind; against listlessness, constancy; against ferocity, mercifulness; against the evilness of the mind, the goodness of the soul.

Against haughtiness, humility; against pride, contemptibleness; against the love of honor, servitude; against praise, reproach.

Against **(23)** wealth, poverty; against possession, renunciation; against enmity, peace; against hatred, love; against anger, reconciliation; against rage, tranquility; against envy, love; against evil jealousy, the love of people; against curses, blessings; against a blow on the cheek, turning the other cheek to the one who strikes us.

Against grief, joy; against presumptions about ourselves, the confident hope that is with God; against physical passions, spiritual passions; against physical sight, spiritual sight.

Against lavish clothing, ragged clothes; against magnificence, asceticism; against obesity, emaciation; against thought that is concerned with food, thinking that dwells on heavenly matters; against the vision of everything visible, the recollection of everything invisible.

Against this world here and now, the search for the world to come; against the love of physical parents, the love of spiritual parents; against attachment to the human family, the attachment of our mind to our heavenly ancestry; against the city and house that is on earth, the dwelling of Jerusalem on high.

Conclusion

14. Therefore, all these [illnesses] and those like them are healed and cured by that which is opposite [to it]. Whoever desires spiritual things needs to renounce physical things. For until one [kind of] desire dies in us, the other [desire] will not live in us. That is, until a physical desire dies, a spiritual desire will not live in our thoughts. The death of each one of them gives life to its companion. When the body **(24)** is alive in us with all of its lusts, the soul dies with all of its desires. When the soul shares in the life in the spirit, and all its parts live with it—that is, its thoughts—then a person rises up from the dead and is alive in the new life of the new world. Until we take off the old [physical] person, we are not able to put on the new spiritual person. But, when we put him on by grace, we do not perceive him.

All these illnesses we have recounted are healed by these medicines. From there it is [the responsibility] of whoever falls sick to know its cure and to become his own physician. Let him ascertain a medicine, its remedy, for every one of these diseases we have recounted. See, a medicinal herb is placed beside a disease that heals [the disease], and with an ulcer is a medicine that cures it. If you seek to heal your diseases, look, the medicines that heal them are right there beside them; just diagnose your diseases and acquire the knowledge of their remedying plants.

By the brief summary I have outlined for you, take notice of the rest by the diligence of your soul. Learning does not teach you everything lest you become sleepy and idle. But if you consider that those things written or about to be written are too difficult and beyond your strength, call on God to assist you and from him you will receive the grace that assists you in the battle in which you are involved. Then, let us draw near with the assistance of God, and with a small number of words (25) we will describe every one of these passions, according to our power, that is, just as grace provides for my personal aid and for the benefit of others, as we set down these discourses in order one after another and show where the disciple needs to begin and how one should progress and ascend all the degrees of the ways of life until one attains the highest degree of love, and from it ascend to the level of perfection. Then he shall receive the spiritual place of the joy of Christ. When he has come to stand in it he is freed from the passions and has escaped from the lusts and has subdued all his enemies under his feet. From then on a person may speak freely the word of the apostle, "Therefore, it is no longer I who live, but Christ lives in me."[16] To him be glory forever. Amen.

The end of the first *mēmrā*, the introduction of the volume.

---

[16] Gal 2:20.

Mēmrā 2

On Faith

(26) Here is the second *mēmrā* in which [Philoxenos] teaches which is the first commandment one should adopt when approaching the discipleship of Christ.

Summary: Everyone should have the kind of faith which accepts God, but neither questions nor challenges him. However, the eye of faith, which one possesses by God's grace, is able to see deeply into the secret things of God. All should approach God with the mind of a child, and so through our second birth, that is, baptism, we are taught by God as infants. Faith is the tongue and command of God the Creator. Sometimes faith does not even offer prayer but gives an authoritative command like God, as was the case with Elijah, Jesus, and others. Jesus made faith the foundation of the Church and we should make faith the beginning of our life in God, for without faith all other spiritual activities are ineffectual.

Faith Sufficient

1. Whoever wishes to approach the way of discipleship of Christ in an orderly fashion should, before all else, take true faith into his soul, which means believing God and not investigating [God]. [Faith] affirms [God's] words but does not investigate regarding his nature. It hears his utterances but does not judge his actions. Faith believes God in everything [God] says, while not seeking witnesses and proofs for the truth of his word. This veritable proof is sufficient for him—that God is the one speaking. Signs and witnesses and demonstrations are necessary when a human being does and says

something. But when God is the one speaking and the Lord of the universe says that he is acting, it is necessary for us to believe— the fact that God is the one speaking and acting being sufficient for the persuasion of our faith.

A person does not have the power to judge [God's] desires. How is it possible for a created human **(27)** being to judge the will of his Maker? Just as a vessel is not able to find fault with its arti- san—"Why did he construct it in this way?"[1]—or judge one of his actions; so also a person who is a rational vessel does not have the right to find fault with the artisan, his Maker. Even if he does have the word of knowledge, it was not given to him so as to judge the will of his Maker by it but to extol the knowledge that has fashioned him. A rational human being is further away from the investigation of his Maker than an [irrational] vessel is from the examination of its artisan. On account of grace we have received reason[2] from God our Creator, and so that we might be astonished at his creatures he placed in us thoughts of knowledge. And so that we might perceive it [God] bestowed in us the perception of wisdom. So that we might receive the taste of its graces, [God] placed in our soul the taste of discernment. And so that we might see him in his deeds, [God] gave us the eye of faith that observes his secrets.

God is greater than the examination of [our] thoughts, and his providence surpasses the investigation of reason. His deeds ac- company his nature, for just as [his] nature is not examined, nei- ther are his natural actions investigated. His desires should not be judged: "Why does he desire this way and act in that way?" Just as he should not be judged by us—"Why did he make us in this fashion or construct [us] in this particular fashion and place us in the world?"—so also not one of his desires should be found at fault by us—"Why did he desire and act **(28)** in this way?"

Whoever approaches God ought to believe that [God] exists, and [God] rewards those who seek him.[3] Paul commended this

[1] See Rom 9:20-21.
[2] Literally, "the word."
[3] Heb 11:6.

law to one who desires to draw near to God and placed this debt on him to pay: to believe only that God exists. Whoever believes that [God] exists and does not investigate "when" and "how," so also if he obeys his will and word and teaching, he will affirm that it is the will of God and will hear and believe the voice and commandment of God. But as for judging "why," and "in which form," and "why thus"—this is an audacious investigation for a soul that has not perceived God.

Mind of a Child

2. Anyone who draws near to God should acquire the mind of a child. Just as a child is with his father and his mother, so also he shall be with God and with his providence. Just as a child receives learning from a teacher and does not investigate his words and examine his teaching, neither does he judge what [the teacher] teaches him by his own ideas, because his own thoughts do not have the capacity to become a judge of what he hears; so a person ought to be with God, not examining him by his words or judging [God's] actions by his secret thoughts. For he is a child, and like a child he should give heed to [God's] teaching and receive [it] with faith.

Because of this, God causes us to be born again in order to teach us to become children, **(29)** so [like] newborn infants from the world we are born to faith. The womb that causes [us] to be born [again] is placed in the middle, which is baptism into which the spirit is mixed, so we are being born by faith. Just as that natural fetus being born from the womb exists completely as a natural child, does not know anything of the world and neither seeks nor investigates, does not disrupt or speak but moves only by natural living movements, and being far from [having] any thoughts, so also this spiritual fetus, which the womb of baptism brings forth instead of a natural womb, ought not be involved with the investigation of the one who has brought him to birth, hearing his words serenely, and being a child with regard to his learning, receiving [his] words, but not approaching their examination.

Just as that natural infant learns the names of worldly things while not understanding their power, so also here let us receive names and words and leave to God the mystery of their meaning. We are children with regard to that knowledge and infants with respect to the ineffable wisdom of God. Because the word of our Savior also summons us in this way, "Let the children come to me and do not hinder them, for the kingdom of God belongs to those who are like these."[4] Moreover, in another passage he said, "Whoever does not receive the kingdom of God like a child shall not enter it."[5]

Faith of a Child

3. Similar to the way the faith of youths is with regard to worldly things, so our faith should **(30)** become toward the utterances spoken to us by God. Because in this way the child also lives with respect to the word he hears from his father. Everything promised to him [the child] believes without a doubt [his father] will give him. He does not distrust his word nor does he also examine or investigate it. He does not test its power [but] counts on its truth and then accepts it. Nor does he know how to distinguish the word promised to him, whether it is greater than the capability of his father, but simply he receives from him everything he tells him and does not doubt.

If he should see purple [robes] on a prince or a diadem placed upon his head, he demands his father to give them to him, believing sincerely that he will give [them] to him, because in this way he puts trust in him that he is able to do everything. If he should see a snake or a scorpion, he is not reluctant to stretch out his hand to [touch] them in his innocence and ask his father or his mother to give [them] to him, making known his childish desire through his crying. His constant impertinence against them, [along with] his shouting and crying, witnesses that he asks with all his natural strength, believing that the authority of his father will stand up even against the injuries of a deadly reptile. There is no doubt in his soul that he will not be given whatever he asks for. Therefore,

[4] Matt 19:14.
[5] Mark 10:15.

through this model of children, our Lord has commanded that all should become recipients of his kingdom, affirming and believing the promises of God to them through the example of children.

Do Not Investigate

4. Our Lord proclaimed and revealed his kingdom to physical beings and said, **(31)** "Repent, for the kingdom of heaven has drawn near."[6] You have heard the voice that preaches about the kingdom, "Believe him and do not doubt," especially when you have learned that the voice is God's. Do not ask yourself, "What is the kingdom like?" Nor should you investigate these spiritual places in your thoughts. Nor should you adopt for yourself a physical meaning whenever you hear about places that are not physical. Do not devise examples from your heart concerning these glorious dwelling places that the ascension of the Son has prepared. Nor should you order by your knowledge what the knowledge of God has previously established. You were not called to the investigation of the kingdom, nor even its preparation or construction, but only that you should become in it an heir and a guest and to take delight in the abundance of its spiritual blessings. You have heard the word Jesus says to you concerning the kingdom, "Repent, the kingdom of heaven has drawn near." He said to you, "Repent," and not "You shall be an investigator of the kingdom." That [kingdom] is near to you, if you are approaching it. The proximity to it is not through examinations of these words that inquire, "how" and "how much" and "what does the kingdom resemble," but so that a person may keep the laws of the kingdom and fulfill the commandments entrusted to us by the authority of the kingdom.

God the Simple

5. All of these things you have heard by faith concerning God who is from everlasting **(32)** and forever and who is in his own essence, not [deriving] from something different. He is not one

[6] Matt 3:2.

person,[7] but a self-existent nature which is believed and acknowledged in three persons. Moreover, the word of faith teaches you
concerning the persons to affirm that That One who has engendered
is not divided, and That One who was born is not separated. But
the Father is substantially with his Son, and eternally with the
Holy Spirit [who is] consubstantial with them. You should profess
only that they exist. But how and since when or how much or up
to where, and in which form and order, and how are they similar,
and how are they three while they are not distinguished from one
another; and how while they are in one another they are named
three; and how is the Son born while he is not separated from the
Father, and how did the Father bring him into being while he did
not go outside of him; and how the three beings are not spoken
of, while from everlasting and forever they are in existence—such
things like these are received by faith and without faith one is not
able to hear them. Not even a simple hearing supports them if faith
is not found prior to them to receive them.

So also concerning spiritual natures and higher orders, faith
is able to receive every word that is spoken about them. How is
faith not **(33)** necessary, for while Scripture calls them genuinely
spiritual ones, in another passage it speaks of them as composite
things and attributes to their composition forms that are different
from one another?

What Faith Can See

6. Concerning seraphim, the word of Scripture has described for
us wings and faces;[8] and concerning cherubim, other likenesses
that are different from one another. Which one should we hold to
be true, for see, the two refute one another according to a literal
hearing of the word? Let us believe that they are spiritual beings,
let us affirm that they are composite ones, let us accept that their

---

[7] *Qnōmā*—ܩܢܘܡܐ. *Qnōmā* is the Syriac translation for *hypostasis*, used in
the christological debates culminating in the Definition of Chalcedon (451).
[8] Isa 6:2.

composition exists in different forms. We receive all these things by faith because they were spoken by God.

"The backs of animals became full of eyes as they were turning around."[9] By this sentence he has taught us that the spiritual nature sees everything, hears everything, senses everything, considers everything, tastes everything, understands everything, and its natural desire desires everything. It is not that it hears through one part, while not hearing through another, or sees with one [part] while not with another. But it hears everything, and sees everything, and is completely self-contained. Its hearing is not troubled by its sight when it sees by the part that hears, and it tastes by that [part] that thinks. While they are not troubling or diminishing of one another, they are believed to exist in this way.

Composite Natures

7. As for composite natures, the opposite of these are found: [nature] hears through one part and sees with another, tastes with [yet] another, smells and senses with others, and thinks through another part. According to the composition of its members, the movement of its passions (34) also divides. But [referring to the] above, with regard to these spiritual natures, every one of them is complete in all of its movements, while the members are not distinguished in it—head and legs and hands and faces, the back and the front, the length and the width, the color and the forms which are different from one another. There is no structure of these members in these natures. Not because there is no eye is there no sight of the eye. Not because there is no ear is there no hearing of the ear. Not because there is no physical palate do they not have the taste of spiritual things. Not because they do not have wings do they not fly. Not because they do not have legs do they not move. Not because they do not have members of the heart, do they not think. But they possess complete function of the members, though they do not have composite members.

[9] Ezek 1:18.

We do not have the capacity in our knowledge to understand how the working of members exists without members, except through this [knowledge] given to us by God. But I say, [it is] through faith that we understand these things; and while these things do not fall at all under the investigation of human thoughts, they are accepted by us without a doubt. In this way we also learn by faith that they exist, and not only those but also the self-existent nature—their Maker—by faith we accept that he exists because the substance of all of our learning is through faith. Even if the sight and conduct of creatures explain and teach discerning ones about **(35)** their Maker, faith, nevertheless, also precedes this. For look, it was considered false by many because [they had] no faith.

Faith as Spiritual Vision

8. To say it briefly, faith sees and senses everything that is spiritual and the entire world of spiritual beings. If we do not take faith into our soul we are not able to comprehend anything outside of what is visible. Faith is not necessary for these visible things because the eye's vision sees them, for they are physical objects and a human being observes them physically. But faith perceives the entire world of the spirit, and if there were no faith it would be as if that world did not exist. Consider how great is the power of faith, for without it all spiritual things are as if they do not exist; and not only living creatures or spiritual places but also the Being that exists, as if it does not exist for us if we do not have faith. Because of this Paul observed the mystery of our teaching and said, "Whoever approaches God must believe that [God] exists."[10] [Paul] commanded the disciple to take faith upon himself and then approach the discipleship of Christ. Since Paul knew that the spiritual nature does not fall below the physical senses—it is not even knowable—since it is not subject to one of the physical senses, **(36)** on account of this he commanded us in his teaching to believe only that [God] exists.

---

[10] Heb 11:6.

Faith Planted in Us by God

9. The Maker has divided all of physical nature into five[11] faculties: some of it visible, some to be heard, some to be smelled, some to be tasted, some to be touched. He gave five senses to a human being so that through them one might experience[12] the world in a multitude of different ways. Then, beyond these five senses of which I have spoken, no one is able to experience anything from the physical world, for even the world itself does not exist beyond these things. As for the rest, everything that is spiritual, whether essence or creature, is not subject to any one of these five faculties and is not experienced by [even] one of these five senses. On account of this also when our Lord gave us this grace to perceive it, at first he delivered faith to us so that through [faith] we might perceive [grace], and then he revealed to us concerning himself. On account of this the blessed Paul said, "Faith is from the hearing of the ear and the hearing of the ear [is] from the word of God."[13] Paul has taught us to receive faith by the hearing of the word of God.

Faith Corrupted and Replanted

10. Even though faith is planted in us by God our Creator, that is, into our constitution, it was corrupted and transformed from faith to error. In a similar manner, we have changed natural wisdom which also was given to us in our constitution, and instead of God's wisdom we have gathered into it the world's wisdom and have exchanged something else outside of God for the wisdom of God. **(37)** As Paul himself said, "In the wisdom of God the world did not know God through wisdom"[14] so also the natural faith in us was changed to error, and these things given to us by our Creator for [our] benefit have been found with us for harm, because we have changed their profitable orders and have used them beyond their

---

[11] Typographical error: read ܐܣܟܡܐ.
[12] Literally, "to taste."
[13] Rom 10:17.
[14] 1 Cor 1:21.

purpose.[15] Our faith believed something that was not proper and our wisdom knew something that was not right. Wherever faith was not necessary, there we used faith. Something that the physical eye sees and all the physical senses perceive, our faith has perceived it as something else and we have imagined one thing instead of [another] thing concerning it. Because the order of faith that was planted into our nature by the Maker was corrupted to such an extent, the Word of God was planted in us a second time and the power in us was awakened by the teaching of Christ. On account of this, above and below, through all his utterances, he urges faith to be in us. "Truly I say to you, if faith is in you like a mustard seed, you will say to this mountain, 'Move from here,' and it will move. Nothing will be [too] difficult for you."[16]

By Faith Nothing Is Too Difficult

11. We have learned by faith that nothing is too difficult for us, and on account of this everything is defeated by the power of faith according to the commandment of the word of Christ. By faith signs occur and miracles are performed and mighty acts are accomplished **(38)** and wonders are performed. Faith alone effects everything that is above nature—whether resurrection of the dead, healing of the sick, cure of the ill, purification of lepers, opening [the eyes] of the blind, the lame running, straightening and restoration of all the other members, or speech of those who stutter, hearing of the deaf, driving away the demons—faith accomplishes all these things. A mountain is moved from its place through faith; the sea and rivers were crossed over on foot through faith; all the natures have obeyed the commandment of a person by the power of faith. Briefly, faith places the power of God in a person, so that when he believes he may do everything he wishes through the power of his faith. Faith reverts the infirmity of the body back to its own strength and makes a human being's contemptible commandment into an obeyed commandment of God.

[15] Typographical error: written ܝܘܡܟܘ, read ܝܘܡܘܟܘ.
[16] Matt 17:20.

Faith Sees the Existence of What Does Not Exist

12. Faith observes something that does not exist as if it did exist, and [faith] counts something that is as if it did not [exist]. This is also the image of God's power, concerning which Paul said, "He calls those things that do not exist as [if] they do exist."[17] The prophet said, "He rebukes the sea and dries it up[18] and empties all the rivers.[19] Then, he looks at the land and it trembles. He rebukes the mountains and they smoke."[20] Again also Isaiah **(39)** said, "All the nations are considered as nothing by him."[21] Therefore, the Spirit of God has said these things concerning the power of God: He calls those things that do not exist into existence, and he calls whatever does exist and changes [it] to nothing. Faith imitates this same power, not only through signs and miracles by which it makes those things that are not in the imitation of God, and by the power of God [faith] uses up and consumes those things that exist, but also those things that are considered as if they did not exist because they are hidden, it sees them openly. We labor in those things that are and are served by them, considering them not to exist, because at first [faith] considers their dissolution. While they do not pass away, [faith] had made them pass away. While they exist [faith] has done away with them. While they are visible [it is] as if they were invisible to [faith]. While their pleasures are being experienced [it is] as if they were nonexistent for [faith]. While all created things run, for faith they are in stillness. While [faith] sees death, it does not affirm that it is death. Wealth is considered [as] poverty. Everything that exists in the world, even in the natural world, [faith] observes as if it were not, because its course will come to an end and its matters will cease.

[17] Rom 4:17.
[18] Ps 106:9.
[19] Ps 74:15.
[20] Ps 104:32.
[21] Isa 40:17.

Faith Already Dwells in the Kingdom

13. But [faith] brings these things that are distant and remote from it and places them nearby in front of it and examines them face-to-face and without a veil observes and considers all hidden and concealed things. The kingdom of heaven is too far for physical vision, **(40)** but the eye of faith examines it. These dwelling places in the house of the Father are physically remote from us, but already faith dwells in them. That spiritual light shines gloriously in its region, and faith walks in it and sees by it. The coat of our glory is in heaven and our faith is already clothed in it. Our spiritual wealth and possession are there and our faith takes it and gives [it to us]. Our true city is in heaven and faith is dwelling in it from now on. Our lineage and our family and our parents are in that [distant] region and faith speaks with them and is in conversation with them at all times. The table of our pleasure is laid out there and faith enjoys it continually. The source of our drink of life flows there and faith drinks from it at all times. The powers of life and the orders of light are in the region of life and faith exults with them.

Distant God Close to Faith

14. What may I say concerning creatures, who, even if they are praised, still are [only] created beings, [and even] if they are great and astonishing they have come into being and were formed [only] recently. If now they are distant from us on account of their secrecy, we shall still draw near them when we become spiritual according to the order of their region. What should we say concerning these [beings]? Wherever the self-existent nature of God is, which is remote and distant from everything, it is near to faith. As much as we might be distant from him, he is not far away. However remote one may be from [faith], he is not far away. While he is far beyond everything, **(41)** he is close[22] to faith; and while he is within all creatures, endowed with speech or silent, living or inanimate, he is everywhere, [and] faith is with him.

---

[22] Written ܡܩܪܒ ܗܘ, read ܗܘ ܡܩܪܒ.

Because this is the nature of faith's vision: we shall see whatever is not visible, and whatever was not known we shall know, and whatever is unperceived we shall perceive. Whatever is infinitely distant, we shall become observer and neighbor. The more that nature which faith seeks to see is subtle and hidden and innermost, spiritual and sublime and ineffable, the more its own vision will triumph. Faith usually shows its proof through these very great things, because it considers it a shame to remain with lesser things and be held back by the work of creatures. On account of this, [faith] passes through everything and is not restrained by anything, except by the Creator. Creaturely existence is not able to endure and retain the power of faith, because there is not one of the creatures in which faith believes. If [faith] believes in it, [it is that] it is created and not that it is. But its own proof is experienced only in God, because [faith] casts out everything and places all the natures to the side and draws near to encounter the Maker.

Faith as God's Tongue

15. Faith makes pass away those things that exist [now] and invokes those that shall come into being. Faith is the tongue of God. Faith is the commandment of the Maker. Faith commands and is obeyed like God in everything. **(42)** [Faith] beckons and all creatures respond to it. The power of God is the power of faith, because from God is received the power of faith. Faith is the mistress of creatures, and like the mistress who commands her servants and they obey her, so also faith commands the creatures and they obey it. This is amazing that not only creatures obey faith, but also the Maker himself does not compel [faith's] will. Everything [faith] seeks, it receives. Whatever [faith] requests from [God], [God] will give it. [Faith] calls him and [God] answers [faith]. The door of the Giver is open before the requests of faith, as he said, "Everything you shall ask and do not doubt, you shall receive."[23] Faith com-

---

[23] Matt 21:22.

mands authoritatively in the house of God, just like the mistress of riches and the stewardess of possessions.

Marvelous and sublime is the mystery of faith and no one is able to interpret its mystery. In the same way, because it is the dwelling place of God, faith, which is not in name [only], is great and [is] not [limited] to the voice and word but is visible by the true testing of the soul, and by the fixed and true stability of thoughts does not renounce itself. Yet through this [faith] imitates God, about which Paul said, "He is not able to renounce himself."[24] In the same way also, since faith does not renounce itself, it does not allow doubt to enter its soul, nor does it allow suspicion to fall into it. Fear does not tread on its authority. Everything that [faith] desires, it accomplishes. Whatever [faith] seeks is given to it. **(43)** It is this faith that the human being who draws near to God ought to take into himself. Faith does not have thoughts that refute one another, nor even opinions that destroy one another. Faith does not regret whatever it does and speaks, nor does it blame itself once it has spoken and asked for what it desires. Just as there is no regret with God concerning anything that he does or says; so also faith has no regret about what it accomplishes, for also through this [faith] imitates God.

Faith as Commandment

16. Faith is a commandment and its commandment is authoritative. [Faith] prays confidently and according to its confidence its prayer is immediately accomplished in actions. But there [are cases] where faith does not [actually] pray, and then commands concerning something, yet speaks with authority, imitating God, and just as there is nothing that is able to resist the commandment of God, so neither [can anything resist] the commandment of faith. There [are cases] where faith prays, and in its prayer it reveals itself. There [are cases] where, without praying, it commands authoritatively and is answered.

---

[24] 2 Tim 2:13.

Elijah did not pray before Ahab and then was obeyed, but the faith that was in him had commanded authoritatively and whatever he said immediately happened. His word ruled over all natures and creatures more than a king's commandment over the cities of his jurisdiction. "[As] the mighty Lord lives, before whom I am standing, if during these years there is to be [any] dew or rain [let it wait] until I speak."[25] It was not written that he prayed [first], and then spoke. But as soon as creation had heard his word, it was bound under the sign of his commandment. As **(44)** the word of God all the creatures obeyed the commandment of a mortal human being. The clouds obeyed him. He summoned the earth and it answered him. He commanded the air and it was no longer visible in its changes. The entire creation came to be a dutiful servant before the faithful word of Elijah, being anxious to perform the commandment of its mistress that she had spoken to it. But in another passage, it was written he commanded the generals of the armies who had risen up to take him, along with the others who were with them. He spoke with divine authority, and the fire of God descended from heaven and burned up all of them. "If I am a prophet as you have said, may fire come down from heaven and devour you and the fifty who are with you."[26] Immediately without delay, the fire from heaven glowed and descended upon the impure, and the word of the prophet had come to fulfillment indeed.

Faith Prayed First

17. Yet in other passages it is written that faith had prayed and then was obeyed, as it is written, "He bent down and placed his face between his knees and sent his disciple to look towards the sea."[27] Moreover, when [Elijah] raised up the son of the widow, he prayed and prostrated himself, and then he raised him.[28] Moreover, through this same prayer faith became evident, for if he did not

[25] 1 Kgs 17:1.
[26] 2 Kgs 1:10.
[27] 1 Kgs 18:42-43.
[28] 1 Kgs 17:17.

believe [he was able to] raise him, he would not have received the youth from his mother and have carried him up and laid him on his couch. Again also to his disciple **(45)** he had said authoritatively, "Ask whatever you desire and I will give [it] to you, while I have not yet been led away from you."[29] Just as the disciple asked, the master commanded. The Spirit ministered indeed, and the gift rested upon Elisha.[30] But when he offered sacrifices on the mountain of Carmel in the presence of Ahab and all of Israel, "Answer me, Lord, answer me, Lord," he called out, "so that this entire people may know that you are the Lord and I am your servant, and by your commandment I have done everything."[31] Until he prayed he was not answered, nor did he bring the fire down.

Weakness and Strength of Faith

18. The reason for this is obvious, why in one passage they had prayed, but in another place they had commanded authoritatively. For in one, their weakness had become evident, and in another the power of God with them was revealed. When they prayed and made petition it was apparent that they were weak people, but when they commanded and were obeyed without prayer, it was evident that the power of God accompanied their command. In one passage they had spoken like human beings, and in [another] passage like servants of God, that is, like gods of the flesh, for the faith that was in them had made them heavenly gods.

Moreover, through this they were imitating Christ God who sometimes had accomplished things as one with authority, and in another passage, he had prayed and then acted. Until he had prayed he did not resurrect Lazarus.[32] Until he looked up into heaven he did not bless the bread and distribute [it] to the crowds.[33] Until he spat and placed his fingers in the ears of that deaf man **(46)**

[29] 2 Kgs 2:9.
[30] 2 Kgs 2:15.
[31] 1 Kgs 18:37.
[32] John 11:41.
[33] Matt 14:19.

and looked up into heaven, he did not command [his ears] to be opened.[34] But as for the rest of the others he was healing through a powerful commandment, without looking up into heaven or asking [anything] from his Father. Through an authoritative commandment he resurrected the young man, the son of the widow.[35] With a [loud] voice he called the daughter of the chief of the synagogue and immediately she stood up.[36] He commanded the sea and it became still, and the wind and it was held back.[37] "Fill the wine jars with water," he said only, "and pour some out and bring it to the head of the feast." His wish took place without delay.[38] "I say to you," he said to the deaf and dumb spirit and immediately [the spirit] departed from the person.[39] "I desire you to become clean," he said to the leper, and as he desired, immediately the leprosy fled from the body.[40]

In this manner also Jesus was performing miracles, for through this he brought himself down to [the level of] those whom he called his brothers by his grace. So that it might not be discouraging for those who are not obeyed until they pray, he also lowered himself and prayed, and then was obeyed. The Lord assumed for himself equality with his servants,[41] so that what was written might be fulfilled, "He should imitate his brothers in everything."[42] He gave them the power to speak with authority and be obeyed, so that through this they might be recognized as being the servants of God, and moreover, to give confidence to [their] faith so that everything it desires, it shall do.

[34] Mark 7:33-34.
[35] Luke 7:14.
[36] Mark 5:41; Matt 9:25.
[37] Matt 8:26.
[38] John 2:7.
[39] Mark 9:25.
[40] Matt 8:3.
[41] See Phil 2:6-7.
[42] Heb 2:17.

Joshua Commands the Sun

19. In the same way Joshua bar Nun commanded with authority the sun and the moon and they were halted. Each one of them
stood [still] **(47)** in the [normal] position on its journey. Joshua
extended his hand and spoke with the authority of faith. "You, sun
in Gibeon, stay! You, moon, in the valley of Aijalon, [stay!]." The
sun was halted and the moon stood still until the nation seized vengeance from its enemies.[43] Why should I speak [only] concerning
the prophets, where also in the entire [Israelite] people, and among
the women and children together, faith has shown triumphs such
as these? Faith has called out as it was commanded, and the walls
were not able to endure before its voice.[44] In every passage such as
these, faith demonstrated triumphs. Throughout the Holy Scriptures it performed these miracles. Whoever is aware of the power
of faith and takes up its experience knows indeed that [faith] has
accomplished these things and believes that it will do such things
as these again.

Faith, Mistress of All Possessions

20. Therefore, you also, O one who desires to become a disciple
of God, acquire faith, the mistress of all sorts of possessions. May
this be for you the start of your discipleship. Place [faith] as the
foundation in the building of your tower, and however high it
may reach, it will not fall. The building of faith is its foundation:
it shall not be shaken by waves or winds. Jesus also established
this faith as the foundation through Simeon.[45] Just as our Lord has
made [faith] the beginning, so also it is appropriate for the disciple
who approaches his education in an orderly fashion to begin with
[faith] first. Jesus laid the foundation for the entire church, but
you, lay the foundation for your own way of life. He built upon
[faith] the virtuous ways of life of the whole world. And you, **(48)**

[43] Josh 10:12
[44] Josh 6:20
[45] Matt 16:18.

build upon [faith] [your] triumphs and your own rules. [Jesus] laid [faith] down firmly so that it might become the foundation for all generations after his coming. As for you, make [faith] the beginning of your life in God.

See how great is [faith's] strength, for it is sufficient to bear all people. Jesus also laid [faith] into the foundation of the building of his church because he foresaw its unconquerable strength, its unfailing truth, its force that does not weaken, its irreproachable triumph, its power that is unwearied, its heroism that is not made feeble, its commandment uncompelled, its irreversible sentence, its word that is not accused of falsehood, and its authority that is not despised.

Jesus Made Faith Foundation of Church

21. Jesus made this faith, a triumphal mistress, the foundation of his church and the beginning of the building of his holy body so that he might teach everyone to begin on it, and that the disciple might lay it as the foundation for all[46] his rules. [It was] not only to show its power that he established [faith] to become the foundation of his church but also to teach everyone who desires to begin in the new building of his discipleship to make [faith] the beginning. With all the rest of his building, [faith] will support and make all the domains of virtues rise up.

Not one of the precious stones will go up into the building of this tower, if faith[47] does not raise it up. There is no life in a single one of the virtues' members **(49)** if the life of faith is not in them. Just as all the body's members are dead without the life of the soul, so without the life of faith, all the ways of righteousness are dead. Just as the members live by the soul, so the works live by faith. Just as the body's members, even if they are healthy and sound, are useless as long as there is no soul in them, and their beauty and their health are of no benefit to them, so also the rules, even if they are wearisome and difficult, and a person is healthy in the pursuit of

---

[46] Typographical error: written ܩܡܘܒ, read ܩܡܘܠܒ.

[47] Typographical error: written ܪܗܝܡܢܘ.ܐ, read ܪܗܝܡܢܘ.ܗ.

righteousness, his labor is empty as long as there is no faith in the members of his works.

Just as all the members receive sensation from the life of the soul, so that through its life every single one of them may be stirred up according to the order of its nature and that faculty accompanying it—the eye for seeing, the ear for hearing, the palate for tasting, the nostrils for breathing, the hand so that it may feel, the foot so that it may walk, the entire body so that it may be stirred up and act and make [the body] throb with living pulses in all the faculties by the service of all its members—in this same manner are also the members of the works of righteousness. As long as there is no life of faith in them, they are dead and useless.[48] For a fast is not a fast if there is no faith with it. Nor also are they considered alms if **(50)** they are not given in faith. Nor also is compassion anything if faith is not with it. Nor [can there be] abstinence and asceticism if faith is not mixed in them. Nor [can there be] humility and submission if faith does not carry them. Nor may narrow confinement[49] [be effective] if faith is not with it. [If] the virtue of faith is not mixed in it, it is not even counted as a good thing. Righteousness that is not mixed with faith loses its name and is emptied of its labors. Just as the body's shadow is not called the body, neither is the hand's shadow or the foot's identified by the name of one of the members; so neither is the body of righteousness, in which there is no life of faith, called the body or is a fast called a fast, or asceticism or abstinence given the names of real members. Without faith, all of them are a shadow and a dead body and are not able to be called a real body because they stand in suspicion of laboring in a foreign vineyard.

Fence of Christ's Commandments

22. Faith is the fence [around] the plants of the commandments of Christ. Every plant found inside this fence belongs to Christ and is planted in his vineyard. Those plants outside this fence are named

---

[48] Typographical error: written ܪܕܝܠܕܐ, read ܪܕܝܠܕܐ.

[49] An ascetical practice of living in a confined space (ܚܒܘܫܝܐ ܐܠܝܨܐ) ḥbūšyā 'alīṣā.

wild plants, because either they did not bear any fruits at all, or if they do bear [fruits] a savage beast or a bird makes them drop and ruins them. If it should happen that they remain, they are spoiled and do not have in them the nutrition of food. This is the vineyard (51) for which the lord of the house hired laborers. Everyone he saw standing outside he considered an idle person and persuaded him to come and labor in his vineyard.[50] Through faith virtues that are discovered are retained, and those that do not exist are acquired. Faith is the gatherer and guardian of treasures. It buries and guards treasures. It is the foundation and the master builder. It is solidified underneath homes and rises up with homes. It forms and enlivens members. It plants and cultivates spiritual plants. It is a fence for the plants and the spring that irrigates them. It is the progenitor and the one who rears. It is the body and the soul that is in the body. It is the sower of seeds and the reaper and gatherer of harvests. It is the planter of trees and picks and harvests fruits. Faith is everything, because it is sufficient to become everything.

Therefore, disciple, take hold of this faith and grasp firmly this truth and do not let go. Everything that you believe, ask and you shall receive from Christ, the one who promised that he would give. To him be praise and to his Father and to his Holy Spirit, forever and ever. Amen.

The end of the second *mēmrā* which is on faith.

---

[50] See Matt 20:1-16.

Mēmrā 3

On Faith

Summary: Faith is the activity of God in the new creation in the same way that wisdom was utilized in the beginning. Faith is required for the efficacy of baptism and communion. Knowledge is external to created things, while faith is within the thing itself, unobservable by the physical senses. Without faith the eyes see the things of the Church as common and poor, while the things of the world are perceived as powerful and rich. If one seeks in faith he believes in God; but if he desires in faith he believes in idols. Faith alone should be the cause of one's departure from the world into the monastery.

Invitation

(52) 1. Come once more and hear, O disciple, the desirable triumphs of faith. Come, give heed to the voice of your mother who through her sweet sounds gives you life. Come, suck the living milk of instruction from the living breast of the mother who has given birth to you. Come, stand at the fountain that gives drink to generations, for anyone who does not drink from it, his thirst is not quenched. Come, sit at the table full of the food of life, for anyone who is not nourished by it has no life in his life. Come, bend your ear and listen. Come, open your eyes and see the miracles that are shown by faith. Come, fashion for yourself new eyes. Come, construct for yourself hidden ears. You are being invited for the hearing of hidden things, [so] hidden ears are necessary for you. You were called to see spiritual things, [so] spiritual eyes are useful to you. Come, see what you are not and renew yourself before you are renewed.

Faith in the Beginning

2. The Creator has made you a new creature, and faith has assisted him in making you. He has brought you to a marvelous transformation and a heavenly establishment. Faith was with him when he was constructing you. **(53)** In the beginning when he was creating the creatures and putting things in order, wisdom was working with him, as Solomon said, "The Lord in his wisdom has set the foundations of the earth and established heaven by his intelligence. And by his knowledge the depths were broken open and the clouds sprinkled water."[1] Again Wisdom said, "When he established heaven, I was with him; and when he made a circle on the faces of the depths, and when he made firm the clouds above and when the fountains of the depths grew strong."[2]

Wisdom was with God in his first works, but in this second creation faith was with him. In this second birth he took faith as an assistant. Faith accompanies God in everything, and without it he does not carry out any new things today.

It would have been easy for him to give birth to you from water and the Spirit without [faith], but he does not give birth to you a second time until [the symbol of faith] is recited. He would have been able to renew you and make you new from someone old, but he does not change you or make you new until he has received from you the pledge of faith. Faith is required of whoever is baptized and then he receives treasures from the water. For without faith everything is ordinary, and [when] faith has come, base things appear glorious. Baptism is [only] water without faith; the life-giving mysteries are [only] bread and wine without faith. The old person appears as he is, if there is no eye of faith that sees him. The mysteries are ordinary and the spiritual miracles are base **(54)** if there is no eye of faith that sees them.

---

[1] Prov 3:19-20.
[2] Prov 8:27-28.

Power of Faith

3. The power of faith is not experienced by reason's testing, but [faith] is experienced by itself and in itself. Faith is not perfected by the ear's hearing but is confirmed within by the power of the soul. The ear receives the hearing of faith only, but the work of faith is born from thoughts. The spring that makes faith flow is a pure mind and a simple thought in which there is neither one thing nor the other. The thought of faith is singular[3] and there is nothing in it that combats against another [thought].

Faith looks in a hidden way, contemplating and considering the power hidden in things. Faith is more interior than knowledge, for whatever knowledge does not see is shown to faith, which is more interior. Because knowledge was not able to do the work of faith, knowledge has departed and faith has entered in its place. Knowledge is outside among creatures, but faith is inside with the Creator.[4] Knowledge investigates the wisdom that is hidden in the creation, and faith investigates the hidden things of the mysteries. Knowledge searches out the power of roots and fruits and of every [kind of] food that is given to the body, but faith searches out the power hidden in the life-giving mysteries that are food for the soul. Knowledge, insofar as it becomes subtle, creeps inside physical things, circulating and wandering in the visible world, but faith **(55)** does not remain in this creation and the power of creatures is not able to receive [faith] so that it might dwell in them.

The tongue is not capable of tasting the power of faith, nor is reason capable of speaking of its beauties, nor describing and depicting its images. Its strength is not experienced by a voice, nor even known by a word, nor by a portion of thoughts that turns toward the body. But within the holy of holies of the inner and spiritual mind, there the mysteries of faith are shown and the secret things are revealed. The portion that is in us alone, the most glorious of every human being, is able to perceive faith. The works of faith are visible on the outside and its words are heard by the

---

[3] ܐܝܕܝܐ, *īḥīdāyā*.

[4] Text written ܒܪܝܐ, read ܒܪܘܝܐ, "the Creator" (Ms. D).

ears. [Faith's] power is experienced within the mind. Even if you see the dead who are being raised up or the blind who[se eyes] are being opened, or the demons who are departing, you have not yet seen the [full] power of faith. Just as you see the power of God in a body that is resurrected, faith also revives the soul from the dead, and just as you experience [faith's] power in the healing of physical eyes, it also creates eyes for the spiritual natures. Just as you see its authority over the demons that depart, it also drives out natural thoughts from the soul.

The power of faith is visible to created beings through external[5] works. A person experiences it through the power of the soul, and faith does not allow the mind to experience it through any other thing, yet without the mediation of another thing it encounters and experiences **(56)** its power. Within the soul, signs from the outside are not mediators of the experiences of faith, but faith itself resides in the soul and pleases it, enlightening and gladdening its thoughts. [Faith] makes its natural light rise within and the soul is surprised at the new light that spreads out over it. Until faith brings back and gathers together the vision of the soul from everywhere it does not show it the beauty of its nature, because the soul is not even able to see [faith] when it divides its vision among other things. The soul's natural vision is impoverished when it is divided and looks outside of itself and is not capable of investigating the purity of the light of faith.

Eye of Faith

4. In just such a way faith gives power to the soul so that it becomes for [faith] a pure dwelling place, for it does not observe things as they are, but as [faith] desires it to see them. For instance, you carry in your hands the consecrated bread of mysteries[6] that is common bread according to its nature, yet faith perceives it [as] the

---

[5] Play on words: "created beings" (*brayyē*) and "external" (*barāyē*).

[6] Lavenant notes that "the consecrated bread" (*gmūrtā* - ܓܡܘܪܬܐ) is "the live coal" of Isa 6:6, a type of Christ.

body of the Only Begotten One.[7] The eye of faith does not observe
as the physical eye observes, but faith compels the body's vision
to see something that is invisible to it. [The body] sees bread and
wine and oil and water, but faith compels its vision to see spiritually something that is not physically visible to it. That is, instead
of bread one shall taste the body. Instead of wine one shall drink
the blood. Instead of water one shall see spiritual baptism. Instead
of oil, [one shall see] the power of Christ.

(57) Faith possesses the power of God, has the will and authority
of God, and gathers profits from wherever it wishes. Faith approaches the bones of the saints, and instead of dead [bones], it
sees them alive and speaks with them as with the living and asks
them concerning its own needs.[8] Faith reveals to the skeletons what
it needs to receive from the giver of requests and pleads with him,
"By your mediation may I receive this gift," while not noticing
that he is deprived of life, silent of word, still of voice, devoid of
conversation, and a stranger to all natural movements. It is not in
the order of these things that [faith] seeks to be a mediator for it.
[Faith] knows that on account of its nature, not only in its death,
but also not in life, this one is not capable of becoming a mediator
between the Creator and his creatures. But because faith looks
at what is above nature and has been mixed in the saints by the
strength of Christ and is with them even while they are laid in
graves, it converses with the dead as if they were living and speaks
with the silent ones as with those who can speak.

The eye of faith sheds the vision of all things visible and puts
on the secret vision of all spiritual things, and everything inside
the body is stirred by it. A person stands in one place and observes
another, dwelling in the lower world physically and residing by
his faith in the higher world. Faith[9] hears about the resurrection of
the dead and about the renewal of human (58) bodies, and in this
way counts [them] as if they had already risen up and had been

---

[7] ܝܚܝܕܝܐ *īḥīdāyā*—Syriac translation of *monogenēs* (John 1:14).
[8] See Ezek 37:1-14.
[9] Typographical error; read ܟܗܝܡܢܘ.

renewed. It has received a promise concerning the world of life and the kingdom of light, concerning the places of glory and spiritual pleasures and tastes of blessings, concerning interpretation of the mysteries and how it should be in imitation of the angels, and [faith] considers true all these things that it has heard.

Faith is in the middle between these things that have passed away and those that are to come. We receive instruction by faith from those things that have happened before us and those that will come to be after us, as it was said by Paul, "By faith we understand that the worlds were established by the word of God, and by those things that are invisible, these which are visible came to be."[10] If a human being does not possess faith, he is able to treat all those things inscribed in the Holy Scriptures as false and to say concerning all these secret things that truly exist that they do not exist, and because of the fact that they are not visible, doubt does not have a refutation at hand.

Faith Needs No Witness

5. Faith also needs no witness to be confirmed in what it hears. Proofs and witnesses are necessary for knowledge, and for whoever desires to see and touch and then affirm. Faith is not from miracles, for just as God does not need to be persuaded by the powers and miracles concerning those things that will come to be from him, for everything is revealed and clear to his foreknowledge, so also faith does not **(59)** have need of miracles, for how does it have need of that thing which it made itself? Look, powers, signs, miracles, and everything such as these take place by faith. Then how would [faith] stand in need of what it makes, so that it may be confirmed by its witness in secret things? In the same way that God does not have need of his works, faith does not have need of miracles that were created by it. Faith does not have need of anything, neither seeing, nor touch, nor signs and miracles, nor arguments and witnesses; but only of hearing the word of God and to know that God

[10] Heb 11:3.

is the one who is speaking, and immediately it receives and does not doubt.

There is no one among the upright who has pleased God without faith, as the instruction of Paul witnesses, for he began with Abel and recited and went down through all of them successively until the revelation of Christ and showed that all of them had pleased God by faith. Setting down a clear standard for all disciples, he said, "Without faith no one is able to please God."[11] Again he said, "All of these have died in faith, but had not received their promises because God foresaw our own benefit so that without us they would not be perfected."[12] According to the word of the Apostle, faith had accompanied them throughout their lives until their death, and by [faith] they had performed powerful acts while they were in the world. By [faith] they had hoped and waited **(60)** to receive the future promises and to obtain what had been promised to them, that one whose word they had followed.

Faith as Land and Sun

6. Faith is the soil that receives the seed of the word of God. Just as the seed of the sower is deprived of harvests if he has no field, so the word of God is void of spiritual profits with us if there is no earth of faith that receives it. Just as the eye [receives] the sun, so the vision of faith receives the spiritual light of the commandments of Christ. And just like the light of the sun, while it makes everything clear, without the eye that receives it nothing is visible; so also the commandment of God—while he is the Maker of everything—does not become confirmed for us without faith. The sun is full of light by its nature, and the Word of God is strong by its speaker, but just as the sun's natural light is dim to the eyes of the blind and does not show anything, so the commandment of God is considered to be weak in a soul in which there is no faith. Faith is the discerning eye that sees and examines everything as it is. Because visible things are insignificant for it to look at, it leaves them behind and observes

[11] Heb 11:6.
[12] Heb 11:13, 40.

those things that are not visible and investigates those things that are above nature and above the senses and recognizes them.

Named by Faith

7. A name is established for us by faith because it has caused us to be born from error to the knowledge of God. On account of **(61)** this, everyone who approaches Christ and becomes a disciple of his Gospel receives his name by faith and is called "a believer."[13] Since faith is our mother and the one that gives birth to us, it is excellent that we should be named by the name of the one that gives birth to us. This is a wondrous thing that the greatness of faith has reached the point that people shall be named by [faith] just as by the name of God and of his Christ. For by the name of God we shall be called godly ones, and by the name of Christ we shall be named Christians, and by the name of faith we shall be named faithful. This is the name that distinguishes us from all [other] religions and makes us strangers to all teachings of error. No one is called faithful except one who has been born out of authentic faith, and [faith] is his mother and the one who has reared [him]. It is right on account of these things [that] we should be called faithful because all of our learning looks at the hope of those future things and eagerly desires the anticipation of invisible things, and these things we have been taught are neither apparent nor evident to these physical senses. Because the hope of all of our virtues exists in faith and if faith should be removed from [our] midst not one of these things of ours will be believable.

Faith Sees Differently Than the World

8. Look, if there are mysteries here and now or if there are benefits that are promised to us above, faith is the one that holds and guards them. If one should consider all the mysteries of the worship of the church with physical eyes without faith, one will believe that they

---

[13] Literally, "one who has faith"—*haymānā* ܪ‍ܝ‍ܡ‍ܢ‍ܐ.

are common and base, and these worldly things will appear by their outer nature to be more powerful **(62)** and glorious than ours.

See, with us [is found] poverty, and with the world, wealth; with us [is] despicableness, with [the world] glory; with us humility, with [the world] pride; with us commonness, with [the world] primacy; with us renunciation, with [the world] possessions; with us hunger, with [the world] satiation; with us needs, with [the world] relief; with us austerities, with [the world] comforts; with us subjugation, with [the world] giving command; with us the narrow road, with [the world] the wide road; with us a single garment determined by commandment, with [the world] the glamour of various clothes; with us the word that inhibits us even from daily food, with [the world] the treasures that are accumulated for generations and years. With us, we appear neglected and disdained, with [the world] there is the appearance of magnificence and honor.

All such things like these show the world that [faith] is more glorious and better in everything than these things of ours, if we lift up from [these two] the faith which is our true wealth, as our teacher Paul also testified in his word, "If we hope in Christ [only] for this life, we are the most wretched of all human beings."[14] In another passage he says, "We are fools for the sake of Christ and sick, insignificant, and disgraced,[15] and having nothing."[16]

Faith Senses What the World Cannot See

9. While we do not possess anything of where we dwell, we hold on to everything that is ours, according to the word again of that same Apostle, "While we have nothing, we hold everything."[17] Briefly, not one of these things of ours **(63)** is visible in this life without the eye of faith which alone sees them. Our wealth is not visible here, and neither is our authority, nor the different degrees of our works, nor our honors, nor our comforts, nor our kingdom, nor

[14] 1 Cor 15:19.
[15] 1 Cor 4:10.
[16] 2 Cor 6:10.
[17] 2 Cor 6:10.

the dwellings of our comforts, nor the blessings hidden and sealed
that are guarded for us, nor the city of our heavenly dwelling, nor
Zion the place of life, which is thirsty[18] and desirous to receive its
children, nor the deposits of our treasures, nor the wealth of our
heavenly possessions, nor our freedom that is above all servitude,
nor the fullness of all our blessings which we shall come to receive.
All these things of ours are hidden in this life and are not visible
to physical human beings. But the faithful have sensed them only
through faith and see everything that is not visible and heed those
voices that are not audible to the physical ear. They touch whatever the hand of the body does not touch and taste those things
that the palate of the mouth does not taste, because the sensation
of the spiritual blessings promised to us is placed within all of the
physical senses. If we do not have their corresponding spiritual
senses and the faith that belong to them, it is as if they do not even
exist.

Seeing the Mysteries

10. If you say, "Look, our mysteries here are glorious," take notice
that without faith their gloriousness is not visible. Everything that
we have received from the world and that we use according to the
tradition which has reached us, if we look at it with the world's eye,
it belongs to the world. But if we investigate it with faith **(64)** it is
above the world. The temples of the house of our prayers are from
the world, because their building is taken and constructed from
the world, but spiritually they are above the world, for they are
types of that "church of the first-born who are inscribed in heaven,"[19]
which is the free Jerusalem, the mother of all of us."[20] All the altars,
along with the rest of the vessels of worship of the mysteries and
everything by which we celebrate the mysteries that have been
transmitted to us, are from the world by nature. On account of the

---

[18] Zion (ṣēhyōn)‿ܐܘܗܨ and "thirsty" (ṣahyā) ܐܝܗܨ are a play on words
in Syriac.
[19] Heb 12:23.
[20] Gal 4:26.

majesty of those things that are ministered to in their course, they are exalted and sublime, and we consider them to be above nature because they are the image of the living and spiritual powers that are in heaven, by which the worship of the hidden mysteries of God and his desires are accomplished.

Even more, those holy mysteries that we perform for the redemption of our life were first received from the world, for from [the world] come the bread and wine that ascend upon the spiritual altar. However, when the altar receives them, just as the womb[21] [receives] the word, it makes them become above the world, the living body and blood of God that are above the world. In the same way also, the water with the oil by which the mystery of our baptism is performed is taken from this very world. But when the time has arrived that through and in them the ones invited to grace will be born, the font of water and common oil have become the womb and the power that give birth to spiritual beings. Just as Christ [rose] from the grave on the third day, the dead sinner who has descended into [the grave] will ascend alive from baptism. **(65)** Because our Lord was resurrected on the third day, [the sinner] is renewed by three immersions with three names. As our Lord after his resurrection moved to the spiritual way of life from the physical way of life that preceded his crucifixion, so also one who is resurrected by baptism as if from the grave walks in new life according to the teaching of Paul.[22] We prepare our departed for burial like anyone else, and the outer appearance of our preparation and of our burial is not distinguishable from pagans and Jews. But we, by the hope of faith and by the expectation of bringing the dead to life, give our departed to life and not to death, and by our faith, they are sent by us to heaven and not to Sheol. But the dead of those who err are being sent to death and destruction because the hope of faith is not found in them.

Great and sublime are the mysteries of the faithful if one draws near to them by the thought of faith. Because the body's eye is too

---

[21] ܪܘܚܐ; reference to the incarnation.
[22] Rom 6:4.

weak for the vision of our mysteries, another eye—that of faith—has been given to us that is capable of examining them, and to see them as they will be, and not as they are, and to see these things that are promised to us and are [still] far from us and are not considered by [faith] distant things, but close by. So then, you have understood, O one who wishes to become a disciple of Christ, that everything that is ours exists by faith, and without faith neither we, nor these things of ours, nor those that come from us, nor those that are promised to be given to us, are not visible, and it is as if they do not exist. So then, in the beginning of **(66)** your discipleship, take faith for yourself and follow God. You will not even [be able to] hear [God's word] to keep his commandments, unless at first you believe in him.

Faith Planted in You by God

11. Faith is planted in your nature and placed in you by the Maker so that you might believe him by the faith which he has placed in us. Therefore, do not reverse the power of faith and believe by it those things that are not, and instead of these things that are true and remain forever, believe what is not true and does not endure. For everything here exists in a form that passes away[23] and is discarded—according to the teaching of Scripture. Everything that shall come to be and was promised to those who are true remains forever while not passing away or being corrupted. So then, do not believe by the faith in you whatever passes away and consider it lasting, but use faith in its order and believe through it the spiritual things. See, faith was also in those [people] who were worshiping idols and considering things of stone and wood and all the natures of creation [to be] gods. But they changed its excellent order and instead of believing by [faith] in God, they believed by it in made-up idols and called on false gods even though they did not exist. Because faith is faith as long as it affirms these things that are suitable for it. But if [faith] should believe other things that are

23 1 Cor 7:31.

contradictory and think concerning them something that they are not, from that point on it is not faith **(67)** but error. On account of this God has placed faith into your nature so that you might believe only him and because of him you might believe what he desires and not something else.

In that same way that the knowledge of God is placed in us naturally, as the blessed Paul said, "The knowledge of God is clear in them, for God has revealed it to them,"[24] faith is likewise fastened naturally into the thoughts of all of us. But just as the knowledge of God was fastened in them, even if they did not worship his nature or honor his being, yet they worshiped his name and honored [him] naturally in all the creatures; so also we believe everything by the faith placed in us, and our will makes our faith turn wherever it desires and causes it to look at the natural movements in us so that it sees [them]. If our will wishes, it could believe in God by faith, and if it desires it could affirm idols and demons by faith. If it wishes to believe that this world of life[25] remains forever, it will yearn for and desire it, and if it wants to believe in this world that is going to be dissolved as if it were real, it will love it and run after it.

Faith against the Will

12. The will is the governor of faith, just as [it governs] all the rest of the natural movements in us, that is to say, [it is] the guide of everything, whether of the outer senses or of the inner thoughts. Just as **(68)** eyes are given to us to see the beauty of creatures, and ears to hear the divine commandments, and hands to stretch out toward the virtues, and feet to run to profitable meetings, the will changes them to the opposite, and instead of virtues for which the members and senses were made, it performs by them evil and despicable things; in the same way also faith is placed into our nature, so that by it we might believe God and affirm the promises of the Spirit; [however,] the power of the will has changed it and

---

[24] Rom 1:19.

[25] Lavenant reads variant (Ms. A): ܕܚܝܐ, *dhayē*, "of life"; instead of written ܕܢܝܚܐ, *danyaḥē*, "of comforts."

instead of God it believes demons, and instead of spiritual things it affirms physical things, and instead of these things that are not visible these things that are visible, and instead of those things that do not pass away, these things that do pass away and are dissolved.

Using Faith to Leave the World

13. But you, O disciple, utilize faith in its excellent order and do not turn it back toward error. Believe God and his promises by [faith] and do not believe by it the world and its pleasures. "For everything that is visible belongs to time; and everything that is invisible is eternal,"[26] as Paul also has taught. So then, believe God and hope that eternal benefits will be given to you by him, and faith shall be for you the beginning of your road. If you do not believe these things that are invisible, you are not able to leave those visible things. If you do not believe that the promise of Christ is true and the good things promised by him to all who follow his Gospel, you have not left what you hold and pursued the blessings he has promised you. **(69)** "If a person does not renounce his father and his mother and his brothers and sisters, and the entire world, and himself as well, he is not able to become my disciple."[27] Hear this voice, O disciple, and depart from the world. Only this Gospel that promises spiritual blessings will distance you from the ways of life and business of the world. You have heard this voice; believe it and become [its] disciple and [a disciple] to no other thing. Let there not be another reason for your departure from the world, otherwise your departure will not prosper. Just as is the first reason, so also will be the rest of those [reasons] that follow it.

Leaving the World for the Wrong Reasons

14. It is the case that many people leave the way of life of the world for different reasons and approach the discipleship of Christ, but not for that one true reason. On account of this, their disciple-

---

[26] 2 Cor 4:18.
[27] Luke 14:26.

ship does not prosper, for they become like sick members in the healthy body of the discipleship of Christ and, moreover, inhibit healthy members from the performance of spiritual ministry and from the work of all the commandments of our Lord. It would have been better for them to remain in the world and not to have been made an example of laxity in the place of the spiritual. The entire way of life of the world is sick and feeble for the spiritual, but the body of the discipleship of Christ is healthy and strong. Whoever cuts off his own members from that sick body and comes to join himself to this living body, **(70)** it is only the love of its way of life that will bring him to union with [this] body.

There should be no other reason for its approach, as many have [done]: whether [to escape] from servitude or from debt, or as a result of the constraint of parents, or from the vexation of a woman, along with all the other unhealthy reasons by which many are forcibly driven to come to be disciples of Christ. When they have arrived, they are with him in appearance, but in truth with the world. Here, only by a false perception, and there by a deed and by thoughts; here on account of habit, and there on account of the will. Forced capitulation leads them here, but discernment of their free will holds them there. In brief, here is their shadow while their body is in the world, and here they exist in picture and image only; there in the true person.

While causing scandal for themselves and also for their broth-ers,[28] they eat the bread of Christ ravenously and not with upright-ness. When they have gone out to hire with him, they work for another and are not ashamed. When he called them, they obeyed another who is his adversary. While everyone accepts them as belonging to [Christ], they treat his grace unjustly and despise his commandments, and create a scandal in the place of edification and a spectacle of losses in the place of profits, an occasion of stumbling in the place of truth and an image full of frauds in the theater of profits. It would have been better for those who are this way, ac-cording to the word of Christ, **(71)** if they had not been born,[29] or if

[28] See Rom 14:13.
[29] Matt 26:24.

they had been born, to have remained in the unhealthy place of the way of the world in which they had lived, and not to have come to make others sick along with them, and while they are dead to God, to kill the living members along with themselves.

Faith as the Reason for Leaving the World

15. But you, O disciple of God, flee from such [people] as these, and may faith only be the cause for your departure from the world, for as you have laid the foundation, so the entire building of your works might ascend. Once your works drain strength from your initial faith that made you depart from the world, by the same faith all things will be accomplished and preserved in health and remain in uprightness, and rush to meet the hidden eye of God, and be accomplished and perfected by the exhortation of faith itself. As long as faith looks upward, it travels urgently the road of asceticism, and one runs quickly the path of labors. That eye of faith which you had opened from the beginning and by which you had seen from a distance the promises of Christ, be careful not to shut it by any of the pretexts that meet you once you have begun on the road of your journey, lest suddenly a stumbling block should [trip] you and make you fall on the path you have been walking. But just as these who begin on a natural road walk on it until the end of the road with that same gaze with which they began, taking care not to close their eyes on their journey and inhibit their guiding vision, so also you, O disciple, who have begun to travel on the heavenly road, guard that vision **(72)** that you have had from the beginning of your road until the end.

The Sleepy Soul

16. As much as the eye of your faith considers future things, so your [ascetical] labors will be light for you and your soul will take delight in the austerities of your good deeds. Just as the foot is guarded from stumbling blocks as long as the eye is open to see, so inattentiveness is seized and distanced from the soul as long as the vision of faith is healthy, and it considers and observes

heavenly things. The soul that deprives itself of the vision of faith is either asleep or is dead. This soul that completely drives faith away from being with it is dead. And that [soul] with whom the name of faith is kept, but its eye is not open at all times to consider spiritual things, this soul is asleep, having plunged into the slumber of inattentiveness. While it labors it is not alert, and while it is justified it does not know, and while it runs it is not aware of its course. Just as one who is asleep does not sense those things beside it, so also whoever shuts off his faith's vision is not aware of the virtues cultivated by it. But in the same way that one blind person is led by another, so also whoever is led astray by force of habit or by the fact that he is not able to change the kinds of labors he has undertaken, travels [aimlessly] in the place in which he is.

Remain in Faith

17. It is not suitable for a disciple of Christ that his virtues should be established by a human law, lest when the laws are broken or **(73)** their legislators wish to change them, his own virtues will be dispersed and scattered. That One who has set for us the struggle is not human. On account of this, it is also not right that human laws should take hold of us in the combat of this struggle, but only the will of him who sets up the struggle—Christ. Therefore, this is the beginning of your departure from the world, O one who begins on the journey of the heavenly road. By faith you have taken off from yourself the garment of the error of thoughts entangled with the affairs of the world [that] deceives one to think about something that does not exist as if it did exist. So then take care not to be altered in your faith. Remember at all times the word of Paul, and by it you will increase your faith and cleanse your thoughts of the dirt of error as he said, "Whoever approaches God ought to believe that God exists."[30] To [God] be glory forever. Amen.

The end of the third *mēmrā* which is on faith.

---

[30] Heb 11:6.

On Simplicity

On faith and how with simplicity one is able to receive the commandments of Christ.

Summary: Philoxenos defines simplicity as the "singleness of one thought." Abraham responded to the call of God with faith and simplicity, as did the apostles, while Adam lived in simplicity until the Enemy made him use cunning and question God's command to him. God is "Simple," for in God there are no structures or parts. The desert is perceived as the source of simplicity: the primary reason for Israel's wandering in the wilderness was to teach them simplicity. If you were cunning you would not have followed God who called you to the monastery and eventually you would have despised instruction.

One Kind of Simplicity

(74) 1. Our Lord has given us an easy and accessible beginning in his Gospel, the genuine and true faith which moves naturally in simple thought, so that through this same faith one may obey him and keep his commandments, just as also all the ancient upright who were called by God had heard his word with simplicity and had affirmed his promises with faith.

I am not speaking about the [kind of] simplicity in the world that is considered to be foolishness, but the singleness of one thought that is simple to obey and not judge, to receive and not scrutinize, in the same manner that an infant also acquires words from its nurse, and even more as a youth who receives book learning from his teacher, neither judging nor scrutinizing those things that were said to him. Because just as the capacity of the infant is inadequate for the inquiry of human books, so the level of our intellect is inadequate to understand the interpretations of divine mysteries.

Simplicity of Abraham

2. It is then by faith alone and by simplicity that a person is able to hear and receive, just as Abraham was called by and followed **(75)** God, and did not become a judge of the voice that came to him,[1] and was not inhibited by family and relatives or by place and friends, along with all the rest of human connections. As soon as he had heard the voice and knew that it was God's, he disdained everything, attached himself[2] to it, listened to it simply, and affirmed it faithfully with the natural simplicity that does not act deceptively by evil deeds. He was running toward the word of God like a child [runs] after its father, while everything [else] had become despicable in his eyes once he had heard the word of God.

He also possessed knowledge and natural discernment, but he showed his discernment here in that he ought to listen to God who had called him, like a servant [who listens] to his master, and like the creature [who listens] to his Maker. Moreover, the knowledge that he has does not give him the authority here to inquire and scrutinize why and for what reason he had been called by God, "Depart from your land and from the members of your family, and come to the land that I will show you."[3]

[God] had not revealed to him in which land his faith specifically would be triumphant and his simplicity would be visible. While it appeared that [God] was leading him to the land of Canaan, [he] had promised to show him another land of life which is in heaven, as Paul also witnesses, "He waits for the city that has a foundation

---

[1] Gen 12:1.

[2] Budge's text is: ܢܗܡ, "depart"; Lavenant opts for variant: ܢܩܦ, "attach oneself" (Mss. C and D).

[3] Gen 12:1.

whose architect and maker is God."[4] Again he said, "It is evident that they were desiring something better than the land **(76)** of Canaan, something which is in heaven."[5] In order that God might teach us this clearly, for it was not the physical Promised Land he had promised to show to Abraham, [God] made him dwell in Haran after he had made him depart from Ur of the Chaldees and did not bring him immediately after his departure to the land of Canaan. Moreover, lest Abraham think he had heard a hint of a reward and for that reason followed the word of God, [God] did not inform him from the beginning of the name of the land to which he was leading him.

A Simple Departure from the World

3. Look, then, O disciple, at this venturing forth and may your venture be like it, and do not delay from the living word of Christ who has called you. Because just as he had called only Abraham there, so here he calls with his Gospel everyone he wishes and invites [him] to follow him. By saying, "All who wish to come after me, let him deny himself and take up his cross and come after me,"[6] he made manifest a general call to all human beings. Instead of choosing there [only] the single [person] Abraham; here he invites every person to live by the example of Abraham.

He also has renewed that [call] of Abraham with the holy apostles. Take notice of their faith which is similar to the faith of Abraham. Because just as Abraham had obeyed as soon as he was called, in the same way at the moment [Jesus] called the apostles, they heard and followed him. He had watched them casting nets into the sea and called them and immediately they left their nets **(77)** and their father and followed him.[7] Before hearing from him, "If a person does not leave his father and his mother, and everything that he has

[4] Heb 11:10.
[5] Heb 11:16.
[6] Matt 16:24; Mark 8:34; Luke 9:28.
[7] Matt 4:18.

and come after me, he is not able to become my disciple,"[8] they had left everything and followed Jesus. A lengthy lesson did not make them disciples, but only the hearing of the word of faith. Because faith was alive in them, as soon as [faith] had received the living word it was obedient to life. They ran immediately after him and did not delay from [being with] him. Through this even before they were called they appeared to have become disciples.

Faith Mixed with Simplicity

4. This is the custom of faith that is mixed with simplicity. It does not receive instruction by many arguments, but just as a healthy and pure eye does not receive a beam of light sent to it by [other] means and devices, as soon as it is opened it investigates by its own power and its own light because its own natural vision is healthy; so also, once the eye of faith that is placed in the pupil of simplicity hears the voice of God, it recognizes it, and the light of his word shines in it and cheerfully reaches out for it and receives it, as our Lord said in his Gospel, "My sheep hear my voice and follow me."[9] Wherever natural faith is maintained in its integrity, the one with whom this faith is kept is the sheep of the pastor.

In the same way it was also written concerning Matthew that our Lord had seen him **(78)** seated at the customs house and called him. Immediately he left his business with all of his possession and followed him.[10] It is also written about Philip that [Jesus] said to him, "Come, follow me,"[11] and immediately he followed him. Therefore, through this purity and simplicity the apostles had followed the word of Christ, and the world was not able to hinder them, nor were human customs [able] to inhibit them, nor were one of those things that are considered something [important] in the world able to impede these souls from perceiving God.

[8] Luke 14:26.
[9] John 10:27.
[10] Mark 2:14; Luke 5:27.
[11] John 1:43.

The Powerful Word

5. Because there is nothing in the world more powerful than the word of God to a person who has in him the life of faith, in whomever the word is weak due to the deadness of his soul, the powerful word becomes weak in him, and the healthy instruction of God falls sick in him. All the activity of one's life orients toward where a person is alive: whoever lives for the world all the activity of his thoughts and senses is turned toward the world; but whoever is alive for God his soul is turned toward the powerful commandments in all its movements.

Because the weight of the love of earthly things was not hung on those who were called, they obeyed at once the voice that had called them. The entanglements of the world are a burden to the mind and [its] thoughts. Everyone who is tied up and bound by them will [only] hear the voice of the summons of God with difficulty. But the apostles are not so, and the upright and the fathers are not in this category, but they have obeyed like **(79)** living ones and have departed as light ones who are not tied down by the weight of anything. Who is able to bind and inhibit the soul that senses God? It is open and prepared, so that whenever the light of the divine call comes it will find [the soul] ready to receive it.

Zacchaeus

6. Our Lord also had called Zacchaeus from the fig tree, and at once he quickly descended and received him in his house[12] because he had been anticipating seeing him and becoming his disciple even before [Jesus] could call him. This is the marvel that while our Lord had not spoken with him and he had not seen him physically, [Zacchaeus] believed in him from the talk of others, because the faith that was in him had been kept alive and in natural health. He had shown his faith through hearing a report of him and believing him; and by his promising that he would give to the poor half of his wealth, and of what he had cheated he would return fourfold, it was through this [demonstration] that he caused the simplicity

---

[12] Luke 19:4.

of his faith to shine in himself. But if the mind of Zacchaeus had not been filled with that simplicity that suited faith at that time, he would not have made this lavish promise to Jesus, and he would [not] have dispersed and distributed in a short time whatever he had collected through labor over the years. Whatever cunning had gathered, simplicity was pouring out. The purity of soul was dispersing those things acquired by sly thoughts, and whatever greed had found and acquired, faith had renounced and was crying out that this did not belong to it. Because God is the only possession of faith, it does not consent to acquire **(80)** other possessions besides him. All our possessions are inferior to faith, aside from that one enduring possession which is God. Also on account of this, faith is placed[13] in us so that it may find and acquire only God, and everything outside of him will be a detriment to it.

Simplicity of Adam and Eve

7. The Holy Scriptures have shown us that in this manner a person should draw near to God in faith and in simplicity. On account of this, as long as Adam and Eve were living in natural simplicity and the faith that was in them was not hardened through physical passions, as soon as they heard the commandment of God, they received and kept it. God had said to Adam, "Do not eat. But if you eat, you will die.[14] And if you keep the commandment, I will give to you eternal life." In faith, [Adam] received and kept [the commandment]. Through simplicity [Adam] had not judged the commandment: "Why did he prohibit us from one tree and give us authority over all the others, and [why did] he promise to give me life if I keep the commandment?" On account of his simplicity Adam did not judge and scrutinize these things. But when the enemy's counsel came and found simplicity, he taught it cunning and slyness and sowed into that one simple thought another thought that was its adversary, his purpose being that a single human being who was worthy of absolutely everything by his simplicity might

---

[13] Typographical error in Budge's text: written ܪܟܘܣ, read ܪܟܘܣ.
[14] Gen 2:17.

be divided into two in [his] thoughts—he desires and does not desire, he judges and is judged, and he is doubtful whether to act or not. **(81)** The advice that was brought to him made that youth and simple one a judge of the commandment of God to him. Because he had lost his simplicity, he also did not prosper by his judgment. He had judged foolishly that he ought to obey an enemy more than a friend, and a murderer more than a life-giver, and that one who had taught vices more than that one who was their teacher of virtues. As long as they were living in simplicity they obeyed the commandment of God. But after they had desired to become cunning, they became recipients of the advice of the accuser, because cunning is on the side of Satan, but simplicity is with those who belong to Christ. For no one desires to become cunning and sly and is able to become a disciple of Christ, as his instruction requires.

Simplicity as the Opposite of Cunning

8. The mind full of cunning at all times refutes and builds up opposing thoughts, binds and lets loose, says the truth and lies. Sometimes it judges this one to be excellent, at another time it rejects it and chooses another in place of it. The mind practiced in cunning is the channel of confused thoughts and does not remain in one [thought] in order to believe and to rely on it. But simplicity, which is the opposite of cunning in everything, as even its name witnesses, does not have in it any thoughts refuting one another. Simplicity has received a name suitable for God, because we also call God "simple" by the word of our profession, because there are no sections and portions of members in him. In the same way also whoever does not plot evil things is called simple by us in normal language, because there is no **(82)** impulse of evil things in his mind, and he does not know how to observe and create an issue for those things that encounter him from the world, nor how to scheme and do evil to his enemies, nor how to refute those things spoken against him, nor how to weave deceits and set ambushes, nor how to contrive and treat others badly. Simplicity does not know how to do such things as these. Because of this at all times the mysteries of God were entrusted to it, and it was worthy of divine revelations.

Apostles the Most Simple

9. Also when the apostles were chosen, it was evident that they were more simple than anyone else. Jesus had chosen them because of this, so that through their simplicity he might mock the wisdom of the world, and through their ignorance he might show the emptiness of the knowledge of the cultivated and the scribes, as Paul also has said, "God has chosen the foolish of the world in order to put to shame its wise."[15] And again he said, "See, has not God despised the wisdom of this world?"[16] And again he said, "Because in the wisdom of God the world does not know God through wisdom, God desired to save those who believe through the folly of preaching."[17] Once more, he had said to some of his disciples who had been glorifying themselves through the worldly knowledge, "Look at your callings, my brothers, for there are not many wise ones in the flesh among you."[18]

Wisdom of Christ

10. By these things I have mentioned, I do not wish to show that there is no wisdom in the teaching of Christ, but that the wisdom which is above the world is the wisdom of Christ and that the wisdom of the world is **(83)** its adversary in everything, as darkness is the opposite of light, and bitter [the opposite] of sweet, and sickness [the opposite] of health. Divine wisdom is not triumphant by these things—by study and reflection of earthly thoughts—but all of its attention is on spiritual matters, and its movements and its thoughts are above the world as also the Apostle himself was testifying concerning himself, "I am foolish with regard to the wisdom of the world, but through my knowledge I acquire wisdom that is above the world."[19] Teaching that not everyone is capable

---

[15] 1 Cor 1:27.
[16] 1 Cor 1:20.
[17] 1 Cor 1:21.
[18] 1 Cor 1:26.
[19] 1 Cor 2:1ff.

of becoming a hearer and recipient of that wisdom which was in him, he was preaching, saying, "The wisdom [of which] we speak among the perfect [is] a wisdom not of this world, nor even of the rulers of this world who come to naught, but we speak of the wisdom of God mysteriously for not even one of the worldly wise is able to be its hearer."[20] The world's wisdom is not capable of becoming the foundation and receiving the building of God's wisdom, and for this our Lord has established simplicity so that it might become the foundation.

Divine Visions and Simplicity

11. Who does not know how much more simple was that first couple, the first ones of the human race, and how they were simple regarding the entire way of the world? They were not tempted or occupied with any of its matters, because even occupation with worldly matters had not yet been revealed. In this way they were close to [experiencing] divine visions **(84)** and God was speaking face-to-face with them continuously and was found with them at all times in intimate conversation, while carrying, bringing, and leading them from where they had been and in which they were created, and escorting and placing them in Paradise. He was showing them everything in detail like a human being, but they had not taken up thought about him in their mind, "Where indeed is the dwelling of That One who was showing them? From when has he existed? If he is the one who makes, was he made? And if he is made, who is the one who made him? Why has he created us? For what reason has he placed us in this Paradise and delivered this law to us?" These things were remote from their minds because simplicity does not consider such things as these but is completely drawn to give heed to whatever it hears, and all its thought is merged entirely into the word of whoever is speaking to it, just like a child [listens] to the word of whoever is speaking with him. Look then also, God had placed simplicity in the ancient leaders of our race, and it became the recipient of the commandment.

[20] 1 Cor 2:6, 8.

Faith, Daughter of Simplicity

12. Simplicity is prior to faith, because faith is the daughter of simplicity. But lack of faith is the child of cunning. Whoever is sly and cunning does not readily affirm what he hears, but the simple one hears and believes all voices. If simplicity possesses natural purity, it receives only these things that are spoken by God, because just as the earth by its natural composition **(85)** has been established by its Creator to receive seeds and plants useful for the needs of humanity, but to produce thorns and thistles is not of its nature, though later on it had received punishment from the Maker, so also simplicity was placed into our nature by the Maker, yet we receive cunning and slyness afterward on account of disputes occurring in us, as every child of humanity can testify.

Simplicity Prior to Cunning

13. Before cunning, simplicity is moving in all those who are born. Those infants and children are full of innocence and purity, yet they learn cunning[21] and slyness once they have lived a while in the world through gradually growing up and by the situations they have encountered. [It is] as if someone should snatch a one-year-old infant and go out to raise him in the wilderness where there is no human activity and instruction in worldly things, and not seeing anything at all of these matters of human activity, [the child] will be found to be living in complete natural simplicity. Also when he has arrived at the stature of adulthood, this one will very readily be able to receive divine visions and spiritual thoughts and become promptly a vessel for the reception of godly wisdom.

The Natural Simplicity of John the Baptist

14. With this type, I believe, was also that remarkable preacher John the Baptist, who because he had lived in the desert, according to the witness of Scripture,[22] up to the day of his manifestation to

---

[21] Typographical error: written ܪܕܐܣܛܘ, read ܪܕܐܣܛܘ.
[22] Luke 1:80.

the children of Israel, he was able to receive and learn the divine mysteries **(86)** and receive the power of spiritual baptism. Through the natural simplicity in which he had been raised he had received in the desert those things that not one of the earlier prophets had experienced—especially before the annulment of the curse and death of sin and before the wall of enmity was broken that was placed in the middle[23] and which was written that it was broken by the cross of Christ—he became the recipient beforehand of these things that were after the cross. On account of this, grace had led him to go out to the wilderness and remain in natural simplicity and be able to receive the knowledge of the mysteries that are above nature.

Simplicity Learned in the Wilderness

15. Therefore, in this same manner when God had delivered the people from Egypt he made [the people] go out into the desert wilderness in which simplicity is acquired.[24] Because of this, I believe he made them go out into the wilderness so that while they were freed from the disputations and customs of humanity, and the worldly cunning and wisdom they had received in the land of Egypt, natural simplicity might become habitual in them so that they might straightforwardly receive godly instruction. Although there were many other reasons for his making them go out into the wilderness, it is apparent that this is the very first [reason] for one who knows how to observe the mysteries of divine providence. Because those who had departed from Egypt had not wished to take off from themselves the evil and cunning they had learned in Egypt, and since they were completely in opposition to the promise of God to them, he held them back forty years in the wilderness so that evil might vanish with its servants, and cunning might perish **(87)** with those who had received it from Egypt. The entire education of the generation born and raised in the desert happened through simplicity according to the law of the place so that it might enter to become the heir of the Promised Land, because this is fitting

[23] See Eph 2:14.
[24] See Deut 8:2.

for those who were raised up in the desert that they might become simple, and this agrees with simplicity, that it should hear and be obedient to the commandments of God.

The Value of Signs and Miracles

16. If one should think that they had believed because they had seen signs and miracles in the desert, and because they feared the punishment that had come on those who were before them, it will be found that those who departed from Egypt saw miracles more than them. For with the rest of all these mighty deeds performed in Egypt, they also had seen the division of the sea,[25] and that awesome crossing over, and moreover that the sea had come back together and had buried the Egyptians who had entered into its midst; and that miracle that had happened at Marah, where through a piece of wood water had become sweet and became their drink.[26] In short, those who had departed from Egypt were witnesses of all the miracles of Egypt and in the wilderness, and of those that had occurred in the middle; but the younger generation born in the desert did not see [any miracles], except only those miracles that were constantly with them—the pillar [of fire] and the cloud[27] and the rock [from which water] flows,[28] and the quail that used to rise up from the sea.[29] Although the miracles they had seen were fewer than [for] those who had departed from Egypt, they had remained in their simplicity in the fear of God even more than those who saw numerous **(88)** great signs.

The Last of the Six Hundred Thousand

17. So that you might know that all the mighty acts that had happened and the miracles that were performed were not able to

[25] Exod 14:21.
[26] Exod 15:25.
[27] Exod 13:21.
[28] Exod 17:6.
[29] Exod 16:13.

uproot and drive away from them the evil things they had learned from Egypt, whereas the generation born in the wilderness became fully removed from [evil things] due to its simplicity—understand from this that after they had arrived at and attained habitable land at the end of these forty years, when they camped opposite Midian and were desiring to enter into the lands of the nations, faced with the sight of women the Midianites had dressed up and made sit facing them, the remainder of the people who had departed from Egypt lusted to commit fornication with them, as also the Holy Scripture explains, "The people saw the daughters of Midian and lusted for fornication and were initiated [into the worship] of Baal-Peor and worshiped idols."[30] Those who had done this, as Scripture said, were these [people] who remained out of the ones who had departed from Egypt. A plague took control over them and twenty-four thousand of them died,[31] and Scripture declared that here the number was completed of those six hundred thousand who had departed from Egypt.[32] God said that they shall not enter to see the promised land.[33] Through this fact that of all the people only those had died, [can] we assume also that only those had committed fornication? Moses and all of Israel were sitting before the Lord at the door of the tabernacle, and Zimri, son of Salu, leader of the tribe **(89)** of Simeon, entered the cell of Cozbi, daughter of the leaders of Midian, in [full] view of Moses and all of Israel.[34] From there Phinehas stood up and showed the triumph of zeal.[35] For by this fact that the plague had taken control over the rest of whoever had remained of the people who had departed from Egypt, we should know that they only had committed that act of wickedness, while the rest of all the people who were born in the wilderness, who had been raised in innocence and simplicity by

[30] Num 25:1-9.
[31] Num 25:9.
[32] Exod 12:37.
[33] Num 14:23.
[34] Num 25:6, 15.
[35] Num 25:7-8.

the fear of God, was sitting at the door of God and asking Moses for mercy in repentance.

Sign of the Calf

18. I am able to believe this by what happened in the casting of the calf, for also there when Moses had descended from the mountain and had seen the people's disorderliness, he knew that this instigation did not involve all of them but [only with] some of them; he sawed down the calf with a file and scattered its dust on the surface of the waters.[36] When the people had drunk from [the waters, the waters] became for them testers of thoughts: those in whose thoughts the calf was previously depicted and had become instigators in doing this evil deed, it is written that the sign of the calf became visible on them—these [are the ones] who were killed by the swords of the Levites. By the finality of their deaths we understand also the beginning of error in them, because they had instigated and had become the first ones in error, and also the punishment **(90)** that the word of Moses had decreed[37] through the sign of the calf overtook them, becoming visible on their person. Likewise here, by the fact that through that sudden plague[38] only twenty-four thousand had fallen,[39] and Scripture has said that with them the number of those who had departed from Egypt was completed, we should know from this that only those people had given themselves over to fornication; and by their judgment let us learn [about] their fornication and by their violent death let us know that fornication had also been their own [fault]—they had remembered the worship[40] of idols that were in Egypt—and as soon as they saw [fornication] in Midian they gave themselves over to it.

---

[36] Exod 32:20.

[37] Exod 32:28.

[38] Budge's text is written: ܟܕܡܘܬܐ—"which through death"; Lavenant opts for variant: ܟܕܡܘܬܐ—"which through a plague" (Ms. A).

[39] Num 25:9.

[40] Literally, "the fear (of idols)."

Simplicity Born in the Desert

19. The simplicity of the innocents born in the desert had kept them with the Lord. They were sitting at the door of the tabernacle, with the simplicity of their heart and with souls distant from cunning and with thoughts free of the cunning of evil, asking the Lord for mercy. On account of this the physical promises to Abraham had also been fulfilled in them, and simplicity had entered and inherited the Promised Land, whereas ignorance came to a standstill at the border of his inheritance that had been promised to the leader of their race. The guilelessness they had with the Lord made them victorious in the battles with the Amorites. Joshua had commanded them after they had crossed over the Jordan to circle around Jericho seven times for seven days, and on the seventh day to circle seven times, while he went ahead of them with the priests who were carrying horns and the ark **(91)** of the Lord.[41] All the people were walking with simplicity behind Joshua and behind the ark like children behind their parents.

Joshua

20. What shall I say concerning the rest of the people, for Scripture also pointed out to us about Joshua that simplicity and innocence were found especially in him? "The young Joshua was not departing from the tabernacle,"[42] for he was constantly there in the service of Moses. He who had kept himself back from going and coming among the multitudes was especially near to simplicity. For if cunning and evil are accumulated by disputation among the multitudes, it is evident that simplicity and innocence are acquired by education and involvement in stillness. In as much as one increases his occupation in stillness, [the more] the possession of simplicity [increases]. Concerning this the customary rules of the world also witness to us that all those who were raised according to stillness and did not go out onto the roads and [did not engage in] dispute

[41] Josh 6:4.
[42] Exod 33:11.

and conversations with the multitudes turned out to be especially innocent and simple ones, and that justice was maintained in them from which uprightness is born.

David's Simplicity Like a Beast

21. Just as the blessed David connected uprightness to innocence in his word, "The innocent and upright have clung to me because I have waited for you,"[43] the prophet testifies concerning the innocence of his soul of how he was with God, "I was innocent and I did not know. I was [like] a beast with you."[44] He had lowered himself down to such great ignorance, **(92)** for just as an animal alongside a human being is not able to judge one of its actions or its occupations because of lack of reason and discernment of its nature, so the knowledge of David was with [respect to] God. Just as an animal is led by a human being, so he has submitted himself that he may be led by the will of God and not become a judge of [God's] will by any means, as he explains after [these] word[s], saying, "Because I was like a beast with you in all innocence, comfort me by your intelligence and lead me after your honor."[45] And again he said, "I have not scrutinized what there is in heaven with you or what is your will on earth."[46] I have not understood the decisions of your providence, for while I am seeking to know if you desire this [one] thing, your will is seeking another. Because I have been troubled by the different forms of your works, I have run to take refuge in simplicity. I was a beast with you that does not know anything, in order that your will alone might become a guide for me, and your knowledge might lead me on the road of life, and you might give me the diligence of your wisdom in everything necessary for spiritual and physical life. Again, he shows in the same psalm that especially with the innocent the grace of God flows, "God is good to

[43] Ps 25:21.
[44] Ps 73:22.
[45] Ps 73:23 (Peshitta).
[46] Ps 73:25.

Israel, to the ones innocent of heart."[47] He has connected innocence to the vision of God, because Israel means "seeing God." Whoever is simple and pure in his heart is able to become a seer of God, just as also **(93)** our Lord has said in his gospel, "Blessed are those who are pure in their heart, for they shall see God."[48]

A Mind Far from Cunning

22. Moreover, the prophet David shows that the mind far away from the cunning of human teachings is especially able to attain the righteousness of God and acquires spiritual courage and the confidence that fights with everything. "Because I did not know the work of a scribe, I will enter into the mighty deeds of the Lord and I will remember your righteousness only."[49] While he was explaining those things in which he was untaught and simple and those things in which he was knowledgeable and wise, he said, "My learning from my youth and up until now [is that] I will show forth your wonders."[50] Again, while showing the purity of his thoughts, he compared them with hands and likened the washing of hands to their purity from iniquity. "I have washed my hands so that they might be pure," that is, "I have cleansed and purified my thoughts, and I have called to mind your altar, Lord."[51] Again he said, "I have walked in the innocence of my heart in my house until the time when you shall come to me."[52] Again he said, "Whoever practices deceit shall not sit in my house."[53] It is apparent that deceit is constructed by cunning. He said again, "Prove me, Lord, and try me, and examine my heart and my mind."[54] And again he said, "I alone have purified my heart, and I have washed my hands in purity."[55]

---

[47] Ps 73:1.
[48] Matt 5:8.
[49] Ps 71:16.
[50] Ps 71:17.
[51] Ps 26:6 (Peshitta).
[52] Ps 101:2.
[53] Ps 101:7.
[54] Ps 26:2.
[55] Ps 73:12 (Peshitta).

David's Simplicity as a Shepherd

23. Along with these, [David's] election testifies that he was chosen from the place where simplicity teaches. Behind the sheep he had been chosen, as he also confesses,[56] remembering his election in one of his psalms, "He chose **(94)** David his servant, and led him from the shearing of the sheep and from behind the nursing sheep."[57] When he teaches also that his kingdom was being guided in simplicity, he said, "He shepherded them by the innocence of his heart."[58] It is clear that innocence is simplicity and also purity. The book of his history points out to us concerning his simplicity: in the business of worldly affairs a counselor of human affairs was constantly with him. Scripture makes it known that Ahithophel was the counselor of David.[59] While it is easy for us to see from other [passages] the simplicity of the blessed David, he also makes this known himself when he was speaking with Jonathan, in which he said, "There is no evil in my heart, but your father plots to take my life."[60] And moreover[61] this [word] that was spoken by Jonathan to his father, "He has put his life in your hands and has made war and has killed the Philistines,"[62] teaches concerning the simplicity of David. When the men who were with him were counseling him to kill Saul,[63] he remained in the same mind of simplicity. The fact that they would counsel him to kill his enemy was one of worldly cunning and slyness, because this is the custom of those full of worldly cunning that they would plot to remove obstacles before them. David remained in his simplicity and in his compassion. There are many things for us to find in the Holy Scriptures that

---

[56] Budge's text is written *mawdā*, ܡܘܕܐ, "makes confess." Lemoine reads *maw'dā*, ܡܘܼܕܥ, "makes known." Lavenant reverts to Budge's text for which there is no variant.

[57] Ps 78:70-71.

[58] Ps 78:72.

[59] 1 Chr 27:33.

[60] 1 Sam 20:1.

[61] Typographical error: written ܠܘܒ, read ܗܘܒ.

[62] 1 Sam 19:5.

[63] 1 Sam 24:4-5.

point to his simplicity and the innocence of heart **(95)** of this man of God. When also this [word] was spoken by the Lord to Samuel, "I have found for myself a man according to my heart,"[64] it was witnessing to David's purity of heart. It is evident that purity of heart is born from simplicity. Moreover, he also was asking through prayer, "Create in me a pure heart, O God."[65]

Other Righteous and Simple Ones

24. Let us see besides these the rest of the other upright and righteous: all of them had pleased God by their simplicity. It was written in this way concerning the first disciples who had become the apostles after the ascension of our Lord to heaven, "All of them were dwelling together,"[66] and "They were of one mind and one soul,"[67] and "in the house they were celebrating the Eucharist and receiving nourishment while rejoicing, and were praising God in the innocence of their hearts,"[68] and "no one was talking about the wealth he had possessed of his own, because everything that they had was [held] in common."[69] It is evident that such equality is born from simplicity. Their praise was ascending to God by the innocence of their heart, and the fact that they might receive food together joyfully—not noticing that whoever had brought a lot would be fed [any] more than another who had not placed anything in common—was happening by the purity of mind.

Simplicity of the Tent

25. Moreover, Scripture has shown that the blessed Joshua had been the most innocent of all the people because his upbringing took place continually in the tent.[70] This one, who was the most

---

[64] 1 Sam 13:14; 16:1.
[65] Ps 51:12.
[66] Acts 1:13; 2:1.
[67] Acts 4:32.
[68] Acts 2:46.
[69] Acts 4:32.
[70] Exod 33:11.

simple and pure of all the people who had been **(96)** reared in the tabernacle in stillness, was chosen for that renowned leadership after the great Moses.[71] The story of Jacob and Esau also witnesses that simplicity is nearest to those who are raised up in the tabernacle or in the home, more than all the others who are instructed in the coming and going [of worldly affairs]. "Esau was a man who knew hunting and a man of the outdoors. And Jacob was an innocent man and was dwelling in a tent."[72]

Cunning and Anger of Esau

26. By their works we are also able to understand the difference of their minds. The Scriptures in every place identify Esau as cunning and sly who retains [his] anger and holds a grudge. "He guards his anger eternally and he keeps his grudge forever."[73] [Scripture] spoke again concerning his anger toward the seed of Jacob. "He became very angry and was jealous of them."[74] This also points out about his prolonged anger when he armed himself to go out to meet his brother with four hundred men. When Jacob returned from Haran after twenty years, [Esau] was seeking vengeance from him for the blessing. But if the humility of Jacob and the hidden providence of God had not changed his anger to gentleness, he would have done what he had gone out [to do].

Jacob's Simplicity in the Deception of Isaac

27. But Jacob appeared in everything to be the opposite of these things, whether with his parents or whether in the house of Laban. For it was shown to us by his deeds that he was simple and obedient. On account of **(97)** this also Holy Scripture declares to us by one phrase all of his simplicity. "Jacob was a guileless man who dwelt in a tent."[75] Moreover, he would not have thought to steal

---

[71] Num 27:18; Deut 1:38; 3:21.
[72] Gen 25:27.
[73] Amos 1:11.
[74] See Ezek 25:12.
[75] Gen 25:27.

the blessing, due to his simplicity, if his mother Rebekah had not instructed him. But when he heard, "the deed will help [you]," he was convinced by the simplicity of his mind and was not troubled. Lest one should think that his simplicity was a natural foolishness, see how he avoids the curses of his father and answers knowledgeably concerning what intervened. "See, Esau my brother is a hairy man, and I am a smooth man. Perhaps my father will touch me and I would become a mocker in his eyes, and curses will be brought on me and not blessings."[76] But his mother, while affirming by faith those first promises revealed to her and what was said to her when she had gone to pray to the Lord, for [God] said to her, "The elder one will become the servant to the younger one,"[77] had responded to him, "May your curses be on me, my son . . . only listen to my voice[78] and do what I am commanding you." Immediately he obeyed his mother like a child, and she obtained and gave to him the food that Isaac was desiring, and she laid skins over his hands and on his neck in those places that were near to the touch. By his simplicity he did not judge anything that was happening to him, but just like a child who is placed before his teacher and does for her whatever she desires, so also that perfect (98) man had been before his mother through his simplicity. Again, when he had taken and brought the food to his father he repeated [the words] Rebekah had placed in his mouth like a child, neither adding nor subtracting. When the time of marriage had arrived he did not proceed to approach [Rachel] by his own will but was observing in his innocence the commandment of his parents.

Cunning and Evil of Esau

28. Yet Esau—being someone crafty for [the sake of] evil—because he wished to grieve and embitter his parents in return for the fact that they had deceived him, went out and took for himself women from the daughters of Canaan who were constantly embit-

[76] Gen 27:11-12.
[77] Gen 25:23.
[78] Gen 27:13.

tering the spirit of Isaac and Rebekah. When he saw that the hatred of his parents had increased toward him on account of the constant vexation of his wives, being afraid[79] lest he would be cut off from the physical inheritance, he saw this also by craftiness and went and took for himself a wife, Basemath, daughter of Ishmael[80]—as one might say, so that with a wound one might receive a bandage. This is not like a prudent son who has regretted those things he had done in the first place, but because he was afraid lest Isaac disinherit him—the one whom [Isaac] had loved [as first-born]—from the inheritance of riches and possessions. In the same way also, concerning the right of the first-born and the blessings for which he had been despondent, [it was] not because he had lost the spiritual promises in them, but because he was cut off from the greater portion of riches that the first-born was accustomed to receive. Because he had seen that the love of his father had changed toward him, on account of it he was thinking that there was something more **(99)** for him to receive in the inheritance.[81] All of these things of Esau instruct whoever knows how to observe them concerning his cunning and his evilness.

Along with these things we find in this same passage the simplicity of Isaac, their father. While all of his love had been turned toward Esau, loving him as a first-born, as soon as he had sensed the providence of God which is above nature and Rebekah had entered to reveal to him what was spoken to her when she had gone to pray to the Lord, at once his love toward Esau was changed and made him look toward Jacob who was worthy of it.

Jacob's Simple Obedience to His Parents

29. Let us look again at the obedience of this same Jacob who like a child was obeying his parents in everything. "If in this way Jacob also should take wives from the daughters of Canaan," Rebekah had

---

[79] Budge's text reads "sees, observes" (*ḥar*) ܚܪ, but Lemoine adopts the variant (*dḥel*) ܕܚܠ "fears" (Mss. C, D).

[80] Gen 26:34-35; 36:3.

[81] See Gen 27:30-40.

said, "why should life continue for me?"[82] Isaac summoned Jacob and commanded him, saying, "Do not take for yourself a wife from the daughters of Canaan, but go to Laban, son of Bethuel, the brother of your mother, and take for yourself a wife from there."[83] [Jacob] obeyed and departed promptly, and suddenly became removed from all the comforts of the house of his father and began on the road of his journey in the same way as a stranger who does not possess a thing. He had not requested from them anything for his use—a beast for carrying, servants for service, and baggage for appearance with other illusory things—which many grasp for today. Nevertheless, he departed from their company with his staff, while **(100)** carrying and being equipped with blessings and excellent promises instead of these human things. His own word explains, while he was praising God concerning these things that were with him and asking to be delivered from his brother, "I have crossed over this Jordan with my staff, and now I have become two camps. Rescue me from the hands of Esau my brother because I fear him."[84] Again, let us listen to his word that he spoke in that place where God was revealed to him, and by it may we especially see his simplicity. "Truly, the Lord is in this place, and I did not know."[85] What have you been thinking, O innocent Jacob, that God is limited only to the place where your parents dwell, and is [God] not revealed and shown in every place to those who are worthy of his revelation?

Jacob's Simplicity with Laban

30. Let us note again how many times his wage was changed in the house of Laban, as his word finally reproached that crafty one. "You have changed my wage ten times, but the Lord has not allowed you to do harm to me."[86] Again, when he had worked with him for his youngest daughter, [Laban] furtively brought to

---

[82] Gen 27:46.
[83] Gen 28:1-2.
[84] Gen 32:11-12.
[85] Gen 28:16.
[86] Gen 31:7.

him the other [daughter] in place of [the youngest] and tricked him unawares through his simplicity. When [Jacob] asked directly why he had tricked him, [Laban] offered him an explanation, and although it was a deception, his simplicity obeyed and accepted immediately. How many times had Laban sought to be a tyrant to him through his evilness? Through [how] many schemes had [Laban] changed toward him through his harshness **(101)** and cunning? The purity of Jacob was not afraid and his simplicity was not shaken, and his innocence did not become inflated. As long as he was attending to these things of his own, God was concerned for him about these [other] things. This is an example of enlightened instruction to all who wish to labor with the Lord: one should not let his thoughts cease from reflection on God nor occupy them with devising schemes by which to harm his enemies.

Purity of Mind and Simplicity

31. But you, O disciple, remain in the purity of your mind. It is the Lord's to know how to guide your life, and which things are beneficial for you that he should do for you. Have you heard about others that are preparing to do harm to you; and others that are lying in ambush to take your life; and others that were made workers for the pulling down of your building; and others that reproach your glory and find fault with your way of life; and others that dig in order to throw you on the earth from the height on which you are standing; and others that make signs, or others that speak against and revile you, and hurl mocking abuses on you; and for others you have been made a proverb and tale and all their conversation is in relating blasphemies about you? But you, in all of these things, remain in your simplicity and do not turn your back from where you have been watching, and do not cease from your secret conversation with God.

Anchor

32. Do not let the coercion of these things outside of you defeat the coercion of the hidden anchor on which your life is suspended, but

hold on to Christ with the hope that is not found false, according to the promise of Paul **(102)** to us, "Let us hold on to the hope that was promised to us, which is to us like an anchor tied onto our soul"[87] so that you may not be moved. For just as an anchor thrown below holds and stops the ship among the waves by means of its weight, lest [the ship] drifts and is battered on a journey outside of its route, so also the hope promised to us in heaven, which is the hidden anchor placed above us, is sunk and hides from us in the heaven of heavens, may it hold our thoughts to itself and tie down our soul's ship lest it wander and be disturbed by storms and waves battering against it from the world and make it depart from its journey route.

Do Not Become Angry

33. Therefore, remain in your simplicity in those things you have heard, and do not let those who talk against you change you so that you become like them. On account of this, the enemy also gathers and arranges these things against you so that he may alter your mind by his gentleness, stir up and disturb your purity, make your simplicity wily, and you become similar to those who are fighting against you, become full of anger like them, a vessel for rage like them, and put on the coat of evil. When your thought has descended from that simplicity that uniquely observes a single thing and you have been watching the crowd and have listened to those who speak against you, through these things the enemy finds you as he wishes and you have become an easy prey for him, prepped and ready at hand. But you, hold fast on to simplicity which is the vessel of righteousness. Just as a natural vessel is **(103)** the recipient of something that falls into it, so also simplicity is the pure and precious vessel that receives the fruits of righteousness.

Remember Jacob

34. So now, may the innocent Jacob become an example for you of these things that I have told you, whose story I have set down for

[87] Heb 6:19.

you. When controversial speech[88] is roused to disturb your simplicity, and you are aware of the enemy's methods that wish to inhibit you, reflect on this blessed man and examine thoroughly his story from beginning to end. For such things like these were written for this [purpose] in the Scriptures, so let them become a support for the soul that is stumbling and falling and a consolation for thoughts full of sadness from the irritation of someone who provokes anger.

Observe how much Esau and Laban had conspired to do evil to Jacob, but the Lord was operating on his behalf in his actions. While he was silent and not anxious to encounter the ways of his enemies, God was reversing their craftiness, and instead of losses he was making him encounter gains. Jacob was occupied with his innocence and God was seeking good things for him. He was occupied in every activity in his simplicity like a child, and the Lord was making his ways prosper in his wisdom. Laban was working and conspiring to harm him, yet Jacob was not noticing. [Being] innocent [he] was not suffering anything; and [being] pure he was unaware. In his place, God was the seer and knower of everything. Whatever **(104)** Laban had bound, God had unbound. [When Laban] had constructed a way to harm Jacob, the Most High dispersed it. [Laban] found the opportunity to increase his possession and to decrease that of Jacob. God found another [opportunity] that was against him, for while Jacob was silent, the Judge was made his advocate. While he was proceeding simply in his actions, God was directing his paths wisely. These affairs of Jacob are written for you and are yours if you remain in the simplicity of the mind of Jacob and in the purity of soul of that innocent man.

Eli and Samuel

35. The simple belong to the Lord: do not be ashamed of simplicity. The crafty and cunning are the instrument of the enemy: do not desire and wish for cunning. Cunning is the soil that brings forth evil. Simplicity is the field that yields righteousness as fruit.

---

[88] Lemoine opts for ms. A (ܪܬ ܬܘܪܟܐ) "of others," but Lavenant returns to Budge's text: (ܪܬ ܬܘܪ) "of controversy."

On account of this the Lord speaks with simplicity in every place, and his desires find rest in [simplicity], and it becomes a dwelling place and recipient of his revelations.

Eli along with his sons were sleeping in the temple of the Lord, and when the Lord desired to speak with human beings he left behind old age that is expert in wisdom and trained in worldly things, as well as the youth who had received the cunning of evil things, and came toward simplicity and was speaking with it and chose to speak and converse with it. The Lord called to Samuel, "Samuel, Samuel!" two times.[89] Simplicity rose up and rushed to old age, for the youth had not known who it was that had called him. Instead of God he ran to respond to Eli. **(105)** He did this three times, because he had not yet experienced the revelations of divinity. But Eli, after he had understood that the Lord had called him, commanded him to give an answer as if it were to the Lord, and not to run back to him [Eli]. "Eli understood that the Lord had called the youth."[90] Old age had sent youth to the Lord so that it might learn his desires, and cunning had need of simplicity so that through [simplicity] it might learn the desires of divinity. Eli was persuading Samuel, asking him to reveal to him everything he heard from the Lord and not to hide from him even a single word. Because he saw that he was not worthy to have the Lord speak to him, he was bringing a request to the boy to reveal to him the divine mystery. Simplicity had become the interpreter between divinity and knowledge, and youth had received and responded [to God].

God Chooses the Naturally Simple

36. The knowledge of God was revealed to a very young boy who was not aware of these things of the human way of life, because the Lord resides with the innocent and speaks with those who are simple. He has chosen the ignorant who once they have learned the word did not think that it is their own but know its speaker and return to him thanksgiving, and the word of God to

[89] 1 Sam 3:4.
[90] 1 Sam 3:8.

them does not become for them an occasion for pride and vain-glory. They do not become exalted in these things of God as if these were their own and do not say, "The word of wisdom that we have is our own." Therefore, the simple and innocent do not think these things but confess through their simplicity that whatever they have belongs to the Lord. Because of **(106)** this we find similarly everywhere that God has rejected cunning and has chosen sim-plicity. Because a spiritually wise person is not easily found who through his own experience manages to taste the knowledge of life, on account of this his natural simplicity is acceptable to God. Because this is [God's] own gift and the first thing formed of our nature: when God had created us he placed simplicity in us from the beginning.

Then simplicity is placed in the middle. Some ascend from it up to the instruction of spiritual matters and become spiritually wise; and some descend from it to the learning and instruction of worldly matters. This [latter] is called crafty and cunning, be-cause if things are spoken of by their own true name, these that are learned—although their instruction is entirely in physical things—are not called wise, nor are these whose simplicity has been instructed in spiritual matters said to be crafty and cunning. But these whose knowledge is gathered from the world are named cunning and crafty, and these who practice in spiritual matters [are named] wise and intelligent, because wisdom belongs only to God and to the person whose request is placed with God. The world's knowledge is not worthy to be called wise in the language of uprightness, nor also should the wisdom of God be called cun-ning and craftiness by discerning knowledge, because there is no contrivance in this wisdom, nor does it consist of the composition of different opinions.

Rejection of the World's Wisdom

37. This also eludes reason: why **(107)** is God pleased with sim-plicity and has chosen it more than the wisdom of the world? In fact, the wisdom of the world is also a gift of God as the Apostle said, "In the wisdom of God, the world did not know God through

wisdom"[91] and account of this is evident that if there were no wisdom in us in the foundation of our formation, and wisdom had not been placed in all the creatures, we would not even be able to gather wisdom from the world. See then, the world's wisdom is also a gift of God. Why then has he rejected it and chosen simplicity? Therefore, it is evident because our own labor is in it, and because while it is being gathered from those who possess it, their view is toward the world and not toward God, and they run after it so that in [their] mind they may be considered to be wise. Briefly said, their souls are full of human passions when they are gleaning and seeking this wisdom among the creatures. Due to the fact that they had applied labors to the search, [as well as]their own affliction and torment for the discovery of this knowledge, they thought it was their own [accomplishment] while examining their labor that they had [done] for it. On account of this the Lord has rejected the wise of the world, and instead of them has chosen the simple.

Again, the wisdom of the world is the opposite in everything to divine wisdom and there is no way that they are to be mixed with one another, in similarity to how light is not mixed with darkness, so that even if one of the wise people of the world should desire **(108)** to become wise in these spiritual matters, he first sheds from himself the thoughts of that wisdom and the entire supposition of his former knowledge and stands at the beginning of the road of the first level which is simplicity, childlikeness, and faith that hears and receives innocently. Then he begins to run ahead on this journey of the road of the wisdom of Christ and if he takes care to travel in front of it, wisdom will show itself to him.

Reproach of Eli

38. Simplicity is a gift of nature, and it belongs to the Maker, and nothing of ours is mixed in it, that is, neither from our will nor from our labor. On account of this, [simplicity's] gift dwells in [God's] gift, and [God's] wisdom dwells in the place he has established.

---

[91] 1 Cor 1:21.

Just as also here he inclined to Samuel and abandoned cunning, and the high priest spoke to him and he came to him. Look, the Holy Book does not accuse Eli of many evil things, except only that he had turned away from and had not rebuked his sons. He was not participating in their iniquity by deeds, and though one could say he had acted like them in his youth, Scripture did not find fault with him in this and did not say, "You have committed iniquity like this in your youth, and now your sons are acting like you." But the Lord said to Samuel, "See, I am doing a thing in Israel, so that both ears of everyone who hears it may burn on account of the iniquity Eli has heard that his sons were doing in the tabernacle and had not rebuked them."[92] But the entire indictment of Eli is because of his neglect and that he had not **(109)** weighted his rebuke against the faults of his sons. It is written that he had rebuked them,[93] but a feeble and weak rebuke, and not like what would be required for that entire offense. This is the only reproach of Eli the priest: his neglect and not his own evil deeds. Notwithstanding this, God had chosen the youth rather than him and had conversed with youth and simplicity.

Tabernacle and Desert

39. Because just as Scripture explains, the education of Samuel had taken place in the temple of the Lord in the same manner as Joshua bar Nun and Jacob, for these too were raised up in the tabernacle as our discourse has demonstrated above. [This is] a remarkable thing, how [it is that] from these two places the Lord had called those he had formed, whether of those who were accustomed to the desert, or of those who were raised up in a tent, because in both of these places simplicity is acquired in them. Look at David and Moses with the rest of the others, God had selected them out of the desert for his providence; and he had chosen Samuel and Joshua and Jacob by the education of the tabernacle. Look then,

---

[92] 1 Sam 3:11-13.
[93] 1 Sam 2:23-25.

we also know from here that simplicity is beloved by God and is the beginning of the road of those who have drawn near to God.

Simplicity of Abel and Cunning of Cain

40. We are also able to see simplicity in Abel, the first righteous person, for Holy Scripture indicates to us that he was more simple than Cain. Both of them had presented offerings to the Lord, and the offering of simplicity was received and that of evil was rejected. Cain was angry against the Lord and against Abel **(110)**—against Abel because he was jealous of him, and against the Lord because he had rejected his offering. If he had been simple he would not have been jealous. And if he had been pure, he would also not have been angry against the Lord. Moreover, we see the cunning of Cain by the excuse that he had found for his evilness, for when he was thinking of killing his brother, Abel, but was not able because he was near to his parents, he said to [Abel], "Let us travel to the valley."[94] Abel in his innocence heard and obeyed like a child, for his simplicity had not considered evil. He had not wondered in his heart why [Cain] was calling him to the valley, nor was he conscious of Cain's hatred toward him, because simplicity does not know how to see these things. Nevertheless, he was dealing with him through the innocence of his heart and through the love of his brother, and wherever he would call him, he would readily obey.

Proper Clothing of Simplicity

41. But look here as well at the works of simplicity and examine the defects of cunning and of evil. Be careful to be on the side of the simple, those who at all times have pleased God and reject cunning as something not proper for you and is not fitting for the discipleship in which you live. Just as the clothing that is suitable for your shape is known, and if you put on something that is the opposite of it you will be laughed at by everyone, so also the clothing of simplicity is proper for your soul, and if you put on that [garment]

[94] Gen 4:8.

of cunning, you will be criticized by those who are discerning—and also the [wedding] feast will not accept you in this garment.[95]

Joseph in Egypt

42. **(111)** Along with these let us look at the pure Joseph whose honor toward his father and his love toward his brothers were born from his simplicity. His brothers were envious of him, but he was not aware; they were considering killing him, but he did not know. His father had commanded him to go visit his brothers and promptly he obeyed him. He had seen dreams that proclaimed his greatness and their servitude. Through his simplicity he had approached and revealed to them their servitude [to him] and [this] innocent had not sensed that cunning was increasing its evilness and through the hearing of these things hatred was increasing in his brothers. But when the old man Jacob had seen the simplicity of Joseph his son, he rebuked him not to reveal [his dreams].[96] [It was] not that he was not affirming that these [things] would come to be, for Scripture says that he was keeping these sayings because he believed that they would come to be, but he reprimanded the simplicity of Joseph, lest his brothers' hatred might increase toward him through the revelation of his dreams. He was transporting food to them and passed from place to place asking for them. He was not aware that he was running toward murderers and not toward his brothers. He saw them and in his simplicity was filled with joy, but those [brothers], on seeing him, [were filled with] gloom and anger. While simplicity was thinking of good things and was increasing his love at the sight of his brothers, the jealousy that had given birth to cunning was becoming increasingly stronger, growing and considering murder. They imagined evil and performed evil. However, observe how both of them ended up, and notice with which one **(112)** God was pleased—simplicity, not knowing how to keep secret its dreams, was being driven about on a chariot of honor, while cunning was

---

[95] Matt 22:12.
[96] See Gen 37:10.

sprawling before it on the ground. Simplicity commands and cunning is obedient to it. Simplicity was being reared in the wisdom of God, but cunning was adding evil. "I have seen that there is no one wiser or more intelligent than you,"[97] the king of Egypt was saying to that simple [person]. Because simplicity is close to wisdom, and the intellect of God is related to innocence, simplicity is the vessel that receives divine revelations.

Paul Rejects Cunning and Deceit

43. The blessed Paul also rightly rejects cunning. "We do not walk in cunning, and we do not deceive the word of God, but by the revelation of truth we show ourselves before all the consciences of human beings."[98] Look, Paul has also taught you that deceit clings to cunning and is the vessel of all evil. On account of this, Paul also flees from it. And which disciple will not reject it if the Apostle has rejected and chased it away and put it outside the pure teaching of Christ? For it was also not suitable for him, just as evil is the opposite of good, so cunning is the opposite of simplicity. Moreover, in another passage Paul writes to his disciples, "Did I cheat you deceitfully like a cunning person?"[99] Here again he joined deceit to cunning. **(113)** In another expression, he accuses the heretics and shows that all of their teaching exists by cunning. "Let us not be children who are greatly disturbed and buffeted by every wind of the deceitful doctrines of people, those who by their cunning contrive to lead us into error, but let us become true by our love so that everything that is ours may increase in Christ."[100]

Wolves in Lambs' Clothing

44. Our Lord also declared to the heretics that they are cunning and sly. For he said, "Watch out for the false prophets, those who

[97] Gen 41:39.
[98] 2 Cor 4:2.
[99] 2 Cor 12:16.
[100] Eph 4:14-15.

come to you in lambs' clothing, but within they are ravenous wolves."[101] This is again the work of cunning that while one is in one thing, he will appear in another, for it is the case that while they are wolves they appear in lambs' clothing; cunning has taught them how to do it in this way. For cunning does two things: it gives rise to evil and increases it and then contrives how it might teach it to others as well. Wherever it is appropriate, it hides, and wherever it knows that it is opportune to reveal, it reveals. Evil is blind, [but] it has eyes of cunning.

The Leaven of Cunning

45. In another passage our Lord was teaching his disciples to guard themselves from the cunning of the Pharisees and of the Sadducees. "Beware of the leaven of the Pharisees and of the Sadducees, and of the leaven of Herod."[102] Know that what he calls "leaven" here [means] cunning and evil. **(114)** In another passage when the Pharisees had told him that Herod wished to kill him, he called [Herod] a fox on account of his cunning, "Go say to this fox . . . "[103] Because he does not have the strength to do with authority that thing he desires, look, he constructs the means of craftiness so that cunning might fill the place of power, just as cunning also filled the place of power for that fox. I live according to my own will, and your cunning is not able to make me depart outside of my will. "I make signs today and tomorrow, but the third day I will finish."[104] See then, our Lord was cautioning his disciples regarding the cunning of Herod and the evilness of the Pharisees who while they were doing certain things were teaching other things.

Our Lord was not cautioning them against the teaching of Moses that the Pharisees were teaching, but against their own traditions, which they had found in their cunning to be an occasion for the pursuit of iniquity. [One can see this] by the fact that they were

[101] Matt 7:15.
[102] Mark 8:15.
[103] Luke 13:32.
[104] Luke 13:32.

presenting themselves as righteous to people and were concerned for the honor of God, while they were dishonoring him in secret by their actions. They were lengthening their prayers in order to devour the houses of widows, and disfiguring their faces so that they might appear to be fasters, and were washing the exterior of a cup and of a dish.[105] That is, they were adorning and making attractive their outer actions, while inwardly they were full of iniquity and all sorts of impurity. They were decorating themselves outwardly with dignity and with modesty in plain view, while secretly they were full of rapaciousness and deceit and licentiousness, and the desire of all **(115)** lusts. Our Lord was commanding his apostles to watch out for this teaching of the Pharisees. All of these things that happen by deceit and which are achieved by a false manner are born out of cunning.

Doves and Serpents

46. Why, instead of these things, does our Lord command the disciples to become innocent like doves toward good things, and wily like serpents toward the bad things?[106] For simplicity is related to faith and wiliness confronts error. They are innocent in order to find their life, and crafty in order not to lose their life. Simplicity is useful for us for the acquisition of virtues, and craftiness is sought by us so that we might not be deprived of them. Purity of mind is [directed] toward God, [while] slyness of thoughts is [aimed] toward people who are crafty to take from us these things of God. Our Lord then has commanded us well to be innocent as doves toward one another and toward him, and crafty like serpents against those who contrive to deprive us of spiritual things, because the craftiness of the serpent is [aimed] toward a person and not toward himself. By the craftiness of his nature he delivers his body to blows, yet guards his head from injury, for from [such an injury] death is absolutely rendered.

[105] Luke 11:39.
[106] Matt 10:16.

As for the disciples who cunningly had asked who among them is the greatest in the kingdom of heaven and with the mind of craftiness had desired to climb one step above the other, he had taught them the simplicity of children in which there is no lust for authority and of dominance, and its thought is not experienced in the love of honor of the world. "Truly, I say **(116)** to you, if you do not turn around and become simple like small children, you shall not enter the kingdom of heaven."[107] And again, "Everyone who does not receive the kingdom of God like a child, in innocence of heart and in simplicity, will not enter it."[108]

Paul's Directions regarding Simplicity

47. Paul also teaches about this simplicity, not only that we should possess it with regard to God and with regard to others, but he also commands ordinary servants to honor their lords through simplicity without deceit and cunning. "Servants, obey your masters in everything, not by flirting like those who please people, but in fear and trembling and in simplicity of heart as if for Christ."[109]

He also commands those who give so that simplicity may be found with them through their gifts. "Whoever gives, [give] in simplicity; and whoever is in leadership, [lead] with diligence."[110] Because if cunning is found in those who give, they will become testers of the actions of those who receive. And for this reason, the gift that simplicity gives is prevented and not counted, because the custom of simplicity is not to calculate and then give but to share liberally and give to everyone. Our Lord has taught this same simplicity, because he said, "Everyone who asks you, give to him."[111] Again, Paul himself prays for those who give so that the fruits of their righteousness may grow and that they may share simply [their] gifts **(117)** with those who are needy. "That God who gives

---

[107] Matt 18:3.
[108] Mark 10:15.
[109] Eph 6:5-6 and Col 3:22.
[110] Rom 12:8.
[111] Matt 5:42.

the seed to the sowers and bread for food will give and multiply your seed and will increase the fruits of your righteousness, in order that you will become rich in everything in all simplicity, for [simplicity] accomplishes through us thanksgiving to God."[112] Here also, Paul had prayed with simplicity for his disciples that they might become rich and said that by [simplicity] thanksgiving toward God might grow and become strong.

Again he said, "You have obeyed the profession of the Gospel of Christ and have submitted yourselves by your simplicity toward them and toward everyone."[113] Again he said, "I am afraid that perhaps, just as the serpent had made Eve err by its deception, in the same way your minds might be corrupted away from the simplicity which is with Christ."[114] He taught us again here that whoever believes in Christ should remain in simplicity with his instruction. He has indicated, moreover, by the word that even Eve had not received the deceit of cunning of the tempter until she had abandoned the simplicity that was with the commandment of God.

Again, simplicity engenders that holy greeting Paul commands his disciples to give to one another at the end of all his letters, and clarity of mind gives it. Again he said, "Let us live by the Spirit and deliver ourselves to the Spirit, and let us not be vainglorious, [lest] we quarrel against each other and contend jealously with one another."[115] This happens by simplicity and purity of mind so that a person may live spiritually and deliver himself to the Spirit.

Reminder to Pursue Simplicity

48. Therefore, it is excellent for the disciples of Christ to pursue simplicity and tend to the clarity of mind, **(118)** and not be envious of those who are cunning for evil things and are crafty to find the honors and comforts of the world. For look, we have learned from all the books of the Old and New [Testaments] that a person

[112] 2 Cor 9:10-11.
[113] 2 Cor 9:13.
[114] 2 Cor 11:3.
[115] Gal 5:25, 26.

should approach God in simplicity and simplicity is the habitation of God. Along with the instruction of the Scriptures, this practical experience shows us that righteousness is much closer to simplicity than to cunning. Even if those cunning and sly have [ascetical] labors and appear [to live] in the ways of righteousness, they are grasped by other passions, and because of this they persevere in [ascetical] labors in order to nourish the evil passions that stir in their souls—whether honor or praise or power—contriving to ensnare it by the way of their labors. But simplicity does not have such thoughts in the practice of its labors, but what drives it is either the excellent law that it has received, while holding it steady, or it is the fear lest it might reject it, or the love of God guarding it in its austerities. If it has attained this up to the level of love, fear guards and supports simplicity.

Do Not Be Ashamed of Simplicity

49. Therefore, do not be ashamed, O disciple, of this good gift, but take hold of it from the beginning of your discipleship, and may it be found with you up to the end and with all the benefits. You have heard God in simplicity and in faith and have departed from the world and have neither judged nor investigated regarding him those things he has told you. If you had been cunning, you would not have heard him. If you had heeded his word with thoughts of wiliness, you would not have followed God who has called you, nor **(119)** would one of those who were called and obeyed God have heard his word, nor would they have followed his commandment when he called them to come follow him, nor would they have become servants of his providence for human beings in some manner [or other]. The bountifulness of the spiritual mind is born from natural simplicity. Notice as well this worldly instruction which a simple mind is able to receive, because a youth is very simple who receives worldly instruction and respects the teachers. Insofar as [youth] grows in stature and becomes cunning in these human matters, it will despise the teachers and treat instruction with contempt. In the same way also, simplicity receives spiritual instruction, being full of respect for the teacher and careful not to

forget the instruction. If one wishes to approach cunning and from it [go on] to lusts, immediately he will treat instruction with contempt and despise God. Therefore, let us take hold and keep guard of this good gift, and may our entire way of life be in purity of heart; let us reject cunning and distance ourselves from wiliness; let us reproach evil and guard against deceit; let us distance ourselves from subtlety and flee from back biting. Let us cast away from us a tongue that lashes back. By a simple intellect and a clear mind, let us praise the holy Trinity of the Father and of the Son and of the Holy Spirit forever. Amen.

The end of the first *mēmrā* on simplicity.

Mēmrā 5

On Simplicity

The second *mēmrā* on simplicity.

Summary: Simplicity is fitting for the life of the solitary and ascetic, those who have forsaken the world and become strangers to it, for in the monastery there is no competition, property or power by which cunning can become involved. In this way of life like the angels, cunning is considered a disease since it encourages wickedness to act out its intentions. A simple person should be called in a positive sense "a child." Jesus chose fishermen who were innocent, but since some sought positions of honor he had to teach them more about childlikeness. Just as a king or person of worldly honor denies knowing about lowly crafts, we should not know about the cunning of the world in our simplicity. The simple are more admired and loved by others than the cunning. Simplicity is the beginning of the path of Christ, but purity of spirit is its end. The apostles, therefore, began as simple ones, but after receiving the Holy Spirit became pure human beings.

The Richness of Simplicity

(120) 1. In this marketplace of riches we should be proclaiming at all times about spiritual riches, because I see that you also are desiring to hear a helpful discourse and not one which is [merely] pleasurable and an occasion for applause. The words that are written for the purpose of pleasurable listening, or to arouse the praise of applause in listeners, are not necessary at all in this chaste place,[1]

---

[1] Typographical error: written ܪܬܐܪܣ, read ܪܬܐܪܣ.

for [what is said] ought to be like the place in which it is spoken, because the place in which we are gathered is [marked by] spiritual riches and benefits. So now let us speak in this place a simple word that bears inner wealth to the one who speaks and to those who listen, because it is written, "May the one who hears the word share in all good things with whoever proclaims [the word]."[2]

Our previous discourse was speaking about simplicity and clarity, and now I also wish to speak again concerning this helpful subject. Simplicity is an appropriate matter for us and our [situation], and there is no way for us to live without it in the cultivation of virtues. **(121)** Just as the members [of the body] are not able to see without the eye, so also virtues are not performable without simplicity. Just as with the blindness of the eye all the members become dark, so by the abolition of simplicity all good things are inhibited.

Simplicity of Monastic Life

2. Simplicity is especially appropriate for the monastic way of life, and clarity of mind greatly agrees with those who have left the world and live apart from it. Wherever there is not one of the ways of the world, the cunning of the world is also not required. We have with us here neither buying nor selling, nor is there with us any bargaining for the sake of transient profits. No one here can become greater than his brothers and be seen with more authority than his companion. No one here surpasses or is surpassed because there are no reasons for superiority among us. No fields and vineyards here are divided, neither are there lands separated by boundaries. No one here wishes to become wealthier than his brother and abound in worldly possession more than his companion. No one here wishes to be seen in resplendent clothes, for every single one of us has the humble clothing of mourning. No one here has been made a servant[3] of his stomach and wishes to find for himself banquets of food, for we are all being fed from one common table.

---

[2] Gal 6:6.
[3] Written: ܥܒܕܐ, "work, act"; read ܥܒܕܐ, "servant."

No one here wishes to violate the honor of his brother, for we are commanded to honor one another. No one here has gone to court against **(122)** his companion, for we all take up one another's cause. No one here wishes to build nor does another desire to sketch [the plans of] palaces, because all of us have a single narrow dwelling in a cloister. No one here wishes to expand his dwelling and construct for himself gilded beds,[4] for all of us sleep on the ground humbly in a small defined space.

Cunning Rejected

3. Wherever these things are completely strange, the cunning of the world should not be found. Wherever the way of the world has been dismissed and discarded, there also its craftiness ought to be rejected. Wherever the physical aspects of the body are despised, there also the cunning that contends on behalf of them should be treated with contempt. Wherever the old person is crucified with all his ways,[5] there also the craftiness that is the defender of the old person ought to be crucified. Wherever falsehood is being rejected, there also cunning—the mother of falsehood—ought to be rejected. Wherever deceit is forced out and discarded, from there its parents and its begetters ought to depart. In a community in which there is no deceit and in which falsehood is not being served, cunning and craftiness, the parents of these things, also ought to be treated with contempt. Wherever there is humble hair clothing, there the simplicity fitting for it should be honored. For linen clothing is not proper for our monastic garb, and neither is decorated and ornate dress right for our order. In that same manner and more than these, cunning is not proper for our discipleship, nor also is craftiness **(123)** for our monastic garb. Ornamentation of the head is not fitting for us: it belongs to decadent and feeble people; nor also that deceit which is the original innovation of the enemy. For

---

[4] Lavenant translates (ܬܠܘܿܡܐ) as "lits"/"beds" rather than "dining rooms."

[5] Rom 6:6.

cunning is the possession of the Accuser and of all his servants. Simplicity [is] the wealth of Christ and of all his disciples.

Usefulness of Cunning

4. Craftiness is useful only for the world's business and for those who have committed themselves to the seizure and plunder of others; and slyness is necessary for oppressing and deceiving relatives. "Wisdom does not dwell in the soul that conspires with evil things," said the wise Solomon, and also, "Spiritual knowledge does not reside in a body that is defeated by sin."[6] The soul that conspires with evil things is full of cunning, because cunning is the deviser of evil things. Whoever desires to cultivate lusts rushes to become a disciple of cunning, so that through what he has learned from it and through the iniquitous malicious deeds [cunning] shows to him, he contrives to conceal his evil deeds and make excuses for the despicable things performed by him. Wherever lusts are being rejected and human passions are being driven far away, one ought to uproot their root and cut off and cast away whatever else makes them grow.

Physical Angels

5. There is no cunning in heaven,[7] nor is there any craftiness of evil things in Gabriel and Michael. There is no slyness or malice of contemptible things in those spiritual places, nor is there any darkness of deceit **(124)** in that luminous Jerusalem, the city of life. There is no one there who conspires to win through falsehood, since falsehood does not even function in that place. There is no one there who is being taught to hide his despicable deeds, nor one who is cunning to conceal his evil works. Just as these things do not exist in that place of spiritual beings, neither should they be found in our location which is a type of that place. This way of life is the image of the spiritual ones. This monastery is a type of the heavenly [residences]. This condition of yours—those clothed in the

---

[6] Wis 1:4.
[7] Typographical error: written ܟܠܒ, read ܟܠܒܐ.

body—is comparable to those higher [beings] who are bodiless. It is appropriate for you to say what Paul preached, "Even if we live in the flesh, we are not laboring according to the flesh."[8] You may appear to be physical to the eyes, but your labor is completely spiritual. You are physical angels and spiritual [beings] clothed in flesh. Your dwelling is pure, refined, sincere and holy, and the image sealed in it [is] of the higher dwelling of those who are spiritual.

Simplicity Is Glory

6. The entire way of life of the disciples of Jesus flourishes in simplicity. If you take simplicity away from them, you have disturbed the rule. With us simplicity is a source of pride, and whoever possesses it is wise. Just as whoever is simple in the world is called a fool by fools, so in this spiritual place it is fitting that someone cunning be named a fool by those who are discerning, for he has acquired in this place a possession not suitable for it and has found in it something that does not belong to it. No one seeks to find trees and seeds and plants among the waves **(125)** of the sea, nor, moreover, does one demand to see the waves and storms on dry land. But each one of them is found in the place where it is needed. In the same way, it is not proper that cunning should be found in the pure place of the spiritual, because the place of cunning is the world, full of evil things. As a singer is not appropriate among mourners, [nor] weeping at a wedding banquet, so it is not appropriate that the craftiness of evil things should be found in a place of simplicity. In a place of spiritual profits, the discovery of cunning is a loss for the spiritual.

Prostitution of Cunning

7. You do not speak deceitfully with your brother, why is cunning necessary for you? You are not perched in the monastery in ambush in order to secretly kill [someone] righteous.[9] Why are craftiness

[8] See 2 Cor 10:3.
[9] Ps 10:8.

and deceit useful to you? Why are you proud, O fool, of whatever condemns you? Why do you glorify yourself by whatever shames you? What is so great for you with whatever reproaches you? Why are you puffed up by a possession that is not yours? From the world you have received cunning, through which you will be accused of having all the vices of the world. For its fruits cling to the tree and the tree of the roots of vices is cunning. Wherever [cunning] is found all the vices are with it. If they are not visible in outward actions, they still exist in secret thoughts. The illness of the soul is cunning, as also its true health is simplicity.

Where **(126)** have you ever seen an ill person who is proud of his disease, or someone suffering who glories in his sufferings? A cunning monk should be ashamed because he has been found in a situation not appropriate for him. Just as he might have had a shameful disgrace—an encounter with a prostitute [for example]— in the same way he ought to be in disgrace if cunning is found with him, which is an image of a prostitute. Cunning is in the soul in the same way a prostitute is in the marketplace, for just as she speaks with all the men and puts on all [kinds of] faces so that she may appear to every person according to his liking, so also cunning is visible in all kinds of minds and acquires borrowed and painted faces through which to show itself to every person according to his liking. What was written straightforwardly by the Apostle, "With everyone I have become all [things] so that I might gain every person,"[10] is accomplished the other way around by cunning, for [cunning] becomes everything with everyone in order to destroy every person and to mock and laugh at every person. If these are the deeds of cunning, how could it be suitable for a disciple of Christ, and how should it be found in simple solitaries?

Cunning, the Companion of Falsehood

8. Observe with the eye of knowledge and understand that all vices spring up from cunning. Deceit is in it, falsehood is found in it, slander is near to it. Mockery is its friend, gossiping is its nest, for

---

[10] 1 Cor 9:22.

its dwelling is an evil hiding place. Deception, as well as transgression, **(127)** is its teaching. It associates with theft, is the advocate for adultery, defends fornication. Hypocrisy is a haughty garment for it. Ambushes are contrived by it. It is ready for false witness [and] is the mother of false disparagement. To state concisely, every evil has raised it up as an advocate to argue on its behalf; for some it hides them, making excuses for others, while prattling that some of these things have not happened and multiplying arguments and pretending an excuse, and making for some evils other facets, saying that not on account of this did these things happen, nor were they done for this purpose. All false speech collects around it. It accompanies the judges when they wish to steal. Officials use it when they wish to receive a bribe. It accompanies those who commit vices when they are being judged. A wife who wishes to transgress the way of the law against her husband takes [cunning] into her company and then departs to the wasteland of depravity. Students are instructed by it and then begin to be unfaithful to their teachers. Advocates who speak before the judges compose their words from [cunning's] wealth, and in [cunning's] furnace their retorts are being forged. It lays out nets of iniquity, lengthening snares on the roads of travelers, hiding traps of deceit, burrowing pits of destruction, demanding of them a second time an already paid for bill of sale. Until falsehood draws near **(128)** to him it does not know how to make excuses for itself. Falsehood is ready to defraud and instructs it how to deceive. An evil will prepares falsehood, and then cunning becomes counsel to it regarding how to make it happen. It begins to walk with falsehood on the path opposed to the truth and calls out to cunning, "Come into my company," and then it sets out.

The Tongue of Evil

9. Cunning is the teacher of all vices, the advocate ready for all kinds of despicable deeds. It adopts the face of all, and pleads the case for all, and makes an excuse. It is as if this is spoken by cunning to evil, "You, evil, do evil as much as you wish, and may all of your members take delight in the comforts of desire. May the

body of all your senses revel in those things it loves. May all your fruits concentrate their tastes in [your senses] and grow and ripen. Revel as much as you desire and do not refrain. Enjoy yourself to the fullest and may your eye not become despondent. Act with iniquity as much as it pleases you. Do evil and fornicate as much as you wish. Become accomplished in iniquity and do not fear. Perfect yourself in all [kinds of] decadent acts and do not tremble. Do not let the report of laws scare you, nor let the threat of judgment shake you. Do not be terrified by the voice of the authorities. Do not let the shout of masters scare you. Against all these, I am arming myself for you. I will make an excuse for you to all who reprove you. It is easy for me to compose praise for you from your faults, and from those things **(129)** which others think to condemn you, I will weave for you a crown of victory. My entire thought is for you with thoughts that are for you. I trouble myself night and day so that whenever it is necessary I will make excuses for you. I will think [of you] at all times. But you, evil, delight in pleasures and I will learn the [kind of] writing that justifies you. Do not be anxious how or what you shall say before the judges. I will compose a speech for you. I will silence those who reprove you. I will defeat justice that speaks against you. I will silence the uprightness of the judges of your faults. I am, O evil one, your tongue. I am prepared to become for you an eloquent mouth. Every tongue that desires to make a case against you, I will stand up and condemn it."

The Evil of Evil

10. These encouragements from cunning are being offered to evil, propounding this [kind of] language in order to provoke it to trespass into iniquity. So then, cunning is the evil of evil and the power of sin and the life of the body of decadent actions. But if cunning did not exist, perhaps evil would have been kept still by fear of condemnation, and by fear of judgment being prepared for it by justice. Cunning then is the most evil of all the evils, for cunning is the tower of sin, so that when it has fallen upon the roads and has robbed every person, [sin] rushes to the refuge of cunning in order that [cunning] will make an excuse for [sin] to

those who reprove it, and [sin] will take shelter in [cunning] as in a fortress from **(130)** the inquisitors of justice who go out to search diligently for its tracks.

Look, in which evil is your glory, O wretched disciple, and in what are you proud, O wolf clad in the skin of a lamb? If your cunning is in you, all of iniquity is with you. If craftiness is in your soul, all of sin dwells in you. If your life consists of deceitful deeds of slyness, all evil resides in you. Your contemptible acts are not openly visible because cunning conceals them. In this way it is confessed by anyone who becomes its disciple that [cunning] is shelter for his sin. This which is the mother of all evils is not suitable for you. Evil does not agree with your spiritual way of life, because it has created a nest for all evils.

The Same Name as God

11. But you, O upright disciple, rejoice in your simplicity for by it you have run the road of righteousness and will not be ashamed to be called a child. This name is fitting for you, and this title is worthy of you, for through it your purity from iniquity is evident. The name of a child is indicative of his purity. The appellation of "simple" proclaims that there is no deceit in him. For just as every one of the craftsmen of the world, or of those who soldier in the military of a human kingdom, has a name by which his position is known that indicates his craft, so also the name of the disciple's [craft] shall be called "simple." Would that you should be named by the [same] name God is called; the name of "simple" is indicative of something singular.

No Deceit in Simplicity

12. The one who is simple has no deceit in him **(131)** and no ambush is devised by him, nor does falsehood prosper in him, nor is plotting found in him, nor does slander dwell in him, nor does he strike his companion in secret. He does not seek to do evil or connive to do harm. There is no deceit in him against his neighbor and he does not consider evil against his brother who sits quietly

with him. But he is a pure and refined vessel and his neighborhood is the neighborhood of light. Just as not one of these evil things is stirred up in a natural child, so also not one of them is aroused in one whose mind is simple; neither does the child consider evil things on account of his childishness, nor does the simple person reflect on hateful deeds on account of his simplicity.

Fertile Land

13. In the name of simplicity all good things are gathered, just as by the title of cunning all evil things are being collected. Simplicity is the plowed field that receives the seed and the plants of all the virtues. Cunning is the soil full of thorns and thistles, that is, divided and empty thoughts. As the growth of the good seed is prevented in a field full of thorns and thistles, so with the divided thoughts of cunning, the simple growth of faith is prevented, and as the growth of the good seed in the soil that is pure of the germination of thorns is sound,[11] so also the growth of the word of truth springs up healthily in a simple mind. Simplicity does not judge the language of faith, nor does it investigate why in this way **(132)** God has commanded. It has no objection against whatever is spoken to it to do but listens attentively and accepts purely and keeps simply. Without effort simplicity is in all of its actions. It is not wearied by thoughts that tie up and untie one another. The cultivation of righteousness is easy for simplicity and without delay it travels on the road of travails.

Simplicity of Little Children

14. On account of this our Lord also taught his disciples the serenity of little children in order that he might enable them to acquire simplicity. He rejected the cunning and chose the simple. He made the crafty and the scribes go away and drew near to him the unlearned and the ignorant. Annas was crafty and Caiaphas was a cunning one. The Pharisees were clever, the scribes were deceitful.

---

[11] Matt 13:7.

The choice of our Savior rejected all of these. Instead of Caiaphas he chose Simeon. Instead of Annas [he chose] John. Instead of the scribes, Andrew; instead of the Pharisees, Matthew; instead of the intellectuals, Philip; instead of the crafty, Bartholomew; instead of the cunning, Jacob (James): a band of those who are simple instead of a congregation of those who are crafty; those who did not know anything instead of those who think concerning themselves that they know everything. For at all times truth has triumphed in simplicity and faith has shone in childhood.

Maintaining a Child's Simplicity

15. Moreover, after our Lord had rejected the congregations of the cultured and the troops of the cunning and crafty and had chosen those fishers and the ignorant and uneducated, he turned again to teach them [how] to add to their simplicity and not remain only on that first level **(133)** of their childhood. He picked up a child and placed him in their midst, and looking at all of them said to them, "Unless you turn yourselves around and become like this child, you shall not enter the kingdom of heaven."[12] Our Lord did this because he had seen that they desired to move away from the mind of their simplicity by a question regarding honor and receive a rank superior to the other. Those who are simple do not ask a question such as this. But the question was born out of a mind desiring to gaze upon cunning and our Lord forbade this utterance of a troublesome question, and said to his disciples, rebuking and admonishing them, "If you are mine, become simple. And if you desire the kingdom of heaven, imitate this child. As you want to receive the life to come, remain in serenity. If you want to become wise in the word of life, remain in your ignorance. I do not wish that you turn into those who are cunning from [being] simple but become wise from [being] simple. Whoever rushes to become cunning from [being] simple will descend below. Whoever rushes to become wise from [being] a child will ascend above. The cunning person does not accept my teaching, and on account of this I have

---

[12] Matt 18:3.

chosen you because you are children. I have rejected the cunning in others. Keep guard that it does not come to be in you and I reject you because of it. May this child be an example for you, for just as he does not desire anything from the world and does not ask for anything of people, neither **(134)** rank, nor honor, nor wealth, nor power, but only his food and his clothing that his childhood has need of, so also you should become children like him, innocent and simple like him, so that you might become my chosen disciples and in order that I will find you as I have chosen you." So see, our Lord Jesus has urged us through this commandment concerning simplicity and has exhorted us to become sincere and innocent.

Necessary for the Kingdom

16. We should not be ashamed of simplicity and abstain from it as from a worldly matter not useful to us, [nor] should those who are simple be despised in our eyes and we consider them not amounting to anything. They are not necessary for this world, but they are useful and necessary for the kingdom of God. Something rejected by human beings is [something] chosen with God, just as the apostles were also being rejected by the entire world. Moreover, our Savior Jesus himself was hated and rejected by all the Jews. Then in this way as well, whoever rejects the simple and for this reason despises and disdains them, the portion of this presumptuous person is placed with the portion of the Jews and the scribes and Pharisees who have rejected Christ and his disciples.

Punishment of Scandalizers

17. See what punishment the word of Christ has exacted upon whoever causes one of them to stumble and take heed not to scandalize them. But even though this saying results in other meanings, "Whoever causes these little ones to stumble, it would have been better for him if a millstone of an ass is hung **(135)** upon his neck, and he is plunged into the depths of the sea,"[13] [it is intended] par-

---

[13] Matt 18:6.

ticularly for this conclusion, that no one should dare to deride the simplicity of the innocent. For when you have derided and mocked and put down his simplicity, and have taken issue with his quietness and have scorned his innocence, and he has been considered by you as idle and useless, the indignation of your blasphemies against him compels him to take off and cast away his clarity and renounce his simplicity, since you have become for him the reason he is derided, and to flee from the childhood by which he was considered to be a fool by the arrogant. Instead of what he had been, he became what he had not been, and through your indignation and blasphemies against him, you have made him stumble in his original way of life so that he might abandon it and take up instead other [ways] that are the opposite of his clarity. While he is living the monastic life,[14] he will reject this [clarity] and honor and choose speech more than stillness, and cunning more than his original simplicity, and craftiness more than his ignorance, and so you will have made him furious and angry rather than gentle and peaceful. Because in this way you have scandalized him and he has been compelled by your indignation to convert his virtues into vices, it would have been better for you that a millstone of an ass be hung around your neck and be cast into the depths of the sea than that you should cause offense to one of these little ones who believe in the Son.

Little Ones

18. Notice that our Lord himself called them "little ones," because they make themselves smaller than everyone, in order to teach you not to despise them because they run toward smallness, but so that they might grow greater in your eyes through [smallness]. **(136)** The appearance of the simple is ordinary and their manner is uncultured and rustic. Whoever wishes to despise them uses their appearance as an excuse to scorn them, because they have no idea how to set in order their outward appearances before people, and to

---

[14] Literally, "he was still"—ܗܘܐ ܫܠܝ.

show themselves publicly before the world as knowledgeable and famous ones. But you, through this especially, take the opportunity to make them great. May their being despised be a reason for you for their honor and their despicableness an occasion for their glory. Wherever faith is guarded in its completeness and is not corrupted by thoughts of cunning, it honors and promotes simplicity, and loves and upholds it even when it may be despicable in its appearance.

Go See the Simple Ones

19. Understand from experience[15] how much those who are simple are beloved to believers, and how much the uncultured and the rustic on account of Christ are loved by every disciple of Christ. Understand as well from this that the crafty of the world run to the uncultured of faith, and the cunning and rulers are bowing down before the simplicity of Christ. Observe and see when those who are great of the world lovingly embrace simplicity and worship and love ignorance. In as far as a person might appear [to have] an abundant portion of simplicity, he then becomes especially great and honored in their eyes. The sons of the world do not go out to see the cunning and crafty, [but] to the spiritual enclaves outside of the world. Lift up your eyes, O disciple, and observe these who are coming to you and are running to your door with love. They are running to see spiritual children and not the learned and those knowledgeable **(137)** of the affairs of the world. For when they desire to see the cunning and crafty who are trained and capable in the wisdom of the world they will be going into the cities and villages.

But when they go outside of the world, they rush to see the youths and the simple and the infants of Christ. May he not come to find you [to be] a serpent instead of a dove, and a hawk instead of an innocent sparrow, and your word [intended] for evil things instead of a wise [word] for good things. May he come to see, O disciple, as he desires to see you, for he has taken off his craftiness and has put on simplicity and draws near to you with it. You have rushed to put on whatever he has taken off and have desired to

---

[15] Literally, "the experience of deeds/works"—ܠܘܣܦܐ ܕܥܒ̈ܕܐ.

acquire whatever he has rejected. He has not carried and brought with him thoughts of cunning, but the simplicity of faith. He has come into your dwelling. May he not come to find in the place of the spiritual what he has abandoned in the world.

As a Sheep in His Suffering

20. Listen to the prophet who also proclaims our Lord through his simple teaching. He compares him with a lamb and a sheep, the animal that is the most simple of all the animals. "Like a lamb led to slaughter, and like a sheep before the shearer, he was silent."[16] The lion, the wolf, and the bear, along with the rest of all the wild beasts, are crafty because craftiness was mixed with their evilness in their creation. But sheep and lambs and ewes are innocent and naive in their behavior and in their movements, and our Lord was compared with them, and believers have been called by their name. Our Lord did not compare himself with a lion while he was being led to suffering and death. He did not call his flocks by the names of animals that are crafty for evil things **(138)** by the nature of their creation, but he was called a lamb and a sheep, for while he was being led to suffering and death he was silent in imitation of them. Just as a sheep before the shearer had been quiet, so he had not opened his mouth in his humility in order to affirm actually the word of prophecy, "when they led him he was silent." When they judged him he was silent. When they scourged him he did not complain. When they convicted him, he did not dispute. When they bound him, he was not indignant. When they struck him on his cheeks, he did not murmur. When he was stripped of his clothing like a sheep of its wool, he did not cry out. When they gave him vinegar and gall, he did not curse them. When they nailed him on a tree, he was not indignant against them. When Simon desired to take off the innocence of a sheep and took the sword for vengeance of the dishonor of his teacher, [Jesus] rebuked him to put back the sword into its place: "Return your sword to its place;[17] I do not

[16] Isa 53:7; Jer 11:19.
[17] Matt 26:52.

have need of your assistance." He was standing before the judge and was being questioned, that one who was learned and teacher of all wisdom, and he did not give an answer. He kept the law of simplicity so that he might affirm this [word]: "Like a lamb he was led to slaughter." They were leading him like a mute, parading him around from one place to another, and dragging him from one spot to another and from one judge to another judge. He stood before Annas and was silent, and until he was adjured he did not speak.[18] He was being questioned by Pilate and was silent,[19] until he had heard from him, "Are you the king of the Jews?"[20]—the question that declares he was being considered a rebel against **(139)** Caesar—he did not give an answer.[21] They brought him to Herod who—so that he might see and hear great things from him—was questioning him as a test. There again he stood silently and was not speaking and an answer was not given to his questioner. He was considered a despicable person who knew nothing and a fool who did not have a response. The Jews and priests thought whatever they wished, but he had not abandoned the innocence of a lamb, nor had he renounced the law of simplicity.

Foolishness of God

21. The Apostle Paul saw that the crucifiers considered him a fool and without intelligence, and his enemies counted him as ignorant and without understanding, so on behalf of Jesus [Paul] said against them that "the foolishness of God is wiser than that of human beings."[22] In order that it will not be a burden to you to be considered by people a fool by your simplicity, God shows himself as a fool, because he was standing before his questioners without giving an answer. He was considered by them ignorant when he did not give back an answer, in order that you may also hold fast on

[18] Matt 26:63.
[19] Matt 27:12.
[20] John 18:33.
[21] Luke 23:11.
[22] 1 Cor 1:25.

to your soul's strength and not transgress the law of simplicity, not even if you are considered a fool by every person and are counted as ignorant and without education. Whoever is irritated if he is considered by someone [to be] simple and unlettered, his mind is tied to this passion of the love of the world's empty knowledge, and if he is considered to be the opposite, grief and sadness rule over his life. You should endure everything in order to complete your road and to attain the end of the road of your journey.

See, **(140)** David the prophet also had pretended to the Philistines to be a madman without sense as a way to protect his life from death. "He let his spit [run down] upon his beard,"[23] in the way of a man without a mind so that he might deliver his life from being murdered. Therefore, if David pretended to be like someone demented, without a mind and discernment, in order not to lose his temporal life, how much more especially should you remain in your simplicity for the sake of eternal life, and not be defeated by the reproach of mockers and depart from the goal which was set by you?

Disciples as Shepherds and Sheep

22. Our Lord had also called the faithful of his flocks the names by which simplicity is known. " 'If you love me,' he says to Simon, chief of the disciples, 'shepherd for me my sheep and my lambs and my ewes.' "[24] As that one was called allegorically by the word of prophecy sheep and lamb, and moreover John had called him "the Lamb of God,"[25] so also he named the disciples of his word[26] by these names that indicate innocence, in order that when all the faithful had heard that those names had been established for them by the shepherd, they would be diligent to remain in all innocence as sheep and lambs and ewes. They should not depart from the law of simplicity. In imitation of these innocent animals who were being led to be killed and dragged off to slaughter, were being bound for

[23] 1 Sam 21:13.
[24] John 21:15-17.
[25] John 1:29.
[26] Typographical error: written ܡܠܬܗ, read ܡܕܠܗ.

shearing, or carried off[27] by animals, yet they were not crying out or complaining, but **(141)** were quiet[28] in the innocence of their nature; in the same way also the disciple of the Lord, in the face of all tests of works and words, of afflictions and abuses, confinements and false accusations, injustices and prisons, the indignations of false witnesses and incriminations, should remain in the innocence of his heart and not renounce the law of his stillness, or take off his innocence, or abandon his simplicity and use craftiness to do evil to his enemies. Evil plots and crafty deeds of iniquity are their own work, and during all their lives they are capable of carrying them out. But you have a work hidden from their knowledge, for your mind's clarity is able to perfect it and secretly you will enjoy it, and those [people] will not sense this pleasure because they have not been worthy of the delights you have tasted.

Joy of Simplicity

23. Simplicity is without anxiety, and, on account of this, persistent joy [accompanies] it at all times. Just as the joy of young children is continual with much laughter on account of their simplicity, because the cares of the world are not beating against the joy stirring childishly in their minds, so joy exists continually in a simple heart because there is no way for it to be filled with grief when [the simple heart] does not bring [this] about. Whoever wishes to do evil to his enemy and is not able, or schemes to become rich but does not become rich, or runs **(142)** to catch up but is not able, sadness and grief rule over his life on account of these things, and all the joy born from simplicity is completely removed from him.

Not Useful for Anything

24. It seems to the world as if one who is simple is not useful for anything. If you believe that you are not useful to the world, O disciple, do not be sad at this, because this is the glory of the

---

[27] Typographical error: written ܟܬܫܝܢ, read ܡܬܟܫܝܢ.

[28] Literally, "in stillness"—ܒܫܠܝܐ.

Christian when one does not practice these worldly things and does not use anything for the physical way of life. If someone should say to you that you do not know carpentry or you do not understand how to work in the craft of tanning or that you do not know one of the common crafts of the world, this is not to laugh at you. Because not even the king is dishonored by the fact that he does not know the work of one of the worldly crafts; but this is an honor for him, for his authority is greater than these [crafts], he does not lower himself to know them. It turns out that not knowing [one of] them is his honor; and knowing [one] is his reproach. Just as we see many people who are in one of the ranks of honor of the world, who while they know the crafts and are acquainted with the rest of those matters beneath their ranks, they deny that they know anything, and this ignorance is accorded in their case as honor. As they run they seek refuge in honor and say that they are not knowledgeable of the crafts. Similarly then this is also the case with the disciple of Christ. Honor is the ignorance **(143)** of worldly things, and his praise is this, that he is neither crafty nor cunning. His good reputation is not to be acquainted with the deceits of evil things, and knowledge of these things is considered by him more despicable than the knowledge of worldly crafts is considered a disgrace to a worldly king.

Interested in the Despicable

25. It is reproachable for a disciple who is enrolled in the higher kingdom that he might know these things that are strangers to his condition and are distant from the way of his discipleship. Is his life not full enough with the encounter with God that he would revert to learn these despicable things and dwell on these fleshly matters and scheme how he might do evil to and deceive his enemies, and how he might become rich and acquire [wealth], and how he might speak or listen against his oppressors, and where he might find profit and by which means will he find it? The relationship of the simple with God does not allow one to revert back to these things and become absorbed in them. He should not descend from the height of knowledge of the kingdom of Christ to the ways

and concerns of these sick passions, which at all times are being stirred up unhealthily in their thoughts. It is not appropriate for a mind in whose simplicity the faith of Christ stirs to turn away and attend to these deceitful acts of the flesh and to those cunning acts of corruption.

Learning Only the Spiritual

26. So then do not consider it disgraceful that you are not acquainted with the cunning ways of the world, but let this be a great honor that you are greater and higher in the likenesses of spiritual things than in those things of the flesh, because also with those who are spiritual there are no devices and strategies to deal with worldly things. If their way of life **(144)** is superior to everything physical, it is evident that also their mind is more elevated than these passions. Their entire conversation is only in the praises of divinity, being educated in spiritual knowledge in these things more sublime than their knowledge, and not lowering themselves to observe what is beneath them, because it is not that they wish to descend from their ranks, but that they are desiring to climb higher and make progress at all times in the mysteries of the [divine] being. Therefore, in the model of these powers are minds that are not being stirred up by physical things. The degree of the spiritual is that they should learn only these things that are above the world, and their thoughts should not lower themselves to the search and learning of these things that are foreign to their [monastic] condition.

Focusing Only on the Spiritual Craft

27. For in the same manner that the training of every one of the crafts is distinct and specific, it is imperative for whoever becomes a student of a craft to be eager to learn it in a school and not in another [place]; so also a disciple: his entire study and conversation should be in the learning of his craft, not distracting the focus of his thoughts through another thing. Our own craft is the learning of spiritual matters, so that our thoughts and our deeds may be above the world, and so that we may progress at all times in those

spiritual matters. The disciple who does not progress quickly at a workshop in the learning of his craft will be found at fault by his teachers and will be laughed at and mocked by his companions. In the same way as this, the disciple of this spiritual craft is worthy even more to be found at fault **(145)** if he does not grow day by day and progress in physical labor and in spiritual thoughts, while the harm that happens to every one of them is evident and certain. Whoever does not receive the learning of a worldly craft has lost the benefits found in that craft. But whoever does not receive the teaching of Christ and does not grow virtuously, the kingdom of heaven is his loss and the blessings confirmed and reserved for the chosen ones of God, [along with] "The thing that the eye has not seen and the ear has not heard and has not ascended up to the heart of a person,"[29] and the relationship that the perfect have with Christ, on account of which Christ had also descended from heaven to earth. Briefly, this is his loss: [he loses] himself along with the rest of the virtues that are above nature.

The Good Earth

28. The mind that is able to receive these things is clear and simple. Just as the mind of an infant is clear and more ready than a mature man to receive the teaching of everything; so it is much easier for a simple mind with regard to the learning of spiritual things than cunning and crafty thoughts. Simplicity is the good soil that easily receives the seeds and plants of this learning, and just as there are properties in natural soils that receive trees and plants and make them so that they might readily produce fruits more than other soils, so also the soils of the thoughts of the simple receive simply the plants of this spiritual learning and swiftly take hold **(146)** of them and produce fruits. But the soil of cunning is the oppressor of this learning, whether it does not receive it at all, or whether, if it does take hold and [learning] is received by it, its growth in [this soil] is choked by thorns and thistles of doubts and

[29] Isa 64:4; 1 Cor 2:9.

thoughts that at all times tear down and build up, which are the opposites of faith and simplicity.[30]

Trusting Children and Simple Ones

29. Rejoice, therefore, in simplicity, O disciple, which not only makes you beloved before God but also makes you dear in the eyes of people. Look and see, if you desire through experience, how the simple are beloved in the eyes of people more than the cunning and crafty. Every person loves simplicity, just as also everyone loves childhood, for the simple and children are both loved. Cunning and evil are hated by everyone, and everyone is wary of it because it is full of deceptions and ambushes and is accustomed to turn the stability of everything upside down. But simplicity, besides being loved, is a source of confidence, and no one is wary of the simple person in what he does, because one is persuaded by its transparency that [simplicity] does not conceive of evil things. Just as no one is wary of a child when he wishes to misbehave secretly in the house, because a child has no ability to observe his misbehavior, so also one is not wary of one who is simple in those things he wishes to do because he bears the image of a child in his thoughts. Who does not desire to be loved by God and to be loved by people? Both **(147)** of these are found in simplicity.

So then, why did you flee, O disciple—to become the beloved of God and dear to people, and to find for yourself free love from the Creator and from all his creation without labor? [You may say,] "But they mock me and consider me a fool and an illiterate, without a brain and without judgment." What good is there that has no opposite, O disciple? If you are afraid of the opposites of virtues, there will not be [anything] good at all [to come] from you. Because opposites are found with all things and labor is involved in the performance of all of them, along with the fact that envy and jealousy also are awakened among people against the rest of the virtues. But more than all the vices, this virtue of simplicity is free

---

[30] Matt 13:3-8.

of adversaries because neither envy nor jealousy are continually against it, and neither hatred nor enmity fight against it. If it is a little bit despised and disdained, it is still found with this love, and even these who despise the simple one love him. Not by hatred is he contemptible in their eyes, but by self-confidence; or they consider him a fool for these worldly things by his not being of use for the things they seek, one who is illiterate [doing] business with people and lacking intelligence for crafty and evil matters.

Ignorance of the World No Disgrace

30. Therefore, it is appropriate for you to rejoice in these things: you are regarded for what you really are and are called whatever **(148)** you should be [called]. If, indeed, anyone says to you, "You do not know how to lie or to commit adultery or to steal," is that considered by you an insult? Or that you do not know how to stand on a chariot to be a charioteer, or that you do not understand the skills of athletics, or that you do not know how to sing or [perform] the routine of dancers, or that you are not able to mock and laugh and to play the part in the playful manner of actors? Do you consider ignorance of these sorts of things a disgrace? I do not think so! Moreover, not a single person should find fault with you because you are a stranger to the knowledge of these skills. In the same way this should not be considered an insult by you, that you are stripped of the craftiness of evil matters and the deception of despicable things. For the blessed David had also said that he was attracted to the innocent and upright,[31] and it is evident that innocence is born from simplicity.

Goal of Spiritual Clarity

31. My word now concerning spiritual clarity is that it occurs in the soul by the uprooting of all vices. One kind of simplicity is natural, and another is the degree of spiritual clarity. Natural simplicity is the beginning of the road of the teaching of Christ; and spiritual clarity is the end of the road of righteousness. Whoever

[31] See Ps 25:21.

begins in simplicity finishes in clarity, just as the blessed apostles were also simple at the beginning of their election. But at the consummation of the providence [of God] after they had received the Holy Spirit they appeared luminous. This is clarity: through labor and fatigue and struggle against all despicable movements, a person sorts out **(149)** the filth of evil things and casts it away from himself. The clarity and lucidity of pure thoughts and of the ideas that are being stirred spiritually above all duplicity remain in him. Simplicity is this: the fact that one is not naturally stirred up by these ideas and does not distinguish them when it enters, nor does it triumph by conflict nor reject and expel them by wisdom beyond the place of its purity. Clarity does these things, but simplicity is the beginning of the road, and the soil clear of thorns so that it may receive the good seed. [It is] one thing that a person may uproot thorns and tear up thistles, and purify the soil and prepare and set it up to receive good seed and beautiful plants. [But it is] another thing that the field is sown, planted, bearing fruits, and anticipating a hand that will gather up the harvests so that the ripe harvest may be stacked and placed in the storehouses.

But clarity—this is its measure—is soil that is complete with seed and filled with plants and bearing fruits of various kinds that have come to maturity and have attained ripeness. Simplicity, however, is a field cultivated and weeded of thorns and is prepared and ready to receive whatever is planted in it. On the other hand, cunning and craftiness is soil full of thorns and thistles and tares, which even if good seed falls into it, its germination will be choked and its growth trampled. Become for Jesus a plowed and prepared field, O disciple, **(150)** and let him sow into you the good seed of his word.[32] May he plant in your soul a new plant of his teaching. If you possess simplicity naturally, rejoice in it and be diligent also to add to it. But if you have not acquired it, as from a natural seed, pursue it by your will and acquire it, because the discovery will be profitable for your life in God. [Simplicity] allows you to live a life without fear with confidence in the dwelling where you are.

[32] Matt 13:18-23.

Simplicity Expects Evil of No One

32. One who is simple does not consider any evil against anyone, nor is he fearful of the evil deeds of others. For as long as he is not plotting to commit evil, he does not conceive that others will be doing evil to him. Simplicity believes that everyone is similar to it and thinks that [another] person considers himself just as he does, and such is the case for everyone. [Simplicity] is the mirror of its soul and the appearance of its self, and according to what is in it, so it observes in everyone else. As it is without deceit, so [simplicity] also believes concerning others. [Even] when those whom it observes are divided by the diverse [ways] of their evilness among themselves—still, to [simplicity] all of them are one. On account of this it resides at all times without storms. Waves and storms are not aroused in it in order to trouble its serenity, because the wind of cunning by which all waves of suspicions are aroused does not blow into [simplicity]. **(151)** Just as in the natural sea, storms are raised up by the activity of the wind beating against its surface, so also the confused thoughts of cunning are born from it and the thought of despicable things is aroused within it through the breath of craftiness that knocks about within it. But the simple mind is a resting place in which there are no storms. Just as the sea is calm from waves without winds, so also the simple mind exists in tranquility, with freedom from all fears beating against it similar to the waves.

Haven from the Storms of Cunning

33. Simplicity is a haven that shelters within it ships fleeing from the storms of cunning, and everything entering it dwells in a resting place. It changes all disturbances into the order of its stillness. The one who is simple not only is simple but also changes whatever happens to him into his state [of simplicity]. Also, obedience clings to simplicity, which is not judging those things spoken to it and does not contend against those who command it. The residence of [someone] simple is pleasing to his neighbors and all those who know him rejoice in it. There is no quarrel in his vicinity, no strife in his neighborhood, no contention in his company, no resistance

in his obedience, no retort against what has been said to him. Everyone is attracted to him by choice and he is chosen by many in the division of tasks and is considered the good portion for whoever encounters him. **(152)** He does not know that he is not being heard and does not try to contend against anyone. Since all of his knowledge is for good and not for evil things, he attempts to please those who command him and does not [seek] to resist their will. Therefore, simplicity is proper for the way of solitaries, and innocence is right for the ascetic life; and clarity is fitting for the life of the monk, and gentleness is suitable for abstinence, and frank openness clings[33] to asceticism.

Wisdom of the Illiterate

34. The chief priests of the Jews were astonished at the apostles, who while they were rustic and did not know how to read or write, were giving answers concerning the life to come like sages. They were being made advocates for Christ through their rustic [nature]. Christ had lifted up fools as advocates to speak for him in order to proclaim especially through them the triumph of his wisdom and so that they might be known to all people that it is not they [who] are speaking, but that it is [Christ] speaking through them. "They understood that they did not know how to read and write and were uneducated, and they remembered that they had been going about with Jesus and were astonished at them."[34] So then this is also astonishing, that simplicity should keep the commandments, and it is a marvel that whatever the wise could not do those uneducated were able to do. If the priests had been aware beforehand that the apostles were sages and spoke wisely, they would not have been greatly astonished by them, for they would have been hearing from them whatever was fitting for their education. But they were astonished at them especially because they had heard from them something they had not imagined, **(153)** and that [the apostles] had answered

---

[33] Typographical error: written ܢܦܩܐ, *napqā*, "to go out," read ܢܩܦܐ, *naqpā*, "to cling, to attach."

[34] Acts 4:13.

them above the level of all the wise. By their simplicity Jesus was triumphant and his wisdom was proclaimed before everyone.

Matthew and Zacchaeus

35. On account of this our Lord also chose the simple and rejected the wise and the righteous in order to teach anyone who would become his disciple to take hold of this beginning and through it progress toward him. And not because cunning is considered to be wisdom in the world should we pursue it, nor because simplicity is despised among people should we decline from possessing it. For look, our Lord has shown us two things by his choice: he has chosen fishers and tax collectors, that is, the uneducated and the iniquitous, the foolish and the evil, the opposite of knowledge and whoever is against righteousness. In this way fishers and tax collectors are those who fish deprived of knowledge and those who collect taxes [deprived] of righteousness, so that when they acquired these two things to which they were both strangers, Jesus would be revealed to every person [as] the one who makes wise and the one who makes righteous. Matthew[35] and Zacchaeus,[36] who had become attached to Christ, had acquired worldly training, but by their being chosen they were found to be simple, their obedience witnessing to their simplicity. Until they had become estranged to worldly training and had become foreigners to human cunning that they had acquired and stood on the level of simplicity of fishers, Christ did not approach them to become recipients of his teaching and did not give them power over the treasures of his knowledge.

Swaddling Clothes of Simplicity

36. Maybe [by] the fact that [Christ] was commanding everywhere regarding simplicity **(154)** that they should imitate young children,[37] he was giving them advice and speaking for the sake of

[35] Matt 9:9.
[36] Luke 19:2-6.
[37] Matt 18:3.

those disciples, along with forbidding others the learning of cunning. He was teaching the simple to remain in their simplicity and admonishing those who were raised up in the learning of cunning to take off from themselves this dirty garment, so that both sides might come to equality, and [so to speak] to begin running the road of virtues with one another's feet. There are some who become a child of simplicity without training, such as Simon and Andrew, James and John.[38] And there are some who by growing up in the world were imprisoned in the womb of cunning, such as Matthew and Zacchaeus and Philip,[39] along with the rest of the others. As for those who were not born, [Jesus] gave them birth from craftiness into the order of childhood and wrapping all of them with the swaddling clothes of simplicity, he then began to make them grow up into the stature of his teaching, bringing them to the level of spiritual strength. If simplicity had appeared to the apostles to be excellent to such an extent, how should it not be found even more with us and that it should be loved in the communities of solitaries where also our labor demands this and those who are coming to us are waiting to see us in this way?

The Cunning Disciple

37. Therefore, the cunning disciple does not prosper and is an example of evil things for all his fellow disciples. He is an instructor of vices and not of virtues, and the image of lost things and not the image of profitable things. He is a teacher of disobedience, the one who shows how to be unwilling. **(155)** He wanders around in vain pursuits. He speaks irrelevant things. A wandering recluse, bound by necessity, led by force to something he does not desire, a laborer full of complaining, a slack hireling who does not earn his own bread, the destroyer of the place of one who is industrious, who seizes [that other's] place and deprives [him] of his labor. [He is] the stone of scandal for the runners, indicating strange paths, misdirecting those who journey steadily into the wasteland, making

[38] Mark 1:16-20.
[39] Mark 3:18.

the way crooked before those who run straight, on the lookout for fallen ones.

He covets powerful people. He is a friend of the wealthy, an acquaintance of the well-known, companion of pleasure seekers. He fasts by necessity, restrained from food by the force of law, toiling ungraciously. A disciple of appearance, not of thought, a nurturer of deceit, a soul desirous of vices, a mocking tongue, prideful, vain, haughty of whatever he does not have, an adversary of every virtue, a face that projects offensive images, a body composed of members of duplicities, a faultfinder about everything, an accuser concerning every action, the avenger of those people that did not consider him, slow for virtues, quick for the race to vices, a child of sleep, a son of laziness, an enemy of the vigil, one who hates prayer, a companion of the prepared table, an anticipator of sweets, on the lookout for delicacies, the right hand of a slanderer, a concealed arm of the enemy. Such things like these are found in a cunning disciple, and these are what is left over of the unsightly things that were mentioned. Whoever is like this should be despised by everyone **(156)** so that his evil may be brought low by his being despised.

Choosing Other Helpers

38. The prophet of God reviles those who are infantile for good things but wise for evil things. "Ephraim became like a young dove in which there was no heart. He came to Egypt and went to Assyria, but he did not walk toward me on the road of repentance."[40] The prophet denounces childhood such as this, because it is not simplicity but foolishness. This is also the impiety of their childhood with respect to virtues: instead of one savior they had chosen for themselves other helpers. They had left the road that leads to God and had pursued the Egyptians and Assyrians so that they might come to their assistance. Even though they had tried numerous times, because they were not able to save them from the evil things among which they had been living, they did not

---

[40] Hos 7:11.

become wise enough by experience to run to the refuge of God. He compared them to doves because others were taking their fruits and the children[41] of their loins were being made servants to others, and he considered them heartless because they had not possessed the discernment through which they might draw near to God.[42] Solomon also reproaches in his writing one who was led after his desire like a child and deprived of the knowledge that fights against his passions: "He was following her like a child, and like a bull that goes to the butcher, and like a dog to the one who leashes [him], and like the deer into whose liver the arrow flies."[43]

This childhood is worthy of accusation because it has not been for the sake of virtues but has served vices. It should not, correctly speaking, be called childhood, even if Scripture has named it this way, **(157)** counter to the purpose established for it, but foolishness, and loss of mind, and lack of discernment, and loss of what is necessary. Our discourse does not advocate this [kind of] simplicity so that an ignorant person may submit to every voice and be obedient to the deceit of all doctrines. The Apostle of God also cautions us by this, "Do not become children who are stirred and troubled by every breath of the false doctrines of people."[44] See, by the word of the Apostle, this mind has been called madness because it is leading to all voices and doctrines and exchanges its virtue through despicable rules and a debauched life. But the point of our discourse encourages that [kind of] simplicity whose application is completely about virtues.

No Other Teachers

39. Examine therefore the simplicity of all the believers, and see the youthfulness of the mind of the disciples of Christ, for while they were not persuaded by the falsehood of the crafty ideas of heretics and did not know the bitterness of their evil teaching,

---

[41] Typographical error: written ܪܒܠ, read ܪܒܝܠ.
[42] Hos 7:13-16.
[43] Prov 7:22-23.
[44] Eph 4:14.

they were being cautioned not to participate in it. They held onto the truth without change on account of their wise simplicity and because the fear of God clung to their simplicity. While they do not know the meaning of [these other] doctrines, they are persuaded by the ideas of their [own] doctrine. Just as a child knows only one master and the fear of him rules over him, and he trembles at his commandment and is terrified only of his rod and does not even know whether there are other teachers; so also **(158)** one who is faithful like a child [allows] only the fear of the lordship of Christ to rule over his life, and other teachers of doctrines are considered as nothing to him. He is not persuaded to seek for himself another instructor and is not obedient to any teacher besides the one. He does not tremble nor is he terrified by the fear of those whose authority he does not recognize, but imitating a natural child his fear pays attention to only one teacher and one instructor. If another teacher wishes to give to him other instruction besides that which he holds, he does not accept [it] because his childhood is natural clarity and not error, the corruptor of ideas.

Running the Path

40. So then let us run as disciples of Christ on the path he has shown us, and let us walk on the road he has paved for us. May the discovery of simplicity be precious in our eyes, and may we become children, infants, in order to receive the excellent teaching. And may one become astute as serpents[45] against the enemy who contrives to injure us. Let us remember at all times what Christ our Lord had said to all the disciples by his word, "Anyone who does not receive the kingdom of God like a child shall not enter it,"[46] [the kingdom] of which we all may become worthy by his grace, and may we become heirs with all the saints, by the mercy of Christ God himself, to him be glory forever. Amen.

The end of the second *mēmrā* on simplicity.

[45] Matt 10:16.
[46] Matt 18:3.

Mēmrā 6

On the Fear of God

The sixth *mēmrā* in which [Philoxenos] explains that after faith, which is born from natural simplicity, the fear of God is stirred up in a person; and how this fear is born and by which things it is established and confirmed in us.

Summary: Meditation on God increases the fear of God in us, by which Philoxenos means an ecstatic feeling in the soul that makes the whole body "tremble." Basic to this fear is the remembrance of God, for if one sins and does not remember or think of God's punishment and disappointment, one's soul is dead. If one is conscious of his sins the fear of God increases continually within himself. The fear of God is born from faith but is also the preserver of faith. Adam and later Cain cast out their fear and as a consequence lost their faith. The commandments are kept by three things: by fear (servants), by reward (hirelings), by love (spiritual beings and friends).

A Mind That Fears God

(159) 1. Now, let us approach the teaching of the concept of the fear of God with a mind that fears God as we have the strength and are able; that is, let us use this concept as the grace of God allows for our own assistance and for the benefit of others. It is not to appear to be knowledgeable [that] we are writing, but we speak because we love [to share] our own benefits with others. It is not because many people have spoken and written before us that we should be silent and not speak. Those who were before us have spoken and written as teachers. But like their students let us rehearse their teaching; just as a child who is commanded to recite at all times the lesson he is taking from his master so that he may not forget it, so also let us repeat those things we have heard, so that by their repetition we might remember them and prevent our thoughts from wandering after vain things without any benefit.

Wandering Thought

2. Because as long as a thought is not retained **(160)** in a worthwhile conception, it wanders outside of itself and goes back and forth in a place beyond the help of God. Just as when [a thought] reflects on virtues it resides in the light of the recollection of God, so when it leads and applies itself[1] to empty and unprofitable thoughts, all its way is in darkness. Whoever lives in darkness does not see nor is seen. He neither discerns nor is discernable. He neither knows nor is he knowable, but is deprived of the beauty of the vision of creatures, and all those who see are also deprived of the sight of him. He neither discerns the road nor does he recognize the path and does not see the trace of his steps.

The Mouth Speaks out of Abundance of Heart

3. In order that it may not happen to us in this way, let us be occupied at all times with the word of God, not only when the tongue sets it in motion by repetition, but also when the heart reflects and studies it thoughtfully, the aim being that our mouth may speak at all times from the abundances of our heart.[2] For whatever a thought reflects on inwardly, the tongue speaks it outwardly. As careful as one might be, if the tongue should be silent through craftiness from whatever it might say, the secrecy of the heart will be revealed to those who are watching through [its] attitudes and movements of other senses, and the face will betray through changes of its expression the hidden mind buried in the soul.

---

[1] Typographical error: Text written ܘܬܘ, read ܘܠܘ.
[2] Luke 6:45.

Tongue and Ear

4. Whoever continually drinks the divine teaching, the plant of his person will yield divine fruits at all times, if he does not listen [only out of] habit to the language of teaching, and [if it is] not for pleasure he heeds the helpful word of God, and [if] he does not receive it in order to grow in human knowledge, **(161)** and [if] he does not hear it to learn how it might be an opportunity for him for the craft of vainglory. The teaching spoken knowledgeably and heard with discernment produces spiritual fruits on both sides—on the tongue of its sower and in the ear of its recipient—because also whoever teaches, along with whoever is learning, listens to his word gladly if he is a genuine teacher and not merely a channel of the learning of others. The constant practice of a craft adds to its knowledge and instructs all the senses by its performance, so also continual reflection on the word of teaching alerts the thoughts to knowledge, sharpens the tongue for the word, and connects the mind with the thinking of God.

Fear of God Protecting

5. The fear of God also grows in whoever reflects at all times on God, and this memory is [guarded] continually in the inner part [of] the soul, becoming for the person a protective wall from all evil things. Just as the wall of a city shelters its inhabitants from the injuries of enemies' advance, so the fear of God protects a person from the coming of marauders and the enemies of our souls. It restrains the body from the cultivation of desires and guards the soul from spiteful thoughts. Because whoever truly is learning to fear God guards not only his body from desires but also his heart from hateful movements.

Orders and Degrees

6. We should show, as we have learned from those who were the seers of knowledge before us and ministers of the word of teaching, of which order is the fear of God, and in which degree does a

person stand who fears God, **(162)** and how is this fear acquired, and by which things does it grow.

Fear out of Faith

7. They taught me that the true fear of God is born out of true faith. Whoever believes truly, also truly fears what he believes. Just as his faith exists not by strategies, so also his fear does not exist by craftsmanship. When a person believes that God exists, he begins to receive the learning of his commandments, for faith is born out of natural simplicity and moreover is established and guarded by this same simplicity. But the commandments that faith hears and receives, the fear of God guards. For in the same way that simplicity guards faith, the fear of God also guards the commandments of God.

True Fear in the Soul

8. The fear [of God], I say, is not so that one may say with a word, "I fear God," or as many appear habitually [to be] ones who fear God, but it is the fear stirred up naturally[3] in the soul, and when the soul trembles and quakes within, it stirs with it as well all the members of the body. The body fears whatever harms it, and the soul, moreover, **(163)** trembles at him who has authority over its destruction. Because just as the fear of the body is of external injuries, or of beasts or of fire, or of swords or of hot irons, or of drowning or of a fall from steep precipices, or a report of robbers or the sight of judges, or painful tortures, or bindings and prisons, so also the fear of the soul is naturally of the hidden judge who is able to punish it along with its body through spiritual afflictions according to its nature.

Just as the body naturally fears all these things we have considered, so also the soul naturally fears the memory of the judgment of God and of the punishments reserved for those who provoke [God's] anger, of Gehenna that is threatening to those who do evil

---

[3] Lavenant adopts variant ms. A: ܚܝܢܐܝܬ, *kyānāīt*.

things, of the hearsay of outer darkness, of the report of the fire that does not extinguish and the worm that does not die. When the body sees things that harm it, it is fearful of them; when the soul observes these things that punish it, it is terrified of them. Not by [any other] means is the body stirred up by these things harmful to it, but as soon as it sees them or reflects on their memory, it is stirred up and is naturally fearful of them. In this same way, when the soul has looked with the eye of faith on future menaces and has seen secretly the fearful things the word of the judge has revealed, immediately it is filled with fear, and all its thoughts—its spiritual members—shake.

Fear Both in Soul and Body

9. By its disturbance [the soul] also shakes with it the body, and by the fear of its thoughts the members of its body also fear. Just as [the soul] shares in the fear of the body, **(164)** so the body is also mixed in with the fear [of the soul]. For even though the nature of the soul is not harmed by these things that harm the body but because [the soul] is mixed into [the body], it fears with [the body]. However, the afflictions and punishments to come are not visible to the eyes of the body, but because the soul sees them secretly and is shaken and terrified by them, [the soul] also shakes the body and makes fear and terror dwell in all its members. It happens in the same way by experience, [for] those who have experienced it and have weathered its trial in their own person know that as soon as the soul reminds itself of the judgment of God and is shaken by its memory, it shakes in common all the members of the body. For as soon as a person reminds himself of God when his soul and body are not pure of sins, at once he is completely filled with fear, and all his members tremble, because in the same way the body also trembles when it sees suddenly something that will destroy and harm it. If someone has not experienced this personally—because not every person has attained the level of the natural fear of God—from the fact that the body is stirred and stirs with it also the soul, this is clear and evident to everyone—let that person understand also that the soul does fear and casts its fear upon the body.

Life and Death of the Soul

10. Only a few have experienced this, that is, those whose souls do not die the death of sin,[4] because sin that occurs contemptuously apart from the memory of God is the absolute death of the soul, as **(165)** the Holy Book also calls the sinner who does not repent "dead." Repentance occurs from a person being mindful of God; so then whoever sins and is not stirred by the memory of the judgment of God, whether by his sin or after the commission of his sin, this one is dead in his soul even though life is visible in his body. Through this it is evident the soul is alive by means of the constant memory of God. If it sins and then repents it is sick. But if it sins contemptuously without repentance and the memory of God, from this it is apparent that [the soul] has been slain by sin. The knowledge of God is the spiritual life of the soul, for just as the body is alive as long as the soul remains in it, its life is evident by its sensing everything that touches it, or which it touches; so also the knowledge of God is the soul's life, and it is evident it is alive from the fact that it senses God.

The Dead Do Not Feel

11. A dead body does not feel injuries, nor also does the slain soul [sense] the memory of the judgment of God. If you inflict on a corpse all [kinds of] afflictions and punishments, it does not suffer. If the soul should participate in all these evil things once it has died to God it does not feel [anything]. A dead body does not feel being struck and does not suffer being cut and pierced; so also the soul dead to God sins and does not feel. It commits evil and does not know. It commits iniquity and does not remember. It is found guilty and its conscience does not disturb it. It acts iniquitously and does not suffer. Just as its conscience is not bothered **(166)** when the discerning one[5] accomplishes justly these things that are naturally

[4] See Rom 6:2.
[5] Lavenant adopts variant (ܟܪܘܬܐ) "discerning one" (Mss. C and D), instead of (ܟܘܬܪܐ) "discernment."

necessary, so also once the soul that has been corrupted by sin[6] has died to God it is no [longer] guilty before its conscience for those things being done by it.

Memory of God

12. Therefore, the memory of God is the life of the soul. Just as all the pulsations of the living body are constant and it pulses and is moved in all its veins and members as long as it participates completely in life, so also the memory of God pulsates and is moved all the time in the soul that has in it the knowledge of God. As long as it is mindful of God it does not sin. But if the light of its knowledge should be covered up for a brief moment by the fumes of desire, the memory of God immediately is stirred up in it and the fear of [God] chases it toward repentance. The fear of God does both of these things in the soul to protect a person lest he may sin, or if he does sin, urges him to heal his own sin through repentance. This is the custom of all those in whom the fear of God or of people is found, whether they do not act foolishly at all, or when, having acted foolishly, they set right their faults. Therefore, the fear of God is a shield against all evil things and guards a person within itself lest he be harmed, and a wall that is a protection from all contemptible things. Sometimes [the fear of God] becomes the healer of evil things, as both of these [roles] **(167)** may be seen in this fear: the healer and the protector. It is a wall protecting against evil things so that they may not come, and the wise healer of evil things that are committed by negligence.

At the Sight of a Judge

13. There are some who are terrified at the sight of a judge, and some others only [need] the report of [a judge] to make one terrified. Whoever is careful not to sin, the sight of a judge inhibits him from evil things. Whoever turns around and repents after he has sinned, the news of a judge [arriving] frightens him and he is

---

[6] Typographical error: written *baḥtīlā*, ܚܣܘܠܬܝ; read *baḥṭīta*, ܚܣܘܠܬܝ.

terrified of his judgment just by hearing [about the judge]. While he is committing sin he is not able to see [the judge], because sin is the blindness of the soul. When sin has been committed and perpetrated in the person of a human being, the vision of his soul is obscured as [if] from much smoke by the fumes of the act of desire and is not able to see the judge but hears the sound of his threats from the mouth of others, that is, from the Holy Scriptures, and trembles at the report and is fearful of what it is hearing. This is when the soul is not completely dead from the knowledge and perception of God. Whoever by his nature is physically blind is not terrified of the vision of harmful things nor is fearful of them, yet [he is afraid] of a report he has heard from others. The lion that has come to tear him up is not visible to him, nor the serpent that has slithered up to bite him, but if he should hear a report from another he is shaken. Moreover, the steep precipice or the pit in front of his steps are not visible to him, but if another person should reveal to him **(168)** about the harm in front of him, he is afraid in advance and at once holds himself back. But one whose vision is naturally healthy does not need others to learn about these things, for his vision teaches him about the harm to his body. By this example, let us also understand one who is warned and does not sin, as well as that other one who after having sinned repents from his iniquity.

Only the Soul Fears God

14. The soul does not fear a vision of bodily injuries, even if it seems that it fears because of its involvement with [its body]. When the soul fears these things, its fear is outside of its nature, that is, the fumes of the body's fear have ascended over it and have darkened its intelligence, and it has become fearful along with the body of those things that do not harm it. But if the soul fears God, it is naturally its fear, because the soul's natural fear is that it should fear only God. The body does not naturally fear God, and neither does the soul naturally fear beasts or the rest of the other sources of harm. See, because cattle and beasts and birds are physical only, and a living soul is not shared with them, there is no fear of God in their nature, except the fear of one another or of the rest of the

other adversaries. In this same manner, the body also, regarding what concerns it, fears only what is harmful to itself. If the soul raises up [the body] to share in its thoughts, [the body] will sense with the [soul] the fear of God, just as [the body] lives **(169)** also with [the soul] in the fear of beasts.

Human Judges Control Only the Body

15. God alone is the judge, the tormenter of the soul, because being more subtle than [the soul] he is able to become its judge. People become judges of the body and even are able to kill it, while in their judgment they do not have any power over the soul, according to the testimony of the word of Christ who said, "Do not fear those who kill the body, but are not able to kill the soul."[7] The power of judges is only over the body, and they judge and torment and kill it. But the nature of the soul is superior to the damage of murderers. It does not burn in their fire, nor do their torments attack the nature of its spiritual state, nor is it cut by their swords, nor is its substance torn by their iron combs. Because whoever judges is a physical being, and the judgment he confers upon offenders he pronounces with a physical tongue, even if the soul stirs secretly the thoughts of punishment, and all the instruments being prepared for tortures are physical ones, and through physical tortures [it is] only the body that receives injuries. But on account of its spiritual state, the soul's nature is greater and more sublime than these. As much as tortures burrow, they burrow [merely] into the sides of the body, and inasmuch as they might penetrate and enter, the soul is far deeper [in the body] than [its sides]. Their death does not reign over its life. Judges are not able to kill the soul, and because of this one should not fear their judgment. "Fear the one who is able to destroy the soul and the body **(170)** in Gehenna."[8]

[7] Matt 10:28; Luke 12:4.
[8] Matt 10:28.

The Soul Fears the Future

16. The Lord alone is the judge of the soul, and That One who has brought it to life is able to bring death on its life and punish its spiritual nature with a spiritual judgment. Because the soul has perceived that the Lord only is its judge, it fears [God] naturally. Just as the memory of the judgment of the world inhibits from their vices those who are alive to the body and dead in their souls, so also with the human being who is alive in his soul: the remembrance of the judgment of God restrains him from his vices. As long as he is mindful of [God's] judgment he will restrain his soul from sins. For it is not an imminent judgment that is depicted right in front of someone intelligent, but that far off [judgment] he is considering at which he trembles and is terrified, because just as external things are revealed to the body's eye, so hidden things are revealed to faith's eye. Just as the living body senses all these things of this worldly body, so also the living soul senses all these spiritual things of that world and observes them spiritually. Therefore, the memory of God is the light that shows what will come in the future, and wherever there are sins, the remembrance of his name is terrifying. But if his conscience has not bothered a person by [his] sins, the fear of the judgment to come will not bother him.

As One Lives, So God Will Live in Him

17. According to how one views himself, so he [views] the memory of God. If he lives on the level of offenders, **(171)** God will be visible to him as a judge. But if he has ascended to the other degree of penitents, [God] will show himself before him as one who forgives. Moreover, if he lives in a merciful fashion, he will discover the wealth of God's mercy, and if he is clothed with humility and gentleness, God's sweetness is visible before him. And if he possesses a knowledgeable mind, he will observe the wealth beyond comprehension of the wisdom of God. If he casts away anger and is free from wrath, peace and quiet moving in him at all times, he will be elevated to see the imperturbable serenity of God. If the movements of faith are continually stirring in his soul, he will observe at all times the incomprehensibility of the works of God and

will affirm even those things which appear to be explicable but that [in fact] are beyond knowledge. But if a human being exists on the higher level of spiritual love, according to the level on which he stands it will be evident to him that God is entirely love.

Seeing the Good of God

18. This is remarkable, that while God is simple in his nature and there are no members or parts in him, he shows himself in many forms to everyone. [God] is visible to anyone who seeks [him] in any aspect one prefers. While he is unique with regard to himself without forms, he appears in [various] forms to minds, according to the passions that are near to the soul. Whoever desires to see that God is good should himself become good, and see, [God] will appear to him as good. Do not imagine that you will see God as the Good while you are living in an evil manner, for this vision causes slackness in you, and you will see [God] as (172) God does not wish to be seen by you. That is, you have not really seen [God] because you have desired to see him outside of his will. [Only] once you become like him in every one of the virtues he has commanded you to keep will he become visible to you as he is. If you believe that you have seen [him], you have seen your imagination and not the reality of his own appearance.

The Problem with Forgiveness

19. So then everyone who lives where there are sins and is aware of evil passions in his soul, and his conscience bothers him in his wrongdoing, ought to see God [as] a judge. He should not dare to see [God] otherwise, so that fear might increase in him, restraining him from evil things. But if you desire to see him [as] one who forgives, leave behind your evil ways and draw near to repentance. Forgive also the offense that others have committed against you, and then lift up your mind's eye and you will see the one who forgives. Whoever consistently sins and offends, and believes that God is the one who forgives, accumulates for himself evil upon evil. "Do not rely upon forgiveness, lest sins increase upon sins."[9]

---

[9] Sir 5:5.

Through trust in forgiveness many people sin constantly without repentance, because they have not felt forgiveness but have heard a rumor of forgiveness. Whoever has forgiven others is able to feel the forgiveness of God, and the same also for every one of the virtues of God. Until we become doers of virtue, we will not perceive that [virtue] is in God. By hearing, every person learns about God that [God] is good, but by knowledge **(173)** of the soul only the good are aware of his grace. By a rumor repeated around, everyone confesses that [God] is merciful and patient and gentle, completely full of love, but by their souls' perception they taste these things in God that they have kept in themselves. Then as long as you live where there are sins, you ought to remember the judgment of God, so that through remembrance of his judgment you may restrain your evil deeds. Do not dare to reflect on any other thing as long as you live where there is fear.

Fear and Joy

20. There is a place of fear and there is [a place] of joy. The place of fear is that of penitents and of those who are aware of their offenses, and of people who have not yet freed themselves from passions. But the place of joy is above debt, and after the defeat of the lusts a person is worthy to attain joy. When he has subdued all his passions under the power of his thoughts, then he will enter to take pleasure in the place of joys, where there is neither fright nor fear. Fear is the opposite of joyousness, and wherever there is fear, joy is not born. Wherever there is joy, fear does not tread, because fear accompanies vices and joy [accompanies] virtues. Just as virtues are the opposites of vices, so joy is the opposite of fear. Whoever is [involved] in vices does not sense spiritual joy when it is born from virtues. Whoever is in joy does not suffer the fear that clings to vices. For a person who desires to be joyous while **(174)** still living in the land of fear is similar to a person who believes about himself that he is good, while he is an evil person full of all contemptible things, or [similar] to a person who believes that he is rich while he is poorer than anyone else.

Sleep of Forgetfulness

21. Therefore, anyone who senses offenses and vices in himself ought to make the fear of God grow in himself at all times, and reflect on it in his coming and going, to dwell on it in his sitting down and in his rising up, and in all his activities his thoughts should be full of the fear of God. While the time for this fear is not determinable, yet for him all times shall be the times of the fear of God. Whenever this fear does not stir in a person, he shall be found negligent in the commandments of God. His thoughts are sinking into the sleep of forgetfulness, and like a vessel without sensation he thinks of evil things and commits contemptible acts, while he is sinning and not knowing that he is sinning. But if he knows, it is the knowledge of hearsay and not of truth.

Sleep of Negligence

22. Because true knowledge of the vices forms fear at once in a person, and just as when one opens his eyes light shines into the pupils, so through the remembrance of God the fear of God shines at once into the mind. It will wake up a person as if from a deep sleep and make him get up. It is like [when] one is disturbed from a deep sleep, while he was preparing to first rise up the light will come to find him on his bed, and when he has opened **(175)** his eyes and has seen it, at once he is astounded and trembles and his trembling suddenly shakes quickly out of him all the weight of sleep in which he was immersed; in the same way, if a person is neglectful and the alertness of the memory of God is taken from him, and he is reduced to the sleep of negligence and the depth of carelessness, if it should happen for some reason or by his will the light of the remembrance of God might shine in his soul, immediately he will be astounded and cast away from himself his initial negligence and be filled with fear, and terror of the memory of the uprightness of the judge will grow stronger. When negligence has departed, at once contrition concerning it enters in its place, and he is full of trembling over those things that were done by him, or over the unprofitable times he had lived away from the memory of God.

When God Always Watches

23. For see, a person who lives in this memory at all times, if even a simple movement of desire should fly over his soul, at once he is full of fear. He is shaken and astonished concerning that thought of desire which has occurred in him. It flees at once and this thought of evil things vanishes before the fear of the soul, like a bird that flies away in front of someone who suddenly has startled its rest. The fear and reverence of people guard the body from lusts, but the fear and shame that a person has before God guard the movements of the soul from thoughts of evil things. Because he sees that God is watching him at all times, he continually scrutinizes himself **(176)** lest he sin and guards his hidden person from hidden flaws that the hidden eye of God perceives.

The Wall of Fear

24. Therefore, surround yourself with a wall, O discerning one, of the fear of God, and evil things will not dare to enter into the city of your soul. Give reverence to God secretly and see, your soul has been guarded in its purity. Stir the fear of [God] in yourself at all times, and see, you have been preserved from the sins of thoughts. May his constant memory dwell in you, and the memory of vices will not reside with it. As long as you are mindful of God, you will not be able to be mindful of vices, because light and darkness do not reside in the eye together, and the memory of God and the memory of vices do not coincide in the soul. Until you have forgotten God you will not be mindful of vices; and until you have forgotten the vices the memory of God will not be stirred up in you. The forgetting of one is the memory of the other, and the entrance of one is the departure of the other. The memory of vices is error, and the memory of God is true knowledge. Error is darkness, but knowledge is light.

Modesty of Soul Hides Vices

25. Just as modesty approaches whoever stands in the light, so also the soul in which the memory of God has shone is constantly

blushing at all times at the nudity of vices. Just as [when] people are watching one hastens to hide his nudity, so when the memory of God gazes **(177)** into the soul, it alarms and astonishes [the soul] to behave modestly and then suddenly extends over it the clothing of modesty. If there is in [the soul] a member of a thought discovered, [the memory of God] hides it. If [the soul] holds something not proper to it, at once it is greatly disturbed and will throw it away. If [the soul] is mixed up, it will set itself in order. If [the soul] is disturbed, it will calm itself down. If [the soul] sins, it will be rectified. If [the soul] is soiled, it will be bleached white. If [the soul] is filthy, it will become cleansed. If [the soul] is impure, it will become sanctified. If [the soul] is polluted, it will be purified. If [the soul] is indecent, it will become chaste. If [the soul] is debauched, it will be made modest. If [the soul] is despicable, it will become wise. If [the soul] is scattered, it will recollect itself. If [the soul] wanders outside of [itself], it will turn [back] toward itself. If [the soul] is poor, it will become wealthy. If [the soul] has lost its life, it will run and seek it. If [the soul] is sick,[10] it will be healed. If [the soul] is weak, it will become strengthened. If [the soul] is infirm, it will be healed. If [the soul] has fractures, it will set them. If [the soul] is full of bruises, it will bind them up. If [the soul] should come to be old and worn out through sin, at once the memory of God makes it new with the fear of him.

Signs of the Memory of God

26. The experience of the fear of God, therefore, is with the soul, and only a human being is able to know[11] whether or not he fears God. Every one of us ought to receive in himself this virtue. If you have remembered God and have trembled, and [if] you have brought him to mind and immediately you have been filled with fear, and [if] your thoughts have shuddered with your members and your soul has trembled with your body, and [if] your mind has bowed down its head and your intellect has become secretly

---

[10] Typographical error: written ܪܟܡ ܬܐ, read ܪܟܡ ܬܐ.
[11] Budge's text written ܐܝܕ, read ܐܝܕ.

modest before God—if these things are happening to you, know **(178)** that the fear of God is in you and the memory of the Lord is truly near to you. It is not one who says, "I fear," who is the one who fears God, but whoever senses in his soul the experience of these things of which I have spoken—this is truly the one who fears God.

Virtues Need to Be Inward and Outward

27. The virtues that are outwardly visible do not demonstrate that their performer is truly one who fears God, because many are the reasons by which good things are done by people. There is another way for the protection of the commandments. Whoever keeps his commandments by the fear of God is a true servant and a godly worker who fears the one who establishes and performs his law. Divine law is not kept perfectly if it is not kept in the body and in the soul. There are many who outwardly bear the burden of [ascetical] labors, but inwardly they are serving all the vices. There are some who bind their members with bonds of austerities but allow their thoughts to wander in contemptible things. There are some who are clothed in modesty on the outside but are arrayed in licentiousness within. There are some who are fasters outwardly but inwardly [are] gluttons and greedy. There are some who appear righteous on the outside but secretly cultivate all kinds of vices. There is one who while he [says he] is a faster is an eater. There is one who appears to renounce [wealth] but is a lover of money. There is one who outwardly is patient but is a wrathful person, whose patience appears on the outside, yet anger dwells secretly in him. There is one who declines comforts publicly but asks for them secretly. There is one who does not lower himself to hear a word of abuse but inwardly in fact perfects [abuse] at all times. **(179)** There is one who prays publicly and there is one who prays secretly. There is one who sings with his tongue, and there is one who sings in his thought. There is one whose body alone is crucified, and there is one whose soul is also [crucified] with his body. There is one who is kept from sins in order not to be reviled by anyone, and there is one who is held back from [sins] on account of the love of righteousness. There is one who is ashamed before the face of God,

and one who is ashamed before the faces of people. There is one who hates to sin because he knows that sin is contemptible of God, and there is one who is mindful lest he commit iniquity because he sees that evil is reprehensible in the eyes of people. There is one who by the fear of future judgment does not commit evil, and one who by the fear of imminent judgment does not offend. There is one who by the memory of imminent fire cools the desire of his members and stills its movements, and one who by the memory of distant Gehenna allays his desire and gets rid of it. So then, the visible labors are not sufficient alone to demonstrate that a person is a fearer of God.

Inner Righteousness Primary

28. But you, O discerning one, examine yourself and may your testimony be from you and in you as to whether the fear of God is in your soul. The righteousness that resides within is made by the fear of God, but that [righteousness] that resides on the outside pursues its deeds in the same place, externally, [and it is] people watching [him] that provokes it. Its operation is outside and not within and is visible only to the eyes of people, and not to the vision of God being performed secretly. The visible austerities are excellent because their aim is to subject **(180)** the members to be obedient to thoughts and to tame the tyranny of the body so that it might be subjected to the will of the soul. However, they do not purge the mind of the movements of sin and do not make the soul fear God if the soul has not learned inwardly to fear God. The inner work belongs to the soul, and the outer labor belongs to the body. The labor of the body is not justified without the labor of the soul, but the labor of the soul is able to be justified even without physical labors, as long as it is not by neglect that a person is abstaining from labors, [nor] is he fleeing from austerities by the love of comforts.

Outer Actions Only Impress People

29. Being watched by people does not guard the outer and inner person from sins, but the vision of the fear of God restrains the

body and the spirit from sins. Just like the person who, standing before the judge to be questioned concerning his faults, would in no way offend before the judge and also would be diligent to hide his former sins, so too a person placed before the vision of God the judge, the fear of [God] drawing at all times on his thoughts, is not able to sin. Day and night he puts on dignity and modesty on the inner person at all times, and every movement of sin that ascends in him, he drives it away from himself by the fear of God. The fear of God makes the inner person attractive, but the fear of people adorns [only] the outer person with virtues. **(181)** Whoever is the judge of your works, may he also be the examiner of your struggle and place the fear of him before you constantly. If the fear of masters is placed before the vision of their servants, and their subjects and subordinates put on the fear of kings and of the judges and of the generals at all times, and moreover [if] the fear of scholars and masters grips and guards the serenity of youth continually, how much more ought whoever becomes a disciple of God and is naturally a servant of that heavenly Lord, and a soldier of the eternal king and a subject of the true judge of the law, should his fear continually rule over his entire way of life, over thoughts in secret and outwardly over the members? The fear of God is a bridle that alters the impetuosity of a person from wandering after evil things and holds him back from running after contemptible lusts, not only for one's public life but especially for one's interior life.

Fear God Interiorly

30. In this way only may the spiritual soldier fear God, not like servants fearing [their] lords or subjects [fearing their] kings and judges. Fear puts on those outer demeanors and is visible on the outside on the members of the body, and when it happens that they hate them inwardly and despise them with their thoughts, they are showing them on the outside a garment of fear. May your own fear of God not be like this, but from wherever [God] is observing, from there show this fear. Wherever [God] sees **(182)** secretly the movements of your soul, may the power of his fear take hold of you. Fear God absolutely, fully, in your interior [person] and in

your exterior [person], for he is the judge of your secret and public actions. May your soul be ashamed before him and not sin, and may your thought be modest and not commit iniquity. If the shame from people restrains us from sins, how much more will shame from God prevent us from vices? But you should remember at all times that God is watching you, and you should observe him also secretly—That One who sees you secretly—and sin will not remain in your thoughts. Just as in that place on which the sun looks down, darkness does not remain, so also in the soul on which God looks down, and [the soul] also senses that he sees[12] it, the thick darkness of vices does not remain. "The eyes of the Lord are ten thousand times brighter than the sun," says the Holy Book, "and he sees all the works of people."[13] Moreover, in another passage it said, "All the actions of people shine like the sun before him, and he examines and knows their ways."[14]

God Watches You

31. The prophet of God reproves by his word the impiety of whoever has committed wickedness upon the mattress of his bed without the fear of God, and reproaching his stupid thought that does not see that God sees him, he introduced to him this argument. "The eyes of the Lord are ten thousand times brighter than the sun," so that through it he may teach every person that God sees our secret things, and that we should be cautious with complete diligence of the sins that are performed in secret. Do not sin in your thought, **(183)** or also stumble in [your] house secretly, because especially in these secret [places] God is the one watching you. As soon as the observation of people turns away from you, the vision of God receives you. When people do not see you as you are, the Lord of creation especially watches you, because as long as people are watching you he knows that you are mindful before them of shameful acts, and the fear and shame from them will prevent you

---

[12] Text written ܕܢܚ ܠ (fem.), read ܕܢܚܐ (masc.) (Ms. A).
[13] Sir 23:19.
[14] Sir 17:15.

from sinful deeds. But when you are alone by yourself, and the walls of the house and the roof shelter you on all sides, here the armor of the fear of God is necessary for you, because in darkness sin is easily accomplished. Here you ought to alert your soul to the memory of God and strengthen your members lest they become subdued before desire and stand up like a champion against the sin that attacks you in order to defeat you, and against the hidden enemy who battles against your life by the movements of your desire.

Faster the Fear of God

32. But the thoughts of the soul are also sheltered in the body's members, and just as the body is sheltered in a house, so also the thoughts of the soul are hidden in the covering of the body, because it is not easy[15] for the inner person to be seen physically, and he sins quickly and commits evil whenever he desires. However, the sin of thoughts is easy and ready, more than that of the members, because the members are inhibited and restrained by many things. But as soon as the thought desires sin, the deed of sin is accomplished through it. **(184)** Neither a time, place, or occasion are necessary for sin, because according to the speed of its movement so is the quickness of his sin. The constancy of the memory of God is required against this speed that thought possesses so that the constant fear of that judge of secret things might dwell in it. That is to say: the movement of the fear of God should be faster than the movement of thought, so that when the thought of sin has been stirred up the memory of God may beat it back right away. For the soul on which this bridle is placed is muzzled in silence by the movements of contemptible thoughts. If it happens [that] all of a sudden [the soul] is seized, this memory will restrain it and make [the thought] retreat so that [the soul] may keep an eye on itself.

---

[15] Typographical error: written ܩܝܢ, read ܩܢܝ.

Protector of the Virtues

33. Therefore, not one of the virtues is not guarded by the fear of God. If one should call the fear of God the protector of the virtues, he is not foolish. Faith is confirmed by it, and [the fear of God] guards fasting. Prayers in its memory are constantly with us. It urges [us to give] alms, silences hateful movements in the soul, quenches desire that burns in the members. It purifies impure thought, uproots reflection on hateful things from the soul, empties thoughts and anger and enmity, and restrains the mind lest one dare to desire what is not one's own. It is the patron so that the laws will not be tread upon [and] it counsels people not to transgress the divine commandments. It is the boundary against **(185)** all evil things and like a shield stands in front of all hateful things, stands against the left hand and pushes excellent things to the right side, and makes evil things cease and stimulates the work of virtues. The fear of God is the inhibiter so that evil things may not be performed, holding a person back from the road of iniquity. It is the good servant on both sides: it holds back a person from the road of vices and advises him to travel on the road of virtues. It pushes him to collect excellent things and turns around to guard whatever has been collected by him. If there had not been any fear, corruption would have ruled over everything. It accompanies the judges and on account of this their commandments are upheld. It surrounds the kings and on account of this their laws are not transgressed. It is attached to the generals and for that reason their authority over those who obey them is [characterized by] fear. It holds all people in the faith of God. Even though fear is born from faith, yet again it is the guardian of faith. Whoever fears God is careful not to transgress the boundary of the faith of God. Whoever believes in God is brought near to the fear of God, and that one in whose soul the fear of God resides becomes the watchful keeper of all the commandments.

Believing In, Yet Not Fearing God

34. Adam believed in God but did not fear God. He believed that [God] exists and received from him the law that [God] had committed to him. Because he had cast away from his mind the fear of

God, he abandoned faith and trampled the law. The establisher of the law also put fear **(186)** around the commandment, "On the day that you eat from the tree you shall surely die."[16] Because Adam had cast out that fear from himself, he believed the deceitful one instead of God and trampled the law that had been established by the judge. Not only did God surround Adam with fear to become a wall guarding his commandments, but in all generations he attached fear to all the commandments he had established.

In the case of Cain, who by his will did not fear God, fear ruled over him by necessity and he was wandering over the earth trembling. Because he had not feared the One who was worthy of fear he was filled with terrors of everything that was visible to him. By the torment of fear itself, he was asking and seeking from God that anyone who would find him should kill him—so that he might escape from a life full of terror and fear. God had also given the law through Moses, being full of various and numerous commandments, and attached fear to all of the commandments because without fear the commandments are not kept. "Do not kill,"[17] and "whoever does kill will be killed."[18] He had established the medicine of fear for the disease, lest one grow and become stronger in iniquity. "Do not commit adultery,"[19] and "whoever commits adultery will be killed."[20] Fear has guarded the commandment so that it might not be despised. By fear he held them back from doing evil things to one another. Because he had seen that they love evil things, he held them back from doing [evil things] by the fear of judgment.

Fear, Reward, and Love

35. Wherever there is no love, **(187)** fear guards the commandments. All the commandments are guarded by three things—by fear, by reward, or by love. The first of all of these is fear. The second

[16] Gen 3:3.
[17] Exod 20:13.
[18] Exod 21:12; Lev 24:17.
[19] Exod 20:14.
[20] Lev 20:10.

is the promises of possessions. The third is true love. The first is that of servants; the second is that of hired laborers; and the third is that of the spiritual and of friends. Fear accompanies him on the beginning of the road of the way of Christ, because the mind of a child accompanies everyone who begins in this learning. Fear is fitting for childhood and urges it to receive learning. Childhood is not able to taste the sweetness of knowledge, and on account of this, fear should accompany it. When the knowledge of Christ has been tasted, and a person has sensed the strength of his commandments, the pleasantness of what he has tasted leads him to the keeping of the commandments. For as long as a person does not reach here, fear—the tutor and reminder of all the commandments—is necessary so that he may be educated. Just as ordinary youths receive instruction from schoolmasters, and a pedagogue receives them next in order to remind them at all times of what they have heard, so a person receives the teaching of the commandments from God, the one who is, so to speak, the schoolmaster and true teacher. At once, fear is useful so that imitating the pedagogue might remind the person of what he has received, so that if he should forget, [fear] would remind him. And if he neglects, [fear] would push him. And if **(188)** he should sleep, [fear] would wake him up. If he should love games, [fear] would rebuke him. If he should wander off into the wasteland, [fear] would make him return to the road. If he should treat [others] with contempt, [fear] would make him remember authority. If he should despise [someone], [fear] would remind him of the one who chastises. The life that fear does not accompany is in the wandering of all vices. Fear is necessary for anyone who has a need to learn, so that it might remind him of his learning. For without fear learning is not completed, and if [learning] is completed without [fear], it is not received. And if [learning] is received without [fear], it is not retained.

Rebels without Fear

36. The prophet of God reviles those who "break the yoke and cut off the bonds"[21] of the fear of God. Again, in another passage,

---

[21] Jer 5:5.

he reviles Israel that has shaken its shoulder free from the yoke of the divine commandments. "Like the cow that has rebelled against the yoke, so the Israelites rebelled,[22] they and their kings and their rulers."[23] [Israel] became a rebel because it had no fear. They had trampled on the commandments because they had not remembered the threat and had despised the law because they had not recalled the sentence of its legislator. That one who established the law by his wisdom, knowing to whom he had given the law, multiplied his threats in relation to his commandments, so that even if the will should despise the law, the fear that accompanies it would urge [people] to its observance. Because whoever has received the law has become a rebellious servant [and] by the fear of torment [the law] forced him to perform service. All the forms of tortures hung before him as an accuser, so that as long **(189)** as he looks at them he might take heed of the commandments and hold on to the law.

Ending Fear through Fear

37. So now, let us take pains to fix the fear of God in our mind, and night and day let us meditate on it. If the fire of desire takes hold in us, let us set the fire of Gehenna opposite it. If the insatiableness of the belly incites us, let us remember that worm that does not die. If beautiful faces allure us, let us remember the outer darkness. If the love of mammon fights with us, let us bring to mind our own ruin. If human profits entice us, let us be afraid, lest we destroy for ourselves the eternal kingdom. If rage pushes us by its impetuosity, let us observe the threat of God against those who are angry. If vainglory troubles us, let us have in mind the shame and disrespect that [we will receive] before our judge. Let us bring to an end fear through fear, and let us defeat death through death. Besides these things, it is necessary for whoever wishes to guard his life with great care from sins to remind himself constantly of death. For whoever is constantly mindful of the day of his departure, and at all times reflects on the hour of his death, does not easily proceed

[22] Hos 4:16 (Peshitta).
[23] Jer 32:32.

to iniquity and does not dare to approach an act of sin. The memory of death causes all lusts to wither and the vision of the memory of death disperses the vices that are amassed against the soul, and the lusts that pile up against the body. Before the death of Gehenna, may approaching death become for us a teacher, and from all sides let us maintain our life with great care **(190)** and let us remember our God. Let us fear his judgment and keep his commandments so that being pure of evil things and adorning ourselves with all kinds of virtues, we may be worthy to enjoy the heavenly blessings with all the saints, and together with them let us praise the Father and the Son and the Holy Spirit forever. Amen.

The end of the *mēmrā* on the fear of God.

Mēmrā 7

On the Fear of God

The seventh *mēmrā* in which he explains that all the ancient upright fulfilled the commandments of God by the fear of God.

Summary: Philoxenos returns to his admonition to climb Jacob's ladder in proper order, as did the upright of old. We should fear God because we have sinned or so that we may not sin. The creation naturally fears God but loves God by the grace which comes down in search of creation. The country of fear is mortal life, while the country of love is the other world of immortal life. As God's graciousness is revealed to us, we are urged to become like the Father. The ancient revelations of God belonged to fear showing us that he is our God, while the latter revelation is of friendship and love showing us that he is our Father. God lifted up humanity from the fear of death that belongs to time and laid on us the fear of death that is for eternity.

Trodden Path

(191) 1. Trodden and smooth is the road of the way of Christ for one who wishes to travel directly on it by the example of the ancient upright. The sight of the steps of those who have walked on the road before us attracts us as well to go on it serenely. Just as signposts and milestones are placed on the side of a natural road in order to comprise the [course of the] journey for walkers, in the same way the examples and models of those ancients, along with divine commandment and law, border this road on which we are traveling and mark out our steps' journey within them, lest one dares to stray from the road to the right or to the left. In that manner we ought not to stray from the clear path of truth to one of the side [paths], lest we wander astray and stumble in our faith; so also let us not depart from the lawful road of the godly way of life that was delivered to us to one of the side [roads]. But as on that road of faith, **(192)** let us also journey straight ahead in this excellent way of life.

Ascending the Ladder

2. We should know the beginning and the end and the middle and should look at the numerous rungs arranged in order one after the other on this ladder that ascends to heaven. This [ladder] is like the one the heavenly dweller first showed mystically to the chosen one of the fathers, the blessed Jacob, and on which the angels are ascending and descending.[1] That ladder was not only for heavenly angels, but the word of Scripture points this out to us through the fact that the angels of God were ascending and descending on it, that every person who approaches its base and begins to climb up and ascend upon it is serving in the order of angels, and is counted among the spiritual elect, and enlists himself to become a heavenly soldier. Just as those people who receive human posts and serve in one of the worldly orders, the name which they had had of peasants is changed for them and instead they are named soldiers; in this way also one who willingly enlists himself in the creation of Christ and serves in this order of the spiritual, the word of Scripture grants him the name of an angel instead of a human being's, and justly so, because having begun in the service of the angels, he also ought to receive their name. From a human being he is named an angel on account of his service and his way of life, and not on account of his nature.

Because of this, the innocent Jacob also saw on that ladder angels ascending and descending—human beings were the ones who were ascending, **(193)** because this [is a matter for] human beings to ascend from the earth to heaven. But those who were descending were angels, because heaven is their place, and from the height of

---

[1] Gen 28:12.

their place they were descending onto the earth. Therefore, angels and human beings were mingling together equally on that ladder so that the Holy Book might teach us that the excellent way of life is common to the spiritual and the physical and keeping the commandments is incumbent on both sides. People in this regard keep the commandments when they are elevated by the degrees of the commandments from the depths to the heights. The angels in this regard serve the will of Majesty when they are sent from above to below for the sake of those who shall come to inherit life.[2] As for those who are lower and physical in their nature, the performance of the commandments has made them higher and spiritual. And as for those who are higher and spiritual in their creation, the Maker's commandment urges them to descend to the place of those lower and be continually with those physical. Just as a single church is gathered from races different from one another in a concord of love that sings the [thrice] holy of the will of God and is moved completely by a single living and spiritual movement, [in the same way] the natural body is moved entirely by the life of the soul.

Beginning with Fear

3. Now therefore, since it is apparent to us from the word of Scripture that this ladder ascending to heaven is composed of many steps, let us step up and go higher according to the order in the steps, as those who rose higher before us on this ladder **(194)** have delivered to us. We are showing that the first step is faith, and the second [is] simplicity which is a clear natural movement, for while faith is being born from [simplicity], it protects faith. Because just as cunning corrupts faith, so simplicity and childlikeness establish faith, for from simplicity is also born the fear of God, since fear is naturally attached to childhood. Children fear, but the crafty despise us. The simple tremble at the announcement of instruction and the cunning prepare a place of escape for themselves.

Just as fear accompanies natural childhood and urges it concerning all the teachings and incites it to accept [education in] writing

---

[2] Heb 1:14.

and learning, so also the fear of God is attached to the infancy of the soul and urges it to guard the commandments and to fulfill the laws, and not to despise and disdain those things delivered to it by the word of God. Until fear guides one to discernment and until the justice of the judge is revealed, [fear] teaches him that he ought to keep the commandments. Terror and fear of the one who establishes the law seizes the disciple to vigilantly keep the laws given to him. When the uprightness that was in him has been revealed, and this virtue that was naturally placed in his soul has sprung forth, it requires him **(195)** that as a debtor he should repay his debt through keeping the commandments. Because just as the creditors of the world [act toward] debtors, afflicting and forcing them to repay something that they owe, so also the uprightness in our soul afflicts us to repay to God the debt of his commandments. Up to this point, it is fear accompanying infancy that leads us, for by this fear all the ancients were pleasing [God].

Fear Accompanying Love

4. Because it is necessary for whoever still stands in the rank of a servant to fear, fear accompanies servitude in all forms. But there is also fear in imperfect love, because the Holy Book says that there is no fear in perfect love.[3] Fear accompanies then whoever begins in love but has not yet been perfected. There is one who fears lest he is struck: this is the fear of servants. There is one who fears lest he suffer loss: this is the fear of hired hands. There is one who fears lest he is saddened: this is the fear of friends. There is one who fears lest he be disinherited: this is the fear of sons. While there is [only] one name for fear, many distinctions are found in it. The fear of God was also with the holy prophets, even with the nation of the Jews from time to time, but the forms of fear were distinctive. The prophets, like friends, were afraid lest **(196)** they might sadden God whom they loved. The Jews, like servants, were afraid of the rod of his discipline.

---

[3] 1 John 4:18.

In order that [God] might increase this fear in them, the rod of his discipline was revealed at once in proportion to the offense, and after the offense the Chastiser gave no opportunity [for mercy]. Because their servitude was not worthy of patience, he had constantly hung the rod of uprightness over their head, and at the instant they were committing an offense they were chastened, and with their offense they were beaten, and barely having started sinning immediately they were receiving admonition. [Showing] patience to the foolish servant teaches him contempt [for his teacher], and so that foolish people residing in the house of God like an offensive servant might not show contempt, [God] the Chastiser removed patience from there, particularly once they had departed from Egypt.

The Purpose of Punishment

5. Let us understand in another way the purpose of this sudden punishment, and that there was no tolerance for the punishment of their faults, because God the master had removed the people from Egypt, its nurse, as if it were a child, so that he might hand down to it the teaching of his knowledge and might teach it the language of his wisdom. But when learning was handed down to the people in its infancy, [the people] forgot [it] and did not retain at all the meditation of the commandments of God in its memory. [God] was consistent with severe punishments so that even if it were by the fear of punishment [the people] might continue to retain memory **(197)** of the teaching.

Instances of Punishment

6. Whoever had collected wood on the day of the Sabbath was stoned by the entire congregation.[4] As for others who were called by Moses but scorned [him] and did not come, the earth was opened up and swallowed them.[5] Others despised his priesthood and sought to usurp honor for themselves, and fire suddenly leapt out

[4] Num 15:32-36.
[5] Num 16:12-32.

and consumed their bodies.[6] Others, who in the appearance of honor brought a strange fire at the wrong time, were burned and perished in a tongue of fire that had leapt out from the tabernacle.[7] Others, because they had desired meat and had rejected the bread of the angels, were tormented by the nausea that they came to have.[8] Others who had erred with the calf were pierced by the swords of the Levites.[9] Others, who had been the reason for the turbulence, were separated out by the waters of testing[10] to the loss of their lives.[11] Others, who had murmured against the Lord, were perishing by vicious snakes.[12] All of them together, because they had quarreled with one another so that they would not enter the Promised Land, perished and passed away in the desert.[13] Therefore, these punishments were attached to these transgressions, and with every one of the vices at once a torment had sprung up at its side so that the vices might be buffeted by torments, and the transgressions by punishments. May the people fear the master like a child who teaches it, and like an offensive servant may [the people] tremble before the judge who inflicts pain on it.

Fear at End of Moses' Commandments

7. Because of this Moses, the pedagogue of the people, was commanding [the people] in every situation that [they] should fear their God. Do such and such a thing, keep the commandments, fulfill the laws, love your neighbor, **(198)** visit the poor of your people, do not lead your brother around with force, do not covet what belongs to your neighbor, honor your father and your mother, do not swear falsely in the name of the Lord, do not trespass the boundary of

[6] Num 16:3-35.
[7] Lev 10:1-2.
[8] Num 11:20.
[9] Exod 32:19-28.
[10] Exod 32:20.
[11] Exod 32:28.
[12] Num 21:6.
[13] Num 14:26-35.

your neighbor, do not plunder or defraud, do not lead by force whoever is weaker than you. At the end of each one of the commandments, he would remind [the people], "Fear your God," so that the fear of God might be in [them]. Moses the teacher had admonished [the people], because he knew that the commandments are guarded by fear, and the fear of God prevents one from iniquity.

Easier to Fear God

8. It was too much for [Israel] to love his God, and because of this [Moses] was urging [Israel] to fear his God. "Love the Lord your God with all your heart and with all your soul and with all your mind."[14] This was the commandment of the righteous among them. But to those who became like servants and were committing faults at all times like servants he had commanded, "Fear your God." Fear holds back vices and love fulfills virtues. Fear cuts off the course of those who are iniquitous and love stimulates the journey of virtues. "Fear your God and love the Lord your God"—both of these [commandments] were placed in the law that was given to the people in order that whoever rises above the commandment of fear may find before him the commandment of love which is more perfect than it. On account of this Paul, while he was showing the distinction between us and them, said regarding the discipline of Christ, "You have not received the spirit **(199)** of servitude for the sake of fear."[15] That is, you were not called to become servants in order that fear will be born to you from servitude, but "you were invited for the adoption of sons,"[16] which in love all good things are perfected.

Therefore, it is well that fear accompanies childhood and this is justly required for the beginning of discipleship, because as long as fear is constant with the one who is learning, it will remind him not to forget what he has learned. Through that example of Moses, he commanded regarding fear to those who had newly begun on

[14] Deut 6:5.
[15] Rom 8:15.
[16] Rom 8:15.

the road of the discipleship of God, so also here, fear should accompany every disciple who begins on the road of righteousness. Whoever fears does not despise, nor does he neglect and scorn [the commandments]. Fear alerts him to keep the commandments and if he should come to despise [them], the memory of fear suddenly alarms him.

Memory and Fear

9. As soon as a human being remembers God, if [God's] memory is truly inscribed in his soul, he is shaken and troubled, and fear and terror fill him, and alarm enters into him suddenly concerning his earlier negligence. As the holy prophet had said, he knew how to fear God and was aware of those things the fear of God does in the soul, "I remembered God and I was troubled."[17] Look, O holy prophet, the memory of God is not a disorder. Why are you troubled by his memory? Why has his beloved memory clothed you (200) with terror? Because I have sinned against him, I have remembered my faults and I have called to mind the judge and I am filled with fear. I have looked at my sins and [their] consequences, and [their] memory has troubled me. Therefore, whoever has founded his heart on God, "his heart is made firm"[18] and he does not fear. This memory of God gladdens the heart established in virtues, and whoever has acquired spiritual health in his inner person, the memory of God makes him exult. Wherever the conscience is assailed by sins, there the memory of the judge makes fear inhabit. The wrongdoer who remembers the judge will be troubled and the wicked one is filled with terror by the memory of chastisement. Concerning this the prophet has said, "At the memory of God, I was troubled. I meditated and my spirit was shaken, and dizziness seized my eyes. I was mute and did not speak. I considered former days and years which were remembered from eternity. I meditated throughout the night and meditated in my heart. I examined my spirit and said, 'O, has the Lord perhaps forgotten me forever and is

[17] Ps 77:4.
[18] Ps 112:7.

not continuing to be pleased with me?' "[19] Through these thoughts the prophet of God was keeping vigil, and he was praying on the couch of his bed as in a church of the saints.

While he was remembering which things he ought to repay to God, he considered the days and generations that had passed, observing how each one of the upright in his time had pleased God, and in what and by which ways of life [the upright] had triumphed before him. The prophet was remembering these things in order to remind all those who would come after him and teach everyone by this example to fear **(201)** God, and that one should make an accounting with himself and observe also with what vigilance others before him were conducting their lives.

Remembering Hours and Seasons

10. To continue, this prophet had also said that he was doing two things. "I have counted my former days and I have remembered the years"[20] long past in which the ancients pleased [God]. By the memory of these two things I was filled with fear: how much the upright have pleased [God] and how much I have made [God] angry. I have brought in my seasons for counting and my hours for calculation. I have meditated about the days that have passed and about the years that I have lived in the world, and I have observed by what I have made [God] angry, and which faults I have committed—which ones I have sinned by actions, which ones by thoughts, which ones by hearing, and which ones by the tongue. While reflecting on these things, I have said, "Do not allow your servant to enter into judgment, for no one who is living will justify himself before you."[21]

The word of the prophet summons us to this example, and he has delivered to us this type of teaching: let us count our hours and seasons in what we have angered [God] and on which matters we are meditating. If those who go out into a worldly market count the

[19] Ps 77:3-7.
[20] Ps 77:5.
[21] Ps 143:2.

incomes and expenses of every day, and of what they have earned and lost, how much more especially is a spiritual merchant who has departed on the search for heavenly wealth bound to do this? The consideration of these things accomplishes two good things with him. The first is that he collects his mind in order to count; and the other is that he is zealous for the gathering of his wealth.

Fear of Making God Angry

11. [What one should] fear, therefore, is that one might make God angry, especially when examining that Majesty, his love and his infinite compassion, those virtues he has made abound upon our race **(202)** and that thing which by our works we are not worthy to receive—his grace—he has given us. When a person looks at himself, who he is and how many are these things he possesses, and who is the Giver of these things, he should remember God and be troubled, as the prophet has taught him. Because of two things it is necessary for us to fear God: either because we have sinned or in order that we might not sin. Whoever remembers the faults that he has already committed, and looks back on his former sins, should be afraid of the punishment of his vices. Whoever believes that he is pure and has no faults in the past to consider and be troubled by their memory should be afraid lest he grieve God by these [faults] that are coming. In this way also the upright were guarding their lives from sins, were healing the wounds that occurred, and were being watchful of those things that had not happened. The first blow that a person receives becomes a lesson to him so that he may not be struck again. The pain of the first illness pushes him to be cautious of another pain.

The God Who Is . . .

12. Who is the human being who could consider God by a vigilant thought and observe his majesty and examine his hiddenness, and see with his mind's eye that serene and holy nature that has no need of anything; whose place is high and his dwelling is elevated, in whom all riches and blessings and treasures are gathered, which

is entirely light and life and delights; who is the One who Pardons and the Merciful One and good; who [is] benevolent, compassionate, and full of love; who is becoming **(203)** and desirable and beautiful; who makes petition and asks and urges every person to live; who is anxious for our lives and seeks our discoveries, and is comforted with our comforts more than we; who is constantly making petition to us to take from his wealth and plunder his treasury and become rich from his treasures and not be poor; who[22] does not rejoice in his life, but in our lives; who because our poverty was not sufficient to ascend to his wealth, he brought down his wealth to our poverty; who because he saw that we did not wish to become rich, he made himself poor in order to enrich us; whose name is beloved and whose title is desirable and whose memory is sweet; who makes the soul that senses him taste the sweetness of the spirit; who rejoices in the rich wealth of his existence that no one among human beings has seen or is even able to see; whose nature is ineffable and his wealth unexplainable, whose gifts resemble him and like him are above the limit of knowledge; who as long as we are evil, in the same way he is good, and moreover, his grace flows more than our evilness; who is the one whose nature alone is the measure of his grace, his love being measured only in him; whose grace is long and whose justice is brief, whose love is [for a] long [time] and whose vengeance is small, ready[23] for forgiveness and slow for refutation; whose punishments are few and whose gifts are many; who also when he travels to us, bears pity for us, and because he loves to possess us, also scourges us on account of this; who has no loss in him except only our loss, and distress does not assail him except **(204)** on account of us; who has put on our sufferings in order to strip us of our sufferings, and wraps himself in our illnesses in order to eliminate our illnesses; who was grieved in order to make us glad, and was saddened in order to fill us with cheerfulness; who was in need of everything so that we might not be needy of anything; who while knowing that we are the ones

---

[22] Typographical error: written ܗܘ, "he," read ܗܘ, "that one (who)."

[23] Budge *'etir* (ܥܬܝܪ); Lemoine reads *'atid* (ܥܬܝܕ) (Ms. A).

inciting anger, he has created our nature as beloved sons who are sought by him; who being aware that we have enlisted ourselves as servants of demons, he has inscribed us as heirs of both his worlds; who while he foresaw in our image that the image of the will of Satan is engraved in it, he has engraved and depicted us in his desirable image; who while he was sensing that we do not guard his ancient [gifts], other things greater than these he prepared in advance for us; who is the wealthy Giver, for this is his loss if we do not receive from him [his gifts]; who while he is giving to us, he returns thanks to us, and while we take from his treasure, it is established as if we are being placed in his treasury; who loves human beings and is good at all times and is a doer of good; who is serene [and] is not troubled, who labors in us by his teaching in order to make us serene in his image; who is wealthy without being impoverished; who devises by his inducements that we might take from his wealth and become rich; who when it is he who possesses, it is as if he is like one who is poor, and when we ourselves possess, it is as if he becomes enriched by us; who without us does not desire to acquire anything, and if he possesses [something] without us, he is like that one who does not rejoice in it; **(205)** whose joy is our joy, and our distress he considers his own, and all our losses he counts as his own; who has given us all our good things and is not satisfied, and has cast on us all sorts of riches, and is not fulfilled until he has given himself to us in his love?

Who Remembering God Does Not Fear?

13. Therefore, this rich and good [God], this one who is overflowing and giving, kind and compassionate, the one who feeds and provides, the benevolent and the forgiver, the one who loves and is full of love, the one who is wealthy and one who makes [others] wealthy, the one who is good and the one who makes [others] good, patient and peaceful, the one who loves our race and loves our nature, our healer and our teacher, our father by his grace and the one who raises us by his pity—what [kind of] human being is not afraid to cause [him] grief and who does not tremble to make him angry? What [kind of] person may observe all these good things that are

given to us, even examines the majesty of their Giver, and his mind is not troubled whenever he remembers him? What [kind of] soul is it that has received all of these gifts without being ashamed before their giver? The fear from this is that a human being may not fear God, and that mortals may not feel ashamed at all this love, and these recipients should not blush at all this wealth of good things.

Imitating the Prophet's Fear

14. Such things as these the prophet has recalled, and on that account he was troubled. Everyone who has possessed the alertness of that holy soul also is troubled in imitation of the prophet and is shaken by the memory of this God in his coming in and going out and in all his activities. **(206)** Whoever fears does not sleep, and if he sleeps, he sees in his dream the cause of his fear. He does not eat or drink. If the necessity of nature forces him, fear is mixed into his eating and in his drinking. Everything that assails a human being full of the fear of God remains outside of him, because fear seizes the location of his knowledge and all the entrances and exits of the city of his soul. In the example of guards who stand at the gates of a city, so the fear of God closes the entrances and exits of the soul and does not allow an action or thought to enter or leave without examining it. Such a thought should not be allowed to depart from within to the outside, nor may an action that is not appropriate enter from outside to within.

Fear of God Elsewhere

15. Moreover, this prophet also explains the fear of God in other passages. "My flesh shrinks from the fear of you and I fear your judgments."[24] Again he said, "I have been like a wineskin in the ice, and your commandments I have not forgotten."[25] Once more he said, "Sadness is in my heart every day,"[26] and "How long will

---

[24] Ps 119:120.
[25] Ps 119:83.
[26] Ps 13:2.

you turn your face from me?"[27] "How long will you forget me, Lord, forever?"[28] "How long will you place sadness in my soul?"[29] Moreover he said, "Heal me, Lord, because my bones are shaken and my soul has been greatly shaken,"[30] and "I am wearied by my groans (207) and every night I have made my bed wet and I have moistened my couch with my tears, and my eye has suffered at your anger."[31] It is evident that all these things are on account of the fear of God. Again he said, "I have been groaning from the disquiet of my heart."[32] Once more he said, "Lead me, Lord, by your fear and by your righteousness."[33] And again he said, "There is no peace for my flesh from your anger, and there is no peace for my bones on account of my sins, because my faults have gone over my head, and they weigh me down like a heavy load. My wounds have become putrid and rotting. I am greatly shaken by my faults. Every day I have walked in mourning because my ankles were filled with shaking. I have trembled and have been very sad."[34] And once more he said, "My heart is upset and my strength has left me, and the light of my eyes is not with me."[35] Again he said, "I have become dumb and have mourned and been bereft of goodness, and my grief was troubled. My heart became hot within me and fire took hold in my body."[36] And moreover he said, "I became dumb and did not open my mouth because you have made and perfected [it] by the rebuking of my sins."[37]

[27] Ps 13:1.
[28] Ps 13:1.
[29] Ps 13:2.
[30] Ps 6:2.
[31] Ps 6:6.
[32] Ps 38:8.
[33] Ps 5:8.
[34] Ps 38:3-8.
[35] Ps 38:10.
[36] Ps 39:2-3.
[37] Ps 39:9.

Virtues from Fear of God

16. In another passage, he called a man blessed who had feared God and [so] informs [us] which virtues the fear of God makes in that one who fears. "Blessed is the man who fears the Lord."[38] Here, a blessing is given to one who fears the Lord, and while our Lord has bestowed blessings on other actions, the prophet David gave a blessing to whoever fears the Lord. **(208)** "Blessed is the man who does not walk on the road of the wicked."[39] It is evident that because he fears God he does not journey on the road of the wicked. Moreover, he said, "Blessed is the person whom you chastise, O Lord, and whom you teach by your law."[40] It is apparent that the fear of God teaches the laws, and a person who fears confesses his punishment. Again he said, "Blessed are those who are without a fault on the road and walk in the law of the Lord."[41] Here again, the fear of God guards from faults and urges one to walk on the road of the law. Again he said, "Blessed is the one whose iniquity has been forgiven and whose sins have been covered."[42] It is also evident here, the fear of God brings one to repentance from which the forgiveness of sins is given, and by means of suffering and tears born from the fear of God the image of his sins is shielded before the eyes of a person. Moreover, he said, "Blessed is everyone who fears the Lord, and walks on his paths."[43] And once more, the prophet David shows that by the fear of God a person walks on the path of the commandments.

In another passage, he said concerning one who fears the Lord, "He takes care of the commandments that were given by the Lord."[44] Moreover, this prophet advises everyone that one should approach God with fear, and he asks every creature to fear the Lord who made it. "May all the earth fear the Lord **(209)** and all

[38] Ps 112:1.
[39] Ps 1:1.
[40] Ps 94:12.
[41] Ps 119:1.
[42] Ps 32:1.
[43] Ps 128:1.
[44] Ps 19:11.

the inhabitants of the world tremble before him."[45] The word of prophecy has cast fear and trembling on all worldly dwellers and has taught all those created that they should journey on this road toward God. Whoever is aware of his servitude ought to fear the lordship of the one who subjects him. Therefore, everything that is created and has the discernment to be aware of its Maker should approach him with fear and trembling.

Loving God by Grace

17. On account of this it is fitting for our nature to fear God. Then [the ability] to love him is given to us by his grace. A human being is not worthy to love God, except that God lowers himself in order to be loved by a human being. The creature naturally is obliged to fear God, yet if it [wishes to] ascend to the degree of love, its nature is not able to ascend there. However, grace descends after [the creature] and makes it rise up onto the height of divine love, so that one who is obliged to fear him by justice may love God by grace. See also, with regard to the kings and rulers of the world—not every person has the authority to show love or reveal before them the profuse and confidential stirrings of compassion—but all the orders beneath their subjection show fear and servitude before them, and not the confidence of friendliness and of love. The habitual pride found with worldly authorities considers loving the poor shameful. Because of this as lords they require fear from everyone, **(210)** and not love as fathers. God, who established himself as our Father by his grace, has given us the authority also to love him. It is not right for us to ascend presumptuously by our will to this but to remain our entire lives under the subjection of his fear. When he himself desires, his grace will elevate us up to the degree of his love. It is not the capacity of our mind to love God, but it is the measure of our creation to fear God. Concerning this the Holy Books in every passage require fear of human beings more than love. Because caution accompanies fear, and confidence [accompanies] love.

[45] Ps 33:8.

Love as the Wage of Fear

18. Love is the result of fear. Until one has labored and toiled and sown in fear, he cannot come to this [level] to harvest love. Just as the harvests of worldly farmers are placed in the hands of God, but the cultivation and sowing is of their will, so also the toils and cultivation of fear are established by our will, but to attain the measure of love and gather its harvests belongs to the will of God. Until the revelation of Christ which love had brought into the world, fear had ministered in this world with all human beings. Until Christ is revealed to a human being in the [proper] place of his soul, he should persist in his life in the cultivation of fear. Even though by grace our Maker named us sons in order to give us pride and make us great, still, it is fitting for us to remain in humility with the fear of servants. **(211)** It was not our [will] that we should have been called sons, but the grace of him who has called us. It is not ours to seek a wage willfully, but this is our [task] to labor in fear. Yet to give the wage of love, this belongs to God. No one is mistaken if he calls love the wage of fear, because just as one receives a wage after his toil, so after the labor of fear, Jesus makes us taste the sweetness of its love, from which joy belongs to us and we live in the confidence of sons.

Joy and Confidence from Fear

19. The inner person finds liberty with God and our mind suckles[46] spiritual joy always. Our intellect revels inwardly at the vision of the heavenly light and gives birth in the soul to the distrust of everything visible. It is as if our dwelling were already in the kingdom prepared for the saints. Such like these belong to that soul that has tasted divine love. The human being who lives in perfect love exists in God. What pleasure is comparable to this, or comfort or luxury that is equal to this—that one may exist in God? The life that is in perfect love is the purification of all vices and the achievement of all virtues. Jesus does not consent to give this wealth of love except to one he knows is worthy of it.

---

[46] Instead of text: ܡܬܩܢ, "sets in order," read variant: ܡܬܩ, "sucks" (Mss. A, C).

While [it is] from love [that] confidence is born, contempt [still] clings to confidence. There is not one of the virtues that does not have a breach near to it from which it could be robbed. In fear there is no **(212)** contempt, but [there is] vigilance and caution and constant vigil guarding the excellent things from the robber. The fear of God pushes a person to gather together the best things and once they have been gathered, fear grows and increases for the one gathering them, for he tends to increase his fear, watching out for his virtues lest they be stolen. He cries out because he fears and takes care of his possession since he is afraid it might be stolen.

From all sides, this [idea] that a person should fear God is useful and necessary for his life in the world. The place of fear is the place of mortal life, but the place of love is the next world of life that does not die. Therefore, let us observe our place and make fear grow in us, and let us examine the dwelling in which we are and increase in us trembling before God, and may the memory to obey him startle us as if from the heaviness of a deep sleep and we become fully awake so that we might keep all his commandments. This is the nature of the fear of God, for it does not push us concerning one thing and not for another but alerts us to perform all the commandments.

Spirit of God Teaches Fear

20. On account of this, the Spirit of God had desired to teach us the fear of God through all the prophets. The prophet David himself has said, "May all the ends of the earth fear the Lord, and may all those who descend into the dust kneel before him."[47] And again he said, "Lead me, O Lord, in your fear and in your righteousness."[48] Because he knew what profit is the fear of God, he was asking for it from God as a gift. **(213)** For the entire conduct of a soul which the fear of God leads consists of righteousness. Again, it is also by his own fear of God that he was stirred to this request to plead

---

[47] Ps 22:29.
[48] Ps 5:8.

with God not to remember the faults of his youthfulness.[49] Again he said, "The beginning of wisdom is the fear of the Lord."[50] Because the end of the road of good deeds is spiritual love, and from love godly wisdom is born, the blessed David taught us well that the beginning of this road of wisdom is the fear of God. Just as there is a beginning and an end to every action in the world, moreover, these paths that were trodden naturally[51] on the journey of travelers also have a beginning and an end; so also there is a beginning and an end for the road of virtues—which is the beginning of the fear of God, and its end, wisdom that is born from love. All who wish to begin in the way of Christianity should start with the fear of God, according to the teaching of the blessed David. Moreover, another prophet said, "The fear of the Lord will open my ears."[52]

Jonah's Fear

21. Concerning Jonah, moreover, it is written, "He feared the Lord and fled to Joppa."[53] For even if his fear had been born from simplicity, he fled like a man who feared God, lest he would be brought back to the task he was thinking was too difficult for his strength. Again, when he was questioned by the sailors where he was from and which **(214)** God he serves, he said, "I fear the Lord, the God of heaven."[54] Moreover, when those who were with him in the ship had seen the miracles that were performed by God in the sea—for the sea, as if it were discerning, aroused itself to exact from them the fleeing servant and after he was given to [the sea], it calmed down and was still from its storms—they saw the power of God through these things that had happened. It was written concerning them, "the people were afraid in the presence of the Lord,

---

[49] Ps 25:7.

[50] Ps 111:10; Prov 1:7.

[51] Typographical error: written ܕܙܕܝܩܐܝܬ, "justly," read ܕܟܝܢܐܝܬ, "naturally"; Lavenant translates "naturellement."

[52] Isa 50:5.

[53] Jonah 1:3.

[54] Jonah 1:9.

and they offered sacrifices to the Lord and they vowed vows."[55]
For God also had required fear of him from the Jews, by means of
Jeremiah, reproaching those who disdain his commandments by
the witness of mute natures, while those who are silent tremble
at his word. "Do you not fear me, says the Lord, and do you not
tremble before me who has placed the sand [as] a boundary for the
sea, an eternal law which it cannot transgress?"[56] Here again, the
Maker seeks fear and trembling from those created, and because
they had abandoned fear of him, they were reproached by mute
natures, those that fear and tremble before the majesty of the Maker,
[yet] his commandments are despised by people.

God Revealing Majesty

22. On account of this in every passage God shows the majesty of
his nature by means of a prophet, so that he might throw the fear of
[Majesty] into his hearers. To those who would have despised his
humility if he had been shown to them, he had revealed to them the
majesty of his nature so that they might tremble before him, and to
the others who upon hearing of his self-abasement had increased
[their] love, **(215)** he showed them his gentleness and humility. For
the fool routinely despises the one who humbles himself before
him, but the wise person on account of his humility loves him even
more. The fool does not have the eye to see love in humility, and
because of this majesty is shown to him, and indignation is written
down for him, and harshness and dread are depicted before him,
so that by these things he might fear all the more that One who
is shown by these things. According to this testimony the will of
God has revealed why it uses these words with people: "the sea
obeys me, and encloses the fury of its waves within the insignificant
boundary of the sand, and its waves rise up but do not cross over
the pathetic gate that surrounds them."[57] Yet you, by your own will,
despise this fearful God!

[55] Jonah 1:16.
[56] Jer 5:22.
[57] See Jer 5:22.

God Has Made Known Majesty

23. Moreover, in another passage [God] explains that he has employed all helpful means with them and has brought to them all the reasons of fear and of love. Yet these [people] neither feared him nor loved him. "If I am the Lord, where are those who fear me? If I am the father, why do you not honor me?[58] Either fear [me] as the Lord, or honor [me] as the Father." On account of this also God, in a certain passage, has repeated before the people the graces he has performed for them: the awesome exodus from Egypt, the abundant gifts in the desert, the entry into the Promised Land, **(216)** the subjugation of foreign nations, the graces that flow abundantly during all the days of their lives, so that in memory of these things, it might arouse them to the love of the Maker. In another passage, he has recited the great deeds he has performed and the works he has raised up by the sign of his will and all the creatures that depend on the power of his word, the natures that guard their limits, and the creation that is yoked under the guidance of his will, the mountains that are placed by him on the balance and the hills on the scale. "He has measured heaven by his [finger] span and the measure of the dust of the earth in the palm of his hand."[59] The peoples and generations of the earth are counted as nothing by him.[60] These things he has spoken through the prophet, for he makes known his majesty through them, and through the hearing of his majesty he instills fear in his hearers.

God Lowers to Love

24. When God speaks to those who live according to the order of servants, he recites before them the great and awesome deeds of his nature. But when he propounds the teaching to those who have become worthy of the rank of love—that of abasement, compassion, and humility—he lowers himself and speaks to them,

[58] Mal 1:6.
[59] Isa 40:12.
[60] Isa 40:17.

because they do not despise him by his smallness, but they love him especially all the more by this. Wherever God does not have confidence in people, on account of the smallness of their mind and the immaturity of their knowledge, there he speaks of violent and dreadful things and does not allow them the freedom to approach the confidence of his love, lest when they have perceived his knowledge and his indulgence, and above all else the love and goodness found in him, by this reason they might despise **(217)** his gentleness and throw themselves carnally to the service of all evil things. This is revealed only to those who have acquired the inheritance of the name of sons,[61] along with that of grace and also by the service of their labors, because the more they taste love, all the more will they love. The more they sense the goodness of the nature of God, the more they will become good. The more his self-abasement and his gentleness are revealed to them, [the more] they will push themselves to imitate their Father.

Later Revelations of Love

25. Through things such as these is why the first revelations of God were all about fear, but this latter [revelation is] of intimacy and of love. For in the first [revelation] he revealed himself to teach us that he is our God. But in this latter [revelation] he appeared and showed us that he is our Father. For in that time he was approaching people [as if they were] in the ranks of servants, but today he has called them to the inheritance of sons. Wherever he had revealed himself to gather servants to him, he was bearing ropes and chains, blows and chastisements, tortures and punishments, fear and terror, indignation and harshness, immediate vengeances, a rod that is constantly extended over the head of the offenders, a tribunal that is open, and a judge who is prepared. There, the wood is upright so that the blasphemer may be crucified on it. There, the stones are gathered for the stoning. There, the fire is made ready to burn for the conflagration. There, the ropes are prepared for the

[61] Rom 8:15; Gal 4:6.

offenses. There, the instruments are acquired to take out a tooth for a tooth. There, eyes are plucked out.[62] There, the branding irons are prepared for the retribution of vengeances. There, **(218)** cheeks are being slapped. There, the condemnations of faults are written down. To such servants, such penalties, in order that the offending servant might not raise his head and rise up against the legislator. He breaks his feet lest he kick. He cuts off his hands lest he strike back. He pulls out his teeth lest he bite. He blinds his eyes lest he see and desire that which is not his own. He inflicts losses on him lest he inflict loss on others.

Fear of Hidden Judges Sufficient

26. By the fear of tortures he has held back the vices of that people, because [the people] were not persuaded that they would be held back from sinister deeds by the fear of [God]. Wherever there is the fear of God, a person does not need the fear of such things as these, because the fear of the hidden judge is sufficient to draw him away from all his vices. Therefore, take hold of this fear in your soul, O disciple, and do not fear any other thing, for the fear of God is not afraid of the world, and the fear of the world does not fear God. At all times, let us be fearful of this lest we anger God. Because of this a portion of fear is placed in you so that you might be fearful of God through it. There is nothing in the world fearful for the soul that has sensed the fear of God. The trembling of tribulations is not considered anything for one who has in him the trembling of the fear of the justice of God. Our Lord has loosed one fear and has raised up another. He has cast from us the fear of temporal death and has laid on us **(219)** the fear of eternal death. Do not fear death yet fear [eternal] death. "Let not those who kill the body cause you to tremble, but tremble at him who destroys the soul and the body."[63] Those are not fearful, for while they were killing, another is resuscitated; but that one is fearful who when he

---

[62] Deut 19:21.
[63] Matt 10:28.

has made [someone] die there is no one to resuscitate, and when he has killed there is no one to bring back to life.

Fear of Eternal Punishment

27. Something that is transitory, its fear also passes away with it. Whatever does not pass away and change, its fear is not shed. "He observes the land and it trembles. He rebukes the mountains and they smoke."[64] Again he said, "They flee from your reprimand and by your thunderous voice they are terrified."[65] Look, according to the word of the prophet, the fear of the Maker is thrown even on the silent natures, because everything is naturally obliged to fear him. If mute creatures fear him, how do reasoning ones not fear? Temporal fire is fearful to human beings, but how far away from the mind is the memory of eternal fire? The vision of visible tortures is disturbing and unsettling, [but] how much do they distance the torments to come from the vision of the soul? Death here is full of terror, inasmuch as the depiction of eternal death is not placed before our eyes. For as soon as the memory of these things that are written enter, the recollection of these things are eliminated from the heart.

Without Fear of God, One Fears Everything

28. As long as our thought is not stirred up by the constant fear of God, every fear that befalls us makes us afraid. As long **(220)** as the king is far away, the judge is feared. [When] the king is visible with his authority, the fear of the judges has ceased. Not only that, but also the judge, along with all the orders below him, is subjected to the fear of the authority of the kingdom, and those who were feared become the ones who are afraid. All these fears are gathered together and absorbed into one fear. All the leaders and commanders, from whom fear had been issuing against the ranks under them, now obey and are subjected to the one fear, the mistress of all fears, so that [God] alone becomes feared, and by the fear of him the

---

[64] Ps 104:32.
[65] Ps 104:7.

power of all fears is dissolved, and the trembling born from all the powers becomes ineffective, and every leader must bow his head before the one head of the kingdom who rules over all of them. So in this same manner, when the fear of God is distant from the soul, [the soul] fears everything—the authorities, the judges, the leaders, the [lower] orders, the generals, the wealthy, the commanders, those mean and ordinary, those little and despised; and with these also, [the soul fears] afflictions and offenses, losses and tortures, illnesses and diseases, indigence and poverty, distance from family and alienation from relations, separation from friends, and exile from [one's] country. Therefore, all these like them are [objects of] fear for a human being who does not fear God.

Soul Full of Fear of God Does Not Fear

29. If the fear of God should enter and dwell **(221)** in the place of the soul and take hold of all aspects of its thoughts, [the soul] is not capable from here on to receive another fear; but every fear that enters to dwell in it, when it has seen that the fear of God dwells in the soul, leaves and moves away because its house is not able to receive another inhabitant. Just as a vessel that is full of something cannot receive another thing to fall into it, unless that first thing with which it is full has been emptied out, so also the soul full of the fear of God is not able to receive the fear of the world or of something in the world, for it is recollected entirely with that one true fear of God.

Therefore, may all of us press to acquire this fear. Let us despise everything and become void of everything in order to be empty for the unique work only of the fear of God. By the recollection of his awesome and venerated name, let us maintain our lives in complete vigilance, and let us raise up[66] praise at all times to the Father and to the Son and to the Holy Spirit forever. Amen.

The end of the seventh *mēmrā* concerning the fear of God which was in the ancient upright.

---

[66] Typographical error: written ܘܢܣܩ, read ܘܢܣܩ.

Mēmrā 8

On Renunciation of the World

The eighth *mēmrā* in which [Philoxenos] teaches that no one is able to become a perfect disciple of Christ unless at first one renounces all human possession and has openly departed from the world, inwardly and outwardly.

Summary: The world is an obstacle to perfection, so commandments were set apart for those in the world (uprightness) and for perfection above the world. Wealth, in particular, is an obstacle to meditation on God. Jesus commanded the wealthy to be masters, not slaves, of their wealth, but the perfect are not to be masters even of inanimate objects. The way to perfection is distinguished through renunciation of the world and its possessions in imitation of Jesus the stranger. The upright are also above the law, not doing evil in order to avoid provoking God to anger. Before baptism Jesus was obedient to his parents and kept the law; after baptism he taught and lived a rule of life more perfect than this and refused to acknowledge his parents. The righteousness of the law is defined as roughly equal to uprightness in this world.

Jesus Teaches through His Own Person

(222) 1. It is necessary for one who wishes to travel on the open road of perfection to start out on his journey well-organized for the road and begin in this discipleship not by the law that appears to be excellent to him but by the law determined from the word of Christ our God that has been handed down to his disciples, just as he has also walked on this road of perfection, has become a law for

us through his own person, and has given us an excellent example so that we might journey in his footsteps. Not by words only has Jesus become our teacher but also by the deeds of perfection which he has fulfilled in himself. On that account, **(223)** he is truly the good teacher who has taught and has acted, for his teaching is his action, and his action is the teaching. In this way also our Lord has depicted and shown to us through the ministry of his own person that after he had performed all righteousness of justice and had kept the law of the commandments being perfected in the world, he then left the world and departed outside of it in order to teach perfection.

No Perfection Living in the World

2. I am not saying that these who are in the world are not able to become righteous, but it is not possible that they can attain perfection because the world is the opposite of perfection, that is, it consists of righteousness and justice that is served in [the world]. One is not able to bear both of these labors and be perfected in both of these virtues while one is in the world. Because of this, the commandments were determined and distinguished for those traveling the world so that by them they may acquire their salvation. Another road of perfection has been trodden that is above the world.

Different Commandments for Life

3. The will of Christ the legislator was that he desired that all people might travel on the road of angels and no one might cease from the example that he has set out in the open; but because not every human being is capable of this and That One desires that every person might live, he has given different commandments to each person so that one might live by them. He has made levels and degrees for his teaching, not because these things are [included] in [the teaching], but for the sake of its recipients and these who are needy and would not be able to be saved **(224)** without them. The way of uprightness is associated with the road of the world; and perfection is associated with the road beyond the world. The

end of the road of righteousness and uprightness is the complete renunciation of riches.

Wealth Chains the Mind

4. As long as a person possesses human wealth, whether a little or a lot, he is not able to travel on the road of perfection because all the wealth he has, according to its measure, is a chain for the mind and a binding for the swift wings of the intellect so that they may not fly on the heavenly road. It is unavoidable for whoever has wealth [not] to think about it, and whoever thinks about wealth does not think about God. If the memory of God is indeed aroused in him, it is not at all times. It is not possible to be mindful of God while one is reflecting on riches. If he believes he is mindful [of God] the memory is a pretense and not authentic. It is not possible for these two memories to reside together in the soul. If they dwell in [the soul] in any way, one of them is a pretense and the other one is authentic. If a person truly believes he is thinking about God while a concern for wealth is in his mind, not with all the strength of his soul is he able to give fully to God whatever is fitting for us. We must not work for God with [one] portion of ourselves and [work] with another portion in the world, and at one time think about [God] and at another time think about mammon, but all of our strength **(225)** we should give to the service of his commandments, and every moment should become for us helpful occasions for the memory of him, so that we might become temples for him only, being empty of all reflection of thought outside him. That a human being is not able to serve God as he deserves while he is in the world and possesses riches and is a lord of wealth, the word of our Savior himself testifies, "You are not able to serve God and mammon."[1]

---

[1] Matt 6:24.

Lords and Slaves of Wealth

5. Perhaps the listener[2] will think that here the door of righteousness was shut before all people, because they are not able to free
themselves completely from concern about wealth. According to
the ordinance of the word of Christ, whoever thinks about [wealth]
does not think about God. It is necessary for us to understand the
saying as it was spoken. With regard to the order of the perfect, a
person who reflects on wealth is not able to reflect on God. In that
other level of righteousness performed in the world, a person is
able to become righteous while he is the possessor of wealth—if
he is not a slave who serves his wealth—but is the master of his
possessions. There are people who are slaves of their possessions,
and there are some who are masters of their wealth. There is one
person whose possession serves him and [another] who serves his
possession.

Therefore, the word of our Lord was spoken concerning whoever is a slave of his possessions, because he is not able to become
a servant of God. "You are not able to serve two masters."[3] You
see **(226)** that he has indicated two masters through his word, and
when he explains which ones they are, he said, "You are not able
to serve God and mammon." Look then, whoever makes mammon
his master is not able to serve God but serves that master whom he
has chosen by his own will, its service being especially beloved to
him, and its lordship over him is loved because he has submitted
himself to it by his own will. People are especially accustomed to
love whatever they choose by their own will, more than whatever
has authority forcibly and naturally over them. If there were a few
who have pleased or are pleasing God, [it is] because they have
been masters of their wealth and were distributing it as a subservient servant for every task, sometimes for the nourishment of the
hungry, sometimes for clothing the naked, sometimes for the redemption of the captives, sometimes in vows and offerings to God,

---

[2] Lemoine notes that this is one of the indicators that this discourse had
been read out loud.

[3] Matt 6:24.

sometimes for freedom of those enslaved by debts. The will that has power over [wealth] was sending [wealth] everywhere it desired like a servant, just as was the case with Abraham, Isaac, Jacob, Job, Joseph, David, and Hezekiah. Some of these were also rich, some were rulers, and some were kings, and collectively all were lords of great wealth and possession. But they were lords of their wealth, and not their wealth **(227)** [the lord] of them. [Wealth] was serving them with all the good things they were desiring, but they were not serving it in all the evil things that mammon demands.

Commandment to the Upright

6. So then, there are distinctions [to be made] in the commandments and it is evident to whom each one is spoken. This commandment, "You are not able to serve two masters, God and mammon," according to the sense of the passage is spoken to those who desire to become righteous while they are in the world. It counsels and instructs them because they have fallen short of the road of perfection not to become totally servants of mammon and abandon the lordship of God, which naturally is set up for their salvation. "Do not set up for yourselves treasures on earth where the worm and rust destroy and where thieves break in and steal, but set up for yourselves treasures in heaven where neither worm nor rust will destroy, and where thieves will neither break in nor steal."[4] It is evident that this commandment is not suitable for the solitaries and the perfect. How could it have been said, "Do not set up for yourself treasure on earth" to that one to whom it was commanded, "Do not be anxious about tomorrow"?[5] How could this be suitable, "Establish for yourselves treasures in heaven by your alms," to one to whom it was said, "Do not acquire two coats, and neither a purse nor a wallet, nor also any bronze [coins] in [one's] purse"?[6] What would there have been for the thief to take or for the worm

---

[4] Matt 6:19.
[5] Matt 6:34.
[6] Matt 10:10.

to destroy with that one who besides himself is commanded to have nothing?

Master or Be Mastered

7. So then, **(228)** "You are not able to serve God and mammon" is a commandment [meant] for those who possess. Because the Teacher saw that they were not progressing to the degree of perfection, he lowered himself to them through his Word and established for them the law suitable for the situation in which they are living, and said, "Since you are not able to renounce [the world], do not become a servant to your wealth and serve it like a slave, but become [its] master in the ministry of all excellent things. When it is your master, it will send you wherever it wishes, sometimes for pillaging, sometimes for robbery, sometimes for false witness, sometimes for fraud and plundering, sometimes for false oaths, and on occasion, even for murder, and wherever there is also association with demons, as long as it is your master and you are its servant it will not allow a single evil action that it does not command you to do. Just as, if you are its master, you will send it for all kinds of good things; so if it is your master, it will send you for all kinds of evil things. The law of the master is to command, and that of the servant [is] to be commanded. As long as a person is the master, he is the commander; but as long as he is the servant, he is the one commanded. Wherever commanders and those who are commanded are found, matters are being accomplished in this way according to the wills of the commanders."

Loving without Knowing

8. Jesus the teacher has not laid a heavy commandment on those who possess, for he commands them to become lords over their wealth; rather, he taught them on this level what **(229)** they desired but did not know how to acquire. Just as a person who would love to become wise, yet does not know how to gather knowledge, finds another [person] to become his teacher regarding how to gather and acquire it, or if there is another who loves wealth but is not acquainted with how it may be gathered, or if there is a person

who loves ornate buildings but does not know how they are built
and decorated, in this same way, people desire to become lords of
wealth, but as a result of ignorance their wealth turns out to become their lord. When the teacher had pity on those who possess,
he taught them, "Become lords of your wealth as you desire," and
with this also he showed them how they might become lords over
[wealth]. Their love of things is one thing, but knowledge of them
is another. There is one who loves but does not know how to find
that thing he loves. There is one who knows how to find and possess but does not love. As for those who were desiring to become
lords of wealth, when they had acquired it, it turned around and
became their lord, Jesus taught them the knowledge of what they
were desiring.

Perfect Commanded Not to Become Lords

9. Therefore, Jesus commanded these people to become lords
over wealth and not to become servants to it. But he commands
the perfect not even to become lords **(230)** and advises them not to
lower themselves to the lordship of dumb things. He had set free
those who possess from the servitude of soulless things, lest while
serving them they might become worshipers of idols, concerning
which it was written, "There is no breath in their mouth and while
they have eyes and ears and hands they neither see nor hear nor
do anything."[7] Concerning this Paul called the love of mammon
idolatry, because just as the heathens bow down to soulless things
in which there is neither life nor sensation, so also the lovers of
wealth serve silent gold and dumb silver, along with all the [other]
possessions that are soulless and lacking knowledge.

Do Not Become a Lord of Wealth

10. Therefore, Jesus commands to one, "Do not become a servant to wealth," and to another he establishes a law, "Do not even
become a lord over wealth." He says to one, "It is a disgrace for

[7] Pss 115:5-6; 135:16-17.

your free will that you might be subservient to gold." And to another he says, "It is despicable for your lordship—you [who] have
authority over the natures—that you should be abased to the possessions of the scabs of [these] natures." He said to one who had
abandoned lordship over all things, yet was seized by the love of
a small possession, "Possess only while you are the possessor of
your possession, and may your possession not become your possessor." He makes that other one whom he saw elevate himself above
this [state] of becoming a servant to wealth ascend even more to
the degree higher than this one, and says, "Do not even become a
lord to [wealth]," because just as **(231)** it is a disgrace for whoever
wishes to become a lord over his possession to become a servant to
his possession, so even more is it a disgrace for that one who has
been freed from the servitude of wealth if he might become a lord
of wealth. A poor person possesses things of poverty, and a wealthy
person [possesses] great and prestigious things of wealth. So then,
because those who possess are the [really] poor, possessing poverty
[which is] wealth and temporal possessions, those who renounce
are the [truly] wealthy ones. It is a disgrace for that honored name
to become a possessor of the things of poverty—gold and silver
and clothing—and to exchange eternal wealth for temporal poverty
and heavenly possession for human mammon.

No Money with God

11. "Do not serve mammon," he said to the one who loves[8] mammon, but, "Become its lord and it will be your slave and servant."
It is evident, therefore, that Jesus commanded this commandment
to the rich of the world. He said to those remaining who wish to
walk on the higher road of perfection, "Possess neither gold nor
silver nor bronze [coins] in your purses, nor two coats, nor shoes
nor staff, for the laborer is worthy of his nourishment."[9] That is to
say, this freedom is suitable for this labor. Therefore, he has stripped
them of the entire world, and then **(232)** made them depart from

---

[8] Typographical error: written ܠܪܚܡ, read ܠܕܪܚܡ.
[9] Matt 10:9-10.

the world. Depart, and leave everything in its place in the world, and do not bring with you dead things to the place of life. You are called to put on the purple [robes]. Take off first "the filthy rags"[10] of the world, and then put on the purple [robes] of the kingdom. Whoever wishes to put on eternal glory, let him first take off the clothes that wear out, and then put on the glory which does not wear out. Whoever asks to be inscribed in the higher Jerusalem, let him not have a dwelling on the earth, and he will become a dweller in that city. Whoever desires not to be received there by grace, let him be received here by grace from every person. Whoever desires to become an inhabitant of the bridal chamber, let him not possess here a purse and a wallet. Whoever wishes to acquire God, let him not acquire bronze [coins] in his purse. It is an endless disgrace that bronze should be possessed [along] with God. Whoever possesses these temporal things with these eternal things is not aware of the grandeur of his possession, and on that account runs to possess poverty alongside wealth. It is not even possible that these two treasures may fall into one vessel, because no one ever places a thistle with gold in one vessel, nor does he equate hay and wood with precious stones.

Worldly Ties Cut Off First

12. This commandment, therefore, was given by the teacher to the disciples when he sent them out to become fishers of people for life. **(233)** At first he had cut off from them all the bonds of the world and had released from them all human ties, and then he sent them to release others. It was not possible that whoever is bound could release another who is tied up. The possession of worldly things ties up all the members and binds all the senses, and the whole person is bound and tied up [by this possession] in his inner and outer selves. Our Lord rightly had first released the ties of the world from his disciples and then sent them to release others who were tied up, so that those who are released might see that those

[10] Zech 3:4.

who are releasing their bonds are bearing the sign of freedom and the emblem of the kingdom, and that they might believe that they [themselves] are released, especially when they see that those who are cutting off the ties of the world from them are free people. Therefore, our Lord had placed this example in this passage of these commandments he had committed to the apostles when he had commanded them not to possess anything. He emptied them, therefore, of everything and then sent them to become ministers of his will in the instruction of others, so that from here he might teach everyone who desires to become a minister of God to become a stranger from any possession of the world and empty himself of everything, following the model of the apostles, and then depart and become a minister of the perfect will of God.

Limited Ministry of Apostles

13. As long as the apostles were with Jesus and were itinerating around with him from place to place, they were not living **(234)** in the order of perfection. On account of this, our Lord was silent before them regarding these commandments as long as the apostles were with him. He had allowed them to do other things that were tied to their continual presence with him and were useful to those who were approaching him; [for instance,] serving the crowds who were seated in the desert,[11] or being sent by him with those things useful for the visible way of life, as in the case when he had sent Simeon to the sea in order to catch a fish and give the poll-tax coin,[12] and when they were physically called with him to a wedding feast.[13] They were wandering from city to city and were itinerating around with him and paying him visible honor in front of the crowds. They held back from him the crush of the crowds, in order that no one could approach him whenever they want, as it is written, "Some people desired to bring to him little children so that he might bless them, but the disciples prevented

[11] Matt 15:35-36.
[12] Matt 17:27.
[13] John 2:2.

them."[14] In every place they were offering him honor such as this, according to the level of their knowledge in that time, but he was lowering himself and received these things from them from time to time because he knew that up to now they were capable only of offering him a visible ministry. Because even if their ministry was imperfect, it was at the level of their knowledge. He was observing [their good] will and in that spirit he accepted its ministry.

Requiring Only What People Can Give

14. This is the custom of Jesus, whether in that time or today, to ask for ministry according to the strength of the will and he does not wish that the work be greater **(235)** than the will of its worker, because if the work appears beyond one's ability to discern, it will either be a law that performs it, or a custom, or an accident. Jesus does not desire to receive ministry from a rational person in [circumstances] such as these as if he were a mute instrument. When he lowers himself to receive from all levels the discernments and ministries they are offering him, he instructs them by his teaching so that they might be elevated from the first [level] to the ministry of the perfect, in order that the first labor might become a path to that one after it, and that the first virtue might become training and a discipline for another virtue more perfect than it.

Mary and Martha

15. Along with the deed the teacher himself propounds the teaching, not only through action, but also through his own word, just as he had done with Mary and Martha. For while both of them were offering him service, the ministry of Mary was more perfect than that of Martha. Both of them were ministering to him, one physically and the other spiritually. Nevertheless, our Lord received both services and gave a blessing to the service that was higher than its companion. "Mary has chosen the better portion which will not

---

[14] Matt 19:13.

be taken from her."[15] As one might say, "You also, O Martha, leave whatever is lesser and lift yourself up by your service to the better degree." Jesus had not rejected at all the service of Martha, because the measure of her ministry had been according to the level of her knowledge and of her love. **(236)** He wished that she would draw near to greater things instead of smaller things and to spiritual ministry instead of physical ministry. The service of Mary and Martha is similar in type to the labor of the holy apostles, the first and last ones, for that ministry they were offering physically in each place was comparable to that of Martha. But that other labor which he had taught them to offer to him through that commandment, "Do not possess anything," was similar to the labor of the blessed Mary. There are many who are justified like Martha and like Zacchaeus,[16] and like those women who were attached to him and served him by their possessions;[17] and there are some whose service is completely spiritual like Mary and the apostles.

That All Be Perfect

16. Through this service Jesus wishes and desires that all people may attain perfection, and on account of this his advent into the world took place so that he might transmit to people this way of the spiritual, as the holy Apostle had also taught, "A person of God should become perfect in all things so that the person of God may become perfect in every good and complete work."[18] Therefore, Jesus had transmitted this perfection to his disciples by those commandments he had given to them concerning renunciation, when he made them strangers from the entire world and from everything in it—not only them, but, by them and with them, all **(237)** who pursue perfection. While he was setting down the law with reference to the apostles, he was transmitting teaching to the

[15] Luke 10:42.
[16] Luke 19:2-10.
[17] Luke 8:3; Mark 15:40-41.
[18] 2 Tim 3:17.

community and the entire race of human beings. He was urging all who wished to obey him concerning this excellent [state].

No Perfection without Denial

17. At the beginning of their election when he had called them to follow him, it was written in this way concerning them, "Immediately when he called them, they left everything and followed him."[19] They were casting nets into the sea, and he saw and called them, and they left their nets and their boat and followed him.[20] Moreover, he saw James and John in the boat with their father, Zebedee, and also called them, and immediately they left the net with Zebedee their father and followed him.[21] See, [here is] the law of the departure after God, and there the righteous rule that was prescribed for us in the Holy Books. Hence anyone who desires to follow God should imitate this departure of the apostles, despising and rejecting everything visible, and renouncing the whole world. But Christ said that whoever wishes to become his perfect disciple should also deny himself.[22] If a person denies his life according to the word of our Savior, then he will become a disciple, but without this there is no way to attain perfection. **(238)** How, while he is neither renouncing worldly possessions nor despising all visible wealth [and] physical comforts, can he attain the perfection that Jesus has transmitted? These things I do not speak of myself, but I follow the will of the Scriptures and support the law that is established by the King. The beginning of Christian discipleship is the apostles, and their calling came to be in this way as it is written concerning them: as soon as they were called, they left everything and followed him.[23] Whoever desires to become a disciple, let him consider this example, and let him see this aim in all his thoughts

---

[19] Mark 1:16-20.
[20] Matt 4:18-20.
[21] Matt 4:21-22.
[22] Matt 16:24.
[23] Matt 4:22.

so as to renounce everything in its interior and exterior aspects, and then he shall begin to travel on this heavenly road.

Let Go First

18. Nothing is full unless at first it has been emptied. One does not lay his hand upon heavenly wealth unless he has let go of the poverty he has held. Nor is one able to hold one thing unless he has let loose of another, especially [when] they are the opposite of one another, for when either one of them is near it negates its neighbor. If, when we have renounced everything and are satisfied only for this—to keep his commandments—our ministry is still not yet worthy of God. When the strength of our soul is divided and despoiled and captured by the love of worldly things, how is it able to offer to God the service **(239)** of love? This commandment is difficult for one who is bound by the love of wealth, and although it is freedom from the world, it is difficult and grievous for those who are captured by the servitude of the world, those who are bound [up in the world] for whom it is pleasing. Their bonds tie them down yet are pleasing to them—people who willingly have cast the bonds of anxiety onto all their members and have taken it upon themselves to become slaves of the world and not servants of Christ.

Desiring Harm

19. Jesus calls you for freedom, but the world prepares you for servitude. If the servitude of the world is pleasing to you, it is not because its nature is this way, but [because] your own desire has been corrupted and you have desired in an evil way. When a person desires something from the world his desire is not healthy, yet like someone sick he desires something that does not profit him, a completely destructive desire. This is the rule for the most part of the sick who desire their harm more than their benefit and [desire] whatever opposes their healing more than whatever heals their illnesses. Because the health in them is changed to illness, and natural desire's strength in them is changed from its natural

order, because by the equilibrium of temperament, and by the
body's health, the health of desire is guarded. When the body's
temperament has been disturbed, the physical desires are also
disturbed with it. **(240)** Whoever burns with fire desires a cold
drink. While it is harmful for him, he asks to drink and becomes
angry with those who do not give it to him. But the wise physician does not answer him because he knows that it is a blind lust
in him that asks for something that is an opponent of his health.
In this example the world's wealth is pleasant and its possession
desirable for those who are sick in their souls. They are deprived
of the health of divine knowledge and ask for everything that is
their destruction. However, our heavenly physician forbids us from
harmful things by his helpful admonitions[24] and commands us not
to do whatever is pleasant for us and by which we are comforted,
but [to do] whatever helps us, even though we are not comforted
by its doing, because the wise physician does not follow the sick
person's will and does not yield to his desires that are harmful to
his health, but forces him to follow the helpful law of healing and
teaches him to struggle with his desire for the sake of his health.

Yoke of Renunciation

20. Therefore, let us receive the yoke of renunciation, as our Savior has commanded us, even if it is heavy for us, for it is not difficult for the will that surrenders to the commandments of Christ.
There is no one who does not desire to be free and liberated from
the yoke of servitude. For everyone the title of "free person" is
more beloved than that of "servant." Our Lord, because he had
commanded us to become strangers from the world, has given
(241) us the true freedom in which he conducted himself while
he was in the world. Although by nature he is free because he is
God, but also because he had taken on the likeness of a servant, he
conducted himself in freedom and was above all the anxiety of the
world. It is written, "Jesus took on the likeness of a servant, and

---

[24] Budge: *zewādē* (ܙܘܵܐܕ̈ܐ) "(by his) provisions"; Lemoine adopts the
alternative reading, *zūhārē* (ܙܘܼܗܵܪ̈ܐ) (Mss. A & B).

he was in the likeness of human beings, and in appearance he was found like a human being."[25] In these things that we are, he truly became. But in whatever is outside of us he did not share, that is, to acquire on earth wealth and riches and mammon, possessions and buildings, or fields and vineyards, for Jesus did not acquire these things in order to teach his own [people] not to acquire them. That free person was not anxious about these [things] in order to free us also from anxiety concerning them and did not bind himself with a yoke of worldly servitude in order to lift up from us also the heavy yoke of worldly servitude. He was not bound by human things so that he might loosen their bonds from us. Corrupting anxiety did not tie him down, so that he might lift up his disciples from anxiety and distress on account of all visible things. Being free, he dwelt freely in the creation in order to teach us also by example to dwell in it in freedom. Therefore, whoever wishes to become a disciple of that teacher, let him observe the way his teacher lived in the world, and may he live like him in the creation. The Lord of the world became a foreigner and a stranger in the world and his servants should also become like the Lord. **(242)** Observe [how] inasmuch as he was renouncing human things, he was gathering complete fullness into himself, for in the creation he was not even acquiring[26] a den for either an animal or bird: "There are holes for foxes, and a shelter for the bird of heaven, but for the Son of Man there is nowhere to lay down his head."[27]

Do Not Possess What Your Teacher Doesn't Possess

21. Look, O disciple, your way of life is inscribed in the word of your teacher. Whatever he did not possess, you [too] should not have. Whatever he had not acquired, you also should not acquire. Disciples are not recognized by external appearance but by the equality and correspondence of deeds, and [the fact] that they travel in the footsteps of their teacher and walk on the path he has

---

[25] Phil 2:7.

[26] Instead of text's ܐܪ, read variant ܪܐܘ (Ms. A).

[27] Matt 8:20.

trodden for them. If the road were not trodden, and the footsteps of our God were not visible on it, there would have been perhaps an excuse for the slothful to whom the bonds of the world are beloved. But look, the path is clear and the road is familiar. The footsteps on it are visible to everyone in the light of the truth. But if a person does not see them and [does not] place his footsteps upon them, it is apparent that since he is deprived of the light, the indicator of faith, and while he imagines he is traveling on the road, his journey strays outside of it. What Jesus said to you—there was no place for him to lay down his head—was intended to teach you that also there should be none for you. He said, "Foxes have holes and a bird of the heaven [has] shelter." Then, if you possess a house **(243)** you are imitating these, and if you have a dwelling in the world, you are the equal of animals and of a bird, because that word has taught plainly in this way. But if you renounce everything in the world and do not have a place to lay down [your] head on the earth, you will resemble God.

Jesus Showed Perfection through Himself

22. Whatever the master was wishing that [his] disciples would become he depicted and showed to them in his own person and affirmed his teaching to us by his deeds, as it is written concerning him. "He began from the baptism of John to do and to teach until that day on which he was taken up."[28] The excellent mode of life that he had demonstrated in himself became these beautiful works. Although raising the dead, cleansing the lepers, opening [the eyes of] the blind and making the lame run, stretching out [the limbs of] the crippled and straightening up those bent over, chasing away the demons, walking on the waves, and silencing the winds are [considered] a work because they are signs and miracles, yet the writer calls the action associated with the teaching the spiritual rule that was visible in the person of Christ. If his coming had been for the sake of good deeds alone and not in order to perform signs, his teaching would have been for the sake of a spiritual rule to which

[28] Acts 1:1-2.

he would have attached action in order to show us in himself the model of complete perfection. He left the world and all the business that exists among human beings immediately after the baptism of John **(244)** and went out into the desert.

Jesus Kept the First Law

23. Because until the baptism, he was fulfilling another way of life. He was keeping all of the first law so that he might repay the debt on account of which our entire race was subjugated to the servitude of sin, the law and death. Everything those who were conducting themselves uprightly in the world should be doing, Jesus had personally kept. It is written concerning him: "He was ascending up to the temple and presenting offerings and submitting himself to the priests, and was accomplishing everything written in the law."[29] These things [are] for two [reasons]: one, in order to repay the debt, and the other, to teach everyone in the world that one should apply oneself to this righteousness of the law and serve God by the observances of the law. He did not neglect even one of the lesser matters of the law without keeping them, in order to teach whoever is still in the world to keep everything commanded to him as if one were still a slave.[30]

Above and under the Law

24. Because anyone who is still bound by that worldly way of life and by the give-and-take of human anxiety is under the law. But whoever empties himself and departs from the world lives above the world, and by necessity he is also above the law, because the law does not have the authority to subject those who are above the world. Whoever lives in a situation of servitude is being led by the force of the law. But whoever lives in a situation **(245)** of freedom, all of his activity is as a free person. By his own will as a free person he has the authority to do good things, not like one who

[29] See Luke 2:42.
[30] Matt 5:17-19.

is tied to the yoke of the law. In brief, wherever vices are practiced, there the law also has the authority to restrain and inhibit them according to the testimony of the teacher Paul who said, "The law is not established for the upright, but for the iniquitous and for the rebellious, and for those who are not pure, and for those who strike their parents, and for murderers and adulterers and fornicators,"[31] and so on. The law then has authority over these.

Motives for Not Sinning

25. So then while our narrative was desiring to show that the perfect who conduct themselves spiritually are the only ones above the law, it is apparent that Paul teaches that the upright who are lower than the perfect are also free of the law, for these also do not do good things as if they were afraid of the law, but in order to fulfill the law. Whoever does not kill because he might be put to death, while being prepared in his mind to kill, is a murderer. Whoever does not commit adultery, while lusting to commit adultery, fearing that he might be condemned by the judge and handed over to the law, is an adulterer. Anyone who thinks of harming [someone], but because of the fear of the punishments commanded by the laws holds himself back and does not harm, is the doer of all sorts of evil things according to his will. The upright who restrain themselves lest they do evil things, [it is] not because they are afraid lest there might be evil things in them, but because they do not want to provoke God to anger by a deed that does not please him. **(246)** Then, there are some who restrain themselves from evil things because they fear evil things; and there are some who restrain themselves from [evil things] in order that they might do good things, because if a person does not cease from evil things, he is not able to do good things.

Righteousness of the Law

26. Therefore, until baptism, our Lord transmitted to people the way of uprightness so that they might do the good things that are

---

[31] 1 Tim 1:9-10.

written in the law and present offerings to God out of their possessions, commit to vows and fulfill [them], be constantly in the temple of God, receive with faith the blessings from the priests, and children might be subservient to parents, serve them and seek also the word of life, ask and learn from teachers everything they are lacking for the learning of good things, and be obedient and subservient to the prophets.

Therefore, our Lord has transmitted in the rule of his Gospel, from the beginning and up to baptism, such things like these and all righteousness fitting for believers to those who possess so that they might accumulate their possessions while they are in the world. He has done everything in order to teach us to act like him. He was purified according to the commandment of the law[32] in order to teach believers to purify themselves from iniquity. He was circumcised[33] so that they also might become circumcised and cast away from themselves the non-circumcision of the heart and cut off from themselves the service of all the lusts. He went up to the temple carrying offerings so that he might prepare for them the road to run to the house of God while carrying their vows and their offerings. **(247)** He was presented to the priest in order that [the priest] might bless him and pray for him. Even if [Jesus] is a priest spiritually, he spoke to [the priest] other great things in order to demonstrate to believers how to ask for the prayer of the priests and to bow their heads and their children's [heads] for the blessing from them.

He was going up every year to the temple, as was written concerning him, in order to teach that believers should go at every hour to the temple of God. He was celebrating the festivals by their rules in order to urge you to perform with discernment the festivals of the church and to fulfill the festivals by all their rules. He was sitting in the midst of the teachers, listening to them and questioning them, inclining his ear and receiving learning,[34] so that you also might hear and question and incline your ear continually

[32] Luke 2:22-23, 27.
[33] Luke 2:21.
[34] See Luke 2:41-52.

to hear the divine commandments, and that you might question and learn which ones are helpful for your life, even from those who are lesser than you in knowledge, just as our Lord himself was questioning those who were less than him in knowledge, and receiving learning from those who had accumulated learning from the law he himself had given [them].

At last, when he had seen all the sinners rushing to the baptism of John the prophet of God,[35] he also went to [John] with them, bowed his head before the hand of the preacher,[36] and accepted to be baptized by him as if it were needed from that one who had need of him. He had left behind human habitation and was running with all the crowds to the desert **(248)** to John. What were these things for, but to teach the wealthy lords and worldly inhabitants to go to the saints and run to the solitaries and honor the prophets and the righteous and obey the admonition of their words by the discernment of their faith? Therefore, our Savior had transmitted this righteousness, had shown this way of life to believers in the interim up until the baptism, and had instructed those who possess to acquire these good things.

How Does a Perfect One Learn?

27. He did not give this rule to the solitaries, nor did he commit it to the perfect. To which temple should the spiritual man go, when he himself is the temple of God? From which dwelling should he run to the house of God, when he does not have even a roof in the world under which to dwell? With what should he offer offerings and fulfill the vows, when he does not possess anything in the creation? With what should he dress the naked and receive strangers, when he himself is a stranger and naked? Which vices should he cut off and throw away from himself, since he is perfect and is accomplished in all good things? Whom should he question and from which one should he learn, that one who does not have any

---

[35] Luke 3:7.
[36] Luke 3:21.

conversation at all with people? If he needs to learn, the Spirit of God teaches him instead of a human being.

Teaching according to One's Level

28. So then, this learning which [continues up to] the baptism was transmitted to the believing **(249)** upright and was given to righteous possessors [of wealth] and to those who have not departed at all from the world, so that they might not be deprived of good things that are appropriate for the situation in which they exist. Because Christ is everything, and everything is in him, and everything is through him and on account of him, Christ has also shown this way of life in himself. While it may be less than that of perfection, nevertheless, in this way he has fulfilled it so that he might give teaching to every person according to his level and offer the excellent way of life according to his rank and his order. Without virtues there is no way for a person to be saved. Virtues are different from one another, and like virtues the commandments given on account of them are different one from another.

Jesus and His Parents

29. Look, it was written that before his baptism he was subservient to his parents. "He returned with them to Nazareth and was obedient to them."[37] Nevertheless, see that after baptism, when he was transmitting to people the way of life more perfect than this one, he would not even consent to acknowledge [his] physical parents. "Who is my mother and who are my brothers?"[38] he was saying to the one who had called him. Before baptism he was obedient and subservient to his parents; later on when he was transmitting the way of life to the spiritual, he said that he did not know them. They called him to come out to [meet] them, but he did not consent. **(250)** His mother had spoken to him, but he did not listen to her, because now he was accomplishing the will of the Father who had sent him,

[37] Luke 2:51.
[38] Matt 12:48; Luke 8:19.

and he was not fulfilling the lowly commandments. But if our Lord had done this thing before baptism, when he was keeping the law, [if] he was called by his mother and did not obey, he would have been transgressing against the law. But now, not so, except to show that he was obeying his natural father more than his parents of grace and to teach also the perfect to obey the father of grace more than the parents of nature. "I do not seek my own will, but the will of the one who has sent me.[39] When I descended from heaven it was not to do my will, but the will of him who sent me."[40] These things were being spoken while he was transmitting perfection so that from here the spiritual who are outside of the world might understand that not only should they be obedient and subservient to natural parents but also to their own will, nor should they consent in anything regarding [their] needs and their own ease, but they should renounce themselves, as it was said by the Savior, "Whoever does not renounce himself is not able to become my disciple."[41]

Authority and Freedom at Cana

30. Therefore, after three days when our Lord had returned from the desert, it is written that Jesus was summoned to a wedding, he and his mother and his brothers and his disciples.[42] **(251)** When the wine was failing for the guests, his mother said to Jesus, "They have no wine."[43] She began here to speak to him authoritatively as a mother would usually do. But Jesus rejected that liberty, teaching that she had been repaid by him the debt of parental honor, and now he is no longer subservient to them as at first. See by which rebuke he removed from her that original authority. "What [does this have to do] with me and you, woman?"[44]—a statement full of rebuke. It is [a statement] completely [full] of indignation, yet

[39] John 5:30.
[40] John 6:38.
[41] Luke 14:26.
[42] John 2:1.
[43] John 2:3.
[44] John 2:4.

excellent because he was giving an example to the perfect through this word, lest they be led by the law of natural parents once they were living outside of the world in which the parents are dwelling. Mary was living in one mode of life and Jesus was in another rule—she according to the law and he according to the spirit. It was not good that he should be commanded—whoever lives in the spiritual rule [should not be commanded] by one who is still conducting oneself according to the law. Mary had commanded as if [she were still] an authoritative person, but Jesus answered her as a free person. "They have no wine." The word is authoritative, like a mother speaking by commandment. "What [does this have to do] with me and you, woman?" as one not subservient gives a reply and he spoke in this way as if with a strange woman who is not his mother. He did not say, "What [does this have to do] with me and you, *my mother*?" but, "What [does this have to do] with me and you, *woman*?" By grace you have been a mother to me, **(252)** and because of providence I was given birth by you. I was subservient and obeyed you, not because I am indebted to you naturally. It was not from you that I have received my beginning, that I should thank you that I came into existence on account of you. Not with pains have you borne me and not with pangs have you given birth to me. You have not raised me as one who is needy so that I should give to you a reward for the supplying of my needs. Everything that you have given me I have given to you. If you had carried me and had borne me and had given birth to me and had taken me up and raised me, these things would have happened to you through my power. That I have obeyed and been subservient to you is not because I should repay you the debt that I do not owe to you, but for the sake of all children who have resisted parents I will repay the debt and fulfill the law. But now that the debt has been paid, and I have fulfilled [divine] providence according to the law, what [does this have to do] with me and you, woman?

Going Up to the Feast

31. This word resembles that one—"Who is my mother?"—and that one in which he said to John, "Look, your mother," and he said

to Mary, "Look, your son."[45] Like that one is another: they sought to bring him along with them to the feast while they were ascending up to Jerusalem, according to the ancient custom before baptism, but when Jesus broke away from them for that custom, he said to them, "You go up to the feast, but I will not go up to the feast."[46] After **(253)** he had sent[47] them on and did not go up with them, he turned around and went up in the middle of the festival. The fact that he did go up is not contrary to what he said, "I will not go up." For he had said, "I will not go up being submissive," because they were going up as servants of the law in order to do the works of the law. But Jesus was going up with authority in order to gather guests to the new feast.

Because he had said, "I will not go up," he showed two things: he was not subject to parents or to the law, because whoever is subject to parents does whatever they command him. Moreover, whoever is under the law and along with all its commandments keeps also its works is obliged to go up from the beginning of the feast, because during this feast they and all the Jews used to go up to the temple. They were also going a few days early in order to purify themselves and arrive the first day of the festival being pure.

But Jesus did not do any of these things. He did not go up with them in order to demonstrate that he was not subject to them, and not from the beginning of the festival in order to teach that he did not go up to keep the feast. But he went up in the middle of the feast, an initiative of his own will. After he had spoken to his parents, "I am not going up," he went up, as he had done at the wedding in Cana, after he had said to Mary, "What [does this have to do] with me and you, woman?"—a word indicating he may be one who does not obey her in what she has said. Nevertheless, he turned around to do **(254)** what she had said, not because she had commanded it, but because of his authority and because the time had then come to begin with signs by which it would be apparent

---

[45] John 19:26.

[46] John 7:8.

[47] Budge's text reads: (ܐܪܕܫ) "after he had dismissed [them]"; Lavenant adopts variant: (ܪܕܫ) "after he had sent [them]" (Ms. A).

who he is and make known his glory and gather disciples to himself, and even more, to show that from then on as a free person he does everything with authority, and not according to the weakness of human nature, and not according to the subjection of parents, and not according to the commandment of the law.

Righteousness in Two Orders

32. We are explaining from Scripture the meaning of these things of which we have spoken. Whoever reads[48] should examine Scripture so that while reading our discourse he may see what the words mean in their passages. In order to emphasize this meaning for us, the words are distinguished one from another, and one mode of life is differentiated from another. Therefore, Jesus has transmitted to us this mystery through his way of life, that [period of time] up to the baptism, and [then] from the baptism to the cross. Because all righteousness is defined in these two orders—whether one should serve [God] through it or serve one's own interests. The service in one's own interest is righteousness external to him, but the service that is in him is the perfection of oneself. One is the righteousness of the law, and the other is that [righteousness] Christ has given. The [righteousness] of the law is [only] until baptism, but that one which is his own, from the baptism until the cross. From [the cross] and beyond, they are the pleasures and life above the world. Jesus had then attained the limit of the righteousness of the law **(255)** up to baptism, and from there until the cross he stood at the limit of spiritual perfection by the perfect good he had brought to the creation.

Righteousness in the World

33. From here we should understand that all people who do good deeds while they are in the world are just like the ancient

---

[48] Lemoine notes that the reference here to "a reader" indicates that what follows is something added to the edition of the *Discourses*. See Lemoine, "Introduction générale," 13.

upright, that is to say, like Abraham, Isaac, and Jacob, along with the rest of all the ancient righteous and prophets. Lawful righteousness is described as this: a person serves [God] while he is in the world, whether he may be clothing the naked, or giving ease to the afflicted, or receiving strangers in his home, or visiting the sick, or running toward the holy ones and solitaries and monks, or organizing for himself the times for prayer, or being continually in the temple of God, or not lending by contract and usury, or not coveting something of his neighbor, or being subject to [one's] parents, or being obedient to and honoring priests and teachers, or doing good things to every person, that is, as he wishes that people may do to him, he does also to them. This is the righteousness that the first law was teaching, and our Lord fulfilled it until baptism, and all believers who have not yet renounced **(256)** their riches are obligated to practice it. But Jesus has transmitted to us the spiritual rule and perfection from baptism and up until the cross so that all of us might become worthy of him by his grace. To him be glory forever. Amen.

The end of the eighth *mēmrā* on renunciation which was composed by the blessed Mar Philoxenos, bishop of Mabbug.

Mēmrā 9

On Renunciation of the World

The ninth *mēmrā* concerning the first goal of renunciation, which is from the testimonies of the Holy Scriptures and from the example of the first disciples, in which [Philoxenos] teaches that if one does not take off the world completely, he is not able to become a perfect disciple of Christ and participate in the mystery of divine knowledge.

Summary: Jesus' departure into the wilderness is the primary example of renunciation for those who wish to be perfect. The analogy is of one leaving the natural womb of this world, renouncing all possessions and going naked into the Christian life. The natural child proceeds out of nonexistence into existence; the child of the Spirit is born into becoming a son of God. An infant cannot be an adult in the womb and so a person cannot be perfect in the world. As the infant casts off the umbilical cord, so the person born from the world must cast off his own passions and physical appetites.

One becomes truly rich by needing nothing, so Philoxenos urges monks to depart from the world possessing nothing. On leaving the world the monk still has temptations and memories of past omissions, as well as concerns for the future hardships of asceticism.

Philoxenos sets out the life of John the Baptist as the model of the solitary and ascetic who received the natural innocence which Adam possessed before he sinned. Monks are to follow his example and not look back on the separation from family life, looking straight ahead to the new world. Those who renounce the world are higher than the upright and are dead to the world, while the upright are still alive in the world.

Jesus' Departure into the Desert

(257) 1. May the departure of our Lord into the desert be the best example for us to learn about renunciation. Through that model in which he moved from dwelling with people to struggling with the power that opposes [him], let us also depart from the world through [that model] in the battle against Satan, while not departing with anything from the world except only our spiritual armor which is not of the world. Jesus departed then immediately after [his] baptism and abandoned the world and everything in it, the dwelling (258) of humanity and everything in it. He departed alone by the power of his soul so that he might wage war with the Slanderer. It is written that the Holy Spirit that was in him had driven him out into the desert. It was not that he was in need of spiritual strength—he who is the equal of the Spirit—for he had given the Spirit to others so that they might be victorious through it; but for the encouragement of these who depart from the world in pursuit of perfection and so that they should learn first of all that the Spirit's strengthening power accompanies their departure and aids their struggle and [is] the one that confers the crown to the struggle in which they are living; for immediately the assistance of the Spirit will cling to those disciples who abandon the world's companionship. When they have despised human assistance, they will find heavenly assistance, and from the moment they reject physical power, spiritual power will immediately accompany them.

Beginning Anew from Baptism

2. So here through baptism our Lord completes the road of the righteousness of the law, and from the Jordan he has made the beginning of the road for his own way of life. Until the Jordan there was servitude, which means he was being subservient to the law like a servant. But from then on, freedom became his rule through his own teaching, and not the commandments of the law. Jesus was born again by baptism and from the belly of the law he received a spiritual place. As he himself said, "If a person is not born again, he will not (259) be able to see the kingdom of God."[1] On account of

---

[1] John 3:3.

this, after his baptism he began to preach the kingdom of heaven. In this pattern everyone who desires to become a perfect disciple of Christ, when one has left the world and is living outside of it, is born again from the physical world to the spiritual world, and from wealth to poverty, from comforts to afflictions, from family to deprivation, from a multitude of friends to solitude, from pleasures to troubles, from the physical mode of life to the spiritual [mode], from a conversation with a human being to a conversation with God, from [one kind of] knowledge to [another kind of] knowledge, and from [one] path to [another] path. To sum it up, a person is born from one thing to another when he moves from the way of the world to the discipleship of Christ, and from being a lord of riches to the renunciation that God commands. Just as when a person is in the world, the way of life in which he lives requires him to perform everything in the world, so when a person moves away from the world and follows Jesus, he is required to do everything in the spiritual mode of life, according to the order of where he has arrived. It is one thing for a person to take off the world, and another for a person to take off the old person. It is one thing to shed personal thoughts and another to shed error, and yet another to shed ignorance.

Leaving Womb and World

3. It is said that a person takes off the world when he distances himself from everything in it and distributes **(260)** his wealth and possession completely to those who are needy. He leaves the world and departs naked alone in the same manner that he has gone out from the womb. Because in this way residence in the world is for a human being just like the natural womb is for the fetus carried in it. Just as he is still in the womb in darkness in a gloomy and damp place, not sensing any of these things of this world, and these things that are in the creation and in the place of the world outside of the womb do not ascend upon his heart, so also a person who is confined in the physical way of the world as in a womb, and his [sense of] discernment being hidden in the darkness of his worries, and his mind enshrouded in the gloom of human anxiety is not able to sense the blessings and riches in the way of Christ. Spiritual things are not apparent to him as long as his discernment

is hidden in the darkness of physical things. Just as that natural fetus does not enter creation unless it is born from the womb, so also here, unless a person moves completely away from the world, he does not arrive at the spiritual way of life. Just as there [the fetus] abandons the womb and exists outside of it, so also here one should leave the world and depart from it, because the world is [configured] in the type of the womb: just as the fetus sheds the womb, a person will shed the world.

Analogy of Fetus and Spiritual Person

4. When the fetus is born it is perfect and complete in its natural structure in all senses and members, yet it cannot use them in their natural function because they have not [yet] **(261)** received growth and become strong. When it has been born into the world, though, its body will receive growth in the world along with all the senses and members in it. Inasmuch as [the fetus] grows and develops in its members and senses and receives the tastes and bears the experience of everything in the world, all its senses will utilize their natural function in a healthy way: the eye in sight, the ear in hearing, the palate in the tastes, the nostrils in smelling, the tongue in speech, the hands in work, the feet in walking, the whole body in touching, the heart in discernment, the liver in anger, the bile in insight, the kidneys in understanding, the spleen in fear, and the brain in intelligence and understanding, along with the rest of all the members that are in the world. Gradually they grow to mature adult stature and acquire full strength of their function in everything. A person becomes physically complete in the world for he is born into [the world] from the womb and receives and is fulfilled in all its knowledge. Therefore, in this same way it is also accomplished with the spiritual person, whoever begins from the image of being a fetus and little by little is fulfilled and becomes "a perfect man according to the measure of the height of the fullness of Christ,"[2] as it was written. But first, at the beginning of his

---

[2] Eph 4:13.

conception he was similar to a natural fetus, for just as [the fetus] is formed from seed and blood in the womb, so also this one is formed from fire and the Spirit after baptism.

Just as **(262)** the natural fetus is born from what is not to what shall [come to] be, so also this spiritual fetus is born from what is not a child to what shall become a child of God and a spiritual [being]. Just as there [in the womb], once it was fashioned from what is not, it was formed gradually, all its members receiving growth according to the measure placed in them to grow in the womb, so also this [spiritual] person who is born from baptism [as] a child of God from being a servant and a physical being begins to grow gradually in the world as in the womb in all these virtues fitting for the faithful to perform in the world. When he has grown up and become mature according to the measure of his infancy in the world just as in the womb, he will [experience] another birth from the world to outside the world, similar to the way that the fetus is born from the womb into the world. Once he has been [re-] born and stands in the place of the way of Christ, as in another world, from there he begins to receive another kind of growth and be fulfilled, not in the body of righteousness which received growth in the world, but in the person of the spirit by which one attains the perfection of the fullness of Christ.

Baptism as Womb

5. Imagine, therefore, baptism as [a kind of] womb, and whoever becomes through [baptism] a child of God from not being a child is like a natural fetus created into existence from not existing, and that baptism which gives birth to the spiritual fetus **(263)** from what is physical to become spiritual is given shape like the fetus from seed and blood and receives the creation of all its members. In this same way this fetus is born here by baptism with all its members and spiritual senses being created and made. Just as there, after he is created and formed, he develops gradually in all his members and senses until he fulfills the term of his infancy, which is limited for him while he is in the womb, and then he comes to be born from the womb, so also here, the spiritual fetus grows in the world after

he is born by baptism until he attains the standard determined for these spiritual fetuses. Just as the fetus is not able to receive in the womb the growth that will happen outside the womb and become a mature man in the womb—because this will be granted him in the world after being born—so a person is not able to become mature in spiritual perfection and live in the stature of a perfect man as long as he still dwells in the world as in the womb, but it is necessary for him first to be born and shed the entire world as a fetus [sheds] the womb, and then he will begin to receive another [kind of] growth that brings [him] to a spiritual nature and perfection.

Worldly Righteousness

6. So then everything one's righteousness performs in the world and all aspects of virtues that happen in it are like the gestation of a fetus in the womb. As much as he might grow **(264)** and become strong in this righteousness while in the world, he is still living like an infant because like a fetus in the womb he is enclosed in the world. Just as a fetus is not able to become a man in the womb, so[3] one is not able to become perfect in the world. As much as a fetus might grow in the womb, the measure of its growth is limited there according to the space of the womb, so however much a person may be justified in the world, the measure of his righteousness is limited according to the womb of the world in which he dwells. Just as whoever is conceived in a natural womb is called a fetus and conceived as long as he is inside it, but when he has been born from the womb he begins to receive other names—newborn, infant, child, youth, and full-grown adult—so also in this same manner this spiritual fetus, as long as he is in the world and all aspects of righteousness are developing in him, inasmuch as he is becoming stronger and coordinated, firm and growing, he is called by these names—righteous, upright, compassionate, and generous—along with [other] names that are appropriate for the excellent way of life in the world. But when he has been born from the world, after

---

[3] Mss. BCD omit the phrase here, ܠܥ ܐܘܗ ܟܬܐ ܪܕܗܢ, "in our natural womb."

his features mature in these first members we have listed, and he has departed to another place of the way of Christ like a fetus who is born from the womb, these titles are designated for him and he is called by these other names that are appropriate for the place **(265)** to which he has departed. He is called in this way one who renounces, free person, abstainer, ascetic, bearer of a burden, crucified to the world, patient, long-suffering, spiritual, imitator of Christ, perfect man, person of God, beloved son, heir of his Father's possession, companion of Jesus, bearer of the cross upon his shoulder, dead to the world, alive to God, clothed in Christ, spiritual person, angel of flesh, knower of the mysteries of Christ, wise person of God. Such names like these are appropriate to name a person who is born from the world so that he may be raised up in the place of the knowledge of Christ.

Shedding the Passions

7. Just as when the natural fetus is born from the womb, even if it sheds the womb, the membrane worn in the womb still accompanies it and goes out with it, but once [the child] has been born [the membrane] is cut off and thrown away along with the rest of the superfluous things adhering to it, and the person of a human being appears by himself, being freed from everything which is not of him—and he is of and for himself; in the same manner also once one has departed from the world, even if it happens that he sheds the world like the womb, he is still wearing his own passions and the lusts of his body that cling to him[4] like a fetus to the membrane. Because just as the membrane is not removed from the fetus while it is in the womb, so a person is not able to shed the old passions, those in which he is clothed **(266)** in the likeness of a membrane while he is in the womb of the world. Just as above, at the moment the fetus is born they will then remove its membrane from him, so also here until a person is born from the physical way of the world, and lives in the other spiritual world beyond the world, [only]

---

[4] Budge's text written: ܘܗܕܡ; Lavenant opts to read the variant: ܗܘܡܬܦܝ ܠܗ (Ms. B).

then is he able to shed and cast away from himself the despicable passions of the old person in the same way as a membrane. Because just as the fetus is not able to receive adult growth as long as it is wrapped in its membrane, once [the membrane] has been peeled off from him and he has appeared free in himself, then he can begin to grow to his natural stature. In this example also a person who while he is still clothed in despicable passions is not able to grow in spiritual stature, but once he has shed and cast them away from him and has cut off all the members of the body of sin[5] that are despicable passions, when his stature begins to grow and other new members of the new spiritual person spring up in place of the old members that were cut off from him, because in place of these original members that were cut off other new and spiritual ones spring up. As long as the old person is finished and vanishes, so the new person will be found and revealed to the light.

Putting On the New Person

8. Even if we have taken off the old person through baptism according to the teaching of Paul and have put on the new [person] in place of it, yet we were aware neither when we have taken [it] off or when we have put [it] on, because grace has accomplished both of them and has taken off **(267)** the old [person] and has put on the new [person]. The mystery we received at that time [of baptism] operates only in the name of faith. But when we desire to take off the old person through our own labor and fatigue, we are aware here that we are taking it off, not only by the hearing of faith, but also [because] an urgent course of the hidden person toward the Lord develops by trials and through sufferings and tears and the love of God, and pure prayers and continual supplications, and astonishment concerning the majesty of the glory of God, and continual wonder concerning it. By such things as these, we are diligently putting on the new person, not [only] by the hearing of the ear, but [also] by our soul's awareness and by an authentic experience of spiritual knowledge.

[5] Rom 6:6.

Taking Off the Physical

9. One begins to grow then in the knowledge above the world in this place, where there is room for one to grow all the way up to the stature of the height of majesty. Because as long as despicable passions surround a person like a membrane and the members of the new person are entangled in them, growth will be prevented and the person will not be able to attain that measure of stature given by Christ, about which Paul said, "May all of us grow and become one in the knowledge of the son of God and [become] a single perfect man by the measure of the stature of the fullness of Christ."[6] But unless one has departed from the world he is not able to attain this level (268) and unless at first one has taken off the entire physical way of life, he is not able to attain this knowledge in order to become aware of the majesty of these things given mysteriously by Christ.

The clothes that we take off and put on are these—in baptism we strip off the old person and put on the new [person]. [We take off] servitude and put on freedom; [we take off] the physical [nature] and put on the spiritual [nature]; [we take off] sin and put on righteousness, and such like these, all of them by the acceptance of faith, all of them really happening with us in the [new] birth of baptism—but all of them are strangers to our senses. When we attain the measure of the body's stature that is able to discern good from bad things by the goodwill and diligence of our soul, we begin to take off evil things and put on good things. [Let us take off] iniquity and put on uprightness. [Let us take off] ingratitude and become generous. [Let us take off] cruelty and become compassionate. [Let us take off] harshness and become gentle. [Let us take off] rapacity and become sympathetic, and many other things like these. All these things happen by a will that fears God, one that struggles with the world so that little by little one may grow by these things until he completely casts off the entire world and empties himself from everything in it and lives freely in himself and is to be seen in another world that belongs to the way of Christ, in the model that the natural fetus sheds the womb and lives outside of it.

[6] Eph 4:13.

Taking Off Passions and Thoughts

10. When a person has taken off **(269)** the world in the way I have described, and completely renounces everything visible, then he begins to take off the evil passions that are in it—the lust of adultery, fornication, gluttony, intemperance, insatiableness, drunkenness—these that are the desires destructive of virtue. When he has effectively taken off all these things from physical members, he then begins to shed also the movements of thoughts. Just as he had alienated them from being with the body, he will also cut off [these thoughts] from the movements of the soul which not only are not served or moved by external members but neither as well by the inner thoughts of the soul. After he takes off from the soul the passions of despicable thoughts, he begins from here to take off also ignorance, error, and illusion, which are born out of the service of lusts, that is, when the heart is hardened through delicacies and delights.

Balance of Body and Soul

11. When a person takes off the body's desires with a pure glance toward God, he also proceeds to reduce his physical needs because the heart is hardened not only by the service of lusts but [also] when the body has fully received its need, hardness of heart [still] exists and the mind is neither cleansed nor purified from physical [nature]. He maintains [his] need at a moderate level, and as long as the body is living in balanced health it is not **(270)** subjugated fully to the wishes of the soul. The middle demonstrates the equality of the two sides. Just as a feather placed in the middle of a scale shows the equality of weight of both balances, so when the body is living in balanced health it is equal on the scale against the soul, and as long as it weighs as much as [the soul], it is not subjugated to the majority of its desires. So then, it is necessary to break the power of the body by the reduction of food, so that in this way it might become subservient and obedient to the soul. But I will cease from this discourse on the reduction of food because I intend to talk about it in the *mēmrā* after this one. We should understand this then, that if a person does not take off, he cannot put on, and

all of us must be diligent to take off from ourselves the physical way of life, so that in this way one might put on the spiritual way of life. One should take off the world and all of its anxiety so that without impediment one may journey on the road of perfection.

The Lightness of Renunciation

12. So then, renunciation is light for those who possess it. If one calls poverty wealth on account of God, that is correct and it is named as it should be. On account of this our Lord has also lifted a heavy yoke from his disciples in making them renounce worldly wealth. "Come to me all you who are weary and burdened with heavy loads **(271)** and I will give you rest."[7] Which [people] are these, except those who are wearied by the excesses of wealth and bear the heavy yoke of worldly anxiety and cares? Which fatigue is as harsh as this one, that when you come to rest you are all the more fatigued? The anxiety of human wealth is a road on which there is no end in life. As long as a person is traveling, [the road] stretches out before his steps and nothing brings it to an end except death. When a person gathers wealth and mammon in order to find ease and enjoy pleasures and be pampered, even his rest is fatiguing.[8] And if the world's ease is fatiguing, what can its fatigue be called? If its pleasures and delicacies are heavy labors, how will its labor be designated? The world is heavy in all its ways, and on account of its love those who bear its burdens do not perceive it and stumble in it like blind people and do not discern [it]. They bear heavy burdens, but they are light to them. They become fatigued and toil after unprofitable business and do not understand. Because our Lord saw them in this empty weariness, he called out to them, "Come to me so that I may give you rest." There is no rest in your fatigue, for fatigue generates fatigue. Labor issues forth labor. Even your wealth amasses poverty and your rest is a vexation, and your pleasure an affliction, your breathing is suffocating. The road of wealth's desire you have willfully trod has no end to it.

[7] Matt 11:28.
[8] Luke 12:18-19.

But if you come to me **(272)** it will have an end. Just as you have experienced [the road] of the world, experience with it this [road] of mine, and if it is not pleasing to you, flee from it. You have carried the heavy burdens of the world and have felt how heavy [they are]; be persuaded to take my yoke upon yourself and learn through experience how gentle and pleasant [it is].[9] I do not make you rich so that you will have need of many things, but truly rich, not lacking anything, because it is not one who possesses many things [who] is wealthy, but whoever is not needful of anything. In the world, as long as you possess, you will be needful. But with me, if you renounce everything, you shall become wealthy. When the first need is fulfilled, a place is prepared in it for the second need. When the discovery that a person wishes to find has been acquired, it investigates some more for the discovery of another possession. When the first desire was accomplished, a wide hole is acquired in it for another desire greater than it, because the satiation of desires creates hunger, and as long as desire eats, hunger keeps making one hungry. As long as a rich person becomes rich, he becomes poor. The more mammon is gathered together, [the more] he will search out something similar. As much as a person increasingly possesses and flourishes, he will desire ardently yet another possession.

If a person should happen to possess half of the world, his desire will not be fulfilled by this possession, but again he will desire to acquire all of it if he is able. And when he has possessed all of it—which is not **(273)** possible—his desire will not be inhibited by the limit of the possession of the entire world, but he will desire to acquire another world like it besides, which does not exist. He begins to be agitated in the quest of something that is not yet created. Who shall not weep concerning this thought, rather, who shall not laugh over it, that he is bound by the love of searching for those things that do not exist? Come, then, to me all you who are weary of wealth and find rest in poverty. Come, lords of riches and possessions, and find pleasure in renunciation. Come, those

[9] See Matt 11:30.

who love the temporal world and receive the taste of the eternal world. You have tried your own [world]; come try also mine. You have borne the examination of your wealth; come also examine my poverty. Your own wealth is wealth; but my poverty is wealth. It is nothing great that wealth should be labeled wealth, but it is remarkable and great when poverty is wealth, for it is proclaimed majesty in reverse. But when you have also tried these things of mine, if they are not sweeter and lighter than your own, go back and bear your original burdens.

Jesus' Renunciation

13. Look again, our Lord has also shown us through this testimony that if a person does not cast away the burden of the world he is not able to bear the yoke of Christ because the two yokes are opposites of one another. Righteousness also is acquired through wealth, but perfection is discovered by the renunciation of possessions. All those who had pursued perfection, whether in the New [Testament] or in the Old [Testament], had renounced **(274)** wealth and then had begun on the road of perfection. When the apostles were called by our Lord, they renounced the entire world and then followed that one who had called them. Moreover, Our Lord himself had depicted and shown us through his person the end and the beginning of the road and had established the boundary of both of them at the Jordan. For there he had finished the lawful road on which he was traveling in order to keep the Law, and from it he began on the road of perfection that he demonstrated in himself for the purpose of instruction of those who love perfection. After he had defeated the world and despised and rejected everything in it, then he went out to battle the god of the world. Just as he subdued the fortress of the enemy, he would subdue also his very person. The Jordan was for him the crossover from one world to the next, from the physical world to the spiritual world, and from the rule of law to the rule of the New Testament. What the sea was for the Hebrews—by it they ended the servitude of Egypt, and the fear of the Egyptians who were against them was removed from them, and from it they had departed to the place of freedom in

which another's lordship would have no power over them, and they would not do the will of others, except only of God—so also at the Jordan Jesus completed the servitude of the Law and from [the Jordan] began the ways of freedom. Just as the wilderness had received the Jews from the sea, so the desert received him from the Jordan. From there he was accomplishing not the weak will of the law but the perfect and complete **(275)** will of his Father, so that he might give healthy commandments and show the spiritual and perfect way that he himself desires.

Jesus Departed without Anything

14. Understand that when Jesus went out to the desert he went out all alone, without accompaniment and without help, without his friends in his wake, nor beloved ones, nor wealth, nor possession, nor clothing, nor ornaments. Nothing of the world went out with him, it is written, except only himself, the Holy Spirit accompanying him. Take this departure of your Lord as a model for your own departure from the world, and go forward also in his example, having nothing with you from the world so that the Holy Spirit may accompany you in the same way. Notice therefore the freedom in which Jesus had departed and you should also depart like him. Observe how far the human way of life came with him, and where he left it, and you should also leave behind the way of the world. Wherever your Lord has left behind the way of the law, go forward with him into the battle against the powers of error, that is, into the struggle with the world. When you have departed from the world, because this is its custom to pursue those who are leaving it and moving away, you should return to the struggle against it and become crucified against it, remembering what Paul said, "I am crucified to the world and the world is crucified to me."[10] Therefore, relieve the world's burden from yourself so that the battle you have prepared against it might be easy for you. Bathe in the waters of knowledge instead of the Jordan and after your bathing continue on in the way of the Spirit.

[10] Gal 6:14.

In the Type of the Hebrews

15. Notice that what **(276)** had happened to the Jews is also the model of these things that will happen to you. For just as all the Egyptians' evil deeds had come to an end for the Hebrews, so also here all the world's evils shall disappear and vanish for you with its excesses and its burden, its anxiety and its cares. Up until the sea the Hebrews were laboring for the Egyptians; but after the sea and beyond they were set apart for God's service by the word of God. The slavery of the Jews in Egypt is a model for your servitude in the world. The freedom that they had taken up in the desert is an example, moreover, of the freedom you will receive after your departure from the world. Egypt was making the Hebrews work with mud and bricks and with toils and harsh labors;[11] and with cares, anxiety, adversities, and groans the world also works against you. The Jews were washed of the mud of Egypt once they had crossed over the sea, and you also have two baptisms. One is of grace that occurs through water, and the other is of your will so that when you have dived from the world into the love of God, you will spring up outside of it, just as the Hebrews after they had departed from the sea[12] had received other rules and were worthy of other food,[13] and new waters had burst forth for their drinking,[14] and other commandments and laws were delivered to them to keep.[15] They received heavenly revelations, were worthy of spiritual visions, and heard the voice of God **(277)** close by while he was speaking with them. The angels also had mixed with them,[16] and [the Hebrews] had attained the company and communion with the spiritual powers, and the tabernacle was pitched among them and they were given the explanation of the worship [that took place] within it, and the crucified serpent was erected for them in the

[11] See Exod 1:14.
[12] Exod 14:29.
[13] Exod 16:14-18.
[14] Exod 17:6.
[15] Deut 5:1.
[16] See Exod 14:19.

desert for healing and health from the bites of venomous snakes.[17]
It is as if their entire way of life[18] already existed in the next world
that is exempt from all worldly custom.

Fear and Vexation after Leaving

16. By this example too when you have departed from the world
as from Egypt, you have crossed over the sea of austerities and lived
in fear and in passions, because those at the edge of the sea and in
the sea were also being filled with fear. The terror of the Egyptians
and the fear of the sea were tormenting them, and until they had
descended into the sea and had turned around and ascended above
it, and had seen the corpses of their enemies floating among the
waves, they were not filled with joy.[19] So also, when the disciple has
departed from the world and wishes to become free of its servitude,
he does not immediately receive joy, nor is he worthy of the taste of
spiritual pleasures, just as neither had those once they had departed
from Egypt received joy or were worthy of spiritual pleasure. But
there will occur to you at first, O disciple, after your transition **(278)**
from the world the fear of austerities and the vexation of thoughts
and repentance concerning your departure from the world, and the
fact that you have dispersed whatever you had possessed, or that
you have abandoned your inheritance and have moved out of the
dwelling of your parents. The demons are gathering secretly against
you in similar fashion to the Egyptians and Satan, their leader like
Pharaoh. Thoughts such as these are disturbing you and burying
you in anxious concerns that ordinarily darken the soul and deprive
you of the vision of light of the knowledge of Christ.

Doubts from the World

17. Such [thoughts] as these begin to agitate in your thoughts:
why have you left the world in which it would have been easier for

---

[17] Num 21:9.
[18] Typographical error: written ܗܘܢܝܗ, read ܗܘܒܪܗ (*dūbārhōn*).
[19] See Exod 15:20.

you to be justified? Why did you decide to disperse your wealth, for while it was with you, you were seen to be through it an especially compassionate person? Now, because you have divided it hastily it happens also that it has been given to those who are not worthy, but if it had been kept with you and had been distributed wisely by you, you would have comforted the weary by it, you would have received strangers through it, you would have clothed the naked by it. The solitaries and the monks would also have been visited by your gifts. You would have supported the widows and the orphans. Your home would have become the haven for all excellent things. With patience, as long as your wealth would have been with you, you would have found ease by it and it would have given ease to many others and your righteousness would have been like Abraham[20] and Job[21] **(279)** and the rest of the faithful who like them have been justified.

Do you wish that your righteousness will become much greater than theirs? Moreover, through this compassion you would be imitating God according to the word of your Lord. Again you would also receive a good reputation among people and would be called by everyone "the father of orphans."[22] All who see and hear [you] would consider you blessed because of your good works. As long as your righteousness would be shining before God, so it would be revealed also to the sight of people. Moreover, it would also be a good example to others so that they might emulate you. As long as the owners of wealth who are like you were watching you distributing your possessions to the needy, they were also being compelled by your example to become generous. From here you would be collecting a double righteousness for yourself, one of your own gift and the other because you have been the cause of compassion to others, for these also have become generous like you.

If you wish to become a faster, it would be easier for you while you are in the world, like the rest of the many fasters whom you

---

[20] Gen 18:19; Rom 4:2.
[21] Job 1:1f.
[22] Ps 68:5.

have seen in the world. In this especially the triumph of your fast would have been all the greater, insofar as foods were near to you and the desires of the belly are arranged before your sight, you would have been victorious over everything by the power of your self-control. In this also you would excel more than the solitaries, because whoever defeats **(280)** things that are found nearby him to make use of if he would so desire them, his triumph is much greater than in the case of one who is lacking because he does not have anything by way of self-control, for even if he desires to find ease and pleasure, the objects of his comfort are not at his convenience.

But if you love prayer, this would also have been easier for you: to pray in your house secretly[23] and go at all times to the temple of God and also take others with you. There was not one excellent deed that you would have wished to accomplish that would not have been all the easier for you in the world. Who is it that rejects ease with royalty? Who is it that declines to take delight here, if he is certain that also future pleasure is being prepared for him, this [pleasure] which was found to be yours on account of your compassion and your alms to the poor?

Future Doubts of Asceticism

18. After these things, these evil demons with their leader Satan are gathering and piling up other things against your soul, depicting before your eyes the labors of asceticism and the harsh diseases that will happen to those who fast and the bitter illnesses that are being engendered from meagerness of food, which also are not easy to heal, nor is it easy for you to cure them, because you have not been able to use these things that are healing and healthy for them. If you agree to offer them human supports on account of the afflictions **(281)** of your diseases, you would become a stumbling block for the others who see you. Moreover, the road of this way of life is long and is not completed except by death. If you desire to put an end to it while you are still living and cease from your

[23] Matt 6:6.

labors, look, you have made yourself a joke and a disgrace for all those who know you. So that you do not cease, see how you are bearing the burden of austerities and increasing your torment with many things, one by the weight of your labors and the other by their length and even more by the diseases and ailments that are engendered by [ascetic] labors. Again, it is not easy for you to offer them remedies, because if you wish to gain rest from your austerities through the supports that you are bringing to them, you will become a laughingstock to those who see you. Moreover, you have become a stranger to your family and your friends and also because the law of your rules does not allow you to approach either conversation or a meeting with them. Again, you will find it necessary to receive favors from others, you who used to be the giver of grace to others. If you agree to receive, see, you have pledged yourself to adulate those from whom you have received, [but if] you do not receive, look, you will be tormented by need's distress.

Demons Mention Virtues First

19. Therefore, the demons gather together and bring such things like these upon the mind of the disciple as soon as he has departed from the world and throw fear and terror on him, disturbing the stability of his thoughts and casting him into uncertainty so that **(282)** he does not know what he will do. They immerse his soul in sadness and make him live between the middle and the end in order that he might remember these things he had abandoned and call to mind these things that will come to be. He pays attention to their advice in his mind, as if they have a case, especially those thoughts that agitate one at first—they are not of luxuries or of depravity or of evil rules, but of compassion and of the love of alms with the rest of all the virtues a person is able to perform while in the world. [The demons] stir up these things in your soul, not as lovers of virtues but in order to lower you from the high level of righteousness to another lower than it. When you have obeyed them and have descended with them, they will also make you descend from that [level] to another level [even] lower than it, and little by little, escorting and inducing, they will bring you down

until they pull [you] down and plunge you into the depths of evil
things. They are cunning in their counsels, for wherever they see
that you are caught, from that spot they will make your passions
grow. [It is] not what you have hated that they will immediately
bring [and] offer you by their counsels, but whatever is beloved by
you. Then, they will persuade you to yield from the rigor of your
rule—only a little bit.

Soul Caught in the Middle

20. And then by all of these [ruses], a misery of thoughts will
weigh heavily upon you and sadness and outcries will be renewed
in your mind, while joy **(283)** dwells far beyond you—the joy of
the world because you have abandoned it and [the joy] of Christ
because you have not attained it. Your soul remains in the middle
of these storms like a ship whose pilot is asleep, being tossed about
here and there, drifting and being buffeted on all sides, and being
dashed against all reefs and all sorts of doubts shaking it, and the
journey on the road of the mind will be troubled. The traces of your
steps' paths will vanish before you and a burden will be piled up
on you. Slumber seizes you in your body and in your soul, and
you will be plunged into the heavy sleep of laziness as during the
night. Just as fear increases during the night for those who are in it,
so fear will increase in you because you have obscured your soul
from the light of knowledge. Instead of light in the world there is
knowledge in the soul from which joy is also born. Just as by the
removal of light darkness is born in the creation, so by the deprivation of spiritual knowledge the darkness of distress and the
gloom of sadness spread out in the place of the soul. From here
fear begins to be born in [the soul] concerning what has passed
and what things are to come: distress, terror and fear, weakness
and smallness of mind and the affliction of thoughts, **(284)** and a
continual agitation that renews itself at all times from it, in it, and
to it. It happens that [the soul] is distressed when there is nothing
to fear, and its mind is troubled not being aware what is the cause
of its trouble, nor are any of its movements agreeable to it at all.

Escaping from Egypt

21. Therefore, you need to pass through this place, O disciple, in order to depart from the world. For like the people from Egypt you also have been called and have followed God. Just as the sea was barring the Hebrews and the Egyptians were pursuing them, so the depth of the power of austerities is laid before you, and the passions, labors, vexations and anxieties, deprivations and poverty, illnesses and diseases, separation from friends, distance from family and remoteness from parents, silence and stillness, and the narrow enclosure, humble clothing and meager food, abstinence and asceticism, as well as reproaches and dishonors if you are slack, and labors and exertions if you are successful, and exhausting vigil, tortuous thirst and extenuated hunger.[24] All such things then are like the fearful sea barring your departure, while demons are pursuing you from behind in imitation of the Egyptians. However, do not fear and do not be alarmed, because instead of Moses, Jesus is with you. In the manner that Moses was attached to the congregation, so also Christ is attached to your soul **(285)** secretly. He also speaks to your afflicted and tormented thoughts what was spoken by Moses to the Jews. "The Lord will fight on your behalf, while you should be still."[25] Do not be in fear as were the people, but be alert and vigilant like Moses, and cry out to the Lord as he had cried out. In the same way it was written that Moses was praying all night with great groaning and with sufferings, and then at the morning watch the Lord said to him, "Why are you crying out to me? Stretch out your hand over the sea and divide it,"[26] and let the Hebrews cross over it and the Egyptians will be swallowed up in it.[27] All of these things that happened are the type of these things that will be done to you.

[24] Lavenant reads (ܟܦܢܐ) *kapnā*, "hunger," instead of (ܟܦܝܐ) *kapyā*, "being bowed over."
[25] Exod 14:14.
[26] Exod 14:15-16.
[27] Exod 14:28.

Abandon Worries and Cry Out to God

22. Therefore, evil demons are the enemies, amassing together against your soul just like the Egyptians who were pursuing [the Israelites] had amassed against the souls of the Jews. But just as Moses had left behind the fear of the Egyptians and had turned himself toward prayer and crying out to God, you also should abandon the worries and thoughts that the enemy demons are stirring up in you and stand up in earnest prayer and cry out passionately from the heart. May the sound of your cry ascend from the depth of the soul's thoughts. Immediately, that word that responded to Moses is also spoken to you, "Why do you cry out to me? Stretch out your hand over the sea and divide it."[28] At once, anxieties will give way and the veil of sadness which had been placed in front of you will be drawn away **(286)**, and the depth of the power of austerities will give way. These things that you had thought could not be traversed by foot, you are treading upon and have crossed over their depth, and the difficult things are easy for you. The wall that was built which you were thinking was impenetrable is torn down immediately before you, while your prayer is penetrating and crossing over the abyss of all evil things, these which were being gathered and placed in your way. Just as the column of old had been behind the Hebrews but went in front of them, and darkness came between them and the Egyptians,[29] so also here the light of salvation shines before you and darkness is placed between you and the devils, your enemies. These [enemies] are swallowed up in that place over which you have crossed and the afflictions from which you have been freed turn around and belong to the demons, your enemies, and your sadness and anxiety are turned against them. The joy that was with them in the type of that column, when they thought they could fight and defeat you, is taken away before them and placed before you. Just as the column of light that was taken from the Egyptians and was in front of the Hebrews, and just as Pharaoh and the Egyptians were swallowed

[28] Exod 14:15-16.
[29] Exod 14:19-20.

up in the sea, so Satan with all his demons is plunged into the abyss
of anxieties into which you were made to plunge. Then you shall
repeat the word of Moses to your thoughts, "The Lord will fight
(287) on your behalf, while you should be still."[30]

Night into Morning

23. Just like the Hebrews with Moses, all of your triumphs will
cross over with you. During the night fear was ruling over the Hebrews so as to be a model for you, that as long as fear is with you,
[it is] as if your life is in the night. But once night has passed away
with the sight of morning and fear is carried away, so also here as
soon as the light of salvation shines on you at the completion of
your prayer your adversities will be wiped away, your thoughts
will be lightened like the limbs in the morning, the gloomy cloud
will be scattered and a cheerful clear sky will shine in your soul, the
sea of your austerities will be crossed over by foot, and the wall of
adversities that was built in front of you will be torn down. You will
be walking in confidence in the region of power, crossing over the
abyss that was not crossable for you, treading upon the region that
the old nature could not tread, escaping from the yoke of servitude,
and entering the region of freedom. You have left Egypt with all
its toil, and the desert full of heavenly blessings is receiving you.
You are conceived and born again into the new world of the spiritual way of life. In the place that conceives and gives birth to you,
there the wheels of your enemies are tied down, the impetuosity
of their rushing about ceases and the advance of their journey is
halted, the clamor of their voices is quieted and silenced, austerities
turn back on them like waves, and at the deepest part of the abyss
they are engulfed, those who had wished to engulf you. But you,
while you are standing at the edge above the sea of affliction and
adversities, after **(288)** a glorious crossing you turn to look back at
your enemies who are being buffeted about in its midst, and the

---

[30] Exod 14:14.

passions are drowning in it with the demons, and the entire way
of the old person is being submerged in it.

Seeing What You Have Never Seen

24. When your soul has seen and taken pleasure in the destruction of those who hate you and you have gained confidence at the
death of your enemies, you shall turn around to look toward the
holy mountain of God and begin to walk where you have never
passed before into the spiritual world that is the spiritual way of
life [that] your journey becomes. From here you will become worthy to see these things above the world and to eat spiritual manna
that your fathers had not eaten, to drink sweet and pleasant water
that flows to you from "the rock [which is] Christ,"[31] to sit in the
cloud of light and the column of the Spirit will enlighten you to see
something that has not been seen by you and hear voices that have
not been heard by you, and by a daily journey to draw near to the
holy mountain of Zion where the Habitation[32] of hidden Existence
resides, to share in the knowledge of angels, and to sense the spiritual things above the world. Your clothing and your sandals shall
grow with your stature, that is, with the daily growth of your new
person the adornments of "your clothing which is Christ"[33] will be
revealed to you and also "your sandals that are the preparation of
the Gospel of peace"[34] will grow with you.

Participating in the Spiritual Mysteries

25. You will enter[35] into the spiritual mysteries **(289)** and participate in the fullness of the knowledge of Christ, while you are
bursting forth at all times with living movements and wonder is
seizing you concerning the majesty of the ineffable God, having

[31] 1 Cor 10:4.
[32] *Shekinta*—ܫܟܝܢܬܐ.
[33] Gal 3:27.
[34] Eph 6:15.
[35] Typographical error: written ܐܠܥܝܐ, read ܐܠܥܣܐ.

departed[36] from the entire visible world, and your dwelling is completely in the spiritual world. Just as you are only visible to those who see you by the shape of the outer part of the body, while all the movement of your hidden person dwells in the heaven of heavens, you will take delight in the places that have no limits and numbers, where there is no physical depiction or corporeal construction, where there is no change of natures and no course of elements, where there is only stillness and quiet, and all the spiritual inhabitants of the place call out the "holies" to the adorable Essence with voices not constructed; where you will taste something one cannot taste by the physical palate, and you will sense something that does not come to corporeal senses and you will know only that you are enjoying, but how you have enjoyed it you are not able to explain; where instead of your conversation with a human being, your conversation will be spiritually with Jesus Christ, while you are bearing the [ascetical] labors and not sensing their affliction, because the awareness of Christ does not allow you to sense your austerities, and your mind's rapture toward God will deprive you of all sensation of physical things. Wherever you see and hear and taste and smell by all the senses **(290)** of the inner person you will perceive the taste of the world of God. Just as [you taste] the natural world your senses will also taste it spiritually.

Tasting the Spiritual World

26. Wherever as with Moses face-to-face [these senses] share divine revelations with you, visions and wonders will receive you into the holy of holies that God—not human beings—has set up, and the hidden glory of God will live in your thoughts. [This is where] your way of life will be among the spiritual powers in the intelligence of the spirit. [This is] where the ark of spiritual signs and of divine knowledge is placed, not symbolically, but in the reality of a knowledge that encounters your knowledge without the mediation of anything. [This is] where there is no altar of gold erected and physical

---

[36] Budge text written: ܚܡܝܬ, "you have dived"; Lavenant reads variant: ܚܠܝ ܐܢܬ (Ms. B), "you have departed."

incense does not ascend from it, but [there is rather] another spiritual altar that receives the pure incense of all holy and rational thoughts. [This is] where no jar of manna as typically provided or food that you have been given by the mediation of angels is kept, but a living table will be constructed which is the person of Christ, so that all his spiritual members will take spiritual food from it like the members of the body. [This is] where no staff that is the sign of the election of Aaron is preserved as a record,[37] but it will be the person of the high priest, Jesus Christ, consecrating living and rational persons before his Father. [This is] where you have died[38] completely from the sensation of these visible things and do not obey anything spoken and sensed artificially, **(291)** while all the members of the old person are dead in you and you have put on the new person who is being made new by knowledge in the imitation of his creator.

Transition to the Spiritual World

27. So then, O disciple, dwell in this rule. Moving from the rule of the physical world, enter this place lawfully, work in it as the rule of the place requires, and do not bring with you into the place of life dead portions from the dead world. I say this because departure from the world is not so that you[39] might appear outwardly to depart from the world, but that you should strip off the world and its entire way of life—in outer deeds as well as in inner deeds—and become a complete stranger to all its memory. Just as one has cut off and cast away from himself physical rules, one should cut off and cast away from himself also dead thoughts that reflect on dead matters. Just as by nature the intellect is tied to the body, so also the intellect itself becomes [tied down] by its worries. When one reflects on the matters of the world, all [the intellect's] movement is dead, but if one's meditation is on matters of the spirit, it moves as if it were alive in living and spiritual matters. Take as a model your body's example concerning the spiritual intelligence in which your thoughts are moving. As long

---

[37] Num 17:2-6.

[38] ܐܬܛܒܥܬ —literally, "you have sunk. "

[39] Text written ܐܢܐ, "I"; context implies ܐܢ̱ܬ, "you."

as the body dwells in the physical world it is physical with all its activities and actions, but when the time has arrived to move on to the spiritual world, it is made new and becomes spiritual and then **(292)** enters the world of spiritual beings; so also as long as a thought dwells in the world, its meditation and attention in [the world] are physical and according to the nature of the world in which it dwells. But if its dwelling is going to be in that spiritual world, and it is stirred up in all its concerns as if [it were] in that place, then a thought will become spiritual according to the order of that place in which its movements circulate. Therefore, every disciple who has departed from the world needs to pursue this portion, because this is our inheritance and in this place is also our rule according to the teaching of Paul who said, "Our own rule is in heaven and from there we await our Life-Giver, our Lord Jesus Christ, who will change our lowly body in order to make it similar to his glorious body, according to his great power, by which all is subservient to him."[40]

Perfect Renunciation Necessary

28. But, as I have said, as long as a person is still trapped in the belly of the world, he is not aware of this way of life. Moreover, if he departs from the world in his outer actions but does not depart from it in his inner actions, he is not able to sense it, because this way of life is not experienced physically, but the mind experiences it spiritually when it is purified from physical thoughts and worries. Therefore, the beginning of this road, as I have said, is the end of the road of the world. Until a person completes that physical road, he will not travel on this spiritual [road]. But the end of the road of the world is this: **(293)** perfect renunciation of everything in the world—not renouncing one thing rather than another, and not letting go of one thing and seizing another—so that he may free and liberate his own members from all the physical things of the world that clutch a person to them.

There are some [people] who are seized in the world by all their members, and some who [are seized] by two parts of themselves,

[40] Phil 3:20-21.

and some one-half of whom is a servant and the other half is a free person. There are some for whom one part stands in freedom and two are in servitude, and there are some of whom a little bit is subservient and all the rest of his members are unleashed and let loose. There is one who is held and bound by only one of his members, and [even though] all of his members are moving, he is still [stuck] standing in his place. But whoever is tied down by one of his members, his whole person belongs to the world, similar to a bird whose claw only is caught in a snare, but its entire being is held down through its claw in that snare. Although its wings are loose from the bonds and it flaps and moves them in order to fly, yet the fastening and the binding on its claw does not allow it to elevate itself to the height of the serenity of air. It falls down at its place and flutters desperately against the earth, loading down its wings and its body completely with the weight of dust. In the same way also is a human being who while all his members are loosed from worldly bindings, he is tied down by one of them. That one by which he is tied down **(294)** ties down all of him, and while he may be bound [only] a little, the strong bindings are thrown completely over his entire person. From there, those who desire to be loosed from worldly ties should set loose their soul completely and take off and cast away the old clothing and put on the new [clothing] which is the way of Christ. Therefore, the clothing of the kingdom is this clothing and all the ornaments of excellent rules should be found in it. Whoever desires to change his clothing should take off [the old] completely and put on [the new] perfectly.

Emptying, Uprooting, Cutting Off

29. These comparisons are set before you as an example of what I am advising you, [so] from physical things understand these that are spiritual. Look, until whoever wishes to place something into a vessel empties it of whatever is in it, he cannot place into [that vessel] what he wants. But if these things are not compatible with one another,[41] that [substance] emptied from the vessel and that

---

[41] Mss. B & C omit here: ܐܦܢ, "even if."

[other substance] poured into it, he will wash and scour the vessel of the smell and taste of that first item, lest the pleasantness of the other taste poured into the vessel may be altered. Moreover, when a farmer wishes to sow into his land good seed and sees that there are thorns and thistles in it, he first uproots and weeds them and then casts the good seed into his field. **(295)** Again, whoever wishes to put on a new vestment first takes off the old one that is on his body and then puts on the new one. In the same way, a physician [treating] an ulcer wisely tries to take off the putrefaction that is on it through voracious and severe medicines and then places a compress [on it] that builds up new flesh. Many things such as these take place in nature, for unless the first things have been cut off and discarded, people are not able to bring other things, especially when these things are the opposite of one another. In the same way here the disciple of Christ also ought to act if he desires to draw near to the perfect way of Christ: to cut off and cast away from himself the entire way of the old world, and then to draw near to the new way of life and cast off ignorance and then put on spiritual knowledge.

True Knowledge

30. Because the matter of being tied down by these things that do not endure happens by means of ignorance, release from them happens by knowledge. Whoever takes off the world takes off ignorance. Whoever puts on the world puts on folly. True knowledge is this: when one does not err with something that does not exist by considering that it did exist. Ignorance is recognized by this: when one is entangled and considers something that does not abide as if it were in fact true. Then those who have put on **(296)** the world wear it as if it were something that endures. Appropriately, they are called ignorant since they mistake the shadow for reality.[42] Justly, those who become strangers from the world are named sages, for they have first taken off the outer vestment before [the world] sheds them. Whoever the world sheds gains no benefit for his achievement, because the

---

[42] Literally, "they mistake the shadow as if it were the body (ܦܓܪܐ)."

world itself has fled from him and has rejected and cast him away as if he were superfluous. Those who by their own good will become strangers from the world and depart outside of it so that it might not be a hindrance to their journey are worthy of blessing and praise.

Veil of Anxiety

31. Like a veil blocking vision, so is the anxiety of the world on the face of divine vision. Just as our vision is not able to look through and over dense bodies in front of it, or [through] a mountain or a building, or something else such as these, and until a person is [standing] above it or advances around it he is not able to see those things that are placed above it, so also our thought is not able to see those things that are outside of the world as long as the wall of the world is built in front of our vision and the heavy shadows and mountains and hills of its anxiety and its concerns pile up on us. But if someone wishes to see the spiritual way of life outside of the world, or to investigate these heavenly things that are above it, let him go outside **(297)** the world or ascend above it. Look, two things are evident to him: the spiritual way of life that consists in the movement of living thoughts and the kingdom of heaven which is above the world. When a person is freed from the passions of the world, it is as if his dwelling is [already] in the kingdom of heaven.

Sweetness of the Kingdom

32. What is the sweetness of the kingdom of heaven? Is it not the elimination of all adversities and the administering of all joys? And is it not, "The miseries and groans are unleashed and flee,"[43] as it is written? We take pleasure in different kinds of spiritual persons, in the pleasure and delicacies of blessings sealed and guarded, having no expectation of miseries, and neither fear nor terror of difficulties that shall come to pass, because that world [consists] entirely of joys, for at all times its inhabitants take pleasure in joys. Life is also

---

[43] Isa 51:11.

found in these things that are a steady joy and a constant pleasure for the soul that is free from passions and makes the shadows of illusions disappear from it. One of the spiritual teachers also correctly said, "The kingdom of heaven is the soul without passions with the knowledge of these things that are in truth,"[44] which are words and incorporeal movements. When the soul becomes free from the passions of evil things—from which are born fear and terror, anxiety and untrustworthiness—immediately [the soul] is filled up with hope and courage—that which is the opposite of these things—(298) and joy and blessedness of thoughts. By what could that one be deeply distressed who has cut off and cast away from himself all the causes of distress and of fear, or of what could he be afraid? Distress is that one might be deprived of the world and its comforts and its delicacies. Fear is that one might become a stranger from contemporary physical life. When a person sheds two things by the philosophy of Christ—the love of the world and the love of life—he will be freed from distress and fear, which are a Gehenna that tortures prior to the Gehenna to come and the judgment that is prepared. If freedom from passions is the kingdom of heaven, according to the word of that wise spiritual [teacher], then also the servitude of passions is a Gehenna that tortures, the outer darkness and the worm that gnaws at the heart and thoughts.

Pledges

33. The taste of two things is given here: the kingdom of thoughts is the sign of that kingdom to come, [and] the torturing Gehenna of fear and of distress is the pledge of that eternal Gehenna, because the pledge that is given in token of a thing has a relationship with what it is given for. Just as even in this world everything that is first given as a pledge for something [tangible] is related to that thing to which it is the pledge, so also the spiritual mysteries that here (299) have been delivered to us instead of a pledge have a

---

[44] *Evagrius Ponticus: The Greek Ascetic Corpus*, ch. 5, "The Monk: A Treatise on the Practical Life," trans. Robert E. Sinkewicz (New York: Oxford University Press, 2003), 97, n. 2.

great affinity with that true physical [nature] of Christ. We receive the body and blood of Christ here in order that we might have a pledge of what we will spiritually eat there of the person of Christ. We receive power and support from it as members of the body and by a spiritual transformation this pledge has an affinity with the person. It is in this way that the body and the blood are also called his own person.

Christ the First Fruit of Future Good

34. Moreover, we receive the Holy Spirit from baptism so that it might be for us the first fruit of perfect participation which we will come to have in the mysteries of the Spirit. For however much this pledge is related to that fulfillment, the name that is unique is witness since the two are called spirits by the word of Scripture. Moreover, it is written about Christ, "He became for us the first fruit of these good things to come."[45] We have an affinity with Christ as a first fruit, and with good things to come [that are the reality]: with us, because he became a human being; and with these things, for in the foreknowledge of the Father [these] things were prepared for us in advance because he is God, and with the Father [Christ] also prepares ahead for us by an unprecedented will these good things. Therefore, by this example there is an affinity of the joy born here of the freedom from passions to that future joy that will be given to those who are worthy (300) of it. Moreover, the Gehenna of distress and sadness born here by the carrying out of evil passions is related by affinity to that future Gehenna. So then, let us be diligent to take off the world, so that we might shed with it also the passions that spring up in us. Again, let us also take off the evil passions so that we might put on after them the living movements of joy and of love.

Example of John the Baptist

35. If you [really] want to know, O disciple, that you are not able to approach the way of perfection without departure from the

---

[45] Heb 9:11; 1 Cor 15:23.

world, learn this from those [words] inscribed in the Holy Books, and remember also the ways of spiritual people that are recorded in these Holy Books. Who among all the ancients was worthy of the exalted and admirable gift like John the Baptist, according to the testimony of Christ in which he said concerning him, "He is the greatest of all the prophets,"[46] and again he said, "Truly, I say to you, none among the children of women has arisen who is greater than John the Baptist"?[47] . . . Let us consider this remarkable man who has attained all of this greatness and see how and where was his way of life and why he was worthy of this whole gift, and by what education, and by how many labors, and after what asceticism, and how long he was separated from association with human beings. When we have seen and understood these things that are his, let us observe the greatness **(301)** of things that apply to him. Let us consider first what belongs to the will and then after them what belongs to grace, because until the will shows its fruits, the Spirit will not grant its gifts.

Therefore, look at the way of life of this remarkable man who while he was still young was separated from dwelling in the world and from association with human beings. He was neither defiled nor impure, and then he was washed and cleansed, but he left childhood being pure before attaining the natural movements that distinguish good things from evil things. He was raised up in the desert, no concerns of the world being in him at all. He had not tasted and thrown up the evilness of people through experience, nor was he troubled at first by lusts and passions, and [only] then had come to quiet thoughts through the labors of his freedom. Because such is the case that before one who would live in this way of life might receive the taste of evil things of the world, he should move away from his vices—it is not a little helpful for the clarity of the soul for those who are worthy of it—just as he might live a little while in the purity of the soul of Adam before he transgressed against the commandment. Because John had come to be

[46] Matt 11:9.
[47] Matt 11:11.

designated for the service of the divine mysteries, and had come to attain the gift that has not been given to human beings, it was appropriate that he was separated from his childhood and had gone out into the desert. For while he did not experience evil things and his mind did not receive the impression of the image of physical memories, and neither was he disturbed nor disquieted by the concerns and anxiety of the world, he would receive through the clarity of his soul spiritual revelations and teachings of divine mysteries and sense something that the entire family **(302)** of mortals does not attain.

On account of this he had also received the Holy Spirit while he was in the womb of his mother so that his soul's thoughts might be stirred spiritually by the urgency of the Spirit, because it was not right that he should be born without intercourse, since this was [the way] of Jesus only, who is God. However, he would come to receive visions and revelations much higher than the old nature, receiving the Spirit while he was in the womb after he was conceived by intercourse. It would have been easy to create him in a new way as [God did] for Adam and Eve, of this there is no doubt. But if that had been the case he would have become a stranger to the old [way of] creation. The Maker was not willing to do this lest it be thought that he was rejecting the first [way of] creation, and that he would be conceived from the same old nature without intercourse, which I have [already] said, was appropriate for Christ only. Moreover, while he was being raised in the world and experiencing its vices he would be worthy at once of the grace that is above the world, by a choice similar to that of the apostles that would come to be given after the cross when the old nature had died and sin and all the evil passions had died with it. But because John would come to be worthy of the knowledge of the apostles before the abolition of the curse and the ceasing of sin and the reality of the cross, it was appropriate that he should also receive the Spirit from the womb and should grow up outside of the world, in order that by these means **(303)** he should obtain the natural clarity of the first human being before he transgressed against the commandment, and by this clarity of soul he should receive knowledge of divine mysteries.

Old Ways Cease

36. Wherever these marvelous things used to happen by grace, they did so by these signs and means.[48] But wherever this salvation is being perfected by the profundity of the love of the ineffable God, it is the person of God himself [who] with power exists in the middle like a free person and with his own hand makes old ways cease and begins new ways. The old man is dead by the cross,[49] according to what was written by Paul, "Our old person was crucified with him,"[50] and the new person has been revealed and made known and visible, not only in the case of whoever is worthy of dwelling [in] paradise according to the model of the first Adam, but whoever is suitable to dwell also in heaven and live among the spiritual [beings] and be like them in everything. Then, after this, grace suddenly seizes the people who are experienced in all evil things, [as well as] tax collectors, adulterers, murderers and thieves, and worshipers of creatures: without means and preparations [grace] makes them worthy of the wealth of its mysteries, and as in a new nature it works in any one that it desires because "the old person has been crucified" and is dead, according to the word of Paul. Moreover, the Apostle himself spoke on behalf of the entire human nature, "Wretched person am I! Who shall rescue me[51] from this body of death?"[52] After he had spoken rhetorically—Who is able[53] to save him?—(304) he revealed while confessing and teaching by his word who is that one who had rescued him from the old and mortal nature. "I confess God through our Lord Jesus Christ who saved me from this body of death."[54] Therefore, after these things have been made known to us—by which the death, rejection, abolition, and dissipation of the

---

[48] Ms. C omits: ܚܫܐ, "passions."

[49] Typographical error: written *bazqīqā*, ܒܙܩܝܩܐ, read *bazqīpā*, ܒܙܩܝܦܐ, "by the cross."

[50] Rom 6:6.

[51] Instead of the written text, ܢܦܨܝܢ, "will save us," Lavenant adopts the variant, ܢܦܨܝܢܝ, "will save me" (Ms. A).

[52] Rom 7:24.

[53] Typographical error: written *mešpaḥ*, ܡܫܦܚ, read *mēškaḥ*, ܡܫܟܚ, "able."

[54] Rom 7:25.

old person take place, and the resurrection and the renewal and the appearance and revelation of the new person [occur]—grace performs authoritatively all works and all powers in anyone whom it desires, and all knowledge and all mysteries and revelations and the entire spiritual economy and the work that is above nature.

Exhortation to Follow John the Baptist

37. We have spoken briefly in order to show the reason for the departure of John the preacher into the desert, why he had received the Spirit from the womb, and why he was reared from his childhood in the desert. But you, O disciple, be diligent in the hearing of these things, take off the world, draw near to the freedom of the pure way of life, love continual conversation with God, and flee urgently from all human talk. See the virtues of this way of life by what had happened with John the Baptist. If the way of solitude, freedom, and estrangement from the world were able to give to John the Baptist apostolic knowledge and through these things he existed with a wisdom higher than human nature long before the cross through which the old ways were abolished and done away with and the new things had appeared, how **(305)** much more now will this spiritual way of life establish you in the knowledge of the mysteries of Christ and give you ineffable pleasure through the sensation of spiritual revelations? Receive it then as proof for the way of life of this righteous [person], and learn also from it that a person may not become a perfect disciple of Christ unless he has become a stranger from the entire world by the example of this upright person.

Serve Only One Thing

38. As the word of Christ has clearly taught us, "Unless a person renounces the whole world, his brothers and his relatives and his family, and his father and his mother, and everything that he possesses, and that which is greater than all of these, his own life, he is not able to become my disciple."[55] Moreover, in another passage,

[55] Luke 14:26.

to one who wishes to serve two things at the same time—honor toward parents and his own discipleship—he inhibited him from this and told him that it is not possible for two opposing things to exist together. "Teacher, allow me to go bury my father and my mother and I will follow you,"[56] that is to say, I will keep the first law that commands me to "honor and obey your parents," and then I will follow you and serve you. And what did Jesus respond against this? "Leave the dead to bury their dead and you, go proclaim the kingdom of God."[57] It is not **(306)** necessary for you to keep the law, because it was kept and dispensed; also [it is not necessary] for you to serve [your] natural parents, because I[58] have obeyed and have served physical parents on behalf of all. So then, the yoke of the law and of nature was taken from you and you have been left a free person by yourself, there being no coercion from the world that subjugates you, because the world is dead to you and you to it. Corpses are not ministered to but only are enshrouded and buried. Leave then the dead to bury their dead, and you, go proclaim the kingdom of God. Look, we also have learned from this testimony that whoever becomes a disciple of Jesus does not even have the authority to serve natural parents, because he has a genuine father who by his grace has enrolled him [as] a son and has set him apart for the service of his wishes.

Plowing Straight

39. Listen to another example that also presents to you instruction like this, and by the type of this testimony urges you to become a stranger to everything and follow Jesus. "One of his disciples approached him and said to Jesus, 'Allow me to go complete the affairs of my house, and [then] I will follow you.' "[59] Listen here to what the teacher responds to the disciple, and receive it as if it were spoken to you through that disciple. "No one laying his hand

---

[56] Luke 9:59.
[57] Luke 9:60.
[58] Budge's text written: ܐܠܐ, "but"; read variant: ܐܢܐ, "I" (Mss. A & B).
[59] Luke 9:61.

upon the plow and looking behind him is useful for the kingdom of God."[60] Whoever carries out this natural labor and drives a yoke of oxen according to human **(307)** custom does not cease to look before him and [does not] look behind him, because in this manner the tillage would not be completed and he would not be able to walk straight ahead, and his furrows would not be cut in a straight line and the oxen would not move straight ahead. Although one is able to see that the labor is physical and is occurring in this same place only, if [the farmer] looks behind him his tillage will be crooked. But here with regard to my discipleship, one labor is different from another, just as one world is different from another and one life from another, and immortals from mortals, and God from human beings. Therefore, if you have taken the yoke of my discipleship on your soul and on your body, you should complete the work of my commandments. Do not turn back to the world, and do not let yourself be concerned about this so that you make peace with your families, and do not be anxious to pay them the debt of physical honor and fulfill the law of the perfection of the world, and [only] then shall you follow me. If you have paid the alms of the world, mine are not being paid. If you are anxious not to make trouble for the world in something, then you have set yourself up to anger me.

Do not allow yourself to be at peace with the world, so that in this way true peace with me may be yours. You will have no house or household servants, why do you rush to greet them? Hostility is set between you and them, why are you anxious to become their friend? "I have not come to establish peace on earth."[61] Why **(308)** are you rushing to be at peace with those who are of the earth? I am calling for a sword and you are rushing to peace? I am proclaiming division and you are rushing to press for reconciliation? "I have come to divide a man against his father and a daughter against her mother and a bride against her mother-in-law,"[62] and you are rushing to greet the members of your house and to patch together

---

[60] Luke 9:62.
[61] Matt 10:34.
[62] Matt 10:35.

the division I have made in the world by your foolishness? I have torn apart this coat of agreement, because it was woven completely by mistake, and in place of it I have woven another garment of heavenly peace, [so] you should also weave this garment and not rush to patch together the old garment. I have brought to an end the peace that was nurturing vices in every person, and I have dispersed that fellowship which was gathering for the accumulation of sins. Do not rush to become a neighbor of those who commit iniquity. "I am going to greet the members of my household," he said to him. Do not greet them. "Do not greet anyone on the road."[63] This is also the sense of this saying by which Christ has alienated his disciples from greeting the world. These things were spoken in the person of one disciple to everyone, that is, to those who were professing discipleship, because it is expedient in order that one might not become a disciple of God in name, but in truth [a disciple] of the world, and to hire out [himself] with one, but to labor with the other.

Outer and Inner Renunciation

40. The world is not required to attain perfection, because neither its dress **(309)** nor its way of life professes perfection. On the other hand, the disciple, by the signs of his dress, proclaims perfection about himself and through these things by which he is outwardly visible to people he personally confesses in order to be inwardly visible to God. The signs of discipleship inscribed on you from the outside urge you so that all the virtues might be written in your soul, because in the manner that you are visible to people by your outer actions, you are required to be visible to God in your inner actions. You have shed the glamour of worldly clothes. Shed also inwardly the love of glamour from your soul. You are far from actual marriage. Distance yourself also from the hidden desire of thoughts. You are abstinent from eating meat and from ease and visible rewards. Become an abstainer in your soul, even from the

---

[63] Luke 10:4.

will that desires these foods. You have taken off from your head
the hair of the secular life of the world. This is a demonstration so
that you might not be entangled by its glamour, nor tied down by
its worries, nor seized by one of its numerous and innumerable
passions. You have departed from the world and have become a
stranger to it through outer appearance. Depart from [the world]
and become a stranger to it also in your hidden thoughts. You
have renounced the outer appearance of wealth. Become one who
also renounces the love of wealth in the inner mind. You have rejected the songs and worldly pleasures. Take delight assiduously
with all **(310)** of your soul in the voices of the spiritual songs of
God. May your discipleship be known more from the inside than
the outside. Just as people discern whether you are a disciple of
Christ by your outward actions, so also may Christ know you by
your inner actions that you are his disciple. Take care lest your
discipleship become for you a business craft. Do not put on the
disciple's honorable garment for the sake of vainglory and passing
comforts. Do not buy physical things with spiritual things, and do
not exchange heavenly things for the corrupting treasures being
placed on the earth. Become a disciple to him alone to whom you
have pledged your life. He taught you first and brought to your
attention this suspect delusion, [saying], "A servant is not able to
serve two masters."[64]

Finish Building Your Tower

41. Through another testimony he further warns you that if you
are not going to become a perfect disciple, you should remain in
the way of life of the world. It would be better for you so that you
would not be laughed at by everyone when you have begun to
build but are not finishing. "Who is the person who begins to build
a tower and does not sit down at first to calculate his expenses,
whether he has [enough] for its completion, lest when he has begun
to build and cannot finish, everyone who passes by and sees him
will mock and laugh at him—'this is the man who began, but was

[64] Luke 16:13.

not able to complete.' Who is the king who goes to battle to fight (311) with his neighboring king, and meets with ten thousand that one who comes with twenty thousand against him, that he does not send messengers and seek a peace if he is not able to meet in battle the multitude of his forces."[65] Look, by these things he who has called you to his discipleship has taught you not to begin on this road unless you are set to complete it, and do not lay foundations to build a tower if you have no intention to finish it, and do not go out to battle against Satan unless you have gathered the forces of powerful thoughts, lest when you go out to battle the enemy might defeat you and [your] discipleship will be reviled. Whoever does not promise is not required by the word of uprightness to do those things that he has not promised. Until the promise, it is [of his own] volition. But from the promise and beyond, it is the law. Because as long as the yoke of promise is not placed upon your soul's freedom, your service is voluntary. But if you receive the sign of discipleship and the promise of the covenant with Christ, then your way of life is not voluntary but is as the law requires that has been established by you by your own will. If while you are in the world you are doing [what is appropriate] for a disciple, this is to your credit. But if in this state of discipleship you perform those things fitting for it, by this you are paying an obligation and are completing whatever is imposed on you. Notice where the tower is going up and with which stones and materials (312) its building is being constructed, then you will be laying its foundation. Do not start on a building that will become for you a laughingstock by those who see it. Do not establish for yourself a sign of despicableness and mockery before the observation of many people. Do not give passersby a reason to speak against you. If you have set yourself to become a disciple, [do so] according to what the will of your teacher requires, and if not, remain in the world. Do not press to be honored by a name of which you are not worthy. Do not grasp the pure pearl with dirty hands nor put on the purple [robes] of discipleship while you do not possess the knowledge that maintains them. Consider in your

[65] Luke 14:28-32.

soul those things that the state of discipleship requires you to do and then place its yoke upon yourself.

Renunciation for Profit

42. Many people become disciples so that they might be honored by the name of Christ, and not to honor Christ himself. They hire on with him in order to have physical comforts, and not to bear the austerities of his commandments. Others on account of the desire of mammon draw near to this way of life that requires renunciation so that whatever they are not able to acquire from the world they may depart to acquire outside of the world. Through that one dissolute disciple of whom it was written in the gospel of our Savior, Jesus reproved this iniquitous thought along with all the related ones. "A certain person came and approached and said to him, 'My teacher, I will follow you wherever you are going.' Jesus said to him, 'Foxes have holes and the bird of heaven has a shelter, but there is nowhere for the Son of Man to lay down his head.' "[66] Get away from me, you disciple of iniquity. I am not able to give **(313)** you what you have desired, and whatever I will give, you will not wish to receive. I know what your will is asking, and what you are desiring I will not give. You have chosen to follow me in love with the thought of wealth. You have departed to seek darkness in light, and poverty in true possession, and death in life. These things that I am commanding everyone to leave behind and cling to me, you have desired to acquire by your coming with me. Through the door by which I wish to make you go out, through that same [door] you have pushed to enter with me. Therefore, I do not receive you. By my outer condition I am poor and on account of this I do not have any outer things to give in the world to which I have come. I am seen as a stranger, for I have neither a house nor a roof, and whoever desires to become my disciple will inherit poverty from me. Why have you desired to obtain from me that thing whose possession I have made you renounce?

[66] Matt 8:20; Luke 9:58.

Renunciation as a Profession

43. Therefore, because many with thoughts of the love of mammon are following Jesus and put on the honorable dress of his discipleship as if it were for a profession, he anticipated this false thought, uncovering it by his word, and through that one person he reproved all the disciples of falsehood and held them back from his discipleship, saying, "[I] do not own [anything], but I will give you what you are desiring, since I do not have even **(314)** a house or a roof." But he impeded those who begin and become slothful and lax, whether by the love of comforts or by the travail of construction, saying, "If you have the resources sufficient for the tower, [begin]; but if not, it would be better that you do not start than that you would start and not finish." Jesus showed us here that he required perfection of all the disciples who follow him, because this tower that takes [one] up to heaven is completed by perfection and is perfected by the gathering of all the virtues. Jesus said, begin if you can finish it, otherwise do not begin it, that is to say, if [so], become a perfect disciple who is accomplished in all exploits, and if not, remain in the world and serve through that other righteousness of uprightness that is lower than the spiritual life.

Therefore, he impeded every one of these who did not seek properly by a response appropriate for them. He spoke to that one who through compassion did [not] want to trouble his family and desired to repay to them a human love, and had asked [Jesus] that he might go say farewell to his relatives and [then] follow him, "A person does not lay his hand upon the plow and look behind him and be useful for the kingdom of God."[67] He said to that one who was seeking to honor [his] physical parents as long as they were alive, and then become a disciple after their death, "Leave the dead to bury their dead."[68] He responded to another who by the perfection of Christ's own teaching had desired to fulfill the desire of his injustice, **(315)** "Who has raised me up over you as a

---

[67] Luke 9:62.
[68] Luke 9:60.

judge and arbiter?"[69] He said to another who by [Jesus'] name was desiring to accumulate wealth and by the powers and signs and miracles he was performing by his authority he was devising to become a master of possessions, "I am poor and there is no place for me to lay down my head." He said to another who was seeking to draw near to this ministry through the skin of outer appearance only, "Do not begin on this tower if you do not have the resources to finish it." Again he said to another, who being weak and lacking strength and not yet having authority over the purity of thoughts and the clarity of soul, had wished to battle with opposing powers, "There is no king who goes out to battle against his neighboring king, unless he gathers together forces that are adequate to meet the enemy that is opposing him."

Being Held Down by the World

44. Through these [words], therefore, Jesus had reproved all sickly thoughts and had made the disciple take hold of the true health of discipleship and the very body of the spiritual way of life. If one is not able to complete worldly things correctly unless one has emptied himself of the work of other things and has occupied himself only with the work that he wishes to do, how much more is one not able **(316)** to complete this spiritual work, unless he has emptied himself of the service of everything visible? Just as the blessed Paul said, "Everyone who wrestles holds back his mind from everything [else]."[70] About which struggle was he speaking, except this physical athleticism of the world, and if the service of physical things is the opposite of that physical struggle, how much more shall it be against the spiritual struggle? Concerning the struggle of the world, the struggle and its battle and its victory, as well as the things that inhibit its triumph, are one in nature and inhabitants of one place, even though these things are totally linked to one another, the world by its anxiety and its concerns is the opponent of those who engage in the struggle. Here, therefore,

[69] Luke 12:14; see Acts 7:27.
[70] 1 Cor 9:25.

the struggle is spiritual, and the labor and way of life are above the world. How is a person able to complete it if he is entangled and held down by worldly matters? Again, Paul himself said, "No one is a soldier and is tied down by worldly things and is able to please the one who has chosen him, and if he does not fight according to his law, he will not be crowned."[71]

Consequently, if soldiers of a worldly kingdom renounce everything in order to learn the crafts of their work, and through this please the king who has chosen them, which disciple who has been chosen for this **(317)** spiritual ministry is able to become a master in it while being tied down by worldly things?

Leaving Everything

45. But again let us see by the word of Simeon to our Lord, and learn from that first disciple how we should become disciples. "Look, we have left everything and have followed you, what now shall become of us?"[72] Did you hear what this disciple has said? How the truth of their perfect renunciation is revealed to you and that they did not possess anything besides Jesus? We have left everything and are following you: see, [this is] the defining law of discipleship. They have not rejected one thing and not another, nor have they left behind one thing and have held on to another, but they have left everything and followed Jesus. May you leave everything and follow him and see that at once the strength of the apostles will clothe you. Try [it] in fact and understand that the word is not false. Do not demand that he make you worthy of the vision of his hidden and spiritual riches while you have not yet renounced everything visible. For as long as you hold on to what is yours, he will not show you what is his. Give everything that you have for his love only, being careful by your giving of the thought that seeks human glory. Go out to travel a little on the road, while bearing the sufferings and travails with the purity of your thoughts. See how as soon as his glory shines in your soul, he will blend you

---

[71] 2 Tim 2:4-5.
[72] Matt 19:27.

spiritually into it so that you may be absorbed completely in his love and forget the weight of your own sufferings, and suddenly he will make you one thing instead of another, that is to say, from the old [he will make you] new.

Being an Old Vessel

46. If not, what **(318)** do you desire? When your purse is full, perhaps you might also come to demand interests and benefits and withhold what is yours and eat by his grace, do you [really] desire to become his disciple and that he give you authority over the treasures of his wealth? [God] forbid that he establish the knowledge of his revelations in a soul that is not worthy of it. Look, if those who are captivated by commerce and by the concerns of human wealth are inhibited from worldly knowledge by many things, do you want to acquire spiritual knowledge together with the concerns of wealth? Did you want to pour out the new wine of the wisdom of his mysteries into the old vessel of yourself punctured by passions and lust, and not spill this knowledge upon the ground if it is poured into you? That means, your old vessel was not even able to receive it. Our Savior previously showed this through his luminous instruction: "No one places new wine into old wineskins lest the wine bursts the skins and the wine is spilled and the skins are destroyed; but the new wine is placed into new skins and both of them are preserved."[73] As long as sin, in deed or in thought, is alive and being performed in you, and physical anxiety rises up from the world in you, you are still an old vessel and are not able to receive the new wine of the wisdom of Christ. Therefore, make yourself new by shedding your passions, and at once you will be capable of taking hold within yourself of the new wine of the instruction of Christ. Leave everything, just as the apostles had left [everything], and then seek **(319)** openly to have authority over the treasures of the spirit.

[73] Matt 9:17; Mark 2:22; Luke 5:27.

Looking Forward and Backward

47. Do not turn behind you, for look, the furrows are straight in front of you. You have placed your hand upon the plow of tilling the difficult and arduous commandments. Do not turn back toward the sight of pleasures. If you have renounced, do not claim again what you have renounced. Even more, do not look sometimes in front of you and sometimes behind you, for there should be for you only one correct perspective straight in front of you. Whoever looks behind and in front of himself resembles one who comes and goes and walks and circles around the same place yet does not move from the spot on which he is standing. No one can say whether he is [still] walking on the road or [about to] complete the path with his steps.

So also is the disciple who sometimes is looking forward and sometimes is turning backward; sometimes he is full of passions and at another time [is full of] mockery; and sometimes he purifies his thoughts and another time they are filthy with iniquitous ideas. Sometimes he bears the weight of austerities and sometimes enjoys pleasures. Sometimes [he is engaged] with much fasting and sometimes with inordinate eating. Sometimes with a prayerful conversation, and sometimes with speech that produces nonsense. Sometimes the memory of God is in him, and sometimes his soul dies from its remembrance. Sometimes he is desirous to shed his pleasures[74] and be with Christ, and sometimes he clothes himself with physical pleasures enjoyable to him. Sometimes all of his thought is spiritually stirred, and sometimes it is agitated by empty worries. Sometimes he is full of wonder at God, **(320)** and sometimes his mind is clouded by physical worry. Sometimes he purifies his thought from a stirring of desire, and sometimes also an act of adultery is enflamed. Sometimes he fasts without measure, and sometimes he eats without control. Sometimes he disperses his possessions out of the love of God, and sometimes he is seized by anxiety over his dispersal. Sometimes he is full of

---

[74] Lemoine reads variant Ms. A: ܢܣܘܗܝ, "his pleasures," instead of ܢܚܘܗܝ, "his life."

the love of people, and sometimes he is tortured because he is not able to avenge himself against his enemies. Sometimes the light of knowledge shines in him, and sometimes his thought is darkened by the world's error. Sometimes he travels forward, and sometimes he walks backward. Sometimes he is united completely with the Spirit, sometimes completely with the body.

Do Not Look Back

48. Therefore, if a person goes and comes, travels and turns around, walks and returns, ascends and descends, becomes thin and becomes fat, is cleansed and is defiled, is shining and is soiled, is purified and is defiled, is modest and is extravagant, renouncing and coveting, denying and affirming, ascetic and desiring—by such things as these the way of discipleship is not completed. But whoever lives by these things stays put on his place and does not move forward from the place on which he stands, and because of this he also does not reach whatever he is pursuing. How does one attain [it] while he is not running [toward it]? Therefore, if this one who has set out to go and travel and walk forward has spent half of his life, so to speak, in the way of discipleship because he has worked in both of them, he will not be **(321)** able to commit himself to either one. Whoever has not sought the good at all, except in name, how shall he find it? Whoever has not experienced, even for a little while, the passion of the love of Christ, how will he attain the ultimate [level] of love? If whoever has been walking like the living has been found dead, what will come from a truly dead [person]? So then, [if] you are following Jesus, walk behind him and do not turn back behind you.

Remember the wife of Lot: because the love of her people and the sound of the howls of her friends had forced her to turn around and look behind her she became a pillar of salt, as it was written concerning her.[75] Because her soul did not become salty by fear of the Most High, she became a [pillar of] corruptible salt. Remember then this woman who was divided in her mind and perished, so

---

[75] Gen 19:26.

do not become divided like her and do not turn around behind you lest you remain on your spot. It will be this way for you, if not in your body, at least in your soul. Whoever turns around and looks behind himself after he has departed on the journey of this road, his soul will become an unfeeling pillar. Just as the wife of Lot had ceased bodily sensation and so became a pillar of salt, so also here the thought that always looks back at corruptible things will cease and be numb to the sensation of spiritual things, because the memory of the world acquires for us the dullness of the heart and soils the clarity and purity **(322)** of the soul, and this physical worry will obscure and darken the pure gaze that renders the mind [capable of] constant vision toward God. If a thought about physical things deprives us of the vision of spiritual things, how much more shall their real possession deprive us? If while we are observing these things in the hands of others they tie us to them, how much more shall they tie us down when[76] they are found in our hands? Therefore, depart from the world, O disciple, by that example in which the apostles had departed, in deed and not [just] in name; by [one's own] thought and not by pretense; by will and not by outer appearance; by desire and not by chance; by discernment and not by tradition; by freedom and not by law. Daily make the desire of this spiritual way of life new in yourself. Taste life while making everything mortal die from you.

Crossing the Fearful Place

49. Find the courage and cross over this fearful place that is placed in the middle, for it is fearful and deep. It is a deep precipice full of evil animals and a harmful and deadly serpent. If you have set your mind to cross over this fearful place, and your will is fully prepared, you will immediately receive grace and it will be your companion. Do you not see that the soul and body are attached to one another and united with each other naturally? But there is a great space **(323)** in their midst and it is a fearful depth that no one is able to explore

---

[76] Lavenant reads variant Ms. A: ܪܡ, "when," instead of written text ܪܡܐ, "how much."

and cross over. If you have afflicted the body in its desires, while suffering and prayer and compassion are accompanying you, you are able to cross over this fearful place. However, since our discourse now is about departure from the world, and not about departure from particular passions, concerning this let us only say, "We have left everything and followed you."[77] Look, receive continually in the memory of your soul the saying that is the common teaching for all disciples. At the beginning of your discipleship may it be your meditation, and by the memory of its exhortation depart from the world. When you are journeying on the road of departure, may it be in your company. Reflect on it at all times, and if something of wealth is pestering to stay with you, or the love of friends or of family ties you to it, remember the word of Simeon. "He left everything" and you also should leave everything like him.

Closer to Jesus

50. Jesus is as close to you as he was to Simeon, and perhaps even closer than him when he had spoken this word, because [the apostles] had not yet received the power to be united spiritually with the love of Jesus. But in the clarity of their faith they pursued the sight of his works and the sweetness of his word. When he made them cling to him by the word, they clung to him in true earnestness. For the word was this one: **(324)** "Follow me." Once they had heard the word they began in earnest. But today your attachment to Jesus is in earnest, because he has integrated you into his spiritual life by baptism. While he was attracting the apostles to himself during that time by the word, in effect he has united you today in himself because he has made you his spiritual member by baptism. As long as you cling to him by your works, his work will precede you. If you run to him, he will have inhabited you first. If you go to him with discernment, he will have come to you first. As long as you are diligent and run, your love and your labor will surpass the apostles—which is not possible—you are below them in many things and are not attaining the level of the union of their

[77] Matt 19:27.

love with Jesus—however, even though your works do not attain [this level], by his grace he will make you attain [this level].

Same Teacher as Simeon

51. The love of the apostles was marvelous, for during the time in which the Holy Spirit had not yet been mingled with their nature, they accompanied Jesus with total fervor. He did not soothe or cajole them—as he flatters you today by all [kinds of] persuasions—but while he was speaking with them condescendingly, it seems as if he were openly driving them away from him. If you wish to go, go, he was saying to them[78] at that time, for by the harshness of his word many had left him and moved away. Simeon said to him, "To whom are we going?[79] Once [and for all] we have followed you, and after you **(325)** we have nowhere to go, for you have the words of eternal life."[80] That is, your words are life, and how shall we abandon life and follow death? For we have left everything and have followed you, because we believe and know that you are the Christ, the son of the living God.[81] Therefore, you also, O disciple, if you believe as Simeon believed, depart just as Simeon departed. Leave everything and follow your wealthy teacher, for he does not lack anything so that you would need to take provisions of wealth from [some other] place. His wealth is not measurable so that you would need to supplement it from the abundance of your wealth so that it may not be insufficient. On account of this, you should endeavor to leave everything, for everything which he will give to you is his, as he had promised to you through Simeon. Look, did Simeon become a disciple of one teacher and you of another, so that you do not have to follow your teacher as he followed? But if you do not depart like him, it is evident that you have become the disciple of another teacher, no matter how much you may imagine about yourself that you are the disciple of Jesus.

[78] John 6:67.
[79] John 6:68.
[80] John 6:68.
[81] John 6:69.

The Reward of Leaving the World

52. In that same passage, two things are recorded for you—the manner of your departure and the reward of your departure. You can learn how you should depart from this [world]: "Look, we have left everything and followed you."[82] But the word of our Lord shows you what is the reward of this departure. "Truly, I say to you, in the new world when the Son of Man sits **(326)** on the throne of his glory, you also will be seated on twelve thrones and judge the twelve tribes of Israel."[83] See, here is the reward of departure: participation with Jesus in the highest honor. He has established the thrones opposite his throne for the disciples, and whatever is not naturally possible, he has shown by his word that it exists. He had promised to honor the disciples who have loved his word not as servants or as subjects but made them worthy of the majesty of the thrones as friends and peers of his honor. This is the marvel of ineffable love.

Concerning angels it is written: "A thousand thousands stand before him and a myriad of myriads are serving him."[84] Concerning the seraphim: they are standing above him and flying and calling out to one another, saying, "Holy, Holy, Holy."[85] Concerning the cherubim, moreover, it is written that they were yoked onto a chariot, and while their faces look downward, the movements of their spiritual [natures] are looking up to meet the Most High, trumpeting, "Blessed be the glory of the Lord from its place."[86] Those who are spiritual function in this ministry, and soldiers and heavenly orders are made obedient to the word of Jesus, as Paul said, "The ministering spirits are those that are sent to serve for the sake of those who shall come to inherit life."[87] Concerning the apostles it was written that they shall sit on the thrones. Through this Paul had indicated to us the majesty of the honor and equality with

---

[82] Matt 19:27.
[83] Matt 19:28; Luke 22:30.
[84] Dan 7:10.
[85] Isa 6:3.
[86] Ezek 3:12.
[87] Heb 1:14.

[Jesus] in inheritance **(327)** as he said, "If we suffer with him, we will also be glorified with him."[88] Again he said, "The heirs of God and the sons of the inheritance of Jesus Christ."[89] Again he said, "If we endure, we will also rule with him."[90] He said again, "He will change the body of our lowly [estate] and make it like his glorious body according to his great power by which everything has been submitted to him."[91] Therefore, the disciple will attain this majesty if he travels precisely in the footsteps of his teacher. Lest you think that this portion of honor was achieved only by the apostles, Paul said, "If we suffer with him, we shall also be glorified with him," and, "If we endure, we shall also rule with him." Our Lord himself said to the apostles, "Not only you, but everyone who leaves homes or family or brothers and sisters or parents or children on account of me and on account of my Gospel shall receive in this world one hundred fold and eternal life in the world to come."[92]

Exchanging Poverty for Wealth

53. Who is so asleep that he does not awaken to the sounds of these promises? Who is so dead that he does not come alive by this breath of spiritual life? Who does not quicken his pace at the indication of this road that ascends to heaven? Who does not desire to be despised and dishonored at the hearing of this unequaled promise? Who does not renounce the whole world, **(328)** even if by chance he has acquired [the world], in order to be seated next to God on a throne? Who is not desirous to exchange these temporary things for these eternal things? Even if these things we have been leaving behind were equal with these things being given to us, we should leave them behind because God has commanded.

But leave aside the fact that they are rejected and despised things, and without our abandoning them on account of the word of Christ,

[88] Rom 8:17.
[89] Rom 8:17.
[90] 2 Tim 2:12.
[91] Phil 3:21.
[92] Matt 19:29.

we can naturally become strangers from them and become aloof to them, and those things that are totally useless do we not exchange for something [useful]? Who does not run to the market in which there is such an exchange? Look, rags are exchanged for purple [robes] and mean little pebbles for pearls, and ordinary stones for gems of beryl; poverty without end for a wealth that has no measure, and false rejected [gold] for true gold; darkness for light, death for life, and bitter for sweet; illness for health, despicableness for authority, and ordinariness for superiority; these things that are corrupted for those that are above corruption, and whatever passes away for something that does not pass away; shadows for the body, hunger for being satisfied, error for knowledge, and the way of animals for the way of angels; the physical state for the spiritual state and endless misery for limitless blessedness.

Even more than this, if we could speak about these things as they deserve, **(329)** who will not exchange these things for these others, and who will not give away all this poverty for all this fullness?[93] Because the spiritual word, even while spoken plainly, is more exalted than all the world's wisdom. Paul has revealed to us by one short phrase the greatness of this exchange, and by a short phrase he points out to us how much lower is ours, and how much greater the things of God. "Those visible things are temporary, but those that are unseen are eternal."[94] Who then does not exchange these temporary things for these eternal things, except us and fools like us?

Renouncing Completely

54. As for you who have renounced visible things, do not ask what sort of wealth you are going to receive in exchange for your poverty. But with regard to this, endeavor to leave your poverty and run to the acquisition of [this wealth]. Of what sort is it and to what is it similar? Paul explains to you not what kind it is since

[93] Lemoine reads the variant from Ms. B: *malyūtā*, ܡܠܝܘܬܐ, "fullness"; instead of *malkūtā*, ܡܠܟܘܬܐ, "kingdom."

[94] 2 Cor 4:18.

nothing is similar to it, nor how much it is since it is immeasurable. "Something that the eye has not seen, and the ear has not heard, and that has not ascended upon the heart of a person, [is] what God has prepared for those who love him."[95] The greatness of the rewards is revealed by these [words] and such like them. Listen to the divine voices urging you concerning the departure after Jesus so that you might become **(330)** one who renounces completely and then becomes a perfect disciple. "Whoever does not renounce everything that he has is not able to become my disciple."[96] After this, what is there for you to say or to reply? For look, with one word all [your] imaginings and your riddles are abolished. The word of truth is the higher path on which you should journey. Moreover, in another passage he said, "Whoever does not leave everything that he has and take up his cross and follow me is not able to become my disciple."[97] When he teaches further that we should leave behind not only our possessions for the sake of his glory and renounce the world for the sake of profession in him, but also our transitory life, he said, "Unless a person renounces himself, he is not able to become my disciple."[98] Again he said, "Whoever wishes to save his soul will lose it. And whoever would lose his soul for my sake, this one will save [his soul]."[99] Moreover, he said, "Whoever loses his soul, this one shall keep life eternal, and whoever serves me the Father will honor him."[100]

Let Us Go from Here

55. Again he said to his disciples, "Stand up, let us go from here."[101] With this [word] he has shown that this is not his place, neither his nor that of his disciples. Where are we going, our Lord?

---

[95] 1 Cor 2:9; Isa 64:4.
[96] Luke 14:33.
[97] Matt 10:38.
[98] Luke 14:26.
[99] Matt 16:25.
[100] John 12:25-26.
[101] John 14:31.

"Wherever I am, my servant shall also be."[102] If Jesus should summon us, "Get up, let us go from here," who will be foolish enough to be persuaded to dwell with the corpses in (331) the tombs and become a dweller among the dead? Therefore, whenever the world desires to take you with it, or the family or lineage or friends, remember the word of Christ who said, "Get up, let us go from here," this voice will be sufficient to alarm you if you are alive. Whenever you desire to sit down in order to rest yourself or to dally in the love of the place in which you are, remember this urgent voice and say to yourself, "Get up, let us go from here."

So by all means, you have to go, but go as Jesus went. Go because he has spoken to you, and not because nature is leading you while you do not desire [to go]. For whether you wish or not, you are standing on the road of travelers. Depart then on account of the word of your Lord, and not by the necessity of force. Get up, let us go from here. This is the voice that awakens those who have fallen asleep. It is the trumpet that with its sound chases away the sleep of indolence. It is power and not [just] a word. Whoever feels it, suddenly a new power clothes him and pushes him from one thing to another at the speed of the blinking of an eye. This word of God makes the disciple jump lest he hesitate in that pleasure of his sitting down. Get up, let us go from here. Look, he will go with you—why are you hesitating? He did not say to you, "Get up [and] go"; but, "Get up, let us, you and me equally." God calls you to go in his company. Who does not burn (332) and is troubled lest he delay from the company of God who has called him? There is on that road neither fright nor fear, neither damages nor injuries, neither brigands nor thieves. If there were on [the road] those who would hinder [you], as long as the Lord is in your company, all of them will flee from before you. Who is the brigand who dares to be seen in his outlaw's garb on the road on which the king crosses? But when evildoers hear a report of him they either flee or hide themselves. Look, from this you will also learn about departure

---

[102] John 12:26.

from the way of the world, if you understand and hear the power of the word with discernment.

The Way of Righteousness

56. Jesus had shown this road of perfection to another, a certain teacher, who with a desire for the perfect way of life was wishing to follow Jesus in a manner that suited him. "A certain person approached him while he was teaching in the temple and said to him, 'Good teacher, what should I do to inherit eternal life?' "[103] And what did Jesus say to this one? "Why are you calling me 'good'? There is no one good except the One God. You know the commandments: Do not kill, do not commit adultery, do not steal, do not give false witness."[104] Look, I have taught you restraint from evil things so that your desire may avoid the paths of sin. But if by this you wish to make progress and not do **(333)** evil things and come to the state of doing good things, keep the commandments of the law: "Honor your father and your mother,"[105] and keep all those [commandments] that are appropriate for this. But if you desire to be above the constraint of the law by the authority of your righteousness, and be led by the will of freedom in virtuous things above the fear of punishment, "Love the Lord your God with all your soul, and with all your strength and with all your mind,[106] and whatever is hateful to you do not do to your neighbor."[107] This is the way of life of the upright that is above the constraint of the law, and Moses and the prophets have taught this righteousness. Whoever keeps this, the law does not have the ability to threaten his righteousness. Go, keep these things that are written[108] and elevate yourself by them to the love of God and to [the love of] your neighbor, which is above the fear of the law because it is love.

---

[103] Matt 19:16; Mark 10:17.

[104] Matt 19:17-18; Mark 10:18-19.

[105] Matt 19:19; Mark 10:19.

[106] Matt 22:37; Mark 12:30.

[107] Tob 4:15.

[108] Typographical error: written ܕܟܬܒܝܢ, read ܕܟܬܝܒܝܢ.

When you have kept these things, you will inherit eternal life. Jesus taught these things for that prideful teacher to do, even if he had not desired to inhibit him, [for the teacher] was seeking greater things than these by a vain mind. However, what he had not taught to that [teacher] is meant to be the true teaching for us disciples.

Moving Away from Evil Things

57. Let us know by [his] word how we should move away from evil things and little by little climb up and become greater in the performance of virtuous things. For what he said to him—do not kill, do not commit adultery, do not **(334)** steal, and do not bear false witness—agrees with what David has said, "Avoid evil and do good."[109] And with what Paul has said, "Do not let evil defeat you."[110] And this [word], "Honor your father and your mother, and whatever is hateful to you, do not do to your neighbor," is like that one, "Do good,"[111] and, "defeat evil by good."[112] And this [word], "Love the Lord your God with all your heart and with all your soul and with all your mind, and your neighbor as yourself," is like that one, "The law was not established for the upright,"[113] because these commandments are above the fear of the law.[114]

Three Orders of Righteousness

58. Therefore, Jesus has established these levels of ways of life through these commandments: first, that a person may avoid evil things and restrain himself from committing all hateful things;

[109] Ps 34:14.
[110] Rom 12:21.
[111] Rom 13:3.
[112] Rom 12:21.
[113] 1 Tim 1:9.
[114] Lemoine's translation omits the following section (**334:10–21**) and relocates it in the middle of **338** because he believes the flow of ideas makes this section more understandable in the later section. This translation and Lavenant's have retained the order of the text as printed in Budge's edition.

second, that he may perform these things that are established under the fear of the law; third, the cultivation of virtues that is above the fear of the law; fourth, the beginning of the road of the discipleship of Christ which is a complete departure from the world; fifth, the [ascetic] labors and austerities by which we make the old person sick; sixth, that we may bear the cross upon our shoulder and attain the fulfillment of the perfection of Christ. Therefore, by these things two ways of life have been discerned for us, and we have learned two forms of righteousness, each one of them existing in three orders. Paul has taught us these things so that we might be held back from **(335)** evil things, so that we might be obedient and fear the law and perform the virtues in order to be above the law in the cultivation of the virtues that we desire. The law has not been established for the upright, and for this reason he has raised those who do [good deeds] above the authority of the law.

Therefore, these three orders of righteousness are practiced in the world, and those who administer them are the upright and the righteous, but not the spiritual or perfect. Two of them are placed above the fear of the law. That third order is above the constraint and fear of the law, because it is fulfilled in the heart and inner mind where the law is not able to observe and see, since the eye of the law sees [only] outer actions and not inner thoughts, and whoever loves God with all his heart and mind and soul, his love is in secret. But especially, "Love your God," [Paul] said, which is above the law, and not, "Fear God," because the law has power over fear and not over love. Love is above the commandment of the law. The law does not have power over those who are being led by love.[115] Therefore, the third order is placed in the middle above the law but is lower than the way of Christ. See from here how much more perfect is the instruction of our Savior because what **(336)** is above the law is the apex of his own instruction. Therefore, our Lord taught these three things that the upright in the world should do. All the virtues are gathered together and are

[115] Lemoine's translation omits the following section **(335:19–336:1)** and relocates it in the middle of **338**. See footnote 97 above.

performed by those who possess [wealth] as an act of compassion by means of their wealth toward those who are needy. In them is placed the complete power of that commandment, "Whatever is hateful to you do not do to your neighbor," just as the Teacher had also explained, "This is the law and the prophets."[116]

The Narrow Door

59. But regarding his own righteousness above the law, he said, "Enter through the narrow door."[117] So then with regard to the law, sometimes you are restricted and sometimes you are given wide berth; sometimes you are laboring and sometimes you are at rest. By such things as these the entire life of your righteousness is woven. But here with regard to the way of Christ it is written, "Enter through the narrow door." It is excellent that like a wise and good teacher, our Lord has gradually delivered to his disciples something old and something new. First, in order to show that he is the Giver of the first and last things; and second, so that from little things he might guide the disciples toward great things, from "Love [another person] as yourself" to "Love more than yourself"; from "Give of what you have" to "Divide everything you have"; from "a little of your possession" to "distribute all of your possession." That which is the easiest of all of these—"a person should not do evil things"—he makes the first thing. For whoever **(337)** is being inhibited from the practice of evil things because of [fear] of legal punishments, it would be easier to approach the practice of virtues that the law commands on account of his fear of the law. Whoever compelled his public actions to perform virtuous [deeds] was also beginning to love God and his neighbor with all of his heart, neither for appearance nor on account of adulation nor on account of fear, but because this is fitting for a person to love God and his kin. After he had established for us these definitions and had explained for us these orders in the righteousness of the upright, he went higher, teaching us perfection by his word. He spoke

[116] Matt 22:40.
[117] Matt 7:13.

to that scribe who was questioning [him]; in fact, he was teaching all the disciples through that one person, "If you desire to become perfect, go, sell all your possession and give to the poor, and you will have treasure in heaven."[118]

Beginning of the Road

60. We have not even begun on the road of righteousness, because for a person to take up his cross and follow Jesus is another way of life. Just as dwelling in the womb is one thing and another is the departure of the infant from the womb, and yet another thing is to become a person in the world after birth from the womb, so it is one thing that a person may be formed and shaped and embodied in the womb of the world[119] with all his senses and members; and it is another thing **(338)** to be born, and still another to be in the world. For righteousness in the world is like the formation of the fetus in the womb. So, "Sell all your possession and give to the poor and you will have treasure in heaven" is the pathway through which one is born from the old womb into the new creation and the door through which one departs from one world into another; and then that saying, "Take up your cross and follow me,"[120] is the way of life of perfection and the road of spiritual life.

A Natural Occurrence

61. It seems that this is a major undertaking for a person to sell everything that he has and give to the poor and depart [as] an apostle[121] from the world. It is still a natural [matter] by which we are entering creation in our first birth and, moreover, the first man also was created in this way. On account of this the upright Job,

---

[118] Matt 19:21.

[119] Lemoine reads variant Ms. B: "womb of the world"—ܪܥܠܝܐ ܪܥܘܬܐ— instead of written text, "womb," ܪܥܘܬܐ.

[120] Matt 16:24.

[121] Sebastian Brock notes the double entendre for "apostle" (ܪܫܠܝܚܐ), which means both "sent one" and "stripped."

when everything he had was taken away and he was deprived of possessions and of heirs because it seemed that something new had happened to him that is above nature, he said, tempering the severity of his suffering by his word, "Naked I came out from the womb of my mother and naked I shall return."[122] What had happened new to me, if not that event when I had departed from the womb? The fact that a person might be deprived of everything he has and be seen by himself alone, [this] is still a natural [occurrence]. But it surpasses nature if it happens through generosity because of God, as in the idea that if our dying is natural, then to die for the sake of God is martyrdom. In this **(339)** example this is also a matter of nature that a person might be visible by himself in the world while not possessing anything. Because Adam was created in this way, and Eve was fashioned in this way, not only were they stripped of the wealth of the world, but also of clothing and the garment of the world. They were similar to the fetus that comes out naked from the womb into creation, as Job had said, "Naked I came out and naked I shall return,"[123] and just as Paul also said, "We did not bring anything into the world, and it is evident that we are not able to depart from it with anything."[124]

Cutting the Cord

62. Such is the case with the membrane in the womb: after the fetus is formed and fashioned, then it surrounds him in order to protect his life, and once he has been born from the womb, [the membrane] is cut off and cast away from him because it is not from his own person, nor is it considered part of the person. So also with regard to wealth and possession with the rest of all human things: after a person is born [possessions] cling to him in the same way as the membrane. Moreover, when he comes to be born from one world to the [next] world through death, his possessions are cut off and thrown away from him just like the membrane that is cut

[122] Job 1:21.
[123] Job 1:21.
[124] 1 Tim 6:7.

off from the body. Just as the fetus is visible by itself without the membrane, so a person will depart from life, being stripped of all his possession. Just as in the case of the person being born while surrounded by its membrane, and when he has entered the world **(340)** they cast it off naturally from him, so also it is natural that a person might depart naked from the world or that he might be deprived of his possession while he is in the world. A person has grace when he anticipates becoming naked from his wealth before nature might strip him of it, and he anticipates the time of his departure by his own free will.

Beginning and End of Roads

63. So then, what difficulty is there in this commandment for one to become a stranger to all his possession, for look, is this commandment [not] natural? Let a person look at his beginning and at his end, and so conduct himself also in the middle of his life. For just as, "Naked he entered and naked he will depart," so he will become naked of his wealth throughout his sojourn in the world. May he praise the One who has appointed that what is natural shall become voluntary. Therefore, it is excellent that our Lord did not make the renunciation of wealth the beginning of the road of his discipleship because it is a natural thing and his own way of life is above nature. Just as our human death is not the beginning of the road of [this] world to come, but our death is the end of the road of the world and our resurrection from death is the beginning of the road of the kingdom of heaven; so also the renunciation of visible wealth and possession is the end of the road of the world, and the shedding of foreign clothing that we put on after we entered into the world.

Freedom and Mammon

64. If this seems difficult, it is not because it is above nature, for look, it is an easy thing for those **(341)** who live in the freedom of nature, but this is difficult for those who are subjugated to passions and serve in bondage to desires. Those who serve mammon as a master are afraid to renounce it, because in advance they have

voluntarily made it their god. Not only are those subservient to it afraid of this passion, but every passion that binds up free will under its power is [freedom's] lord. The coercion of [mammon's] fear imposes on it, and [free will] is not easily able to shed it. Take from this the testimony that it is not the passions that forcefully subjugate us, but our freedom has subjugated itself under the passions, and [the passions] have become lords over it. For look, those who have control over themselves and take off this clothing of anxiety of possessions, if one should compel them to be subjugated to wealth, they would fear to become its masters more than the masters of wealth fear to lose it. If the renunciation of possessions were naturally fearful or difficult, everyone would be afraid of it, and its power would rule over all naturally. But look, free people are above its subjugation, and it would be considered by their sovereign freedom a bitter servitude.

The Second Birth

65. Therefore, all the commandments of righteousness and of compassion that a person cultivates while he is in the world are still this side of the bounds of nature. That is why all the old law (342) and its commandments were being placed under nature because it was not possible that the law could be above nature. Yet our Lord said when he was asked by Nicodemus, the scribe of the law—"What is your teaching?"—"I am proclaiming to people a second birth."[125] Although he also signified the fact of baptism through the word, still, he is demonstrating mightily about this that a person is born from [this] world to [the next] world with the power of the grace of God, [and] also by the power of his will. The womb that gives birth to him is the perfect renunciation of everything that the eye sees.

Therefore, three births are evident by which a person of God is born. The first birth is from the womb into creation. The second is from slavery to freedom, and from being human to becoming a son of God, which is what happens by means of grace through baptism.

---

[125] See John 3:3-8.

The third birth is this one by which a person is born voluntarily from the physical to the spiritual way of life, and the renunciation of everything becomes for him a womb that gives birth to him.

Plenty of Room

66. Moreover, along with the rest of the births that [follow] this one of renunciation, a person is born when he has departed outside of the world, as is the case [when he is born] from the physical [nature] to the spiritual [nature], and from passions to passion-lessness,[126] and [when he] moves perfectly from all the old person's agitating movements to the living movements of the spiritual person. For these degrees and levels and births **(343)** are in this way of life, and as long as a person desires to walk straight ahead, there is room for his steps because the place of spirituality is spacious without end. Now, if in this physical world there is room for his steps as much as he [desires] to walk, and if one travels his entire life [but] is not able to circumscribe the world by his steps, how in that spiritual world will we not [be able to] travel even more so since our journey in it is endless? As long as a person penetrates and ascends and enters, a place will receive him within a place and a degree above a degree because the world is without end. This [physical] world, even as big as it is, is still placed under an end and a limit. But that [spiritual] world is above a limit and is beyond end.

The New Birth

67. Blessed is the one who has become worthy and has entered [the spiritual world] through a transformation from the old person to the new [person], making all physical movement die from himself and being moved by other living and spiritual movements. [Our Lord] wisely said, "If a person is not born again, he is not able to see the kingdom of God."[127] Because unless a person renounces everything he has in the world and sheds the entire physical way

---

[126] ܪ̈ܚܡܐ ܠܐ; *lā ḥašūšūtā*, Greek *apatheia*.
[127] John 3:3.

of life in his hidden and public actions—through the example
by which the fetus sheds the natural womb and is born into this
world—he is not able to see the kingdom of God, that is to say,
to sense the living movements (344) of the Spirit that are within
physical awareness. This shall be a model for you: just as the fetus
is enclosed in the stomach's womb, so is a person enclosed in the
world in its physical way of life with all its heaviness and its gloom,
its dullness, anxiety, and cares. Just as the fetus itself is born from
the womb through the door of the womb into the light of this creation, and when it has been born into this light that it finds in front
of it, it sees all things and the world's excellence, all the different
kinds of creatures, and the variety of the natures of this composite
creation, and receives this vision and perceives these tastes through
the growth of its physical stature, little by little; so also whoever is
born again from his worldly way of life, and departs to the other
spiritual world through the door of renunciation, the moment he is
born and receives that world, the light of knowledge begins to be
evident to him. Just as the things of this world are visible in natural
light, and everything in it is distinguishable from its neighbor, so
also by that spiritual knowledge that a person begins to receive he
will see all spiritual matters, boundaries, places, orders and ranks,
and everything above the body's awareness. Because just as the
body senses these things of its [own] nature, for the sensations
of its senses have an affinity[128] to worldly things, so also the soul
(345) senses by the mediation of the Spirit all these things that
have an affinity to its nature above the world, which is then being
born again, along with that of baptism, which our Lord declared
to Nicodemus.

Inheritance for the Righteous

68. Let us examine the answer of our Lord that [he had given]
to that young man who had approached him and asked to learn
the concept of perfection, so that from it we might also receive

---

[128] Lavenant reads ܪܚܝܡܐ, "related"; instead of written text ܪܡܚܝܠܐ,
"weak."

perfect knowledge and be born from one way of life to another. So then, when he asks to learn, "What I should do to inherit eternal life?"[129] Jesus said to him, "Do not kill, do not commit adultery, do not steal, do not give false witness,"[130] which distances one from evil things. After these is the cultivation of good deeds, by means of that word he said, "Honor your father and your mother,[131] and "Whatever is hateful to you do not do to your neighbor."[132] And he said, "If one keeps these things, he will inherit eternal life,"[133] because the inheritance of eternal life is for all of the righteous and upright and compassionate and doers of good deeds while they are in the world, those who have been called "blessed" by the living word of our Lord. Because he said to them, "Come, the blessed of my Father, and inherit the kingdom which has been prepared for you from before the foundations of the world, because I was hungry and you gave me [something] to eat, I was thirsty and you gave me drink,"[134] with the rest of these things spoken by our Lord to them. All of these are appropriate for the first righteous ones who were in the world and for the upright (346) who are also owners of wealth. Whoever clothes the naked and receives strangers, who sets out a table for the hungry and sustains those who are needy with all physical things, it is evident that he is a lord of possessions, for without wealth these things would not be able to happen. Those who have renounced have no wealth to perform these good deeds—how much more so for the spiritual and the perfect? So then, this advice that was given here by our Lord is not only inappropriate for the perfect and the spiritual but also for those who have renounced [worldly things], because they do not have the wealth to do these good deeds.

[129] Matt 19:16.
[130] Matt 19:18.
[131] Matt 19:19.
[132] Tob 4:15.
[133] Matt 19:17.
[134] Matt 25:34.

The Spiritual and the Perfect

69. It is apparent how much higher is the degree of those who have renounced from that of the upright by what everyone professes. For whoever does not possess anything at all, who by the love of God has completely renounced his wealth, is higher than whoever has kept his wealth with him and does good deeds with it. Moreover, those who are spiritual are higher than those who renounce, and the perfect [are higher] than the spiritual because spiritual [nature] is commensurate with spiritual powers. Now perfection is the type of the fulfillment of Christ, through which all those who attain the stature of the knowledge of the fulfillment of Christ are perfected spiritually, as Paul has said.[135] How much higher is this degree of the perfect and the spiritual than that of the upright and compassionate who are in the world, the word of our Savior himself spoken to the possessors of worldly wealth is sufficient. "Be diligent to make for yourself friends from the mammon of iniquity, so that when it has been depleted they might receive you into their eternal (347) tents."[136] So then look, the perfect are like the lords of the region and the citizens of the city, receiving upright strangers who are entering their world, because they are fellow heirs of Christ and heirs of the Father who is in heaven. As Paul said concerning them, "The heirs of God and fellow heirs of Jesus Christ."[137]

Becoming Dead

70. While explaining that they have attained this level since they are bearing the cross of Christ, [Paul] said, "If we suffer with him we shall also be glorified with him."[138] Participation in the sufferings of Christ is not by making alms and showing compassion to those who are needy but by dying completely to the world and to the body and the lusts and the passions, and crucifying the

[135] Eph 4:13.
[136] Luke 16:9.
[137] Rom 8:17.
[138] Rom 8:17.

old man[139] with all of his lusts, just as Paul also said concerning himself, that he was being crucified to the world,[140] and the entire sensation of the world was eliminated from him in the same way it is eliminated from those naturally dead. For just as a corpse does not suffer from any one of those things that approach it; so also neither in that person who has been crucified with Christ and has made the old person completely dead in himself is there any sensation of one of these worldly things. Concerning this Paul also called "dead" those who live in this way of perfection. That upright [person] who dwells in the world and has a wife, children, wealth, and possessions **(348)** cannot be called dead because his entire way of life is like that of one living. Someone dead is not married and does not give birth, but with these others there is marriage and giving birth, along with the rest that belong to these things. "You have died," cries out Paul to the perfect, "and your lives are hidden with Christ in God."[141] Again he said, "You are dead to the world, but alive to God in our Lord Jesus Christ."[142] Again he said, "If you have died with Christ from the elements of the world, why do you receive the commandments as if you were living in the world?"[143]

Renouncing Wealth to Be Perfect

71. A person will attain this way of life after renouncing possessions and beginning to cultivate virtues in his own members, because as long as he has wealth, he will justify himself by wealth and will not empty himself of the anxiety of wealth he is cultivating in himself. If he believes that he may [still] work with these things while being wealthy, his work will be confused, that is to say, he will find himself coming and going [without direction]. With that

---

[139] Rom 6:6.
[140] See Gal 6:14.
[141] Col 3:3.
[142] Rom 6:11.
[143] Col 2:20.

other one, even if he should work hard in the [ascetical] labors[144] of the body, it is not possible for this person to live in the purity of thoughts, which is the absence of passion[145] in the soul, in order to enter by it into spiritual love from which knowledge is born that sees everything and from there the mind climbs by degrees and ascends **(349)** to divine conversation. So then, on account of this, those who desire perfection divest themselves of wealth in order to become fit for service in their own person. Being free from everything in the world they will make war with the body's lusts and [each will] become a soldier [of God] on his own and not by those things outside of himself. When he has uprooted the desires of the body and then[146] the passions of the soul, he will begin to sow in himself the seed of living knowledge. Therefore, whoever has desired to approach this way of life, let him renounce wealth and be born again and then enter it. For a person is not able to enter it without it being this way, according to the testimony of Christ himself. "If you desire to become perfect, go, sell your possessions and give to the poor and you will have treasure in heaven,"[147] and "take up your cross and follow me."[148]

Wages and Rewards

72. Look, therefore, how perfect is the instruction of Christ, for not even when a person renounces everything that he has, he still will not begin on the road of his instruction, because renunciation is the end of the road of righteousness that is practiced in the world. That [saying], "Take up your cross and follow me," is the beginning of the road of the spiritual way of life. Jesus has placed the reward in the middle between the righteous and the perfect, "Go, sell your possessions and give to the poor and you will have

---

[144] Typographical error: written ܥܠܡ̈ܐ, *'almē*, "worlds," read ܥܡ̈ܠܐ, *'amlē*, "labors."

[145] See note 126 above. ܠܐ ܚܫܘܫܘܬܐ, *lā ḥašūšūtā*.

[146] Lemoine opts for the variant ܥܕ *'ad* (instead of ܟܕ *kad*) in Mss. A and B.

[147] Matt 19:21; Mark 10:21; Luke 12:33.

[148] Matt 16:24; Mark 8:34; Luke 9:23.

treasure in heaven." See, [this is] the reward for righteousness. He calls this wage a treasure because those **(350)** who function in the world's righteousness perform good deeds on the condition of a wage. In his saying Jesus has rightly placed the treasure at the end of the road of righteousness in the world, for when their reward is set out before them, they will run from afar toward it like those who wrestle for sport, and the crown of their triumph is placed in their full view. But our Lord did not allow a wage to enter into the place of the perfect because it is an insult to the perfect that they might serve on account of a reward in the spiritual way of life. See, the spiritual [life] in which the perfect live is the reward of the righteous and of the upright, because when they have performed good deeds in the world [it is] on the condition that they might be transformed and become spiritual and free from everything physical and the passions and subjugations of the world.

Way of the Perfect

73. This is the way of the perfect, because they are stirred up spiritually, work spiritually, and have already been transformed from physical [life] to spiritual [life] while they are in this visible world. How then would they wait to have for a reward something that is in fact now their labor? Just as an angel does not look to have its [own] spiritual nature as a reward or to be sent to serve the wills of Essence, because it is [already] in [the Essence] and serves it naturally, so also the perfect [person] does not look to have a reward in a spiritual transformation because he is already living in the spiritual transformation, and his movement is exactly like the heavenly hosts, and his entire way of life **(351)** is in their imitation. Like them, he chants the "Holy" [Trisagion] spiritually and sings [the Psalms] spiritually, and serves God in spirit and in truth, as was said by the word of God concerning the perfect, "God is spirit and those who worship, worship him in spirit and in truth."[149] God is spirit and the work of the perfect is spiritual. So now look, they

---

[149] John 4:24.

work in a godly manner and have been elevated also from the order of the spiritual so that they might also work in imitation of God with an authority and a freedom that is not subservient, which is higher than the laws and the commandments in imitation of God.

Indescribable Work

74. We are not able to tell the story through our word of the work of the living movements of the perfect, because unless a person has attained their level he is not able to speak concerning the perfection of their work. For even if they desire to describe their living movements and their godly work, they are not capable because this work is not physical, so that one might speak with a physical tongue, but they are sensing him only and are working in a godly manner in their inner person, while neither their work, nor their movements, nor their sensation, nor their continual contemplation, nor the visions and revelations that [come] to them can be described. This is the end of the road of Christ, O disciple, and on account of this perspective your journey will continue **(352)** if you run. This is the way of life delivered to us by Christ.

Depart therefore from the world and empty yourself of everything in it, in your body and in your soul, so that you may find these things that are beyond description and through them take pleasure with all the orders of light in the world of truth through Jesus Christ, to whom be glory from all generations, forever and ever. Amen.

The end of the second *mēmrā* on renunciation and on the cultivation of the spiritual commandments.

Mēmrā 10

On Gluttony

The tenth *mēmrā* against the lust of the belly in which [Philox-enos] denounces gluttony while revealing and showing all its aspects; moreover, he also finds fault with those who subject their lives to this passion and explains that it is not possible for those people who cultivate slavery for their pleasures to approach knowledge and the accomplishment of even one of the triumphs of virtue.

Summary: The lust of the belly is the filthiest passion, inhibiting rational thought and being the entrance for all evil, enslaving the soul as well as the body. It inhibits compassion, and as the opposite of fasting destroys prayer and is the source of sloth. The glutton considers doctrine and Scripture idle and irrelevant, and blaspheming those who practice faith calls virtues "vices." Yet he criticizes unduly anyone who breaks a fast for necessity. Philoxenos cautions about the conniving of the glutton who tries to counsel an ascetic to be moderate and who hears only those Scriptures that support his eating. Philoxenos exhorts the disciples not to be lax in their strenuous asceticism and to beware of falling into the trap of the lust of the belly which will lead to all sorts of vices. Gluttony is the sin of Adam's fall in Eden.

This Foul Passion

(353) 1. While all the passions of evil things and the cultivation of pleasures are reproached and rejected by the word of divine knowledge, this abhorrent passion of the lust of the belly is rejected

and reproached more than all of them, that [passion] that usually renders people who subject themselves to it [into] the image of animals, because it takes from them the movements of knowledge appropriate to rational beings and submerges and darkens their mind under the weight of food. The door for all evil things is this foul and abhorrent passion, and wherever it has power it is like a great door, wide open to the entrance (354) of all despicable things. It destroys every virtue, inhibits all righteousness, and in all forms opposes all divine labors. A person who is humbled under this despicable desire is not able to receive the yoke of the discipleship of Christ.

Mistress of the Body

2. Because once the stomach has become the mistress over the body, it commands and subdues all its wills, and instead of the road that ascends to heaven, it shows [the body] that other road that lowers [it] down into Sheol. It hangs the weight of food and excessive nourishments upon him, and moistens and weighs him down with too much drink, so that when he has borne the weight of food and it has weighed down his lightness and has piled on [his] body another body of desire, it will easily tip the scales on the road that takes one down to Sheol.

Lust of the Belly

3. This passion of the lust of the belly is more despicable than all of the passions. Once one becomes its servant and carries its heavy yoke upon his shoulder, it no longer allows him rest from its service. He serves it night and day, and it sends him everywhere it wishes like a weary servant, not on clear paths but on roads full of stumbling blocks and to a place where harmful things are found. The lover of desirable things does not have eyes that see the light, because even if [he does] they are darkened by the weight of food. Day is night to him, and night is a double death. His intelligence is swallowed up in the heaviness of sleep. His thoughts are scattered by the erratic nature of the humidity (355) of the body. The natural fire in him is cold because it is extinguished by abnormal humidity.

His thoughts are obscured from knowledge because his soul's eye that seeks knowledge is shut. A heavy weight is hung on him at all times, because twinned with his body is another body of food.

Therefore, the lust of the belly is the adversary of everything and is the enemy of all valiant struggles. It destroys a good reputation and inhibits all victories, not only spiritual triumphs, but also physical triumphs. The lust of the belly is also the adversary for these things that are in the world with courage and with strength, because courage is useful for everything that is of renown and of praise, and health is necessary, and lightness of the members is needed as well as a healthy strength. An insatiable lust is the adversary of all these things. When strength is diminished by too much food, and by it the vigor of the members has left, no longer are they ready for actions or for the works of righteousness. If a person with a knowledgeable eye should investigate everything just as I have said, the weight of food is an adversary for physical strength and for the knowledge of the soul, for labors of righteousness and deeds of mercy, and for gifts of alms. Whoever is enslaved to his belly is an animal without discretion. His entire way of life imitates animals and his entire existence being stirred up by the physical passions, he is completely void **(356)** of these [passions] of the soul.

Adversary

4. Understand from these actions that the lust of the belly is the adversary of all these triumphs of which I have spoken: teaching, knowledge, worldly courage, labors of righteousness, mercy toward people, love, and the knowledge of God. Even the world testifies that [the lust of the belly] is the adversary of learning by a tradition circulating that children who are set apart to receive instruction are guarded from too much food by their parents. Because gluttony is a fence around knowledge, so that when the members have borne the weight of food they are not able to bear the lightness of learning because lightness is the opposite of heaviness—therefore, children who are being educated receive measured nourishment so that their mind may be [alert], their thoughts ready, and

their memory purified to receive and to retain, because [too much] food inhibits both of these things.

Thick Fume of Food

5. [It is] not only children who receive formal education [who] are inhibited from too much food but[1] also those who receive **(357)** learning and are instructed through confrontation with worldly realities; these others who possess worldly knowledge are also in need of this [discipline]. There is no one who has approached knowledge or composition or speech without understanding that too much food is the adversary of these things. The dense fume of food, when it grows and is not purified, clouds the heart and darkens the mind, troubles discernment and closes the door at the birth of a word. Similar to a covering it is spread out over all the faculties of knowledge, inhibiting and destroying the power of their activity. An orator is not able to speak if he is weighed down by food; and neither is the scholar [able to] know, nor the wise one [able to] understand. And, so to speak, the entire inner person is darkened by the density of the fume of food.

Lightness of Being

6. Because the spiritual and light nature mixed in us seeks spirituality and lightness, inasmuch as the body becomes thin through asceticism, so there will be participation with its spiritual [nature].

---

[1] After "but" (ܐܠܐ) Mss. E & F insert the following lines: "Also the rest of the people who learn one of the other crafts of the world, masters being attentive to them and teachers encouraging [them], every one becomes a watcher and guard of excessive food and of unregulated drink. Those who learn the vain crafts of the world eat and drink by measure—dancers or charioteers or athletes or those learning the craft of war, or others who are receiving the art of reading and writing. If these crafts that are performed physically and the knowledge received from the world are in need of abstinence from food, and if food should increase, it becomes their adversary, how much more does too much food become the adversary to actions that are accomplished spiritually?"

As long as a heavy weight is not placed upon it, it acquires lightness by which it participates with the lightness of the soul. Therefore, by a wise economy a spiritual portion was placed into a physical portion. **(358)** Inasmuch as the body is thickened by foods, it pulls down the soul toward it and suspends its heaviness upon it, and ties up and snares the wings of its thoughts. But if its life is engaged in the continual reduction of food, it is light, clear and purified, the heaviness of its nature is diminished, and it enlightens and gladdens the soul that is in it. Moreover, it is readily obedient to its will, and because it is light and thin the soul draws to itself everything as it desires and does not resist it, nor does its thickness inhibit [the soul] from establishing it where it desires.

Heaviness of the Lust of the Belly

7. Each one, whether the soul or the body, draws one another to its will, because [each] is the adversary of the other by its nature or by its will, according to the word of the Apostle who said, "The body desires something that harms the spirit, and the spirit desires something that harms the body, and both of them are adversaries of one another."[2] But if all of the lusts of the body, according to the word of the wise Apostle, are an adversary of the soul, then more than all of these is this lust of the belly because it is the door of all the lusts and there is not in any of them [one] that is heavy like it. Just like a weight hung on to a light and flighty nature tips the scales downward, so is this desire of the belly because its constitution [derives] from moisture and weight. Although the body is naturally heavy because thus is its nature, by the increase of food still another weight is added to it. When [one] weight is added on to [another] weight, and the body **(359)** is doubled in size, that is, the body of food [is added] on that natural [body], the weight prevails over the soul and the mistress becomes a submissive handmaid, so that then the soul cannot lead the body freely but carries its weight like a slave.

[2] Gal 5:17.

Adversary of Mercy

8. The lust of the belly is also the adversary of compassion because it retrieves and makes everything distributed by the gift of compassion its own. Just as the lust of the belly cannot make the lustful person merciful (for the thought of compassion does not occur to such a person unless his belly is full), so it is for a greedy person who gives a gift: he only gives a gift when his belly is full. But this is not compassion but rather the imitation of an animal and of a beast. Even a beast leaves its manger and lies down when its stomach is full. In the same way, until the greedy [person] fills his stomach from the table of his desires, he is not convinced to look at another with a merciful eye. He does not offer from what is placed before him to another who is in need, because he believes in this way by the servitude of his lust, that there is no one in need like him.

Neediness of Greed

9. In reality, there is no one who is needy as one [who is] a slave to his lust, because as long as one gives to lust its needs, it will remain ever needy. Never by the accumulation of food is it filled, but as long as one eats one will long for other foods. Moreover, as long as one drinks clear wines **(360)** he will be desirous; just as his food becomes his hunger and not his satisfaction, so his drink [becomes] his thirst and not his refreshment. As long as the greedy [person] eats, the more he will become hungry. As long as he drinks, [the more] he will be thirsty, and there is no end to the lust of the belly. For when he is filled up with the first meal, because it is not his need he sets to fill but his desire, he seeks another [meal] better than the first one. Moreover, when he has taken from this [meal] according to [his] desire's pleasure, he looks at another one that is sweeter and tastier than it. In this way, his gluttony passes through every single one of the foods yet is not filled by any of them. If it seems that he is satisfied and his hand is drawn away from eating, it is not that his lust has been satisfied, but his stomach is full and cannot contain anymore.

A Stomach Never Too Large

10. However, [the glutton] was desiring that his stomach might become as large as his lust, and his stomach might become [as big] as his eye, so that he might be able to gather into his broken-down pantry everything he desires. One who loves to possess is a foolish glutton who gathers the treasures of his pleasures to place into an open house that does not guard anything that enters it. For the Maker—in order to restrain the lust of the gluttons—has made the stomach of a limited capacity, so that by necessity even though they do not wish, they will be inhibited from their lusts. When the will wishes to amass many things, but the cavity of the stomach [is] not [able to] receive them, look, is he not forcibly inhibited from his lust's searching? When the will lusts, the small cavity that is not able to hold [more] inhibits him. If the cavity that receives their lusts [were as big] as **(361)** the will of the gluttons, the sea and the dry land would not be sufficient for them. The mountains and the hills are not enough for them, and the air and the sun with every [kind of] creature would not [be able to] fulfill their lusts. But now that a smaller vessel has been given to their vast will, look, the sea and the dry land would [still] not be sufficient for them and they would gather all sorts of provisions and not be filled, and they would [still] satisfy every lust [but] not be satisfied, and they would be asking and investigating about all exotic foods: if only they had the stomach in proportion to their will, what would they have not done?

Food for Tomorrow

11. Therefore, the glutton is even worse than the animals, for when a beast's stomach is full it rejects the rest of its food in the manger and does not know that it should keep [some] for another time or day. This is not the case with the glutton, because it is not with his stomach that his desire is filled. When the capacity established naturally in [the stomach] to receive food is full, lust has taken and kept aside the rest for another day, that is to say, for days and months. The glutton, seated at the table of his need

and reflecting about the times to come, is anxious not only to be fed what is found [before him] but wonders about what he shall eat tomorrow, his hand upon the nearby basket and his mind at a distant table. He carries [food] in his right [hand] and in his left, but both of them are not sufficient to offer fuel for the fire within him. All his members are not sufficient to serve the harsh mistress whom he has voluntarily placed over himself. **(362)** He serves it completely yet does not satisfy [it]. His eyes and hands and legs are made slaves to it, but they are not adequate. He reflects on it in his inner [thoughts], and in his public [actions] he runs on its behalf, and it is served like a mistress, but never satisfied. Like Sheol it receives what is fuel but is never filled. Like fire it takes up the fuel of food and does not say "enough," and in imitation of the soil it drinks but is never quenched. Like the eye it desires everything but is not filled by anything. The glutton was wishing he might have other members so that they might be adequate for the service of the iniquitous mistress he has acquired.

Envy for Other People's Food

12. The glutton's eye is also envious of whoever is seated with him at the table and looks at him with an envious eye lest he might be eating more. Perhaps in his thought he even counts his bites or whether the portion that has been placed before [his neighbor] is greater than his. His belly receives food and his thought reflects on the neighbor who is seated with him. Because the malevolence of the lust of the belly is expanded over everything, its eye is malevolent also for whoever is near to him. But how does its eye not harm whoever is its companion at the table, indeed, if it keeps [it on him] for days and months? It is also jealous with others who are far away from it. Concerning every person [the lust of the belly] asks, "What is his food? Which meals are arranged on his table? And how large are his meals?" When it has inquired and measured its pleasures with whomever it hears about, if its own are more numerous than **(363)** [those] of that [other] one, see, it will rejoice. If [the pleasures] of that [other] person are more than its own, it will be filled at once with grief, and along with grief also with

envy, and with envy a contemptuous mind: why is there someone superior to it with regard to food? So then, if the gluttonous eater is jealous of those who are far away, is not his eye [more] envious of one who is with him at the table? Not because he speaks to him openly, "Do not eat," for he is prevented from saying this by his shame, but his thought desires this: if only[3] [his neighbor] had held back his hand, so that what is found on the table might be enough only for his own gluttony.

Mother of All Passions

13. Therefore, the lust of the belly is the most disgraceful and abominable of all the lusts, and there is nothing similar to it among the rest of the other passions, but only in this: it is the mother and nurturer of all of them. Just as a root bears the branches of the tree with everything in them, so also the belly's gluttony is the root of all evil things. Like branches and shoots from the roots, all the passions of desirable things sprout from it. It gives birth, raises up, nourishes, and makes [one] act, and through it all evil things are fulfilled. From it a person begins on the road of evil[4] and his first step is to depart from the path of uprightness. Just as abstinence—that is, fasting from all foods—is the beginning of **(364)** the road of righteous struggles, so also lust of the belly is the beginning of shameful deeds. If you observe with the eye of knowledge, O disciple, you will see that all evil things follow after it, one after the other.

Removing the Memory of God

14. In the first place, [the lust of the belly] darkens the intellect from reflection on God and clouds the mind from the remembrance of Christ. When the memory of God has been lifted out of the soul, there is no doubt that a person will not consider doing all [manner of] evil things. Just as the beginning of everything accomplished in

---

[3] Written *dedalōī*, ܕܕܠܘܝ; Lemoine opts for variant (Ms. E) *dalōī*, ܕܠܘܝ.
[4] Literally, "the road of the left [hand]."

the world is our memory of it, and until we take up the memory of matters in our mind, we do not approach doing them, so also the beginning of all good things is the memory of God. Therefore, a person mindful of God becomes involved in performing excellent deeds. If one should do something good while not remembering God in his action, his good deed is not of God, but of that thing his memory was receiving in his mind while he performed it. Look then at this good thing that is the beginning of all good things—I am speaking about the memory of God; the desire of the belly is its opposite, along with the fact that it is the beginning of all evil things. Therefore, as in the beginning of the road of good things stands the memory of God, so in the beginning of the road of all evil things stands the lust of the belly. When the two beginnings become opponents of one another and one of them is victorious over its companion, with that first one being defeated, **(365)** all those things that come after it are defeated as well. Just as it is not possible that a house can be built without foundations, so good things are not able to happen without the memory of God. Just as a building that is not established on a firm foundation is on the verge of falling, so also virtues not built upon the memory of God are necessarily associated with an imminent change and do not remain consistent in their work because they do not have a firm foundation supporting them. Therefore, gluttony and the fullness of the belly first of all extract the memory of God out of the soul. When it has uprooted the foundation, all good things are uprooted with it.

Gluttony as Defiler

15. Gluttony is also the adversary of fasting and the destroyer of prayer, the defiler of the purity of thoughts, the obscurer of the mind and the darkener of intelligence. It is the defiler of the conscience, the destroyer of learning, the annihilator of knowledge, the one that harms wisdom. It makes memory forget and paints images. It is the mother of illusions, the intoxication of the soul, that which overwhelms the mind. It is the one that brings about sleep, the multiplier of troubled dreams. It engenders fornication, pollutes the body, manufactures strange emissions, the fire of desire, the

one that commands adultery. It commits fornication by thoughts even without the members. It is the eye that desires everything, the relative of depression, the mother of laziness, the cause of the love of mammon, the despiser of sages. **(366)** It looks askance at teachers. It is the channel of all despicable deeds, the nurturer of jealousy. It is the illness of health, that which weakens strength, the enfeebler of the body, the tapeworm of the members, the moth of the body. It diminishes the strength of the senses and wanders in empty concerns. It is the relative of animals, the society of the beast. It despises the valiant and is jealous of the diligent. It is the destroyer of labors, the stumbling block of rules [of life]. It loves empty conversations, seeking pleasure at all hours, but silences sacred song. Deficient in all good things, it is zealous for all evil things, the image of harmful things, the stone that is placed in the middle for the stumbling of many, the model of injuries. It induces laxity in all those who see it. It counsels evil things, flees from austerities, loves comforts, tracks down meals and tables. It is equally an illness of the soul and of the body, a vessel of decay, a stinking smell, the source of the excrement of the body, a friend of darkness, a relative of gloom. It eats by itself, the enemy of those who do not give it [anything], an abominable image, a vile resemblance that is not describable. It is the enemy of God, one that uproots faith, the beginning of the road of error, the door that allows all despicable deeds to enter. It demands tribute from all, subjugates everyone, enables fear to grow, and destroys courageousness. It is the cause of sadness and depression, nourishment for dullness of the heart, the yoke fellow of an avaricious dog returning to its vomit.[5] It has many diseases, a nest of illnesses. It seizes **(367)** the results from labors. It is the first cause of the forgetting of God [and] worships idols.

If someone should collect and name the lust of the belly with tens of thousands of names like these, it would still be too few, and it would not have been called by the names worthy of it. This mistress is the adversary of God, and just as if God should be called by all [manner of] glorious and great names, still they would be too few and not sufficient to show the splendor and beauty of [God's] nature; in the same way, the lust of the belly if it is called by all sorts of names, they are not sufficient to demonstrate its abomination and its obscene appearance. For which virtue is this evil thing not its destroyer? One justly calls it the evil of evils, the iniquity of iniquities, and the sin of sins.

Made for Only One Thing

16. Therefore, the glutton is not capable of any other thing, except only this [business] of eating, for all actions, aside from this one, are considered empty to him. He does not think a human being was made for any other thing, except only for this [one] thing: to fulfill his desires. The conversation of a glutton is completely on his belly and all the subjects[6] of his speech focus on this. Whatever subject you might bring up to him, he will excuse himself from it and will bring you [around] to conversation about the belly. Before food, the memory of food is pleasant to him, and while he has not yet sat down at the table, his attention is completely [focused] on the table. While he has not **(368)** yet actually dined, his thought and his word are entirely with food. The beginning and the end of his conversation are taken from his belly. For with it he begins and with it he ends—it is the reason for all of his conversation. If you should repeat before him something you have learned, he considers it emptiness. If you should speak or read to him spiritual matters, he thinks he is seeing a dream. If he should hear the triumphs of the saints and the labors and ways of life and courage of upright people, he does not believe that they are true. The explanations of the Holy Scriptures are considered by him as frivolous fairy tales. For the word of interpretation is his soporific device: [hearing] a homily[7] brings sleep upon him. Those who read and teach are considered by him without anything to do because he thinks that there is no work better than his own.

---

[6] Lavenant suggests reading *nīšē* (ܢܝܫܐ) "subjects," rather than *ḥaššē* (ܚܫܐ) "passions."

[7] Literally, "an account of admonition" (ܡܠܬܐ ܕܡܪܬܝܢܘܬܐ).

The Glutton Despises Wisdom

17. He labels the search for truth a disputation, and he calls conversation about faith an investigation. [If] a person should have his mind in the Scriptures, he considers him a brash and garrulous person. If he should see someone who is persistent in reading, he will say to him, "Have you nothing [better] to do?" If he observes another one who rushes about asking, seeking to gather and store up[8] in himself the knowledge of Christ, [the glutton] considers his life to be a life of emptiness. He inserts evil names for good ones, so that while reviling them, he might free himself from accusation. Lest he be blamed for why he was not persistent in these better things, he inserts lesser things for better things, so that his own obscenity will not be denounced by those who see [him]. He renders odious by his word the beauty of good things and reviles the works of praise along with **(369)** those who have done them. He reproaches divine teaching along with its teachers. He denounces the wisdom of Christ along with those who seek it. He maliciously repeats [denunciations] against knowledge along with its disciples because it is not easy for him to speak maliciously of these matters openly—of wisdom and knowledge, of reading and learning, of faith and the search for truth, of constant meditation on the words of the Spirit, of spiritual conversation with the Holy Scriptures, of the inner conversation with the mysteries of the Essence, of the word of God which is the nourishment of the soul—for since it is not easy for him to revile these things openly, he reviles those who do them, casting insult upon praiseworthy things by the abuse of these [people]. He also openly reviles these things, calling speech about faith an inquiry and the search for truth a dispute, and the teaching of the Holy Scriptures a frivolous investigation. Look, is it not obvious that he names virtues vices and calls excellent things despicable?

---

[8] Lemoine opts for secondary reading: Ms. F—*na'sīm* (ܢܩܣܝܡ), "to establish, accumulate, store up."

Belly First

18. Zeal for God is deemed by him to be a disputation, and he considers whoever fights for the sake of truth a troublemaker. For a person [who] on account of God does not show favor to people is called by him "audacious." If someone should counsel him, "Stand up and show [some] zeal for God," he cries out, "I was not made for this, and I was not intended for such as these, for I consider these things vain, and I do not intend to be involved with vain things." If he is asked by someone, "What do you want?" he gives back **(370)** an answer and is not ashamed, "Let us eat something that God has provided for us and be quiet." That is to say, "Let us serve our belly and get rid of faith." This is the sense of his word, even if he clothes it with a form that is more humble than this. He is not ashamed to ask for the bread of God and renounce its truth, to look for [God's] grace and curse his faith, to appear as one who loves peace and flees from controversy and tumult while it is not so, but he is afraid lest he disturb with something that mistress of evil things he serves and be deprived of a single one of the occasions of physical comforts to which he has pledged himself once and for all.

Quieting Faith

19. The abolition of teaching is considered wisdom by him; for a person to be silent from knowing faith he himself thinks is faith, saying, "It is not necessary for us to learn anything else. It is sufficient for us that we should believe and be silent." While he is not a believer, he takes refuge in faith, not because he loves it, but because he loves his stomach and loves his life. He stills the direction of faith so that the search for his pleasures might go forward. Outwardly, his word is on behalf of the truth, but inwardly he speaks against the truth, and his struggle is for himself. Wherever he is called to show diligence he brings quiet into play. Wherever courage and zeal for the sake of faith are required, he teaches and advises that everyone should be still and be by himself. Should a useful conversation happen, he falls asleep; [but when] harmful stories come up, he wakes up. If examples **(371)** of exegeses enter, he slumbers. If riddles and stories and foolish worldly proverbs

and the frivolous conversation of old women are stirred up, see, he is the first one ready and prepared to repeat them, and he will usually be the first one to tell them. He does not know what subjugates his desire, unless it is only bragging. His soul is empty of fruits and full of the collection of the leaves of insipid stories. He runs to take refuge in simplicity when he hears that truths are being spoken. While he is shrewd with regard to evil things and astute with regard to malice, he identifies simplicity as the reality that no one knows the truth, faith being considered something belonging to himself [alone] that transmits his faith to those who are in error. He commands everyone to be silent from spiritual matters so that he might have an opportunity to repeat the vain things he loves. Above and below this is his story, the lusts of his belly and the pleasures of his body. He neither knows nor senses that there is anything else besides the service of his stomach.

Image of Animals

20. Therefore, the glutton bears the image of animals in all his aspects, while his soul is more wretched and debased than they. Animals are made by the Creator for these two things: while their life consists in their eating,[9] they may carry out work and service for the human race; but the glutton eats and does not work. While he is zealous for the table, he is bereft of all works of diligence. The soul that serves the belly does not perceive God because it is asleep from (372) all thoughts of knowledge and from meditation on God, since the soul's knowledge springs up with the lightness of the senses and members of the body. The body's lightness comes from the lessening of food, but it is certain that the glutton is doubly yoked, both with the obscurity of thoughts and with the heaviness of the body.

Maligning Ascetics Who Eat

21. The stories of the labors of the courageous also weigh heavily upon him because they are the opposites of his way of life. If

---

[9] Typographical error: written ܩܘܬܠܗܘܢ ܚܝܐ, read ܩܘܬܠܗܘܢܚܝܐ.

it happens he has heard about one of them who on account of the love of his brother has broken his abstinence, or as a free person due to the fear of illness or [due to] the necessity of weakness in order to support his body performing labors [he had relaxed] a little of his asceticism for a short time, [the glutton] has grabbed hold of this and repeats at all times that "so and so" used to eat, mentioning it before everyone so that it might be an excuse for his laxity and through it hide his despicable lusts. It is not this way, O glutton, as you have imagined. It is not with [the same] intention that you have eaten [that] the diligent are taking nourishment. Their desires are not being fulfilled through their food, nor are they making themselves slaves to their stomachs by your example, but as free people they take up sustenance for need only. Do not take from them that they have lowered themselves to eating only for the sake of need, but observe as well their asceticism and consider the prolonged time of their abstinence, and that while they are eating [it is] not lust they are fulfilling, but need.

It is one thing that one should eat for desire and another that one should gain nourishment for need. Whoever eats on account of his need, eats for his soul and not for his body, because **(373)** he nourishes his body in order that it might be found to be ready and prepared at all times for the soul that requires it. But whoever eats with desire, his food is for his body and not for his soul. It does not even occur to him that he has a spiritual nature, for only as if from far away does he hear the word of others that he has a soul.

Dead Soul

22. The soul of a glutton is dead, and while it does exist in him, it is as if it were not [there]. When [the soul] is not stirred up or active or operating by one of its own [faculties] but is dead[10] to all movements of knowledge, all its conduct and way of life is only physical. Look, is it not as if—while it does exist—that it does not, and while dwelling in the body it appears that it is not in it? The

---

[10] Lemoine reads *mḥtā* (ܡܚܬܐ) as *mītā* (ܡܝܬܐ), "is dead."

body is known by two things: by its appearance and by its works. But the soul is known only by its works, because its nature is inside the appearance. From here also, while there is a soul in the glutton, as it is from the Maker, it is not in him according to [God's] will, because the deeds by which it is known are not found with him. Therefore, the glutton's soul accuses and complains against him, even though he is not aware of its complaint because he is dead to it. Just as a living body accompanies someone dead while he is not aware of it, so the glutton's soul is attached to his body while he is not aware of it. It bears and leads around a cadaver, because he lives only for pleasures and not for [the soul].

Enemy of God and of Fasting

23. While all the passions, as I have said, are worthy of blame by the word of justice, more than **(374)** all of them this passion is the most blameworthy from the normal, not only because it is the opposite of knowledge, but even more because it is the enemy of God. A person who degrades himself beneath a useless life of the lust of the belly does not consider a thing for the world or for God and does not receive [either] one of them, because diligence is required for the world, and God, moreover, seeks from human beings labors, austerities, and purity of soul. If these are not in him, [God] does not receive him. Gluttony is the opposite of these things and flees from labors and from austerities.

I do not think that one is able to describe [completely] this evil of the lust of the belly, especially one who has not experienced its passions. The fast is its enemy, and hearing about asceticism and abstinence disquiets and troubles it. The glutton does not live for any other thing except only this—to conduct himself like the animals. If someone should call him thus by name—even though in fact he is [one]—it will anger him. The fool does not comprehend that what the other said verbally to him is in fact the case with himself. [It is] not that the other person insults him, but he himself is an insult. When his insults are derived from himself and he is the root of his wrongs, who is there for this despicable person to be blamed, and how shall he find fault with those who speak against [gluttony], for look, he has placed **(375)** himself in the very middle so that he might become conversation for others? Every person thinks about him, and everyone speaks about him: one puckers a lip; another, a wink of his eye; another, giving [a gesture] with his finger; and others murmur and relate his dissoluteness. But the soul of a glutton has been selected as the most enduring, and even though he endures all these things happening to him and rejoices, the only consolation being made for him [is] the pleasure of his belly. Lacking in intelligence, he does not comprehend that ever since toil and trouble have encountered him on all sides, he should accept to bear the labors of asceticism rather than the reproaches of the lust of the belly.

The Tired Glutton

24. Therefore, from all sides fatigue encounters a person, whether with dissoluteness or asceticism. It would be much better to endure labors with praises for asceticism than to endure fatigue with reproaches and shames for gluttony. However, the glutton is more [fatigued] than the ascetic, not in containing his lusts, but in serving his lusts; not in acquiring perseverance, but in performing slavery for his belly; and not in being brave in the austerities fitting for courage, but in serving the desires of [his] dissoluteness while being wearied and tired;[11] or while he is gathering and collecting for himself the fullness of his desires like dry twigs gathered for the fire, or while bearing the weight of foods after being fed them, because the eating of heavy foods is heavier for the stomach than lead is as a weight for the shoulder. As soon as a person eats beyond the norm, weight is heaped upon his entire [body]. All his members become feeble, **(376)** the power of his senses is weakened, the sight of his eye also becomes dark by an excessive flow of humidity, and moreover the ear's hearing becomes more dull, and the tongue's word becomes impeded, and the mind, the source of words, clouds over. The intellect, the pilot of wisdom, becomes agitated. Also its

---

[11] Lemoine reads Ms. F, *welā'ē* (ܪܪܕܐ), "tired, wearied," instead of text's *wla* (ܪܕܐ), "and not."

flow of words becomes confused and stumbling. The joints are dislocated, the knees are quivering and the hands are trembling, and the vessel of the glutton's person is completely wasting away and growing old prematurely by the excessive weight of the food that he carries.

Health and Meager Food

25. Therefore, innumerable are the ailments engendered by too much food, [while] asceticism does not create disease in the body as does gluttony. Under the pretext that gluttons do not become sick—so they say—gluttons devote themselves to food, and the fools are not aware that they are fleeing from what will happen to them. Wherever they run to receive health, they find there an ailment facing them. Wherever they try to escape from diseases, there diseases will be gathered for them. Who does not know that a reduction in food along with meager nourishment gives health to the body, especially when moderate labor accompanies it? The teaching of doctors who are more knowledgeable than all the [other] professions also testifies about this matter of the body's health and the sickness, that is, their teaching is the art that **(377)** has been found for the body's support. If these [doctors] are asked, they will always prescribe a reduction in food, and along with this, one's food should be meager, and they are extremely cautious of drinking too much wine. If they permit a person to drink [wine] on account of necessity, they dilute its strength by a lot of water and then allow him to drink; on the other hand, prescribing that a person should be completely wary of idleness, love weariness, and be busy[12] with work, and [that] in all cases laboring in close connection with exercises will keep the physical health of people. These are, as they say, so that the arteries of the body might not be filled with vital fluids that come from too much food and become stopped up and do not let the living power of food continually pass through

---

[12] Lemoine reads Ms. F, *wnet'ne* (ܪܠܫܕܘ), "to be busy," instead of text's *wnetb'e* (ܪܠܕܘ).

them, which is the strengthener of the body. They also wrote this down: the cause of all the diseases of the body is food. If it should happen and [diseases] should be engendered from other causes, if there should be too much food, [food] increases [their problems] and holds them back completely from the benefits of medicine.

Ailments from Too Much Food

26. Besides the word of doctors, we should understand from experience as wise people that the cause of all evils, diseases, and ailments of the body is from too much food. If you wish, consider the rich and the poor, those who are comfortable and those who are harassed, those who do nothing and those who labor, and see who has kept **(378)** his body healthy and who has numerous and frequent illnesses, and with their great number [of illnesses] do they not risk losing their life? Is it not [the case] with the rich, whose stomachs are bursting from too much eating, who before they digest and clear out their first meal are hastening for another on account of their gluttony? [With them] these diseases are obstinate and stubborn. This is the wage their gluttony gives to them, for they are also worthy to receive this reward from that mistress of iniquity whom they serve: to some a disease of hands and of feet; to some tumors and ulcers that occur from too much [weight] of the body; to some trembling of the members and shaking of the head, and an ailment of the intestines, with the rest of the other afflictions, because it is from this that thorns come to sprout in them; to some heavy sleep at all times; to some continual slumber at all hours; to some the weight of the entire body, sneezing, and frequent hiccups, while also whatever the glutton may say is obviously sent out from heavy members, being born from a mind plunged into [the depths of] the flesh. All these things happen to gluttons, even while they constantly bring other remedies to their bodies—discharges and purgatives, and other means for the assistance of the body, blood-letting, drugs, purging, and continual ablutions at all hours. But too much food defeats all these means of assistance and creates for them dangerous diseases and harsh illnesses **(379)** in their bodies, whose healing is difficult even for wise doctors.

Poor Person's Health

27. But the poor person who conducts his life in labor and with fatigue acquires a healthy body. His body is light and ready for all work. He does not hang on it excessive weight, and if he should eat more than his allotment of his meager food by his own ignorance, immediately his labor's work accepts the weight of his food, his labor acting for him as a constant doctor, and without the means of medicines he receives health from it. Which doctor knows [how] to heal the body in the same manner that the work of labor heals him, and what is more, without injuries and without medicines? Labor does not take medicines and bring aids from outside itself like a doctor, but it is the doctor and it is the medicine. It is the one that binds up [wounds] and it is the bandage. It is the healer and the cure. The assistance [it gives] derives from itself, and it gathers into it the health of all the members. Therefore, through this [labor] from which dissoluteness flees because of the love of pleasures, poverty finds health.

I am not saying that diseases do not also happen to the poor, and that there are no ailments for laborers and those fatigued, but that the diseases of the rich are more numerous and more difficult to heal because they are lazy throughout all their lives and have been made servants of their pampered body while serving its desires or subtracting surplus from it, or healing the diseases born from being too full. They devote their entire life to the elimination of these things, and beyond it they are unaware there is anything else. On the other hand, the disease of a poor person **(380)** is easy to heal, and [any] excessiveness of his body is minor and of little concern. Quickly he receives health from the medicines brought to him because these causes that are cut off from him increase excessive things in his body.

Associate of a Murderer

28. If this is the way things are, who would not love the reduction of food that is the mother of health? But I know that these [words] are considered irrelevant by gluttons, because his ear is stopped up by his desire and is not able to hear sound teaching. It is as if food were made a curtain in front of all his senses, preventing them from their natural function. Who will not weep over this seeing that he

damages a beautiful work of God by his laxity? That is, he is justly worthy of a punishment, not only on account of the fact that he serves his lusts and enrages God by his desire, but also on account of the fact that he damages by his gluttony healthy members that were beautifully fashioned by the Maker. Whoever corrupts the members of his body by means of his gluttony is the associate of a murderer and a companion of a corrupting thief. What is written in the Law is appropriate for him, "Every murderer shall be put to death,"[13] and "Whoever cuts off the member of his neighbor shall have his [own] member cut off."[14] The glutton corrupts the members of his own body and little by little destroys and consumes the strength of his body and of his members. He damages the beautiful creation of God and tears down the building of his body that the will of the architect had previously built.

By all [kinds of] reasons he incurs punishments **(381)** on himself, according to the word of uprightness; first, because he had transgressed against the commandment of God who has commanded that a person should not become a servant to his desires; and then because he is inhibited from beautiful actions and the work of all virtues that the Holy Scriptures are continually urging us to do; and, moreover, [because] he has willfully driven away from himself the memory of spiritual things; and again, because almsgiving for the poor is despised by him, his gluttony also provokes him to depart from it to greed; and along with these things, because he damages his beautiful constitution by his own hands and corrupts the desirable members of the creation of God that [God] had created by his grace for the service of his desires. See, therefore, the cause of your [broken-down] constitution, O glutton, and tremble before God, and do not damage yourself.

Why Make Your Belly God?

29. There is another hope that is not visible—why is your hope tied to your belly? There is another [kind of] food that is spiri-

---

[13] Exod 21:12; Lev 24:17.
[14] Exod 21:24; Lev 24:19-20.

tual—why are you crazy for worthless foods? Christ has a table that has been promised to his friends—why do you suspend your attention to look at the time for the table? There is another world with its heavenly blessings—why have you confined your life's confidence in the visible world? Have you counted as benefits the losses [included] in it? Not for this has the Creator created you, to eat like animals, but to take nourishment as a rational being and to glorify him as a living being. Not for this did he make you live, to eat, but to allow you to take measured nourishment in order to live. Not for food was your life ordained, **(382)** O miserable one, but in order to be sustained by measured nourishment. Distinguish your life from the life of animals. Do not become a servant to your stomach and offer it for the service of corrupting desires. You are a wise person; do not bind your soul by your own volition with an animal's yoke. You are a beautiful image of your creator. Why have you inscribed on yourself the likeness of animals? The word of the One who has called you has invited you to be equal with spiritual beings. Why do you roll about and fall down to be defiled with hogs in the mire of lusts?

You have been ordained to [sing] the Holy [Trisagion] with the seraphim. Why do you compare your life with a mute beast by your feebleness? You are the master of creation by the will of your Maker. Why have you voluntarily been made the servant of your belly? The will of your Creator has committed all of creation to you, and have you subjected yourself to your small belly? All the natures are bound to the yoke of your subjection, but have you placed upon your neck the yoke of a corrupting mistress? All the species and works [of creation] obey your word, yet have you made yourself a feeble servant to a stinking desire? You have been made a god by the true God, but have you made your belly a god? You have authority, glorious one, over his work, but by your wretchedness are you lowering yourself to this completely despicable desire? He has created everything for your glory, but are you exchanging his glory for your belly? God calls you to conversation with him, but is your own thought tied down to the table? You have been made a rational instrument of the holy praises, but are you wearing yourself out and cutting off the strings of your lyre by your wretchedness?

Your Lord has loved you to such an extent that he should become food for you, but for his love should you not have abstained from vile **(383)** foods? The Living One died and was buried in order to save you, yet have you made yourself a tomb for food? He has not spared his life and has given it to death for your life, but are you not acquiring a little food for your life on account of his love? Look at the life that is promised to you, O wretched one, and see this life you are living in the world and at least be ashamed of yourself. Therefore, do not become by your life a tomb for your soul and corrupt yourself before you are corrupted naturally in the tomb. Look, your soul is buried in your body like a body in the tomb, the body being a glorious instrument ordained by the Creator to belong to the soul and associate with all good things. Why have you made [your body] become a tomb for [your soul] and enclosed yourself[15] in it as if in a place of filth? The glutton's body is corrupted by his eating before natural death might corrupt it. It becomes worn out and wastes away little by little before dwelling in Sheol wears it out. The glutton's diseases are from the will and not from nature, because even if they flourish in his corporal nature, still their cause is his will and by his freedom they are born in him by too much food.

Scandalous Presence

30. Therefore, the life of whoever loves desires is a scandal and he sins not only in himself but also is the cause of harm for those who see him. He is a disease placed in the center and everyone who passes by him is scandalized by him—the dissolute and the vigorous, those living in luxury and the chaste, the pampered and the ascetics, those who eat and those who abstain; some are offended and some increase their dissoluteness. **(384)** The glutton, seeing his companion, adds more unto his own dissoluteness. The dissolute person looks at him and puts on his dissoluteness again like one coat over [another] coat. Whoever is grasped by the desire of his belly sees him and remains even more with his love. But

---

[15] Written: ܬܬܚܫܒ, *teṭḥšab*, "consider yourself"; read: ܬܬܚܒܫ, *teṭḥbaš*, "enclose oneself."

the valiant and ascetics suffer loss because they are scandalized by him, and his story draws them into a conversation they do not like. From all sides he stirs up war against them, whether [it be] not to lower themselves at the sight of his dissoluteness and become like him, or not to cease conversation with God at the narration of his dissoluteness, or not to become prideful by their tenacity comparing their virtuous life with his dissoluteness. In that manner that the courageous and the diligent assist themselves as well as their companions, in the very same way the dissolute and friends of lusts cause harm to themselves and to those who see them, and their life in the world is found to be in all ways a cause of harm for [other] people.

Alert Like a Dog

31. The youth of the glutton is something despicable and his adolescence is something ridiculous, and his old age is a matter of reproach. His youth is dissolute; his adolescence, licentious; his old age, indulgent. Games and pleasures are plentiful for his youth, adultery and fornication for his adolescence, eating and vain conversations for his old age. Not only does he hate doing good things, but also hearing their narration. Not only doing them weighs heavily upon him, but also if he should hear conversation about them. On that account, if one should repeat to him a triumph of the saints, **(385)** immediately deep sleep and yawning seize him. His entire body bears the weight of sloth, while showing signs of the death of his soul by the stretching of his limbs and the conduct of his body. If he is able to depart, he moves away, and if not he immediately falls asleep on the spot. The soul of a glutton is like a dog and justly one ought to give him this name. In that same way a dog is asleep amidst all events, and the conversation and speech of human beings is strange to its hearing, for only the sound of the table and the sight of food awakens him, so also the glutton is like him, immersed in the slumber of sloth, and all profitable subjects are considered irrelevant to him. Divine words pour over his ear like water over a rock. But, [if] someone repeats before him a story about the stomach or a conversation about food, at once his soul is

awakened, his thoughts are alerted, his body immediately becomes light, and he jumps into a conversation of what he loves, like a dog before his beckoning.

Calling by Name

32. Therefore, one ought to call a glutton by names such as these so that he may hear his names and be ashamed of his desire. Since [he is] like a hog rolling around in the mire of [its] desires, one should call [him] by its name. Since, like a dog who wakes up suddenly at the sound of the table, the tales of the belly also awaken him, it is fitting that he should also be named a dog. Since he runs quickly to the table like a beast to [its] manger, he can be justly called by the name of a beast. Since like an animal he is deprived of all conversations of wisdom **(386)** and of knowledge, and lives only for his body, he should be called by that name that suits him by his deeds. If there were, moreover, other names more disreputable and abominable than these, it would be suitable that he should be called by them. The speech that calls him by names such as these is not shameful to him, because his shame comes from within. Just as names are derived from things and are called by names derived from them, so the glutton's names are rightly taken from him, and appropriately he is called by names that are taken from him. A person who dishonors himself—who will honor him? A person who pursues his own despicableness—who will praise him? A person who attracts mockery and hateful speech upon himself—who will be deprived of his good name more than him?

The Glutton's Friends

33. I should speak again, besides these things I have already said, and show the characteristics of gluttons so that by them [gluttons] may be known to all those who are discerning, and so that they may be despised and disdained as is fitting by all those who see [them]. These are the laws for one who is subservient to his belly. He does not really love anyone. If it happens that he loves one who has been made a servant and minister for the desire he loves, [he will love] this person [only] as long as he fulfills his pleasures. But

if for some reason [his friend] should happen to be changed and neglect and reduce his honors a little, at once [the glutton] will also change his love, and his praises that [he gives] to his friend will be turned around **(387)** into reproach. Because his own love is tied to the belly, anyone who serves [his belly] is his friend. Whoever neglects it is perceived by him as an enemy.

Again he starts to look for those friends who will be useful to him, those who are capable of becoming servants to his desire. Steadfast people he does not like. The pure he does not love. Those who are hard-working he considers rustics. The righteous are counted by him as fools. Those constant in prayer are said by him to be without work. Seeing a stranger, he passes by him at a distance. He hears a report about one of those he believes could become stewards for his desire; look, he flies with the speed of the love of his desire, his belly carrying his feet. He circles all around, becoming a friend of the wealthy and a servant and minister to the great people. Their conversation is considered by him glorious and talking with them a [matter of] pride. Hearing the Gospel is not as dear to him as the conversation of one whom he believes[16] has borne and brought the fulfillment of his desire. Perhaps the feet of Abraham—while bearing for them the love [of God] and running to the herd so that he might bring a calf to the angels[17]—were not as light as the feet of the glutton rushing toward one who is bringing him food. His entire love is in order to receive. If it happens that he gives, [he does so] in order that more might be given back.

Telling Stories

34. He does not know how to acquire a friend without the belly, for he wishes that what he loves should also be loved by others. If there is murmuring against him, he thinks that he can appease it with a gift of the stomach. If he has angered someone by his foolishness and his jealousy, he runs with a gift of food **(388)** to

---

[16] Lemoine reads variant (Ms. F): *dmesabbar* (ܕܡܣܒܪ), instead of written text: *dmesaybar* (ܕܡܣܝܒܪ).

[17] Gen 18:7.

reconcile him. His hope is based on [food], and through it he thinks the bonds of his deeds can be released. As for that god he serves, he believes madly that everyone is bound like him in its servitude, and by his example his belly is his god. He waits anxiously for the visit of a friend, but if he has arrived and has not brought [anything], [his] soul's expectation and his face's appearance are changed. The glutton's hand is stretched out to receive and closed [to give] gifts. If he should happen to give, it is to set up for himself an occasion to be rewarded even more. Wherever[18] he knows that the law leads to a gift [which] usually will be given to him, there he does not bother to honor [the donor], for he knows that even while he might not be rewarded [as a result], custom and law will lead to a gift. He rewards wherever he is rewarded and lays a foundation of debt where it was not laid. Moreover, he repeats before new friends the tales of his old friends and recalls to memory also the gifts that he had received from them. "Such a one sent to me [such a thing], and such a one forced me, and while I did not desire [it] he compelled me by oaths and I took [it]." As one might say, "Listen and learn, and do likewise!" He teaches new friends the deeds of old acquaintances and makes them disciples of the first laws of the ancients.

He ignores all [other] stories and makes his own the center of attention. If a story should be told, whether of a work of labor or of a divine teaching, he craftily twists and disposes of it in order to bring about a tale of the stomach into the middle. He does not live for any other thing, neither in his conversation **(389)** nor in his language, his occupation, his accomplishments, his concerns, nor in his thoughts. The blessing of blessings is considered by him the lust of the belly and all of his questions are stirred up by this. He knows the different kinds of foods and knows also the tastes of [different] places, from which garden the fruits are most pleasing, and from which river the catch is most tasty, and who knows [better] how to season and arrange tasty foods. These are his questions and his explanations.

---

[18] Lemoine reads Ms. F variant: *'aikā* (ܐܝܟܐ), "wherever," instead of written *'ainā* (ܐܝܢܐ), "that, who."

The Ennui of the Glutton's Prayer

35. Two eggs are more dear to him than the New and Old [Testaments]. Hearing about a vigil terrifies him. Prolonged prayer is a torture for him. If you lengthen [the time] of genuflection, he grumbles about it. If you lengthen a prayer, he mumbles to himself, turns the gaze of his eye all the time toward the windows, looks at the trajectory of the sun. He sets limits for it. He marks the hours. One day is considered two in his eyes. Prayer is short, but the time of his eating is long. There is nothing that he accepts for himself except only to fulfill the lusts of his belly. Everything else is considered by him to be irrelevant—reading and learning, fasting and abstinence, prayer and psalms, ministry and genuflections. If he should perform them by customary law out of shame, he will do them with abhorrence and grumbling. What pretexts will he use to cease prayer? He will seek to have conversations with such and such people, along with other distracting activities, so that he might be held back from worship and singing. These things of God are [performed] by him carelessly, but those things that he desires, [he does] with complete **(390)** diligence and love. If a tiny sore should be on his body, he takes it to be a harsh ulcer. If he should be a little sluggish, he considers it a dangerous and obstinate illness. He seizes anything of profit as a pretext to bring an end to the only reason for his life. He is zealous in everything aside from this, [that is] to serve God. Also while he is not sick, he schemes to show himself as being sick, so that when he ceases from worship and fasting, he is not greatly censured. He recites his diseases before everyone, and while the cause of his illness [may be] small and insignificant, he makes it greater and enlarges it. He calls on God as a witness so that through this [action] he may convince those who hear him that he is applying himself forcefully to the labor of the monastery.

Only Cure Is by Eating

36. The glutton tinkers with the health of his body, and while he has with him the means to block the source of his illnesses—to suppress his gluttony a little—he wanders and seeks help outside

of himself. If you advise him, "Reduce your eating a little and keep yourself from oil and from wine," you will be considered by him as an enemy of his life. "It would be better for me[19] [to suffer] diseases and not to deprive the belly of something. I will accept protracted illnesses and only my desires will I fulfill. If one wishes [to give me] medicine in order to cure me with eating, [good], but if not, it would be better for me to eat more than to be healed."

Use and Abuse of Friends

37. Therefore, the glutton has many corporeal friends to accumulate for him from all sides the needs of his desire. He is cunning and crafty in his planning, knowing which friends to choose and [what] to do [with them]. **(391)** For not even by mistake does he consent to acquire [as] friends one of the blessed or one of those who have renounced or one of those who are bearing the labors [of asceticism] or the lovers of the [highest] virtue or one of those who are acquiring the knowledge of Christ. Not even by chance or by name does he consent to become a friend of these [people]. Not only this, but he is also their secret enemy because by their appearance and by their word and deeds they confute his gluttony. On account of this, he begrudges and hates them. If you see him honoring one of the sages or one of the upright, he does this for show lest he be accused by the faithful who love these good things and, moreover, to silence the murmuring of many and deflect from himself the eager zeal of those who honor the good things.

Seduction of the Zealous

39. If he sees a young disciple dressed with the discernment of faithful zeal, like a benevolent person he calms him down and advises him as one having compassion for him, "Be silent and do not dishonor your family and do not abandon your stillness. Be silent and, look, you will be loved. Be occupied only with fasting and with

---

[19] Lavenant reads (ܠܝ) "for me" instead of text's (ܠܟ) "for you" to fit the sense.

prayer, and do not approach anything that does not pertain to you."
He counsels here these things in order to calm down the zeal of the
disciple and not because he is well pleased with the cultivation of
virtues. After bringing him down from this good thing—consisting
of a person struggling for God—he begins to pull down as well the
virtues that follow this, that is, the weight of labors and austerities
(392) that are for God, and fasts of asceticism and protracted prayers.

Self-Justification

39. It is not that these things are necessary, he says, but so that a
person may purify himself and acquire a good mind. He finds a reason in hidden actions in order to nullify public actions and makes
himself righteous in those things that are not required because his
dissoluteness rebukes his public actions. Wherever it is not easy
for people to see, there he makes himself out to be righteous, and
whatever austerities and labors are visible, he schemes to slander
them, giving other explanations for them. It is not this that God
requires of us, he usually says, that one should kill himself and
afflict his body more than the standard, but that we should become
righteous in our souls and purified from evil things in our thought.
While his way of life is beneath the level of animals, the wretched
man will speak about spiritual things like a perfect one.

Manipulation of Scripture

40. His explanations are long in favor of his method. If he hears
a word from Scripture useful to him, he seizes it with all prudence
so that it might be useful for him at the right time when he becomes
involved in a verbal battle against those who are reproaching his
gluttony. When he wishes to eat everything and not hold himself
back from eating any of the foods, he begins to repeat what was
written by our Lord, "It is not what enters the stomach [that] defiles
the person."[20] His ear is alert[21] for this only, to hear those things

---

[20] Matt 15:11.
[21] Literally, "his ear is pierced."

that appear to give a hand to his desire, and before hearing other things he closes the door of his hearing. He is not pleased to hear that other [word], "Whoever wishes to become my disciple **(393)** let him renounce himself and take up his cross and follow me."[22] Nor that other [saying], "Whoever wishes to save his soul must lose it,"[23] nor that one which moreover [Jesus] said to his disciples, "In the world you will have afflictions,"[24] nor that one, "When the bridegroom has been taken from the sons of the bridal feast, then they shall fast."[25] Maybe also that meal of our Lord where it is written concerning him that he had performed the feast and had eaten the Pascha, or where it is said that "they set before him a portion of roasted fish"[26] and a honeycomb, or where it is also written, "They had upon them fish with bread,"[27] the glutton presents to them an example such as these when he simply wishes to eat everything. He establishes for himself the way of freedom of Christ, who, as God, was above the laws and commandments, to be the stumbling block for his life, but does not understand the reason of that way of life and does not sense that other types were being inscribed there. Moreover, when the Apostle is read and he hears from him, "Everything created by God is holy and there is nothing that is rejected if it is received with thanksgiving because it is made holy by the word of God and by prayer,"[28] or this other [saying], "The stomach is [meant for] food and the food is [meant for] the stomach,"[29] or that one in which he says again, "He who does not eat should not judge that one who does eat,"[30] and in such things as these inscribed in the teaching of Paul **(394)** he rejoices and receives them excessively, although the fool does not under-

---

[22] Matt 16:24.
[23] Matt 16:25.
[24] John 16:33.
[25] Luke 5:35.
[26] Luke 24:42.
[27] John 6:9.
[28] 1 Tim 4:4.
[29] 1 Cor 6:13.
[30] Rom 14:3.

stand the rationale of the words. Nor does he wish to hear the other [sayings] that were written on valor and on asceticism by Paul, whether [Paul] relates about his numerous fasts, or crying out to his disciples, "You are dead to the world,"[31] or when he writes, "It is good that one should not eat meat or drink wine,"[32] or where he warns, "through many tribulations it is necessary for a person to enter the kingdom of God,"[33] or where he says, "But God will bring both of them to an end, the belly and the food."[34] Therefore, on the reading of such things like these, the glutton ignores the literal [meaning] and does not even desire to hear them.

Memories of Food

41. Therefore, the life of one who is a friend of pleasures consists of these ways. Just as the memory of God is near to the perfect, so at all times concern for his belly is near to him. He sings and worries about it. Its memory is borne at all times through his prayer and his service. He worries about it constantly, because there is no other life outside of it. The memory of [the stomach] makes light of his prayers, and its continual worry causes him to cease from all appropriate things. The times of his eating are not distinguished for the glutton, but by night and by day he eats and eats [again]. While he may not [appear to be] eat[ing], he is eating. For you do not observe him eating [more than] once or twice [a day]; nevertheless, notice that all times of night and day (395) it is his concern. While his body is not eating, his thought eats. Not even for animals are the times for eating distinguished, because an animal, even if it eats all the time, night and day, it is without a set time, but [an animal] does not worry all the time about its eating. But the glutton is eating all the time because he is thinking all the time about his belly, perhaps even while he is asleep because he sees [himself] eating in his dream. Shame is removed from the eyes of

[31] Rom 6:3ff.
[32] Rom 14:21.
[33] Acts 14:22.
[34] 1 Cor 6:13.

the glutton because impudence has made his face appear that he is not ashamed. He hears its taunts and ignores [them]. It shames him, yet he does not pay any attention. The love of his belly defeats in him all the violent forces that batter him. He is bereft of spiritual things, that is, he does not even know that they exist. He chooses the most excellent oils, requests the purest wines, asks for the tastiest foods. There is no work for him in the world except this. As long as we tell his story, we will not have come to an end of the story of his dissoluteness. From what we have said, we have given [only] a small taste of the kinds of his dissoluteness, so that from this those who see him might come to recognize him.

Imitate Ascetics, Not Gluttons

42. But you, O valiant disciple, flee from the example of this [glutton], and do not slack off from the rigorousness of your way of life by the sight of him. Know to whom you have become a disciple, and may your discipleship become the reason for your course [of life]. Do not imitate the sluggish person, but emulate the industriousness of the valiant. Do not let a person who is the model of an animal become a model for you. Do not count that one eats and drinks and fulfills his desires to be a good thing, but [as an] evil thing more evil than all the [other] evils. Hear also the word (396) of prophecy, the woe that was accorded to the gluttons, "Woe to those who are up early in the morning and run to strong drink and tarry in the evening and wine sets them on fire. With harps and lyres, tambourines and timbrels, they drink wine and do not understand the works of God."[35] Look, the spirit has also taught you that someone serving his [own] desires is not able to understand the works of God. As we are not able to speak in our sleep and act like those wide awake, so also a person who is plunged deep into pleasurable sleep does not understand the living works of God or know [how] to gauge his direction [in life] and admire the varieties of his providence, and does not know through it [what is] marvelous concerning the majesty of his glory or [how to] be alert

---

[35] Isa 5:11.

to his knowledge and ready to respond to his wisdom. Whoever is submerged in desire does not sense these things, because these memories belong to those who are awake and are living. A blessing is given to whoever understands these things. For if a curse is given to those who eat and drink and do not understand the works of God, a blessing, the opposite of these, is given to ascetics and abstainers who at all times meditate on the works of God. But you, O disciple, run to be worthy of a blessing and flee from the curse promised to gluttons, and may those who are diligent become an example to you for good and not those who are lazy, and [may] those who fast [be an example] and not those who eat, and the ascetics and not the gluttons, the abstainers and not those who are greedy, those who serve God and not those who serve their stomach, and those who are valiant and not dissolute, those who are good and not those who are evil.

Good people are not **(397)** lacking from the world to be an example for you of virtues. Let us imitate them and not those who are evil. Therefore, do not consider these people who stand below you, but lift your eyes above and observe those people who are greater than you, and rise up to them. Just as with worldly matters every person chooses greater things, so also with these godly matters, let us choose for ourselves greater and more elevated things. So then, there is no one in the world who loves poverty more than wealth, for everyone declines it and pursues wealth, and flees from diseases and pursues physical health. Through this example here let us pursue these things of the spirit and love the wealth of valor and not the poverty of gluttony. Let us love the health of our souls and of our thoughts more than the ailments of desires.

No Power over Spiritual Health

43. The soul of the person who serves desires is sick all the time and does not have control over his spiritual strength and health. Just as one whose body is sick does not have control over his health in order to eat what he desires, nor over his strength to do what he wishes, so also a person whose soul is sick through gluttony does not have the power over the strength and health of his soul to

occupy himself with his works and [do] everything as he wishes and desires. Through that example in which the limbs do not respond to the sick person when he wishes to move them for a particular action, so also his thoughts do not respond to a glutton when he wishes to perform through them a particular good deed. All **(398)** the virtues are difficult for one who is subservient to his belly, because he is the servant of all these desires. If the passion of food is stirred up in him, he is not easily able to defeat it because he is its subject; neither [is he able to defeat] the desire of fornication if it stirs in his members, nor rage and anger, nor jealousy and evil intention; nor is it easy for him to defeat [even] one of the despicable passions because he is the servant and subject of all of them.

One Passion Hard to Defeat

44. [The passions] are difficult to be subdued, especially when there are many of them. If a single passion should have power over our life and subject us for a long time with the work of its slavery, it is difficult for us to defeat it; how much more will we be defeated by numerous masters? Through gluttony, as I have spoken, all the rest of the passions enter because it is the entrance of all the lusts. But our Savior said in his Gospel, "You are not able to serve God and mammon."[36] And if by our subjection to a single master, that is, to mammon alone, we are not able to serve God with it, when there are many masters subjecting us and every one of them is directing us forcefully to its will, how are we able to serve God, that One who does not accept that a human being should serve any other thing besides him? Therefore, if all these sins together are the adversary of the uprightness of God, each one of them opposing its neighbor in its service, **(399)** how will they not all become, in their being served, hindrances to the commandments of God? They are different from one another in their actions, and the will of God is the opponent of all of them, especially of this lust of gluttony by which each one of the rest of the other lusts are escorted and enter little by little.

---

[36] Matt 6:24.

Varieties of Foods as Test of Desire

45. Therefore, when a person is forced to perform slavery to his belly, it throws him into great turmoil[37] so that he may gather from all sides and bring to it its needs, because it seeks not only to eat but how it should eat. If it had reclined at table only to satisfy its needs, the belly's need would have been satisfied with something small and with ordinary and lowly things worthy of their prices. How often have many people made use of roots and herbs, because they sought their need and not the satisfaction of their desires? Even if God as a wealthy creator had given everything abundantly to our use, we should observe his will and conduct ourselves in this way. For on that account he increased foods and the varieties of tastes in the world to be a vessel for the testing of desire and to examine by them the mind of people. What do they desire and what are they pursuing? Wherever there are no objects desirable, there is no examination of desire. But as for the disciple, he should know himself and not become subservient to the desire of his body **(400)** and not open the door that allows destructive animals to enter.

A Door Left Open

46. Just as a fortified door is closed, keeping evil beasts and poisonous serpents outside, if it should be opened for some reason, all who dwell inside the place will be liable to harm; in the same way, when the door of the lust of the belly is shut, all the murderous passions of the destructive lusts of the soul are outside and do not enter and harm and destroy the spiritual nature of the soul. But if this door should be opened before them through our dissoluteness, and the will does for our stomach what it desires, immediately all vices gather together and enter into our soul and destroy all thoughts of excellence in it.

---

[37] Read Ms. F, *b'amlā* (ܒܥܡܠܐ), "labor," "travail," instead of written text *b'almā* (ܒܥܠܡܐ), "in the world."

Other Lusts Enter

47. At the very moment you open this door, the destructive beast of fornication enters, eating and destroying equally soul and body, and afterward the lust of money[38] [enters] for which both of them are in need, the lust of the belly and fornication, and whatever is born from them. Grief is born from the lust of money, whether concerning what we do not possess, or if we should lose what we have collected, whether completely or a little bit of it. From here again the passion of anger is born in us, being enraged or angry against those who do not allow themselves to be defrauded by us according to our desire, or against those who are not obedient in fulfilling their service to us, and sometimes against servants, sometimes against hired hands, and sometimes against those who are **(401)** more despised and inferior to us. Against these, we become full of rage and anger because of [particular] reasons that confront us. Moreover, we are filled with jealousy against those who are greater and richer than us, and [that is] robbery and fraud. How many times are we led to murder by this reason? Through this wealth pride also grasps us and we desire vainglory from people through the appearance of wealth. From here we learn to accept slander from those who are less than us, and, moreover, we also slander others who are greater than us. From these we also venture continually into lies and oaths and blasphemy against God. When the memory of judgment has completely disappeared from the soul, from then on it will commit all kinds of evil things without fear.

Fornication Fueled by Gluttony

48. Therefore, for such things like these, gluttony becomes the first cause. Who does not realize that the lust of fornication burns in the body that eats and drinks and lives luxuriously? While it may not be performed openly and be visible to people by action, yet it makes thoughts burn continually and the person seeks to

---

[38] Text has *karsā* (ܟܪܣܐ), "belly"; Lemoine reads *kespā* (ܟܣܦܐ), "silver, money," which is referred to below.

contrive a situation for the fire that is in him. He desires all sorts of beautiful things and stumbles on all forms that are seemly by their appearance. For as long as the fire of desire is in his members, his thoughts fly over all the faces and fornicates secretly with every figure. While one does not fornicate publicly, he continually is fornicating secretly. While he is not an adulterer in his body, he commits adultery in his soul at all times and always. **(402)** Therefore, food and drink are the fuel for the fire of lust. Whoever wishes to extinguish from his members this secret fire, let him hold himself back from this fuel, and see, it has been extinguished. Fasting and abstinence and asceticism are water that extinguishes the fire of desire. As oil is for fire, wine is for desire. As dung encourages the soil to yield fruits, so also the stink of foods entices the members by despicable desires.

Food Obscures the Mind

49. The veil of the intellect is too much food. Prior to thoughts of fornication, food by itself also obscures the intellect. For as long as the tumult of desire agitates pure thoughts—on account of this there is no doubt—especially those who have experienced it know, yet before this desire, the lust of the belly is the one that overwhelms the mind and sees the veil of the mind and the clouding of the thoughts that possess the light of knowledge. The darkness of an enlightened mind is the vapor of food. Just as thick fog and smoke disturb the pure and clear air, so also the vapor of food agitates the clarity of the intellect. The disciple of Christ should not only refuse foods that are expensive in their prices but also those things that are considered to be less [expensive]. It is not because food is expensive in costs [that] it disturbs the intellect and clouds the mind, but on account of its abundance, **(403)** and this harm is also found in those [foods] that are cheap, as well as in those that are expensive.

Memory of Food

50. The Scriptures correctly warn people of gluttony in every place. According to the teaching of Paul, "Those who occupy

themselves with food are not aided by it."[39] Not only that they are deprived of help, but they have accumulated for themselves losses and harm. "Neither the intemperate nor the drunkards shall inherit the kingdom of God."[40] Read in this passage, O disciple, and see with which vices the Apostle compares this evil thing: with [magical] charmers and corrupters and other ones like these. Even if the lust of the belly is not [like] these, it will lead to these [kinds of evil]. When the heart has become hard from food, immediately it drives away from it the memory of God. When the memory of God moves away from a person, which evil does he not do and by which iniquity is he not pushed?

Forgetting God and Remembering Food

51. As also the prophet Moses has taught us: by this reason the people had forgotten its God, and by the lust of the belly they had gone out to the worship of idols and were led from food to blasphemies, and from pleasures they attained all kinds of evils. "He made him [Israel] reside on a fertile land and allowed him to eat the harvests of the field. He allowed him to suck honey from a rock and oil from flint rock, the butter of cows and the milk of sheep, with the fat **(404)** of fattened animals, rams, the sons of ibexes, and kids, with the fat and the best of the wheat, and he has allowed him to drink the juice of grapes [for] wine. Israel became fat and resisted; he became fat and strong and acquired riches."[41] What happened to [Israel] as a result of these things? Where did [Israel] arrive on account of these pleasures? In which situation did he find himself on account of the delicacies with which he enjoyed himself? To which illnesses had gluttony and too much food cast him? Moses has explained and made known to us clearly what the people had acquired from these possessions. "He has forgotten the God who made him and reviled the Strength that had rescued him. He had made [God] jealous by foreign [deities] and had made him angry by idols. They sacrificed

---

[39] Heb 13:9.
[40] 1 Cor 6:9-10.
[41] Deut 32:13-15.

to the demons who were not gods, to the gods that had not known them."[42] These things the people had acquired from delicacies: this inheritance of the worship of demons they had inherited from the body's excess. By a table rich in its foods they were seduced to the impure tables of idols. By delicacies they had gone out to cast cakes before engraved [images]. By the desire that receives strength from nature, they had come to impure thoughts that are strange to nature.

Uprooting Source of Gluttony

52. So look, O disciple, from where that people came and went, and uproot from yourself by perseverance the root that sprouts the worship of idols, the plant that beginning from the stomach finishes with the worship of demons. The prophet did not say literally to you that the people bowed down to idols, but he informed you first of the reason for which [the people] bowed down. He did not relate to you only about its difficult and obstinate illness before he informed you of the cause of the illness, **(405)** from where it comes. "He [Israel] ate and drank" and lived lavishly and from here on "he forgot God who had made him."[43] Because error had entered, it brought into being abuses and blasphemies. "He reviled the strong one who had rescued him."[44] This was not sufficient for him. But moreover he made gods for himself against God, and instead of one he fashioned for himself many. "He made [God] jealous with strange [gods] and provoked him to anger by superstitions."[45] Let us see, along with the testimony of the word, also by the deed, from where they had come offering praise before the calf in the wilderness. "The people sat down to eat and drink and stood up to play."[46] Until food entered, blasphemies had not issued forth, and until the wine was poured into them, they did not put on [the clothes of] fornication against God.

[42] Deut 32:15-17.
[43] Deut 32:18b.
[44] Deut 32:18a.
[45] Deut 32:16.
[46] Exod 32:6.

Corruption Always Gluttonous

53. Since food has made these misfortunes, who then will not flee from its overabundance? Whoever sets himself up to become a corrupt person will become an eater. The glutton adopts vain thoughts for himself and then approaches delicate foods. By the love of the body a person is led to become a servant to his stomach. Whoever loves desire, it is clear that this one hates the glory of Christ, for physical desire is the opposite of spiritual desire. As long as one is alive, that other one is not able to live. When the body's desire is alive in someone, spiritual desire is dead in him. Just as the body is deprived of all **(406)** its pleasures when it becomes a stranger to its own life, so the soul becomes a stranger from all good things when spiritual desire is deprived of it. Because spiritual desire is the beginning of the entrance to all the virtues, the desire of the body, on the other hand, is the entrance of all the vices. It was right that even while the lust of the belly does not inhibit us in one of the virtues, for its sake alone it is necessary to reject it, lest it make us similar to animals, inasmuch as it is the entrance for all vices and the field that ordinarily produces thorns and thistles.

Heaviness of the Body

54. If those who achieve worldly victories and desire to become famous through physical skill maintain their life through a modicum of food, how much more should spiritual athletes have need of this to acquire valor and run the road of their labors? If the body, which is sustained [in] its natural life by food, when it wishes to become famous in one of the physical endeavors, the law of asceticism takes hold of it, how much more is the soul in need of asceticism which ordinarily diminishes the weight of the body and makes it lighter and obedient to the soul that dwells in it? For inasmuch as the body is heavy through too much meat, so it has made its work difficult for the soul. But when it is light and diminished by asceticism, the soul also easily accomplishes in it **(407)** all that it wills because [the body] is related to it in its lightness. As long as [the body] is heavy and fat, it is [soul's] opposite because [the soul] is subtle and rational. Inasmuch as [the soul] loves a higher place

suitable to its spirituality, so also the body loves the denseness of the earth and the weightiness of the dust. When [the soul] leaps to ascend above, through its heaviness [the body] tilts [the soul] so that it descends downward and crawls with [the body] on the earth of desires like a reptile. The voracious body makes the soul irrational and forcibly takes from it all its movements of wisdom. Because the vessel of discernments and thoughts of the soul is the heart, when it is made heavy through too much food, all the soul's thoughts stirred up by it become heavy with it. Because [the body] makes [the soul] heavy and cold, the fire naturally mixed in it diminishes, as also does the warmth of the soul's knowledge and its thoughts' light movement comes to an end.

Soul Uses Bodily Members

55. Because even if the gift of rationality begins from the soul, still, its activity is visible through the mediation of the members of the body, and all its natural parts are in need of all the [other] parts of the members of the body.[47] Look, we see that when [the soul] desires to investigate in the world, it observes through the eyes of the body. When it desires to hear a physical voice, it receives it by hearing. Or if it still seeks to broadcast its natural word, it makes it pass over to us by the tongue, **(408)** the bridge of words. Briefly, whenever it wishes to feel something from the world, it is through the mediation of these physical senses that it goes out or enters in. But when it desires to see the region of the spiritual or to hear the living words of their spiritual [nature] or seeks to investigate by a vision that is above nature, it does not have need of these senses at all but sheds them, and only through its own parts is it stirred by living movements that are above nature. Then, just as we have learned that the soul has need of external senses, so also is the case with the inner members, in order that [the soul] might be stirred through them in all of its parts, whether for wisdom, for comprehension, for enlightenment, for thoughts, for discernment, for intelligence and instruction, for the fear of God. Therefore, through

[47] See 1 Cor 12:12-31.

all of these things, it uses the mediation of these members. As long as they are light and the weight of food is not placed upon them and they are not disturbed by the excessive vapor of the food, so also it works lightly in them. Just as light that is mixed with light, and through their mixture the light shines even more, so also the illuminated soul is mixed with illuminated members when they are light and pure from the filth of food. But if they are fat and heavy, it is as if they have a fat body and there is a veil made in front of its illumination, and instead of receiving from them helpful things, they become for them harmful things and obstacles for the lightness of its work.

Don't Eat Too Much Food

56. Such things as these are recognized by those who perceptively view the knowledge of nature. **(409)** But if you really desire, O disciple, to share this natural knowledge and be elevated from it to spiritual knowledge, keep yourself away from the weightiness of food and may your body's natural density be sufficient for you and do not make it fatter and heavier with too much food. If, moreover, you eat too much on the pretext of health, you are very mistaken to think in this way. Too much food does not create health but gives birth to diseases and illnesses in the body, making healthy only desire's body, and as long as all the members are sick and becoming feeble and diminishing of strength, so the desire of hallucinations flourishes and is strengthened in the soul and in the body.

Foolishness, Gloom of the Soul

57. With desire, foolishness also becomes stronger because the lust of the belly increases this despicable passion of foolishness more than all the lusts, since foolishness is the gloom of the soul, just as also knowledge is the light of its nature. Just as a lamp is extinguished by winds and gusts or is obscured so that it might not spread out readily in a house in which there is heavy and moist air, so the light of the soul's knowledge is obscured in a heart darkened by the weight and moisture of foods. Look also at the sun whose light is established in its nature and not by causes gathered from

outside similar to a lamp, its rays are obscured in air **(410)** that is disturbed and troubled. While light exists in the richness of its fullness in the nature of its sphere, it is dark and obscured in the body of the world. In the same way also consider the soul in which the light of knowledge is gathered like natural light in the sphere of the sun, but when the heart is disturbed like the air and all the interior members are shaken by the fumes of food, the rays of the soul's knowledge are inhibited from being distributed perfectly into all the parts of the body. All the movements of a human being, whether of the outer senses or of the inner members, are stirred up foolishly and confusedly. For the soul's knowledge is a hidden pilot for the entire body: it holds the eye in modesty, the tongue[48] in order, the ear in safekeeping, the hand in caution, the tongue in proper balance, and the feet in a measured walk. Just like a chari-oteer for bridled horses, so also is the soul. It holds and leads all the senses with reins of knowledge, and just like a driver for horses it is also the controller of the senses and the director of the inner members. This good thing is the light of the body, and the order of all the members dissipates through gluttony with one who does not keep watch and is not careful.

Cannot Serve God and Belly

58. Therefore, let us flee from this foolish passion and may the disciple of Christ not become a servant of his stomach. If we are not able to serve together God and mammon, **(411)** according to the word of Christ, it is apparent that also [we are not able to serve together] the belly and God, because [the belly] has also been called a god like mammon, and just as Jesus called mammon "master," in the same way also his Apostle called the stomach "a god": "Those whose stomach is their god and their shame is their glory."[49] He mocks those who take hold of the word of God as a craft and because of their stomach they hire out their soul with Christ, not

---

[48] Budge's text written: *l'aynā* (ܠܥܝܢܐ) "eye." Mss. A & B read: *llēshanā* (ܠܠܫܢܐ) "tongue."

[49] Phil 3:19.

for the love of him, as there is also today with many people who wear the honorable robes of discipleship and present themselves as teachers and good servants of God, neither on account of love, nor even with discernment and fear, but only to serve their stomach which they have made for themselves a god and serve. But the Apostle of God teaches openly that the stomach's heaviness lowers the soul's vision from heaven down to earth, "Those whose mind is completely on earth."[50] He established first that their god is their stomach and their glory is their shame. Then he said that their mind is completely on the earth in order to explain that the reason they are bound on the earth and their mind is rolling around in the dust has become for them the lust of the belly. Just as its lust has bound those on the earth, it also binds in this way anyone who serves it. What difference is there for someone who rolls around in the pleasures of his belly from tapeworms that swarm in the filth, or from hogs that wallow **(412)** in the mud? Here also it is proper that this foul desire should be named[51] filth and mud and shame. For if Paul called it thus, how can we not call it like him?

Beginning of Shame

59. But we are able to see that [gluttony] is the beginning of all evil things—and for the fall of Adam. Through it [Adam] had transgressed against the commandment of God and through it he had despised and rejected the law that [was given] to him. The slanderer seized it to become his assistant because he had seen that it was more powerful than all the desires and through its door it is able to enter into the rest of all the vices. Neither through fornication nor through the love of money, nor through vainglory, nor through the adornment of clothes, nor through envy and pride, nor through any of the other passions did this enemy struggle with the leaders of our race, but only through the lust of the belly, because he saw that it is sufficient to be an instigator to all the desires. Because he

---

[50] Phil 3:19.
[51] Text written: *detešmešteh,* ⲙⲇⲭⲁⲭⲏ, "of his service"; read: *dteštamah,* ⲙⲍⲇⲭⲏ, "that it should be named."

is a cunning tempter, he saw which passion is strongest and primary in us, and he approached and enticed it and after it, it sowed slackness and after this, desire, then also concerning the passion of fornication, "As soon as they had eaten, the eyes of both of them were opened and they knew that they were naked."[52] It is evident that because the lust of copulation has swarmed in the members of union, they also perceived and were ashamed of the sight of one another. Until food had entered, **(413)** lust was not awakened; and shame and fear had not reigned until[53] lust was awakened. See, then, the beginning of shame is the lust of the belly, and the blessed Apostle also correctly called it shame.

Lust of the Belly Beginning of All Sin

60. "The woman saw the tree was beautiful and desirable to the eyes, and it was desirable to look at it. She took from its fruits and ate and gave also to her husband with her and he ate."[54] Do you see that the beginning of inner sin and the transgression of the first commandment was the lust of the belly, and through it all sins and all punishments were generated and entered into us? Just as with Satan jealousy was the beginning of evil, so also with the house of Adam the stomach was the beginning of the transgression of the commandment, and through it sins have entered and all punishments have been generated. It was the beginning of diseases and illnesses. Through it the travails of birth have entered. On account of it the land was cursed[55] and produced thorns and thistles. It has distanced us from the pleasures of Paradise. It has cast us away as if in exile to a land of curses. On account of it we have become slaves to demons. Through its lordship over us we serve in slavery to Satan. On account of it the evil spirits mock and laugh at us. It has made death enter, the destroyer[56] and disperser of our constitution

---

[52] Gen 3:7.
[53] Written: ܪܡܐ, *dmā*, "when"; read: ܕܡܐ, '*damā*, "until."
[54] Gen 3:6.
[55] Typographical error: written ܐܬܠܛܬ, read ܐܬܠܛܬ.
[56] Typographical error: written ܡܚܒܠܐ, read ܡܚܒܠܐ.

and through which this attractive and beautiful image has been made despicable and abominable. It has given us the bread of diseases to eat. It has gathered for us food by the sweat of our brows.

A Simple Fruit

61. The lust of the belly is foolish and blind. It sought to eat but was deprived of food. It desired comforts, but it has lost the comfort and luxury **(414)** of Paradise. While it has loved to eat, it has not known how to eat. Perseverance has not taken hold because this is the nature of this desire, hasty and impatient. It rushed and picked [only] one fruit and was deprived of the table of all the delicacies of Paradise. That desire that was with the house of Adam shall be the type for this one that is with us. Just as there, due to the eating of a single fruit,[57] they were deprived of the food of all of Paradise, so also here a full table deprives us of the table of the kingdom of heaven. As long as the stomach is full and suffering from too much food, the memory of blessings to come is eliminated from the soul, and as long as the eye considers these foods and desires them, the mind's eye is closed from the vision of spiritual pleasures. Therefore, if Adam, because he desired a single fruit has lost the delicacy[58] of all of Paradise, whoever is weighed down by the desire of too much food, how much more will he be deprived of the table of the kingdom?

Losses of Eating

62. On account of his eating Adam lost Paradise and inherited death with all the curses, and Esau on account of his eating let go of [his] birthright with the blessings[59] and became a servant to sin and subservient under the hand of his brother. On account of eating the people forgot God and instead of God served the image

---

[57] Typographical error: written ܐܪܙܐ, read ܐܪܬܐ.

[58] Typographical error: written ܐܘ ܒܐܣܘܡܪܐ, read ܐܟܪܐ ܒܐܣܘܡܪܐ, "had lost the delicacy" (words incorrectly divided).

[59] Gen 25:33.

of a mute animal.[60] Moreover, on account of eating the anger of
God **(415)** rose up against them.[61] Again, after eating they slipped
down into fornication with the Midianite women, after which a
plague suddenly ruled over them.[62] It is written concerning them,
"While the meat was still between their teeth, the anger of God rose
up over them."[63] Again, after eating and luxuries, the Sodomites
also defiled themselves through filthy action, and comforts and
the lust of the belly brought them to that evil without end, as the
prophet of God explains concerning them. "This was the iniquity
of Sodom, your decadent sister, who became satiated with bread
and sat down in silence."[64] After [their] fill of bread and comforts
they defiled themselves by an unnatural desire.

Caution against Simple Food

63. May such things like these become a reminder for you, O
one who desires to travel on the road to heaven. Cut off and cast
away from yourself the hole of the stomach that like a millstone
in the sea plunges the soul into the depth of evil things. Do not
suppose that only through rich foods is gluttony reckoned. Look,
the gluttony of Esau was revealed through the eating of lentils:
it was not by too much meat or even too much wine or with any
other preparations of food, but only because he was gluttonous
concerning the eating of lentils [that] the word of God rejected and
cast him away. Through that food which is near to you, show your
self-control. Struggle with whatever is close. Against the worthless
and despicable things that are prepared before you, let there be
a battle for you lest you use them for filling up the stomach. For
no one **(416)** concedes to nearby opponents and fights with those
who are far away. There is no one who can neglect a recent illness
and [while still] suffering [from] it bring healing to a disease not

---

[60] Exod 32:1ff.
[61] Exod 32:9-10.
[62] Num 25:1-9.
[63] Num 11:33.
[64] Ezek 16:49.

yet apparent. Because the delicacies of food that the wealthy and the famous people of the world use are not near to you, abstain from these little things [of value] that are placed before you. If you conquer these things that are of little value, you can be sure that you will also be a conqueror against greater things and will seize the victory as well from those that are costly.

Slumbering Prayer

64. A full stomach does not give birth to pure prayer, and the stomach that is distended by too much food does not sing the psalms alertly. If its ruin were found only in gluttony, it would be blameworthy, [and] perhaps his culpability[65] would not be as bad, yet on account of other evil things that spring out from it, the disciple ought to be cautious of it. The sleep of the eater is great, his dreams are disturbed, his visions are troubled, great is the flow of his desire. His sleep is deep and not a healthy sleep. If he stands to sing a psalm, count him as one not standing, for just as he was immersed in his lying down, so he is submerged also in his standing up. He collapses against walls, grabs the posts, leans on the stalls in order they might support his heavy body, that is to say, that they might lessen the weight of the food he is carrying around. It happens that he begins and ends his worship and does not sense where he is. Many voices cry out into his ears and he vanquishes all of them by the depth of his sleep, his ear **(417)** blocked by the weight of food. His eye is shut by sleep. His entire body is fatigued and wearied since he has not eaten by measure. The people [who are] living are standing at his side and look at him like someone dead. Those who are alert look at him and deride and mock him by his sleeping.[66] He does not know which psalm he is singing. He is angry against whoever awakens him; he is full of anger and threats against whoever chases away his torpor. It can happen that he falls down while standing up and disturbs

---

[65] Written: *dšyānah*, صليحة, "of his peace"; read: *rešyāneh*, صليحة, "his culpability."

[66] Written: *ba-dmūteh*, ةامحد, "by his example"; Lavenant reads: *b-dam-kūteh*, ةكمحد, "by his sleeping."

the liturgy by the noise of his falling. At the moment of silence he creates a commotion. At the time when God is sung by those living and alert, he stands before him like a corpse without a soul. And with someone who says that he is not ashamed and [does not] blush, how could he feel ashamed when he is not even aware? He despises God in his standing up. He sows jealousy in those who see him and moreover, abuses those who wake him up. He becomes a scandal and a stumbling block for those who stand at his side, because they leave their psalmody and talk about him and are annoyed at the sight of his torpor. If the glutton is [still] asleep, he is sound [asleep]. If he should be awakened while he is asleep, and if he should sing, he is dumb. If he should stand up, he will lie down on his side.

Do Not Forget God

65. Take note then of these harmful things, O one who loves spiritual benefits, and renounce this vice lest through it you forget God and forget also yourself and your discernment is obscured by all the things that are convenient. Remember, moreover, along with these things what was also spoken by Moses the prophet to the Jews. "Be careful not to **(418)** eat or be satisfied and forget the Lord your God who brought you up out of the land of Egypt."[67] See, clearly, the Spirit of God has taught you that forgetfulness is born from satiety. When a person has forgotten God, he advances without fear into all [kinds of] evil things and participates in all [kinds of] wicked matters. Just as the sight of a harsh lord is [fearful] for disorderly slaves, so the memory of God chastens the unruliness of thoughts, and as soon as the thought of him falls into the mind all the unruly movements rush to the orderliness of fear, and the soul at once becomes a peaceful house and a temple of orderliness, a dwelling of purity and the holy habitation of the Trinity. Therefore, whoever wishes to travel on the road of heaven must untie the fetter of desires from his feet and take the weight from the wings of his intellect, so that he may travel lightly into the assembly of majesty and hear the advice of Saint Paul to us, teaching and instructing us, "Be cautious lest there be someone

[67] Deut 6:12-19.

among you who is licentious and slack like Esau who has sold his birthright for one meal, because afterward he had wished to inherit the blessings and was rejected. He did not find an opportunity for repentance even though he asked for it with tears."[68]

Lightness of Being

66. Therefore, let these things be a reminder for us and let testimonies such as these be inscribed into our heart. Let us be light so that we might become spiritual. Let us close the door of the lust of the belly so that all evil things might be kept outside. Let us mortify the desire of the body from us so that the desire of the Spirit might live in our soul. Let us reduce by self-control **(419)** even the needs of our life in order to be worthy of grace for the life of glory. Let us renounce the foolish mistress in order to confess fully the Holy Being. Let us free the members from weight so that the members might be made lighter for pure prayer. Let us get rid of the fumes of desire, so that our soul's eye might be cleansed for the vision of knowledge. Let us not desire a full table with too much food so that the table of the kingdom might receive us as ones who are famished. Let us despise and reject the body's health in order to attain the health of our hidden person. The fear of diseases should not make us approach food, lest from here on we may increase bruises in our soul. Let us praise the one who provides for little food, so that it may be apparent that we are the children and not the slaves hired by their stomach. Let us conquer through self-control the first desire so that from here on we might become stronger for the conquering of all the lusts. Let us speak to one another what was said to all of us by the Apostle, "The stomach is for food and food for the stomach, but God destroys them both. The body is not for fornication, but for our Lord and our Lord for the body."[69] To him be the glory from us all, forever. Amen.

The end of the first *mēmrā* on the lust of the belly by the holy Philoxenos, bishop of Mabbug.

---

[68] Heb 12:16.
[69] 1 Cor 6:13.

Mēmrā 11

On Asceticism

The eleventh *mēmrā* concerning the asceticism and discipline of the body, in which is explained that through austerities one is able to enter the spiritual realm of the delights of the knowledge of Christ.

Summary: One is not completely worthy of the life of Christ until he extinguishes all appetite for worldly foods. Abstinence gives us birth into the blessing of Christ and is the beginning of our becoming like angels. The lust of the belly contends that food and hunger have been given to you by the Creator. Natural hunger needs the power food supplies but should not foster a lust for food. You are god over your own lusts, willing whether they exist or not. If you defeat the first lust (gluttony) you will increase your strength against other lusts. But if you only conquer the rare and expensive foods, you are not completely victorious; defeat common foods as well. If possible eat like a dead man; if you eat like one alive, do not taste your food with pleasure which would mean that lust is still alive. Also overcome lust for common garden vegetables, for lust knows it cannot tempt monks with fancy foods. Food itself is not reprehensible, only the lust which eats it. Philoxenos encourages monks to abstain from all kinds of food and to eat without the sensation of taste, seeing the table as a place of struggle rather than pleasure. The apostles did not receive the Holy Spirit until they led a life of abstinence after leading a life of freedom in Christ.

Uprooting Evil First

(420) 1. "Enter through the narrow door"[1] proclaims the word of our Savior to all true disciples of his word, because without this door one is not able to enter the kingdom of God. A human being is not fully worthy of the taste of the way of Christ until he eliminates from himself every sensation of the world's tastes. He is not able to cut off and cast away this sense from himself unless he cuts off the pleasure of all the lusts through the power of self-control. When a person cuts off a vice and casts it away from himself, virtues and excellent things spring up in him in place of them—that is, in the same place from which the evil is cut off the good thing at once springs up and takes its place. Just as all the soul's strength has turned toward watering and making grow **(421)** this plant of evil, so the strength of all the thoughts is turned fully to make the tree of good grow that is planted in the soul after evil is uprooted from it. Because unless vices have been uprooted, the virtues do not take [their] place; and unless evil habits have been cut off and cast away from us, the tradition of excellent ways will not take hold of us. If we have not abandoned dissoluteness, tenacity cannot take hold of us. Unless gluttony has died, asceticism cannot live in us.

Summoning Death and Life

2. Death and life are ministered to us by both—the death of the old person that is the despicable lusts, and the life of the new person that is the stable ways of life. Because death [resulting] from the condemnation of a person introduces the commandment to him, yet the desire of every one of us summons this death of lusts, because from the beginning the death of sin enters through the will, and then after it comes the death of condemnation by the will of God. In the same way here, before the dissolution of one's physical nature that condemnation dissolves, the will of every one of us is able to dissipate the structure of the old person of lusts. When this death has been dissolved, not even that natural [death] is solid.

---

[1] Matt 7:13.

Dying before Death

3. Because the death of sin has made natural death enter, with the dissolution of [sin] [natural death] is also destroyed. Those who do not die beforehand die in truth. But those who by their own will make the person of lusts die from them through the death of this [sin], the death of a natural person **(422)** is dissolved. Therefore, it is excellent that we should die before our death so that we might also live before our life. Wherever death of the will precedes, it also dissolves natural death. Wherever natural death is first destroyed by the power of freedom whoever is dead is alive before he lives.

Removing Putrefaction

4. Because these[2] destructions and restorations of all kinds happen prior to us, it is appropriate for us in the first place to uproot vices and then to establish in ourselves a foundation for the building of virtues in order that the rock may accept our foundation, as it is written,[3] and the solid rock for our building, as it was said.[4] Through this we are also imitating natural physicians who do not apply a bandage that builds up and renews the living flesh until they remove and cleanse the putrefaction from the abscess. In the same way, once we have rooted out the putrefaction of the lust of the belly and denounced its foul-smelling and abominable forms, we are showing the profit of asceticism now by our word and exhorting the disciples by helpful teaching to take hold of this self-control in themselves.

Birth through Travails of Asceticism

5. While this is believed to be difficult in [the performance of the] labors, yet it is the travail that gives birth for us to the taste of the blessings of Christ. Just as a fetus is born into the world

---

[2] Read (ܗܠܝܢ) *hālēyn*, typographical error in Budge's edition.
[3] Matt 7:24-25.
[4] *Mēmrā* 1; 4:3–9.

through the travails of birth, so a person is born into the world of the knowledge of Christ through the travails of austerities and the endurance of labors. If one should call asceticism the purifying of the lusts of the body he is not mistaken, because just as **(423)** the body is washed by an ablution of these things splashed upon it and obscures the appearance and color of its nature, so through asceticism the scars of the old person are cleansed[5] and scoured. While it is being scoured and purified the beauty of the new person is being revealed. When it has been revealed and reestablished in its natural appearance, then it is easy for it to see and be seen in the beauty of its soul, because from here it receives the garment of knowledge. The beginning of asceticism is bitter and harsh, but its conclusion is pleasant and sweet. Its burden is heavy for those who do not perceive its lightness. Its load is difficult for those who have not beheld the spiritual riches inside it. It is the narrow door that ushers one into the expansive realm of the spiritual.

Asceticism: Beginning of the Gospel

6. Just as the end of the road of the world is renunciation from possessions, so asceticism is the beginning of the road of the way of the Gospel. It is right that we, after the discourse concerning renunciation, should embark on instruction concerning asceticism, because as long as a person possesses something outside of himself, he will cultivate it and reap harvests from it. While good and compassion begin by his will, yet he will carry the seed outside of himself and cast [it] into the fields of the afflicted. As one might say, he receives from the world and gives back to [the world]. Even if the fruits of this righteousness are gathered with regard to the person of this human being, the labors are still outside of his person. What labor and austerity does that person exert in his [own] body when the righteousness of his alms consists of wealth outside of himself, **(424)** apart from this alone: he resists the thought of the lust of the belly and subjugates it under the will of compassion? But when he has renounced everything and lives freely in the world on

---

[5] Read Ms. B (ܚܣܘܠܠ) instead of written ܚܣܢܢܠܡ.

his own, he has his own person for the field of his cultivation. He cultivates [himself] and sows himself, and from himself austerities begin and through himself they are completed. From then on he does not sow strange lands with the seed of alms, but the rational field of his person, and through it he begins the cultivation of the labors of righteousness.

Angels Deprived of Food

7. But the first rule of this field is the cultivation of fasting and asceticism. For without this, all the virtues of a person are feebly cultivated and their strength in us is diminished and weakened. Neither is our prayer nor our psalm singing pure, nor are our thoughts sanctified, nor our knowledge increased, nor our intellect purified, nor our mind lightened, nor is our inner person made new by wonder at the greatness of the glory of God without the cultivation of fasting and the observance of asceticism. We are ascending from these things to those [other] things and from this degree we ascend to others greater than it. From this in order to resist food we attain the image of angels, because in the case of angels they are completely deprived of food. Let us estrange ourselves willingly from the food of lust and reduce a little the needs of the body. Through this **(425)** we are demonstrating that we have the earnest desire in us to imitate those who are spiritual.

Two Stomachs

8. On account of this our Lord who came for our salvation would have been able through his own authority, as soon as he was revealed, to make us into the image of angels, which at the end he was going to give to us according to the wealth of his grace. He did not make us in this way but taught us how we could imitate the angels and left this to our will so that we might pursue their likeness, and that by the strength of our freedom we ourselves might take off our old physical [nature] and put on the newness of the image of angels, and exchange food for food, desire for desire, table for table, nourishment for nourishment, fruits for fruits, and

meals for meals. Because we have [two kinds of] stomach[s] which receive the various kinds of food, and when someone has closed the openings of one, then he opens the other in order to receive spiritual foods and delight in and enjoy spiritual fruits that are above nature. Because our nature is too weak by its own power to cut off and cast away these things from it, the gift of the Spirit has come to our aid in order to perfect with grace whatever nature is not able to do by itself.

Heavenly Banquet

9. Therefore, fight against the lusts of your body, O disciple, with all of your soul and cultivate virtues in your personal field that has remained for you from the world, because of all there is in the world you alone will be found **(426)** for life. The bridal chamber is open for you, the kingdom is prepared, the couch is made, the rooms are arranged, and the table of delicacies is prepared in that living banquet in which God has made himself the server, just as he also cried out to you through his true word, "Truly, I say to you, he will make his chosen ones sit down and will gird up his loins and cross over to serve them."[6] Remember this table at all times so that you will take strength from its memory and despise a normal table. There is no one who exchanges the delicious table of the kingdom for the decadent and plain table of barley bread. More than this, this table of the body's foods is comparably less and inferior to that spiritual table.

Struggle with Hunger

10. Therefore, be alert and watch out for yourself when this desire begins to fight with you and gather all the strength of your thoughts [with] an alert intellect standing at their head [as] commander, [for this desire] resembles a leader of bandits that is the passion of the lust of the belly. Because this desire—knowing that it is too weak to fight with the thought of self-control—directs hunger against

[6] Luke 12:37.

[the intellect] so that it might become its ally to show you that your fault is not as great if you are being pressured by hunger.

It presents to you arguments such as these, for example: need is placed in you by the Maker and hunger naturally reigns over your body; the sustenance of your human life consists of nourishment; without these things you cannot remain **(427)** in the world, and if you wish to live outside of these things, you are resisting the will of the Maker, the one who wishes in this way that your bodily life be supported in the world; a moderate meal is neither blamable [nor is] drink taken in measure. When this desire has led you into these enticements and has brought you from the fact that you do not eat to the reality that you do eat, it draws you further from this [situation] to how you should eat and what you should eat. It does not counsel you from the beginning that you should eat with desire but convinces you to eat on account of need and then takes you from need to desire. One is supported by the strength of self-control while one is struggling to conquer natural hunger. If weakness exerts power over him during the time of his strength, it will be easily defeated so that it may come to complete debility when a lighter portion of weakness has control over him.

Varieties of Hunger

11. Observe in detail the prudent knowledge that not all hunger is natural hunger, nor is all food the food that fills a need. Observe the varieties of hunger and distinguish them and make your own hunger depart through knowledge. There is a [kind of] hunger that occurs in infancy. There is a [kind of] hunger that [comes] from weakness. There is a [kind of hunger] that [comes] from illness. There is [a kind of hunger] that is from an excessive discharge. There is [a kind of hunger] from habit and from the laziness of thoughts that do not have anything with which to be busy. There is [a kind of hunger] that is from the weakness of the thoughts themselves. There is [a kind of hunger] that is from a midday listlessness that happens to the body. There is [a kind of hunger] that the coldness of the body seeks in order to be warmed **(428)** by food. There is a [kind of hunger] to which too much labor gives birth.

For such things as these are the cause of hunger, along with others in which hunger is not a healthy hunger.

On account of this you will find many who are hungry from the beginning of the day, and some who are hungry in the second hour, and others in the fourth hour and in the sixth, and others in the ninth, and others in the evening. There are also some who prevail over hunger at the end of the day by a vigil. There are some who bypass even the third [hour]. When they have reached the number of the double vigil, natural hunger is completely elimi-nated from them because instead of food they have natural warmth for nourishment that is awakened in the body. While you should understand from this the various types of hungers engendered in you, distinguish and put away the hunger of your need from all of them, while from time to time you ought to resist this one so that the endurance of your austerity may be especially revealed and so that through it your love for God may be known.

Natural Hunger

12. Keep watch lest desire's hunger causes you to err and con-sider that it is natural hunger. This is true natural hunger: not the stomach's emptiness from food, but the absence of the strength of nourishment from all the members. When the members have shed the strength from food and instead have put on weakness, you will call on[7] them and they will not answer you for the service you desire. This is natural hunger, and it is necessary **(429)** then that you should cautiously receive such nourishment that will restore to the members their strength. Keep guard of your thought lest it becomes mixed with the body in eating. Put the desire in you to sleep lest it be aroused, and instead of need, desire should grab nourishment from you. Because if this should be [the case], your eating shall become blameworthy, even while you are enduring hunger and eating simply.

---

[7] Written: ܦܢܐ, "possesses"; read: ܩܢܐ, "calls (on)."

Abstinence against Hunger

13. Therefore, your thought should be watching all your actions at all times, whether these are in the world or in your body, or whether all the others are being cultivated in the soul. A human being is not an animal who eats whenever he is hungry, but as a rational being the soul ought to demonstrate appropriate self-control even when the body shows its natural hunger and to use what belongs to it, as [does] the body with these things of its nature. May the body's hunger become a reminder of [the soul's] own hunger, and may it take its need as a testimony of the need of its spiritual life. The vibrant soul ought not to be subjugated to the feminine passions of the body but be aroused against them for battle, subjugate and tie up, prevail over and defeat [them], and give birth through it [to] plans[8] and preparations against these desires that ascend from below to above in order to humble its majesty and defile its elegant beauty. Whenever the body by its needs or by its desires' hunger fights against you, defeat the battle of that moment by self-control, while giving birth in yourself to another hunger against hunger **(430)** and turning your mind from concern regarding the body's hunger to meditation and conversation with God. In the same way you will be able to vanquish the worrisome suffering of its hunger.

Hunger of Desire

14. If natural hunger were to have power over every one of us, all of us would be equally hungry, a little bit more or less. But because hunger is also engendered by the passion of desire, we are hungry at different times. Who does not know that it is not natural hunger that occurs at the beginning of the day or in the third hour, or indeed not that [hunger] that is in the sixth [hour]? Because as I have said, natural hunger is the emptying of the strength of food from the joints; but especially when passion is defeated by the power of self-control it proves that it is not natural hunger. Moreover, if it

---

[8] Lemoine translates (ܪ̈ܕܐܣ) as "les préparatifs," indicating he has emended the text to (ܪ̈ܕܐܣ).

should be natural [hunger], even here we should persevere[9] because our way of life is above nature and our struggle is against nature. Look, the human life in us does not [consist of] natural passions, but is itself nature. Even so, we struggle for the sake of truth against human life, for there are distinct boundaries laid down: until the boundary of death we [must] struggle for righteousness against these desires, but the battle on account of the faith is against natural life. We were not commanded by our Savior to kill ourselves voluntarily through self-control for the labors of righteousness, but we were commanded to die[10] for the truth. So then even through ways that are **(431)** within faith, we should struggle against all natural needs for the sake of truth against the life of nature [itself].

Resist Passion of Hunger

15. Resist, therefore, the passion of your hunger whenever this desire is aroused in you and put in order all the powers of your thoughts for the battle against it. If it is not defeated by one, it will be defeated by many. For how is [hunger] not able to be defeated by the power of many thoughts, which ordinarily is defeated by a single living movement for God, if this movement should be in us full of health as if from a living and healthy nature? Because just as a hand has strength,[11] so also is a stone thrown by it. According to the strength of the arm, so is the strength of the arrow shot by it. According to the strength and health of the soul, so also is the strength of the movement by which it is sent into battle against desire. Desire is not able to persist before it, not even if it has lasted a long time in us by habit, that is, [it is] no [longer] a need.

Different Needs

16. Notice that there is also a distinction among needs, because there is a need of desire and there is [a need] of health. There is [a

---

[9] Lemoine has adopted the reading ܡܣܝܒܪܢ (Ms. E) instead of written ܡܣܝܒܪܢ.

[10] Lavenant reads variant *da-nmut,* ܕܢܡܘܬ (Ms. E), instead of written ܪܚܡܬܐ.

[11] Read variant (Ms. F): ܐܝܟ ܐܪܐ ܚܝܠ ܕܐܝܬ ܥܡ ܐܪܐ.

need] of strength and there is a need of one's own life. Therefore, let us let go of the first needs and let us use that other one, because while we are compelled to fulfill a need, let us neither fulfill that of desire nor that of health nor that of strength, but only of one's own **(432)** life, just as also we have learned from the testimony of the ancient upright that they were not speaking of the need of any of these [first] three. For those who were determinedly persisting in fasting, some of them forty days, and some of them three weeks, is it not evident that they were only fulfilling the requirements for life? Moreover, the limit of our Savior's fasting points this out to us, and his reply against the Accuser has taught us this clearly. "It is written: a person shall not live by bread alone, but by every word that comes from the mouth of God."[12] "He is living," he said, and not, "he is cured" or "he is strong" or "the need of his desire is fulfilled." While the saying is brief to read, yet an important distinction is apparent in it. He has taught us clearly through that saying that "not by bread alone does a person live," for he should be sustained only in order to live—and not for desire, nor for strength, nor for health. For a life such as this a person lives in the world, being [alive] in illness and weakness. Just as [in the case of] one who has a serious disease in his body, for instance, in the intestines that are the recipients of nourishment, the food he receives nourishes his disease and not his strength; so also whoever is nourished by the desire in him, his food is the nourishment of his desire and not of his human life. It is evident that whoever nourishes desire **(433)** will give birth to lusts, because according to the nature of the land is also the taste of the trees that spring up from it.

Eat Like a Free Person

17. So then do not eat like a servant, but sustain yourself like a free person. May your food not be for others but for yourself. Instead of offering servitude to a desire, become a servant to yourself. Who would be so absolutely foolish [as] to take away [food

---

[12] Matt 4:4; Deut 8:3.

from] his mouth and place it into the mouth of others? Perhaps [you would do that] for a helpful friend, but [would you do it] for an enemy who is the opponent of your true life? Desire does not have the power to subjugate your life, but it will wrest strength from your strength in order to subjugate you. Therefore, do not allow your strength to give to it, so that with [your strength] you will be struggling against yourself. Do not clothe your enemy with the armor with which you should be fighting against him. Do not be divided against yourself, that is, do not be totally on the side of your enemy and turn around and make war with yourself. This desire is sick, if you wish. How is it not sick, because without you it does not even exist? But if you create it, you also are the one strengthening it. If it begins to exist from you, it will also strengthen itself because it takes strength from you against you. Just as God [rules] over creatures, you are a god over your lusts, and just as by the will of the Maker creatures exist, and if he should wish they do not exist, so by your will do the lusts exist, and by your will they are reduced to nothing. "God calls **(434)** those things that do not exist into existence,"[13] so also your will creates the lusts that do not exist in order that they might come to exist. God looks at everything and it becomes nothing; so also your will [sees] all the passions and immediately they will vanish and be reduced to nothing. If you wish, your passions may exist, and if you wish they do not exist. The cause of your lust shoots up from you, and from you is born its destruction. If you make it live, you can make it die. If you make desire live in you, you will make your life that is in God die. There is no way for a person to live with God and with lust, just as also neither with the Accuser and with Christ. The body's desire is a hindrance for the spiritual person in the same way that the Slanderer is also the opponent of your entire being. The beautiful passions spring up in you from the soul with the assistance of grace, but the cause of despicable lusts is from the body, while it is the enemy pushing them.

---

[13] Rom 4:17.

Defeat the First Lust

18. Therefore, defeat whatever is necessary to be defeated so that
the One to whom victory [belongs] may triumph in you. Fight and
defeat the first lust so that from here on the victory over all of them
will be easy for you. For if one defeats you, then how much more
will many defeat you? Even when all of the lusts have been gathered together they are still weak. But how much weaker will they
be when you defeat each one by the perseverance of self-control!
You should also separate them from one another so that the victory
against them might be easier (435) for you. When the lusts desire to
be amassed against your self-control, do not give them what they
are seeking and do [not] fight at the same time with all of them, but
separate and distinguish one from another and struggle individually
against each one of them and seize the victory. Do not allow them
to accomplish their will in you, not only so that they do not defeat
you, but also that through this they may not congregate together.
Their weakness is visible in them by the fact of their moving around
in troops. If their feebleness has been revealed to you through their
gathering together, how much more will their profound weakness
be visible in the isolated arrival of each one of them?

Guard the Desire for Truth in You

19. Therefore, guard the portion of the desire of truth in you that
yearns for life, longs for virtues, and desires a healthy and incorruptible desire. Corrupting desire is placed under corruption and
whoever wishes to acquire the power of self-control will destroy it
easily. But incorruptible desire, even when its enemies believe they
are defeating it, is not disrupted due to the authentic solidity of its
nature. If it seems that it is defeated, it is not utterly defeated but
separates itself from a thought not worthy of it: even while being
held by it, it fights against despicable desire.

Defeat the First Desire

20. Therefore, it is excellent for us to defeat all the lusts, especially
(436) this first desire, which if we defeat it, we will receive the

strength of victory from it against other lusts. When this evil desire is defeated in us, the others after it will fail with it. Inasmuch as we see that our work has increased because through one we defeat many, so let us apply ourselves concerning [this] task, because if we delay, not only in that place is there defeat, but [also] in the rest of the struggles that will come after this one. Just as if we should win our first victory, it is the victory for all struggles—so if we are defeated, it is the defeat for all conflicts. Therefore, we should become victors at all times, because victory belongs to our nature, but to be defeated is outside of our nature. On account of our will and the flatteries of our enemies, let us then fulfill by our will the will of God our Maker who has established us in the struggle to become victors. May the king who has chosen us therefore not become ashamed of us and may he not be accused to have chosen and mixed into his army dissolute soldiers, for our defeat displays the ignorance of that one who has chosen us. Therefore, lest the Wise One appear ignorant through us, let us become victors.

Sweet Taste of Victory

21. Therefore, see, by the experience of your fighting, that whenever this lust of the belly disturbs you by which thoughts it will be defeated, and by this routine whenever it lines up in battle against you, you also should line up these thoughts against it. After victory the pleasure of victory will be received by you. For as long as you are troubled by the allurement **(437)** of lust, the sweetness of victory will not be tasted by you. After a little while, when you are clothed in the armor of self-control, depart with victory from the battle's struggle, and then[14] the sweetness of victory will meet you. It is not even possible that ease would encounter you during labor,[15] for ease is born after labor. You are not able, while holding the seed in your hand, to have the harvest be born in the palm of your [hand], but [it is] from the seed after [the seed] has been sown that crops will be harvested. Again, while you are still involved in a

---

[14] Written: *kad*, ܟܕ, "when, while"; read *hāydēn*, ܗܝܕܝܢ, "then" (Ms. F).
[15] Lavenant reads *'amlā* (ܥܡܠܐ) "labor"; instead of *'almā* (ܥܠܡܐ) "world."

battle of war, and victory has not been revealed to whom it belongs, your triumph is not [yet] proclaimed in the cities; but [only] after the battle is finished and victory is apparent, then the victory of the warrior will be proclaimed in the towns. Take such examples as these for this spiritual war in which you are involved. If you are disturbed while you are fighting, know that this is normal. If you are fatigued and sweating profusely, moreover, this will be a [consequent] part of your work. If there is struggle, there is labor in it, and if there is a struggle, those who enter into it run with fatigue and sweat. But you, do not look at these things that are near, but look ahead to the pleasures that follow the austerities. May your thought not be tied to your body, but may it run to see those things to come in order to strengthen the members engaged in war by the memory of victory.

The Spiritual One Must Conquer Stomach

22. You are spiritual, yet you are fighting with the body's desire. It is ridiculous for [someone] spiritual to be defeated by the body, and for one **(438)** who is invited to heaven it is shameful that the belly fights with and defeats him. If you are marked by grace to fight and defeat the principalities and spiritual authorities, that is, the powers and opposing armies, how much more is it necessary for you to conquer the stomach. Look, this is what your garment confesses, and the sight of your discipline proclaims the victory for you against the opposing powers. Who will not laugh at one who is prepared for these things when he sees that the stomach is defeating him, especially when it is not a necessity of life forcing you to [do] this, but desire born from the weakness of your will and being born from you it stood up in battle against you and brought you down?

Smash the Infants

23. Although[16] he is strong, he is still but an infant and a boy, and it would be easy for you to place him under your heel. See,

---

[16] Written: ‌‌‌‌،ܠܗ; Lavenant reads variant: ‌‌‌،ܗܠܐ (Ms. F).

therefore, how the Spirit advises you, "Smash the children of Babylon upon a stone while they are infants."[17] It is excellent that the word of prophecy has called these passions "children," in order to show their weakness and to encourage you to victory. [The word] had not called them "your children," lest it would cause you dishonor that such children as these have appeared to be from you, but [Scripture] has named them "the children of Babylon," that is, those who are born out of slavery and not out of freedom. Because the mother who gives birth to desires is slavery, which the word of prophecy has described as Babel the pillager, because hastily as in a robbery it robs the power of **(439)** our spiritual person and seizes his wealth.

Despise the Lust of the Belly

24. Therefore, when desire is married with hunger for war against you, marry your thought with grace and stand up in prayer, and despising the desire, do not [allow] your thought to turn back toward it. But I say—and this is of great [importance]—even when you fight and win, your victory is still beset with defects because you had need of combat, and [only] then did you conquer the stomach; you should have disdained it, and since it is so despicable in your eyes your thought should not even attach itself to it, but you should disdain it in the way a powerful person [disdains] a weak one, and as a mighty and strong man [disdains] a despised and fallen person. In this way also it is the custom of valorous soldiers when they see the weak coming toward them for combat, they disdain, despise, and mock their approach as it is written also concerning that mighty blasphemer whose pride resided in the power of his body. "When [Goliath] saw David, he despised him."[18] If he, by confidence in the flesh, had in him such great disdain of David, how can you by the spiritual power in you not despise and disdain the lust of the belly?

---

[17] Ps 137:9.
[18] 1 Sam 17:42.

Lust of the Belly First Afflicts Infants

25. Who does [the lust of the belly] usually defeat, if not the infants and very young children? As soon as the lust of the belly afflicts them with its need, they begin to cry and annoy their parents, demanding from them their needs, and [this is] because these [children] have not yet reached the stature in which the strength of self-control is born from **(440)** the soul. But you have reached the vigorous stature and your soul's power has been revealed to you if you wish to use it. Why are you defeated by the stomach like an infant and become a mockery by which a childhood's passion will laugh at you? For in that stage in which a defeat by the stomach is near to the nature of an infant's stature, in the same stage the victory against it is closer to you. Just as his infancy is subject to defeat, in the same way victory clings to the maturity of your stature. Understand also from this the weakness of the lust of the belly, because its battle is with the stage of infancy. As for the rest of the other desires, we see that they are renewed in our life at the various [stages] of age afterward, but this lust of the belly is stirred up in infancy. Recognize that because it is weak it wrestles with an infant. But when it fights against you, it comes as a temptation and not as a victory. So then, be victorious by the strength of your perseverance. The fact is that even when it has been defeated its defeat is not great, since it is a battle of infancy.

Other Passions Weakened by Defeat of Lust of Belly

26. However, the assistance that is born from it is not weak in the same way as it is weak. While [this desire] is small and despicable, when it has been defeated its defeat is not an amazing thing, but it opens a door for us to triumphs against all sorts of passions. The rest of the lusts that come after it are weakened when they see [it defeated] so that they do not come to a battle. **(441)** Or if they do approach to fight, [it is] with fear and terror, and on account of this they come with half their strength and not with full strength, because fear usually diminishes and disperses [one's] strength. Therefore, fight, O disciple, and be victorious like an adult so that you will be crowned successfully like a powerful person. Do not be defeated because it is not for this that you are set apart. Do not fall

because it is not on account of this that you were chosen. Do not give up because a powerful hand is with you. The hand of Christ is with you in all these battles in which you are engaged, if you sense the right [hand] that has taken your right [hand] and the powerful arm holding your weak hand.

Fight against Desire, Not Eating

27. However, because it is necessary for me to teach you as well these initial kinds of this victory, listen and I will tell you. Do not consider it a victory when you defeat only the lust of quantities of expensive foods; however, when you have defeated the lesser and more common [foods], consider this more so as a victory. It is not only from eating meat and drinking wine that a disciple ought to refrain, but from everything that he desires. Therefore, do not fight against eating, but against desire. If then you fight against eating, when you have won the battle with one [food], another will fight with you. But if it is against lust, you will be victorious in one [case] over many.

Advice to a Monk on Eating

28. With this is another matter: there are foods whose reprehensive [nature] is obvious when a solitary or **(442)** a monk uses them. What will aid you in battle here is the discretion that comes from many people [watching you]. How many times do you restrain yourself not to eat out of shame in the presence of those who are watching you? Because in this battle assistance comes to you from the outside, its victory indeed is small. But, you, like [someone] wise [on the lookout] for profits and someone crafty toward [his] assistants, struggle with these things that are permitted to be eaten and make war against their desire. In short, this is a hint I will give to you: everything that is placed upon your dinner table and your eye sees and desires, do not think about it, but say silently to your stomach, "Because you have desired it, you will not taste it."[19] When it has accepted this law from you, it will occupy itself

---

[19] Written: ܐܠ ܟܪܨܟ ܐܟܘܠ ܗܘ ܐ.; read Ms. F, ܐܠ ܬܛܥܡ ܐ.

with its need, and the eye of its desire will not extend itself broadly over foods.

But I say—the fact that perhaps because it appears new, not everyone will accept it, and those who understand it are few, and rare are those capable of it—it would be a lot better for you to eat meat without lust than lentils with lust. Why? Because passion is not born with eating meat. But here with what is of no value the passion of desire for food precedes eating. Eating is accused on account of its passion, and not on account of its nature. Or have you forgotten what Paul cried out: "Everything that is created by God is holy and there is nothing that is rejected if it is received with thanksgiving"?[20]

Eating Like a Dead Person

29. However, **(443)** pay attention to me here as well: do not take this word of freedom as a reason for [eating] meat and use it to serve your desires, for it is written for free people. If you have tested yourself to stand on the heights of the freedom of Christ and have subdued the servitude that is in you by the power of your self-control, use this saying. If you have felt that when you have eaten you had not eaten, and when you have drunk, you did not taste your drink, if then you are eating like a dead person, eat. But if you are eating like a living person, take care not to taste, for the sensation of taste of whatever you are eating is a testimony against you that you are still alive to lust and you will eat [just] in order to eat and not so that you may live. Saint Paul, when he was standing at the peak of this freedom, said, "One who does not eat should not judge one who does eat, and one who eats—on account of freedom—should not despise that one who does not eat"[21]—on account of the slavery of the law. Because whoever the law controls is still a slave and has not reached the perfect freedom of Christ. So then, see from here, and do not consider that you are standing in a place of freedom while you are still serving slavery and eat everything

[20] 1 Tim 4:4.
[21] Rom 14:3.

when it is not permitted to you. The blessed Apostle also has cautioned you of this, not to be enticed by thoughts of freedom while you are still a slave. "You have been called to freedom, my brothers; only, may your freedom not become an occasion for the flesh."[22]

Pay Attention to Your Own Discernment

30. If you are still a slave, do not be directed **(444)** only by laws external to you, but also by the laws you discern. For external laws are maintained for many reasons: for the sake of visibility or on account of fear, on account of praise or for the love of honor, for opinion[23] and for the growth of other passions, so that one might humiliate his enemies, or to show others to be dissolute in comparison to his evilness. There are many reasons such as these for an external law. But as for the law of your discernment, let this be yours: if you desire something, hold yourself back lest you use it. Moreover, through the fact that you desire, know that you are still a slave. When you have sensed your slavery is like this, recognize that the law is necessary for you. You then ought to surround all the movements of your thoughts with the law. Every thought that is stirred up in you by the desire of something, hold it back by the fear of the law, while considering minutely also the movements of nature as well as the movements of desire. If the movement is natural, subdue it; but if it is of desire, uproot it. You have the power to uproot the movements of desire, but of nature you should subdue and calm them down, because desire also receives movement from nature. For [desire] is intent on watching nature [to see if] it might be stirred up and when it has seen that [nature] has been stirred up, [desire] takes [nature's] movement and makes it its own. [Desire] makes it leave [nature and] gives it to your will in order to accomplish it in fact. But you, understand as an observer of your passions that if something desirous is mixed into **(445)** the movement, say, "I am receiving the movement from nature in order

---

[22] Gal 5:13.

[23] Lemoine apparently omitted 444:4 in his translation. Lavenant adopts variant (ܪܕܢܝܣܐ —"opinion") Ms. F, instead of text's ܪܕܢܝܣܐ —"illusion".

that it may receive its need and hunger. But I am distinguishing that [movement] of desire lest I eat to condemnation through it."

Despise the Cheap Foods

31. Defeat therefore the desire of vegetables so that you may also defeat through it the desire of fornication.[24] Do not let ordinary food entice you, lest an attractive face allure you. Despise cheap [foods] so that they will not amass the desire of better [foods] against you. Desire does not offer you anything except what is related to your way of life. Because you are far away from worldly foods, from home-cooked meals, and from eating meat and drinking fine wines, [desire] avoids offering you these things because it knows that they are foreign to you and have no affinity with your vows to [be able to] use them. You are cut off from them due to both habit and law, and on account of [your] abode and [your] rule. Wherever desire sees something fighting with it, it ceases from the battle against these things and entices by means of other things that are ordinary foods: desire of fine grain, desire of vegetables, desire of cold [water] instead of fine wines. Through these things that do not seem to you very culpable, because in fact their ordinariness is an excuse for them, [desire] advises you, "Eat and you will not be blamed; drink and you will not be accused. These things are necessities and it is not necessary for you to hold yourself back from necessities, and especially **(446)** in the evening or the one day in two you approach a meal, eat everything placed before you. Moreover, eat to satisfy [yourself] so that your body might become strong and bear the [ascetical] labors." By the appearance of righteousness it advises laxity for you, because it sees how often you are terrified of the advice of open laxity. But do not be enticed by the pretense of these things and do not disdain the commonness of things. Do not think food is naturally blameworthy, but [only] when one eats it with desire. For a person to eat meat and vegetables with desire,

---

[24] ܪܚܡܬܐ, "fornication"—Lemoine translates as "la viande," "meat." The following sentence and *mēmrā* confirm the sense of "fornication" as Philoxenos' intended subject.

eating both of them is equal and they are blameworthy because
desire has eaten them.

Not the Fig, But the Desire

32. It is not the fruit that Eve had eaten that gave birth to death,
but the desire of the fruit gave birth to death. If [Eve] had kept the
law and had not eaten with desire at that time, how many times
afterward would she have eaten of it and not have been blamed,
when simply she would have approached it like any other tree? It
is written, "She desired and then she ate."[25] On account of this she
was guilty. What indeed is the nature of this fruit that was able to
engender death along with all bad things? Look, as many say, and
as even the Book indicates to us [by] a little sign, the fruit Eve ate
was a fig.[26] It is evident that the nature of a fig does not engender
death. [It is,] then, desire that has engendered death that also engenders [death] in every generation in everyone. The root **(447)** of
death is desire, and the root of desire is copulation. Because of this
all those who are born from copulation are stirred up with desire
and are subjugated to death, aside from the one who was not born
by copulation. On account of this he was also freed from the stirring of desire and from here on he appeared above natural death,
he who while he received [death], it was willful and not natural.

Jewish Dietary Laws

33. Therefore, the nature of food is not blameworthy, but it is
blamable whenever desire is eating it. Also in the case of those
foods set apart in the law, the reason why they were set apart and
forbidden for the Jews was in order to teach them to defeat their
desire even if [just] in certain things. [If] the law had inhibited them
from all foods the commandment would have been too burdensome on them and they would not have accepted it; and [if] the
commandment had not inhibited them from anything, they would

---

[25] Gen 3:6.

[26] ܬܐܬܐ, *tēthā.*

have been stirred up like animals to all the lusts without discretion and would not have been able to learn that it is excellent for a rational being to be victorious over his desire. Because of this he permitted them to eat on account of weakness but held them back from eating many things so that the discernment of their rational nature might be apparent and they might learn to fight against the lusts. Because they would not gladly accept the war against lusts, [the law] pronounced unclean for them [certain] foods, so that, even if it was [just] because [certain foods] are impure, they might hold back from their use.

Discerning Abstinence

34. As for your own [situation], it does not work this way, but (448) purify and sanctify everything as it is written, "Everything is sanctified by the word of God and by prayer,"[27] so that from here your discernment's endurance may be visible. It is not because you should not eat unclean things but because of what was said, "It is good that one should not eat meat and not drink wine, nor anything [else] that would scandalize our brother,"[28] and also so that you may be victorious over desire by your will and not on account of the constraint of the impurity of foods. Desire is not awakened against these things that are unclean by nature. On account of this everything before you is holy so that—when from all sides the occasions that arouse your desire may be seen—you may overcome all of them and be victorious by the love of God. Moreover, on account of this it is appropriate that you should be seen as one [who has] self-control. Therefore, with what concerns you the discernment of foods is this: everything that you desire shall be impure to you. Whatever you approach without desire for its need, this is permissible for you to eat without reproach. The law that inhibits and permits[29] you is not written outside of you as for those [Jews], but it is that [law] which is written on your heart and

---

[27] 1 Tim 4:5.
[28] Rom 14:21.
[29] Written: ܩܒܐܪܘܐ; read ܩܒܪܘܐ.

your conscience testifies concerning it and is read by you alone, but others outside of you do not see it.

Freedom to Eat or Not to Eat

35. Your freedom will not be prevented from eating, as in the law, nor will it transgress against the law if you should eat. For freedom is above the law **(449)** and on account of this it does not matter whether you eat or do not eat, as Paul also said concerning this spiritual freedom: "Whoever is mindful for today is mindful for his Lord. Whoever is not mindful for today is not mindful for the sake of his Lord. Whoever does not eat, it is for God he does not eat; and whoever eats, eats for God and thanks the Lord."[30] Through this, then, freedom is with us [whether] we eat or do not eat. On account of this [Paul] does not distinguish for us foods by the law—they should be separated before us into what is and what is not desirous, and whatever we desire let us refrain from its eating as if from something impure, whether it be expensive or cheap, whether it is permitted to be eaten according to custom or not; but whenever we have no desire in its eating, let us eat it as if it were pure, while our conscience does not bother us with its eating. The bothering of the conscience is a transgression of the law, as was also said by the Apostle, "If someone doubts and eats, he is condemned."[31]

Meat in the Wilderness

36. The Jews ate meat in the wilderness, and it was written concerning them, "While the meat was still between their teeth, the wrath of God ruled over them."[32] It was not because they had eaten meat, but because they had sought to eat it with desire. If simply eating meat had brought on wrath, wherever else they were eating they would have received a punishment such as this. The priests,

---

[30] Rom 14:6 (Peshitta).
[31] Rom 14:23.
[32] Num 11:33.

moreover, who were eating meat continually **(450)** in the temple would have been worthy of the same condemnation. However, it is not written anywhere that wrath ruled over them on account of eating meat except only in this passage in which they had sought meat desirously. That they had sought desirously, David testifies: "They lusted greatly in the wilderness and tested God in the desert, and he granted them their requests and sent fullness to their souls."[33] In that same passage where they had asked for meat, it is written, "The people said to Moses, 'It was better for us when we were in Egypt, for we were sitting beside pots of meat and were eating and were full, everything as our soul desired.'"[34] Moses, when he had seen that they had lusted and defiled themselves through their lust, said to them, "Sanctify yourselves tomorrow so that you may eat meat."[35] As one might say, because they had defiled themselves by their lusts the gift of God does not approach the impure. "Sanctify yourselves from that desire in order that you may be worthy of the gift of meat. And you will eat it, not one day or ten or twenty. You will eat it up to one month, until it comes out from your nostrils and you will be sick of it, because you have rejected the Lord who is among you, for you have said, 'But who will let us eat meat?'"[36] Look then, everyone who eats with desire according to the word of Moses to the Jews **(451)** rejects the Lord through it and enjoys himself on account of his desire's will. It is excellent that nausea became the limit for that eating which desire had demanded, because need guards the limit, but there is no limit and end for desire.

Elijah Ate Meat

37. Understand from another angle that they were guilty because they had desired and not because they had eaten meat. For see, Elijah,

---

[33] Ps 106:14-15 (Peshitta). Note that the Hebrew psalmist writes that God sent "a wasting disease" (NRSV), the opposite of the Peshitta's and Philoxenos' "fullness."

[34] Exod 16:3.

[35] Num 11:18.

[36] Num 11:19-20.

while he was not asking desirously, ravens were sustaining him with bread and with meat in the evening and in the morning.[37] He was drinking water from a brook, and when meat was sent to the prophet by the Giver, he received it with the authority of his freedom, as if it had been a meal of vegetables. Moreover, in another situation, understand that it is desire that is blameworthy. Every day, from morning to morning, the people were picking up the manna that had come down to [the people]. As long as they were picking it up according to the commandment, they were neither blamable nor condemned. But when they desired to pick up more, it bred worms and became putrid to the shame of the desire that had picked it up.[38] Moreover, when they were eating it, it was changed to the taste of all the foods in their mouth. It is apparent that also the taste of meat was filling them, for it is written: "It was like a honeycomb and its taste like that of [flour] kneaded in oil."[39] Although it was changing into all these varieties of tastes, those who ate it were not condemned for this, because **(452)** it was a gift of grace and not a demand of their desire.

Yet Esau Ate Lentils

38. But in order to understand that everything eaten with desire is what is blameworthy, even though it is plain, place before your eyes these two [instances]: the eating of Esau and the eating of Elijah. Esau was condemned because he had eaten lentils, and Paul calls him on account of this a dissolute person and a fornicator. "For a single [portion] of food [Esau] sold his birthright."[40] Elijah, although he ate meat, was a pure and holy spiritual person and as a spiritual [being] was taken up to the place of the spiritual beings. So now, understand from these examples of Elijah and Esau that it is desire that is guilty and not eating. Therefore, seek to eat everything and do not be guilty; be above desire in everything and [you may] eat everything. But if you are not above desire, everything you eat will

[37] 1 Kgs 17:4.
[38] Exod 16:20.
[39] Exod 16:31; Num 11:9 (Peshitta).
[40] Heb 12:16.

be a condemnation for you, even if it is something plain, just as Eve was guilty eating fruits, and the Jews were accused gathering up manna, and also Esau was condemned by eating lentils, and again did not the people perish because they had eaten and drunk with desire before the calf?[41]

David Almost Drank Water

39. David, the sage of God, should persuade you that even drinking cold [water] was blameworthy when it was [drunk] with desire, because when he had desired to drink water from the great well in Bethlehem, and those who heard obeyed and brought [water] to him,[42] he defeated his desire and poured out [the water] before the Lord, as if **(453)** through [the water] he was pouring out the desire that was in him. It is not the nature of water that made him sin, supposing he had used it for drinking either because it was cold or sweet, but because he had sensed in himself that he had sought it with desire, he overcame his desire and did not give to it its request. Moreover, in order to vex those who had become ministers to his desire, he was ungrateful to them in order to teach everyone not to become subservient to desire and not to gladden the faces of those who have become ministers to our desire.

And Noah Drank Wine

40. God had also permitted Noah to eat everything as if it were green vegetables, and while Adam was condemned because he had eaten a fruit, Noah, by a generous covenant, was given authority over all foods. But wherever he used it with desire he too was also blamed.[43] When he was receiving the pleasure of wine with a desirous taste and had gone beyond the acceptable norm with his drinking, he committed here an offense. God had permitted him to eat all the meat that his soul desired.

[41] Exod 32:6; 1 Cor 10:7.
[42] 2 Sam 23:16.
[43] Gen 9:21.

Free People Eating without Desire

41. While food was burdensome for those discerning people, it was given to Noah through a promise, it was sent to Elijah through a gift, Abraham received [with hospitality] God and his angels with it,[44] Isaac in his old age agreed with it and spread [his] blessings on Jacob,[45] Samuel offered in advance this gift to Saul as to a king.[46] David and all the righteous kings have used food in such ways, and with all the numerous upright its usage was **(454)** [the norm], and they were not blamed on account of [food] because they were above desire. They were eating not as slaves with desire, but as free persons they were using everything with authority, and while they were eating fancy foods they were praised, yet others while they were eating those [foods] that are plain and despicable were rejected and reproached. Paul cries out to us, " 'May your hearts not become heavy'[47] through the eating of meat and the drinking of wine,"[48] in order to teach us that this food weighs down the heart. [But] they ate and were not weighed down. Perhaps on account of this they ate it in order to show that their lightness is stronger than its heaviness, and their intellect was all the more purified by what [usually] thickens the heart, and the lightness of their mind was enlightened by whatever makes the body heavy and clouds the thoughts. They did not consider it a very great thing that while abstaining they might become serene, pure, and holy; rather [they considered] to become pure from those things that thicken the heart, that is to say, to become pure of those things that are the opposites of purity, so that as strong people they might be victorious over what was opposing [them] and as authoritative and free people they might avoid harm in those things that caused harm.

[44] Gen 18:7.
[45] Gen 27:27.
[46] 1 Sam 9:24.
[47] See Luke 21:34.
[48] Rom 14:21; Eph 5:18.

Measured Eating

42. But you have not [yet] reached and ascended here to this degree. On account of this it is necessary for you to abstain from everything and to eat by measure so that you might become pure, and eat and drink by weight and by measure so that you might be cleansed, because just as you are promising to pursue the clarity **(455)** of the soul, you will be diligent to come to the likeness of angels. However, you are not able to stand in the freedom of spiritual [beings] until you completely take off the servitude of physical beings. When you have cast off this servitude as a spiritual and free person you will be blameless in everything that you eat. Eating meat does not make your heart heavy and the drinking of wine does not cloud your thoughts, as it is also written concerning the angels, "They ate meat and drank wine at the home of Abraham,"[49] and their spiritual nature was not made heavy by this meal. All the upright who are inscribed in the Scriptures were similar to them, for they were eating and did not become heavy and thick because they were eating without passion. Become passionless and eat like the angels at Abraham's home, and like all the righteous in the Old Testament you will not be blamed.

Freedom Not Always Used

43. But this is the situation: you are obligated to guard the sobriety of your way of life because this is appropriate for your promise and for the profit of others, because we are not permitted to become involved with everything we have with regard to freedom and authority, for even if freedom has authority over everything, it is not used with everything in order not to destroy its freedom. The fact that a free person is not bound by the desire of something shows through this his freedom, and though he has authority he does not use it; and he will double its freedom all the more and guard it lest it become undone, as also Paul has written concerning **(456)** this freedom, "Everything is permitted to me, but not everything

---

[49] Gen 18:8.

edifies."⁵⁰ In order that you might learn in particular about this along with everything else—[whether] to eat or not to eat—he explained the authority of his freedom [and] said immediately after these things, "Food belongs to the belly and the belly [belongs] to food. But God brings both of them to an end."⁵¹

Abstain in Order to Be Free

44. Therefore, O disciple, keep the law of asceticism so that you may also attain the authority of freedom, and restrain yourself and do not eat so that you may approach that situation in which you are not aware you are eating. Abstain from nourishment by the authority of your own soul so that the lusts mixed in your members may be brought low. Do not eat in order not to sin, nor drink in order not to err. Be constant in fasting so that by it you might be worthy of the purity of prayer. Reduce your nourishment at the time of your meal so that the wing of your mind might be light in running toward God. Calculate with your body down to the smallest things so that through these your soul might have authority over the abundant wealth of divine knowledge, and may that One who has revealed to you the treasures of his wisdom and of his knowledge not calculate with you. Close your eyes a little from the lusts and see, you have crossed over the dangerous place. For the time of passion⁵² is very short, but the time without passion⁵³ is without end.

Eagerly Attack Desire

45. Therefore, do not be defeated in the time of victory. Seize the war of desire as an opportunity that [some] work may be found for your soul. As long as the lusts accomplish their work **(457)** in

⁵⁰ 1 Cor 6:12.

⁵¹ 1 Cor 6:13.

⁵² Typographical error: written ܪܚܘܫܚܘ, "need"; Lavenant reads ܪܚܫܚܘ, "passion."

⁵³ ܪܚܫܚܘ ܪܠܐ, "without passion" (= *apatheia*).

you, there is no work in you for your soul, and while it is in you, it is as if it were not, because it is empty and bereft of the actions of its nature. Has the body begun to stir its lusts in you? Jump right up[54] and be astonished at the sight of your desire, just like someone lazy for whom some task has been found, and say to your soul, "Why are you afflicted, my soul, and why are you sad for yourself"[55] seeing that you are deprived of [anything] beneficial? Look, a task has fallen into your hands, prosper by it. Look, desire strips down in order to confront you in the contest. Show the skill of your athleticism and the strength of your arms. Look, here is an opportunity for rewards, because you love rewards. Look, your enemies have gathered at the field of battle. Scream at them at the top of your lungs, rebuke severely and scatter the armies of the lusts. The diligent in this place do not garner losses; you who are diligent, reap the benefits. Through this especially your victory is proclaimed that wherever others were defeated, you have taken the victory. Desire is the reason for defeat for those who are lax, but for you because you are diligent it will be a cause for triumphs. Just as a warrior who is confident in his strength and is established in his craft rejoices at the sight of enemies, so also you should rejoice at the coming of the lusts, because without these your triumphs will disappear and you will not have an opportunity for conflict from which victory is born. Let these things be spoken by you to your soul whenever it happens **(458)** that lusts are aroused against you, and especially against this stupid desire of the lust of the belly that ordinarily sprouts up from childhood. It enters and destroys on its own, because it loves to be seen by itself, and lays the foundation of dissoluteness from the beginning of the growth of a child[56] in order that when it begins from there it will be discovered to be the assistant to all the desires that sprout up on all levels.

---

[54] Lemoine opts for variant Mss. EF: ܬܘܕܝܟ, "jump up," "bondis."

[55] Ps 43:5.

[56] ܪܒܘܬܐ.

The First Desire

46. This then is the first desire that has been victorious over the world, and because of it the transgression of the first command-ment happened.[57] Perhaps also with Cain, when he turned toward this, contemplated killing his brother in order to inherit the land for himself alone.[58] It placed a blemish on the righteous Noah.[59] It stripped Esau of his birthright[60] and his blessings.[61] It also brought the Sodomites to the act of impurity.[62] In its company the sons of Seth also came to the passion of fornication, on account of which they were rejected from the household of God.[63] It had slain the people in the wilderness by punishments of all kinds. They stood up from the table of lust and bowed down to a dead calf.[64] Through its enticement they denied all the graces that [were given] to them. "Because Israel had become fat and had kicked against it," through this desire it is written, "[Israel] had forgotten God its Maker."[65] Because the priests desired and drank and were unruly in the place of atonement, fire consumed their bodies.[66] Also through it the prophet was reproaching **(459)** the people, giving "Woe" to those who rose early in the morning and ran toward [desire].[67] Another prophet, moreover, was accusing them of this same desire: "They were eating the fatted lambs from the flock and the calves from within the herds."[68] Because of this the scribes and Pharisees re-ceived "Woe" from our Savior since [desire] had taught them also

[57] Gen 3:6.
[58] Gen 4:8.
[59] Gen 9:21.
[60] Gen 25:30-34.
[61] Gen 27:30-38.
[62] Gen 19:4-5.
[63] Num 24:17.
[64] Exod 32:1-20.
[65] Deut 32:15.
[66] Ps 106:14, 18.
[67] Isa 5:11.
[68] Deut 32:14.

to perform the feast and the Sabbath and [tithe] the cummin.[69] [Desire] required taxes regarding the priests so that with no [legitimate] right they would be receiving from the offerings of those making offerings. [Desire] had stripped the sons of Eli of their priesthood.[70] By too many delicacies Solomon also was led into the error of idols.[71]

Desire Corrupts All

47. Today [desire] corrupts everyone. The world is fatigued on account of it. Because of its pleasure creation pursues its course. All people fulfill servitude to it. And if it did not exist, the door would have been shut in the face of all evil deeds. Examine and see with knowledge that the course of all people and the labor and fatigue and sweat of all who enter into the world exists only on account of it. With its intent and on account of its need, merchants travel on roads, sailors journey on terrible seas, farmers and laborers endure labor and fatigue, craftsmen work in cities, hired hands rush to those who hire, slaves serve masters, masters, moreover, sell and acquire their slaves. On account of it treasures are accumulated and treasuries are guarded for years. By its pretext gold and silver and revenues of all kinds are accumulated and put aside.

From the Heights of Knowledge

48. Climb up, **(460)** therefore, and stand on the heights of knowledge and look out on the entire world from there and see its course, its lightness and its agitation, and the promise of its dwellers on all sides. See those who are ascending and others who are descending, those who are going and others who are coming, that one who is crying out and the other one who is shouting, that one who is quarreling and another who is struggling, that one seizing what is not his own and that other one who is plundering his companion,

[69] Matt 23:23.
[70] 1 Sam 2:34.
[71] 1 Kgs 11:1-5.

that one who like a thief takes the spoil and the other one who like a brigand seizes those who approach from the roads, warriors[72] being lined up on the borders, kingdoms being divided against themselves, generals rebelling[73] against kings, kings battling lest their powers be taken away, judges receiving a bribe, lawyers selling victory unjustly, students learning on account of it, scribes teaching on account of it. When you have seen all these things and many like them and the varieties of disturbance and the tumult that fill the world, turn around and seek the reason for all these things. You will find that it is only the lust of the belly.

If Gluttony Were Defeated

49. But if [the lust of the belly] were defeated, everything would be in silence and tranquility, and you would not be able to see anything in the world resisting the will of God or leading us to transgress the commandment and trample on the law. If someone were to say that there are other causes of the passions serving all these things in the world, let whoever says this know **(461)** that the lust of the belly is the initial cause of these other evil things. Although the passions are very numerous and varied and are stirred up differently in all people, and hence the world is disturbed and creation is upset, however, the great source from which these troubled streams flow to all sides is this desire of the lust of the belly. If one should plug up this source by the strength of his self-control, he will see at once that all the streams of evil things being discharged from it are drying up, and there is silence over everything and "peace reigns over all flesh,"[74] and tranquility will spring up in the disturbed places, and all the minds will be filled with pleasure and joy. In a manner of speaking, if there is nothing in the middle, you will not be able to see in the world a single one of the evil things, because

---

[72] Lemoine considers ܪܒܐ to be a haplography since "those who approach" and "warriors/soldiers" have the same consonants.

[73] Lemoine reads variant (Ms. F): ܡܬܒ, rather than written ܡܬܒ.

[74] See Jer 12:12.

all evil things are gathered near it, and all labors and exhausting works run on account of it.

All Evil Linked with Lust of Belly

50. Our eating bread by the sweat of [our] brows is born from it. It has made thorns and thistles grow. By its fault the punishment of death rules over all. It is the general of those on the left side and through it all the armies of sin are tied down, and just like generals who go out to battle at the head of armies against enemies, so also the general of all vices goes out to battle against the virtues, and thoughts and deeds of iniquity accompany it, and movements and actions of sin and all the occupations of vices journey in its perverse footsteps. All the works of sin **(462)** are made for it, and like members [of the body], they receive power from it and are nourished by it. In a similar manner the senses are linked with the head, error and the worship of idols, doubt, suspicion and falsehood are also tied with the lust of the belly. In the way that all the members of the body receive strength and support, so also all the vices are strengthened by it, for they have brought along fornication and adultery and the other passions of corruption, decorative clothes and empty pleasures of the lust of the belly, sadness and vainglory and pride, anger and despair, bitterness, evil, hatred, enmity, resentment, rage and sharpness, anger and jealousy, bitterness and agitation, false pretenses and preeminence, power, backbiting and slander, and the tongue that continually strikes behind someone's back, mockery and ridicule, oppression, fraud and murder, magic, drunkenness and blows, with all the other despicable passions that are like these, because all of them are linked together with the lust of the belly. But I allow myself to say that of the labors and austerities and diseases and illnesses, and of such things like these that physically afflict us, that of all of them, [the lust of the belly] is the cause.

Victory over Gluttony is Victory over All Sin

51. Whoever struggles by the strength of his self-control and is victorious over this first evil is able to defeat all sin by [his] victory over it. It is right as well **(463)** that godly people have passed

down to us that whoever wishes to become perfect on the road of Christ must first struggle against this passion. Then also those who depart from the world after perfection, if they do not begin at first with asceticism, they will not begin legitimately on the road of the commandments; and maybe they will not even be able to finish because the lust of the belly deceives them, and even while they may use it in an orderly fashion in the beginning, it will bring them to illusory thoughts and to fantasies of the mind. This veil that stands in front of the intellect and darkens it from the sight of God and clouds it even more, for until it is torn away from before the face of the mind, one is not able to look upon the Holy of Holies of the knowledge of Christ, not even while a person is bearing austerities and labors. If he does not tear away that veil of the heart's cloudiness the heavenly light will not be visible to him and he will not labor in the way of Christ with his own self-awareness. For when this has been torn away, then one will begin to sense the renewal of himself and to know by his mind's knowledge that there is something else outside of whatever is visible and tangible, and receive moreover the sensation of these things above the world, and the wonders and living movements that concern God, so that one might move himself toward God in a living manner like him, and not in a mortal manner according to the nature of his body. **(464)** Briefly, following the victory against this desire a person is worthy of the entire spiritual vision.

Soul Is Weakened as Body Is Nourished

52. If those who are in the world and cultivate uprightness are in need of fasting and asceticism, how much more do those who have departed outside of it [have need of] a covenant of the spiritual ways of life? The definition of this asceticism is this: we struggle against all the foods used by the belly, not by perseverance of the members only, but also by steadfastness of thoughts. If one is compelled to eat on account of his need, let him eat from these things that are despicable, despised and common, inexpensive and little in demand; but let him also be cautious of a full belly, because just as it was said by one of the spiritual teachers, "a big stomach is not

able to give birth to a refined intellect,"[75] the exorbitant fullness of the stomach, without a doubt, is the darkener of the intellect. This is why no one among these who have experienced with knowledge is able to doubt. If fools doubt about it, they doubt because they do not know about it by experience, or while they do know, it is too hard for them to renounce their pleasures. Therefore, a perfect testimony will show you this, that inasmuch as the body is nourished, so the soul will be weakened, and as much as [the body] becomes heavy and adds [one] body upon [another] body through nourishment, the soul will vanish and come to an end. While it exists, it seems as if it were not in [the body]. As long as the body increases in the strength and vitality of its stature, [the soul] lowers its own **(465)** stature and diminishes its members— which are its thoughts—and its knowledge vanishes and the light of teaching is inhibited from it. As much as the body finds itself, [the soul] becomes lost; and as much as [the body] heals itself, [the soul] becomes ill. But whoever wishes to find himself, his body will deliver [him] to the destruction of all afflictions. Look, he has found his soul in the destruction of his body, and the health of the spiritual person in the illness of the physical human being, just as Paul also testifies, "When I am sick, then I am strong."[76]

Body and Spirit as Constant Adversaries

53. When two sides opposing one another are engaged in conflict, as long as they are equal in the number of soldiers and equal in the skill of war the battle is endless for them, because at all times they are [either] victorious [or] are vanquished, capturing and surrendering victory to one another, and seizing by force triumphs from one another and giving back one to the other, and from their equality continual war is born to them. So then, the soul and the body are also like this with regard to one another, and as their natures are opposites of one another, so also are their wills. On

---

[75] A proverb found in several Greek writers: Basil of Ancyra, Gregory Nazianzen, John Chrysostom, John of Damascus, and Gregory Palamas.
[76] 2 Cor 12:10.

account of this Paul also has said, "The body desires something that harms the spirit and the spirit desires something that harms the body and the two of them are adversaries to one another."[77] As long as they exist in this measure of equality, they will have constant war without peace. Sometimes the body is victorious over the soul and sometimes the soul defeats the body. Whoever (466) battles in this way remains [fixed] in his place, for even if he moves to take a little step forward by means of the soul, the body adheres to him and makes him turn backward. Furthermore, [the body] draws [him] away from [his] place and makes him descend into the depths of sin. By these rises and falls, goings and comings, a person does not move from his location and is not able to grow according to the stature given to him by God, so that through it he may grow to spiritual life.

Tomb for the Soul

54. Therefore, if these movements of their life, consisting equally of soul and of body, are not able to take the victory and set out ahead on the journey of their way of life, how are those who are living in the body and are continually nourishing the body, granting it the fullness of its needs, giving it food in order to satiate[78] it, giving it as much as it desires to drink, and submerging it into the heaviness of sleep able to take the victory against the passions and complete this Christian road on which they are traveling? These who nourish themselves in this way and type are anxious about their bodies, for not only are they not able to be victorious over the sin in them, but to such an extent does their soul die and perish [that] their bodies become tombs for their souls, and like bodies their souls are buried in tombs, since they do not sense anything at all in their own life, (467) and if there is any movement of life in them it is entirely for the body. When the soul makes the body die, it does it all by itself. If the body should make the soul die, it

---

[77] Gal 5:17 (Lemoine notes that in the Letter to Galatians it is "the flesh" not "the body").

[78] Lemoine reads variant Ms. E: ܐܠܗܘܡ, rather than written ܐܠܗܡ.

thinks and acts and speaks like one living, but the soul dwells in [the body] like [something] dead that does not sense [anything]; and if it seems that it is alive, because its nature is immortal, it lives for the body and not for the soul.

Soul Raises Body to Resurrection

55. Therefore, take away from the body and give to the soul, and do not take away from the soul and give to the body. As it was promised to be for you from your Creator, so you should also do to yourself. This hope was given to you: your body shall be lifted up to the level of your soul at the resurrection, not that the soul should be lowered to the dead state of the body and to its corruption. It was said to you that half of you lives with your [other] half, not so that the better portion in you might be destroyed along with what is inferior. So then, lift up the power of your body above your soul and change [it], mixing its life with the life of the soul so that mortal life may be preserved along with [the soul's] immortal life and [the body's] feeble strength may be mixed in with spiritual force's power. Instead of the tomb consuming your body and dissolving and dispersing the composition of your members, take portions of its members by means of common labors that are in all the members and place them next to the soul. When [the soul] departs from you by the dissolution of death, it will not **(468)** depart by itself but will carry with it all that belongs to the body: [the body's] strength with [the soul's] strength, its life with its life, its physical nature with its spiritual nature, its members and its senses and all of the labor of their functions with all the spiritual portions of the soul.

Different Strategies for Different Generations

56. This struggle is useful to us, especially so that we may be victorious through it from the beginning of our childhood, because from the beginning of the planting of human infancy this passion clings to their life and makes these passions grow in all the stages of life suitable for them. With infants and with old men, with youth and those old of days, this passion engenders anger and indignation, constant impertinence and rage. But with the rest

of the middle ages—adolescence, adulthood, and middle-age—it engenders fornication and vainglories, the love of money and the love of power, along with others such as these. According to the characteristics of these ages, it is necessary in this manner that the forms of combat should also be adjusted. For with the age of infants, since it is beneath discerning knowledge, it is necessary that they should be prevented from the practice of this desire by the constraint of law and should be commanded to fulfill this regimen of asceticism by teachers and masters, and even though it is burdensome on them and they do not find pleasure in it, so they should also be compelled to complete it in order to adopt a good routine and become trained in self-control from **(469)** their childhood. When they have attained those ages that produce knowledge, they will sense by the taste of self-control and will taste the sweetness of this victory. The childhood that from the beginning is learning the virtues and being instructed in the practice of self-control [is] like the field that is first plowed and seeded so that in the appropriate time it will produce the fruits of knowledge. What should I say to children? Just as with all ages, even that of mature people and of accomplished men, the knowledge of struggle is not apparent to them during the periods when their thoughts are agitated by the battle of struggle. But once they have ceased from war, then they will be aware of knowledge. If, on the other hand, knowledge is found with them while they are fighting, their knowledge is concerning how they should fight, that is, the knowledge that is the transmission of the law, [the knowledge] that consists of hearing and of tradition, of learning and the word, but not that spiritual knowledge that naturally rises up in the soul and engenders words without the memory of transmission.

Simplicity of Spiritual Knowledge

57. Just as the eye receives through its rapid [movements] the vision of the simplicity of light, so also the soul's vision receives the clarity and simplicity of spiritual knowledge after the victory over these physical passions. Just as the ordinary sun falling on natures and various bodies seems to them **(470)** to be cut and divided, while

its single nature is simple in which there is no division, in the same way also is spiritual knowledge when it has risen on the ways of life and labors: it seems to them that it is separated and divided, while with its soul it is a unique and simple [knowledge]. The soul is not worthy to receive the rising of this light, unless one has first been born from the physical nature to the spiritual nature, [one's] birth being completed through labors and austerities. "Flesh and blood are not able to inherit the kingdom of heaven,"[79] the blessed Paul teaches us. As one might say, as long as the movements of a person consist of flesh and blood, he is not able to inherit the spiritual knowledge of Christ, which [Paul] calls allegorically[80] the kingdom of heaven. [While] there are other meanings for this passage with respect to other passions,[81] with regard to the matter set before us it is appropriate for us to relate it also in this sense because the true kingdom is this: the knowledge that does not err or does not appear [illusionary] but sees clearly everything in its place—these things that are natural and these that are above nature—according to the level that has been given to those that are created. A person whose life consists of movements of flesh and blood is not able to become an heir of this knowledge. If he should happen to receive [spiritual knowledge] by oral transmission, he is hearing the words from others, but it is not **(471)** the same knowledge that has revealed itself in his soul.

Daniel and the Pure Young Men in Babylon

58. Because this knowledge exists within the words and inside the readings and names as the example of these pure young men who were raised in Babylon testifies to us,[82] who while they were receiving human learning by an instructive word, they were desiring

---

[79] 1 Cor 15:50.

[80] ܐܟ ܕܒܡܬܠܐ; literally, "as with a parable."

[81] ܚܫܐ, "passions." Lemoine translates "évêques/bishops"; Lavenant: "contextes."

[82] See Dan 1:4-7.

to receive divine knowledge above the transmission of words. That [knowledge] revealed itself in them at the right time and this knowledge was teaching the youths what human knowledge was not able to know. It demonstrated itself in them because they had also journeyed lawfully toward it on the same road of this knowledge. When their nourishment was given to them from the table of the kings, they were commanded to take food fitting for those receiving the education of the kingdom. They rejected this table because they sensed it was making worldly knowledge grow. Cleansing and purifying foods are required for those who receive human education, so that their physical senses might become clear and made light, according to the purity of the food.

Yet spiritual knowledge does not have need of these things because it does not take hold in the soul by the illumination of the physical senses, but when all the soul's parts have been purified and made clear from the passions of the vices, then this knowledge will rise up in it. Pure foods are helpful and are not a little beneficial to the lightness of the senses of these who receive human[83] knowledge, [but] those who are spiritual **(472)** do not have need of something like this. And so that you may know that this is the case, take the testimony of these pure young men. In place of clear and purified foods of the [earthly] kingdom that give fattening and heavy nourishment to the body, they chose for themselves dry vegetables and drinking water.[84] The strength of this eating of vegetables is contrary to those who were receiving the knowledge of human education, yet since those were not purifying their bodies, but their souls, they had chosen for themselves the eating of vegetables in order that the body may be defeated and the power and natural strength of the members should be humbled, and that the living parts of the soul may be revealed after these things for the perception and sight of divine knowledge.

---

[83] ܢܦܫܬܐ , literally, "(related to) the soul."
[84] Dan 1:12.

That is what happened: after three years[85] because they had eaten vegetables and had drunk water, knowledge was revealed to them, not that [knowledge] born from words, but that which is born from works. They were performing works that engender spiritual knowledge and were learning words that engender human knowledge. Yet because their own purpose was observing the revelation of that knowledge [that comes] from deeds, and not that [knowledge] from words, wherever they were looking, there they saw; and from wherever they were hoping, from there they received. They became a channel for words and receptacles for spiritual knowledge. There is something for you to understand from what happened—that not only were they eating vegetables and drinking water, but also after an extended fast they were receiving this nourishment of asceticism. Because whoever **(473)** eats vegetables also perseveres in fasting, and whoever drinks water also is disposed at all times to pure prayer, if that is the purpose of his asceticism.

Understand this from the reading [of Scripture] that when the time arrived that knowledge would show itself in them, they had applied themselves to asceticism and fasting and prayer, and then the revelations for which they were asking were shown to them. "Daniel told his companions to ask from the God of heaven that this mystery might be revealed to them, in order that Daniel and his companions might not perish, along with the rest of the sages of Babylon. And then the mystery was revealed to Daniel in a night vision."[86] This then is the gift asceticism had given to the young men and this is the harvest they had reaped from these fields from which vegetables were sown and water had been drunk.

Fast In Order to See

59. Run then, O disciple, like them, in order that you will find [spiritual revelations] like them. Restrain yourself so that you may depart to the wide open [spaces]. Make yourself small so that you may enter through the narrow door. Drink water so that you may

[85] Dan 1:5ff.
[86] Dan 2:18.

drink in knowledge. Nourish yourself with vegetables so that you may become wise in the mysteries. Eat according to limits so that you may love without limit. Become a faster so that you may become a seer. This is your food because it is also your discipleship, for such as this is promised. Eating delicacies and filling the stomach are not your [behaviors], but of these who live in the vices in the world that make thorns and thistles of sin spring up at all times—because a person who is sown with delicacies and drinks wines normally produces fruits such as these. The harvest of eating vegetables and drinking (474) water is visions and heavenly revelations, spiritual knowledge and divine wisdom, and the explanation of hidden things. The soul that works with such as these will sense something that human knowledge does not sense.

Milk of Two Mothers

60. Begin in the way of [ascetical] labors from your childhood, and do not say, "I am [just] a child," because your rationale is taken up from the example of youth. For those attractive [youths], as the story of Scripture indicates, were very young of age when they began in this divine service and they discovered this [knowledge] without teachers. But you are doing it while you have teachers. There were those who were persuading them to do the opposite— that is, to eat and to drink—but for you, divine teaching counsels you [to do] the opposite, to love the way of asceticism and to take hold of self-control. While they were not obliged or required, they chose this for themselves by their discernment. But, if you act like them, you will repay a debt and fulfill your promise by the word of God that is with you.

Therefore, awaken your soul and look at these children of the Old [Testament] who, while they were born from a single mother, were suckling from the milk of another. While the Old Testament had given them birth to the faith of God, they were fulfilling the spiritual way of the New [Testament]. The milk of their mother was not sweet to them, but they were yearning earnestly to suckle from the breasts that are giving suckle to you, (475) and desiring your table. But when you do these things, you are doing what belongs to you, and you will grow up from where you have been born and keep the laws to which you are obliged.

Kingdom Within and Near

61. This is what your choice proclaims: labors, austerities, asceticism, and subjugation of the body; and after these, pleasures born from these things encounter you: delight, joy, and confidence—all of which are above the world. Before the kingdom you will inherit the kingdom. A human being who with the austerities of his body and with heavy labors also cleanses and purifies his soul from vices will inherit the kingdom before the time of the kingdom. Before the revelation of universal glory, its glory will reveal itself to him from his soul. He himself will become the source of his knowledge, because there is one who will come to be worthy of the kingdom in heaven, and there is one who finds the kingdom in himself: "Look, the kingdom of God is within you."[87] In another passage he said, "Repent, for the kingdom of heaven has drawn near."[88] Both of these [statements] are true. [First,] the upright will come to inherit the kingdom of heaven at the end of the world above in heaven, and [second,] the kingdom is within you, because it is the spiritual knowledge revealed to those who are spiritual, as if they already are in the kingdom of heaven with an ineffable pleasure.

Joy and Hope of Affliction

62. But it is not possible to find one of these without the austerities and labors of the body, for those who bear the labors physically are heirs of the kingdom (476) of heaven. Those who with labors acquire the clarity of soul will discover the kingdom within them and enjoy its blessings and delight themselves in a continual joy over which sadness cannot rule. Because they are rejoicing at all times, joy is born from them, as Paul has also said, "You should

[87] Luke 17:21.
[88] Matt 3:2.

rejoice at all times."[89] Again in another passage he said, "Rejoice in your hope and endure your afflictions."[90] Hope grows in us concerning these things which are to come by the endurance of austerities, as Paul himself said in another passage: "Affliction perfects in us endurance, and endurance trial, and trial hope; but hope does not dishonor."[91] Whoever does not bear austerities by his own strength, it is evident that he does not even have a memory of hope. Because if he were hoping, he would also be afflicting himself for the sake of his hope, just as all the upright who have entered the world have afflicted themselves through all sorts of labors. Through many austerities they have traveled on this road that leads them to the kingdom of God, and because they were traveling by hope, the taste of austerities was sweet to them.

Two Roads from the Belly

63. The beginning of the road of austerities for all of them was asceticism, just as the beginning of all vices is the gluttony of the belly. For from the same place two roads begin: from the lust of the belly is the road to the left, and from hatred of the belly **(477)**, the road to the right. Whoever desires to begin in good order on the road of discipleship should begin from here, so that, by afflicting and subduing his body, reducing food and drink from it, and bearing the labors of vigil, austerities, and fasting, its pleasures are cut down and he becomes agile and light of soul for his occupations. But the work of austerities is not as difficult as they are reputed to be, because what one hears from a distance usually causes everyone to be afraid. But when it has been investigated and one has actually experienced these matters, from there they are easier matters for those who do them.

[89] 1 Thess 5:16.
[90] Rom 12:12.
[91] Rom 5:3.

Subdue the Body

64. But as for you, O one who has taken off the world, there are some things that will be greatly helpful to you and will give you a hand for the excellent way of life. The fact that you are removed from seeing and hearing worldly things guards your life not just a little in holiness. But these illustrious youths, about whom I have brought you their example, when the royal table was placed before their sight, they were rejecting its delights and choosing for themselves austerities instead of comforts.[92] Consider from here the power of their self-control, that while there was no teacher to instruct [them], nor to offer a hand and encourage [them], nor the example of others before them, nor fear of the law on them, nor want and poverty, and neither fright nor fear inhibiting them, nor the fact that they were far away from the vision of these things, which is also an assistance to endurance, and while there was not one of these, **(478)** they had filled their soul with the strength of their self-control. But in your case, even while all these things are helping you, persevere in the self-control that is fitting for your discipleship and defeat the evil mistress, the mistress of all iniquities, and subdue your body and afflict your members, just as Paul also had said, "I subdue and subjugate my body lest, having preached to others, I myself am rejected."[93] If Paul, even though he has taken the victory against the passions by the power of grace, has need yet for subduing the body, how much more for those in whom the desires of the flesh still live is it necessary for them to subdue their bodies through fasting and asceticism and to struggle and be victorious?

Table as a Place for Struggle

65. But as for you, O disciple, if you wish to become excellent in your discipleship, may that table, which is for others a place of pleasure, become for you a place of struggle. Arrange on [that

[92] Dan 1:8.
[93] 1 Cor 9:27.

table] a battle against all foods, whether large or small [portions], whether rich or plain. Do not dismiss desire because it has limited itself with small matters, and do [not] think[94] that it is not worthy of reproach. But you are all the more blameworthy if you are defeated by little things, even more than by great things. Because if desire defeats you by little things, how much more will it defeat you by great things? If by vegetables **(479)** it defeats you, how much more will it defeat you by eating meat? "Whoever is iniquitous in a little also is iniquitous in much."[95] Be victorious over whatever desire [uses] to fight with you. If [it is] in eating meat and by different and tasty meals, fight against these things and defeat the lust of the belly. But if [it is] by dry vegetables, herbs, fruit, and ordinary and plain fruits, gain[96] the victory against it by means of what it fights with. Do not say, "The victory I win over these things is not a [great] thing," but consider that a defeat would be [even] greater if you are defeated by these things. Therefore, if that desire that normally desires always the great things has lowered itself and desired lesser things in order to subjugate you, do not lower yourself with it and you will defeat it wherever it seeks to defeat you. Wherever [desire] calls you, there you ought to pursue it, and in whatever it desires arrange a battle against its enticements, imitating in this Christ your Lord.

Imitate Christ

66. For wherever the Tempter sought to tempt him, there [Christ] would find himself. Wherever [the Tempter] wished to begin in conflict, from there also [Christ] answered him. Having begun with the battle against the insatiableness of the belly, [Christ] defeated this desire by the endurance of fasting in order to give us also an example and establish for us a clear law so that if we also wish to begin in the spiritual ways, we should begin **(480)** by fasting and after it little by little we will be led into all the triumphs. Because

---

[94] Written: ܬܣܒܕܐ; read ܬܚܫܒܕܐ (Ms. F).

[95] Luke 16:10.

[96] Text reads ܢܣ, "place," read ܣܒ "take" (Ms. E).

our Lord was also victorious at first over the lust of the belly and after it over the lust of money and over the vainglory of the world and over [the love of] leadership and power,[97] which are engendered from this. After these things he was victorious over vainglory, the hateful passion that is born from appealing things. By these three things he defeated and brought to an end all the passions that cling to them, then began to preach with authority the kingdom of his Father, and to deliver the teaching of perfection to people. Therefore, just as when Christ our Lord was fulfilling the work of the law and commenced with the spiritual way of life, he began by fasting, so also by his example you ought to make a start by [fasting] for your discipleship which is above the world.

Christ Fasted to Our Limits

67. Which asceticism was there as perfect as Jesus', who not only had distanced himself from the tastes of food but also from their smell and their appearance, in that he had abandoned the cultivated land in which these things are found and had gone out into the desert?[98] He deprived himself of everything so that he might cut off all the senses and discard this despicable desire, because unless one has departed from the world, he is not able to journey on the road of perfection. Consider also this: how long did our Savior extend his fasting? As long as our [human] nature is able to manage, Moses[99] and Elijah[100] also have journeyed and reached this number. If our nature had been able to advance more, our Savior would have fasted more. If our[101] strength were too little **(481)** to attain this number, [Christ] would have reduced the number of the days he had fasted, and he would have measured the time up to where human nature was able to attain. For not according to his strength

---

[97] See Matt 4:1-11; Luke 4:1-13.

[98] Matt 4:1-2.

[99] Exod 24:18.

[100] 1 Kgs 19:8.

[101] Lemoine translates "our strength" to fit the context, instead of written ܡܚܝܠܗ—"his strength."

did our Savior fast, but according to our strength. If our Savior were fasting according to his strength he would not have been hungry at all, because the nature of his spirituality is not to be hungry. He fasted physically according to the measure of the strength of physical beings, lowered himself toward us, and revealed to us the limits of the endurance of our nature. Because by a great number of delicacies the power of self-control was weakened in us and we were thinking that without these things there is no way for our nature to live, and if one were to reduce these delicacies and the sustenance of foods it would perish. Our Lord fasted forty days and taught us that the strength of our natural endurance extends up to here, if barriers of desire are not placed in the way and do not cut off the road of self-control. But our Savior has broken and surpassed all the barriers of the desires and endurances of illnesses and sicknesses and has reached up to the end of forty days. On that account many people also have attained up to here, but no one has surpassed this limit that our Savior has fixed because it is natural. If it has been heard or spoken that someone has surpassed this boundary, this is beyond natural human strength and **(482)** was accomplished solely by grace for many reasons, some of which are hidden from us and some of which are revealed to us.

Freedom after Gluttony

68. Therefore, the disciple should set this example before him if he wishes to become diligent in the spiritual way of life. Just as our Lord was victorious over all the other passions, so also after asceticism it will be easy for you to be victorious over the rest of the lusts. Just as after all the lusts were defeated, Jesus then began with authoritative teaching and with the ways of freedom to eat with everyone and be invited by everyone and to mingle and speak with all [kinds of] persons—these things being the sign of authoritative freedom—so also you when you have defeated the lust of the belly and from this the rest of the passions that follow after it, you will stand in the freedom of Christ and mix authoritatively with all [people] and speak with all, and eat and drink with the publicans and the prostitutes. Your conversation with women will be without

fear while your freedom does not distinguish a male from a female because you have left behind that thought by which the passions see differences. When the mind is not agitated by passion, there is no difference between the face of a man and that of a woman, nor a beautiful appearance and an ugly one, but one will encounter without passion all [people] and will observe everything. You will enter every house[102] without fear, greet every person, and be all [things] with all [people], while you are one without being changed for the profit of everyone. The examples of these things **(483)** were evident in Christ and in his apostles.

Asceticism of John the Baptist

69. Understand that our Savior came to such things as these by asceticism, and not only he, but also the holy apostles and the divine prophets, and also that one who is the intermediary of the two Testaments, John the Baptist. Remember how Scripture recounts to you concerning the ways of his asceticism, that it was new and different from the way of all [other] people. His dress was that of camels' hair,[103] the belt of his loins was leather similar to the prophets. His food [was] locusts and wild honey, his dwelling the arid desert deprived of cultivated land, and his occupation [was] among wild animals. In all this profound asceticism he was perfect from his childhood. After these things, he then became worthy to receive revelation and become a preacher before the coming of the Most High One, and to be equal before the cross of these who are after the cross. While human nature was not yet born to spiritual [nature], he would be uniquely born before the birth of all. He was worthy as a result of his stringent asceticism of this ineffable vision and this marvelous and admirable change, with the strength of that grace for which everything is easy. This is the nature of this way of life when it is close to the serenity of the soul that gives birth to a person to live in the spiritual world and become the equal of angels, while still residing in the physical world.

---

[102] ܒ, contracted form of ܒܝܬܐ, "house."
[103] Matt 3:4.

The Apostles Needed to Practice Asceticism First

70. Understand along with this that even the blessed apostles, although they were chosen **(484)** by grace, were not worthy of the spiritual gift until the way of asceticism was first visible in them. Look, while they were living in the world with Jesus it is not written concerning them that they conducted themselves by the laws of asceticism because by the pouring forth of grace they were conducting themselves in the way of the freedom of Christ to which our Savior came after his temptation in the wilderness. Although they had not yet attained this [freedom] from the experience of their own conduct, Christ himself by his grace associated them with his perfection. While the Pharisees and disciples of John had not understood the authority of this freedom they were finding fault presumptuously with Christ, "Why do we fast a lot, but your disciples do not fast?"[104] Jesus responded with a saying whose meaning was higher than the strength of their hearing: "'The sons of the bridal chamber are not able to fast as long as the bridegroom is with them.'[105] But just as in a wedding feast not only is the bridegroom dressed in white clothes and engaged in pleasurable activities but also all the guests of the feast,[106] so in this same way not only do I, who after the victory and the payment of the debt of all passions have come to this freedom of the feast, rejoice and enjoy myself, but also I associate with me my invited disciples to the kingdom. 'The days are coming when I shall be lifted up from them, and then they shall fast in those days.'[107] That is to say, **(485)** when the bountiful light of free authority has been gathered [back] to me." Then they will also light the lamps of their endurance, and there will be an opportunity for the Spirit so that instead of the light of Jesus, [the Spirit] itself will shine on them inwardly. That is what also happened after the ascension to heaven. Although as by a pledge they had gone beforehand in the way of freedom, yet they did not

---

[104] Mark 2:18.
[105] Mark 2:19.
[106] Matt 22:11.
[107] Mark 2:20.

receive this freedom in themselves until they had first labored in the ways of asceticism. Therefore, as soon as our Savior had ascended it is written concerning them, "They returned to the upper [room] in which they had been."[108] They remained there in a long fast and in close quarters, in pure prayers and with continuous tears, and then they became worthy to receive the Paraclete.

The Apostles Continued Asceticism after Pentecost

71. If the days of their asceticism were few, from the ascension of Christ to the coming of the Spirit, let us learn that after they had received the Spirit they were persisting in this cultivation of fasting and asceticism. Everywhere it is written concerning them that they were fasting and praying. "While these were fasting and praying, the Holy Spirit said to them, 'Set apart for me Saul and Barnabas for the work to which I have called them.' "[109] Again, when they wished to choose seven deacons, the apostles said to them, "We will persevere in prayer **(486)** and in the ministry of the Word."[110] Again, when Simeon was confined in prison, it is written: "The entire church was praying."[111] Moreover, before Paul was baptized and received the Holy Spirit, it was written concerning him in this way: "For three days he did not eat or drink,"[112] and he did not stand up from his place on which he had thrown himself down upon his face to pray, and in this way he received the Holy Spirit. The rest of his life after his election, he devoted himself to fasting and prayers, just as in every place he remembered his fasting and his prayer and was bearing many austerities for the Gospel. With the rest of all his labors and austerities, he counted also his great amount of fasting: "With much fasting and much vigil, with much hunger, in the cold and in nakedness."[113] Again, he said, "In everything I am trained in satiety

---

[108] Acts 1:13.
[109] Acts 13:2.
[110] Acts 6:4.
[111] Acts 12:5.
[112] Acts 9:9.
[113] 2 Cor 11:27.

as well as in hunger, in abundance and in poverty."[114] Yet how much he was indigent and poor is testified by the fact that once he [was reduced] to selling his garment,[115] [since] they were not able to buy nourishment for him and for those who were with him—besides the constant labor he was performing with his hands during the nights in order not to be a burden upon [another] person.[116]

Simeon's Providential Hunger

72. Moreover, it is written concerning Simeon, "He was going up to the roof to pray at the ninth hour, and he was hungry and wished to eat and he asked [them] to prepare [something] for him."[117] From this he has taught you that besides continual teaching **(487)** and prayers at every hour, also in the specific hours that are the worship of the community he was constantly praying. Along with his prayer his fasting was constant. The fact that he was hungry during the ninth hour and was desiring to eat, the hunger was providential and not normal, [for] he did not have a routine at that time to take nourishment. It is evident from what [Scripture] said that when he had gone up to the roof to pray, suddenly hunger had fallen upon him and he abandoned his prayer and asked that they prepare nourishment for him. If that had been the time at which it was usual to eat, his hosts would have been customarily preparing [something to eat]. But from the fact that he commanded them to prepare [food] for him, it is evident he was hungry by providence, so that by the passion of his hunger he might receive the instruction of these things that would be said to him, while his own fasting was constant.

The Apostles' Perfection

73. Consider [the fact] that the apostles did not fast, and their way of life was not fitting to bring you testimony because after

---

[114] Phil 4:12.

[115] 2 Tim 4:13; Lemoine wonders whether this refers to the coat left with Carpus at Troas.

[116] Acts 18:3; 1 Cor 4:12; 2 Thess 3:8.

[117] Acts 10:9-10.

they had received the Spirit, the Paraclete, they became perfect, and just as our Lord did not fast after his temptation, so also it was not appropriate that they should fast, according to the way of freedom and perfection in which they were living. However, although their way of life in the spirit was superior to [ascetical] labors, they were descending to labors and austerities, first, in order to give us an excellent example so that we might imitate them and, another [reason], because austerities and labors became the comfort of their pleasure. But what was the nourishment of **(488)** these great [apostles] who had attained perfection? When did they find it? It was not bread and vegetables and olives only. If the apostles had need of the ways of asceticism, and in the time of perfection they were acting like those who are fearful, who will not tremble and abstain from dissoluteness and run to adopt a tenacious way?

Angelic Visions Come Only after Fasting

74. Understand also from the testimony of the prophets that whenever they were worthy of the vision of God or of angels, they were engaging themselves in much fasting, and then they became worthy of the vision of revelations. As it is written concerning the "man of desire,"[118] Daniel, who after three weeks of his fasting[119] then became worthy of the vision of angels. If such a fast were required for one who was looking for the coming of an angel, and then he became worthy to receive spiritual revelations, how in your case, when you are waiting for the spiritual vision of Christ and receive into your soul a sensation above nature, is not a long fast, asceticism, and discipline of the body all the more necessary for you so that you may attain these things that are greater than what Daniel had seen?

In the same way also, after his fast of forty days and forty nights, Elijah then received the vision of God on the mountain of Horeb while he was alone in the desert.[120] With an extended fast he was

---

[118] Dan 9:23.
[119] Dan 10:2.
[120] 1 Kgs 19:8.

also bearing the fatigue of his journey, and besides these things isolation from people and the stillness that is **(489)** purification of prayer. After these things he heard the voice of God speaking with him. Similar to this holy man, the blessed Moses was twice worthy to enter the cloud and receive the law on tablets. He had purified himself by a fast such as this,[121] and then became worthy of that awesome vision. In the same way also when the prophet Ezekiel was about to receive the prophetic revelation of the razing of the city and the pulling down of the temple, the word of God made him enter arduous austerities, eat bread by weight, drink water by measure, and sleep on his side in austerity,[122] then he came to the prophetic visions. In the same way you will find all the upright and the prophets that whether by their own will, or whether by the commandment of God to them, they were bearing at all times austerities and travails.

David's Fasting

75. As the blessed David made known, the members of his body were weakened by the arduousness of his fasting: "My knees have become enfeebled from fasting and my flesh has wasted away due to oil."[123] Moreover, he said: "Because I have forgotten the eating of my bread and as a result of the sound of my groans my flesh cleaves to my bones."[124] He was not bereft of the memory of God in order to turn toward natural nourishment, but he had forgotten completely this corruptible nourishment, because what is spiritual had occupied his mind and by the arduousness of his travails and austerities, and by the passion and distress of his groans, his flesh was clinging to his bones. Moreover, he teaches you concerning **(490)** the meals he was taking for his nourishment: "Because I have eaten ashes like bread."[125] These were the seasonings and tasty things being placed

---

[121] Exod 24:18; Exod 34:28; Deut 9:9, 18.
[122] Ezek 4:4ff.
[123] Ps 109:24.
[124] Ps 102:4-5.
[125] Ps 102:10.

upon the table of this righteous king at the time of his meal. But hear again regarding the refined wines he was drinking: "I have mixed my drink with tears."[126] See the food and drink of the upright king: his eating is ashes and his drink is the tears of suffering. What disciple hears these things without his heart being broken by the suffering concerning his dissolute life, if he is a disciple?

He said again, "I have humbled myself through fasting. I have become for them [an object of] reproach.[127] I have made sackcloth my clothing and I have become for them a [mocking] word."[128] Through this he has taught us that not only did he endure the labor of virtues but also the shameful things and indignations he was hearing on account of them. He bore [them] with patience so that you also might learn from here that if your labors are despised by those who are lax, and your austerities are recounted mockingly by those who love comforts, you should remember this word of the prophet and be consoled. May it become a pillow for your soul when a reproach by those who are evil encounters you.

David's Further Austerities

76. In another passage, he spoke of the arduous extent of labors that he had attained through the perseverance of his austerities: "I have become like a wineskin in ice and I have not forgotten your commandments."[129] He has taught you **(491)** through this that by great emaciation and thirst the humidity of his body had evaporated and disappeared. Moreover, in another passage, listen to what he teaches you, that before one enters the austerities and is tested in the furnace of the endurance of labors, one is not able to go out to the open space of spiritual pleasures: "You have made me enter into fire and water, and you have brought me out into the open spaces."[130] He is comparing with fire and water the austerities,

---

[126] Ps 102:10.
[127] Ps 35:13.
[128] Ps 69:12.
[129] Ps 119:83.
[130] Ps 66:12.

vices, and labors that were surrounding him on all sides, whether by his voluntary austerities, or by the chastisement of God which was [for the purpose of] testing him, or by those evil ones who were jealous of his virtues.

Job's Afflictions

77. Listen again along with this upright king to the word of a spiritual athlete, Job. Before every one of his meals, which fruit did the medicine of the Spirit teach him to place upon his table? "Because my groans came before my bread and my moans are poured out like water."[131] These are the fruits he was receiving at first, groaning and weeping, and then was drawing near to natural nourishment. He was eating at first passions and was drinking the tears of his groans, and then he was receiving physical nourishment, because from then on whatever he was nourishing himself with was for holiness and not for eating. Hear again from him of those afflictions he was bearing, yet he was not departing from the love of God. "Why do I take my flesh in my teeth and my soul is placed in my hands? If he kills me, it is for him only I wait."[132] (492) As one might say, even if he may not love me, I will not move away from his love. God chastised him like an enemy and he was crying out, "By a friend I am wounded." He did not renounce the love of the one who chastises [him].

Straight and Narrow Road of Afflictions

78. If you are seeking, O disciple, you will find everywhere that not one of the upright had pleased God in the world without austerities and labors, because this is the street of the city of the kingdom above. "The road that leads to life is straight and narrow."[133] So then, let us travel on the straight path that God has paved for us, and let us walk on the road of austerities that he has

---

[131] Job 3:24.
[132] Job 13:14-15.
[133] Matt 7:14.

shown us. Let us be in the narrow way here so that we may be in the broad way there. Let us be hungry here so that we may be satisfied there. Let us reduce our eating and our drinking so that there spiritual nourishment may overflow in us. Let us bring our soul into the furnace of austerities, so that we may be given to the kingdom as pure gold in which there is no blemish. Let us not refrain concerning the destruction of our body, so that our hidden person may be made new day by day. Let us not think about the diseases and illnesses that happen to us, but let us consider that the soul's wounds are not healed without such as this. Let us be filled with joy in our course so that we might be certain we are running toward hope. Let us work as the sons of grace in the house of the true Father in order to be worthy of that inheritance, full of the blessings promised to the children. Let us remember at all times the word of the Apostle, "Through tribulation we must enter the kingdom of God."[134] With the Apostle, let us say to one another, "If we suffer with Christ, **(493)** we shall be glorified with Christ."[135] If we endure [with him], we shall also reign with him. To him be the glory of all of us forever. Amen.

The end of the eleventh *mēmrā* on asceticism.

[134] Acts 14:22.
[135] Rom 8:17.

Mēmrā 12

On Fornication

The twelfth *mēmrā* against the passions of fornication in which [Philoxenos] explains that not only is fornication considered an act of desire when it is satisfied in the body, but also when it remains in the thought and causes the soul to fornicate with a person far away.

Summary: Philoxenos sees the corrupt conversations and stories associated with lustful meals fueling the fire of lust. This lust is placed by God into our bodies for the continuation of the race and in marriage is good, but not for disciples. Defeating this lust is the source of victory and spiritual accomplishments for the disciples.

The analogy is given of a person lured into loving an ugly blind woman, who then sees the king's beautiful daughter, which is the beauty of Christ. Jesus prohibited disciples from intercourse since God did not place us in the world to perpetuate it, but as a place for spiritual contest in order to gain the crown of victory. The lust of intercourse is left in our members as an adversary. If we lose, it is because of our weakness, not the strength of lust.

The soul must not be mingled with the body and become subject to its lusts. Philoxenos contrasts fornication of body, soul, and spirit with intercourse of the same three. It is not good for the mind to have intercourse with the body, but it is good that the body be an associate with the soul in fortitude. When physical lust arises, the soul must counter with the desire of the soul as an antidote. No crown of glory is achieved if there is no adversary.

Like a Wise Physician

(494) 1. Wise physicians, who wish to approach knowledgeably the healing of diseases that occur in the body of human beings first learn the causes of the diseases and analyze them. Then without difficulty they prescribe the [correct] treatment to the sick because when the cause out of which diseases and illnesses have germinated has been removed, along with the cause the illnesses that it has generated are uprooted. It is not possible that shoots or fruits can remain when the root that causes their growth is lifted up from (495) the earth. It may happen that plants can survive for a little while because of their natural moisture, yet they will inevitably wither inasmuch as their roots are disturbed and removed from the earth. In the same way also with diseases and illnesses that occur in the bodies of people, [for] once physicians have first removed the causes by which diseases are engendered, little by little the disease is finished and disappears once the cause that has engendered it is cut out from the body.

Learning First the Causes

2. We should act this same way toward the passions of sins, whether they are born from the soul or from the body. At first one must remove the causes that produce these passions in order that from here on our lives may be preserved in holiness from evil things and our personal way of life might be [kept] in freedom from iniquity. Let the human being who wishes to become a free person in God first become free from the desires stirred up in him, and then draw near to the way of the freedom of Christ, because that region of free persons does not allow him to enter as long as the shameful sign of servitude is visible on his person. From then on while we are considering through this what we were and what we are, and from where and to where we are called, and which life we have exchanged for which, let us be mindful of ourselves at all times and continually take on ourselves the knowledge of our way of life. Let us first learn the causes of the passions of sins (496) that continually torment our life by their enticements in order that without difficulty we may find the healing of our soul, while

our example for the healing of our soul is this natural healing that heals human bodies. Like doctors, let us first observe the causes from which sinful enticements against our life are born so that we may be able to attain spiritual healing.

The Passion of Fornication

3. Since in the discourse previous to this one we confuted the desire of the lust of the belly, our word should now be stirred up in an orderly way against the evil passion of fornication, whose cause and generator and nurturer is the lust of the belly. It is easy to defeat once a person is victorious over its first cause. By eating and drinking this passion of fornication grows stronger and becomes inflamed in our members, and along with this, by dissolute conversations and by human speech and by the memory of faces of attractive appearance that are etched in our soul, by the recital of stories of desire when they are spoken and listened to willingly, and by the constant sight of faces, which by the passion of their sight dissolute souls first become captive. For when the lust of the belly makes the fire of fornication increase in the body, harmful conversations will come and awaken it.

A Natural Desire Not for Disciples

4. This desire is placed naturally into the members of our body by the Maker for the fruitfulness of marriage and the establishment of the world. However, with the disciples, it is not kept **(497)** for this use, but in order to be for them the cause for spiritual crowns and the occasion for heavenly conflicts, so that while fighting and being victorious they might be counted as victors. By the triumphs that they wrest from the place of struggle against it they will be recorded as triumphant in the heavenly Jerusalem. It is not so that the disciples may become married that the desire of marriage remains in them, but so that by the heat of natural desire they may experience the strength of the heat of spiritual desire. When the fire that transgresses the law burns in their members, let them try out the burning fire of Jesus that is mixed in their souls. Through a pleasure outside of nature, let them taste the pleasure of true

nature. Through the movement which fulfills itself with its beginning, let them receive the taste of pleasure of the living movement that begins to desire the attractive vision of Christ's beauty which endures without end in the soul in which it started, if it is purified in order to become his habitation.

The Usefulness of an Enemy

5. The fire of this natural desire burns hotter than the rest of the other desires, and with its heat is mixed also a corrupted pleasure in order that we might learn two things, one after another: the sweetness of the love of Christ and the approaching end of corrupting desire. Spiritual fire, which has been mixed in us, would have been able to bring to an end and get rid of this fire of natural desire, but the will would be without fruits and the freedom in us [would be] without the labors of courage. It is excellent **(498)** then that an enemy has been set against freedom, because when [the enemy] is vanquished in the struggle of self-control this freedom will be evident, its strength will be known, and its authority will be proven. Therefore, as for this [desire] kept within us as a source of profits, let us not be slack so that it may be for us a source of losses. Whoever changes profits into losses is foolish and ignorant, and whoever takes whatever is given to us as an opportunity for good things as a sign of evil things, he is evil and an opponent of good things.

Worldly Practices, Solitary Vices

6. Therefore, let us be courageous in the battle against this evil desire. While [desire] is a good thing with respect to worldly marriage, it is considered evil if it is done by the disciples, because not everything is excellent with every person, even though it may be excellent and good in its nature. Wealth is excellent in the nature of its creation by the Creator, unless the solitaries who are commanded not to have two tunics and not to be anxious about tomorrow acquire it—with them its possession is evil. Also eating meat and drinking wine is pure for those who are [living] in the promise of the way of the world. But it is not good for those who willingly offer their soul to the covenant of the vocation of Christ's

discipleship to use these things without some reason of necessity. Good **(499)** and even excellent are also the rulers and authorities of this world, because it is written, "There is no authority that does not come from God."[1] But for those who have been separated from a human dwelling and have committed themselves to great and lofty things, it is [a matter] of shame and of criticism that they should desire human honors. Dwelling in cities and villages is also not blamable, [nor] residence in the world and the way of life among human beings. However, for those who have renounced [the world] by the love of God, once they have taken off the world by the will of their freedom and have departed to live outside of [the world] as solitaries and ascetics, dwelling and occupation among people [is a matter] of reprehension and of reproach to them. Many things such as these, while there is no reprehension in doing them by those who have not already committed to a covenant against them, are reproachable for those who have committed themselves to abstinence[2] if they do these things.

The Place of Marriage

7. Therefore, this desire of marriage falls into the same pattern. It has been well placed in nature by the Creator. It is the upholder of the world and has become the root and fruit of human nature; it turns around and gives back to the human race whatever the punishment of death seizes and takes from them. However, take notice, O disciple, that even though it is placed in nature, it was awakened by the transgression of the commandment **(500)** and after eating the fruit its movement is apparent. As in a parable let us first recognize that it has power only in the world of physical beings, not being useful for anything in the world of those who are spiritual. The types of two ways of life are seen in the leaders of our race: the spiritual and the physical, the spiritual world and the physical world, and [the world] of the first Adam and of the second Adam.

---

[1] Rom 13:1.
[2] ܢܙܝܪܘܬܐ (*nzīrūtā*).

Fruit in Eden

8. Before they ate the food by which they transgressed the commandment and by which also the desire hidden in the members was stirred, their way of life was completely spiritual and they were stirred up spiritually in everything—in holy thoughts, in pure intellects, in a mind worthy of God, in reason that is pure and strained clear of the despicable movements of desire, and their dwelling was in Paradise in the model of spiritual hosts. While they were visible only through the vision of the body, yet in the spiritual mind they were secretly residing in heaven. At first the Creator made Adam taste spiritual things because [the Creator] wished that he become the heir of these things. Even though all these worldly things came to be and were established by the word of the Maker, yet the freedom of Adam desired [worldly things], and his will wished to pursue them. This much is certain by eating the fruit in transgression of the commandment: the eating of that fruit is the beginning of all our lusts, according to the word that the Apostle teaches us when he said, "I would not have known desire if the Law had not said, 'You shall not desire,' and it is in this **(501)** commandment that sin has found an occasion and perfected in me every desire."[3] So then with us spiritual desire is prior to physical desire, just as the story of the leader of our race shows. Adam descended from above to below, and from spiritual desire he departed to physical desire, and from the heavenly ways of life he lowered himself to earthly ways. From the vision of the beauty of God which is never filled up he turned to examine the vision of the beauty of his wife. Until Adam had turned aside, these external things were not apparent to him. Until he turned his soul around toward the world, the desires of the world were not arrayed before his sight—these things that became the cause and beginning to all their [desires] was eating the fruit. In the same way there that all our desires were engendered from the belly, so also here all evils begin from it.

---

[3] Rom 7:7-8.

The First Thorn from the Belly

9. The first thorn that sprouts from the field of the lust of the belly is fornication. As soon as it germinates, it becomes for the mind's sight like a thorn to the eye and inhibits it from gazing toward God. For not only does this desire obscure the vision of these who have not seen [the beauties of God] but also of those who have seen the divine beauties for a long time. If they should be held down by this passion, their movements will be blind. Like a curtain it stands in front of them and inhibits them from the vision of that desirable beauty of Christ. **(502)** They will be exhausted finding whatever they have lost, but they will find it [only] with difficulty and with travail. There are some who are completely blind, like those who are born blind from their mothers' wombs; and there are some who after they were born and saw light became blind through an accident that happened later on; the clear sight of their thoughts has been blinded. With these the memory of the heavenly light is kept. Also in that time when they incurred the damage, like that one who became blind remembers natural light he had seen before his blindness, so also this one who is blinded by the passions remembers the spiritual light he had seen before this. He does not receive this light as if from a report, one that is worthy of his sight, but as one who remembers its original clarity. Comparing his current blindness against it, he groans: from where has he descended [and] to where [has he now gone]? Which desire has he exchanged for which [other] one?

Vigilance Required

10. So then more [important] than for those who have never seen at all and have not sensed this spiritual light, vigilance is necessary for those who have seen and sensed. Just as when a rich person has greater vigilance for the sake of his wealth than someone poor who does not possess anything, so also whoever finds in the clarity of his soul the beauty of divine vision, continual alertness is necessary for him lest he lose what he has found. For just as a person might turn **(503)** his eye from in front of him and look behind him, or [turn away] from what he is looking at in the sun and observe darkness,

so it happens for the thought that sees God, when it turns away from [God] and observes a despicable desire. Until the soul loses the beauty of Being, it does not give way to desire the corrupted beauty of the body. For without beauty [the soul] desires beauty, and without sight it looks for vision. Because the desirable elegance of Christ's beauty is not inscribed before it, [the soul] becomes tied down by the sight of the body's elegance. Because alertness is not awake in it, sleep is awake in it. Because the fire of spiritual love is cooled in it, the fire of physical love is excited in it.

Desire for the Beauty of Christ

11. Until a person perceives his soul's beauty, he does not begin to perceive the inexhaustible beauty of Christ, which is his nature, for every soul that perceives and sees it naturally takes hold of it by its love. Just as those who desire the body's beauty, its love stirring naturally in their members, so also whoever attains to the beauty of the desire of Christ is stirred by his love as if by natural coercion and nothing is able to cut him off from that link of love. For if that one who is held captive by the body's desire and by the attractive sight of a corruptible body, who is surrounded on all sides by the causes of his destruction, abomination, **(504)** and corruption, despising everything and treating admonition and everyone's refutation contemptuously, yet the physical love in him is victorious over the coercion of every fear struggling with him on all sides, how much more will the soul that has loved Christ and ardently desired the vision of his elegant beauty be released from all yokes of fear and cut off and transcend the coercion of all laws, and all beautiful things are hateful in its eyes when comparing them to the vision of the beauty of that One who loves?

Beauty over Ugliness

12. It is as if a person should be seized by a natural desire, and without the proximity of an attractive face should [then] love a blind woman, despicable of features and misshapen of face; and if one should happen to gaze upon an attractive face and look upon the desirable beauty of another body, comparing the beauty that he

has found with that first unattractive woman by whose love he was captured, he will despise and reject that first desire, and reprimand himself— with what had he tied down his love? Henceforth, the passion of the second beauty has authority over all his movements and takes everything captive, and he is wounded by that passion, especially when he compares it with that first despicable [nature] he was loving. In the same way also it may happen that the mind will be seized by physical beauty when it lacks beauty—that is, without the vision of Christ's beauty—(505) it will be ensnared by the vision of physical beauty, desire whatever is not worthy of desire, and be enflamed with the fire of a love of a corruptible nature, which is not even appropriate to be called love, but a hideous and abominable passion. But if, whether by his will's love, by the indication of others, or by an action of grace, the desirable beauty of that uncreated Being should happen to be shown to this person, and [when] he senses this incorruptible beauty, immediately he will forget natural beauty and that attractiveness will come back before his vision as complete abomination,[4] and he will rebuke himself: by what [kind of] love was he tied down, by which constraint was he subjugated, and which weakness prevailed over his strength? He will reprimand himself on account of the dissoluteness by which he was subjugated to the love of the corruptible body.

Exchanging for the Superior

13. For everything changes itself into that which is its opposite— one pleasure into [another] pleasure, one honor into [another] honor, one wealth into [another] wealth, one glory into [another] glory, one delight into [another] delight, one desire into [another] desire, one beauty into [another] beauty. All of these things are comparable with one another, these that are higher along with those that are lower, those who sense the higher things reject the choice of all those things lower than they and are desirous of these higher, these more glorious, more attractive, more elevated, more excellent, because this is the nature of the soul's desire, that it will desire those things

---

[4] Text written: ⲕⲑⲁⲧⲩ, "abstinence"; Lemoine reads ⲕⲑⲁⲧⲩ (Ms. EG).

higher than it. **(506)** When it desires in this way, it desires naturally; but when it desires those things inferior to it, its desire is outside of its nature. That means its discernment has been overcome by participation with what is contrary to it, and then it has desired whatever is its opposite. Or if it desires it, it is lacking [the soul's true] desire. None who have seen the sun neglect it and yearn to change it to darkness, unless those works worthy of darkness were stirred up in him, and when he associates the gloom of sin with natural darkness he desires darkness in the darkness. It is evident that his desire is blind, because without sight he cannot discern what he is desiring instead of something else.

Physical Beauty Always Imperfect

14. This is debilitating that one might be seized by the sight of physical desire, especially if those from whom the passions were dispelled revert back to become subservient to them [again], and after they had become worthy of the vision of spiritual beauty, they are [then] seized by the love of physical beauty. These are also worthy to be hated with good cause because they have changed one thing into another. Instead of the beauty of the king's daughter,[5] more comely than all, they desired a poor blind [woman], more unsightly than all. So then, if one who is worthy to perceive the soul's beauty is no [longer] satisfied [by it], how much longer would the beauty of Christ remain without satisfying the soul, which is naturally the desirable and lovable beauty? **(507)** There is no beauty comparable with his beauty, no vision similar to his vision, no elegance more beloved like his, no image more beloved as its depiction, and no traits as desirable as his own because he is completely an [object] of desire. There is not in him one portion that is excellent and another that is its opposite, despicable and hideous, as when something like this exists in the corruptible body—one member in it is beautiful, another through its despicableness lessens its beauty. There is a situation when the face is comely but the feet are disfigured, or it may be that the eyes are lovely but the rest of

---

[5] Ps 45:13-14.

the other senses are inferior, lesser, or injured. The constitution of
the members is put together well, but in something else it is found
faulty in stature. In short, physical beauty is not able to become
completely perfect, free and pure of blemishes.

Beauty Swallows Up Ugliness

15. This was also wisely established by the Maker so that physical
beauty might not be perfect in its beauty, so that whoever is seized
by its desire must rid himself of it when it is near. When an ugly
member is placed with a beautiful one, and an unsightly one with a
comely one, whoever has been seized by the desire of the beautiful
will be repulsed[6] by the ugly sight of that one coupled to it. The
desire of this beauty will cease from him and in him, and it will
be a reproach next to that one seized by its passion. There shall be
mixed with **(508)** the disease also its remedy, and beside the illness
shall be found the cure, and within the beauty you will observe
the ugliness. These things were constructed in this way by divine
wisdom because that One [who is] cause of all, the beauty of all
beauties, does not wish that the beauty of our soul might desire
alien beauty outside of him. If from the mind's deep slumber ugliness should appear to us in a beautiful place, and by the sight
of attractive members we may be ensnared by corruptible desire,
this ceasing of desire shall come to be from two causes: from the
ugliness of hideous members and from the attractive beauty of the
higher vision—ugliness driving us far away from underneath and
the contemplation of the desirable vision receiving us from above,
we will be mixed and swallowed up into this insatiable beauty
[which] will completely spread out inside us and be mixed in us,
and the image of his spiritual nature will be embodied in our soul.
Therefore, let us not err and desire those things unworthy of desire,
and let us not lose the spiritual desire mixed into our soul. Adam
desired the fruit's beauty and from it he was led to the sight of Eve's

---

[6] Written: ܩܡܨܕܬܘ; read ܩܨܕܬܘ.

beauty. The lust of the belly entered and awakened the body's lust. With the lust of copulation, other lusts also will spring up in us.

The Purpose of Solitaries

16. This desire was planted in us for the perpetuity of the human race. Those who are not established to perpetuate the world should be victorious over the movement of this desire. For the promise **(509)** of the disciples sets them outside of the world. They have become superfluous to [the world] and strangers in everything by their covenant, that is to say, they have become above the world as they live in the heights of righteousness, according to the promise of our Savior to them. These who once they have departed from the world should also be beyond desire, which is the perpetuator of the world. These two lusts that adhere to one another, I mean the lust of the belly and the lust of copulation, their actions are perceived differently to us. One perpetuates the life of our person, and the other guards the life of nature. The desire of the belly maintains the life of our person; and the desire of marriage guards nature by the succession of generations. If it were possible that we could sustain our life in the world without physical needs, the commandment of the One who makes us live would be also preventing us from eating and drinking; but because this is not possible, in this way a limit for the maintenance of our life has been established by the commandment of the Maker. With regard to marriage, he inhibits us because he did not place us in the world as perpetuators of the world, but only that it may be for us a place of struggle, so that in spiritual combat we may seize from it a crown of triumphs.

Desire as the Necessary Enemy

17. Since an enemy is necessary for whoever fights—for without one such a combat does not happen—[God] has left desire in our members so that it might become for us an enemy while fighting and being defeated in order that the athlete's victory will be seen. **(510)** But if he should be defeated, his feebleness will be charged that he was defeated by his weakness and not by the strength of the enemy. Desire is victorious over us, not because it is stronger than

we, but on account of our own weakness and feebleness. If desire had it in its nature to be victorious, it would have defeated everyone and would be victorious all the time. But now that is not the case, for sometimes it is victorious and sometimes it is vanquished, and sometimes it is defeated and at another time it defeats [others]. Our will's strength should be evident by the fact that [desire] is defeated, but our freedom's feebleness will be apparent by the fact that [desire] is victorious and defeats us, [as well as] the disdain and negligence we have concerning our person.

The Soul's Strength

18. Until a desire takes [your] strength away from you, it is not able to defeat you, that is, it does not [dare] to stand up against you in battle until your will permits it. Take your own experience of this, for as long as you wish it will be dormant, but when you are seeking [it] you will awaken it. But if a natural movement outside of your will should awaken [a desire], it would be easy for you to extinguish its fire by a small puff of air, if there is such strength in your soul to emit a breath against it. Yet [a desire] will not be extinguished by the powerful breath of a body, which when [a desire] is moved in [the body] [desire] makes [the body] subservient under its will to all its senses. That body defeated by [desire] is not [even] able to puff at it. And if it does puff, it does not extinguish [desire], but when the soul exists **(511)** in its natural power, has control over the discernment of its thoughts, and has gathered with its person all its movements, so that they may be moved by [the soul] and not by the body, then with great strength it will emit a breath of rebuke against[7] desire whenever [the soul] wishes, and as quickly as the blinking of an eye it will extinguish the natural fire throbbing in the members.

Distinguishing Soul from Body

19. When the body is directed by the soul, their entire way of life is solid and healthy, and as is proper for a person he is directed in

---

[7] Typographical error: written ܠܥܘܒ, read ܠܥܘܒ.

the stability appropriate for rational beings. But when the body's wills direct the soul, a person conducts himself into the ways of animals. When also those movements of its desires are performed without feeling, on account of this it is deprived of the penitence attached to discernment. For as long as the soul is mixed with the body in its thoughts, [the soul] is not able to direct [the body], neither to be able to see itself nor to observe the body's desires, nor to accuse its own passions, but like a blind person deprived of his own sight and of the sight of everything, so also the soul when it has become blind through sinful passions does not see its own self or anything outside of it.

So then it is necessary for us to distinguish the soul from the body before the body separates from the soul, for the Maker has established a natural mingling in us. It is not our own [prerogative] to separate it unless one wishes to be deprived of divine life. But this distinction of the thoughts of the soul from **(512)** the body has been placed into the hand of our freedom.

The Solitary Thought

20. Whenever we desire, it is easy for us to distinguish the thoughts of our soul from our body, having learned this distinction from the Scriptures and receiving from them the power to make the soul dwell solitarily in the house of the body. Indeed, the Spirit of God has explained this in a parable, saying, "He makes the solitary reside in a house."[8] For as is appropriate, he calls there a good thought "solitary," so that while it resides in the body, it does not share its passions and does not tie the mystery of love with those things not worthy of its love, but while being moved by it, solitarily, and by the wonder of the grandeur of God's glory, it dwells in the house of silence. He has attributed the name of the solitary to a holy thought such as this, because just as a person who becomes a stranger to the entire world is called a solitary and being aloof to its give-and-take, to its wealth and its pleasures, and to everything that is in it, so also that thought dwelling in the body [which] makes

---

[8] Ps 68:6 (Peshitta).

[itself] foreign and distant from all desires and services of its pleasures is called "solitary," for with itself it is only reflecting on itself,
and his soul's beauty is revealed to him by the constancy of this
study, and the beauty and splendor of its own being.

Solitariness of God and Thought

21. The prophet illustrated superbly the solitariness of this
thought by that solitariness that belongs to God with [regard to]
everything. **(513)** Just as God, while he is mixed into everything,
is distant and remote from everything in the solitariness of his
nature, so also this solitary thought while mixed in the body is
remote from the body. "God is in his holy dwelling."[9] And then he
introduced after it, "God makes the solitary reside in a house."[10]
Why was it necessary to place this [word] beside that one, if not
to give testimony concerning the solitariness of the thought from
that one of God? Just as God is in his holy dwelling, that is, he is in
himself, while everything is separated and distant from him, even
while he is near to everything, so also the solitary mind, while it is
near to everything, everything is distant from it.

The Necessity of the Solitary Thought

22. It is fitting also in this way that thought should approach
everything by the authority of its nature, so that it might be an
observer and discoverer of the knowledge sown into everything.
But it does not allow anything [else] to approach it, because God
also is near to everything by the infinitude of his nature, while
everything is distant from him because it is finite. In the same way
also the mind should act authoritatively so that when it is near to
everything on account of its freedom, everything shall be distant
from it because it is not suitable for it, that is, these things that are
physical, because unless a thought exists in its solitariness, it is also
not able to gather to it its natural strength. As much as [thought] is

---

[9] Ps 68:5.
[10] Ps 68:6.

mixed with the body, its power over the members of the body will be stolen and dispersed. It will be impoverished and abandoned by the strength of its soul, becoming subservient to desires and in a state of being commanded, and not the one that commands. When (514) the soul is associated with the body and gives heed to the enticements of its will, it will be subservient to [the body's] desire and not to its own. That is, [the body] desires with [the soul] these corruptible things that it itself desires and becomes estranged from the healthy desire of its nature.

The Soul's Natural Desire

23. However, this is the soul's healthy desire and we experience it when the soul is stirred through its natural desire. Whenever we desire good things and excellent movements are aroused in our soul, the soul is stirred by its natural desire, and on that account it desires virtuous and spiritual matters in the cultivation of excellent works. The body's desire is not strong enough to confine spiritual desire, but this desire takes away strength from the soul in order to fight with it. Desire by itself is weak and on account of this it snatches the assistance of other things so whatever it is not able to do by its own strength, it finds by the aid of other things. These are the things that assist this desire: lust of the belly, pleasures, games, adornment of clothes, profane conversations, talk about lusts, recitation of acts of fornication, beauty of faces, sight of the elegance of the body, wandering of the mind, the memory of things. Desire calls such things as these to its assistance and then begins to fight with the soul and sets up against it a battle (515) of enticements. These things make the weakness of desire known, because if it were able to be victorious by itself, it would not have had need of these [other] things.

How to Defeat Desire

24. But you, O disciple, what is necessary if you wish to be victorious over the desire that fights with you? First, you must pluck its wings, forcefully seize the forces that [desire] has called to its aid, cut off its limbs, and expose, lift up and pull out its roots. When it

remains alone by itself, you will be victorious over it without any difficulty. When desire begins to fight with you, do not bring to it tinder through which it could be set on fire, but gather far away from it everything that feeds it. When it has burned itself up in the fullness of time, it will rot and cool off on its spot. Therefore, take away from it at first food and drink. Eat bread by weight, drink water by measure. Drive away from yourself bodily pleasures. Bear on yourself the austerities of discernment. Subjugate your body under the weight of [ascetic] labors. Let it be tormented by hunger, afflicted by thirst, exhausted by vigil. [If the body] seeks to sleep, do not allow it. If it wants to grab some sleep, drive [sleep] away from [the body]. Resist its need to be fed, count out [the measures] with it and then give to it, and in brief, do not give it pleasure with anything at all, because pleasures, without a doubt, are the progenitors of desire.

Stop the First Causes of Desire

25. Again, along with these things, cut off these first causes **(516)** of which I have spoken to you. Do not listen in on a conversation about an encounter with desire. Do not delight in the stories of its exploits repeated before you. May you not continually retain the vision of a face that has passionately taken hold of you. Extract the enticing depiction of its elegance from within your mind. Uproot fully from your soul the memory of the beauty that has captured you, because as long as its memory lives in you, it will enflame you. For just as fire catches hold of tinder when close to it, so also desire seizes and ignites itself in the members by the sight and encounter of these matters, and when [desire] has seized it, no one is able to extinguish it. Fight and be victorious over little things so that big things will not defeat you. Therefore, if you become a stranger from contact with these things of which I have spoken to you, and drive away from yourself the things that are the instigators of desire, you will shut the door in the face of desire and it will not enter to have power over you. But if you should be overcome and defeated by these things that are weak, how much more will you be defeated and brought low by desire?

Stay Away from Contentious Things

26. However, in order not to increase the travail for you and plummet you into battle, whether you have departed from it or not, distance yourself from these things that cast you down and make you enter into the midst of battle, and become a stranger to them so that you might become a stranger to desire. Trample the daughters [of desire] so that you might also trample [down] the mother. Cut off the limbs so that you may cut off also the head. (517) Pluck the wings so that the body may remain in the depths of defeat. Do not speak the language of fornication lest you come to the deed of fornication. Do not accept a memory of desire into your soul lest you be handed over to desire by [some] action. Do not load up your stomach with too much food, lest you light the fire of desire in your members. Do not let too much wine flow in your members, lest something too alluring is poured into all of you. Do not let tasty foods be pleasing to you lest the sweetness of desire becomes agreeable to you. Cause your eye to avoid a comely sight so that your soul may be emptied of distractions. Close the door of your hearing from the conversation of desire lest the house of your soul becomes a continual dwelling for it. Do not admire the comely sight of your body, and do not examine the elegance of the sight of others. Do not compare and you will not be compared. Do not offend and you will not be offended. Do not corrupt and you will not be corrupted. Do not cling [to someone] and you will not be clung to [by someone else]. Flee in order that they will flee from you.

Anger against Desire

27. Put on anger against desire and drive it away like an enemy from your soul's house. In the time of desire, use anger instead of love because love usually becomes a path to desire. There are many who were snagged by spiritual love in order to be changed to physical love. While the beginning of their love was excellent, its conclusion was hideous and abominable. Let your passions fight with your passions, those that you sense are opponents (518) of one another. When you sense that one of the evil passions is

disturbing you, set up against it that passion that is its enemy. And especially against this abominable passion of desire, you ought to fight by means of passions that are its opponents. The passion of anger is bad, but in the time of desire it is very necessary. Harsh also is the rapaciousness of hatred, but in that hour of battle it can be very useful to you. Along with these, do not refuse what stirs up hatred in you, because it will help tremendously when physical love entices [you]. By all means, place this passion before you when desire is stirred up so that you may rescue your life from death and your soul from absolute destruction.

Take as an example for your battle at this time people who fight to the death for their physical lives. There are many who out of the fear of death will fight until death, whether with an animal or with bandits or with enemies or with a venomous serpent. They are not simply standing around in this battle but are converting all of their strength toward this in order to preserve their life. At that moment they are stimulating in themselves every faculty that stirs up strength in the soul and in the body. **(519)** They put on menace, anger, fury, and the battle cry. They project also a fearful voice, become indignant, and alter the peacefulness of their faces into menacing anger. Their fighting is with hands and feet, with thought and with members, that is, fully with the soul and the body. Because they are afraid lest they die, they will fight on account of the fear of [death] up to the edge of death. All these things happen in order that mortal lives may be delivered from death. Therefore, by the example of these things you also should be diligent for the sake of your soul's life and become menacing and full of rage, harsh and furious in the time of desire. Do not say, "These things do not attract me," for at that moment they are very menacing to you. There is no war without fury, nor is a struggle completed without indignation. If you are engaged in a battle, you should put on fury so that the enemy who is fighting with you will be troubled at the sight of you and flee. Whoever presents a cheerful face to his enemy is an enemy of himself. Therefore, do not present a happy face to desire lest it sleep with you. Look at it with an eye [full of] hate and immediately it will flee from you like a prostitute in the marketplace.

Carrying the Prostitute

28. Desire is also [seen] in the example of the prostitute, for when **(520)** it has been stirred up in the members, if a thought appears to present to it a cheerful face, immediately [desire] will seize and confine it to an association with it. It takes and places on [the thought] its polluted yoke in order that he might become a slave to it, subservient and not one who commands. But if a thought remembers itself, assumes an exterior of seriousness, puts on a coat of chastity against the licentiousness of desire, and is visible to [desire] with a serious and fearful face, immediately desire will leave and move away, not only from being with [the thought], but also from the place in which it was stirred up, that is, from all the members of the body as from a house that is not its own, [and] being ashamed it will flee and depart.

However, because the obscenity of this action is not apparent to every person when a pure thought becomes subservient to a defiled desire and is trampled under its feet, let the disciple observe and understand by a small example that I shall give. [It is] as if one of those who is renowned in purity, either through disciplines or heavy [ascetical] labors, should carry upon his shoulder one of the women prostitutes into the marketplaces of the city and with an air of licentiousness should stroll through the markets and the porticoes of the city—all who see this would shudder and everyone would be grief-stricken concerning what is happening, and the story would become conversation and gossip wherever it is heard. By this clear example one should also examine the hidden thought when its purity is subservient to a licentious desire and allows itself to become a residence and dwelling place **(521)** in which [desire] may reside. Now, this sight is more obscene and abominable than what happens in the marketplaces of the city. For there [one] body carries [another] body and [one] body accompanies the [other] body, its companion. Yet here it is not so, but a spiritual thought is defiled in accompanying the flesh's desire, and an association occurs outside of the law and a liaison not normally achieved.

Fornication outside the Law

29. When a thought fornicates with desire, this is fornication outside the law. There are different kinds of fornication: there is a physical fornication, a fornication of the soul, and a spiritual fornication. There is also a physical intercourse, an intercourse of the soul, and a spiritual intercourse. Physical fornication is an act of adultery that happens outside of the law with a foreign woman. The fornication of the soul is when its thoughts communicate secretly with the desire of fornication itself, although a public action is not performed. But spiritual fornication is when the soul participates with demons or accepts agreement with foreign doctrines. Moreover, physical intercourse is with a lawful wife, but intercourse of the soul is when it receives and mixes in [itself] that knowledge of the nature of things and the meanings of the conduct of everything that happens in this life below. Spiritual intercourse is when divine doctrine and all spiritual things are mixed together.

Keeping the Soul Free

30. Let us then be diligent so that we become free **(522)** first of all from the fornication of thoughts that is the fornication of the soul and we will be freed also from the fornication of the body. It is not good that a thought should participate with the body, but that the body should become a participant with the soul through courage. Suspend your soul to the height of its nature above association with the body so that while it is raised up to the height of the serene ways of life, it will also make the body ascend with it from the depth of desires. The soul has been established as queen in order that she might [reign] over the body and take hold of the reins of all its senses like a driver and a wise charioteer. It is not appropriate that your soul should do something your body loves, but that your body should be subservient to those works the soul loves, which are the acceptable will of God, while changing [the body] from all of its heaviness to the lightness of [the soul's] pure ways of life and taking pleasure in the pure air of its holiness, changing its dissoluteness for [the soul's] courage and its heaviness for its lightness, its love for the love of [the soul], its desire

for [the soul's] desire, its needs for [the soul's] needs, its fatness for [the soul's] thinness, its physical [nature] for [the soul's] spiritual [nature], its hunger for its satiety, and finally, changing all which belongs to [the body] by knowledge by means of all that is spiritual moving in [the soul]. When the soul participates with the body, this participation is adultery and fornication. But if the body should attach itself to the soul with one accord and be raised up from below to above **(523)** by a stable marriage, this is legitimate intercourse, which was established naturally by the Maker in the person of every one of us.

Legitimate and Adulterous Unions

31. Look, this natural union of men with women was also established by the commandment of the Maker in the beginning. When it happens according to the will of the Maker, it is called a legitimate union. But if it is serving another model, it is called adultery and fornication. This analogy is symbolically depicted in the soul and body, for if the soul should unite with the body it is fornication, but if the body should unite with the soul it is a legitimate union. A word of Scripture points to this meaning in which it says, "A man should leave his father and his mother and cleave to his wife."[11] It did not say regarding the woman that she should leave her parents and cleave to the man, even though in worldly custom this is what is done—women leave behind [their] natural parents and cleave to their husbands—so it is customary that the opposite of the word of Scripture is carried out naturally. Then, since the saying mentioned concerning the person of the man is an analogy based on the body, [the body] should leave everything it finds pleasurable and be joined to the soul. If Scripture had said that the woman should leave her parents and be joined to the man, it would teach the soul that it should be in union with the body. But since it said concerning the man that he should leave his parents and be joined **(524)** to his wife, the saying depicts to us the mystery of the teaching and exhorts the body to be diligent in renouncing

---

[11] Gen 2:24.

its pleasures, despise its desires, and be in union with the soul in all good things. When the body is united to the soul, and the soul to the spirit, and through the spirit with the Trinity, it is perfected indeed with [that saying], "The Lord is above everything and in all of us,"[12] as well as this one, "You are the temple of the Lord and the spirit of God dwells in you."[13]

The Soul Not to Permit Body to Corrupt Itself

32. Again, Paul made the soul fear that which allows the body to become a servant to fornication, saying, "Whoever destroys the temple of God, God will destroy him."[14] Therefore, he teaches the soul here not to allow the body to corrupt itself by the union of fornication, because the damage from this will end up with [the soul]. When [the body] corrupts itself by its natural desires, [the soul] also is condemned by eternal judgment. God had rightly placed this retribution upon the soul, even though it was decreed on both the soul and the body, because the soul had also corrupted [the body] since it had allowed [the body] to lower itself to its natural desires. While it would have been possible to prevent it, it did not hold [the body] back. While [the soul] could have made [the body] taste the pleasure of its own desire, what was agreeable to it was the pleasure of [the body's] corruptible desire, of which also its movements and its passions and its ways are [a matter] of shame.

Desire Prefers to Work in the Dark

33. Desire is unsettling when it stirs up every organ of the body and lowers and brings down the valor of a person beneath a work (525) of sin, abolishes its knowledge, obscures its discernment, and darkens its judgment. For until the soul has surrendered its will in order to be subservient to the pleasure of desire, desire is not able to defeat it or to obscure the light of its judgment from it. Desire

---

[12] Eph 4:6.
[13] 2 Cor 6:16.
[14] 1 Cor 3:17.

also has a concern—just as does the enemy that is its assistant—to extinguish the light of knowledge from the house of the soul, for it is easier for desire to perform its works of shame in the dark, because just as virtue eagerly awaits the light, in the same way, desire rejoices at the onset of darkness and on account of this sends out its fumes, blowing on the light of the soul and extinguishing it. When the entire person remains in obscurity, he or she does everything as if in darkness, both public as well as private actions.

The Light of God's Vision

34. In that example in which the body's eye is ashamed of light and extinguishes it, then approaches the works of sin, so also the soul's vision is ashamed of the hidden gaze of God upon it. On account of this, desire extinguishes this light by which the soul usually sees God and then leads the soul to participate in its work. The soul is ashamed to approach the works of sin as long as the light of God's vision is shining in it. Just as the body is also ashamed of its companion and vision is ashamed of sight as long as natural light is placed before the vision, and just as sin is performed willfully in darkness without shame, so boldly without shame the soul commits fornication with the body when the light of the memory of God has been extinguished from it. **(526)** Since this sin is agreeable to the soul, it extinguishes the light, for as long as it remembers God it does not sin. If in a deep sleep it should lower itself to a work of sin, it does not enjoy its desire, because the fear of God seizes and takes away from it the pleasure of what it is doing.

Therefore, this light of the memory of God accomplishes two things in the soul: for one, it restrains [the soul] so that it may not sin; and for the other, if it desires and does sin, it performs the works of sin with fear, trembling, and trepidation. Just as the body is disquieted in the doing of sin when it knows that eyewitnesses are coming near, so also the soul is disquieted and is afraid of the coming of the vision of God. Because this is the only light that is able to restrain the soul from this fault, [the soul] should take it with it at all times and let [the light] shine constantly in it. Let [the soul] not allow the memory of God to move away from being with it, and let it be captured by the pleasantness of his encounter. For as long as [the soul] is engaged in the encounter with [God], it does not lower itself to an encounter with desire. As long as this light of God's vision blazes in it, darkness does not enter with authority into its enlightened boundaries. As long as the soul's desire is mixed within the spirit's desire, its thoughts will not mix with the body's desire.

The Desire of the Soul

35. The soul that neglects to desire its own nature and descends to desire whatever is not its own is worthy to be laughed at. The body's desire becomes a lesson for the wise soul so that [only] its own desire may be stirred **(527)** in it. Now, if the body desires [what belongs to itself], does not the soul desire its own? If [the body] is alive in its natural movements, is not [the soul] alive in its living movements? If [the body's] desire is hindered by many things but prevails over all of them, and [the body] is stirred up by [desire], that is, [the desire] in itself, is not the soul freed from all adversaries, stirred up by the excellent desire of its own nature?

The Knowledgeable Spectator

36. Therefore, should not the disciple move away from the stirring of this body's desire without receiving knowledge from it? But when he has seen that [desire] has been awakened, he will awaken his soul with knowledge and become its observer. If he is the master of his freedom and lives in the power of the soul's nature, not even when [desire] has been awakened in the members is he disturbed and afraid of it, but he stands on high and looks out and observes it: how was it aroused and from which causes; how long ago did it begin and how was it raised up? Will he [then] allow its heat to have control over the member of his body and be spread out fully in everything? During that age in which [heat] increases in the members, he will also make courageous thoughts increase in the soul. The more [desire] is enflamed, [the more] he lights up the soul's desire against it, places it as if in a wrestling arena, and sits down and becomes a spectator from the height of knowledge.

Intelligence the Spectator

37. Desire stretches out [its] hands and grabs hold of all the body's members and like an athlete wrestles with its counterpart, while intelligence **(528)** sits down and is made a spectator [sitting] from the height of knowledge. He gathers information from the struggle and learns of the victory of both sides, and the defeat that is found with both of them. When he is freed from [being involved in] the battle, he possesses the knowledge of the struggle. Intelligence like this does not allow itself to enter and be confined by the desire that fights with the body. Otherwise, it is not able to become a spectator of the battle, nor is it able to gather and acquire from it [any] learning. Just as the body is not able to become the spectator of its [own] battle as long as it engages in the struggle of the battle, neither is desire a spectator of itself as long as it is engaged in the fight against the body; in the same way, not even a thought is able to become a spectator of this battle if it allows itself to be mixed into the passion of desire, because the passion of desire is blind and makes one blind who is seized by it. Desire blinds the eye of thought lest being a spectator it may not release its soul from its yoke.

Do Not Shy Away from the Battle

38. Therefore, if you have confidence in the strength of your thought, do not be afraid that desire is moving in your members. It will be an occasion of many good things for you if you acquire knowledge that reaps profits out of losses. In the first place, it will be an occasion for you for battle, because if you do not have an enemy, there will be no battle. If **(529)** there is no battle, victory will not be realized. If victory is not declared at the conclusion of the struggle, the glorious crown of triumphs will not be given. So then, be encouraged in your war and do not succumb from the fact that desire is stirring up in you.

However, take care that things do not spew forth into a foreign stream and, moreover, that a thought may not take pleasure secretly and fornicate without a body with an incorporeal image, because this is the custom of desire. For when a real body is not near to it, it will fornicate with the shadow of an image, and instead of a person, with the image of a person. Whoever [thus] fornicates, embracing by his thought something that is not near to him, unites his soul to the image instead of to its body, instead of with his members he commits adultery in his thoughts, and instead of its body he defiles himself. When the passion of fornication has taken hold to entice him in [his] thoughts by [over-]abundance, it will expand its satisfaction without a pretext. While there is no external seducer, desire through its abundance forces it to go out. It searches for means and finds ways and enflames the fire of destructive excitation in the body. For in that [same] way divine desire seeks for itself means by which it might serve its wills and please God. In that same way also the desire of fornication seeks for itself ways through which to serve its pleasures and enrage God.

Spiritual More Powerful Than Physical

39. Nevertheless, raise up **(530)** in battle [one] desire against [another] desire, O discerning mind, and that [desire] of the body will shortly be defeated by that [desire] of the spirit, because spiritual things are more powerful in everything than physical things. Hold the reins of desire and of the body while they are quarreling one with another, and you will be sitting consciously on high as a spectator of their conflict. Snatch the crown from the midst of them both, that is, the body that is united with the soul takes the crown—[the body] for which incorruptible life is also preserved by its union with [the soul].

Desire Enters the Body from Outside

40. The body naturally is mixed with the soul, but desire enters from the outside by the transgression of the commandment. On account of this we are not able to separate the body from the soul, but we are able, if we wish, to cut off and cast away desire from the body. It is not the case that just as the body is constructed in order to be a dwelling place for the soul, so the body was created to be a house for evil desire. If the body had been made by the Maker to be a dwelling for desire, there would not be any divine command-

ments to drive desire out from it anywhere, while different voices are shouting menacingly from all sides. From here judgment, from there menaces; here torture, there Gehenna; here retribution, there gnashing of teeth; from here endless scourging, from there chastisement without end. Besides this, [the body] is also chastised by nearby diseases and scourged by occasional illnesses, **(531)** while ravenous death suddenly makes [the body] cross over from life, and fear accompanies it and terror surrounds it and damages and losses go to meet it. While in the beginning desire was of no effect in [the body] because of childhood and adolescence, at the end [desire] is extinguished in him because of old age.

Desire Extinguished by Asceticism

41. Divine wisdom has constructed such ways as these for the abolition of evil desire from the body. For when [the body] has seen afflictions on one side and continual tortures attached to life, it should extinguish seductive desire from its members, that is, it should cool down and douse from it the fire kindled in all its members in the manner of a flame that catches hold of dry stubble and like a fire showing its ardor in much tinder. Just as rubbish before fire, so the members are before desire. In that manner, once fire has control over tinder, it destroys it; in the same way also when desire has power over the members of the body, it will destroy them. The result of the burning of a fire is ashes, and the result of desire in the members is annihilation. Therefore, do not hide the fire in the wood nor desire in the members. In the same way that naphtha and oil increase the burning of fire, so food and drink strengthen the ardor of desire. Just as fire is extinguished by water, so also desire is extinguished by asceticism. If you throw a lot of water on the fire, [the water] will extinguish it. But if you should pour on it **(532)** naphtha or oil, it will inflame it. In the same way, if you throw the provisions of desire on the eating of food and the drinking of wine, you will be adding fire upon fire and will place a flame upon a flame. But if you reduce food and drink from the body, its natural desire will be cooled down and all its desires will be extinguished and become cold.

Desire Is an Occasion for Victory

42. Therefore, may desire be stirred up in your body, not for your defeat, but for your victory. May it not be an excuse for your reproach, but may it become for you the crowns of triumphs. Not so that you may appear by it foolish and ignorant, but so that you may gather from it meaning and wisdom. Not so that it may be stirred up in you in order to blind your discernment's sight, but so that it might become for you a little salve that cleanses the eye of your thoughts, so that, O intelligence, what was written to you might be accomplished. "The wise one will sit on a great height, but fools will fall into a pit."[15] Therefore, when you are sitting at the height of knowledge, may desire be confined underneath you with the body. Be a spectator of their fighting and not a participant in their desire. Be watchful of your natural desire, O intelligence, while you are a spectator of the battle of flesh's desire. May it be subordinate to you in all things just as the earth is confined below the mountains. May it stir up your will and may your will reject it. May its course also be in the line of your vision. The movement of desire with the wise becomes a reason for learning and an occasion for knowledge, for they stir up the passions **(533)** in them in order to experience the passions and test their strength by them, in order that they may establish the pattern for the ways of their knowledge, when these things are happening, and at which stage [of life] they are being performed. When the mind is in its natural freedom above the passions, and like a master commanding his servants—they obey him when he places the yoke of his lordship upon them and cues their vision to his gestures so that they might be disposed to his word and prepared to hear what he has commanded, when he remains in his natural freedom—those [passions] will serve the will of his word like servants.

Which teaching could be better than this one by which a person may find himself victorious over his passions? These passions not only create triumph for you but also a wise and knowledgeable person if you become their spectator and not their performer and

[15] Lemoine/Lavenant do not know the source of this citation.

are freed from their pleasure and [not] tied down by the knowledge that is from them. As long as a thought is seized by the sweetness of desire, it is not capable of being a spectator of conflict and a collector of knowledge but turns toward corrupting pleasure. Desire is placed in us for wrestling and not for defeat, in order to be defeated by us and not so that it might be victorious over us, and in order that we might become sages by its instruction and not that it might show us to be fools and simpletons.

The Better Truth of One's Own Experience

43. For everything we learn that we find outside of ourselves, we compile its content through the word. Yet the learning of knowledge that we acquire by the defeat of our passions establishes the truth of his wisdom toward us by actual experience. Because of this, this learning is also believable and true. **(534)** The soul finds this wisdom more agreeable than what is outside, because it is at home and by it the soul is at rest upon itself, and its delight comes from within and not from causes outside of it. When we gather knowledge from outside, the possession of our knowledge is outside of us. But when we find learning such as this by the experience of our own passions, the learning gathered for us is true and believable. There is confidence concerning it and it preserves itself. If things outside of us become an opportunity for our knowledge, how much more are these things that are stirred up by us and in us and become for us an occasion for the learning of wisdom, if we allow the desire to be moving in us for this aim,[16] and not for the pleasure of its own desire?

Be a Spectator of Yourself

44. Therefore, be a spectator of yourself by discerning knowledge, and discern and understand between yourself and your passion, so that you may run to find the purity of your person. May desire not find pleasure in you, lest it demands its pleasure from you at all times. Do not grant it fulfillment when you are starting, lest

---

[16] Written: ܟܐܘ, "passion"; read ܟܐܘ, "aim/purpose."

by granting this it will demand another beginning of you. Cut off its course and look, its source will be stopped up. Inhibit it from the road of its journey, and immediately its engendering movement will cease. Desire is never satisfied. On account of this, by its eating it is hungry all the more, and while drinking it becomes especially thirsty. As long as desire satisfies its wills through you, its enticements of you are not completed. Do not say, "Now I will do its will and at another time I will fight against it." For if you are defeated once by it, it will defeat you at all times. Inasmuch as it (535) becomes stronger in its doing, your own strength will become weaker. Do not allow yourself to give your strength to desire so that it is thereby strengthened, but use your natural strength and it will persist in the weakness appropriate to it.

Awakening Spiritual Desire

45. May desire's heat be an instructive example for you so that by comparison spiritual desire will awaken and warm you. In that same manner in which the body is enticed by its natural desire, so also the natural desire of its spiritual nature is enticed and heated up. As long as the spirit's desire is warm in you, there is no way for the body's desire to be awakened in you. If this is not actually experienced by you, receive teaching from what is the opposite. Look, when the body's desire is fervent in you, you should be aware that the spirit's desire will disappear from you completely at that moment. For that [desire] of the body would not have been awakened if it had not found [the spirit's desire] asleep. For it is by the sleep of one that its companion is awakened. Because of this they constantly keep guard of one another, so that when the movements of the first one were done [for the night], the [movements of] its adversary might enter in after it. Just as a thief keeps watch of the sleep of the master of the house, so the body's desire watches the sleep of the spirit's desires. When it has noticed a little bit of negligence and carelessness and that the taste of the sensation of divine desire has been taken from a person, at once the flesh's desire is awakened and begins to move and ascend upon all the members, and if a person is negligent (536) and succumbs to it, it

will spread itself out into the house of his person and it will become dark to him like the night.

Darkness of the Flesh's Desire

46. Inasmuch as the sun sets in the west on its journey, shadows increase and multiply over the earth until it goes down and its rays are cut off, and then the shades of the night will ascend completely and cover the creation; even so, the darkness of the flesh's desire looks constantly at the journey of the light of spiritual desire. Inasmuch that it sees that [spiritual desire] is proceeding to descend, so also it will be stirred up to ascend, degree by degree, level by level, section by section, until this light is completely immersed and obscured and the rays of its spiritual nature have been drawn back toward it. Then the cloud of desire ascends to conceal the soul completely and it will be a gloomy night in a lighted house. From then on a person begins to stumble over everything because he cannot see to make out the things placed in front of him. Just as in the obscurity of night the distinguishing of everything is concealed, so in the obscurity of desire, all the discernments of the soul will become dark and the vitality of its knowledge will be impoverished, especially if it has sensed spiritual knowledge. In the same way that darkness is the opposite of light, so this passion of desire is the adversary of spiritual knowledge.

Looking at God Spiritually

47. Not even when the mind turns itself around to become a spectator of the movements of desire does it look with a spiritual eye, but (537) with the part [of the mind] that sees, examining things with the knowledge of the soul [and] watching in this manner, it collects knowledge from the struggle. Because when the intellect looks at God spiritually, something that is its opposite is not visible to it, nor also does it lower itself to look at desire. The wonder of the grandeur of the glory of God does not allow it to turn around and look back at those things left behind it, because the pleasurable vision it tastes is sufficient to bind it to itself without disturbance. Moreover, one might say that he will look at desire in order to

gather information, but a mind does not gather information such as this from opposing things, but through the simple movement of the knowledge that it has found after freedom from passions. Just as also the angels know everything—they are not comparing one thing with another and bringing to one another matters that are the opposites of each other—but they are moved consciously by a simple and singular thought.

Be Careful of Observing Desire

48. The mind should also be careful of this: one who wishes to become a spectator of desire while not yet having been freed completely[17] from the passions, when he has lowered himself to receive knowledge he may be seized by the pleasure of despicable passions. Because the mind at that time is engaged in a contest and just as the body and desire are fighting [one another], [the mind] is also in conflict not to be seized by the love of something that it sees. If the mind is confident concerning this—that it may examine the passion of desire without passion— [well and good], otherwise it would be advantageous **(538)** for it to flee and not watch. It would be better to flee if one senses his weakness rather than to become subservient to one's enemies. It is an example of strength and a sign of courage to fight and to take the victory. But if one is seized by passion's pleasure and is seduced by the love of knowledge, it would be better to be free at least from passion and not to be subjected to it while not receiving knowledge. It is not even possible he will find knowledge if he is seized by passion, because its nature's eye that rushes to inquire about the knowledge of things will become blind and will be seized by passion's pleasure and not by the pleasure of discernment.

Victory through Divine Knowledge

49. Just as virtues are different from one another, so their tastes differ from one another, and everyone chooses what he wishes and

---

[17] Typographical error: written ܕܬܚܙܐ read ܕܢܬܚܙܐ.

is seized by the passion he seeks. There are some who are seized by the passion of desire, and some by the passion of knowledge. Whoever is seized by passion in desire's pleasure is not concerned to gather knowledge from it. In this way also, whoever is seized by the delight of knowledge does not return to the pleasure of desire, for he captures the thing which captures and all the parts of the soul and of the body gather to that powerful passion in order to make it grow and to serve it. Because of this you will find many people among the lovers of knowledge who are freed from this passion **(539)** of desire. But their victory is not a complete victory because by passion they are victorious over passion, and not by the discernment of divine knowledge.

But as for us, not only is victory necessary against desire, but it is also proper for us to know the reason by which we are victorious, so that in this way the victory also may be identified by the cause. If the cause is from God, the victory is also divine. If [the cause] is with the world, or from the love of knowledge, or from vainglory, or so that a person may not impoverish one of the other passions when he is victorious over the passion of fornication, it is proper to consider this victory weak because it is obvious as to its cause, whether weak or strong. Those who are victorious over passions by passions repress them but do not transcend them. Whoever is victorious over passions without passion receives a victory untouched by passion.[18] How should it be called a victory over passions when it is constructed from passions? How should it be described as the oppressor [of passions] when it springs up from the root of their germination? If you defeat the passion of fornication because the yearning for knowledge is strong in you, the time will arrive for the passion to defeat its companion, but another time will come and [one passion] will defeat [the other], and while they are defeating and being defeated by one another in this way, a just victory will be taken away from the middle.

---

[18] ܠܐ ܚܫܘܫܘܬܐ —*lā ḥašūšūtā*, "passionlessness" or *apatheia*.

One Passion Defeats Another

50. This is the victory that happens through justice when a virtue **(540)** defeats a vice, spiritual desire defeats physical desire, [that which is] illuminated [defeats] darkness, knowledge [defeats] folly, and in this sense all of the rest. But a victory happening through iniquity is this—when something evil shall defeat something good, the dark one [will defeat] the enlightened, and folly [will defeat] knowledge. The victory standing in the middle is that of their own passions against one another and not a victory of divine triumph— when these passions defeat and are defeated by one another, and as the status of one becomes the destruction of the other. Just as there are people who for the passion of the love of money fight against the lust of the belly, there are some who for vainglory defeat this desire of fornication, and there are some who for the desire for human praises fight with the desire of possessions. There are some who for the passion of the lust of honor restrain themselves from the passion of lengthy conversations. There are some who make war with the love of pleasures for the desire of power. While both are evil things, they are victorious over one another and are defeated by one another, but it is not considered strictly victory when one passion fights with another passion and is victorious over it.

Opposite Desires

51. Therefore, desires are moving in the body and evil passions are also stirring in the soul, and just as their natures are opposites of one another, so also are their passions the opposites of one another. All the body's desires, so to speak, are the opposites of the soul's passions. For the most part, **(541)** all the evil passions that spring up from the soul are the opposite of the body's desires. Because there are physical passions and there are passions of the soul: the physical ones are those that spring up from the body and [the passions of] the soul are those that shoot up from the soul.

All the physical passions, if one examines [them] closely, are helpers of one another. The passion of the lust of the belly has its germination from the body and is a helper of the passion of fornication, which is also a physical passion. In the same way also, the adornment of clothes, the passion of human pleasures, and all those things that are found after these with the body are the assistants of the passion of fornication.

Love of Money as Mediator

52. The passion of the love of money is in the middle. Sometimes it helps the body's desires, and sometimes it assists the soul's passions. For through too many expenditures it helps the lust of the belly, fornication, the adornment of clothes, the pleasures and sounds of singing, and the pleasure of human conversations, which are all children of the body. But also with others it is the assistant of the soul's passions: aiding the love of power, and even more the passion of vainglory, if someone wishes to be glorified in this way for the honor and praise of the world. But there is still one who nurtures boasting and gives a hand to jealousy, along with other things similar to these. The cause of their being stirred up is from the soul. Therefore, this passion of the love of money **(542)** is the binder and gatherer of divided passions. It is found in yet another way to be the opponent of the passions of the soul and body, if one examines knowledge minutely in order to nurture and strengthen, it holds back desires from the body and, moreover, the passions of the soul from the soul.

Passions: Helpers of One Another

53. All these passions of the soul, again, are helpers of one another. For in the same way that the word has shown that they are assisting the physical desires one with another, the same is also being found with the soul's passions. Look, honor is the assistant of vainglory and vainglory, moreover, is the assistant of boasting, and boasting is the instigator of power and authority.

All these things assist one another in this order. Yet there are other examples and aspects that are the opposite of these. However, [our] discourse is now journeying on this path, these passions are aides and assistants of one another, because just as the good assists the good, so also the evil one nurtures evil. Because the paths of the passions are narrow and have exits, movements, ends, and different forms, no one should judge my word while observing the goals of others, for through them are these passions that are the adversary of one another of the body and of the soul, and that middle one of the love of money. However, may the one who becomes the judge of our word examine this point of view placed before us, and he will find that this is just as we have written. **(543)** A human being's person from whom all the passions spring forth is one because sin is also one, even if it is divided into many forms and its composition consists of the members of opposing passions.

Passion of Fornication

54. However, let us speak now concerning the passion of fornication that our discourse has stirred up in order that we might be vigilant and become its spectators, because it is obvious whoever is defeated by it is not truly vigilant. For in that same manner that happens to those sleeping who dream without the discernment of knowledge and sense also desire's pleasure in their sleep, so also whoever allows himself to serve through it his wills' passion, it is as if he falls into a deep sleep and does not have then a healthy understanding, a vigilant discernment, an enlightened knowledge, or a firm intellect. Yet in that same way, his body's senses are disturbed and his constituent members are made slack by the enticements of desire, so also his soul's thoughts are disturbed, his mind is cloudy, and his discernment is taken away. Just as all the members of the body turn around to become servants of desire, so also all the soul's thoughts lower themselves, are immersed with the body's pleasure, and are swallowed up in the sweetness of the corruptible body. During that time a person does everything like one asleep.

The Awakening of Penitence

55. Understand by these actions that he is immersed in sleep. When, without the fear of God, the respect of people, the memory of distant torment, the memory of an approaching judgment, remorse, or shame, [these things] are placed before his eyes during

that time and he neither reflects nor does one of these ascend **(544)** upon his heart, is it not evident that he is submersed as in a deep sleep and does everything without sensation as in a daze? Moreover, there is something we should know from another thing, because at the end of its work of desire, penitence at once enters into the soul and suffering is born into it on account of those things it has done. The conscience, in which there was nothing during the time of passion, becomes grieved, mournful, and sad after a time of passion, repenting for the sake of shameful deeds and sensing that what it had done is reprehensible. The memory of judgment and condemnation stirs it up, and future punishments are depicted in its presence, as though in the light and a wakeful state. Whatever was not apparent to it while it was asleep in passion is [now] apparent to it. It thinks about God, reminds itself of judgment, calls to mind torment, despises desire, and blames itself for what it had transgressed that by the impact of a dream it has been vanquished, and by the course of a shadow it has been defeated, and being something, it has been subjected to nothing. Such beautiful memories like these that happen to it after the fulfillment of desire make known that it has turned from sleep to vigilance and has stood in the healthy memory of itself, and from heavy slumber and from the death of sin it has returned to the house of life.

Vigilance and the Speed of Desire

56. Vigilance, then, is useful to a person during the time of desire more than anything else in order to observe how[19] despicable and vile is that thing victorious over him. A short time is sufficient for the fulfillment of desire or to be restrained from the performance of its despicable deed. Look, we see that there is not one of the desires whose action is fulfilled as quickly in this way as the pleasure **(545)** of desire. The fact that its comfort lasts only a short blink of an eye and its pleasure a split second ought to make us despise it and not agree to its destructive enticement. I do not know that there is another desire without profit like this desire, whose weak-

---

[19] Typographical error: written ܟܡܐ, read ܐܝܟܢܐ.

ness is visible from all sides. If its profit does not exist, and if the
duration of its pleasure is short, if its delight is like a shadow, if
the movements of its refreshments are vile, if the causes that entice
it are weak, if its conduct is similar to that of animals, if its ways
are types of beasts, if remorse is near to it, if fear accompanies it, if
shame is the bedfellow of its dwelling, if fright is found with it, if
terror is its companion, if something hurtful accompanies it, if harm
is near to it, if an evil name is crowned by it, if reproach accompanies it at all times, if it is mockery it is laughed at by everyone—in
whatever ways you might observe desire, something harmful will
accompany it. Indeed, by which [weakness] will it be victorious
over us? Why should it subdue us? If[20] its enticement is strong, we
ought to despise this all the more.

Desire Diminishes One's Strength

57. However, on account of our feebleness it will defeat us—it
appears—through whatever was specifically required for us to
defeat it, and if it seems that it is powerful in us, it is because our
soul's strength is weak in us. The strength that is in desire is taken
from the soul. **(546)** When strength has been snatched[21] from the
soul, weakness remains with it. Which soul is sadder than this one,
whose strength is being used by other things and is dressed in the
weakness of other things? The spiritual nature of our soul naturally
possesses the strength that is the opposite of the desires, and it is
easy for it to be victorious over them if it wishes. Just as weakness
is naturally close to the nature of the body, [along with] dissolution
and destruction, so also strength is near to the spiritual and true
nature in good things. If [a person] uses his natural strength, and
if he fulfills [the soul's] good intention along with this [strength],
spiritual grace will accompany the soul, giving it assistance and
strength. Just as a powerful man might seize the hand of a child
and compel its weakness to accompany his strength, in the same
way also the Holy Spirit takes hold of the soul's thoughts and

---

[20] Lavenant adopts variant reading (Ms. E): ܡܕܘܚܐ ܗܢܐ.
[21] Written: ܕܐܬܚܠܨ; read ܕܐܬܚܠܨ.

picks it up as if by the hand in order that it might be elevated to spiritual things.

The Assistance of the Spirit

58. By its union with the Spirit [the soul] acquires lightness more than its nature [ordinarily possesses]. Whoever entrusts his soul to the Spirit to become his mentor, the entire conduct of his life is above harm. On account of this Paul also teaches us to live in the Spirit and to deliver ourselves to the Spirit.[22] Whoever lives in the Spirit and entrusts [himself] to it, his entire conduct becomes spiritual, and by the movements of the Spirit he and his thoughts and actions are being led according to the will of the Spirit. It is not for want of assistance we are defeated by desire, but **(547)** because we do not seek the assistance of the One who assists. Just as when desire, wishing to be victorious over us, will call others to its aid, and then fight and defeat us, so also if it is set for us to fight and be victorious over it, let us call to our aid the divine power and assistance of grace that is in us, and we will easily defeat the desire that fights with us. As long as our soul is pure from the thoughts of desire, it thrives in its natural strength, and as long as [the soul] is ascending to live in its natural strength, it is worthy to receive divine strength that will become its assistant. When it has become its companion in this way, it is not readily defeated by desires that fight with it.

Drying Out Desire and Disease

59. Therefore, guard your soul from the causes that lead you on toward desire and block the watery aqueducts from which a strange flow is gathering against you on all sides. When you have cut off the causes by which diseases are nurtured, even though you are not bringing them medicines for your ulcers, they will dry out by themselves, and little by little the pus in them will be eliminated and dispersed. This desire is nurtured in us by causes outside of

[22] See Rom 8:14.

us. They are numerous and different one from another, and each one of them extends a unique strength to desire. If you cut off these causes, desire will also cease and vanish. For desire does not exist without these things, and it does not remain in us if **(548)** its causes are abolished.

Desire sometimes begins from the body, sometimes from the movements of thoughts, and sometimes by causes outside of us— whether by vision or by hearing or by such as these. We should astutely observe from where it begins and cut it off from there in advance. If it is awakened in us by external causes, let us cut off from ourselves human encounters and estrange ourselves from the sight of those faces that are its assistants. By this way we will block its entrance into us. But if its movement occurs from discharging the heat of the body, we should weaken the body and reduce its strength by less food and emaciation, by drinking water, doing it by measure with the rest of the other austerities that usually cool down the heat of the body. But if we sense through a thought that the beginning of desire is about to happen, we should know that the mind is empty of the reflection of God, because [if] its own movements are not in it, strange movements outside of it will fall into it. If it is apparent to us that a desirous thought was stirred up in us by the elimination of reflection on good things, let us be concerned to seal the mind by reflection on spiritual things and by the study of divine knowledge. Let us be persistent at this time with the reading of the Scriptures and with the hearing of the stories of valiant and strong people, depicting their images at all times before **(549)** our eyes, and awakening in us a desire to imitate them. Let us be persistent, moreover, in prayer which more than anything else acquires strength for the mind, because this is the particular work of prayer, to put on invincible strength for the mind. Just as when we are far removed from encounters with vain minds and have made ourselves strangers from visions of dissoluteness, we are purifying our thoughts and are withdrawing from this into ourselves; in the same way, after the recollection of the mind let us be constant when in prayer, our thought receiving the strength to defeat decisively the passions fighting with [the thought].

The Unconquered Mind

60. Therefore, these three are the ways by which desire takes control over our lives, and if we know wisely how to shut the door in their face and set up a fitting[23] strategy against every one of them, we will be casting desire outside of ourselves, remaining in the purity of our souls, and led by the strength of the unconquered mind, because after this the soul will be worthy of the blessing of a higher vision and a sensation that belongs to it above the body in spiritual things. Just as the body is stirred up and is comforted by these things of its nature, so the soul will be pleased with spiritual movements and exult in the light of living knowledge that is above the world, of which all the disciples of faith shall be worthy **(550)** by the grace of Christ, our[24] God, to whom be glory forever. Amen.

The end of the *mēmrā* on the desire of fornication.

---

[23] Lavenant reads variant (Ms. G): ܗܠ ܫܢܝܠܐܙ, "that is fitting for it" / "le moyen approprié"; instead of the written text ܗܠ ܐܘܚܬܗܡܙܙ.

[24] Lavenant adopts variant (Ms. G): ܢ ܗܠܐ ܐܘܚܡܙܙ.

Mēmrā 13

On Fornication

The thirteenth *mēmrā* on fornication and on the evil passion of the desire of the body, describing how much great athleticism is required of us who are fighting in this battle: how the outer passions will be exposed before the hidden movements in order that they might also be freed in this way from [the body's] outer passions, until they are delivered in all ways from it and from its passions in their interior and exterior [forms].

Summary: The passion of fornication obscures the soul's discernment so that the mind no longer recognizes that fornication is a passion. Jesus advised uprooting lust from the soul by not lusting after a woman in one's heart. Young adulthood is the primary period of fornication. God allowed marriage, lust, riches, and power to remain as originally constituted but commanded the monk to become a stranger to the world. Whoever defeats his lusts in early adulthood will become mighty in his soul in old age, but one who has lived entirely in the body will come to a complete end in old age. The best defense against fornication is very little water. Gideon choosing his soldiers through the lapping up of water is an example of using water sparingly to fight against the sin of fornication, symbolized by the Midianites.

The Heat of This Passion

(551) 1. While examining those despicable passions that inhibit the soul from divine knowledge and purity of prayer, I have found

that this passion of fornication more than many [others] is the inhibitor of virtues, ruling and enticing especially persons deprived of self-control. When the cause for this passion occurs from the heat of the body, it will find thoughts that are devoid of the reflection of God and the search of superior knowledge, [and] like a flame in wood, this passion's fire also catches hold and takes control over all the members. Hotter **(552)** and swifter than all the others is this destructive passion. Great valor is required of the soul when it sets up a battle with [fornication] in order to fight and be victorious over it, while also calling on the grace of God for its assistance in this struggle. A person who fights this battle is concerned to fight and to uproot this passion from [his] thought, and to pull up the roots of its germination from the depths of the heart. For it is there that it enters to take hold and make for itself a dwelling. When it is uprooted from there, all its branches stretched out over the rest of the members will dry out.

Recognizing the Fact of Sin

2. If this passion should rule in the soul for a long time and take bodily form in it by constant occupation, it will obscure [the soul's] judgments and not allow it to see that [fornication] is also a passion. However, like all the other things not blameworthy in their doing, this desire is also not considered by the mind as something of reproach. This is the concern that sin has: to uproot the thought from the soul that sees that it is sin, so that without fear and terror it might be served by thoughts within and by actions without. As long as sin is visible to us in others and not being performed in ourselves, we assess that it is a sin by an examination of the justice in us. But if it should actually come to be from us, [our] knowledge of its performance will be uprooted from our soul and the eye of discernment—by which its despicable action is visible to us—will become blind. Let us take care then not to slip and fall into this desire. But if by the allurement of [particular] situations we should become ensnared in it, may this not be hidden from us so that we may know how to discern that it is sin, especially when **(553)** it is hidden secretly in us in [our] thoughts.

Desire of Thoughts

3. The desire of thoughts is considered by many as if it were not a sin, although it is plainly not only a sin but the root of all sinful actions. The heart is the source of all thoughts and from it are born the movements of good and bad things. Whatever takes root and holds on to it in himself, whether good or evil, its external fruits are visible as well. The heart, [even] when desire is being choked in it, could awaken it whenever [it wishes]. Like a tree that is cut down with its root [still] remaining in the ground begins to sprout again from[1] water's humidity, so also when desire is cut off, its root will remain in the mind by the humidity of food and drink [and] it will begin to grow again in the thoughts and members.

Fighting Hidden Desire

4. Here the war against this hidden desire is more useful for us than whatever is done outwardly, because there [outwardly] many causes will inhibit it: many people watching [us], shame, decency, and the laws of punishment. It happens, moreover, that the passion of desire is no longer acceptable to those persons whom it [normally] seizes, because an act of desire will be prevented by all these things, as though the war in its outward [actions] is not too hard for us, for we do fight with it not by ourselves, but we have all these assistants. Whenever we **(554)** wish to commit an act of sin and devise many ways of committing it, these and others like these will prevent us. While desire is being performed within us on account of our will, it is held back from the outside due to circumstances that inhibit us, and although we are considered pure by people from our outward actions, we are considered fornicators on account of our will by God who examines our inner actions. While we do not sin before one another, our sin is apparent before the knowledge of God.

---

[1] Written: ܡܢ, "what"; "when"; read ܡܢ, "from," "by."

The Heart as Source

5. So then, let us be careful regarding both of these things in order not to be ashamed in the eyes of people or be ashamed before God, being concerned first to please God, for from [this concern] is also born freedom in the presence of people. The fact that one does not fornicate in public does not guarantee that one is not considered a fornicator in private. But so that one might be freed from thoughts of fornication, this will prove him also to be pure in public matters, because action is not the root of thoughts, but a thought is the root and cause of deeds. The will of everything resides there in the heart, the source of thoughts, just as the will of God is also resting there. Because the streams of deeds are distributed from [the heart], as from a great source, we should maintain [its] clarity so that it may not be troubled. Just as when the head of the source is troubled all streams flowing from it are also troubled and become impure, in the same way, when the heart is bothered by desire, all the senses are troubled, all the members are disturbed, the entire person is upset, ideas are troubled, thoughts are confused, and every one of the members **(555)** of the body makes known by its appearance that it is subject to a secret desire in the heart. [It is] whatever starts from the heart, whether good or evil things, which is counted as sin or righteousness by the examination of divine knowledge.

Uprooting Desire

6. Concerning this, when our Lord wished to tear out desire from its root, and not just to cut off [its] outer effects, he said, "Anyone who looks at a woman as if to desire her has already committed adultery with her in his heart."[2] He set down the idea there, comparing one adultery with [another] adultery, and a legal examination concerning aspects of sin's deeds with the particularity of his own knowledge. "You have heard that it was said to people of old, 'Do not commit adultery.' "[3] The law had forbidden the ancients

---

[2] Matt 5:28.
[3] Matt 5:27.

from acting out desire, and so that their fornication might be not visible in external members, the commandment was prescribed to them. Because they did not have the strength to uproot the thoughts of fornication from within the heart, the Lawgiver left alone that first [statement of Jesus] and moved on to the second one. Because they were not capable of purifying the heart from the thought of adultery, he compelled them by the force of commandment so that at least they might guard the body from its action. He established righteousness for them in an external place where many causes are found that support this perseverance. However, our Lord did not seek [only] to remove adultery from the outside, but from wherever he sees it.

God's Vision

7. The vision of God is unique, and wherever he sees, human vision cannot see, because **(556)** [human beings] are not able to understand secret thoughts in the soul. [He says,] Just as [when] people are watching inhibits you from the external act of adultery, let my vision also prevent you from the thought that desires adultery and purify the spiritual place of your soul in order that it might be similar to my[4] vision that observes it. Just as my watching you is pure from error and from supposition, so let the place that receives this vision also be pure from the passion of fornication. As for myself, desire is adultery, and for a thought to wish something is the [same] as the body ministering [to it], because I do not need to see desire actually being carried out and then consider it adultery, for the thought that desires adultery has already committed adultery. "Anyone who looks at a woman as if to desire her, already he has committed adultery with her in his heart."[5] Wherever it is easy for him to commit adultery he performs adultery. The fact that the deed is not outwardly visible is not [from] the will holding it back, but [that] it was prevented by other factors. Hence, it is

---

[4] Written: ܕܝܠܕ, "which engendered"; read ܕܝܠܝ, "my."
[5] Matt 5:28.

apparent that triumph is not from the will, but from the results of its impediments.

The Evil Will of Sin

8. The observation of the knowledge of God looks at the causes within our thoughts and inquires into the depth of the mind where it is not easy for human beings to see or easily understand if they seek to examine, because only God is able to explore the heart and know hidden things. Just as this belongs to [God] to know our secret things, so this is our [task] to purify our hearts before his sight. Many (557) who do not actually commit adultery are adulterers in the will and in their souls, continually performing fornication. They continually conceive and bear images of all sorts, and continually fornicate with beautiful faces without bodily union. It does not occur to them that even if people do not see [them], God is examining the secrets of their thoughts, for wherever the thought is, [there is] the sin, and wherever the performance of the action, [there is the sin]. The thought that folly wishes something evil, this is sin according to its will, even while it does not actually do anything in practice.

Not Looking to Desire

9. But as for the strong, our Lord established for us this commandment, "Anyone who looks at a woman as if to desire her has committed adultery with her in his heart," in order to pull up sin by its root and to cut off and extract the destructive desire from the depth of the heart. He did not say to you, "Do not look," but that you should not look so as if to desire. The eye observes everything but does not desire everything. In this same manner, may the beauty of a woman be before your eye like the sight of anything [in general], and do not let yourself be trapped in this beauty. If her nature's beauty were visible to the soul, it would not have yearned for the body's beauty, because its own [natural] beauty would be sufficient to connect the thought with the pleasure of its vision. When it had seen her and looked upon her nature's beauty, desire

would be aroused in it to acquire for itself what her soul possesses more than anything else, and be associated with it in all purity.

Adultery of the Soul

10. Do not **(558)** desire in your heart a foreign desire. Do not let the eye of your thought observe the beauty that is outside of you. It is dishonorable for the soul to be tied down to the flesh's desire. If it is bound by this [desire], its chain is outside of its [true] nature. Because it had taken upon itself the sense of the flesh, its sight also had desired [something] outside of its nature. There is an adultery of the body and an adultery of the soul. When the soul desires by means of a thought, this is adultery unique in itself. Just as with the body, the name "adultery" is the action, so with the soul, the action of adultery is the thought. There is no excuse for one who is considering committing adultery that he is not an adulterer because he has performed the deed of sin in his soul, for insofar as the nature of the soul is higher than that of the body, in this way the fornication of the soul is more serious than that of the body.

Moreover, it is apparent on another level that this iniquity is bitter, because it is not in the body in which desire is naturally mixed that he has committed fornication, but he has subjected the soul to something foreign to its nature; out of ignorance of its own desire [the soul] has lowered itself to desire[6] that which is not its own. Moreover, the fornication of the body has certain occasions, and distinctions and divisions exist in desire. At times a person sins and at times he ceases from his sin. But there is no cessation from the activity of this iniquity for whoever fornicates in his soul, because desire is constantly being mixed in his soul. If one should depart from its thought, it is not on account of his repentance concerning it but because another passion has become stronger in him and has led him away **(559)** to that thought.

---

[6] Lemoine reads E,ܡܕܥ, "to know," instead of written ܡܪܓ, "to desire"; but the written text fits the context better.

Hiding in the Dark

11. The victory against desire is understood in this way: not when we cease from considering fornication upon encountering another thought, but when we are victorious over it specifically, first establishing in us the preparation for victory over it. There are many in whom the thoughts of fornication cease because other thoughts come along and put them to sleep. When also these thoughts that have come are completed and have ceased from their work, the thought of fornication is found in its place, because it does not move from there before this, but like a body in the dark it has veiled itself in the shadow of another passion. After the shadow of its concealment has turned away, then the body of fornication is visible being installed in the soul.

Recognizing Sin in the Dark

12. Therefore, my brothers, let us flee from this fornication, especially in that it is not considered to be fornication. Many flee from the evil whose effect is evident, but people are caught all the more unawares by what is not considered to be sin. It is not only whatever does not appear to be evil that is evil, but whatever God has decided is evil let us especially consider evil. Look, the evilness of every one of sin's works is also apparent to a person before he is seized by it, but when he has become enslaved to it and served it personally a long time without repentance, the awareness of its evilness is taken away from him for he does not recognize and see **(560)** its despicableness. The fact is that his discernment has been destroyed, because sin not only defiles the person but also blinds [one's] discernment. [Sin] makes one who sees become one who does not see, and one who knows become someone who does not know, and one who discerns become someone who does not discern. When the darkness of sin was poured into the soul, the sight of what readily was visible and understandable in the light is obscured by [the darkness]. Just as everything is hidden from sight in darkness, even the form of darkness, so also the obscurity of sin is spread out in it, hiding everything from the soul, even sin itself, so that [the sin] is not recognized as being a sin. [The ability] to recognize one's

sin is the first step of detachment from sin, because after one has
sensed that he is bound, he will figure out how to detach himself.
But if he does not even know this—that he is tied and bound—how
can he scheme to seek to detach himself?

A Beautiful Work of God

13. "Do not look at a woman as if to desire her, otherwise, you
are her adulterer."[7] Observe her with a clear eye as a beautiful work
of God, and praise the wise Fashioner whose will has composed
and adorned her from the following: from a despised nature, what
beauty; from ordinary dust, a beauty that captivates those who
see it. See from the beauty of the work the beauty of its Fashioner.
And while you are astonished at this despised [creature] that has
been to such an extent adorned and become glorious, marvel and
be astonished at that One glorious by its nature, for the beauty
of her appearance will not satisfy those who are worthy to look
upon [God].

Pure Soul, Pure Body

14. Apply yourself, then, to purifying your soul, so that your
body becomes pure along with your [soul]. Be **(561)** holy in body
and spirit because you are the house of the Spirit of God's habitation. Your prayer is also pure and light when your thought is
pure from the passion of fornication. With this the light of Christ's
knowledge shines all the more in you when your soul's eye is
purified [for the light] to reside in it. Just as it is easy for a healthy
body to do anything, so it is easy for the mind pure of evil things
to become the dwelling place for divine movements. Just as illness
weakens the body and makes it not useful for anything, so also the
thought of sin weakens the soul's strength and renders it bereft of
divine movements. This thought of fornication emits a foul odor
into the soul so that it will be changed from that sweetness and
delightfulness that it possessed and will exhale a putrid odor from

---

[7] Matt 5:28.

then on. The treasure of divine thoughts will not fall into a soul like this. Just as things naturally possessing a sweet smell shall fall into pure vessels fitting for them, so also divine knowledge resides in the soul pure from thoughts of sin, especially in a soul freed from this passion, because greater than the rest of the other passions [this passion] causes wandering and troubling of thoughts.

Adulterous Woman

15. Solomon depicted this passion of fornication through these similar things, "Three things are hidden from me and four things I do not know: The way of an eagle in the sky, **(562)** the way of a serpent on a rock, the way of a ship in the heart of the sea, and the way of a man in his youth. Such is the way of the adulterous woman: she eats and wipes her mouth clean, saying, 'I have not done a thing.'"[8] He compared the lust of fornication with an adulterous woman whose roads and paths are not known because she casts her sight indiscreetly upon all and stumbles on all, and she fornicates with everything outside of the natural order. The intoxication of desire works in the same way when it has control over thoughts yet does not have a known way or a path that is clear and distinct. You seek to trace[9] its footsteps, but you are not able. For this lust of fornication wanders in the soul and is turned around easily to any place while the tracks of its footsteps are not distinct and its way is not clear to those who see it, just as an eagle in the sky, a serpent on a rock, and the way of a ship in the heart of the sea.

Age of Adolescence

16. The wise Solomon also excellently placed the young man in the role of an example similar to these first three. Because as the sea is to a ship, the air to an eagle, and a rock to a serpent, so also is a young man to desire. An eagle powerfully tears asunder the air, and without hindrance a serpent glides on the rock, and a ship

---

[8] Prov 30:18-20.
[9] Literally, "to stand upon," ܠܡܩܡ.

travels swiftly in the heart of the sea. In the same way also thoughts of fornication during the time of adolescence are easily fulfilled in the soul. If someone should call adolescence **(563)** the way of fornication, he would not be mistaken. That is, just as Solomon called it, he will also call it. The easy road of a serpent is a rock for it does not stumble over anything, nor does the heaviness of the dust inhibit his journey there. Again, the way of an eagle is the air and of a ship the sea. So also the way of fornication is adolescence, for as with wings it flies wherever it wishes and runs swiftly to every place. Because the heat of the body is great during adolescence, it becomes a great occasion for the inflammation of desire. When fire originates from fire, that is, desire [originates] from that natural [desire], it stokes the harsh flame of sin. From here on constant warfare will be found with this age—mortifications, labors and austerities, the minimizing of food and reduction of drink—so that when an opportunity is brought up in which desire takes hold, it will be consumed and perish. Anyone who wishes to become a witness of such things as these will sense this from practical experience.

Removing Tinder from Desire

17. Henceforth, everyone who seeks to be victorious over this desire, let him attempt to remove the tinder before it [along with] the occasion that sets it afire, and see, it will not take [hold of him]. With these causes desire enters: either at the sight of women, or with a conversation of constantly telling stories about it, or by eating and drinking given **(564)** to the body beyond need. If you take these three things out of the mix and meditate on divine knowledge, even a thought of desire will not trouble you. For as long as the body does not stir it up on account of heat, and the soul does not reflect on it due to idleness, from where can it be aroused? Either the body ignites it by its heat, or the soul meditates on it without any thought [regarding] knowledge. Outside of these two things, desire has no place for support. When it has found a body dead from labor and a soul alive in divine meditation, it goes back at once to [its] tracks but cannot find a dwelling. If the disease of desire makes you suffer, know its cause and cut it off. Why should you

be tormented in your ignorance by an illness that is easy to heal? I am not convinced that there is another passion easier to cure than this one. Food does not make you sin when it is taken in an orderly way for the maintenance of your life. But it is sin when it brings you to desire. As long as you eat for yourself there is no sin in your eating. But if you eat for desire, your eating is sinful. How do you know when you are eating for sin, and when [you are eating] for yourself? Inasmuch as desire is stirred up in the body's members and shakes you, if you are eating, your nourishment is of [sin] and [sin] will grow and become stronger through [nourishment], and not your strength and your life.

Not Your Life, But Christ's

18. Desire is mixed into your life for the maintenance of your life, that is, **(565)** so through your mediation your life may be given to others, but how much more will that which is victorious over the love of life defeat and subjugate desire? You do not have the authority to give your life to others, because it is not yours, but Christ's.[10] The intercourse and marriage of the world maintain the human race and transmit life from one person to another, so that from one human being [another] human being will come to exist, and from one who is living will be born one living like it. This was when our life was our own. In that time, we had the authority to share [life] with others by the union of marriage. But now because we are living in the spiritual life of Christ, we do not have the authority to give life that is not our own to others, because [our life] does not belong to ourselves. "You do not belong to yourselves," said the Apostle to us, "You have been bought at a [great] price. Glorify God, therefore, in your body and in your spirit which belong to God."[11] You see that the spirit, as well as the body, belongs to God and we do not have power over either of them. Whoever does not have power over his life, how will he give [life] to others

[10] See Gal 2:20.
[11] 1 Cor 6:20.

by desire's union, that is to say, how will there come to be with them another person through human generation?

Creating Another Creation

19. Therefore, a spiritual birth was revealed in the world in order to eliminate physical birth, and another womb of baptism was created in order to make the natural womb cease from giving birth. If all of human nature had been capable of keeping this commandment **(566)** the will of Majesty would have wished to take pleasure in this. But because our Savior saw the weakness of humanity, that it was not capable of this work, he established his will in the middle of things so that perhaps a small number might become doers. Do not look at this only, for the womb of the mother is established by God first, but consider this also, that instead of the first one, another womb was created that will give birth to those who are spiritual instead of the physical, according to the perfect will of God, because this is "the good and perfect and acceptable will with [respect to] God,"[12] so that all physical [beings] might become spiritual. This [is the reason] he came into the world: that he might create for humanity another creation.

The Usefulness of Worldly Desires

20. But you, do not look at this, for [while] he has not eliminated marriage and has not stopped the flow of desire, do not think that perhaps he takes pleasure in these things. Look, he has not made this entire world pass away, nor has he taken away its pleasure, its wealth, and its power, but he leaves it as it is in its original arrangement. He commanded you to become a stranger to it and to take it off like a worn-out coat. The fact that things remain as they are, the world or its pleasures or your desire that is in you should not be an occasion for your error, and your soul should not be bound up with something from which you had once detached yourself. These things have been left behind so that they should be

---

[12] Rom 12:2.

an occasion for your struggle and not for your desire, in order that your strong will and your intelligence—the friend of God—may examine them. The world has persisted in order to inflame you with the desire of another world. Wealth and power have remained in order to create (567) in you an eager longing for that incorruptible possession and for that indissoluble honor. Pleasures also remain in the world in order that you may be desirous of that taste of the spiritual life. Desire has also remained in your body in order to be an occasion for your goodwill, so that little by little you might receive it from the body and place it upon the soul.

Transfer Bodily Desire to the Soul

21. Therefore, do not give your desire a portion with the body, nor allow your natural pleasure to be dissolved, and the joy and sweetness in you to be eliminated, but bear them as from one house to another house, from body to soul. Just as one who takes out precious vessels from a house that he knows is going to fall down and carries them to another [house], new and solid, that he is confident will not fall down and be damaged, in the same way take all the passions that are with the body, for by their names they are an occasion for good things, and bring them to place in the dwelling place of your soul, in that house that does not fall or is destroyed or corrupted. Take the heat from the body and place it upon the soul. Take desire away from it and mix it in with the [desire] of the soul. Take its strength and mix [it] with the strength of the soul. Change everything that belongs to it so that they might belong to the soul.

Especially during Adolescence

22. Be diligent in doing these things, especially during the age of adolescence. When the passions begin to exhibit themselves—because neither in childhood nor in old age do you have [these]—how can it be easy for you to take and give to others something that does not exist? The time of passions is the time of adolescence. This is also the time of [great] strength. It is excellent that strength has been revealed along with the passions so that you might fight

with it and deliver **(568)** the good things from your body and bear and carry your wealth from one place to another. Whoever during his adolescence fights and is victorious over his desires is able to become strong in his soul, and this one alone is able to progress in the complete growth of virtues because he is able to give and receive. Old age is bereft of both of them, and childhood has not yet attained either of them.

Do Not Wait for Desire to Cool Down

23. Do not wait for desire to cool down by itself and diminish little by little naturally, for through this there is no grace for you. Just as your natural death is not said to be a testimony for God, because you are receiving a punishment placed upon your life and you do not have reputation or glory through this, so also through this there is no pride for you when desire should cease with strength, old age, or illness. However, your triumph is when you cool it down during the time it is warm and extinguish it during the time it is inflamed in [the body]. As soon as [desire] begins to stir in the members you should prepare the shoulder of your thought and bear and carry it to place upon the desire of the soul.

Speak to it in this way: "Why are you moving to where you will be corrupted and the sense of your pleasure will suddenly cease? So come, be stirred up in your natural place, where the sweetness of your desire does not dissolve and come to an end, and, moreover, regret does not come near your satisfaction, weakness does not follow you into the soul, **(569)** the nature of your warmth does not cool after the completion of your work, but at all times you are standing strong, your sweet taste is kept without change, liberty and confidence are being strengthened in you while you are desiring, not those things worthy of reproach and blame that are not attractive to you but those things by whose desire you are stirred up naturally. Moreover, the desire for them is glory, and daily virtuous desire becomes stronger and grows, and you will progress forward. For with the body, your time is short, but with the soul, there is no end for you. And with the life of the soul your pleasure will remain immortally. With the body, the union with another body will inflame you. Yet with the soul, the union with the Holy Spirit will set you on fire. Therefore, do not be united to a corrupt body, [for] there will be no room there for you to be stirred up unless the soul has lost its discernments, and the corruption and marred things of the body are hidden from its face. But if at the moment you are searching for your pleasure discernment should shine upon the soul, at once your work will cease and there will be no outlet for your corrupting pleasures."

Soul Desires Better Things

24. You[13] should speak such things like these to desire when you are bringing it from the body to the place of the soul. Therefore, may [desire] accept from you the promises and good advice, and it will come to receive something better than what it is leaving. In the same way that desire is placed in the body naturally, so the desire of virtues is placed in the soul, **(570)** and when the soul desires naturally, its desires are spiritual things. When there is a lawful union, it is united with the Spirit. From this union holy and pure children will be engendered. Just as the union of the body creates pleasure in the members and corruptible heat stirs throughout the body, so also when the soul is united to the Spirit, it will receive spiritual pleasure and acquire heat rapidly and mightily in order to fight against the vices that are the opponent of its pleasure. When its soul has tasted this sweetness that it will have from the union with the Spirit, the desire of marriage will completely die in it.

Only One Desire Possible

25. Know from experience that it is as a result of the absence of the sensation of the Spirit's desire that the flesh's desire is aroused in your members. It is not possible that both of them could enter into you together. As long as the warmth of the Spirit is in you, the [desire] of the body is cold. And as long as the heat of the body

---

[13] Lavenant reads the variant (Mss. B and E) ܡܢܟܘܢ—"spoken by you," instead of text ܡܢܢ—"spoken by us."

is in you, [the desire] of the Spirit is cold. These two desires are set one against the other: against the desire of the Spirit [is] the desire of the body. Just as these [desires] are different from one another, all their actions are also different one from the other. This one takes hold of members and that [other] one sets thoughts on fire. The instrument of one is the form of the body, and that of the other is the nature of the soul. Agitation accompanies the one and orderliness [accompanies] that [other] one. The one, during the time it is being satisfied, obscures the light of thoughts and eliminates from the mind **(571)** knowledge and wisdom. But that other one fills the mind with light and gathers into the soul the knowledge and wisdom of the Spirit. That [desire] of the body, once it has been satisfied, makes a person weak and contrite, so that he is ashamed before every person, even before himself, and fears everything. But that [desire] of the Spirit places strength and valor in the soul, contempt concerning everything visible, self-assurance with people, and the pure observation of God. The confidence in him with regard to human beings he [already] has with regard to himself. That [desire] of the body is the teacher of folly, for a person who continually serves this desire is not able to become wise. But that desire of the Spirit not only acquires for human beings the knowledge of the world's soul but also delves the mind into the living movements of the Spirit and dresses the human being with readiness and preparation toward everything that is good. It stimulates his mind [to respond] quickly to every deed of the Spirit, and all his soul's movements are stirred up with vitality, strength, and virility. While this desire does not even allow the body's laziness to approach a person, yet if the body should tolerate laziness by its natural coldness or by reason of diseases and weakness, at once the ferment of this desire will warm it up and with its heat drive away the coldness of the body, and from here, a person is awake **(572)** and prepared for divine activities.

Spiritual Fervency

26. Those [who are] spiritual accomplish the way of their deeds, not by the natural heat of the body but because they are spiritually

fervent, being light and ready for deeds such as these, as also Paul commands that we should arouse this fervency of the Spirit in ourselves, for by it all spiritual activities are accomplished and by its strength we will complete the course of this road. "Be spiritually fervent."[14] Because there is also fervency for the desire of the body, Paul distinguishes for us by his word and teaches us in which desire we should be fervent. Be fervent in the desire of the Spirit, so that your every orientation and all your work may be spiritual.

Just as the blood's heat chases laziness from the body that the coldness of phlegm produces, so does the spirit's fervency chase from the soul and the body the negligence born from error and the lack of the love of God. Just as when natural heat rises up and approaches the heart and is mixed in, it makes a person eager and ready, alert and light with regard to the activities of the world, so also [does] the Spirit's heat, when it approaches the soul's mind and makes a person eager for his own edification regarding these heavenly things instead of the world—for the gathering of spiritual commerce, to utter judgment against those who pillage his inheritance, to desire an incorruptible union, to become the father to immortal children, **(573)** to be anxious and acquire, reflect and gather together, to amass and to guard.

Therefore, a person is prepared for all these spiritual and heavenly things by the fervency of the Spirit, and Paul has taught us well that we should become spiritually fervent, because just as coldness is dissolved and eliminated in the presence of heat, so in the presence of the fervency of this spiritual heat laziness will flee and negligence will be chased away, listlessness will cease, supposition will be dissolved, error will be taken away, and all the shadows of sin will turn away to hide themselves completely. Just as natural strength is born from heat, and weakness has control over the members through coldness, so by spiritual heat the soul acquires strength, courage, and valor, and chases away completely by excellent actions every [kind of] laziness that occurs to the soul or to the body. Just as the magnitude of its flame and intensity of

[14] Rom 12:11.

its light are in proportion to [its] flame, so according to the level of heat found in the soul is its fervency in spiritual things, and knowledge and wisdom that has power over the divine treasures.

Spiritual Strength in Old Age

27. Therefore, insofar as there is still heat in your body, and natural desire is living in your members, be diligent and ignite spiritual heat in yourself and awaken divine desire in your thoughts, so that while [one] desire is jealous of [another] desire, and one flame contends with [another] flame, the desire of the Spirit will be strengthened and take the victory, since victory is naturally appropriate to it. For during the time **(574)** you have strength for the service of the body's desire, be eager to make your strength become the servant of the Spirit's desire, because the Holy Spirit does not work its effects in idle bodies, nor also in persons who are cold from old age does it show clearly the discernments of divine wisdom. Whoever during his adolescence engages his strength in the service of evil desires, in the time of illness of his old age he will not receive divine knowledge. However, when natural health ceases from him and he attains the level of old age, he will be completely useless and [become] cold and feeble equally in his soul and in his body. But if you wish that the heat of your adolescence may be available for you during your old age, labor with your strength in the time of your adolescence and entrust this heat into the hands of your soul. Because the soul does not grow old with the body, when the body is weak in old age you will bring forth from the treasure house of your soul and nourish yourself during your old age by these deposits you have committed to the soul. When the body's strength has weakened, you will find strength with [the soul]. When [the body's] heat has become cold, by [the soul's] own fervency you will be warmed up by your works. When the strength of the members has dissipated, you will be fortified with your works by your thoughts, and when natural desire has ceased with the body's heat, the Spirit's desire will remain with you, which at all times is shared and spiritual children are engendered.

[One age] is the time to sow and another is [the time] of harvest.[15] Therefore, sow virtues into your soul during your adolescence, so that you may reap them from [the soul] during your old age. **(575)** Therefore, if you desire to live in marriage, try to place in yourself this desire that conceives and engenders even in old age. Physical union is not powerful enough at all times and natural desire is not retained in the members at every age. Yet this [desire] of the Spirit is not like this, for all ages [share in] it, if the same age of adolescence is known to it. Therefore, while there is a bridge that crosses over from the body to the soul, cross over while there still is strength in your legs to walk, while there still is light for you to walk by, while the shadows of old age are not yet looming over you and you are remaining in the place of the body.

Anger Useful against Desire

28. Therefore, stir up anger in yourself against desire, because when love is stirred up desire accompanies it. Take on anger and rage so that they may become an opportunity for you to set out against [desire]. Just as love is necessary for you against anger, so anger is useful for you against desire. Desire is peaceful and tranquil on its arrival, while dissoluteness accompanies it [along with] lukewarmness, negligence, ways of licentiousness, and movements and shameful ways that are the adversaries of courage. But when desire looks upon you through these means, put on the armor of anger and confront it. Just as the fragility of infants' sleep is connected to how fast one who gazes upon them with a fearful face runs away, terrifying them, so also you will chase away the infancy and importunity of desire if **(576)** you show it faces full of anger and indignation.

Picking Flowers of Virtue

29. Therefore, pick from the midday of adolescence the flowers of the virtues, and gather and collect for yourself fruits of all kinds[16]

---

[15] Eccl 3:1-2.
[16] Typographical error: written ܪܟܐܪ, read ܪܟܐܪ, "kinds."

in order that they may be kept for you for the winter of old age. One who lives completely in the body, in the time of his old age completely loses it. But whoever in his adolescence is fervent in the desire of the Spirit will remain without change until the end of his life. There is no body that retains its natural [faculties] without end. But[17] some of them cease before the end of life and some disappear with life. But all of them are pillaged and taken away from the body and return to the soul, if there is a discerning mind that knows how to make them return. Look, although natural life is clearly dissolved by natural death, yet it is retained spiritually with the soul; so also in this same manner the rest of the natural things of the body cease—these which are from old age and from the body—when they are committed into the hands of the soul, they will remain with the life of the soul without end.

No Idle Soul

30. Therefore, desire does not have the strength to persuade you if your will does not accept an advocate with it. On account of this, it is like one who knowing his weakness does not approach you without your consent. However, when it has received a thought to become its guide, then it will enter to light its fire in the members. But as soon as you have sensed the corruptible fire that takes control in your body, light the living fire that is in your soul. When you have sensed your members are devoted to the service of desire, occupy your thoughts with the worship of the knowledge of the divine mysteries. Therefore, do not let desire come to find you idle, and see, it will not accomplish its wills in you. Find yourself living **(577)** before it in the Spirit so that by the fire in you, you may extinguish its fire. Wherever it seizes an opportunity, cut it off there, and wherever it begins to enter you, close the door there before it and shut it out.

---

[17] Typographical error: written ܐܝܐ, "I," read ܐܠܐ, "but."

The Body Created for the Soul

31. A despicable desire enters into us from the outside, for that which is attached to us naturally, whether of the soul or of the body, is placed in us for the service of virtues. Because the soul is also able to desire God and the body is able to be moved by its natural desire, it is excellent that [one] desire was established against [another] desire, so that when they are mixed into one another they will establish a single action of pure and holy desire. The causes that stir up the soul's desire are from above, but those of the body are from below where the body's nature is. However, [God] did not create it to desire these things, but that in union with the soul [the body] might desire spiritual things. Look, even if [the body] is formed from the earth[18] and consists of various ingredients, nevertheless, it is not formed by the earth, that is, in order to be named or called an earthly body, but it was created by the Creator to exist for the soul, that is, to be the minister of its wills in everything and to be associated with all the virtues. We ought to consider then that its actions are not from where our body is, but to observe there the purpose of its works, where it was made. It was made for the spirit and not for the earth. It was ordained to become spiritual and not corruptible. It is called the body so that through this name it might be known that it was taken from the earth. He is still called a human being so that through this it might be revealed that he is united to a living soul.

Three Names of a Person

32. It is excellent that this person of the human being is called by three names: by [two] unique ones[19] and by a name **(578)** that is common—body and soul and human being—so that by that [name] of the body its physical nature might be known because it is from the earth, by the name of the soul the living nature that dwells in it might be shown, [and] by the title of human being, let us learn

---

[18] Gen 2:7.
[19] ܟܢܫܐ.

the mixture of the person that was constituted from both of them. Because the body does not have thoughts, and the soul has no visible actions, they were correctly merged with one another, one that is the fount of thoughts along with that [other] one which is the vessel of active service, so that by both of them a virtuous body might be established. Whoever seeks to degrade the body because it has no thoughts, let him honor it because it is the minister of [good] works. Whoever seeks to disparage the soul because it does not perform good works through public actions, may it grow in his eyes because it is the source of our thoughts of virtues.

Warm Desire of the Spirit

33. The Spirit's desire is warm in that case in which the body's desire is also warm, but they are not on the same level, for according to the subtlety of the soul is also the warmth of its desire; and according to the heaviness of the body, so is the fire of its desire cold. If it seems that it is warm in those things that are physical and lax, it is not because its nature is strong and warm but because their will is dissolute and cold. Understand that as long as the heat of the body's desire is cold and as long as the soul's desire is warm, by those things that happen to both of them, look, whenever the body's desire is stirred up in the members, people watching will also make it cold. If one should hear a rumor of a threat, if some kind of threat is uttered **(579)** against him—a sudden shock, another passion contrary to it if it should be aroused in him by a person, an admonition and reproof of friends or neighbors, the memory of judgment by people, the memory of the impotence of nature, thinking about the disfigurements of that face by which desire is captivated, hunger and thirst, heat and cold outside of the norm, illness and disease—if these occur, and many other things such as these, whenever they happen, they will quickly extinguish and eliminate the heat of the body's desire. Yet nothing is able to extinguish the warm and spiritual desire of the soul when it catches fire completely in the thoughts of the soul, as those testify through their acts in whom the divine fire of this desire burns. The entire world has fought with them and was not able to extinguish their

desire—kings and rulers and authorities—not by a threat of words only, but also by afflictions and harsh punishments, imprisonments and torments, prisons and severe punishments of all sorts, fire and combs [for torture], swords and wild animals, and everything that causes suffering and makes [one] ill through temporal afflictions. Not one of all such things has been able to cool down and make the warm power of this desire cold. However, the contrary has happened, and these things have become the fuel for the fire of their desire. As a fire is fed by wood, rubbish, and fatty oils, so also the good desire in them was acceptable nourishment **(580)** from afflictions and torments. When fire was approaching their bodies, that fire of divine desire in them was becoming increasingly stronger and all the more on fire, especially because it was victorious over contrary things.

The Return of Strength

34. Because ordinarily that victory that takes place over harmful things affirms and strengthens the person in the love of what he loves. When he has removed the obstacles in front of him and has taken away the splinters before his feet, he walks more easily and runs without hindrance. When he has crushed his enemies under his strength, his strength will become all the more powerful, because that strength taken from those who hate him will be added to him and that strength subtracted from them will revert to him. But when the soul's desire fights with the flesh's desire, not only does it cool down its heat, but [the soul's desire] reverts [the flesh's] heat back to itself so that [the flesh] might become a servant of its will and be mixed in it with spiritual fervency, and not serve the body's desire by union with another [body].

On account of this, the Creator also made the body's desire warm, because the desire placed in the soul is warm. From here whenever the soul wishes to be stirred up by its own natural desire, it shares the heat of the body's desire, reverting back to its goodwill, and in this way will perform an excellent work. Not only through this, but also in every one of the natural portions whenever the soul wishes to be stirred up for the service of these external things, it approaches the members that are related to its secret portions, while seeing through the eye and hearing through the ear with the rest of all the senses and members that are servants of its inner will. Just as with these things **(581)** when it also wishes to desire, it will share the body's desire with its spiritual desire, perform the work of divine love, and ignite itself with the love of the life of righteousness, just as the signs of the inflammation of this desire are visible in the external members of the body, not for hideous movements or for work of the service of foolish desire, but because while they are warm they are tranquil, and while they are fervent they are calm.

The Warmth of Physical Desire

35. Then, may the heat of the desire mixed in our members not be a reason for guilt, but let us observe that purpose for which the Maker has mixed it in us and let us use it according to this order. But whenever the body's desire is warm in the body, it is the opponent of purity, yet when it is mixed with the soul's desire it is an assistant to virginity. Then it is proper that the strength of desire not be distributed outside, but let it be gathered up and the soul's desire accumulated inwardly, so that being mixed one into the other, like light into light, they will burn one light that is perfected in purity.

Strengthening of the Soul through Asceticism

36. The nourishments that belong to every one of these desires are different from one another. With fasting, asceticism, vigil, prayer, mortifications,[20] and physical labors, the desire of the soul is increased and strengthened. By these things that are the opposite—comforts, delights, pleasures, food and drink, ornate clothing, and conversation with licentious and dissolute people—the desire of the body grows and is ignited in us. Look, it is not as a result of the body becoming enfeebled through labors that the soul also becomes weak with [the body]; rather inasmuch as [the body] is weakened, the soul will become even more virile and stronger.

---

[20] Typographical error: written ܟܘܦܢܐ, read ܟܘܒܫܐ.

Due to this it will make [the body] even weaker so that it might become stronger. There is a distinction between the body becoming naturally enfeebled (582) and the soul weakening itself with this purpose to live by its natural strength. When in this sense the soul weakens the body and reduces the power of its strength through austerities, what Paul said is accomplished with them, "As much as the outer person is disintegrating, that which is inside is being renewed day by day."[21]

Gather Provisions for Old Age

37. On account of this Solomon also counsels us to commence from our youth with [ascetical] labors for the sake of good things, and from the beginning of our life to be instructed in this learning so that we might be victorious over whatever is in us and does not agree with us, and be subject to the desire that is contrary to our [soul's] desire. From here every person who in the time of his strength is victorious over the weakness in him, in the time of his weakness he will be found strong. That is to say, if he takes upon himself in his adolescence the stability of old men, he will find for himself the strength of young men in his old age.

Therefore, take provisions for yourself for the time of your old age, O disciple, from the field of your adolescence, so that when you have ceased from your body's labor, you will find the soul's rest for yourself. For you will not be at war all during your life. As for this, your Maker, having pity on you, has limited your conflict only during a determined period. But he has made your pleasure endless. In the beginning and at the end you are without war, either because the desire has not yet been stirred or it has grown cold after being stirred up. Whether you wish or not, in the time of your old age you will find yourself empty and will not be able to fulfill your desire on account of the weakness of the body, not because you have extinguished the desire, but [the desire] extinguishes itself in you.

[21] 2 Cor 4:16.

Ageless Soul

38. The fire of desire that the Maker has placed in the body's nature for the procreation of the human race ceases toward the end of the life of **(583)** a person during his old age, because he is not a progenitor his entire life, for neither in his youth nor in his old age is he able to do this. In this he resembles not only himself but also beasts and animals, birds and plants. In the same way are also these species that do not show the fruits of their types in their youth or in their old age, because every one of the species is limited, and its propagation is also placed under a limit, especially since it is engendered in the body and through the body it is perpetuated. On account of this it is limited like the body. Just as the life of the body is limited, so also is its strength limited, while not even its strength is evident in every period of its life. As I have said, neither in the beginning nor at the end of his life is procreative strength with him.

But in the soul, because there is no structure, there is no old age, and the warmth of its desire never dissipates unless an evil illness happens to it. Just as the body grows old or becomes weak by the mixture of its components, so also the soul becomes sick and weakens by sin and by evilness. Through its weakness the heat of its desire is extinguished, so that from here it is not even able to show its fruits. Therefore, whoever weakens desire in his adolescence, this one will be found strong in his soul during his old age, and after completing his war his strength will remain with him. This is also what happens to worldly warriors, that not only when they are standing in the line of battle and fighting with their enemies do they possess their strength, but also after the battle has come to an end, their strength **(584)** will be visible within them. Their strength does not vanish with their combat, even if in the time of conflict itself its energy is more evident because it is assisted and comes to be by zeal.

Building Purity

39. In the same way also you whose soul is clothed with the power of purity in order to be for you a weapon for war against fornication, do not think that with the end of your battle the time

of your strength has also ended, but at the end of the battle you will become new all the more, although not to fight but to cultivate virtues. With this strength you accomplish two things: you are fighting with fornication and are completing an edifice of purity. Just as when a craftsman is given an old building to renovate, he pulls it down with his strength and with his strength builds it back up, so also is your own new building and the tearing down of your old building, both of which are accomplished by your own strength, when you have torn down fornication—the way of all evils—and have built modesty—the pure way ascending to heaven.

Fornication Accompanies All Evils

40. In which evil is there not fornication? Which is the despicable thing that does not enter through its door? If the lust of the belly is its fortifier and if the lust of gold serves it, rage and anger are attached to it, and through these it fights against its opponents. Sadness travels in its footsteps and shame accompanies the end of its action. Perhaps also vainglory which is considered to be its opposite is the assistant of its despicable deed. How many times have they returned because of it to the passion of fornication after the end of their labors, believing they had arrived at the haven of rest? Because they were seized by it through their negligence, it hardened their intelligence and clouded their vision, which had been made pure **(585)** through the victory over the desires of the body, and made them return to the desire of fornication which they had defeated at the beginning of their struggle. So then, one is not mistaken who calls fornication the way of all evil things.

Fornication of Thoughts

41. But fornication, I say, is not a matter of the body alone, but more than that, it is a matter of the soul. Because with the layman, adultery is in the action, but with the monk [it is] in the thoughts. It was spoken to the worldly person, "You shall not commit adultery"; but to the monk, "You shall not desire." The war of thoughts is not at all evident to the layman. On account of this he is not victorious over his desire through strength but serves it lawfully,

this being natural. But the monk does not have this authority and his victory is not visible in the absence of action, but his triumph is proclaimed through his victory over thought. Because he is a spiritual soldier for Christ, his victory is also spiritually perfected by inner thoughts. He purifies the place of his soul through his self-control, so that when he has chased away the thought from there, his soul's entire house is visible in light. Wherever there is light the cloud of sin does not enter, because sin is committed in darkness even as righteousness [is performed out] in the light.

Beautiful Faces

42. Therefore, may this destructive passion not entice you, and may it not subtly have control over your thoughts. Great is its opportunity with you, especially when you are dwelling among people; it becomes greater in the memory of different persons, and by means of the beauty and the sight of the body. The desire of fornication, because it is born from the flesh, also desires the flesh. Just as the desire of the belly longs for different tastes, **(586)** in the same way the passion of fornication desires [different] faces beautiful of appearance. Its love does not remain watching [only] one of them, because it is not people it loves, but beauty for [the sake of] passion. But when its enticement is great, it is also not based on vision's beauty but grows and becomes stronger by itself. When it has constrained the soul's strength in a hidden way, it is openly victorious over the self-control of the body. But if it should be defeated by the body while it is wide awake, it will turn to fight it during sleep. The memories of those faces driven away by the soul wide-awake are defiled and replenished during sleep and cause the person to be defeated forcefully during his sleep. On account of this, asceticism is necessary for you in order to reduce the oversaturation of the body, so that fornication might not find an opportunity in your members during sleep.

Dangers during Sleep

43. This is the custom of this passion that fights first through the members of the body and [then] moves toward desire, as [is

the case] with an animal. But if one should acquire discernment and prevent the stirring of his members from acting, it will turn around to enter him with a thought and entice him secretly so that through [a thought] it might awaken also the members to an act of desire. But if [the passion] also is defeated by thoughts, it will be defeated in every way when the thought observes God, and patience and asceticism are also found with him. Then this evil passion will come to him with sleep, and during sleep it will fight with the self-control of the soul. But if this should happen to us we should not let it go without remorse; especially if a vision (587) of faces is depicted in our mind, this makes clearly known that it is something left over from the waking state. If a bodily emission happens without the sight of faces, it is the oversaturation found in the members. Because the body is not brought low by asceticism, an occasion for desire is found in its members, and if [the body] is not fully aware of what is happening, [it is because] it is plunged into excessive sleep.

Therefore, the disciple ought to defeat the passion in all ways in [one's] action and in thought and in the emission during sleep. Yet the fact that he might be defeated in sleep is proof that he was not victorious in thought; and the fact that he was not victorious in thought is a testimony to the fact that he was defeated in action. On account of this, reduction of food and lessening of sleep are useful in order that excess not fight with the body and so that we might not be defeated in a dream outside of our will. Just as this too will not happen during sleep to those who are weak and old in years, because now the emission of fornication has vanished and dried up from their members, in the same way nocturnal fornication no longer happens to a body that becomes weak through the labors of asceticism, because if thoughts should stir up and demons should be enticing, an opportunity will not be found for the emission of desire in the members. The solitaries also fight with sleep as with desire and eating, because like these it makes the mind dense and increases desire. If one should bring nourishment to the body only on account of its need, and likewise give it sleep, insofar as it is possible it will become free from the passion of fornication. If its waking state does not result in the wandering of thoughts, but (588) with a mind that is recollected and sings and prays, it will drive away this passion from thoughts, and if it departs from the soul, it will no longer remain with the body.

Mortifying Your Members

44. "Therefore, mortify your members that are on earth,"[22] the blessed Paul commands us. If the members die according to the teaching of the Apostle, you will have no place in them for the stirring of desire. What can a desire do in a dead body? The word of the Apostle shows that it is possible for the members to die because he was not commanding something that is not able to exist. In particular he said, "Your members that are on earth," as if it were that we have other members in heaven or from heaven. This then is the meaning of "Make your members die that are on earth." Because the desires are from the earth, they will have power over the members that are from the earth. But if we should make these members die through enduring fasting and abstinence and asceticism, and along with these through constant vigil and the vigilance of prayer, then desires from the earth will not be received. What can passions do to dead members? [The Apostle] calls the members that are in heaven [members] of the new person and told them that they are from heaven. Just as is the case with the earthly person, so also are the earthly [members], and just as the heavenly person so also are the heavenly [members].[23] Therefore, he called these [members] of the new person heavenly. With these things, the old passions should not have power over them, because it is not **(589)** fitting for them and they are not their own. Therefore, how can the passion of fornication have authority over the member of the new person, one who has become one body with Christ?

---

[22] Col 3:5.
[23] 1 Cor 15:48.

The Limit of Words

45. But I—not by the grandeur of a gift that is with us only and by the abundance of our honor—I say that we should be victorious over this passion of fornication, but also over these things attached to the passion—a confused face, sadness, remorse, deprivation of liberty, obscuring of the mind, hardening of thoughts, and confusion of opinions. Therefore, all such things like these enter into the soul following the passion of fornication. But if we endure, are victorious, and establish in our soul the beautiful image of purity after victory over this passion, the soul will immediately be filled with joy and liberty with God and with people. It will enjoy the pleasure of its thoughts and receive the light of divine knowledge. It will also put on strength and be filled with confidence.

The soul receives from this victory such a pleasure as this that we are not able to explain by word because even the soul no longer can find the words. Whatever is found through action is pleasing also in the literal sense. These things that are acquired verbally will also bring joy verbally. Therefore, because the victory over desire came to be through the soul's strength with the assistance of grace, so also the pleasure that happens to it after this is performed in the same order because it is from [the soul's] natural health and from the gift of the grace of God. For in that order which is **(590)** twice the pleasure and comfort of the body—because sometimes one takes pleasure from natural health, sometimes one receives pleasures from foods and desirable things that are external—so it also happens to the soul that sometimes when it stands in the purity of its mind and acquires its natural health it senses its pleasure. Sometimes when it is worthy of the grace of God and the contemplation of spiritual revelations, it will receive this pleasure. Because [the soul] takes pleasure in it, it knows and senses spiritual pleasure spread out into all its parts. But there is no way that it might put into words or verbal teaching this sweetness and spiritual pleasure it has sensed, because it has received a taste of this sweetness in a spiritual manner. When the body receives the pleasure of eating from physical tastes and from seasonings, or is moved by the sight of a face in the pleasure of desire, or its hearing is delighted by the sweet sounds of singing in different kinds of tuneful songs, or the body receives the pleasure of comfort from a gentle touch—because all these things are physical and bodily and are actually[24] pleasing to the body—a person is able to speak of this pleasure by a word, and because bodily things have pleased the body and assuaged [it] with a complex and incarnate sound, he [can] speak concerning their pleasure as much as a person wishes. Because the pleasure of the soul is not from bodies, nor from their physical actions, **(591)** nor from their corruptible tastes, but its pleasure is from the spiritual contemplation of everything it is able to sense once it has found its natural health, it is not able to describe this pleasure happening to it by a word. However, it finds pleasure in a hidden way and rejoices invisibly because its joy is not from itself.

Soul's Natural Pleasure

46. Just as the soul is inside the body, which by the strength of its life allows it to sense the sweetness of everything, so within the soul is spiritual contemplation that customarily pleases the soul. When the soul finds enjoyment in this way its pleasure is natural. According to the order of its nature it receives pleasure because the world of the soul is within it, just as the world of the body is outside of it. But when the soul derives pleasure outside of its nature, [the soul] takes pleasure from the body or from the world. For a pleasure like this happens when it enjoys satisfying the body's desires, whether by the lust of the belly, or by the performance of the passion of fornication, or from these worldly things, it receives honors, praises, singing voices, and the pleasure of the physical sight of visible things. All these things, whether of the body or of the world in which the soul finds pleasure, give it pleasure outside of its nature. It does not find pleasure on account of its health, **(592)** but on account of its illness.

---

[24] Typographical error: written ܐܬܒܣܡܬ, read ܐܬܪܓܪܓܬ.

Unhealthy Pleasures outside Natural Order

47. Therefore, there are pleasures that serve the health of the soul or of the body, just as [there are also pleasures that serve] their illness. It is evident then that when the soul delights in evil pleasures, its delight is outside of its nature. It finds comfort not in what is appropriate for it, but in something foreign to its natural health. Look, when its body commits adultery and performs this action that transgresses the law, pleasure comes, as it seems, to the soul from this. However, when [the soul] fights and is victorious over its body's desire and completes the victory with an excellent purpose and with discernment acceptable to God, after this victory [the soul] also receives pleasure. Just as from the fulfillment of desire and from the victory over desire, it receives pleasure from both of them together. However, that pleasure which it has received from the body—as I have mentioned how many times—is outside the order of nature, and that [pleasure] which it has by the victory over desire is natural pleasure, and just as a healthy person perceives this sweetness, this pleasure will be enjoyed legitimately and naturally.

Ineffable Pleasures of the Soul

48. These who are victorious over the battle of desire by a spiritual goal perceive this thing of which I am speaking, yet while perceiving their pleasure are not able to articulate their pleasure. How shall they describe it, for they do not take pleasure in it bodily? Because everything belonging to the Spirit is not from the body, let us seek [these pleasures] in their place and there they shall be found. Where **(593)** they are found, there they will be enjoyed. Where their pleasure is, there will be also their joy, a joy that rejoices and is not visible, a joy in which there is also strength. Just as above, when desire is victorious over the soul it shows it to be weak and miserable, clothed with shame, so also here when the soul defeats desire it becomes full of strength, joy, and confidence after this victory and acquires a clear eye so that it may perceive authoritatively the spiritual knowledge mixed into all visible things. However, just as these things that satisfy the body's desires sense the body's pleasure, so also these things that serve the spiritual

desires of the soul enjoy the spirit's desire. Just as the soul's illness
senses the pleasure that comes from the body's desires, so also the
soul's health senses this pleasure [of the spirit]. If one should seek
to perceive something said by the words written down, he will be
seeking a matter outside of its place and time, and he will not find
the fruit he seeks because it is not from the tree he seeks to pick.
Just as every fruit is found in its [own] tree and is picked from
there, so also spiritual matters are visible in their [proper] places,
and these rational and spiritual fruits that are naturally sweet are
found in their [own] tree.

The War against Foreign Rule

49. Then after its victory over the passion of fornication, the
soul picks the spiritual fruit that pleases **(594)** and enlightens it.
Whoever seeks [spiritual fruit] will find it after the victory over this
passion, a victory occurring not only in the body but also in the
soul. Sometimes this desire fights with the body and sometimes it
battles with the thoughts of the soul, for as long as its fire ignites the
[body's] members it will not fight with thoughts. How can it fight
with something that does not contend with it? As long as thoughts
are subjugated to desire and serve its will, [desire] will command
all the members like a mistress, and it will satisfy with authority
all its comforts in the body's location with which it dwells. But if
the mind should become the seer of its soul and perceive that a
foreign regime dwells in its body's space, and thieving and pillaging passions are residing in its members, it prepares then to drive
them out and begins to stir up a war to make the foreigners depart
who have been found inside his house. Because their dwelling is
pleasing to the desires, they will also fight them in order not to be
expelled, so that from here on a war of thoughts will be stirred up
against passions, and that of passions against thoughts, and victory
will be found wherever the strength is greater.

Nothing Secret before God

50. Therefore, desire in the members is completed by action,
but it is not served at all times as it wishes. But there is nothing

that prevents whatever is hidden in thoughts from materializing into a deed, except only the vision of God. On account of this the prophet also declares "woe" to those who defile themselves upon their beds and uncovers the foolish thoughts they are thinking and saying: " 'The walls of my house surround **(595)** me, and the roof of my house protects me'; but he does know that the eyes of the Lord are brighter, ten thousand times more than the sun, and see all the ideas of human beings."[25] While the saying seems in its revelation to be [reproving] that person who is iniquitous upon his bed in his house in secret [and] those who fulfill their desires in darkness in their homes hidden from the sight of people, nevertheless, the word of that prophet is reproving all the more that thought that is secretly fornicating in the soul; for instead of walls, the members of the body are surrounding it, and instead of a roof, the vessel of the heart covers it, and while dwelling in this concealed and hidden place, fulfilling here his adultery, believing that he is not visible to anyone, fleeing not from sin but from the sight of people, he does not understand that before the luminous vision of God there is nothing hidden. The vision of God that examines hidden things is ten thousand times brighter than the light of the sun. Just as nothing is hidden before the light of the sun, but it reveals and displays before view everything on which it shines, so also the seeing eye of the knowledge of God examines the hidden [actions] of people and observes the thoughts that are hidden in the mind, and while a thought has not yet committed adultery through actions, [God] considers him an adulterer by his will and judges him by his intention[26] and not by his actions.

Thoughts the Root of Actions

51. There are some who find pleasure in action and some who find pleasure in the shadow, and there is an adultery that exists in the body and one that is fulfilled **(596)** in the soul. Therefore,

---

[25] Sir 23:18-19.

[26] Lavenant suggests reading "his intention"—*nīšēh* (ܢܝܫܗ), rather than "his pleasure"—*neyāḥēh* (ܢܝܚܗ).

464 The Discourses of Philoxenos of Mabbug

whoever drives away adultery from the heart, it is apparent that also he does not allow it into the body. Thoughts are the root of actions. Just as if a tree is disturbed from its root and its growth that is solidly established in the earth is weakened its leaves will become shriveled at once and its fruits will wither and its whole appearance will be changed, in the same way also, if the root of desire is disturbed from the heart and weakened, at once the external actions begin to dry up; for just as the root is in the earth, a thought is also in the heart and makes external actions increase, whether of good or of evil, and just as trees are grown by means of water, so also are actions by the watering of thoughts. Just as plants will dry up that are placed by a spring if the spring should dry up, so the works of desires that are placed by the source of the heart from which they drink[27] and grow will wither if someone plugs up its own spring of evil thought. The fact that a person may cut off desire from thought is the perfect victory through actions. There are no evident times for this desire of thoughts, but it is stirred up and satisfied at all times, especially whenever there are occasions from the outside that serve it. So then let us be especially careful and consider wisely, and from wherever desire is looking upon us, from there let us shut the door before it.

Subduing the Body

52. Desire is mixed into the movement of our life, and as long as life stirs in our body, so also desire **(597)** is stirred up and pulsates in it. However, just as death makes the movement of natural life cease, it will likewise silence the movements of desire in the killing of the old person. Therefore, if from natural movements of the body desire confronts us, let us know that mortification and constraint are necessary for the body, and let us remember the helpful word of the Apostle, who said to us with regard to his own person, "I constrain and I subdue my body."[28] While we are examining this, let us subdue our body and constrain the animal desire that stirs and

---

[27] Written: ܘܫܬܐ; read ܘܫܬܝ.
[28] 1 Cor 9:27.

leaps around in it, while we place upon it the weight of an extended fast and the reduction of eating and the lessening of drinking; if these things are sufficient for its constraint when we approach it in measure, [well and good], but if not, then let us double and increase them, and if such things are not sufficient by themselves to subdue it, let us look for other things that are harder for it, and let us use them with it.

The Danger of Too Much Water

53. More than anything else, reduction of drink is necessary for this battle due to the desires, especially this desire of fornication [which] is nourished by moisture. If moisture nourishes it, then the dryness that happens from the reduction of drinking will dry it out and heat it up. It is just as when Gideon the warrior turned away from the battle those who went down on their knees and drank [their] fill of water, yet those who drank a little, lapping water with their hands to their mouth, he led them with him into battle against **(598)** the Midianites.[29] These things were discovered and accomplished not simply by [Gideon], but God had commanded him that he should do it this way. While he was gathering a large [number of] people for battle to go against the camp of Midian—which is compared with the passion of fornication—God commanded him to sound the horn and to warn the people and say before them: "Anyone who is afraid and trembling, let him turn back."[30] The majority of the people who were with him turned back at this word. It is evident by this that not everyone who was summoned to battle was suitable for battle, and because there were still among them some who by their fervent mind were desiring victory while being afraid of the weariness [to be encountered] on its behalf, God told him to examine those [people] again. After he tested them by water, he turned back from the battle those who, kneeling down on their knees, used too much water in drinking, because being saturated with water is not suitable for the battle against desire. He

[29] Judg 7:2ff.
[30] Judg 7:3.

led with him to the conflict against the camp that is compared with fornication the few who hastily drank a little bit, lapping [water] with their hands to their mouths. That this was the case, as it was reported, the narrative of the book of Moses testifies, saying, "The people fornicated with the daughters of Midian and were initiated into the idols of their gods."[31]

Gideon against the Midianites

54. Because everything that was happening to them is a type of our own spiritual way of life, everything that is written regarding them demonstrates our own concerns, just as Paul also said, **(599)** "Let us not fornicate as some of them have fornicated, and in one day twenty four thousand fell."[32] Therefore, when the battle of fornication encountered this dissolute generation that went out from Egypt, they were not able to withstand it but were defeated by the beauty of the women of Midian and fornicated with them, and on the heels of this fornication, at that time a plague suddenly overwhelmed them. However, because there the fornicators had perished through the punishment suddenly inflicted on them, it was not the passion of fornication that was caused to cease, as it should have been. Here through the guidance of Gideon, he was not slaying the fornicators, but making fornication perish. On account of this, when he was about to destroy this camp that had caused that first people to sin because, as I have said, the model of fornication is shown in it, [Gideon] led a few people with him to battle against this passion, those who had drunk in haste a little bit of water, and through this they showed themselves to be competent to engage in this battle, which did in fact happen.

The Battle against Fornication

55. While he was preparing them for the conflict he made them take hold of pitchers, horns, and lamps, and they hid the lamps

[31] Num 25:1-2.
[32] 1 Cor 10:8.

inside the pitchers. They held the horns in their right hands and the pitchers in their left hands. At the instant they sounded the horns, they broke open the pitchers and the light of the lamps was visible because the sound of the trumpet is the signal of the commandment of God, that One who cries out in all his scriptures against this passion of fornication, such as: "Let us not fornicate as some of them have fornicated," as well as: "May no (600) one be found among you who fornicates and is dissolute like Esau, for with one meal he sold his birthright,"[33] or like this: "Do not err, because neither fornicators, nor adulterers, nor idol-worshipers, nor those who are corrupted, nor those who lie down with men, nor thieves, nor gluttons, nor drunkards, nor rapacious ones shall inherit the kingdom of God."[34] Or like this other one in which [Paul] said: "Everyone who is a fornicator or impure or an oppressor who is an idol-worshiper, there is no inheritance for him in the kingdom of Christ and of God."[35] And like this one in which our Lord said: "Everyone who looks at a woman in order to desire her, at once he has committed adultery with her in his heart."[36] Moreover, the apostle James said in his letter: "From where are there wars and strife in you, but from the desires that are battling in your members?"[37] Again, Peter said: "If a murderous desire comes upon you, do not suppose that something strange has happened to you because you are being sorely tested."[38] Moreover, God called out through his word to the nation of Jews: "Do not desire the wife of your neighbor."[39]

Therefore, those trumpets sounding against the camp of Midian were the type of these holy words spoken against the passion of fornication. Just as there[40] at the sound of trumpets the pitchers were broken at once because the entire people was commanded

[33] Heb 12:16.
[34] 1 Cor 6:9.
[35] Eph 5:5.
[36] Matt 5:28.
[37] Jas 4:1.
[38] 1 Pet 4:12.
[39] Exod 20:17.
[40] Written: ܒܬ ܐܘܠܬ; read ܩܐܪܝܒܘ ܩܕܬܗ ܒܬ (Ms. F).

by Gideon in this way, "As soon as you hear that I make the sound **(601)** with the trumpet,[41] you also should shout with trumpets and break the pitchers and the light of the lamps that was hidden in the pitchers will be visible."[42]

Our Spiritual Type

56. All these things are the type of our own spiritual way of life. With the sound of the trumpets the divine commandments are being made known that the moment a person makes use of them by the sound of his soul, crying out mightily against the passion of fornication, at once this desire will be chased away and destroyed by the divine voice. Just as there with the sound of the trumpets the pitchers were broken, so also here with the hearing of the commandment this desire of fornication will be broken and destroyed. Just as there with the breaking of a pitcher the light that was hidden in it became visible, so also here with the elimination of fornication the light of the knowledge of Christ will shine in the soul. In this way three things become apparent: the commandment of God is compared with the sound of the trumpet, the passion of fornication [is compared] with the pitcher that was broken, which was light and easy to break, and the light of divine knowledge that will shine in the soul with the elimination of fornication [is compared] with the lamp that was visible in the breaking of the pitcher. These things are especially known to those who have experienced them.

Control of Drink and Food

57. Therefore, this teaching shows us the battle of Gideon and informs us of these models. On account of this, [only] those who drank a little water actually went into this battle, so that while considering them, we should imitate them. Let whoever fights this battle not bloat himself with water or fill his belly with food. **(602)** Let him also not be defeated by the desire of plain foods and deal

[41] Judg 7:18.
[42] Judg 7:20.

with a full stomach, but may he remember Esau who is accused by Paul's word and is called a fornicator and a dissolute person who sold his birthright for a single meal. While Esau was not censured in this passage by the weightiness or great expense of the food, it was on account of his decadence [that he was censured], for that meal was of lentils. Because he was defeated by his desire and he ate them in a gluttonous way, he was called a fornicator and dissolute. Paul justly named this defeat fornication, for whoever was defeated by the sight of a meal of lentils, how much more would he be defeated by an attractive, beautiful person?

Against Desire

58. Let us consider also the word of God that was spoken to the Jewish nation that not only eliminates adulterous action but also the desire of thoughts. He did not say, "Do not commit adultery with the wife of your neighbor," but "do not desire the wife of your neighbor."[43] While their election was recent, the commandment that he spoke to them was mature and perfect, by which he cautions them of the desire of thoughts more than of adulterous behavior. "Do not desire."[44] If you do not desire, you also will not commit adultery. Our Lord said, "Anyone who looks at a woman in order to desire her, immediately he has committed adultery with her in his heart,"[45] because there are some who look, but not for adultery, yet simply to look and see. Whoever looks in order to commit adultery, this one is an adulterer with regard to his will and his desire. Both of the sayings suit **(603)** one another: that one, "Do not desire the wife of your neighbor," and this one that was spoken by our Lord against the adultery of thoughts, for he said above, "Do not desire." Here he said, "Do not look as if to desire," because vision in and of itself does not cause one to sin if the inner will does not agree with it.

There are some who look in order to commit adultery, and some who look in order to see. Simple vision, then, is the eye's nature,

[43] Exod 20:17; Deut 5:21.
[44] Rom 7:7.
[45] Matt 5:28.

but the vision of desire is not of the eye only, but of the will and of the thought. For if David had not looked, he also would not have desired; and if he had not desired, he would not have committed adultery. "He ascended to the roof of his palace and saw a woman bathing and he desired her. He sent [for her] and had her brought [to him] and committed adultery with her."[46] If he had but simply looked, he would not have desired, and if he had not desired, he also would not have committed adultery.

So then let us shut the door of vision before desire, for vision is not insignificant in depicting illusions in the soul. Because of this also, desire is stirred up in different ways in our members and desiring different persons. This happens to it when the vision of God is not placed before the eyes of the soul. If the memory of God is found in [the soul], all the memories of evil desire will vanish from it quickly and it will not be deprived of the vision of that insatiable beauty in order to consider a corruptible beauty.

Reminding the Soul

59. It greatly helps us for the mortification of desire to observe the corruption of nature and other things that are **(604)** dirty and filthy, for the conscience abhors these things that adhere to the body's nature. If one should consider their prodigious defilements, these too will extinguish the heat of desire. Just as the prophet of God David was mortifying the pride of human nature, he said to him, "A human being resembles a vapor, and his days pass like a shadow."[47] Moreover, while destroying confidence that [one human being] has in [another], in order that no one, whatever his condition, should tie his hope to a person, his neighbor, he said: "Do not be confident concerning a person or a ruler, for there is no redemption through him because his breath goes out and returns to his earth, and on that day all of his thoughts are destroyed."[48]

[46] 2 Sam 11:2.
[47] Ps 144:4.
[48] Ps 146:3-4.

Let us act the same way with the passion of fornication, for when it heats up inside us and disturbs our thoughts let us set against it either the memory of God and the fear of his judgment, or let us employ against it repetition of the words of the Scriptures, or let us examine its corruptibility, its weakness, and its own natural human diseases. For when one examines these things wisely and observes their end with the power of his soul and sees the emission, defilement, diseases that happen to the body, the superfluity of putrefaction in the members, and things such as these adhering to the body, one can also extinguish its desire through these things, despising and disdaining [the body], for one sees what things the desire makes him need. However, let the thought be wary when one examines the filthiness and abomination of [human] nature, lest [nature] be rejected in its eyes. For it is not in order to despise [human nature] that he should stir up these matters in himself, **(605)** but in order to mortify his desire.

Celibacy of the First Upright [People]

60. If an empowering example and an encouraging image is still necessary, let us remember the first upright [people], not only those who came after the revelation of our Savior and later, but especially those who lived before his arrival, for although perfection had not yet been transmitted to humanity, and they were not yet worthy[49] of the way of the world to come, even so purity was more honored in their eyes[50] than marriage, and everyone of them was honoring holiness[51] more than [marital] union. For Abraham, Isaac, and Jacob, who are the patriarchs of the faithful nation and the acceptable dwelling places of all the upright whose faith and compassion they have emulated, it is apparent that more than marriage—which is the perpetuator of a generation of people—they were desiring purity and separation [rather] than marriage.

---

[49] Typographical error: written ܐܘܬܕܪܐ; read ܐܘܕܪܐ.

[50] Typographical error: written ܒܣܘܬܝܗܘܢ, "in their foundations," read ܒܥܝܢܝܗܘܢ, "in their eyes."

[51] "Holiness" in Syriac asceticism is the state of celibacy.

Joseph's Remembrance of God

61. After them [came] the pure Joseph, who when he was a child of few years demonstrated by his self-control the discernment of those much older, while he had no teacher to instruct [him], no pedagogue to enlighten [him], nor a father to protect [him], nor a good example to assist [him]. Instead of all these the remembrance of God was sufficient for him. He was accomplishing beforehand by himself[52] the action of what was said finally through the word, "I have placed the Lord in front [of me] at all times in order that I may not be disturbed."[53] When his master's wife was infatuated with him due to his beautiful body and was endeavoring to entice him into an act of sin, he had been learning beforehand the philosophy of Christ's teaching **(606)** and was holding on so as not to be defeated by his desire; he was encountering a double battle from within and without. On the outside, his master's wife was fighting with him with her beauty, her words, and the enticement of her [physical] intimacy. From within, the body's desire was fighting vehemently, and while he was standing between these two tremendous struggles, he was victorious over both of them by the power of his self-control.

Therefore, consider in what straits his soul was situated at that time, when waves upon waves of desire aroused by flatteries from outside were beating against him. However, they were not turning back the strong rock of his self-control. Just like a ship that is vibrating and being shaken by the waves against it, so also the ship of Joseph's soul was being shaken. Nevertheless, because the anchor of his soul was placed above in heaven, according to the word of Paul,[54] and was not thrown down into the depths, at all times his thought was elevated to the heights. Against the desire aroused against him, he awakened also the memory of God and was terrified by the vision of his judgment. He said to that [woman] who was enticing him impurely, "My lord has given me authority over

---

[52] Written: ܡܣܩܒܗ; read ܒܩܠܡܣܗ (Ms. F).
[53] Ps 16:8.
[54] Heb 6:19.

his entire house and has not restrained me from anything, except only you who are his wife. Therefore, how can I do this great evil thing and sin against the Lord?"[55] To sin against God was more for him than all the severe judgments and violent and cruel torments, and maybe it was not by the judgment of God that he was inhibited from sinning, but by this [principle]—that one should not sin against God.

Natural Law Written on the Heart

(607) 62. For if there is in [the soul] a sense of divine life, what is the torment that will make the soul suffer like this when it acts foolishly against God? Joseph called this a great evil for one to sin against God. And truly, because it is a great fall and there is no cure for it, except by the grace of God, that a person might sin against God, as also the divine book said, "If a man should sin against the Lord, who will pray for him?"[56] But the wise and pure Joseph, regarding the fact that he might sin against his lord—for was this not his wife?—establishes it as a sin against God, because the commandment of God was violated in the transgression of natural law.

For even while that word had not yet been heard, "Do not desire" and "Do not commit adultery with your neighbor's wife," however, the action of the word was mixed into nature, because [the saying], "Whatever is hateful to you, do not do to your neighbor,"[57] is written into nature, and with signs and creative acts of God it was inscribed upon the conscience of every person so that the law of every person might be inside him. No one is able to say, "I have not yet learned to read, and I have neither read nor have come to know the letters of what is written," because the creative act of God has been drawn on the tablets of the heart.[58] As long as a person is growing in the stature of his body, he is studying in this book. Joseph, when he was only twenty years old—for he was

---

[55] Gen 39:8.
[56] 1 Sam 2:25.
[57] Matt 7:12; Tob 4:15; Acts 15:29.
[58] Prov 7:3.

standing in this season of years when this battle rose up against him—was studying inwardly these writings, **(608)** and the learning which he had received from them he was reading to his master's wife, "How can I do this evil thing and sin against God?" How will I judge myself in that matter which I have already decided? How will I condemn myself by what I have previously seen is a condemnation? That blessing which Paul gave to whoever had not judged himself by something he had discerned was delivered in fact to Joseph, and in a few years, he was demonstrating a victory that surpasses his years. Perhaps this is what Moses had received from him when he said, "May all who are registered in the census, from a twenty-year-old and up, give an offering to the Lord."[59]

Joseph an Example for the Monk

63. Look, a helpful and encouraging example [is given] to the disciple who is struggling with the desire of the flesh, although matters are neither equal nor comparable, because the promise of Joseph does not resemble your own. Providence had not determined that he should become a virgin or a solitary, but to become a father to a numerous people, as the Exodus has shown. Moreover, there was no model available before him there, no example of another person who might be of help, and no law was written that was preventing him from this, because Moses had not yet been named, and not one of the prophets had spoken, and no commandments of those who teach the perfection of Christ our Savior were as yet heard in the world. Moreover, the way of asceticism that powerfully smites desire was not found with him, and he was not exempted from the sight of and conversation with women that also inflame desire. But in a manner of speaking, he was fighting rampant desire, **(609)** that is, he was dwelling with an untethered lion.[60] In a new struggle inside the struggle of self-control, he has taken the victory.

But as for a monk or a solitary, or someone who has separated himself [from society] by a promise of God to whom these things

[59] Exod 30:14.
[60] See Sir 25:16.

are spoken, there are many things helpful to him. First is the covenant that they had committed to with God, for this memory by itself is sufficient to teach us divine philosophy. But along with these things is also dwelling in the desert, removed and exempt from all disturbing encounters. Moreover, if [one resides] in the monastery, whether of many or of few [monks], these walls surrounding [the monastery] protect the one enclosed from wandering in the world.

The Purpose of a Monastery

64. It is necessary for whoever wishes to be seen as a victor in the battle against this passion that he should be exempt also from encounters with women and from the sight of faces that stir up desire in him. Because just as the lust of the belly desires different foods, so also this defiled passion of fornication desires faces beautiful of appearance, and its desire is fettered to attractive flesh. As long as the sight of [a face like] this is distant from him, the memory of its appearance will die within him, and when he has forgotten the images, then he no longer will commit adultery with them in his soul. Therefore, the monasteries of those cloistered and the dwellings of solitaries are not simply established in order to guard many from the sight and encounter with women, but so that through the lack of these things the intellect may become pure and discover its strength. When he has been confirmed in his own strength, he will confront the war of fornication **(610)** with courage—if it should happen to confront him—whether from natural stimulation or from the inducement of demons.

Further Models for the Monk

65. Now, the memory of Joseph, who was an adolescent and a youth and was enticed by his mistress for this despicable deed of adultery, was it not sufficient for him to become a powerful [model] for every disciple with whom desire[61] does battle? If there should be victory here [with us] is its praise less than that of Joseph because

---

[61] Written: ܪܚܡܬܗ; read ܪܚܡܬܐ.

[we have] many supporters? The weakness of whoever is fighting will become known by how many supporters he has. After the story of Joseph, the holiness of Moses was written down, the chastity of Joshua, the naziriteship of Samson[62] and his fall that dissipated his strength,[63] the education of Samuel,[64] the sin of David and the chastisement concerning it,[65] the virginity of Elijah, the renunciation and purity of Elisha, and the famous gatherings of the sons of the prophets who were dwelling in the mountains[66] in the manner of monks and through self-control were living a life of estrangement to the world. Every example that is an instruction of chastity and of virginity was written down and came to be known after Joseph's exploits in order that he might be seen as a victor and triumphant because he fought and was victorious without an example, and if after all these examples we should slip and fall, we are weak and worthy of all torments.

The Veil of Fornication

66. The passion of fornication, according to the teaching[67] of the fathers, is a veil before the intellect's vision so that it may not investigate the things of God. Just as a person may extend a cloth over the letters and they would not be visible to the eye that would read them, so also this passion becomes a veil before the intellect so that it may not examine spiritual matters. It is not only when it is actually satisfied **(611)** that it darkens the intellect, but even if it [simply] remains in the thought while the soul takes pleasure in it. We should first purify the place of the intellect, and then the external members as well will be preserved, because the desire of the members is placed in the middle and inside it is the discernment of the intellect and outside of it the vision that excites. If

---

[62] Judg 13:5.
[63] Judg 16:19-21.
[64] 1 Sam 2-3.
[65] 2 Sam 11:2-4.
[66] 1 Kgs 18:4.
[67] Written: ܚܠܦ; read ܚܠܦܝ.

[desire] should obey and submit itself to the intellect, [the intellect] will change [desire] to the order of spiritual desire. But if it should receive memories from the outside and nurture [them], it will instigate a war and trouble the clarity of thoughts. Inasmuch as [desire] weakens the intellect, it will strengthen itself. All physical and tangible things will become strong, those which are from the world will make [desire] grow.

Being Dead

67. Some fight and are defeated, and some do not fight at all. That one who fulfills his desires will not fight, nor that one who is completely victorious over his desire—that first one, because he does not begin, and the other because he has concluded—but all the warfare [is in] the middle. On account of this Paul also called "dead" those who had finished this conflict. "You have died to the law in the body of Christ, so that you may belong to another one who has risen up from the house of the dead in order that you may bear fruits for God."[68] While showing the reason for war that happens between the two, he said, "When we were in the flesh, the passions of sins that are in the law were working in our members to bear fruits for death."[69] Those who live in the flesh are defeated at all times by desire and are bearing fruits for death. But those who are directed by the law stand up in the place of war, the law being made **(612)** for them an assistant and a fortifier in which they stand. When also in this middle place they fulfill the law and take hold of victory, Paul said to them, "Now we have been discharged from the law and we are dead to that which had hold of us, so that henceforth we might serve in the newness of the Spirit and not in the oldness of the book,"[70] because there is no desire in the new life. Wherever there is no desire, there is no war. And wherever there is no war, there the peace is known that our Savior brought to the world. Then the new peace will be visible to the new person,

[68] Rom 7:4.
[69] Rom 7:5.
[70] Rom 7:6.

because this is one who is led into the new life, and in this place there is no war of desires, but just as one who lives in the flesh lacks the awareness that it is sinful, so also whoever conducts himself spiritually will live without being subject to the passion of sin. Because lack of awareness does not know that it has sinned, but impassibility does not remember sin.

Beyond "Do Not Desire"

68. In both of these passages the old person sheds his desires in baptism and in the tomb. Whoever sheds his desires in baptism is called to the adoption of sons, but whoever serves them his entire life and leaves them in the tomb[71] is called to judgment with the trepidation of the resurrection. Whoever conducts himself in the spiritual way of life after his baptism is truly a new person who does not put on the old ways that he had shed through baptism, and for him there is no war with desire because he is dead to the world. Paul said, "I would not have known desire if the law had not said to me, 'Do not desire.'"[72] **(613)** So then, whoever conducts himself in the new person will not know desire, not living through abstention from desire but through the impassibility of desire. Just as Adam had been before that law was established for [desire], he had not known desire because [desire] was not [yet] alive with movement [in him], the commandment brought [it] to movement and the movement received the law. The law said, "Do not desire." Because he heard, "Do not desire," he was brought to know desire. He learned of sin through the commandment that inhibits sin. That is what happened to those who are defeated by the desire of the body, for when the saying against desire was said to them, repeating its ignominious forms, its impudent orders, and its violent movements, by these things that were spoken for its elimination, through them [desire] was especially set on fire in them because its opposites were being led to its aid and inflaming its passion.

---

[71] Lavenant, instead of written ܟܬܒܐ, "in battle," read ܩܒܪܐ, "in the tomb."

[72] Rom 7:7.

This is also what happened to Adam or to any human being who is defeated by desire when that [command], "Do not desire," is spoken to him.

Dead to the Law, Living Free

69. Thoughts habitually receive memories and memories stir up desire. It is then necessary that the disciple should distance himself from conversations and sights lest he receive memories and the memories should stir up desires and disturb the thoughts. But once a thought is disturbed, he is then not able to see God. "Let not sin rule in your dead body so that [as a result] you obey its desires."[73] If, according to the teaching of Paul, they are dead, I mean **(614)** those people who are alive in the Spirit, it is evident that also desire is dead in them. It is dishonorable for the intellect, not [so much] to be defeated, but just to fight. How does one who is dead fight?

However, for those who have not experienced [them] these things are difficult to listen to. But we are writing these things not from [our own] experience, but following the authority of the teaching of Paul. "The law has power over a man as long as he is living. A wife is bound with her husband as long as he is alive according to the law. But if her husband dies, she is freed from the law of her husband. But if while her husband is alive she should join with another man, she would be an adulterer. But if her husband should die she is freed from the law and is not an adulterer if she should belong to another man."[74] Therefore, what does the sense of this example seek, and what is the Apostle teaching us through these [words]? "You also have died to the law in the body of Christ in order that you might belong to another who has risen up from the dead."[75] As long as you are members of the first Adam who received the first commandment, you are subservient to the law. But now that you have become members of Another, that is, of Christ who has risen from the grave, the law no longer has authority over you

[73] Rom 6:12.
[74] Rom 7:1-3.
[75] Rom 7:4.

because that one of whom you are members is not subject to the law. Because just as God is above the law, when he became a human being who is subject to the law he kept the law and fulfilled all of its commandments. He departed to freedom that is above the law, that was spoken by our Lord, "If the Son frees you **(615)** truly you will become free people."[76] "Now that we have ceased from the law, and we are dead to that one who had seized us, let us serve then with newness of spirit and not by the ancient book."[77]

The Way of the New Person

70. But as I imagine, these words of the apostles are known and clear to whoever lives in the way of life of the new person. Whoever is in this way of life is not a hearer of words [only] but sees their meaning because vision is much more believable to perceive and comprehend actions. We are able to know these things clearly that are visible to the eye. In the same way also these who are found in the way of the new person will see the words of the Apostle, and not [be] hearers only, because it is not from the hearsay of others he was writing. He did not receive this learning "from a human being nor through a person" but, as he said, "through the revelation of Jesus Christ."[78] It is evident that revelation shows hidden things, for just as one's eyesight sees what is revealed [to it], so also the pure intellect examines spiritual things. The purity of the intellect, as I have said many times, is acquired by the mortification of all the works of the old person.

Freedom of the Soul from Law

71. Then Paul said excellently, "The woman is bound by the law as long as her husband is alive," calling the soul "the woman" as a type that is not freed from the works of the old person, and "her husband," the law to which [the soul] is subservient. It is through

---

[76] John 8:32.
[77] Rom 7:6.
[78] Gal 1:12.

attachment and obedience to [the law] [that the soul] is protected
(616) from foreign adulterers. But if the husband of this [woman]
should die, that one to whom she was tied by the law of his marriage, she will be free to belong to whomsoever she wishes, as also
it has happened to the law through the freedom of Christ: every
soul that was subservient to [the law] because it was bound by
works of sin was freed by means of the way of Christ. It is not that
the law protects [the soul so that] it does not sin, but because it is
united with Christ. Since it is not inhibited from evil things by the
fear of punishment, it will perform [good] genuinely by the love
of good, because the fear of the law is not as powerful to hold the
soul back from vices as the good [soul] is strong enough to bind
itself to [Christ] once it has sensed the pleasure of its taste.

Alive in a New Body

72. "You have died to the law in the body of Christ," which is
to say, because you have been placed in another body you have
become free from the servitude of the law, because the authority of
the law is over the old person whose beginning came to be after the
transgression of the commandment by the first Adam, as Paul said,
"The first Adam was a living soul, the second Adam a life-giving
Spirit."[79] Therefore, because there are two Adams according to the
teaching of Paul—one who was conducting himself by a living soul
over which the law has authority, and the other a life-giving spirit
that is above the law—Paul said excellently, "The woman, as long
as her husband is alive, **(617)** is bound by the law." Therefore, the
soul that conducts itself according to nature is subservient to the
law, but that one that is stirred up by the living Spirit is above the
law, because that spirit that is the giver of the law is not subservient to the law. Those who are worthy to conduct themselves by
the Spirit are above thoughts, movements, and the actions of sin.
It is not because they are afraid of the law that they do not serve
sin, but because they are dead[80] to sin. "You have died to the law

[79] 1 Cor 15:45.
[80] Typographical error: written ܡܝܬܝܢ, read ܡܝܬܝܢ.

in the body of Christ so that you may belong to another who rose up from the dead."[81] Just as these members that are connected in the natural body sense only the sickness or suffering that happens in their body—and if their body is healthy, they will enjoy its health—but they neither suffer nor sense the illness that is in the body of others, so also the new members that were placed in the body of that one who rose up from the dead, Christ our Lord, will sense the spiritual life and true health that the body in which they are connected has naturally acquired, while not sensing the passion of sins that are in the body of the old person, just as the body of every person does not sense the diseases and illnesses of the body of another [person].

No Fornication in the Body of Christ

73. Although all the works of the old person inhibit the intellect from sensing the way of the new person, more than all is this passion of fornication. On account of this Paul said, "Every sin that a person may commit **(618)** is outside his body. But whoever fornicates sins in his own body,"[82] the body here being called the body of Christ in which he was worthy to become a member, as he said, "You have died to the law in the body of Christ so that you might become members of another who rose up from the dead."[83] And again he said, "The body is not for fornication, but for our Lord, and our Lord is for the body."[84] So then, the body of that one who is alive in the ways of the new person, according to the word of Paul belongs to our Lord. Just as in the very body of our Lord there was no passion of fornication, so also the passion of fornication should not be stirred up in one whose body has become a member in the body of Christ, because the body which belongs to our Lord came into being through a new structure, and from this it has come to be that the body shall not be for fornication but for our Lord, and

---

[81] Rom 7:4.
[82] 1 Cor 6:18.
[83] Rom 7:4.
[84] 1 Cor 6:13.

our Lord for the body. He said, "But God raised up our Lord and raised up us by his power."[85] Just as God the Father raised up his Son from death to the immortality of the next life, so also all of us are raised up with him by his power. For just as [Christ] after his resurrection did not conduct himself according to our way of life, so also we, who have been raised up with him by his power, no longer live[86] a life subservient to the passions of the old person.

Members of Christ

74. Is this not how we should conduct ourselves in the new life? [The Apostle] introduced at the same time a word full of rebuke and teaching, saying, "Do you not know that your bodies are members of Christ?"[87] Here, Paul is not **(619)** only teaching us, but he finds fault with us and shows that just as there is no way for a member to live outside of its body, for all the members placed in the natural body exist in it and live by it, so also you, whose bodies have become members in the body of Christ and are receiving from him your entire stature—life, joy, purity, holiness, righteousness from all evil things, impassibility with respect to sin, gentleness, tranquility, peace, love, the movement in all things of the Spirit, and finally, all those things that this body possesses to give to its members—[cannot live outside of Christ].

If this is the lawful way of the new person, then one does not work for good by constraint of the law that inhibits evil things, but because this is appropriate for his position's rank. Through the incarnation from the Virgin Christ came to possess the members of his own body. This has shown and brought to light the fact that he became a human being. By the birth from baptism, which imitates the birth from the Virgin, these members that are baptized do not come through his incarnation, but through his guidance. Every one of these who are baptized, who with regard to his person is a body and a soul and an integral human being, becomes a member in the

---

[85] 1 Cor 6:14.

[86] Written: ܣܝ̈ܡ, read ܣܝ̈ܡ.

[87] 1 Cor 6:15.

body of Christ. This structure is not visible to people, as that which happened in the incarnation from the Virgin was visible (where what had been hidden was revealed, the Son of God became visible, and from the incorporeal the structure became visible). Rather, in this case from corporeal people [the baptized ones] become spiritual people. And from the fact that every one of them who is himself a body **(620)** of many members is counted in the body of Christ as a member, [the body of Christ] is constructed invisibly and [each person is] established in the body ineffably and becomes a spiritual member in the body of God, according to the word of the Apostle, "Your bodies are the members of Christ." How then will a member of Christ fight to defeat desire?

Members of Fornication in the Body of Christ

75. If there were a battle of this desire in the holy body of Christ, there would be an excuse for those who are disturbed by desire while they are members of that body. But the apostolic word not only commands us not to commit adultery, but not to become recipients of the passion of fornication, or to be disturbed at all by desire, or to fall into a battle, because a dead person does not fight. Those living receive sensation and sensation stirs up desire. If there is no old life [there is] also no sensation, and if there is no sensation, no desire is received. Therefore, no battle is stirred up any longer against desire. How can a person fight with something that does not exist? "Shall I take a member of Christ and make him a member of a prostitute?"[88] "Shall I take," he said in a manner of speaking, because as long as he is situated in the body, there is no way to become a member of fornication, just as a member placed in the natural body, as long as it is in its [proper] place, there is no way that it might receive life from another foreign body, but only from its own body. If one should cut off [a member] from there, he will not be able **(621)** to unite it with another body, even while it is alive, but with its being amputated it lets go of its life with its body, and it remains dead and without sensation in the hand of the one who

[88] 1 Cor 6:15.

holds it. For this reason Paul said, "Shall I take a member of Christ and make him a member of fornication?" as if to say, if he is not taken from there, he will not become a member of fornication. But if he should fornicate while he is in the body, this means he will become a recipient of this passion of fornication and will sin in his entire body, that is to say, he will make his entire body suffer.

Just as when one of the members of the body receives a wound its pain runs throughout all the rest of the members of the body, so also the member that receives the passion of fornication, when placed in the body of Christ it will infect and make his entire body suffer. This is what he said: "He sins in his body,"[89] as if to say [that his] sin is not only in that he himself is sick through the passion of fornication but [also in] his causing the entire body to suffer. If one wounds the body of another, his wound will be assigned to him under the condemnation of sin, and the law commands [him] at once to be avenged as someone guilty, saying, "A blow for a blow, a burn for a burn, and a fracture for a fracture";[90] [so] it is evident also that a member placed in the body of Christ, if it should be seized by the passion of fornication, will infect the entire body. Because of this Paul said justly, "He sins in his body."

Vigilance against the Worst Sin

76. There is no other sin that knows in the same way **(622)** [how] to defile the soul and the body like the passion of fornication. Because of this Moses, showing special vigilance against this passion, said, "The man from whom seed is emitted while he is sleeping shall be impure."[91] He made his reproaches so strongly [saying] that he makes himself impure not only when he is stirred up by the will and comes to the act of adultery of fornication, but [even] if some way or other the seed should be emitted from him while he is sleeping.

---

[89] 1 Cor 6:18.
[90] Exod 21:25.
[91] Lev 15:16.

Moreover with that other matter, where he commands concerning those members that are separated from sacrificial animals to be offered to God, he vigorously cautions that the two kidneys and the fat that is upon them should be burned, while not in any place does he designate them for the eating of priests and senior priests, but he submits them to a burning fire with the rest of the other members that are being compared with the works of sin: "Take the fat and the tail and all of the skin that covers over the inner [organs] and the caul and both of the kidneys and their fat, and burn all of these in the fire,"[92] and with all of these and before all of them, the two kidneys and their fat, which are these passions of fornication and of adultery. Let them burn the kidneys with their fat—which is the sign of the heaviness of the intellect—because it does not allow the despicable aspect of these passions to be seen.

Overseers of Passion

77. Therefore, if the old[93] law burns the passion of fornication in the fire, and designates as contaminated anyone whose seed somehow or other is emitted from him while he is sleeping, and burns the adulterer and adulteress **(623)** in the fire; and [if] our Lord in the teaching of his Gospel cuts off not[94] only the adulterer but also the thought that brings him to adultery; and [if] Paul said, "Neither fornicators nor adulterers will inherit the kingdom of God,"[95] and moreover, "Whoever unites with a prostitute will become one body with her,"[96] and "whoever fornicates sins in his body," and again he said, "Shall I take a member of Christ [and] make him a member of fornication?"[97]; and along with the words of the Scriptures practical experience also teaches this to those who are observers of

---

[92] Lev 3:4, 9.

[93] Lemoine reads typographical error: "old" (ܥܬܝܩ) instead of "silent" (ܫܬܝܩ).

[94] Written: ܠܗ, "(to) him"; read ܠܐ, "not."

[95] 1 Cor 6:9.

[96] 1 Cor 6:16.

[97] 1 Cor 6:15.

their passions—which disciple who wishing to live justly and in a holy way would not be wary of falling into this passion and [not] receive through a living and vigilant hearing the voice of God that cries out to us, "Become holy, just as I also am holy"?[98]

Yearning for Holiness

78. Therefore, a holiness that imitates [God's] holiness would not be required of us by the commandment of God if he had not also given us the Spirit that makes us holy, which is a soul for our soul, the purifier and sanctifier of its thoughts, and makes it so that it conducts itself not by its own thoughts and descends toward the pleasure of the body's desires, but so that it may be elevated toward purity and its own holiness and receive the splendor of its glory. If old age and illnesses become the suppressors and extinguishers of this desire, how much more will a healthy will that loves spiritual things and yearns for divine holiness! Old age [and] illness do not uproot desire but weaken and put [it] to sleep. But this will **(624)** made perfect by the power of the spirit[99] of sanctity completely eradicates desire, establishes the person in impassibility, and causes it to be stirred up in all his thoughts and spiritual matters, eliminating from him [not] only the disturbance of passions but also the sensation of tangible things. Just as in that one who is seized violently by the love of this passion the love of other things is extinguished, so also that one who sheds it completely and is bound perfectly to the love of spiritual things does not receive the sensation of the things that stir up this passion.

Closing the Entrances

79. But you, O disciple, because you have not yet attained these things, meditate on these things that I have written to you above and put them into practice, closing the entrances of desire that are the spectacles and external conversations and blocking its source

---

[98] Lev 19:2.

[99] Typographical error: repetition of word—ܟܘܬܗ, "of the spirit."

which is passion and the natural health of the body, as well as purifying thoughts which how many times have become its assistants and disturbers in the members. If you cut off [desire] through these three things—a thought does not reflect on it, the members are not stirred up by it, and there shall be for [desire] no entryway from the outside—you shall remain in stillness without agitation, and the journey of your ship will be without waves and storms toward the haven of peace, while the rest of its profits are guarded inside it.

Conducting Oneself into Another World

80. Through this you will become like the heavenly hosts, and while you are living in the body you will be stirred up by the Spirit. While you are in one world, you will be acting [as if] in another, and sensing also the reason for the coming of Christ to the world, which all of those who live corporeally do not comprehend. They only hear the voice **(625)** about his mysteries, while not sensing the meaning of his mysteries. But let us not be deprived of the knowledge that comprehends the meaning of these holy mysteries, and let us [not] become strangers to the cultivation of the divine commandments, and let us not be deprived of spiritual contemplation[100] of the visible and spiritual things.

By the grace of him who came for the salvation, liberation, and renewal of everything, Jesus Christ, the Only Begotten One, God the Word, to him be glory from all those who have received and have perceived his salvation, and have become the mediators of his gifts in all the generations of the worlds of light and of the regions of the Spirit, forever and ever. Amen.

The end of the thirteenth *mēmrā*, which is on fornication and the desire of the body.

---

[100] ܪ ܬܐܪܬܐ, *te'āwrīya.*

Bibliography

This is not an exhaustive bibliography, which would be beyond the scope of this volume. There are three excellent current and comprehensive bibliographies that deal with Philoxenos of Mabbug and the Syriac-speaking church, its literature and history.

Michelson, David Allen. "A Bibliographic Clavis to the Works of Philoxenos of Mabbug." *Hugoye* 13, no. 2 (2010): 273–338. http://www.bethmardutho .org/index.php/hugoye/volume-index/443.html.

Kessel, Grigory M., and Karl Pinggéra. *A Bibliography of Syriac Ascetic and Mystical Literature*. Eastern Christian Studies 11. Leuven / Paris / Walpole, MA: Peeters, 2011.

Minov, Sergey. *A Comprehensive Bibliography on Syriac Christianity*. Online http://www.csc.org.il/db/db.aspx?db=SB at The Center for the Study of Christianity, Hebrew University of Jerusalem (http://www.csc.org .il/).

General Articles and Monographs on Syriac Christianity

Baumstark, A. "Die Evangelienexegese der syrischen Monophysiten." *Oriens Christianus* 2 (1902): 151–69, 358–89.

Brock, S. P. "Iconoclasm and the Monophysites." In *Iconoclasm: Papers Given at the Ninth Spring Symposium of Byzantine Studies, University of Birmingham, March 1975*, edited by A. Bryer and J. Herrin, 53–57. Birmingham: Centre for Byzantine Studies, University of Birmingham, 1977.

Brock, S. P. "Hebrews 2:9B in Syriac Tradition." *Novum Testamentum* 27, no. 3 (1985): 236–44.

———. "*Notulae syriacae*: Some Miscellaneous Identifications." *Le Muséon* 108, no. 1–2 (1995): 69–78.

———. "The Transmission of Ephrem's *Madrashe* in the Syriac Liturgical Tradition." *Studia Patristica* 33 (1997): 490–505.

Connolly, R. H. "A Negative Form of the Golden Rule in the Diatessaron?" *Journal of Theological Studies* OS 35 [140] (1934): 351–57.

———. "Die Genealogie des Nestorianismus nach der frühmonophysitischen Theologie." *Oriens Christianus* 66 (1982): 1–14.

Frothingham, A. L. *Stephen bar Sudaili, the Syrian Mystic, and the Book of Hierotheos*. Leiden: E. J. Brill, 1886.

Hausherr, I. "De doctrina spirituali Christianorum Orientalium. Quaestiones et scripta." *Orientalia Christiana* 30 (1933): 147–216.

———. *Hésychasme et prière*. Orientalia Christiana Analecta 176. Roma: Pontificium Institutum Orientalium Studiorum, 1966.

Lebon, J. *Le monophysisme sévérien. Étude historique, littéraire et théologique sur la résistance monophysite au Concile de Chalcédoine jusqu'à la constitution de l'église jacobite*. Universitas Catholica Lovaniensis, Dissertationes ad gradum doctoris in Facultate Theologica consequendum conscriptae 2.4. Louvain: J. Van Linthout, 1909.

Mingana, A. "The Early Spread of Christianity in Central Asia and the Far East: A New Document." *Bulletin of the John Rylands University Library of Manchester* 9, no. 2 (1925): 297–371.

Palmer, Andrew N. *Monk and Mason on the Tigris Frontier: The Early History of Tur 'Abdin*. Cambridge: Cambridge University Press, 1990.

Stewart, C. *'Working the Earth of the Heart': The Messalian Controversy in History, Texts, and Language to AD 431*. Oxford Theological Monographs. Oxford: Clarendon Press, 1991.

Vööbus, A. *Studies in the History of the Gospel Text in Syriac*. CSCO 128, Subs. 3. Louvain: L. Durbecq, 1951.

———. *History of Asceticism in the Syrian Orient: A Contribution to the History of Culture in the Near East*. 3 vols. CSCO 184, 197, 500, Subs. 14, 17, 81. Louvain: Secrétariat du Corpus Scriptorum Christianorum Orientalium, 1958, 1960, 1988.

———. *Syriac and Arabic Documents Regarding Legislation Relative to Syrian Asceticism*. Papers of the Estonian Theological Society in Exile 11. Stockholm: Estonian Theological Society in Exile, 1960.

Text and Translations of *The Discourses* of Philoxenos of Mabbug

Budge, E. A.Wallis, ed. *The Discourses of Philoxenus Bishop of Mabbôgh, A.D. 485–519*. Edited from Syriac Manuscripts of the Sixth and Seventh Centuries, in the British Museum, with an English Translation. 2 vols. London: Asher & Co., 1894.

Lemoine, Eugène, trans. *Philoxène de Mabboug. Homélies. Sources Chrétiennes* 44. Paris, 1956; Nouvelle edition revue par René Lavenant. *Sources Chrétiennes* 44bis. Paris, 2007.

Editions and Translations of Other Works of Philoxenos of Mabbug

Brière, C. M., ed. *Sancti Philoxeni episcopi Mabbugensis dissertationes decem de Uno e sancta Trinitate incorporato et passo. Dissertatio 1ª et 2ª.* Patrologia Orientalis 15.4. Paris: Firmin-Didot, 1920.

Brière, C. M., and F. Graffin, eds. *Sancti Philoxeni episcopi Mabbugensis dissertationes decem de Uno e sancta Trinitate incorporato et passo. II. Dissertationes 3ª, 4ª, 5ª. Patrologia Orientalis* 38.3 [176]. Turnhout: Brepols, 1977.

———, eds. *Sancti Philoxeni episcopi Mabbugensis dissertationes decem de Uno e sancta Trinitate incorporato et passo (Mêmrê contre Habib). III. Dissertationes 6ª, 7ª, 8ª. Patrologia Orientalis* 39.4 [181]. Turnhout: Brepols, 1979.

———, eds. *Sancti Philoxeni episcopi Mabbugensis dissertationes decem de Uno e sancta Trinitate incorporato et passo (Mêmrê contre Habib). IV. Dissertationes 9ª, 10ª. Patrologia Orientalis* 40.2 [183]. Turnhout: Brepols, 1980.

———, eds. *Sancti Philoxeni episcopi Mabbugensis dissertationes decem de Uno e sancta Trinitate incorporato et passo (Mêmrê contre Habib). V. Appendices: I. Tractatus; II. Refutatio; III. Epistula dogmatica; IV. Florilegium. Patrologia Orientalis* 41.1 [186]. Turnhout: Brepols, 1982.

Brock, S. P., trans. *The Syriac Fathers on Prayer and the Spiritual Life.* Cistercian Studies Series 101. Kalamazoo, MI: Cistercian Publications, 1987. See Philoxenos of Mabbug, 101–33.

Chialà, S., trans *Filosseno di Mabbug. I sensi dello Spirito: Lettera a un suo discepolo, Lettera parenetica a un ebreo diventato discepolo.* Testi dei Padri della Chiesa 48. Monastero di Bose: Qiqajon, 2000.

Cody, A. "An Instruction of Philoxenus of Mabbug on Gestures and Prayer When One Receives Communion in the Hand, with a History of the Manner of Receiving the Eucharistic Bread in the West Syrian Church." In *Rule of Prayer, Rule of Faith: Essays in Honor of Aidan Kavanagh, O.S.B.,* edited by N. Mitchell and J. F. Baldovin, 56–79. Collegeville, MN: Liturgical Press, 1996.

de Halleux, A. "Nouveaux textes inédits de Philoxène de Mabbog. I: Lettre aux moines de Palestine; Lettre liminaire au synodicon d'Éphèse." *Le Muséon* 75, nos. 1–2 (1962): 31–62.

———, ed. *Éli de Qartamin. Memra sur S. Mar Philoxène de Mabbog.* 2 vols. CSCO 233–34, Syr. 100–101. Louvain: Secrétariat du CorpusSCO, 1963.

————. "Nouveaux textes inédits de Philoxène de Mabbog. II: Lettre aux moines orthodoxes d'Orient." *Le Muséon* 76, nos. 1–2 (1963): 5–26.

————, ed. *Philoxène de Mabbog. Lettre aux moines de Senoun.* 2 vols. CSCO 231–32, Syr. 98–99. Louvain: Secrétariat du CorpusSCO, 1963.

————, ed. *Philoxène de Mabbog. Commentaire du prologue johannique (Ms. Br. Mus. Add. 14, 534).* 2 vols. CSCO 380–81, Syr. 165–66. Louvain: Secrétariat du CorpusSCO, 1977.

————. "La deuxième Lettre de Philoxène aux Monastères du Beit Gaugal." *Le Muséon* 96, nos. 1–2 (1983): 5–79.

Fox, D. J., ed. *The "Matthew-Luke Commentary" of Philoxenus: Text, Translation, and Critical Analysis.* SBL Dissertation Series 43. Missoula, MT: Scholars Press, 1979.

Graffin, F. "Une lettre inédite de Philoxène de Mabboug à un avocat, devenu moine, tenté par Satan." *L'Orient Syrien* 5 (1960): 183–96.

————. "La lettre de Philoxène de Mabboug à un supérieur de monastère sur la vie monastique." *L'Orient Syrien* 6 (1961): 317–52, 455–86; 7 (1962): 77–102.

Harb, P. "Lettre de Philoxène de Mabbug au Phylarque Abu Ya'fur de Hirta de Betna'man (selon le manuscrit no 115 du fonds patriarcal de Sarfet)." *Melto* 3 (1967): 183–222.

Krüger, P. "Der Sermo des Philoxenos von Mabbug de annuntiatione Dei Genitricis Mariae. Zum ersten Male herausgegeben mit einer Einleitung und Übersetzung." *Orientalia Christiana Periodica* 20 (1954): 153–65.

————. "Philoxeniana inedita." *Oriens Christianus* 48 (1964): 153–65.

Lavenant, R., ed. *La lettre à Patricius de Philoxène de Mabboug. Patrologia Orientalis* 30.5. Paris: Firmin-Didot, 1963.

Lebon, J. "Textes inédits de Philoxène de Mabboug." *Le Muséon* 43 (1930): 17–84, 149–220.

Nau, F. "Note inédite sur Philoxène, évêque de Maboug (485–519)." *Revue de l'Orient chrétien* I 8, no. 4 (1903): 630–33.

————. trans. *Concile d'Antioche; lettre d'Italie; canons "des saints Pères", de Philoxène, de Théodose, d'Anthime, d'Athanase. Textes et traductions d'après le ms. syriaque nº 62 de Paris et le ms. 12155 de Londres, avec un fragment syriaque des voyages de saint Pierre.* Ancienne littérature canonique syriaque 3. Paris: Lethielleux, 1909.

————. "Littérature canonique syriaque inédite. Concile d'Antioche; lettre d'Italie; canons 'des saints Pères', de Philoxène, de Théodose, d'Anthime, d'Athanase." *Revue de l'Orient chrétien* 14 (1909): 1–49, 113–30.

————, ed. *Documents pour servir à l'histoire de l'Église nestorienne: I. Quatre Homélies de saint Jean Chrysostome; II. Textes monophysites: Homélies d'Érech-*

thios; Fragments divers; Extraits de Timothée Ælure, de Philoxène, de Bar Hébraeus; III. Histoire de Nestorius, d'après la lettre à Cosme et l'hymne de Sliba de Mansourya; Conjuration de Nestorius contre les migraines. Patrologia Orientalis 13.2 [63]. Paris: Firmin-Didot, 1916.

Olinder, G., ed. A Letter of Philoxenus of Mabbug Sent to a Novice. Göteborgs Högskolas Årsskrift 47.21. Göteborg: Elanders Boktryckeri Aktiebolag, 1941.

———, ed. A Letter of Philoxenus of Mabbug Sent to a Friend. Göteborgs Högskolas Årsskrift 56.1. Göteborg: Elanders Boktryckeri Aktiebolag, 1950.

Parmentier, M. F. G. "Pseudo-Gregory of Nyssa's Homily on Poverty." ARAM 5 (1993): 401–26.

Tanghe, A. "Memra de Philoxène de Mabboug sur l'inhabitation du Saint Esprit." Le Muséon 73 (1960): 39–71.

Tixeront, L.-J. "La lettre de Philoxène de Mabboug à 'Abou-Niphir." Revue de l'Orient chrétien I 8, no. 4 (1903): 623–30.

Vaschalde, A. A., ed. Three Letters of Philoxenus Bishop of Mabbôgh (485–519), Being the Letter to the Monks, the First Letter to the Monks of Beth-Gaugal, and the Letter to Emperor Zeno. Facultas Philosophiae 2. Roma: Tipografia della R. Accademia dei Lincei, 1902.

———, ed. Philoxeni Mabbugensis tractatus tres de Trinitate et Incarnatione. 2 vols. CSCO Syr. 2.27 [9–10]. Paris: Typographeo Reipublicae, 1907.

Watt, J. W., ed. Philoxenus of Mabbug: Fragments of the Commentary on Matthew and Luke. 2 vols. CSCO 392–93, Syr. 171–72. Louvain: Secrétariat du CorpusSCO, 1978.

Monographs on Philoxenos

Bergsträsser, E. Monophysitismus und Paulustradition bei Philoxenus von Mabbug. ThD diss.; Universität Erlangen-Nürnberg, 1953.

De Halleux, A. Philoxène de Mabbog. Sa vie, ses écrits, sa théologie. Universitas Catholica Louvaniensis, Dissertationes ad gradum magistri in Facultate Theologica vel in Facultate Iuris Canonici consequendum conscriptae 3.8. Louvain: Imprimerie orientaliste, 1963.

Frend, W. H. C. The Rise of the Monophysite Movement: Chapters in the History of the Church in the Fifth and Sixth Centuries. Cambridge: Cambridge University Press, 1972.

Jenkins, R. G. The Old Testament Quotations of Philoxenus of Mabbug. CSCO 514, Subs. 84. Leuven: Peeters, 1989.

Kitchen, R. A. *The Just and Perfect in the Ascetical Homilies of Philoxenus of Mabbug and the Liber Graduum*. MA thesis; The Catholic University of America, 1978.

————. *The Development of the Status of Perfection in Early Syriac Asceticism, with Special Reference to the* Liber Graduum *and Philoxenus of Mabbug*. DPhil diss.; University of Oxford, 1997.

Martikainen, J. *Gerechtigkeit und Güte Gottes. Studien zur Theologie von Ephräm dem Syrer und Philoxenos von Mabbug*. Göttinger Orientforschungen, I. Reihe: Syriaca, Bd. 20. Wiesbaden: Otto Harrassowitz, 1981.

Merton, Thomas. *Pre-Benedictine Monasticism: Initiation into the Monastic Tradition 2*. Kalamazoo, MI: Cistercian Publications, 2006.

Michelson, David A. *Practice Leads to Theory: Orthodoxy and the Spiritual Struggle in the World of Philoxenos of Mabbug (470–523)*. PhD diss.; Princeton University, 2007.

Articles on Philoxenos

Abramowski, L. "[Review of] A. de Halleux, *Philoxène de Mabbog. Sa vie, ses écrits, sa théologie* (Louvain, 1963)." *Revue d'histoire ecclésiastique* 60 (1965): 859–66.

————. "Ps.-Nestorius und Philoxenus von Mabbug." *Zeitschrift für Kirchengeschichte* 77 (1966): 122–25.

————. "Die Schrift Gregors des Lehrers 'Ad Theopompum' und Philoxenus von Mabbug." *Zeitschrift für Kirchengeschichte* 89 (1978): 273–90.

————. "Gregory the Teacher's 'Ad Theopompum' and Philoxenus of Mabbug." In *Formula and Context: Studies in Early Christian Thought*, edited by L. Abramowski, no. 8, 1–19. Collected Studies 365. Hampshire: Variorum, 1992.

————. "Aus dem Streit um das 'Unus ex trinitate passus est': Der Protest des Ḥabib gegen die Epistula dogmatica des Philoxenus an die Mönche." In *Jesus der Christus im Glauben der Kirche. Bd. 2.3: Die Kirchen von Jerusalem und Antiochien nach 451 bis 600*, edited by A. Grillmeier and T. Hainthaler, 570–647. Freiburg im Breisgau / Basel / Vienna: Herder, 2002.

Akhrass, R.-Y. "La Vierge Mère de Dieu dans la pensée de Philoxène deMabboug." *Hugoye* 13, no. 1 (2010): 31–48.

Aland, B. "Die philoxenianisch-harklensische Übersetzungstradition. Ergebnisse einer Untersuchng der neutestamentlichen Zitate in der syrischen Literatur." *Le Muséon* 94, nos. 3–4 (1981): 321–83.

———. "Monophysitismus und Schriftauslegung. Der Kommentar zum Matthäus- und Lukasevangelium des Philoxenus von Mabbug." In *Unser ganzes Leben Christus unserm Gott überantworten. Studien zur ostkirchlichen Spiritualität Fairy v. Lilienfeld zum 65. Geburtstag*, edited by P. Hauptmann, 142–66. Kirche im Osten, Monographienreihe 17. Göttingen: Vandenhoeck & Ruprecht, 1982.

Albert, M. "Une lettre inédite de Philoxène de Mabboug à l'un de ses disciples." *L'Orient Syrien* 6 (1961): 243–54.

———. "Une lettre inédite de Philoxène de Mabboug à un Juif converti, engagé dans la vie parfaite." *L'Orient Syrien* 6 (1961): 41–50.

Baarda, T. "'He Holds the Fan in His Hand . . .' (Mt 3:12, Lk 3:17) and Philoxenus, or How to Reconstruct the Original Diatessaron Text of the Saying of John the Baptist?" *Le Muséon* 105, nos. 1–2 (1992): 63–86.

———. "Philoxenus and the Parable of the Fisherman: Concerning the Diatessaron Text of Mt 13,47-50." In *The Four Gospels 1992: Festschrift Frans Neirynck*, edited by F. van Segbroeck, C. M. Tuckett, G. van Belle, and J. Verheyden, 2:1403–23. Bibliotheca Ephemeridum Theologicarum Lovaniensium 100.2. Leuven: Leuven University Press / Peeters, 1992.

Baethgen, F. W. A. "Philoxenus von Mabug über den Glauben." *Zeitschrift für Kirchengeschichte* 5, no. 1 (1882): 122–38.

Beck, E. "Philoxenos und Ephräm." *Oriens Christianus* 46 (1962): 61–76.

Bergsträsser, E. "Philoxenus von Mabbug. Zur Frage einer monophysitischen Soteriologie." In *Gedenkschrift für D. Werner Elert. Beiträge zur historischen und systematischen Theologie*, edited by F. Hübner, 42–61. Berlin: Lutherisches Verlagshaus, 1955.

Bettiolo, P. "Sulla Preghiera: Filosseno o Giovanni?" *Le Muséon* 94, nos. 1–2 (1981): 75–89.

Bou Mansour, T. "Die Christologie des Philoxenus von Mabbug." In *Jesus der Christus im Glauben der Kirche. Bd. 2.3: Die Kirchen vonJerusalem und Antiochien nach 451 bis 600*, edited by A. Grillmeier and T. Hainthaler, 500–568. Freiburg im Breisgau / Basel / Vienna: Herder, 2002.

Brock, S. P. "Alphonse Mingana and the Letter of Philoxenus to Abu Afr." *Bulletin of the John Rylands University Library of Manchester* 50 (1967): 199–206.

———. "The Syriac Euthalian Material and the Philoxenian Version of the NT." *Zeitschrift für die neutestamentliche Wissenschaft* 70, nos. 1–2 (1979): 120–30.

———. "The Resolution of the Philoxenian/Harklean Problem." In *New Testament Textual Criticism: Its Significance for Exegesis; Essays in Honour of Bruce M. Metzger*, edited by E. J. Epp and G. D. Fee, 325–43. Oxford: Clarendon Press, 1981.

Cowe, S. P. "Philoxenus of Mabbug and the Synod of Manazkert." *ARAM* 5 (1993): 115–29.

De Halleux, A. "A la source d'une biographie expurgée de Philoxène de Mabbog." *Orientalia Lovaniensia Periodica* 6–7 (1975–76): 253–66.

———. "La philoxènienne du symbole." In *Symposium Syriacum, 1976: célebré du 13 au 17 septembre 1976 au Centre Culturel "Les Fontaines" de Chantilly (France)*, edited by F. Graffin and A. Guillaumont, 295–315. Orientalia Christiana Analecta 205. Roma: Pontificium Institutum Orientalium Studiorum, 1978.

———. "Monophysitismus und Spiritualität nach dem Johanneskommentar des Philoxenus von Mabbug." *Theologie und Philosophie* 53, no. 1 (1978): 353–66.

———. "Le commentaire de Philoxène sur Matthieu et Luc. Deux éditions récentes." *Le Muséon* 93, nos. 1–2 (1980): 5–35.

———. "Monophysitismus und Spiritualität nach dem Johanneskommentar des Philoxenus von Mabbog." In *XX. Deutscher Orientalistentag vom 3. bis 8. Oktober 1977 in Erlangen: Vorträge*, edited by W. Voigt, 66–67. Zeitschrift der Deutschen Morgenländischen Gesellschaft, Supplement 4. Wiesbaden: Franz Steiner, 1980.

———. "Un fragment philoxénien inédit de polémique anti-chalcédonienne." In *Von Kanaan bis Kerala: Festschrift für Prof. Mag. Dr. J.P.M. van der Ploeg O.P. zur Vollendung des siebzigsten Lebensjahres am 4. Juli 1979 überreicht von Kollegen, Freunden und Schülern*, edited by W. C. Delsman, J. T. Nelis, J. R. T. M. Peters, W. H. P. Römer, and A. S. van der Woude, 431–41. Alter Orient und Altes Testament 211. Kevelaer: Butzon & Bercker / Neukirchen-Vluyn: Neukirchener Verlag, 1982.

———. "Le *Mamlelā* de 'Habbib' contre Aksenāyā. Aspects textuels d'une polémique christologique dans l'Église syriaque de la première génération post-chalcédonienne." In *After Chalcedon: Studies in Theology and Church History Offered to Professor Albert Van Roey for His Seventieth Birthday*, edited by C. Laga, J. A. Munitiz, and L. van Rompay, 67–82. *Orientalia Lovaniensia Analecta* 18. Leuven: Peeters, 1985.

Graffin, F. "Le florilège patristique de Philoxène de Mabbog." In *Symposium Syriacum, 1972: célebré dans les jours 26–31 octobre 1972 à l'Institut Pontifical Oriental de Rome*, edited by I. Ortiz de Urbina, 267–90. Orientalia Christiana Analecta 197. Roma: Pontificium Institutum Orientalium Studiorum, 1974.

———. "Note sur l'exégèse de Philoxène de Mabboug à l'occasion du discours de S. Paul aux Athéniens (Actes 17, 31)." *Parole de l'Orient* 9 (1979–80): 105–11.

Grillmeier, A. "Die Taufe Christi und die Taufe der Christen. Zur Tauftheologie des Philoxenus von Mabbug und ihre Bedeutung für die christliche Spiritualität." In *Fides Sacramenti Sacramentum Fidei: Studies in Honour of Pieter Smulders*, edited by H. J. Auf der Maur, 137–75. Assen: Van Gorcum, 1981.

Guillaumont, A. "[La diffusion des opinions relatives à l'apocatastase chez Jacques de Saroug († 521) et Philoxène de Mabboug († 523)]." *Annuaire de l'École Pratique des Hautes Études, Ve Section: Sciences Religieuses* 88 (1979–80): 369–71.

Hainthaler, T. "Philoxenus von Mabbug." In *Syrische Kirchenväter*, edited by W. Klein, 180–90. Urban-Taschenbücher 587. Stuttgart: W. Kohlhammer, 2004.

Harb, P. "Lettre de Philoxène de Mabbug au Phylarque Abu Ya'fur de Hirta de Betna'man (selon le manuscrit no 115 du fonds patriarcal de Sarfet)." *Melto* 3 (1967): 183–222.

———. "Faut-il restituer à Joseph Hazzâyâ la Lettre sur les trois degrés de la vie monastique attribuée à Philoxène de Mabbug?" *Melto* 4 (1968): 13–36.

———. "Die Unechtheit des Philoxenos-Briefes über die drei Stufen des monastischen Lebens." In *XVII. Deutscher Orientalistentag vom 21. bis 27. Juli 1968 in Würzburg: Vorträge*, edited by W. Voigt, 380–84. Zeitschrift der Deutschen Morgenländischen Gesellschaft, Supplement 1.2. Wiesbaden: Franz Steiner, 1969.

———. "L'attitude de Philoxène de Mabboug à l'égard de la spiritualité 'savante' d'Évagre le Pontique." In *Mémorial Mgr Gabriel Khouri-Sarkis (1898–1968), fondateur et directeur de L'Orient Syrien, 1956–1967*, edited by F. Graffin, 135–55. Louvain: Imprimerie orientaliste, 1969.

———. "La conception pneumatologique chez Philoxène de Mabbùg." *Melto* 5 (1969): 5–15.

———. "Le rôle exercé par Philoxène de Mabbug sur l'évolution de la morale dans l'Église syrienne." *Parole de l'Orient* 1 (1970): 27–48.

———. "Les origines de la doctrine de la 'la-hašušuta' (apatheia) chez Philoxène de Mabbug." *Parole de l'Orient* 5 (1974): 227–41.

Hatem, J. "Le moine et l'un chez Philoxene de Mabboug." In *Le monachisme syriaque aux premiers siècles de l'Eglise, IIe – debut VIIe siècle. I: Textes français*, 219–234. Patrimoine Syriaque, Actes du Colloque V. Antélias, Liban: Centre d'Études et de Recherches Orientales, 1998.

498   *The* Discourses *of Philoxenos of Mabbug*

Hausherr, I. "Contemplation et sainteté. Une remarquable mise au point par Philoxène de Mabboug (✝ 523)." *Revue d'ascétique et de mystique* 14 (1933): 171–95.

Jansma, T. "Philoxenus' Letter to Abraham and Orestes concerning Stephen bar Sudaili: Some Proposals with Regard to the Correction of the Syriac Text and the English Translation." *Le Muséon* 87, nos. 1–2 (1974): 79–86.

Jenkins, R. G. "Some Quotations from Isaiah in the Philoxenian Version." *Abr-Nahrain* 20 (1981–82): 20–36.

King, D. "New Evidence on the Philoxenian Version of the New Testament and Nicene Creed." *Hugoye* 13, no. 1 (2010): 9–30.

Kofsky, A., and S. Ruzer. "Christology and Hermeneutics in Philoxenus' Commentary on John 1:14." *Orientalia Christiana Periodica* 71, no. 2 (2005): 343–62.

Lehto, A. I. "Aphrahat and Philoxenus on Faith." *Journal of the Canadian Society for Syriac Studies* 4 (2004): 47–59.

Martikainen, J. "Erkenntnistheorie bei Philoxenos von Mabbug." In *XXI. Deutscher Orientalistentag vom 24. bis 29. März 1980 in Berlin: Vorträge*, edited by F. Steppat, 133–36. Zeitschrift der Deutschen Morgenländischen Gesellschaft, Supplement 5. Wiesbaden: Franz Steiner, 1983.

Mar Severios, Mathews. "The Suffering, Death and Resurrection of Christ—A Philoxenian View." *The Harp* 4 (1991): 59–65.

Mathai, M. A. "The Concept of 'Becoming' in the Christology of Philoxenos of Mabbug." *The Harp* 2 (1989): 71–77.

McCollum, A. "An Arabic Scholion to Genesis 9:18–21 (Noah's Drunkenness) Attributed to Philoxenos of Mabbug." *Hugoye* 13, no. 2 (2010): 7–30.

Michelson, David A. "'Though He Cannot Be Eaten, We Consume Him': Appeals to Liturgical Practice in the Christological Polemic of Philoxenos of Mabbug." In *Malphono w-Rabo d-Malphone: Studies in Honor of Sebastian P. Brock*, G. A. Kiraz, 439–76. Gorgias Eastern Christian Studies 3. Piscataway, NJ: Gorgias Press, 2008.

Mingana, A. "New Documents on Philoxenus of Hierapolis, and on the Philoxenian Version of the Bible." *The Expositor* 8, 19 [110] (1920): 149–60.

Molina Prieto, A. "La Theotókos en las 'Dissertationes' de Filoxeno de Mabbug." *Marianum* 44 (1982): 390–424.

Nin, M. "La *Lettera ai monaci di Senun* di Filosseno di Mabbug: un esempio di cristologia anticalcedoniana in ambiente siriaco nel VI secolo." In *La tradizione cristiana Siro-occidentale (V–VII secolo). Atti del 4° Incontro sull'Oriente Cristiano di tradizione siriaca (Milano, Biblioteca Ambrosiana, 13 maggio 2005)*, edited by E. Vergani and S. Chialà, 83–108. Ecumenismo e dialogo. Milano: Centro Ambrosiano, 2007.

Odorisio, D. M. "Thomas Merton's Novitiate Conferences on Philoxenos of Mabbug (April–June 1965): Philoxenos on the Foundations of the Spiritual Life and the Recovery of Simplicity by Thomas Merton, OCSO, introduced and transcribed by David M. Odorisio." *Hugoye* 13, no. 2 (2010): 133–53.

Pinggéra, K. "Christi Seele und die Seelen der Gerechten. Zum fünften Fragment aus dem Johanneskommentar des Philoxenus von Mabbug." *Studia Patristica* 41 (2006): 65–70.

Ruzer, Serge, and Aryeh Kofsky. "Philoxenus of Mabbug: Hermenutics of Incarnation." In *Syriac Idiosyncrasies: Theology and Hermenutic in Early Syriac Literature*, 121–40. Leiden: Brill, 2010.

Tisserant, E. "Philoxène de Mabboug." In *Dictionnaire de théologie catholique*, 12:1509–32. Paris: Letouzey et Ané, 1935.

Tsirpanlis, C. N. "Some Reflections on Philoxenos' Christology." *Greek Orthodox Theological Review* 25 (1980): 152–62.

van Rompay, L. "*Mallpânâ dilan Suryâyâ*. Ephrem in the Works of Philoxenus of Mabbog: Respect and Distance." *Hugoye* 7, no. 1 (2004).

———. "Bardaisan and Mani in Philoxenus of Mabbog's *Mēmrē against Habbib*." In *Syriac Polemics: Studies in Honour of Gerrit Jan Reinink*, edited by W. J. van Bekkum, J. W. Drijvers, and A. C. Klugkist, 77–90. Orientalia Lovaniensia Analecta 170. Leuven: Peeters, 2007.

Viezure, I. "Argumentative Strategies in Philoxenos of Mabbug's Correspondence: From the Syriac Model to the Greek Model." *Hugoye* 13, no. 2 (2010): 31–57.

———. "Philoxenos of Mabbug and the Controversies over the 'Theopaschite Trisagion.'" *Studia Patristica* 48 (2010): 137–46.

Vööbus, A. "La biographie de Philoxène. Tradition des manuscrits." *Analecta Bollandiana* 93 (1975): 111–14.

Watt, J. W. "Philoxenus and the Old Syriac Version of Evagrius' *Centuries*." *Oriens Christianus* 64 (1980): 65–81.

———. "The Syriac Adapter of Evagrius' *Centuries*." *Studia Patristica* 17, no. 3 (1982): 1388–95.

———. "The Rhetorical Structure of the Memra of Eli of Qartamin on Philoxenus of Mabbug." In *V Symposium Syriacum, 1988: Katholieke Universiteit, Leuven, 29-31 août 1988*, edited by R. Lavenant, 299–306. Orientalia Christiana Analecta 236. Roma: Pontificium Institutum Studiorum Orientalium, 1990.

————. "Two Syriac Writers from the Reign of Anastasius: Philoxenus of Mabbug and Joshua the Stylite." *The Harp* 20 (2006): 275–93.

Young, Robin Darling. "Philoxenos of Mabbugh and the Syrian Patristic Understanding of Justification." *Communio* 27 (2000): 688–700.

————. "The Influence of Evagrius of Pontus." In *To Train His Soul in Books: Syriac Asceticism in Early Christianity*, edited by Robin Darling Young and Monica J. Blanchard, 157–75. *CUA Studies in Early Christianity* 5. Washington, DC: The Catholic University of America Press, 2011.

Monographs and Articles Principally on *The Discourses*

Chesnut, R. C. *Three Monophysite Christologies: Severus of Antioch, Philoxenus of Mabbug, and Jacob of Sarug*, 57–112. Oxford Theological Monographs. Oxford: Oxford University Press, 1976.

Gribomont, J. "Les homélies ascétiques de Philoxène de Mabboug et l'écho du messalianisme." *L'Orient Syrien* 2 (1957): 419–32.

Hausherr, I. "Spiritualité Syrienne: Philoxène de Mabboug en version française." *Orientalia Christiana Periodica* 23 (1957): 171–85.

Jansma, T. "[Review of] E. Lemoine, *Philoxène de Mabboug. Homélies* (Sources chrétiennes 44; Paris: Cerf, 1956)." *Vigiliae Christianae* 12, no. 4 (1958): 233–37.

————. "Quotations from Genesis and Exodus in the Writings of Philoxenus of Mabbug." *Studia Patristica* 18, no. 4 (1990): 245–48.

Kitchen, R. A. "Syriac Additions to Anderson: The Garden of Eden in the Book of Steps and Philoxenus of Mabbug." *Hugoye* 6, no. 1 (2003).

————. "The Lust of the Belly Is the Beginning of All Sin: Practical Theology of Asceticism in the Discourses of Philoxenos of Mabbug." *Hugoye* 13, no. 1 (2010): 49–63.

————. "Review of Lemoine, E. and Lavenant, R., trans., Philoxène de Mabboug. *Homélies* (1956 and 2007)." *Hugoye* 13, no. 1 (2010): 65–73.

Lardreau, Guy. *Discours philosophique et discours spirituel: autour de la philosophie spirituelle de Philoxène de Mabboug*. L'ordre philosophique. Paris: Éditions du Seuil, 1985.

Lemoine, E. "Philoxène de Mabboug. Homélies sur la foi et sur la crainte de Dieu." *La vie spirituelle* 94 (1956): 252–61.

————. "La spiritualité de Philoxène de Mabboug." *L'Orient Syrien* 2 (1957): 351–66.

————. "Physionomie d'un moine syrien: Philoxène de Mabboug." *L'Orient Syrien* 3 (1958): 91–102.

Mathew, J. P. "Philoxenus of Mabbug. The Eighth Discourse on Poverty." *The Harp* 13 (2000): 173–76.

van Peursen, W. T. "Sirach Quotations in the *Discourses* of Philoxenus of Mabbug: Text and Context." In *The Peshitta: Its Use in Literature and Liturgy. Papers Read at the Third Peshitta Symposium*, edited by R. B. ter Haar Romeny, 243–58. Monographs of the Peshitta Institute Leiden 15. Leiden / Boston: Brill, 2006.

Biblical References

21:9	218	16:19-21	476	**Job**	
24:17	358			1:1	219
25:1-2	466	**1 Samuel**		1:21	264
25:1-9	68, 323	2–3	476	3:24	384
25:6	68	2:23-25	85	13:14-15	384
25:7-8	68	2:25	473		
25:9	68, 69	2:34	359	**Psalms**	
25:15	68	3:4	82	1:1	165
27:18	75	3:8	82	5:8	164, 168
		3:11-13	85	6:2	164
Deuteronomy		9:24	354	6:6	164
1:38	75	13:14	74	10:8	99
3:21	75	16:1	74	13:1	164
5:1	217	17:42	342	13:2	164
5:21	469	19:5	73	16:8	472
6:5	157	20:1	73	19:11	165
6:12-19	325	21:13	111	22:29	168
8:2	66	24:4-5	73	25:7	169
8:3	337			25:21	71, 117
9:9	382	**2 Samuel**		26:2	72
9:18	382	11:2	470	26:6	72
19:21	173	11:2-4	476	32:1	165
32:13-15	314	23:16	353	33:8	166
32:14	358			34:14	260
32:15	358	**1 Kings**		35:13	383
32:15-17	315	11:1-5	359	38:3-8	164
32:16	315	17:1	32	38:8	164
32:18a	315	17:4	352	38:10	164
32:18b	315	17:17	32	39:2-3	164
		18:37	33	39:9	164
Joshua		18:42-43	32	43:5	357
6:4	70	19:8	375	45:13-14	395
6:20	35			50:16-17	3
10:12	35	**2 Kings**		51:12	95
		1:10	32	66:12	383
Judges		2:9	33	68:5	219, 400
7:2ff.	465	2:15	33	68:6	399, 400
7:3	465			69:12	383
7:18	468	**1 Chronicles**		71:16	72
7:20	468	27:33	73	71:17	72
13:5	476				

Index of Topics